The Musical Companion

For this new and extensively revised edition of *The Musical Companion*, the general shape conceived by the original editor A. L. Bacharach has been largely retained.

'The ABC of Music' has been rewritten by Roger North, the composer, who teaches at Morley College.

'The Instruments of the Orchestra' has been brought up to date by John Gardner, composer, conductor and a professor at the Royal Academy of Music. Extra material on electronic music has been contributed by Michael Graubart of Morley College.

'Orchestral Music' is presented by Robert Layton of the BBC.

'Opera' has been revised, from Dent's original version, by Charles Osborne, author of many books on opera.

'The Human Voice' has been revised and extended by Alan Blyth of *The Times*.

'Chamber Music' has been taken over by Hugo Cole of *The Guardian*, himself a former student of Nadia Boulanger.

'The Solo Instrument' has been rewritten by John McCabe, the well-known composer and pianist.

Eric Blom's 'An Essay on Listening and Performance' has been retained, and the conductor David Atherton has contributed a new section on 'Listening and Performance Now'.

Edited by
A. L. BACHARACH & J. R. PEARCE

The Musical
COMPANION

REVISED EDITION

W. R. Anderson John Gardner
David Atherton Julius Harrison Eric Blom
Dyneley Hussey Alan Blyth Robert Layton F. Bonavia
John McCabe Hugo Cole Colin Mason Edward J. Dent
Roger North Edwin Evans Charles Osborne
Francis Toye

Pan Books London and Sydney

First published 1957 by Victor Gollancz Ltd
Revised edition published 1977
This edition published 1979 by Pan Books Ltd,
Cavaye Place, London SW10 9PG
© Victor Gollancz Ltd 1957, 1977
ISBN 0 330 25670 X
Printed and bound in Great Britain by
Richard Clay (The Chaucer Press) Ltd, Bungay, Suffolk

The Musical Companion
was first published in 1934
The nineteenth impression was published in 1954

The New Musical Companion
was first published in 1957
The fifth impression was published in 1973

ACKNOWLEDGEMENTS

The publishers acknowledge the following holders of copyright material:
Universal Edition London Ltd, for extracts from *New Sounds in Class* by
George Self, *Here and Now* by John Paynter, *Tempi Concertati* by Luciano
Berio and *Verses for Ensembles* by Harrison Birtwistle, all reproduced
by permission. Boosey & Hawkes Ltd, London, for an extract from *The
Young Person's Guide to the Orchestra* by Benjamin Britten, Universal
Edition London Ltd and Boosey & Hawkes Inc., for an extract from
Music for Strings, Percussion and Celesta by Bartók, reproduced by per-
mission. Durand et Cie, Paris and United Music Publisher's London,
for an extract from the *Turangalila* symphony by Oliver Messiaen, reproduced by permission. Harvard University Press, Cambridge, Mass., for
Poetics of Music by Igor Stravinsky. The *Sunday Herald*, Boston, Mass.,
for a short passage by Charles Munch. The frontispiece is reproduced by
permission of the British Library Board.

CONTENTS

Introduction by Livia Gollancz   12

Book 1 The ABC of Music
by Roger North, incorporating material by W. R. Anderson

PRELUDE   17

A TABLE OF ORCHESTRAL AND VOCAL COMPASSES   18

PART 1 MUSICAL NOTATION
1 What is Music?   19
2 The Rise of the Art of Music   22
3 The Rise of Polyphony   28
4 The Development of Music Notation   33
5 Secular Monody   39
6 The Growth and Progress of Musical Form   40

PART 2 THE ELEMENTS
1 Rhythm   51
2 Melody   62
3 Timbre   68
4 Harmony   74
5 Form   81

PART 3
1 Scales; Modes; Keys   94
2 Sonata Form   100
3 The Rest of the Classical Sonata   104
4 The Fugue   106
5 Programme Music   108
6 Some Definitions and Technicalities   111
7 Instruments   112
8 The Reading of Music   117
9 Glossary   122

Book 2 The Instruments of the Orchestra   137
by Julius Harrison, revised and expanded by John Gardner, with
additional material by Michael Graubart

PART 1 THE RISE OF THE ORCHESTRA
1 Introduction   139
2 First Beginnings   140
3 The Strings   146
4 Woodwind   149

5 Brass   154
6 Percussion. Balance. Six Typical Orchestras   158

PART 2 THE EXPANSION OF THE ORCHESTRA
1 Trombones and Horns   163
2 The Orchestral Revolution   166
3 Post-Wagnerian Growth and Later Trends   171
4 A note on Electronic Music   180

PART 3 THE ORCHESTRA AS AN INSTRUMENT
1 Arrangement of Instruments in a Full Score   183
2 The Orchestra on the Platform   186
3 The Conductor's Role   191
4 A Glance at Orchestration   199
5 Some String Devices in Orchestration   204
6 Woodwind Devices in Orchestration   209
7 Brass Devices in Orchestration   214
8 Percussion and Harp in Orchestration   224
9 Percussion in the 20th Century   228
10 A Postscript on the 20th Century Orchestra   229

Book 3 Orchestral Music   233
by Julius Harrison, with new material by Robert Layton

PART 1 'ABSOLUTE' MUSIC AND THE SYMPHONIES
1 Introduction   235
2 The Symphony   236
3 Haydn and Mozart   240
4 Beethoven   246
5 Schubert and Dvořák   252
6 The Symphony after Beethoven   262
7 France after Berlioz   266
8 Bruckner and Mahler   269
9 Brahms   277
10 Russia   282
11 Scandinavia   301
12 The Symphony in Britain   312
13 The United States   322

PART 2 ORCHESTRAL MUSIC OF MANY KINDS
1 Mainly of Suites   328
2 Overtures, Variations and Rhapsodies   331
3 Miscellaneous Music   334
4 Programme Music   335*

5 Key Developments 1900–1950 339
6 What of the Future? 349

Book 4 Opera 355
by Edward J. Dent, with revisions and a section on Modern Opera by
Charles Osborne

PART 1 HOW OPERA AROSE
1 The Operatic Convention 357
2 Origins 359
3 The Renaissance 361
4 Early Italian Opera: Monteverdi 362
5 Standardisation 364
6 Vienna and Paris: Lully 365
7 England: Purcell. Germany 367
8 Survey of the 17th Century 369

PART 2 THE EIGHTEENTH CENTURY
1 Italian Influence: Scarlatti 372
2 More about Conventions 374
3 The Castrati 375
4 Metastasio. The French School: Rameau 376
5 Comic Opera in Italy and France 377
6 English Comic Opera. The European Position 379
7 Gluck 380
8 Mozart 383

PART 3 FROM MOZART TO WAGNER
1 Cherubini. Beethoven 387
2 Cimarosa. Rossini 389
3 Bellini. Donizetti. Auber 391
4 Romanticism and Weber 393
5 Wagner 396
6 Wagnerianism 399
7 Operetta 400

PART 4 FROM VERDI TO THE PRESENT DAY
1 Verdi 403
2 French Opera 405
3 Mascagni. Leoncavallo. Puccini 407
4 From Wagner to Strauss 409
5 The Russians 411
6 A Note on Some English Operas 413

PART 5 MODERN OPERA

1	France	415
2	Italy	417
3	Germany and Austria	418
4	Russia	423
5	Other European Countries and Latin America	425
6	The English Language	427

PART 6 A RETROSPECT AND A PROSPECT   431

Book 5 The Human Voice   435
by Alan Blyth, incorporating material by Francis Toye and Dyneley
Hussey

1	Modes, Plainsong and Polyphony	437
2	Minstrels and Troubadours	439
3	The New Art and Machaut	441
4	England and Flanders	442
5	Flanders and Italy: Lassus, Palestrina and Victoria	446
6	England: Tudor Era and Purcell	450
7	Italian and German Baroque	458
8	Bach and Handel	460
9	The Classical Tradition	465
10	Mostly of Requiems (1835–1900)	468
11	Folk-song	471
12	European Song in the 19th Century	476
13	Change in the Air	490
14	Revival of English Song	493
15	New Developments	498

Book 6 Chamber Music   503
by Hugo Cole, incorporating material by Edwin Evans

PART 1 BEFORE BEETHOVEN

1	Early Beginnings in England and Abroad	505
2	Chamber Music of the 16th and 17th Centuries	506
3	The Coming of the Violin	512
4	The New Art is Born	514
5	A Pause for Definition	515
6	Chamber Music and Sonata Form	518
7	Haydn: First Period	519
8	Mozart	521
9	Haydn: Second Period	523
10	Boccherini	525

PART 2 FROM BEETHOVEN TO BRAHMS
1 Beethoven: First Period   527
2 Beethoven: Second and Third Periods   530
3 The Romantic Dawn   533
4 Schubert   535
5 From Spohr to Schumann   537
6 Brahms   540
7 Germany and Austria after Brahms   542

PART 3 NATIONAL SCHOOLS
1 Nationalism and Chamber Music   544
2 Bohemia   545
3 Scandinavia   548
4 Russia   549
5 France   552
6 Britain: Early Beginnings   557
7 Britain: From Elgar to Britten   559
8 The United States   562
9 Nationalists of Other Countries   565

PART 4 INTERNATIONALISTS, CONTEMPORARY AND AVANT-
GARDE
1 Schoenberg to Stravinsky   568
2 Bartók and Shostakovich   572
3 The Sixties and Seventies   575
4 Chamber Music in a Changing World   583

Book 7 The Solo Instrument   585
by John McCabe, with an opening section by F. Bonavia
KEYBOARD INSTRUMENTS INTRODUCTORY   587

  1 Virginal and Harpsichord
     (a) The English School   588
     (b) The French School   591
     (c) The Italian School   592
     (d) Bach and Handel   593
  2 Music for Solo Piano
     (a) Haydn   597
     (b) Mozart   600
     (c) Beethoven and the Early Romantics   602
     (d) Schubert and Weber   607
     (e) The Romantics   609
     (f) The Romantics outside Germany   614
     (g) France   616

(h) Italy and Spain 618
(i) The Slavs 619
(j) Scandinavia 621
(k) Russia 622
3 Solo Piano: 20th-century Developments
(a) Twelve-tone Technique 625
(b) The Schoenberg Tradition 626
(c) The Avant-garde 627
(d) Neo-classic 629
(e) America and Britain 630
(f) France 631
4 Piano and Orchestra: Piano Duo, Organ, Harpsichord
(a) Bach and Haydn 632
(b) Mozart 634
(c) Beethoven 636
(d) Mendelssohn, Chopin, Schumann, Liszt 638
(e) Lesser Romantics and Shorter Works 640
(f) Brahms, Tchaikovsky 641
(g) Lesser Romantics 643
(h) France and Germany 644
(i) Britain 645
(j) Bartók, Stravinsky, Schoenberg 646
(k) The United States of America 647
(l) Russia 648
(m) Piano Duo 649
(n) Organ Repertoire 651
(o) Modern Harpsichord 654
5 Violin Sonatas
(a) The Italian School 654
(b) Bach, Handel, Mozart 655
(c) Beethoven 657
(d) The Romantics 658
(e) The 20th Century 659
(f) Violin Unaccompanied and Two Violins 662
6 Violin Concertos
(a) Bach 664
(b) Mozart and Beethoven 666
(c) The Romantics 667
(d) The 20th Century 670
7 Viola, Cello, Double-Bass, Harp, Guitar
(a) Viola 674
(b) Cello 676
(c) Double-Bass 680

(d) Harp		680
(e) Guitar		681
8 Wind Instruments		
(a) Flute		682
(b) Oboe		685
(c) Clarinet		686
(d) Bassoon		688
(e) Horn		688
(f) Trumpet, Trombone, Tuba, Harmonica		690
9 Percussion		692
10 Concertos for More than One Instrument		693

Book 8 An Essay on Listening and Performance   697
by Eric Blom

Listening and Performance Now   745
by David Atherton
INDEX   763

A note on the use of §

§ denotes an extract largely from the original *Musical Companion*. This sign appears also at the close of each extract, but not at the close of sections within an extract. In many cases these extracts have been revised and updated by the authors of this new edition, and in some cases the present authors have incorporated a few words from the original into their own material. It has not been found practicable to indicate the exact provenance of very short passages.

INTRODUCTION

Livia Gollancz

As a publisher I am particularly pleased to be presenting this completely revised and largely rewritten edition of a book that I first knew in childhood, and which greatly influenced the formation of my own musical taste and interests. It has also proved widely popular for nearly half a century. I grew up with *The Musical Companion*, one of the books in which my father, Victor Gollancz, took an especial pride. Music and his home background were the dual elements of spiritual and physical renewal in his life; and they made his many other activities possible – publishing, politics, social reform etc. It was therefore not surprising that his home was filled with music and that a book such as this was very close to his heart.

The first edition included a prefatory letter from the Editor, A. L. Bacharach, to the Publisher. The following few phrases are as relevant today as they were in 1934:

My dear Gollancz,
I think you will agree with me that neither of us can claim credit for having first envisaged this book. That we have co-operated in its production is simply the direct result of something that is going on today all around us.

Both of us have been for many years lovers of music in all its manifold forms. If you have been the more ardent supporter of opera, and I the more passionate devotee of chamber music, we have had a common meeting ground in the Queen's Hall. Both of us number among our friends composers, performers and musical critics; both of us, because of our known musical affiliations, must have been asked over and over again by other friends where they could learn more about the art and its exponents.

It was not, therefore, surprising that a casual remark from me, foreshadowing the possibility of producing a book such as this one, should have elicited from you something more than ready sympathy . . .

May I give two pieces of advice to the reader? First, do not necessarily attempt to read *The Musical Companion* straight through. If you are a novice, begin by taking Book 1 slowly and thoughtfully, and then read Blom's delightful concluding Essay. After that, go as you please. And if you are not a novice, start anywhere you like and read backwards or forwards, as you will. The index may help your browsing. Secondly, though I would beg you to read with sympathy, do so with reasoned scepticism. *The Musical Companion* contains very many facts but by no means a few opinions. The former may be safely held to be as accurate as scholarship and erudition can make them; the latter deserve the respect due to their holders, all of them musicians and music lovers. But it would be a fatal mistake to take them or accept them as dogma.

Music is not a science, but an art; in music an instant of true appreciation and perception is worth an age of learning and lore. You and I have the hope that *The Musical Companion* may help its readers to add to their musical experience and sensibility, not because its authors are pundits or mandarins, but because they are scholars and musicians, and because for those very authors, learned though they are, the Music's the thing.

When the book came up for reprinting in its twentieth impression, the editor and several of the original contributors being still alive, it was decided to make slight revisions to the original text and generally to update it, and issue it under the title *The New Musical Companion*. A. L. Bacharach contributed a second preface, which told how, at the time he wrote his original, 'neither Editor nor Publisher in his most hopeful moments would have dared forecast that during its first twenty-one years it would go into nineteen impressions and that the number sold would then have passed the 180,000 mark. Except at those times during and just after World War II when printing, paper and other factors made re-issue impossible anyhow, these new impressions have followed each other so regularly, and always been so urgently needed, as to make attempts at revision seem at any rate unmanageable, if not unnecessary.

'Nevertheless, we took the occasion of the book's "coming of age" to look back to 1934 and then again to scan *The Musical Companion*, especially those parts surveying the more or less contemporary scene; we both found it clear that something would just have to be done. Besides the need to give mention to the chief musical works composed during the ten years before the outbreak of war, during the war years themselves and during the ten years after its end, the more important recent results of musicographical research had to be incorporated; further, there were the inevitable revisions of judgment to which the individual contributors were themselves becoming anxious to confess . . .

'There was the further sad complication that two of the contributors were no longer alive. The gap so created has been gallantly filled by Colin Mason.' At that time Colin Mason was a critic on the *Guardian*; but was to die soon afterwards.

And now we must consider this new volume which again takes the original title, *The Musical Companion*. Since 1930 – and indeed even since 1957 – musical life in Britain has undergone what can only be described as a revolution. It is not just that more and more people attend concerts, recitals, the opera, and listen on record, television and radio; it is that audiences have become vastly more knowledgeable and expert than formerly. This high standard has been borne in mind in the revisions made for this edition. Material that remained applicable to present-day standards and judgments has been retained, and enclosed between § § for identification; but all has been carefully considered by the new authors who have themselves contributed more, or less, according to their own views as to what would be attractive, and indeed necessary, for today's music lovers. Thus, one contributor will have recast totally his section, whereas others will have used differing amounts of the earlier material. Eric Blom's famous 'Essay on Listening and Performance' (for countless numbers, the concertgoer's *vade mecum*) has been retained uncut, and David Atherton's piece follows, bringing it up to date.

Each new contributor is expert in his particular field. Roger North (The ABC of Music) is a composer, and a teacher experienced with pupils of all ages and particularly in the field of adult education – mainly at Morley College. He has also given many Radio 3 talks of an instructional nature. As a boy he played the piano and showed a talent for improvising. This led to study at the Royal Academy of Music. Roger North writes of his career: 'I started talking about music in the early 1950s and haven't left off yet. I am still discovering new depths in great musical works I thought I knew inside out.' In his contribution to this book, he presents musical details, in relation to a musical whole, without recourse to musical notation, something a composer is in a particularly good position to do.

John Gardner (The Instruments of the Orchestra) is a composer, teacher and conductor. He has written many orchestral and choral works, music for the theatre (Stratford and the Old Vic) and for festivals. He is Professor of Harmony and Composition at the Royal Academy of Music, was, until recently, Director of Music at St Paul's Girls' School and, for a while, Director of Music at Morley College. He is an excellent conductor, particularly popular with amateur musicians, but with much professional experience, including a stint on the staff at Covent Garden in his younger days.

Robert Layton (Orchestral Music) was born in London and studied at Oxford – composition with Edmund Rubbra, and history of music with Egon Wellesz. He completed his studies with a visit to Sweden 1953–5 where he attended the Universities of Uppsala and Stockholm. On returning to London, he taught for a while until joining the BBC in 1959. Since 1960 he has been in charge of all talks emanating from the Music Department. He is general editor of the BBC Music Guides and has contributed one volume himself, on Dvořák (1977). He writes regularly in *The Gramophone* and is part-author of the Penguin *Stereo Record Guide*. His full-length books include one on *Berwald* (1956), and *Sibelius* in Dent's Master Musicians series (1965). He has always specialized in Scandinavian music and is currently translating Erik Tawaststjerna's biography of *Sibelius*, volume I of which appeared in 1976.

Charles Osborne (Opera) is the author of numerous books on operatic subjects, has contributed criticism to most of the more important London newspapers and journals, and broadcasts frequently. He came to England from his native Australia in 1953, His *The Complete Operas of Verdi* (1969) is perhaps his most successful book to date, and is shortly to be followed by *The Complete Operas of Mozart*. Over future years he intends to write similar books dealing with the work of all the most important operatic composers. He is Literature Director of the Arts Council of Great Britain.

Alan Blyth (The Human Voice) sang as a tenor at school and Oxford, and is now an Associate Editor of *Opera* magazine. Since 1963 he has written music criticism for several newspapers and journals including *The Times*, *New Statesman*, *Listener* and *The Gramophone*, and is now on the music staff of the *Daily Telegraph*. He was music editor for the recently published new edition of the Encyclopaedia Britannica, has contributed to the latest Grove's Dictionary and has written biographies of Colin Davis and Janet Baker. Since 1952 he has attended almost every new opera production and almost all Lieder recitals in London, and has travelled widely in Europe and the USA for the same purpose. He broadcasts frequently on vocal subjects.

Hugo Cole (Chamber Music) originally worked as a research zoologist at Cambridge but soon switched to music, playing both cello and horn. He studied instrumental playing and composition at the Royal College of Music, and later composition with Nadia Boulanger in Paris. Although he divides most of his time between composition and journalism he has been a confirmed chamber music player, on the cello, ever since leaving school. He no longer plays the horn, but acquainted himself with the wind chamber-music repertoire at first hand in his younger days. He still plays string quartets whenever he gets the chance. His compositions include songs, chamber music and several children's operas, a medium in which he has been particularly successful. He is one of the *Guardian*'s music critics and writes a weekly page for *Country Life*. He also contributes to *The Listener* and various specialist journals. Until now he has written one book, *Sounds and Signs* (1974).

John McCabe (The Solo Instrument) is a composer and pianist who studied at Liverpool and Manchester universities, the Royal Manchester College of Music and later at the Hochschule für Musik at Munich. For a while he was pianist in residence at the University College of Cardiff, but solo work and composition made it inevitable that he should gravitate to London. As a pianist he has made many recordings (he is currently engaged on a 16-record cycle of Haydn's piano music for Decca) and given numerous concerts not only in Britain but also in other European countries, the USA and Canada, and appears often on television. His major compositions include two operas, many orchestral, vocal and piano works, and *Mary, Queen of Scots* commissioned for Scottish Ballet. He is the author of the BBC Music Guide, *Bartók's Orchestral Music*, and of a biography of Rachmaninov (both 1974).

David Atherton (Listening and Performance Now) hardly needs mention as he is so well known as an orchestral and operatic conductor. Since 1968 he has been resident conductor at Covent Garden, and was founder (in 1967) of the London Sinfonietta and remained its musical director until 1973. He has edited books on Schoenberg and Roberto Gerhard, and has also arranged orchestral suites and a ballet from Gerhard's music. He is a contributor to the new edition of Grove's Dictionary.

I cannot close this introductory note without paying tribute to John R. Pearce, who gave so much time and energy to the organisation and initial editing of this new edition. Without his vision and tenacity it would have remained a pipe-dream. He undertook all the early work on the project and saw it through as far as the detailed editing on all contributions. For personal reasons he left this country shortly before the book went to press, and now makes his contribution to the Canadian publishing scene.

Recently I told Sir Adrian Boult, an old friend of my father's, that this new edition would soon be before the public. He wrote: 'It is splendid to hear that the excellent *Musical Companion* is reappearing with a fine new list of contributors who will most certainly bring it up to date, and will, I believe, retain the best parts of the excellent first edition. Interest in music, both live and recorded, seems to be steadily increasing as the years go by, and I know *The Musical Companion* will find many eager readers who will use it to further their own musicianship.'

London 1977   L.G.

Book 1

The ABC of Music

by Roger North
incorporating material by W. R. Anderson

PRELUDE

Of the three sections 1 looks at music in general and in historical perspective, 2 at its 'elements' – rhythm, melody, timbre, harmony and form – while 3 fills in some of the details. I have tried to steer a middle course between, on the one hand the boring details of the 'rudiments' of music, and on the other the smooth, shallow waters of oversimplification and evasion. If it has been necessary now and then to encompass a few dull technicalities – and some readers may choose to dodge these – the far more dangerous shallows have been avoided, I hope, successfully.

A TABLE OF ORCHESTRAL AND VOCAL COMPASSES
(REAL SOUNDS)

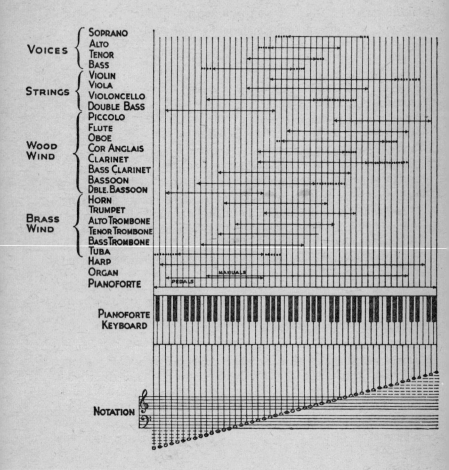

The practicable or useful orchestral or choral compass is shown by the continuous line: extra, possible, notes by dots

PART 1

1 WHAT IS MUSIC?

'Is this music yes or no? If I am answered in the affirmative, I would say . . . that it does not belong at all to the art which I am in the habit of considering as music.'[1]

That was written, not in the 20th century about some avant-garde piece of music heard for the first time, but in 1857 about – amazingly enough – Beethoven's Fifth Symphony, which was by then half a century old. The writer was referring specifically to one of the finest passages in the whole symphony – the shadowy music linking the tiptoeing hush of the end of the scherzo to the noisy blazing glory of the finale. Well if that was not music in 1857, what was? And if the question needed an answer then, how much more now in the last quarter of the 20th century, with composers of electronic music having all possible sounds at their disposal, with music composed by throwing dice, by switching on radios at random, by instrumentalists playing not from notated music but from strip cartoons, with singers imitating motorcycles and audiences being asked to listen to the ambient sounds of an auditorium and to make their own music out of them.

Many of us will be tempted to say that of course none of this is music, but might not *we* be thus dismissing another Beethoven Fifth? No wise critic today is willingly going to take that risk. Hence the non-committal nature of so much present-day criticism. At least our 1857 critic was sincere.

A typical dictionary definition of music is 'the art of combining sounds so as to please the ear', which is all right as far as it goes, and as long as we interpret the phrase 'please the ear' sufficiently broadly. Any attempt to go further, however, is beset with pitfalls. A phrase often used is 'the rhythmic combination of tones'. This embraces a lot of music but excludes non-pitched sounds like hand-clapping and a huge array of percussion sounds – cymbals, gongs, many drums etc. – which have played a big part in music from the earliest days. For the same reason it excludes a large amount of electronic music.

Similarly any definition which assumes there must be harmony is at fault since it rules out, for instance, unaccompanied song, and it rules out more and more European music the further one goes back in time

[1] A. Oulibicheff, *Beethoven, ses critiques et ses glossateurs*, Paris 1857; taken from Nicolas Slonimsky's *Lexicon of Musical Invective* Coleman-Ross, New York, 1953.

beyond the Middle Ages, to say nothing of those non-European musics which do not use harmony.

There is even music without melody, which must be a sad thought to those people for whom music *is* melody. We hear the complaint often enough: 'I don't like it because it hasn't got a tune.' The same listener will, however, ascribe a tune to a piece of music which he likes, but which may lack the tune he fancies he hears. A piece of music which is rich in harmony and instrumental colour might have next to no melody. A piece for percussion only might have no melody at all and an electronic piece is unlikely to have any melody.

The Shorter Oxford English Dictionary, presumably aware of all these pitfalls, defines music thus: 'That one of the fine arts which is concerned with the combination of sounds with a view to beauty of form and the expression of thought or feeling.'[1]

Now we are getting warmer. Form in music is how a piece of music goes on after the first few sounds have been uttered. Do we hear those first few sounds again at once, or do we hear them again after something else? Do we not hear the first sounds again, but something like them? Or do we never hear those first sounds again nor anything like them? In that last instance our feeling for form in music prompts us to ask, if not, why not? Beauty of form can be said to exist when we enjoy the relationship between what we are hearing now and what we heard seconds or minutes ago. This applies especially to our appreciation of a good tune, as any careful analysis of such a tune will show. We recognize patterns of notes which recur and we notice to what extent they are the same and to what extent they are different. This kind of beauty of form is present in nearly all music whether it be a string quartet or a sea shanty. Even a musician improvising and not knowing what he will be playing in the next moment will be intuitively exploring this relationship between the now and the just now.

A composer may more easily achieve a music in which no recognizable patterns are likely to recur by throwing dice, using a roulette wheel, tables of random numbers or a computer, all of which have been done. This need not necessarily rule out beauty of form since the sophisticated listener may enjoy the absolute unpredictability of the music, although probably not for very long since the unpredictability will itself become too predictable. Or the listener may even in some strange way impose his own form on the music. In practice, composers who employ random techniques will rarely use them to disorganize every aspect of their composition.

[1] S.O.E.D., reprinted with corrections 1972.

How about the Oxford Dictionary's 'the expression of thought or feeling'? It seems very doubtful whether music can *express* thought at all. Once a thought has been put into the listener's mind by, say, the words of a song or just the title of a piece of instrumental music, then the music can certainly add poignancy to the thought, partly by matching the mood associated with the thought, sometimes partly by a vague imitation, more accurately an analogy (e.g. a 'leaping' figure in the piano accompaniment to Schubert's song 'The Trout'), but mainly by just being music. Music *can* express a mood but it tends to be rather unspecific. A general raising of the emotional temperature is something every film-maker can rely on music to bring about, and it is surprising how little the mood of the music matters. We have sad music and happy music, to be sure. We also have great music, but not great because of being sadder or happier than other music, nor really because of being a subtle blend of different emotions. A great composer is something more than an expert chef. Great music is great because of its beauty of form and because of the emotions engendered by listening to it, which are largely a function of its beauty of form. A piece by Mozart may pass through a variety of moods which will be reflected in the listener but his delight and excitement will be mainly derived from Mozart's masterly handling of the form. This is what makes Mozart a greater composer than Tchaikovsky.

We always speak of music as if it is the sounds themselves; in fact it is the *experience* of them, the experience of composing them, of performing them and of listening to them, all of which are different, but must share a common delight. They must also share an attitude. Unwanted music is something of a contradiction in terms. 'Turn that row off,' we say, whether it is pop or Palestrina, Verdi or a vacuum cleaner. Conversely an attitude in the listener can create music where none has been composed or intended. We like to think that a bird 'singing' is taking delight in making music and expressing its joy in being alive. But ornithologists tell us that he is a defiant 'king of the castle' warning the other 'dirty rascals' off his territory. The endless variations on a few 'themes' which characterize the more beautiful songsters could easily be produced by a very simple computer, and therefore need not be a conscious selection of sounds by the bird, in which case it is we who create the music by our attitude to what the bird utters.

A fault in a long-distance telephone line in the United States resulted in a series of sounds which an engineer recorded. The sounds are very beautiful. To me they are music. Not a complete piece but nonetheless music, or we should have to deny the name of music to the few existing bars of the scherzo of Schubert's 'Unfinished' Symphony and to the final fugue of Bach's *The Art of Fugue*. Whether they considered them to be music or not, most people would agree that bird-song and the telephone-line sounds were pleasant sounds. They would not feel the same about, say, the noise of traffic in a busy street. Yet it is possible, although far from easy, for a listener to think of any sounds as music. To do this he must suspend his normal reactions to everyday sounds, which is to ignore those which do not concern him. He must concentrate on all the sounds *as sounds* – continuous – spasmodic – increasing – recurring – deep – rich – thin and so on. As for form, certain sounds will tend to recur in more or less the same order. For example different people going through the same doorway and up the same steps will provide 'variations' on a 'theme'.

Of course this is very far from being everybody's kind of music. It is perhaps the end of the road, for the listener has become his own composer. Since music is not the sounds themselves, but the experience of them, anybody who says 'This isn't music,' is saying 'I am not having that experience,' which he has every right to say. What he has no right to say is: 'Neither are *you* having that experience.'

Our 1857 critic was absolutely right, then, when he very carefully spoke only for himself in saying, of part of Beethoven's Fifth Symphony, '. . . it does not belong at all to that art which *I am in the habit of considering as* music' (my italics). He would probably not disagree with the definition of music which ran thus: the pleasurable, satisfying, sometimes uplifting, sometimes awe-inspiring, sometimes devastating experience brought about by certain successive and simultaneous combinations of sounds. He would not disagree because the definition makes no attempt to say *what* sounds and how combined.

That will be the task of the rest of this book.

2 THE RISE OF THE ART OF MUSIC
The earliest beginnings

When we look at reproductions of the life-like pictures that palaeolithic man engraved and painted on the walls of his dwelling caves, we may well wonder whether he possessed an art of sound equally advanced. A wall painting of c. 15,000 BC in the Trois Frères cave in France shows a man, dressed apparently in the skin and horns of a bison, playing a 'mouth-bow'. This instrument, which exists in primitive tribes today (or did until recently), is like a small hunting bow, the string of which is plucked or struck and held in or very close to the open mouth, which can act as a changeable resonating cavity producing the notes of the harmonic series (q.v.). In principle it works like a Jew's (jaw's) harp, and anyone with a stick, a piece of string and palaeolithic technology can make one in a few minutes. The bison-man in the picture appears to be dancing and it is tempting to suppose that he is playing a tune on his mouth-bow and dancing or stamping his feet in time to it. But there would probably be no rhythmic relationship between his stamping feet and the sounds upon his mouth-bow, which we could barely call a tune even in the vaguest sense.

If he had a word for his 'music', it would probably be something like 'sound-magic'. Curt Sachs distinguishes between the obvious expected sounds produced by stamping, hand-clapping and hitting most objects, and the less expected sounds produced by stretched strings, reed pipes, etc. 'In the former group a motor impulse finds an expected audible result; in the latter an action . . . is unexpectedly followed by a sound which consequently has an unexplained and frightening character. . . . Something living, a spirit or demon has answered.'[1] A mouth-bow, incidentally, is an instrument which is virtually inaudible to anybody other than its player, and therefore could not take an effective part in communal music-making in any modern sense.

Music, unlike painting, is a non-representational art. The equivalent in sound of a life-like pictorial representation of an animal would not be music (in our sense), but an equally life-like imitation of an animal's cries, something primitive hunting man is invariably highly adept at. He is equally skilful at imitating an animal's movements, which he does in his mimetic animal dances, accompanied by the appropriate animal cries. Many primitive cultures are totemistic. The totem gods (who were the ancestors of man) each created one type of animal or object in which his spirit still resides. A man's skilful imitation of an animal's cries and movements is not then just showing off, but a being-at-one with his particular totem god. The sounds are especially important, since to primitive man they *are* the spirit, the soul of the dead ancestor, whether he resides in a bison or a mouth-bow, a kookaburra or a bull-roarer.

When man learned to sow and reap, he had to make noises with clappers and rattles and such to scare away the birds and other

[1] C. Sachs, *The History of Musical Instruments*, p. 37 Dent, 1942, orig. Dutton 1940.

animals from the crops. He used similar instruments to scare away the demons, others to woo the rain god, others to appease the hailstorm god and so on. A particular instrument would represent a particular god. In fertility rites and initiation ceremonies (as with peoples at similar stages of development today and recently), the obvious sexual associations of particular instruments and instrumental playing would dictate their roles, feminine for drums played with the hands, gourd instruments etc, masculine for wind instruments, drumsticks etc.

Early music is thus inextricably bound up with ritual, and it would seem that it was through ritualistic sound-making that man first assumed the special attitude to sounds which gives rise to the experience we call music. Music-making today is not without its ritual. The applause and the taking of bows at a concert, the high-priest conductor, the formal dress, the strict protocol – woe betide the second fiddle player who leaves the platform before the leader (concert master)!

The early civilizations

Man's earliest known civilization was in Mesopotamia between the rivers Tigris and Euphrates. This was well under way by 4000 BC. By between 3000 and 2000 BC the Sumerian peoples were performing elaborate temple rituals with chanting of hymns and playing of flutes, reed pipes, lyres, harps and various sorts of drum. Each hymn had its own 'tune', usually associated with a particular instrument. Some of the music of the early Indian civilizations of c. 1500 BC has survived to this day probably almost unchanged. The hymns of the *Rigveda* (literally 'Book of knowledge of hymns') are still chanted in a particular way in many Indian temples, apparently just as they were over 3000 years ago. The ritualistic magical element is strong in Indian classical music today. The player improvises, basing his music on a particular *raga*, which is something more than a scale or mode and less than a theme. The ragas (and there are over sixty of them) are very ancient, are assigned to particular times of the day or night and have particular associations, e.g. peace, youth, colours, etc.

The early Chinese civilization of c. 2000 BC went in for seasonal agricultural festivals. These would involve choirs of boys and girls singing alternately and then together, and two groups of instrumentalists playing likewise. They were supposed to symbolize *Yang* and *Yin*, the two opposite poles of the universe, which would be thus

24

united in 'harmony'. Sexual rites would follow. Chinese music right down to the present day has generally confined itself to a five-note or pentatonic scale. This scale is to be found today on the extreme fringes of the Europe–Asia land mass, in China, Lapland and Scotland. This suggests that it was perhaps universal before two more notes were added to make the seven-note scale (heptatonic) which was the basis of virtually all Western music right up to the 20th century, and still is of a great deal of it. (The black notes on a piano keyboard will give a pentatonic scale.) But counting the number of different notes in a tune does not always give us the right answer. 'Auld Lang Syne' is one of the very few Scots tunes that really are completely pentatonic. A great many more of them confine themselves at first to the five notes but then stick in a sixth one just to be difficult – 'Loch Lomond'; 'The Eriskay love lilt'; 'Comin' through the rye', etc. Very primitive cultures have tunes made up of a group of three notes which is later repeated higher or lower giving six notes in all. Or a two-note group may be repeated many times getting steadily higher or lower giving a total of six or seven. So it would be wrong to regard the five-note scale as necessarily being any older than the six- or seven-note scale. I shall have more to say about scales later on (p 94).

Ancient Egyptian civilization is nearly as old as Mesopotamian, and there was probably some contact between the two well before c. 2500 BC, since at that time they had many instruments in common, although the Egyptian instruments were at an earlier stage of development. Various invading tribes brought in other instruments between c. 2000 and 1500 BC when the Pharaohs, pushing eastward, came into contact again with Mesopotamia. By c. 1200 BC or earlier, the Egyptians had far surpassed the Mesopotamians in the use and technique of all kinds of instruments – many types of harp; lyres; pandores (long-necked lutes); flutes; double reed-pipes; trumpets; clappers; bells; drums; sistra (rattles with metal plates probably sounding very like their name which is not unlike the name of the god Osiris, whose special instrument and therefore whose voice they were).

From the tombs we have numerous highly accurate pictures of music-making and of some of the instruments themselves but not a single note of the music, for the Egyptians made no attempt to write it down If the music of the songs was anywhere near as beautiful as some of the words, it was fine indeed. There were professional musicians of both sexes, the art often being handed down from father to son (or daughter). The general word for music was *hy* which meant 'joy', and it seems that music was enjoyed by everyone except a few fuddy-duddies who, according to a writer of the first century BC considered music useless, immoral and effeminate. That sort of person existed even then. But perhaps the fuddy-duddies had a point. Herodotus (c. 484–425 BC) tells us of a crowd of 700,000 pilgrims led by flute or reed-pipe players, some of the women frenziedly jingling their sistra, while others exposed themselves.

The Egyptians had a more 'classical' side to their music though. Plato (c. 429–347 BC) approved of their strict keeping to the rules (*nomoi*) – whatever those rules were, for no Egyptian book on the theory of music has come down to us. But the first of a long line of Greek music theorists spent many years of study in Egypt and later in Babylon in Mesopotamia. This was Pythagoras (c. 585–474 BC), the Greek philosopher and mathematician. Some of the theories and discoveries attributed to him (for he left no writings) are very probably of Egyptian or Mesopotamian origin.

Pythagoras and his followers were seeking a simple mathematical relationship between the different notes used in various musical scales, in order to relate this to other 'sciences', mainly astronomy – 'the Music of the Spheres'. As a result we know quite a lot about the scales and modes of ancient Greek music but very little about the music itself. The Greeks had a music notation from quite an early date – the notes were given the letters of the alphabet just as we talk about the notes C, D, E etc. – but they apparently made very little use of it. The earliest example we have is a papyrus of c. 250 BC. A hundred years before that Plato was writing of a great art in decline. Music was becoming mere entertainment. Of the later music most of the examples we have (all vocal) do not indicate the rhythm, which can only be very vaguely guessed at from the words. One piece, the 'Epitaph of Seikilos', has rhythmic indications which rather surprisingly show it to have a rhythm – *short* long *short* long – very prevalent in mediaeval times a thousand years on. But of the notes, as in all Greek pieces, we can never be very sure, so any modern performance should be taken with a large pinch of salt. This is mainly because it might be in one of a number of different modes (Phrygian; Dorian, etc.) which were named after different regions of Greece and determined not only the notes used but also the style and emotional quality, although the latter two distinctions were breaking down in Plato's day.

The main instruments of ancient Greece were the lyre (*kithara*) and the reed-pipe (*aulos*). The lyre was the more 'classical' instrument associated with Phoebus ('shining') Apollo, the god of youthful manly beauty. Being a plucked stringed instrument it was ideal for accompanying the voice. The louder, less refined, more 'romantic' *aulos* was the instrument of Dionysus, the god of wine. Each god had his cult, the Apollonian more intellectual, formal and controlled; the Dionysian, sensuous, more abandoned – two dispositions which have vied with one another throughout musical history. At various times one or the other has been more in the ascendant, for example the Apollonian in Mozart and the Dionysian in Wagner. Or sometimes the battle rages within the one individual, as in Beethoven. The modern pop festival is highly Dionysian, although the instrument is not the reed-pipe but the plucked string, a reversal of role made possible by electronic amplification. Apollo is suitably appalled in the many who disapprove. Guitar and kithara are obviously the same word if not precisely the same instrument.

The musical legacy to us from the ancient Greeks is not through their music itself but through their literature which inspired, for instance, the humanistic individualism which was the basis of the Renaissance. Opera began as an attempt to re-create Greek drama in the way it was believed to have been performed, namely sung throughout. We now know that this was not so, although music played a vital part in it. The music theorist has usually been an observer of what the practical musician already does, but although Pythagoras and his followers probably did not contribute much to the advancement of Greek music, the experiments and measurements they made were necessary to the understanding of the mathematics of the tuning of instruments, without which many later developments like harmony (q.v.), chromaticism (q.v.) etc. would have been impossible. But for the music itself we must look a little further to the East.

The Jews and the early Christian Church

By the rivers of Babylon, there we sat down, yea we wept, when we remembered Zion.

We hanged our harps upon the willows in the midst thereof.

For there they that carried us away captive required of us a song; and they that wasted us required of us mirth, saying, Sing us one of the songs of Zion.

How shall we sing the Lord's song in a strange land?

(from Psalm 137)

That piece of ancient Jewish history (c. 600 BC) is particularly well known because the song is sung or spoken in churches all over

Christendom as well as in synagogues world-wide. The captivity of the Jews in Babylon would not have been the first Jewish contact with Mesopotamian culture and we know well, from earlier in the Bible, of the Jews' sojourn in Egypt. With all this ancient Jewish literature in continuous use in the Christian church, much of it sung, it is more than possible that some of the music would come down to us as well. And indeed there are strong similarities between some of the melodies the Oriental Jews sing their psalms to, and the old Plainsong melodies, which were the sole music of the Christian church up till about the 10th century and the basis of church music for another 300 years, and which are still very widely used.

Plainsong or Plainchant is often called Gregorian chant, after Pope St Gregory (540–604) who until very recently was thought to have been the composer or at any rate the original compiler of the chants. In fact several popes before Gregory are said to have made editions. These have not survived, nor have Gregory's, but in any case, if the music was written down, the notation of the period was not precise enough to have been much more than an *aide-mémoire*; we cannot therefore be sure of the antiquity of any particular Plainsong melody. It is a fair assumption, however, that the general nature of Plainsong is very old indeed, although we should not assume that modern performances make it sound as it did a thousand or more years ago. *The Pelican History of Music* (vol. 1) has an excellent section on Plainsong.

3 THE RISE OF POLYPHONY

In its literal sense of many simultaneous different sounds, polyphony is as old as communal music-making. Primitive peoples will tend to sing or play *more or less* the same tune together, with resulting occasional divergences into more than one note at a time. This heterophony, as it is called, is something not often found in our Western music today. A rare example was formerly practised at community singings (perhaps still is) by singing the two First World War songs, 'It's a long way to Tipperary' and 'Pack up your Troubles' simultaneously. The two tunes are so alike that the notes do not part company for too long at a time. At the time of writing (1975) there is an orchestra in the South of England where, I believe, the qualifications for joining are that you must have an instrument, but not really be able to play it. The result is an interesting degree of heterophony. Long may it survive.

But heterophony need not be a primitive device at all. Accompanying the voice with a plucked stringed instrument goes back to the earliest civilizations. The method almost certainly employed was that the stringed instrument (harp, lyre, pandore or whatever) played a decorated version of the tune the singer sang. Solo song was probably accompanied in this manner from the Mesopotamians to the Middle Ages. The nature of our Western development of harmony has rather ruled heterophony out of court (although it is with us again in some modern works) but it is extensively employed in other musics the world over. So also is another very ancient device, the drone, which is a continuous unchanging note sounding all the time, perhaps best known to our ears through the bagpipes, a very old instrument. One of the pipes of the Egyptian double reed-pipe was often a drone and it is likely that the harp and lyre players sounded one or two of their strings more or less continuously, as Indian sitar players do today. The drone is highly significant in relation to the development of tonality or key (see p 42), there being a tendency for a tune to 'home' on to the drone note, although this is something of a chicken and egg situation, since it could have been the 'homing' tendency which is tonality, that first suggested the idea of the drone.

Another device of polyphony which would be likely to happen in the first instance more or less by chance, is what we would now drily call a canon. Two or more people or groups of people sing or play the same song or tune, but start at different times. In a sense the first voice (or voices) is pursued by the others. Hunting songs were sung in this way probably from prehistoric times, a practice which survived into the Middle Ages and beyond as something actually called a 'chase', although by then composers were taking great care over how the different notes sounding together 'fitted' with one another. Polyphony in the sense we usually use the word had arrived.

The frontispiece of this book shows the manuscript of the famous round 'Sumer is icumen in'. It is not strictly a chase because the words are not about hunting, but it is a canon. Notice the Maltese cross quite near the beginning. The second voice starts the song when the first voice gets to that point, the third voice starts when the second voice gets there and the fourth voice when the third gets there. Put together, probably by a monk of Reading Abbey c. 1280, it is not quite the extraordinarily precocious phenomenon it was once supposed to be but it is a remarkable piece for its time, having in addition two more voices singing a sort of two-chord accompaniment, not unlike the blow-suck chords of a mouth-organ or concertina.

Men and women or men and boys singing the same song together will not be singing the same notes. They will be singing in 'octaves', always keeping eight notes apart, that is eight notes apart in *pitch* (q.v.), the women or boys always eight notes or an octave above the men. This makes no polyphony or harmony, because notes an octave apart sounded together sound strangely like one note. We often call it unison (one sound, i.e. the same note) singing which, strictly speaking, it is not. Singing any other number of notes apart produces some sort of harmony, yet it is something that could easily happen by chance (and does) if two or more people start the same tune on different notes. The practice of singing or playing four or five notes apart (we usually talk about 'parallel fourths or fifths') is probably very old indeed. It is often called 'organum' although the word can be applied to most early polyphony. It appears in Western music in the 10th century which is about the time from which Western polyphony in general *appears* to date, but what really dates from that time is a practical means of notation, and therefore of preservation of an art that almost certainly goes back further.

In the early Middle Ages the church exercised a very strict control over its music. Only in certain parts of the liturgy were composers permitted to adorn the Plainsong with additional notes. Parallel fourths and fifths which added new notes but no new melody were the most readily allowed. A little naughtier was the addition of notes keeping the same rhythm as the Plainsong, but no longer keeping parallel, so that there were now two tunes stepping strictly together but diverging, converging and sometimes passing through one another. The intervals between the voices, that is the differences in pitch between them, were still mainly fourths, fifths, octaves and unisons. Composers soon went further, setting more than one note against each note of the Plainsong. Here now we have true 'counterpoint' – two (or more) simultaneous melodies each with its own distinct rhythm. The word 'organum' originally meant any musical *instrument*, perhaps especially including the organ. There were organs in the 10th century. Winchester cathedral had one with 400 pipes and three simultaneous players called 'strikers', for it probably took a heavy fist to put down one key. It is possible that the three of them 'struck' some notes simultaneously but more likely, I think, that they operated consecutively like bell-ringers. An organ of this nature would be well suited to the slow rendering of a Plainsong melody, while voices (and perhaps other instruments played with fingers rather than fists) wove around it a relatively florid counterpoint.

There is an element of the very ancient device of the drone here. Since instruments were certainly employed as well as voices, I shall from now on refer to the simultaneous different strands of melody as 'parts', although the word 'voices' can be used to mean exactly the same thing even with instruments.

Plainsong is neither in two-time nor three-time, or rather it is continuously changing from the one to the other, and its pulse rate or tempo tends to surge, to get faster or slower. Where the other parts have the same rhythm, there is no problem, but where the parts have different rhythms these rhythms have to be comparatively simple, and all have to share a steady, rigid common tempo in order for them to be able to keep together. This caused the whole special rhythmic quality of the Plainsong to go straight out of the chancel window. It led later to two practices – the removal of the rhythm altogether, by stretching out the Plainsong (now called the cantus firmus or 'fixed song') into immensely long notes like rocks in the flowing stream of the other parts (this would suit the early organs); and the technique of isorhythm (literally 'the same rhythm'), which deliberately imposes on the Plainsong an unchanging repeated rhythm of a fixed number of notes, which is unrelated to the number of notes in the Plainsong, and so does not fit. The Plainsong is thus arbitrarily chopped into equal-sized pieces, rather like cutting a picture into equal-sized triangles. At first isorhythm always went with another chopping-up device, the 'hocket' (see p 54). These devices are not composers' ways of paying lip-service to their early masters, for they did it to secular tunes as well, but of using the Plainsong as a theme rather than as an expressive melody.

Nevertheless the church did not approve. In a famous bull of 1322, the eighty-two-year-old Pope John XXII scorned those 'disciples of the new school who chop up the melodies with hockets, lubricate them with discants and even insert popular songs in the upper voices'. The multitudinous notes, he says, 'run about unceasingly, inebriating, not soothing the ears . . . devotion is disregarded, lasciviousness promoted'.[1] All he was prepared to allow on pain of punishment were the old parallel fourths, fifths and octaves, which would be putting the clock back some 200 years. Luckily for us, composers seem not to have taken much notice. There had long been a practice tolerated by the church of 'troping' the liturgy – adding extra words to existing music, for instance in the long-drawn-out alleluias and

[1] My own translation from the Latin as quoted in *The Oxford History of Music*, vol. I, 1929.

then sometimes adding new music to the new words. Here was a chance for a composer to write something entirely his own, as was also the *conductus*, a piece to be sung as the priest was 'conducted' from one part of the church to another. But the practice of building on the old foundations died very hard, and it was not until the 15th century that really freely imaginative polyphonic composition got off the ground.

In the history of music, the only Englishman to point the way forward to his European colleagues was John Dunstable, who died in 1453. His motets are still based on Plainsong and one cannot fully appreciate them without knowing the particular Plainsong melody involved, but instead of this being only rigorously plodded through as a cantus firmus in a middle voice to an arbitrary rhythm, it is now the theme of a free-ranging melodic variation in the top voice. This incidentally releases the Plainsong from its rhythmic strait-jacket, restoring a lot of its spiritual quality. At the same time, with all the voices free, the composer's imagination can take wing. Dunstable's harmony makes full use of parallel thirds and sixths, which had been in use in the British Isles for centuries, although not usually written down.

Continental composers seem to have been far more conservative in sticking to the fourths and fifths, probably not so much because of Pope John as of Pythagoras who, because he could not fit thirds and sixths into his simplistic mathematical 'perfect' scheme of things, therefore called *them* 'imperfect'. Not the only example in music of progress being delayed by faulty theories. Dunstable's innovations were avidly taken up by composers on the Continent. Great names appear – Dufay; Josquin des Près; Isaac. This is the early Renaissance. Humanity and imaginative expression are coming to the fore – composers are freely writing both religious and secular music and the cross-fertilization of the two is complete. Settings for the Mass still often use a cantus firmus, but this itself may be a popular secular song. The famous 'L'homme armé' ('The armed man') was a great favourite. Where mediaeval polyphony employed one singer to each line of melody (part), Renaissance polyphony employed many, thereby enriching the sheer sensuous sound of the music.

In the next century (the 16th) we find more familiar, but not greater names – Lassus; Byrd; Palestrina – writing in a polyphonic style generally a little simpler and certainly more familiar, since the underlying harmonic formulae are still in use in a lot of music today. Polyphony continued for another century and a half, notably in the great

German tradition which culminated and ended with J. S. Bach. But the arrival of opera in about 1600 had marked the re-emergence of monody (one main melody) into the main stream of music. No good composer, though, however monodic his style, could afford not to have studied the great polyphonic composers of the Renaissance, for a good accompaniment (certainly up to 1900) is not hewn or cast, but woven from a number of melodic strands. Mozart knew it well, and Wagner, but so did Johann Strauss and John Philip Sousa.

4 THE DEVELOPMENT OF MUSIC NOTATION

The problem of communicating music in writing – notation – was for long tangled up, and even now remains, in some of its elements, foolishly illogical and unnecessarily complicated. That is not to frighten anyone from learning it: to read music, even a little, gives one a great advantage as a music-lover, and should be attempted by all amateurs who want to make progress through the many attractive mansions of the art. It should (but even yet does not) go without saying that all children ought to learn to read music at school. It is a sad and odd reflection on our educational system that young men and women can leave a university unable to read the simplest song tune: as odd as if one were to profess oneself a lover of books, and be entirely dependent for the enjoyment of literature on hearing somebody else read them.

Nowadays so much of our music is written down that we are surprised to find ancient civilizations either apparently having no music notation or, when they had it, not bothering to use it much. However, with a little thought we can see that they simply did not need it. We all learn music in the very first instance, whether singing or playing an instrument, by imitating the sounds others make. Rather as we learn to talk, which we do long before we learn to read. One of the reasons the Suzuki method of violin teaching leads so quickly to astonishing results, is that the children learn by heart and retain tune after tune without all the added problems of trying to read the music, which in itself is a highly complex intellectual process. The process of learning to sing or play in the ancient world was probably much the same. Complicated dexterous embellishments, which might be difficult to remember, would be improvised anyway and there would be no point in even trying to write them down any more than there would be in jazz today. With no harmony in our sense, a composer would not need to give carefully notated instructions to the different instruments in an orchestra, since they would all be playing more or less the same tune, and the percussion instruments would probably be struck according to some well-known rhythmic pattern. Nevertheless a composer/performer (and the non-performing composer must have been a rarity until fairly modern times) would occasionally need an *aide-mémoire*, and this is really all that the earliest forms of notation were.

If the Mesopotamians and the ancient Egyptians had any music notation, it was very far from being in general use. The Greeks used the letters of the alphabet to denote the notes of the scale, at first only for instruments in a fairly simple and direct form that was closer to tablature (see below), and later for voices in a form which became more and more complicated and impractical as time went on. The Chinese probably used something similar, for they gave names with corresponding characters to each note. In about 100 BC a master is known to have written down a zither tune for his pupil – maybe in the character notation, but more probably in tablature, which is a word for any notation system which tells the player not what notes he is to play, but where to put his fingers on the instrument. Tablature has been used in many periods, mainly for keyboard and plucked string instruments – especially the lute. Today guitar chords are sometimes shown as a picture of part of the guitar finger-board with blobs for the finger positions.

Plainsong was at one time notated according to the Greek alphabetical notation, simplified and adapted to Roman letters. Later from Byzantium came an entirely different system – neumes. In their simplest form these were short sloping lines like acute and grave accents, placed above the words of the text to indicate how many notes there should be to a syllable, and very roughly the rise and fall of the melody. There were additional signs – dots, short horizontal lines, curved lines etc. to indicate certain types of melodic movement. Neumes could enable a singer to remember and perform expressively a tune he already knew, but could do little more than that, since neither the rhythm nor the exact pitch of the notes was indicated. For centuries, scribes had been scratching a horizontal line across the parchment to keep their writing straight, but it was a long time before anyone saw that such a line could be used to represent a note of a specific pitch, so that neumes on, above or below the line would refer to notes on, above or below that specific note.

In the 11th century, probably as a result of the innovations of Guido d'Arezzo (died 1050), this line which had been vaguely used here and there before, was first inked in in red (neumes were black) to refer to the note F. Obviously one line was not enough and very soon another one, a yellow one, appeared for the note C and finally two more (uninked at first) to make the four lines the neumes move about on in the notation still used for Plainsong today. The different colours were soon replaced by the more flexible clef system, which meant putting a letter (C, F, G, or in the early days D) on one of the lines to fix it as representing that note. Our modern staff notation does just this although the signs we put on the lines for G = 𝄞, F = 𝄢 and C = 𝄡 do not look much like the letters any more (see p 120). It is worth noticing that in doing this we are using the adapted Greek alphabetical system, as we do when we talk about the notes C, D, E etc, although we do not actually read music from them.

Guido d'Arezzo did two important things. He arranged matters so that if a certain note is on a line, the next note up or down the scale is in the space between that line and the next, and so on up or down – line – space – line – space etc. Not an ideal arrangement, but in nearly a thousand years no one has come up with anything better. The standard grouping of the lines in sets of five called the staff or stave came in a good deal later. 'Sumer is icumen in' (c. 1280) on the frontispiece of this book has a stave of six lines. These notational niceties were becoming necessary because as we saw in chapter three (p 30) organized polyphony was coming into use. It was now very important that the different voices should keep on the right notes in relation to each other. Very important too that they should get their different rhythms right.

It is, on the face of it, odd that the longest note normally used in our notation today is called a semibreve, which literally means 'half a short one', and that the next longest note is called a minim, which comes from *minima* (literally 'the smallest'), but at one time these really were the shortest notes. This does not mean that the music was all terribly slow. In that papal bull of 1322, which I quoted in chapter three (p 31), Pope John complains about the multitude of notes 'running about unceasingly'. He goes on: 'the liturgy is sung in semibreves and minims peppered with even smaller notelets'. These 'notelets' were presumably the ultra-high-speed crotchets! I am reminded of a certain organization representing musicians' interests which apparently issued, not so long ago, some similar sort of bull, requiring composers not to write so many semiquavers! Mediaeval rhythmic notation was excessively complicated, being tied up with things called rhythmic modes, which meant that the same rhythmic notation could mean different things. Many attempts were made to sort this out and there were treatises galore, but it was not until the 17th century that the notation we still use was standardized. The movement towards the use of shorter note values, making the semibreve (𝆺) the longest note in general use, probably arose because notes with tails (minim 𝅗𝅥; crotchet 𝅘𝅥) are easier to read, and notes which can be grouped together (quavers 𝅘𝅥𝅮; semiquavers 𝅘𝅥𝅯) are even easier. Keyboard instruments which could be played very fast indeed were being developed from the late 16th century.

Bar-lines, the upright lines drawn across the stave at regular intervals of time, originated as indications of the ends of sections. In 16th-century polyphony they acted as guides at *irregular* intervals, to keep the voices together. It is this freer use of the now strait-jacketing bar-line that gives such rhythmic suppleness to the earlier music. One should always listen to madrigals, for example, bearing it in mind. The 17th century saw the standardization of our present use of barlines, of time signatures and of key signatures (the placing of the key's necessary sharps or flats together at the start of the line). The flat sign (♭) on the note B at the start of each line of 'Sumer is icumen in' on the frontispiece does in practice work as a key signature, but no such thing existed in the 13th century. It is, in fact, telling the singers to use the hexachord (six-note scale) with the 'soft' B (B molle) sometimes called the 'round' B, written b and corresponding to our B flat (B♭). The other kind of B was the 'hard' B (B durum) or 'square' B, written ♮ and corresponding to our B natural (B♮). So there were two kinds of B. This shows that the fundamental deficiency of our system was there from the start. One position on the stave could mean either of two notes, thus necessitating an additional hieroglyph to tell us which. As composers used more notes, so more alternatives appeared until each of the lines and spaces could refer to at least four different notes. Performers have been putting up with this for a long time now, as the twelve notes of the chromatic scale have been in use since the 16th century, but tremendous problems arise when, in the 20th century, composers start to divide up the octave into twenty-four notes (quarter tones) and more. One way with quarter tones is to write half sharps, half flats, one-and-a-half sharps and one-and-a-half flats giving *eight* possible pitches for one position on the stave. The American composer Harry Partch, who divides the octave into forty-two unequal parts, uses what becomes a sort of keyboard tablature, since his microtonal harmonium has a conventional keyboard, which means that to play two notes sounding an octave apart, two keys forty-three notes apart, i.e. visually three-and-a-half octaves apart, have to be depressed and the music notated accordingly.

Many 20th-century composers have found conventional notation unsatisfactory rhythmically. The so-called 'tyranny' of the bar-line, forcing every bar into the same number of beats, is easily dealt with by leaving the bar-line out altogether, as Charles Ives did early in the century, or by changing the time signature, if necessary every bar, as Stravinsky did in, for instance, the *Rite of Spring*. The French conductor Roger Desormière devised a system of open boxes ($\sqcup$) and triangles ($\triangle$), which are much easier for conductors to read than the $\frac{5}{16}$s, $\frac{7}{8}$s or $\frac{11}{14}$s etc. of much 20th-century music. Many conductors and some composers (e.g. Messiaen) add them to their scores.

The absolute serialists of the 1950s demanded absolute precision from their performers. In order to control mathematically all the variables (parameters) of their music, they could ask for twelve different degrees of loudness, twelve different ways of attacking each note as well as rhythms nearly impossible to play accurately (see p 60). With a few additional hieroglyphics, traditional staff notation was sufficiently precise for this, but the performers were not. So they had to go and make way for the electronic studio and the tape recorder. Electronic music which is recorded on magnetic tape needs no notation, except possibly for study purposes. The composer has in a sense already been the performer. In another sense, we can say that the notation has become so definitive that the piece can be played by a machine. This was the watershed – absolute precision, absolute control, but only one immutable, albeit authoritative, pickled version of the music. It was dead, and so the imprecise no-two-exactly-alike live musicians had to be brought back to play together with the tape. Musicians playing with the tape will need some form of notation, traditional or otherwise, for the music they play, as well as something to keep them synchronized with the electronic music on the tape. Timings in seconds and minutes will have to appear on the score, and except for very short sections, a stop-watch will probably be needed. For some pieces a graphic representation of the sounds on the tape can be used – squiggles, dots, lines, hailstorms etc.

Since the 1950s the movement in music has been generally *away* from precision, or rather away from precision in those areas where precision was previously important. Conventional notation, arising as it did with organized polyphony, concentrated on precisely notating the *relationships* of pitch and rhythm between the different voices and instruments. Until the appearance of the metronome in the early 19th century, indications of tempo (the speed at which a piece is played or sung) were either non-existent or in words like *allegro* ('gay'), *adagio* ('slowly'), *andante* ('at a walking pace') and so on, all fairly vague indications. Metronome marks could tell the performers exactly how many crotchets, minims or whatever were to go by in one minute. Composers soon found that this was *too precise*. The tempo we play a piece in will vary (within limits) according to the circumstances of its performance, the mood of the performer, the size of the hall, the audience, the nature of the previous piece and so on. A composer's own recording of his work will often depart widely from his own metronome markings.

For quite a lot of the music composed since about 1960, traditional notation is too precise. For instance, a composer may want a number of violins to play high up, but not any particular note. He may want a number of instruments to play certain notes at *approximately* a certain moment. For the one he needs to be able to show high and low but does not need a five-line stave, for the other he needs the stave, but cannot use any conventional rhythmic notation. The notation used for this sort of music is called 'graphic' notation, sometimes 'visual' notation. On it the passage of time usually moves from left to right not in beats and bars, but in such a way that, say, five centimetres on the page represent one second of time. Notes are likely to be represented as horizontal lines of length proportional to the duration of the note. They can slope upwards or downwards at different angles or go up or down stepwise depending whether a glissando (sliding note) or a scalewise movement is asked for. (Back to the old neumes. See p 34.) A line can be narrow, representing a single note at a time, or thick, representing a number of adjacent notes in a cluster, the exact composition of which may or may not be designated. Stave lines can come and go as needed, and various hieroglyphics indicate special ways of playing an instrument – plucking the strings of a piano – bowing a stringed instrument on the 'wrong' side of the bridge – blowing down a clarinet without the reed sounding and so on. Some of these may be mere fashionable gimmicks, in which case their hieroglyphics will perish with them, but it is clear that, for a large and probably increasing body of music from now on, the traditional barred staff notation will not suffice.

We must not suppose that once organized polyphony had arrived, other forms of music just stopped. A more or less continuous tradition of solo song with instrumental accompaniment probably ran down through Greek and Roman times to the Middle Ages, dividing up and being modified by the different European peoples and languages. But we cannot have any real idea what any of it sounded like until, in the 12th century in Provence, the troubadours started to write down the notes of just a few of their many songs. Even then the rhythm has largely to be guessed at from the words. The troubadours (literally 'finders') wrote mostly songs of courtly love, but also political songs and even devotional songs to the Virgin Mary, a fusion of Christianity and chivalry which was to inspire composers for hundreds of years, and particularly during the Renaissance. The art spread northwards where the trouvères (the same word as troubadour in the language of northern France) wrote similar songs although more formal. There were more professionals among the trouvères, some of whom wrote in polyphonic forms as well. In Germany the Minnesingers (literally 'love-singers'), mostly noblemen, practised their courtly art of making and singing love lyrics. Wagner's Tannhäuser was a Minnesinger. With the changing political system and the decline of the power of the nobility, the city guilds began to flourish with their musical societies. Guilds of Meistersinger (Master singers, i.e. poet-composer-singers) with their song contests and pious insistence on strict rule, existed not only in the Nuremberg of Wagner's opera. Hans Sachs, a central character in that opera, was a notable Meistersinger in the 16th century.

Mediaeval songs were often danced to as well as sung. Some of the troubadour and trouvère songs are very dance-like. Since there was no harmony (except probably a drone; see p 29), accompanying instrumentalists would be playing the tune anyway and they certainly played very often on their own without the voice. A song followed by a dance and vice versa was common in mediaeval plays. Purely instrumental dances began to be written down in the 13th century, but they must have existed long before that. The French-speaking English court imported the troubadour and trouvère art, and Richard I (Coeur de Lion) actually practised both. Probably because of this, English song was able to carry on more or less unaffected by the more formal courtly art, and it may be that this greater freedom – possibly allied to a tradition of spontaneous polyphonic singing, which certainly the Welsh had as early as the 12th century – had something to do with John Dunstable's emancipation of the process of composition in the 15th century (see p 32).

6 THE GROWTH AND PROGRESS OF MUSICAL FORM

Music cannot exist without form any more than a potato can have no shape. A single note has form, but what we usually mean by form in music is the perceptible logical progression from the beginning to the end of a piece, usually by means of a balanced amount of repetition and non-repetition.

Some primitive music will seem too repetitive to our ears – for instance a child's incessant reiteration of the same few notes or even of the same single note. But much primitive music is more subtle, repeating a fragment higher up or lower down, repeating it after something different, repeating it with alterations, even repeating it by different voices before the first voices have finished. These represent in embryo most of the formal devices of sophisticated composers – sequence, development, ternary form, rondo, canon, all of which we shall look at later.

With vocal music the form the words take is bound to be reflected in the music. Very old indeed must be the strophic song, where the same music is repeated to different words for each stanza. A strophic song might have a refrain as well, where the same music will recur to the *same* words. This also goes far into the past. Some examples, though not so old, are 'Rule Britannia'; 'Dashing away with the smoothing iron'; 'Marching through Georgia'. The trouvères were very fond of highly organized relationships between words and music. In the *rondeau* for instance the tune falls into two sections, both repeated while the lyric has five different lines, the first two repeated. The pattern is:

music	A	B	A	A	A	B	A	B
words	a	b	c	a	d	e	a	b

Plainsong structures are multifarious, depending not always so much on the words as on their original ritualistic manner of performance. For example some of the chants are antiphonal, that is to be sung by two groups of singers alternately. Others are responsorial, meaning that a chorus 'responds' to a solo singer. A cruder responsorial form occurs in some work-songs like this well-known sea shanty (chanty).

solo	Boney was a warrior
chorus (as they haul)	Way-ay-ah
solo	Boney was a warrior
chorus	John François

From this sort of thing probably stems the tendency for musical phrases to group themselves in matching or opposing pairs. Think of or listen to the opening of Beethoven's Fifth Symphony, or the first prelude of Bach's '48', where not only does very nearly everything happen twice, but the pairs so formed fall into pairs themselves.

Organized polyphony as we have seen began as an adornment of Plainsong, but soon destroyed the Plainsong's rhythmic character. The theorists were hard at work and mediaeval polyphonic structures were highly mathematical, with the figure three (the 'perfect' number because of the Trinity) looming large. If a two appeared it was as two sets of three or three sets of two. Isorhythms usually came in three sets of three. And the music was usually in three parts (three solo voices). Two-time eventually crept in up the back stairs from secular music in the 14th century.

During the Renaissance the greater expressiveness and melodiousness of the different parts in a polyphonic composition gave them a form of their own, more like solo song, but without any of the predetermined structural restraints, repeats, etc. Little figures of a few notes (often suggested by a Plainsong or other cantus firmus melody) would reappear here and there higher up or lower down or at the same pitch, but not according to any rigid plan. Canti firmi (see pp 31–32) were still used but far more imaginatively and, as we have seen, they no longer had to be Plainsong melodies. The counterpoint between the other parts would probably be either canonic, which meant that some of the parts would have the same melodies as others but start them a few notes later; or it would be imitative, which meant they would imitate each other with similar, but not exactly the same melodies, often starting much the same, and then going their own way. Commonly the two were mixed, possibly two parts in canon, the others imitative. The melodies often changed their rhythmic nature in the middle, perhaps starting with long notes and then changing to a stream of shorter ones. Canon or imitation ensure that both rhythmic qualities happen simultaneously, or the same effect might be achieved by having two different melodies from the start. The words were set phrase by phrase – new phrase, new melody(ies), but a single phrase of the words might be drawn out to a considerable length by having many notes to a syllable (melisma), or by repeating words (commoner in the later Renaissance). The good composer ensured an over-all unity by giving some of the different melodies certain common features. Great variety could be had by different groupings – the high voices might tend to alternate with the low voices, or a six-part piece might reduce to two or three parts only for a middle section (a common practice later on). The whole sound was thus richer than mediaeval polyphony, with several voices to each part as well as the instruments.

The music of this period (15th and early 16th century) is immensely rewarding, particularly that of its greatest masters, Josquin des Près (died 1521) and Heinrich Isaac (died 1577), easier to approach perhaps if you can follow a score, and certainly very exciting to sing. Any choir that sings Byrd, Lassus and Palestrina is missing some of the greatest and most rewarding music ever composed if it does not have a go at Josquin and Isaac.

Secular polyphonic forms (part songs, madrigals etc.) – and Renaissance composers wrote freely both sacred and secular pieces – would naturally tend in some cases to be shorter and more dance-like – more 'bouncy' and often more *homophonic*, which means that the parts move together in the same rhythm, although on different notes – in other words in chords. We are now approaching the harmonized single melody, which was to dominate music from about 1600 on. The later Renaissance did not change the polyphonic forms all that much, apart from throwing out the cantus firmus, but it did standardize the *cadence* (see below). And this meant that they were approaching something else too – the key system.

On page 29 in connection with the ancient device of the drone, I mentioned the tendency of a tune to 'home' on to a certain note. We can call this note the 'final'. Up to the end of the 16th century composers were working with a system of modes. Any tune in a mode has to end on its final, and it is largely the relationship of the other notes in the mode to this note that gives each mode its different character. There were originally considered to be eight modes (later twelve), but really only six different ones (see Part 3, Chapter 1). The key system narrowed the six down to two called major and minor, the major being identical with one of the modes and the minor being a mixture of that mode and another.

Although the key system established itself in the 17th century, it was really only the acknowledgement of what had been happening anyway, through something called *musica ficta* ('falsified music'). This took place mainly at the *cadences*, which are musical endings, equivalent to the inflexions we use in speech to indicate the ends of sentences and clauses. At the end of a sentence for instance we let our voice drop. Although a drop in pitch *is* a cadential device in music (especially Russian music), it is rather limiting. In polyphony from the earliest days composers did the obvious thing to achieve a feeling of finality. They made the parts converge step by step on to the final – a principle which has survived in cadences to this day. And there was a tendency from very early days for the part moving upwards to the final to make it a small step (a semitone) even where the mode demanded a larger (whole tone) step. This is probably because, like a magnet, the nearer one approaches the final the stronger its 'pull', and therefore the greater release of tension and consequently greater finality when one actually arrives. The part moving downwards to the final would not need any alteration, since it would have the natural finality and relaxation of the falling voice as in speech. The result of this was that in polyphony composers tended to use the same cadence whatever the mode, and since cadences came pretty often, some modes were virtually squeezed out of existence. In the latter part of the 16th century the only mode unaffected by musica ficta was the Ionian mode, which is the same as a major key. Two other modes were in effect transformed into the Ionian mode, and the other three became in effect the same thing as a minor key. (See Modes and Scales p 94.)

One interesting consequence of the fact that the modes were altered from a very early date, is that in this century composers like Vaughan Williams were able to find an unexploited area of music, and compose polyphonically in the modes *without* musica ficta, although they rarely do this exclusively. On page 42 I mentioned the tendency of some secular polyphonic pieces to be more homophonic, amounting to a succession of chords. Josquin's 'El Grillo' (the Cricket) and Thomas Morley's 'Now is the month of maying' of a good deal later are fairly well-known examples. These successions of chords tend to form themselves into various characteristic patterns ending with the two chords that make a cadence. Such chord patterns can be used as an accompaniment to a single main melody. I say *main* melody because the chords themselves are made up of a number of simultaneous melodies, which are still there although we do not really hear them as such. A composer or arranger knows when he harmonizes a melody with chords in a traditional manner, that he must think of his chords

43

in this way if his harmony is not to sound stilted and weak ('voice leading' or 'part writing', it is called).

If we simplify the modes to two and we simplify polyphony to a single main melody with chords, we hardly have a richer music, but we certainly have one which is lucid. Just what we need for opera which began with the invention of the new 'recitative style' just before 1600. In recitative the words are sung more or less in their normal speech rhythm, to an entirely free melody, which is given some shape and direction by the accompanying instrumental chords. This is true of early recitative, but it soon began to acquire its own particular melodic patterns. As its counterpart, the formal aria (extended solo song) developed in importance, so recitative declined and became more stereotyped. Both recitative and aria are monody, i.e. a single main accompanied melody, although the accompaniment to an aria would normally be expected to be something more than merely a succession of chords. Polyphony continued for another century and a half and was adapted to the key system, finally succumbing more or less to monody with the death of J. S. Bach conveniently in 1750.

The key system added a new dimension to musical form (although it was not until the 18th century that it was fully exploited). This was the facility to move from one key to others and back, thereby adding a new 'home away and back home again' element which could operate on a larger scale than the home and away element of the final and other notes within a mode. Of course it had previously been possible to move from one *mode* to another. Late 16th-century composers were constantly doing it, often for structural purposes too, but changing mode is likely to be changing mood as well, which might not be desirable. However, because of musica ficta the effect was usually not so much a change of mode as a change of final. And this amounts to the same thing as a change of key. (See p 97.)

Instrumental form
Before the key system, instrumental pieces of any extended length were either instrumental equivalents of vocal polyphony or they were variations (see p 87) – variations usually of dance or popular song tunes. Both types lasted into the period of the key system, the polyphony becoming, in its most highly organized form, the fugue (see p 106) and virtually dying with its greatest master J. S. Bach, while variation form continued in use right through the period and beyond, in spite of the fact that changes of key play no part in variation form as such.

In the late 16th and early 17th centuries, dance tunes were tending more and more to end their different sections on different finals. This gradually crystallized into something called binary form, which came to be used more and more, at first only in quick movements, for example in Corelli's concertos and sonatas, but later in many sorts of movements until by the mid-18th century it was probably the commonest instrumental form. (See p 85.) As its name suggests, it is in two sections, each of which is repeated (or should be). The first section closes in a new key, while the second section starts from there and moves back to the home key. In shorter pieces the second section may go straight back to the home key and stay there. Countless pieces are in binary form, among them most of Domenico Scarlatti's huge number of harpsichord sonatas, and probably nearly every dance tune composed in the 18th century. The rondeau is an exception (see below).

It is interesting to notice how the rhythms of the dance (which were also generally speaking the rhythms of monody) had invaded even vocal polyphony by the 18th century. Compare any of the choruses of Bach's B minor Mass with any 16th-century Mass. I can imagine Lassus or Palestrina saying of the B minor Mass, 'This isn't a Mass, it's a suite of dances. The "Gloria" is a *bassedanse*, the "cum Sancto Spiritu" is a *réjouissance*, the "et resurrexit" a *courante*, the "et expecto" a *bourrée* and the "Sanctus" a *gigue*.' They resemble these dances in rhythm but not in form.

We shall see later on (p 100) how binary form came to be more closely organized into something called sonata form or 'first movement form' and later vastly expanded, although the original binary form was kept for dance movements and shorter pieces. In Beethoven's 'Eroica' Symphony the first movement is a huge sonata-form structure, while the main funeral march tune of the slow movement is in binary form.

Although binary form in one guise or another tended to permeate most instrumental forms (and some vocal ones), there were others, among them variation form, which we have mentioned, and those forms working on the recurring refrain principle A B A C A D A (etc.) which probably goes back to very early communal music-making, where perhaps a solo singer or instrumentalist (or a succession of different ones) sang or played the differing B, C, D etc. sections (the 'episodes'), and a chorus or band or both joined in the refrain, A. (A refrain is often called a chorus.) The refrain principle was most happily applied in the rather short-lived *ritornello* ('refrain') form which Vivaldi and his followers (who included J. S. Bach) used in their concertos. Perhaps the best-known examples are the six Brandenburg concertos of Bach, of which all the first movements are in ritornello form. The ritornello, which is a complete tune, is first played by the full band, out of which subsequently emerge the various soloists to play the episodes. The ritornello is played again several times, usually by the full band in various keys at 'key points' in the movement (is this the origin of that phrase?), but rarely in its entirety until its final appearance back in the home key at the end. Fragments of the ritornello may be used for accompanying the soloists in the episodes, and the ritornello itself may be interrupted by short episodes. The form is really only suited to instrumental polyphony and so it, too, more or less died with Bach.

Rondo form, which follows the same refrain principle, comes straight from the rondeau, a dance which was simply A B A C A. This was rather neatly interwoven with sonata form to become sonata-rondo (see p 105), something which incidentally brought it closer to the more highly organized trouvère song of the same name and lineage. Last movements, particularly of concertos, are often in sonata-rondo form, which tends to be gay, tuneful and dance-like.

So far we have been considering single movements, but most sonatas, symphonies, concertos and the like consist of three or four movements. The number and nature of the movements within various types of musical works has depended more on tradition than on absolute necessity, or perhaps we should say on a necessity born of tradition. The symphony for instance was originally, in baroque times, an orchestral piece in three very short movements (quick, slow, quick) which was played at the beginning of an Italian opera. In other words it was the overture – but it was called *sinfonia*. In due course the movements became longer and the piece was detached from the opera and performed on its own. Somewhere along the line another movement – a dance movement, a minuet – was inserted. Why? The reason can only be that the symphony had another baroque ancestor, this time of French origin: the orchestral suite. (Bach's four orchestral suites – called 'overtures' – are good examples.) The suite was also originally an overture (and called such since the word is French). It began slow and dignified, in a jerky or 'dotted' rhythm (q.v.). This would lead to some quick music, followed usually by a return of the slow music. A number of dances would follow, among which would probably be a minuet. The last dance would be quick and gay – a jig (*gigue*) or some such. The last movement of a symphony was invariably quick and gay and commonly dance-like. Many were jig-like. So it would seem quite natural to insert a minuet as last movement but one. By the time of Haydn and Mozart (classical period), many symphonies had slow, dignified introductions to their first movements. These could have come from the suite, or possibly from one of the two earlier types of sonata, often called a 'church sonata', which had four movements (slow–quick–slow–quick), each slow one acting as a sort of introduction to its succeeding quick one. Handel favours this type of sonata. The other earlier kind of sonata, the chamber (room) sonata (sonata *da camera*) was more like a suite.

It would seem to be desirable that an abstract piece of music, by which is meant a piece of music not relating to or expressing any particular literary or other extra-musical idea, should generally end on an optimistic note. There is thus a need for a quick last movement. But apart from that and the necessity for a variety of mood and tempo between successive movements, there would seem to be no good reason why one sort of succession of movements should be better than another.

The Romantic composers of the 19th century were more interested in what they put into their music than in how they put it together. Some (e.g. Mendelssohn, Brahms) were content to take the forms as Mozart and Beethoven had left them. Others – in particular Liszt, Wagner and to a smaller extent Berlioz – with their strong literary proclivities, needed something looser, something which could follow the changing moods of a poem, story or drama and still remain one piece of music. They used a device already present in Beethoven (e.g. the Fifth Symphony), although for not quite the same purpose. This was to transform a theme, i.e. a tune or just a musical phrase or motif, to suit the mood of the moment. It is not a complete substitute for other forms, being more a means of linking up or inserting smaller forms into a whole, without destroying its cohesive qualities. Liszt used the form for what he called (and what he meant to be) his 'symphonic poems', and also for some of his more abstract pieces like his two piano concertos, in which the purpose is closer to Beethoven's although less subtle. In opera, in the traditional so-called accompanied recitatives, the orchestra either interpolated expressive fragments of music, mainly between the singer's phrases of recitative or, more rarely, played continuous pieces of instrumental music, expressing the mood of the singer, whose recitative went along with it. Wagner carried this instrumental form to its ultimate conclusion, so that each act of his music dramas is an immense symphonic poem, in which the singers happen to be taking part.

Pieces of music lengthened in the 19th century, but after Beethoven the forms did not really *grow* – they just became looser and more elastic. Some composers continued this process of transformation of themes: Sibelius, an inveterate symphonic poet, composed a great symphony in one movement, by tugging at both ends of the one movement and dropping two others into the gaps that opened in the middle. But by then (1924) other composers, led by Stravinsky, had moved into the 20th century in a rather paradoxical way – by looking back at the 18th. Neo-classicism, as it was called, did not produce any new forms to speak of. Ritornello form had a fresh airing in some of Stravinsky's Bach- and Vivaldi-based concertos. Anything which smacked of the 19th century was at first studiously avoided. Thematic development (see p 88) which had been elevated in importance by Beethoven, and made an almost continuous process by Wagner, was replaced by new musical material, so that the forms became more sectional and more static. At the same time, far from rejecting Wagner's continuous development process, Schoenberg and his followers took one aspect of it – that of continual shifting between keys – a stage further, by never allowing any key to establish itself. With key going overboard, so also went the forms dependent upon it. In their place, though not a complete substitute, came the twelve-note (or -tone) row, series or set. Something which could be transformed in certain ways without losing its identity, and which could control both the melody and the harmony throughout a composition, and thereby achieve a great unity. Variations, never dependent upon key, became again a frequently-used form, as were also some rigorous polyphonic forms resuscitated from the Middle Ages, such as 'crab' canons, where one part is the same as the other in reverse, and palindromes, melodies which like the palindrome 'madam I'm Adam' get halfway and then retrace their steps. Eventually composers wanted to control every aspect of their composition with the series – rhythm, the loudness, the manner of playing the instrument(s) etc. This meant turning the series into a set of numbers which could then determine the whole piece (total serialism). Presumably the intention was to achieve a tremendous unity, but the result is surprisingly similar to music in which the process is the precise opposite – namely complete *dis*organization, where the notes, the rhythm, loudness etc. are determined by random processes. The reason for this must be that the highly organized totally serial music has failed to communicate its organization to the listener. Both processes appeared on opposite sides of the Atlantic at the beginning of the second half of the 20th century, which may mean something.

Ever since the days of the cantus firmus, European composers (some more than others) have been concerned with unifying an extended work, often with some single element running right through it. Maybe the concept of 'one God'. Born in America in the same year as Schoenberg (1874) and working for his whole creative life in a climate of total incomprehension, Charles Ives turned the idea of unity on its head. A staunch believer in the Emersonian doctrine of transcendentalism, he saw (and heard) everything around him as manifestations of God in His infinite variety, and he sought not to reconcile them, nor just to observe and record them – at which he was a master – but to unify them by putting them together simultaneously: sometimes a conductor's nightmare, but always a moving experience. The resulting enormously complex polyphony works, because the individual scraps of music which go to make it up are highly familiar, so that we can actually fill in for ourselves the bits we cannot hear.

In the movement away from the absolute precision of total serialism (see p 37), composers have sought ways of exercising less control over the traditionally more precise aspects of music, which are rhythm, melody, harmony and form (which is our concern here). One simple expedient is to leave it to the performer to choose the order in which he plays the movements. He could be allowed to repeat some movements – even leave some out altogether (a good idea where the music is bad). Another way of achieving this 'indeterminacy', as it is called, is to have a game going on offstage – or on, if it is music theatre (see p 92) – to determine who plays what and when. This is chance as opposed to choice – an important distinction, since in the latter the performer has merely taken over some of the composing, as is the case when a performer improvises on a composer's theme. One hugely welcome trend today is the re-emergence of the art of improvisation, which was dying in Mozart's day, rare indeed in the 19th century and confined to jazz for a large part of the 20th. In some improvised pieces today the 'composer' has merely issued a verbal directive called a 'text' (possibly to give it the authority of Holy Writ) which might be: 'Play a note – hold it until the shell of the universe falls away and you become one with all things that ever were or ever shall be.' We of little faith might add, 'or until your breath runs out and your knees drop off.' With or without a 'text' (and some directives are much more down-to-earth and practical) some beautiful music has been made. The form will vary greatly in detail, but the age-old tendency towards a climax some time after halfway seems to operate, and the listener knows that the over-all structure does not depend on an intellectual process which he may not be able to follow.

Musical form has grown and it has dwindled and grown again.

Bruckner's Eighth Symphony is well over an hour long. Webern's symphony lasts for under ten minutes, yet I should say Webern's is more highly organized, although not necessarily the greater for that. As with all Webern's music, a lot happens in a very short time, and it makes considerably larger intellectual demands on its listeners than does Bruckner's. In the 16th century there were polyphonic pieces in as many as forty parts. 17th-century forms, often dance-based, were generally monodic and much simpler. The new form grew until in the mid-18th century the generation after Bach and Handel again went for something simpler, which in its turn developed through Mozart to Beethoven (both of whom were latterly re-discovering Handel and Bach). 19th-century composers after Beethoven, in general, simplified the forms a little (without shortening them), and it was left to the first half of the 20th century to produce some of the most complex and concentrated forms yet.

Today is a time of searching. Some composers are painstakingly building on the past, others are equally busy demolishing one traditional structure after another. Trends and fashions change so quickly with radio and all the other means of instant communication, that if there is a movement away from the complexities of yesterday – as there seems to be, now, in 1975 – it may well have gone into reverse by the time this book is printed. In any case only some of the leading composers will subscribe to it.

PART 2 THE 'ELEMENTS'

When dealing with the basic elements of music, it is not enough to say that something is so; it must be shown to be so. To this end a number of musical works are cited below. I have taken care to confine any more detailed probings to easily found and identified parts of works with which most music-lovers will be very familiar, e.g. Beethoven's Fifth Symphony, Mozart's G minor, Handel's *Messiah* etc. Records of the works mentioned are all readily available.

1 RHYTHM

Beats, bars and metre

John Philip Sousa said that a march tune should make you simply have to get up and march about. His tunes certainly do – or if we are a little too inhibited for that perhaps we just tap our feet. If we refrain from even doing that, something still seems to jump up and down inside us. It is the rhythm that is doing this to us, and rhythm is a very physical thing. We can call rhythm 'the legs of music' but it can be more subtle than that suggests, and so we might extend the metaphor to 'the arms, the fingers and even the eyelids of music'. One need not be very bright to realize that rhythm has something to do with time. It is really the chopping of time into bits. Chopping time into equal bits will give us a steady pulse or beat like the ticking of a clock. Chopping it into unequal bits will give an irregular rhythm like gunfire or spasmodic hammering. Most music has both kinds of rhythm.

Take the words, 'run away', 'ship ahoy', 'riding high'. In each case if we speak the words normally the last syllable takes longer than either of the others. So we could say that each of those phrases has a rhythm which goes, short–short–long. Now take the first three lines of the song 'Dashing away with the smoothing iron':

T'was on a Monday morning
That I beheld my darling.
She looked so sweet and charming

The first syllables of 'morning', 'darling' and 'charming' are long, and I mean long, not louder or more stressed, although this may be so as well, as we shall see in a moment. But these are not the only longer syllables. Carefully noticing the rhythm as we say the words in the same way as we would sing the song, it turns out to be like this, with the same rhythm to each line:

short	long	short	long	short	long	long
T'was	on	a	Mon-	day	mor-	ning
That	I	be-	held	my	dar-	ling
She	looked	so	sweet	and	char-	ming

A clear pattern of alternate shorts and longs with two longs together at the end of each line. This pattern is the result of hanging the uneven shorts and longs on a framework of the other kind of rhythm, the steady, even pulse or beat. If we say the words and at the same time on each long syllable tap with our fingers on anything handy like this:

	beat		beat		beat	beat
T'was on	a	Mon-	day	mor-	ning	
That I	be-	held	my	dar-	ling etc.	

we should be beating evenly and steadily, which will feel quite normal and natural and *musical*, provided we do not beat too strongly and thereby make it more like a march and much less 'sweet and charming'. If we want to beat more strongly we can do it on *alternate* long syllables:

	beat			beat
T'was on	a	Mon-day	mor-ning	
That I	be-	held my	dar-ling etc.	

These are in fact called the strong beats. What is really happening is that there are two pulse-rates superimposed. In this case one is half the rate of the other. If we imagine two people beating, one at each rate, the result will be:

	BEAT			BEAT	
	beat		beat	beat	beat
T'was	on	a	Mon- day	mor	- ning
That	I	be -	held my	dar	- ling etc.

It is not too difficult for one person to beat the two rates, one in each hand. The strong beats are where the beats coincide. I put a vertical line before each strong beat because this is also what we mean by two beats in a bar or two-time. In written music such a vertical 'bar-line', as it is called, measures off every two beats in two-time, every three beats in three-time, and so on. 'Measure' is the more self-explanatory American word for 'bar'.

52

Throughout the verses of the song the beats come on the longer syllables, which is fairly natural since in speech we often stress a syllable by lengthening it rather than making it louder. But this does not have to be so. The refrain begins with six short syllables in a row, which fit in with the two pulse-rates like this:

BEAT						BEAT		
beat		*beat*				*beat*		*beat*
Dash -	ing a -	way		with	the	smooth -	ing	iron
short	*short short*	*short*		*short*	*short*	*long*	*short*	*long*

The six short syllables fit in one bar or measure. Saying them over will show that they are all of equal length, which means that in that bar there is a third much quicker pulse-rate, three times the rate of the quicker beats and six times the rate of the slower beats. In fact this high speed pulse-rate is running through the whole song, and through our minds, whether there is a separate syllable or note to each pulse or not. One note or syllable might stretch over two or three or more of the shortest pulses, but we can still feel them to be there, and we could beat out any of the three pulse-rates right through the tune. They remain in the proportion of one, two and six to a bar, and we call this the 'metre'. If we suddenly throw in an extra one of the quick pulses (or take one out), in other words if we vary the metre, it puts the music out of gear. Try singing and beating this:

beat	*beat*	*beat*	*or beat*	*beat*
Dash - ing a - way with se - ven			smooth - ing irons	

The slower beats either have to get out of step with the quicker pulses or they have to become uneven.

Stravinsky was very fond of doing this, particularly in the highly rhythmic works he composed at about the time of the First World War. In *The Soldier's Tale* and *The Wedding* it happens every so often, with a resulting hiatus throwing us temporarily off balance. But in the latter part of the *Rite of Spring* it is going on more or less continuously, with the frenetic, convulsive result of never allowing us to establish a fixed relationship between the quick and the slower pulses. In a work of this kind the conductor (who will be beating time at one of the slower pulse-rates) cannot beat evenly. With these works conducting suddenly became much more technically difficult, and Toscanini's famous dictum, 'any fool can conduct' needed some qualification.

Syncopation

Varying the metre occasionally is in some ways preferable to doing it continuously. In order to knock something down you have first to set it up. Rhythmic anarchy has its place in music, but much commoner – as in life – is the struggle against an existing order. Far older than variable metre is the device of syncopation. Mediaeval composers used a device called 'hocket', which may be the same word as 'hiccup'. This was a fast and highly rhythmic interplay between two voices produced by staggering their movement from note to note. It came from the chase (see p 29), a canonic hunting song, in which the hocketing to words like, 'Ho! Catch him there! Up he goes, now!' brilliantly evokes the excitement of the hunt, but it was used in church music as well, much to a certain pope's disgust (see p 31). Hocket rhythms are often surprisingly like those characteristic of cakewalk and ragtime – two early forms of jazz. To 'rag the time' was to delay (or anticipate) some of the notes of the tune which would normally be expected to fall on the strong beats, and so make them fall on the weakest pulses of all, which are the quick ones immediately before and after the strong beats. Ragtime was piano music and it set a thus rebellious right hand against a rigid, plodding left hand keeping strictly on the beats. Syncopation seeks to disrupt a metre, but it depends for its effect on failing to do this. And so it tends to be at its most effective when fighting against an authoritarian regime. Traditional jazz sets its syncopation against a clearly stated beat, almost invariably four or eight to a bar.

Jazz musicians often admire the music of J. S. Bach, much of which has a strongly stated metre, sometimes with highly effective syncopation. In his D minor harpsichord concerto the seventh note is far more prominent than any of the preceding six. It is the highest and longest yet, and it is leapt up to. But it comes on a weak pulse. In the next bar there is another much wider leap up to the most prominent note in the bar, which is again on a weak pulse. And in the third bar there are two such leaps, each wider and to a higher and consequently more prominent note, the last one being the highest note in the tune. This powerfully rhythmic, athletic tune is the refrain or ritornello mentioned on page 45, so it will keep on reappearing, mainly in the orchestra. Also highly syncopated is the last movement of Bach's Sixth (and last) Brandenburg Concerto. If we beat time to the beginning of this movement (and there are few easier pieces to beat time to), for the first two bars (8 beats) the tune – again a ritornello – fits comfortably with the beats. Then the syncopation starts and for the next six bars or so hardly any of the notes of the tune coincide with the beat.

The first movement of Beethoven's 'Eroica' Symphony gives the impression of a super-human struggle. The metre is in fact an easy-going three in a bar – something between a waltz and a minuet, but against this Beethoven constantly struggles. Before the first tune is over he is busy putting strong accents on weak beats, and very nearly all the other tunes in the movement start strongly on the weak second beat of the bar, with a strong first beat often going by in silence. Another device he uses is the age-old hemiola. At the tremendous climax in the middle of the movement there is what amounts to a syncopated hemiola.

Hemiola; cross-rhythm; polyrhythm
The hemiola, which was common enough in mediaeval music, depends on the fact that we can divide six into two groups of three or three groups of two. The effect is of two bars of three-time being made to sound like one bar of three-time going at half the rate:

ONE two three FOUR five six

ONE two THREE four FIVE six

ONE   TWO   THREE

A particularly clear-cut example of the hemiola at work in alternate bars is the song 'America' in Leonard Bernstein's *West Side Story*. Exactly the same thing is happening in Orpheus's song 'Vi ricordo o brosch'ombrosi' in the second act of Monteverdi's *Orfeo* of some 350 years earlier. In the first half of the 18th century the hemiola was used a great deal at the ends of sections of pieces in three-time, giving a slowing-up effect without actually changing the tempo. Handel does it constantly. Very well-known examples are 'I know that my Redeemer liveth' and 'The trumpet shall sound', both from Part Three of the *Messiah*, and that splendid dance in three-time in the *Water Music* where the horns always answer the trumpets.

In all of the above examples there is a change from one rhythm to another. If the two rhythms were to happen simultaneously, we could call it a cross-rhythm. In Chopin's waltz in A flat, opus 42 (be careful to get the right one – Chopin wrote several in that key) the first tune is in two-time and so is not a waltz tune at all. Yet the left hand is all the time giving out the characteristic oom-cha-cha waltz vamp in three-time. A most effective and highly exciting use of cross-rhythm occurs in Britten's *Young Person's Guide to the Orchestra*. Towards the end of the final fugue, Britten re-introduces against it the theme by Purcell on which the whole work is based. The theme is in a slow three-time, the fugue in a quick two-time. The rhythmic relationship between the two is further complicated by the fact that the beats of the theme are three times slower than the beats of the fugue. No one is expected to divine the actual mathematical relationship by just listening. The effect, which is of course what matters, is of the theme striding majestically and purposefully forward at its own dignified pace, while the fugue, now seeming hurried and fussy by comparison, dances attendance.

Cross-rhythms play a vital part in a lot of African music, although we should here call them polyrhythms, since there will usually be more than two conflicting rhythms. Twelve short pulses can be grouped as 12 ones, 6 twos, 4 threes, 3 fours and 2 sixes, and any or all of these can happen simultaneously. In addition there can be unequal divisions say, of twelve pulses into five and seven, and these, being prime numbers, will again only break down unequally into, say, $3 + 2$ and $3 + 2 + 2$. Polyrhythmic techniques have not figured greatly in Western music, probably because they tend to build up an exciting but rather inflexible, complex musical texture. The French composer, Messiaen, has made successful use of polyrhythmic techniques, among many others, and has constructed sounds of a fantastic richness. The influence here is not of African music but of the Balinese gamelan orchestras. Messiaen is himself a highly influential composer and is father of the recent trend towards the use of a large array of tuned percussion instruments.

Five-time; seven-time etc

The use of metres of five and seven and larger prime numbers which can only be divided unequally into smaller parts was rare before the 20th century. The second movement of Tchaikovsky's 'Pathétique' Symphony stands out for this reason. His five in a bar is $2 + 3$ throughout. It is really a waltz in which every other bar has lost one beat. Instead of oom-cha-cha, oom-cha-cha, it is oom-cha, oom-cha-cha. In the 20th century there are numerous examples. 'Mars, the bringer of war' and the first of Holst's *Planets* menacingly hammers out a relentless rhythm, made more uncomfortable by being in five $(3 + 2)$. Bartók ends his 153 pieces called *Mikrokosmos* with 'six dances in Bulgarian rhythm'. The metres are not necessarily prime numbers, but the sub-divisions are all unequal. Thus the first three are nine $(4 + 2 + 3)$; seven $(2 + 2 + 3)$; and five $(2 + 3)$. All are very exciting if well played. Such rhythms come naturally to the peoples of South East Europe. In a restaurant not long ago I asked a Greek trio if they would play again an interesting piece in seven they had played earlier, but although it was the only piece in such a metre they did not know which one it was.

Continuous fives, sevens and so on are splendid for some dances, short pieces and relentless hammerings, but in extended pieces they become something of a strait-jacket, and are much more likely to occur among other metres in a piece where the metre is being varied. An unequal sub-division *is* a varied metre anyway. There is no real difference between a bar of five (3 + 2) and a bar of three followed by a bar of two.

'Serial' rhythm

The German composer Boris Blacher has written a number of pieces in what he calls 'serial' rhythm. Serial metre would be a better phrase since the principle is to vary the metre bar by bar according to a numerical pattern or series. Thus the bars might be successively 2, 3, 4, 5, 6 and so on, or going the other way 11, 10, 9, 8, 7 and so on, or something a little less straightforward, 2, 5, 3, 6, 4, 7. The effect can be satisfying or exciting, constructing as it does a rhythmic pattern of decelerating, or accelerating (or both alternately) strong beats. A fragment of melody can be repeated many times, each time losing or gaining a note or two, which is of course repetition with a difference – one of the age-old basic principles of musical construction.

Before 1600

Before the 17th century the bar-line as we know it did not exist. In pre-17th century dances and solo songs, neither of which differ much rhythmically from later music, it is usually fairly easy to put in bar-lines for modern performance, but in many polyphonic pieces it is difficult and often undesirable. Each part will have its own metre, which might be different from the others, or more likely the same but staggered, so that what *we* would call the strong beats do not always coincide. The over-all rhythmic effect is one of flow rather than metre, but we must listen to this music most intently, trying to hear as many of the individual parts as possible, so that we can detect the rhythmic as well as the melodic and harmonic relationships between them, which is a large part of what it is all about.

Further back in the Middle Ages the polyphony was made up of parts added above and below a cantus firmus (see p 30) which imposed a certain mathematical rigidity on the rhythmic structure. The cantus firmus may have an isorhythm (see pp 31 and 41) imposed upon it. Putting in bar-lines for modern performance is easy. The metre is nearly always three-time.

Rhythms

So far this chapter has concentrated on metre, but the other aspect of rhythm, the patterns made up of different combinations of long and short, slow and quick sounds are just as important. There is the obvious distinction between an even rhythm of equal-length sounds like, say, most of the notes of 'Good King Wenceslas' or the first line of 'Frère Jacques' or the pizzicato (plucked strings) section of the third movement of Tchaikovsky's Fourth Symphony, and an uneven jerky rhythm of unequal length sounds such as 'Charlie is my darling' or the main march tune from the third movement of Tchaikovsky's 'Pathétique' (Sixth) Symphony. The jerky, uneven sort of rhythm is often called a dotted rhythm because of the way it may be written down (see p 119).

These two kinds of rhythm are effectively contrasted in Part Two of Handel's *Messiah*. In the chorus, 'Surely He hath borne our grief', a dotted rhythm evokes agitation and the chastisement of Jesus, while smoother flowing, even rhythms are just right for the following chorus, 'And with His stripes we are healed'. But uneven rhythms do not necessarily evoke agitation. The tempo, the speed of the music is important.

Tempo

A little earlier in the *Messiah*, near the end of Part One, is the aria 'He shall feed His flock'. The rhythm here is an uneven short–long–short–long–short–long, but the music is the opposite to agitated. The tempo is slow – about forty beats to the minute or just about baby-in-arms-rocking-to-sleep tempo. Compare 'Silent Night', 'Rock-a-bye baby', the pastoral symphonies in Bach's Christmas Oratorio (Part Two) and Handel's *Messiah* and the *pastorale* at the end of Corelli's Christmas concerto. The three latter are examples of the 18th-century tradition stemming from the *pifferari* – pipers who used to play a tune in that rhythm in the streets of Naples and Rome at Christmas time. The rhythm is that of a dance, the *pastorale*, which is virtually identical with the *siciliana*. Here it is clearly related to the rocking of the baby Jesus, just as the *pifferari* represented the shepherds with their pipes. Hence Handel's choice of that rhythm for 'He shall feed His flock'. Incidentally if you speed up the latter half of 'Rock-a-bye baby' it turns into 'Lilliburlero'. A lullaby has turned into a march simply by increasing the tempo. The tempo therefore is vital to the quality of a rhythm. This is the main reason why performances or interpretations of a work can and do differ so much. Furthermore with a very old piece which has no words to help us guess the tempo, we could easily be so wrong as to mistake a lullaby for a march or a joyful dance for a dirge.

Accent

Dynamic, i.e. loudness and softness, is not in itself an aspect of rhythm, but it does affect it greatly. An accented note, a loud note among other quiet ones, will be isolated, and the listener will automatically relate it to any other accented notes there may be. This could produce syncopation or cross-rhythm, depending on the rhythmic pattern the accented notes make in relation to *all* the notes. As we saw on page 53, the longer sounds of a rhythm tend to carry more weight and to occur on the strong beats. There will of course be more sound in a long sound than in a short one of equal loudness, and this will make the long sound *seem* louder, which is what matters. For this reason dynamic cannot be separated from rhythm.

A performer may automatically reinforce the strong beats a little (not a lot or he is insulting his audience), either by playing the notes on those beats fractionally louder, or making them fractionally longer. In the latter case he will need to make the succeeding note or notes fractionally shorter, if the music is not to become slower and slower.

Rubato

This brings us to the practice of *tempo rubato* (literally 'stolen time'), which every performer uses to some degree, and some to too great a degree. Rubato is a variation in the tempo and hence in the rhythm. An important, eagerly awaited moment may be delayed a little by slowing the tempo, or a certain brilliant passage taken slightly faster. The tempo is made to ebb and flow. The most expressive and effective form of rubato is where a tune's tempo ebbs and flows, but the accompaniment stays rock steady, which means that any stolen time has to be given back before too long, or tune and accompaniment will part company for good. The 'crooners' of the 1940s (their descendants are still around) were good at this, if perhaps they tended to overdo it sometimes. Chopin's music is usually treated to almost continuous rubato. Unfortunately Mendelssohn once said something like, 'I don't think this fellow Chopin *can* play in time'. I suspect though that Chopin, a great pianist as well as composer, used mainly the steady-accompaniment type of rubato, which is much more difficult and comparatively rarely used in modern performance.

The rhythmic series

Schoenberg's twelve-note system related the melody and the harmony of a piece to a row or series of twelve notes. Around 1950 composers were trying to relate the rhythm (and in some cases everything else) to the series as well. So they used a rhythmic series, a series of durations (note-lengths) as well as a series of pitches (notes). The method of relating the rhythmic series to the pitch series was arbitrary and did not work very well; it is virtually impossible for the listener, contending with twelve different durations unrelated to any particular metre, to perceive any recognizable and memorable rhythmic pattern, let alone relate it to the melodic and harmonic patterns. More recently the American composer Milton Babbitt has devised a way of relating a rhythmic series to the metre of a piece, but I think it will always be difficult for the listener to appreciate a relationship between pitch and rhythm, except in a crude way such as speeding up or slowing down a gramophone record.

Random rhythm

Recognizable rhythmic patterns help us to predict what is likely to happen next. This is the situation in most of the music we hear. Sometimes, though, a composer wishes to put us in a state of not knowing quite what to expect. Near the end of the *Rite of Spring* – the second passage in the 'Danse Sacrale', which is (to begin with) the last quiet passage in the work – Stravinsky repeats the same stabbing chord many times. The stabs come singly or in pairs or in threes, but we have no idea which grouping will come next. There are only three 'possibilities', but no one possibility is any more likely to occur than any other. This uncertainty sets up fear, and when muted trombones call out like an animal in the jungle, and then call out again, to be answered *unexpectedly soon* by the same call on high shrill muted trumpets, we nearly jump out of our skins. Stravinsky's use of variable metre in this work (see p 53) is for similar purposes. In the middle of the second movement of Bartók's *Music for Stringed Instruments, Percussion and Celesta* is a passage where, in front of a running, pulsating pizzicato background, the piano and celesta stab out in high, pinging chords the main tune (fugue subject) from the first movement, in what seems to be a completely haphazard rhythm. The effect is of great excitement. Syncopation is part of it since the background is in a rigid metre.

Both Stravinsky's and Bartók's music have a beat or pulse framework which their random rhythms stand against. More recently music has been composed using tables of random numbers, or by putting the notes where the imperfections of the paper suggest. There is no tempo, metre or steady pulse-rate, but this does not mean that the listener can have no worthwhile musical experience. If an unchanging metre was becoming a strait-jacket in the early 20th century, so for many composers is a steady pulse-rate in the later 20th century. We are, after all, capable of feeling the passage of time without having it marked off for us like inches on a tape measure.

Statistical rhythm

Traditional music demands of its performers precise ensemble. They must play their notes at exactly the right moment. A pizzicato chord on a string orchestra, like the one that ends Elgar's *Introduction and Allegro*, is expected to sound as one clear 'pong', and not a sort of 'splitter-splatterong'. The latter, which happens often enough (though usually unintentionally), can be said to be a 'statistical' event, there being no exact moment of the chord, just an average of all the players' different moments. A number of composers today have composed and are composing music in which many of the events are deliberately so timed. (c.f. statistical sound pp. 61 and 81.)

Electronic music

The rhythms of electronic music are not usually related to a beat or a pulse framework, although any sound which occurs regularly and often enough will automatically set up such a framework. A certain complex sound may contain a throbbing, which is, of course, a regular rhythm. A sound like burning sticks will contain a random rhythm of cracks. An electronic piece might take two rhythmic patterns, identical in every way, except that one is a tiny fraction slower, so that they very gradually move out of step with one another. Two (or more) sequences of sounds can be made to recur at differing rates, with a resultant changing rhythmic interaction between them.

Rhythm, as stated at the beginning of this chapter, is the chopping of time into bits. In electronic music we can speed up our chopper, until a rhythm becomes a continuous sound. If the speeded-up rhythm is a random one, the continuous sound is noise. If it is regular, the continuous sound has pitch.

2 MELODY

Melody is obviously a succession of notes. *A* melody, *a* tune, is a succession of notes going somewhere. A succession of notes cannot fail to have some sort of rhythm. By 'going somewhere' we mean having form. Without form no tune would seem to end or to progress towards its end. A melody is therefore compounded of more than one element.

Certain aspects of the rhythmic element of melody have already been discussed in the previous chapter under Beats, Bars and Metre (pp 51–53). Certain aspects of the formal element of melody will be discussed in chapters eleven and twelve.

The element that melody brings to rhythm and form is pitch, which is simply the highness or lowness of a note, and depends on the frequency (the number in every second) of the vibrations set up in the air by the instrument or voice producing the note. This is why, if we play a gramophone record or a tape at too fast a speed, not only is the music faster but all the notes are higher in pitch. The notes of a melody will differ in pitch, but they need not all be different. The first half of 'God Save the Queen' keeps coming back to its first note, as do 'Good King Wenceslas', 'All Through the Night' and many others. 'Dashing away with the smoothing iron' has three attempts at getting away from its second note. Tunes like 'For He's a Jolly Good Fellow' and 'Lilliburlero' contain quite a lot of notes but are in fact 'worrying' a fairly small number of notes.

All the tunes mentioned repeat the same rhythm to different notes, which is usually the case with simple tunes and perhaps the reason for the popularity of certain works which start with such tunes – for example Tchaikovsky's piano concerto no. 1 in B flat minor, Mozart's G minor Symphony (no. 40) and Beethoven's Fifth Symphony, where the one rhythm permeates the whole first movement. Songs can and usually do repeat exactly a lot of the music, since the words can be different, but this is something to be avoided on the whole in instrumental music. At the beginning of the slow second movement of Mozart's Prague Symphony (no. 38), the first phrase of the melody is immediately repeated, but with extra notes by way of decoration, which alters the rhythm as well. The next bit of tune does repeat the rhythm exactly, but the notes are changing just a little each time, and there is a dialogue between violins and cellos. Brahms is doing the same sort of thing to the tune on the oboe which starts the slow middle movement of his violin concerto. Here one must listen more closely and intelligently in order to notice what is a decorated repeat and what is new, but the reward is the greater. Greater still if one can manage to apprehend the much more extensive embellishments the solo violin then adds to that melody.

These are all examples of the basic principle of musical form – repetition with a difference. Repetition is something we expect. We expect things to go on either as they are doing in the piece we are listening to at the time, or as they usually do in similar pieces we have heard. A complete change is surprising, and it has its place. Much more interesting is a change which can be seen to relate to what has gone before, but in an unexpected way. A splendid example is the first phrase of the 'Marseillaise'. This begins in a very ordinary way by a jump (of a fourth) up to its key note, as do 'The British Grenadiers'; 'O Waly Waly'; 'Begone Dull Care'; 'Rule Britannia' (verse); 'On Ilkla Moor' (refrain); 'The Red Flag' (*Der Tannenbaum*) and thousands of others. After their initial jump all these go up the scale by steps, but the 'Marseillaise' takes just one step up as if it is going to do the same, and then jumps up another fourth to match the jump it started with. We do not expect the second jump, but once it has happened, we subconsciously relate it to the first jump, and are pleased with the logic of it. One can say so often about fine music, 'I didn't expect that to happen, but now it has it seems inevitable.' This is constantly the case with Mozart's music. His melodies (and no great composer relies more on melody, not even Schubert) are usually made up of musical clichés, but joined together in such an original and meaningful manner that they are a perpetual delight to the most sophisticated ears. Apparently unrelated tunes nevertheless seem absolutely right when strung together. Careful analysis will tell us what our ears were telling us all along. In other words, we do not have to analyse and discover the subtle inter-relationships born of Mozart's incredibly fertile imagination in order to appreciate the beauty of his music. We do this intuitively, although just how intuitively Mozart composed, we can never know. I myself feel certain that the subtle inter-relationships *are* intuitive.

Every performer worth his salt knows that although Mozart's music is not difficult to play, it is very difficult to play well. This is because any slight blemish will be obvious, particularly in the phrasing. Phrasing, which is important in all melody, is the way notes are played in relation to their neighbours – whether one note follows another without any silence in between or, if there is a silence, is it barely perceptible or quite long – is the latter note louder or softer? In general, phrasing will underline the structure of a melody, putting a little breathing space (literally with wind instruments and voices and hence probably the origin of phrasing) at the ends of the phrases. Smaller fragments will be given shape by phrasing: a group of four quick notes may well have the first note passing to the second without any silence in between (legato), the other three all shortened a little (staccato) to leave tiny silences between them. This will give a slight stress to the first note, since it is the only one to be given its full value. There are obviously many ways in which melodies can be shaped by the phrasing – one of the finer points of music that the listener will do well to pay special attention to. Niceties of phrasing will quickly sort out the good performer from the indifferent.

Most of the music most people hear has melody. The oft-heard complaint, 'It hasn't got a tune', is usually unjustified. It used to be said of the music of Bartók, one of the more tuneful of composers. But the same people did not say so about the far less tuneful, slower music of Debussy. They were familiar with Debussy's idiom but not with Bartók's, which made it difficult for them to follow the logical progress of his tunes. Similarly people unfamiliar with the special rhythmic qualities of Plainsong may find it hard to appreciate the great beauty of some of those melodies.

Polyphony began, as we have seen, by the addition of parts above and below the Plainsong. This soon gave rise to new kinds of melodies. Such melodies, for instance, would not necessarily end on the final or key note, but on one of the notes of the final chord. Different kinds of cadences will thus affect the music melodically. The melodic quality of much of the music of Dufay and Josquin is greatly affected by their use of a particular kind of cadence known as the 'Landani' cadence. From the harmony affecting the melody, it is not a large step to harmony becoming part of the melody. Bach often writes a tune which jumps about in such a way that we can think of it as two simultaneous tunes going on one above the other. The first tune the solo first violin plays in his Concerto for Two Violins in D minor is a good example. Yodelling is doing the same thing. Any tune which sounds the notes of a chord consecutively is implying a harmony, e.g. the beginnings of 'The Star-Spangled Banner'; 'The Blue Danube'; Mozart's *Eine Kleine Nachtmusik*; Beethoven's 'Eroica' Symphony; Wagner's *Tannhäuser*, although the tune can be harmonized in such a way as to contradict the implied harmony. This happens to some extent in the first and last examples.

The invention of recitative just before 1600 brought simplified speech rhythms to sung melody, with harmony (simple chords) giving it some musical direction. Recitative can be highly expressive, but we sense its lack of musical structure, and so await the formal aria which usually follows. The only way in which recitative can be given cohesive musical form is by giving that form to the accompaniment – usually a melody for the orchestra. Wagner carried this to its ultimate conclusion. Schoenberg's *Sprechgesang* ('speaking-song') tries, like recitative, to achieve something between speech and song. It keeps the formal rhythms of song, but makes use of the fact that in speech we never stay on a note, but are always sliding up or down. It takes little or no account of when we go up and when down, or by how much. That is left to the singer, with very varied results. Schoenberg directs that each note of the song should be sung and then immediately slid away from. It works extremely well in *Pierrot Lunaire* – the first work to employ it throughout – where its melodramatic quality is well suited to the highly-charged, surrealistic atmosphere of grotesque, moonlit and bloodstained imagery. It is effective too in a more negative way in Schoenberg's opera *Moses and Aaron*, where it is used for the part of the introverted, tongue-tied Moses, as against the normally sung, eloquent, smooth-tongued Aaron. But although Schoenberg has exerted a huge influence over 20th-century music, comparatively few other composers have employed *Sprechgesang*.

Chromaticism (see p 98) has affected melody greatly. The change from the modes to the key system was really a narrowing process, certainly as far as melody was concerned. Around 1600, the time of the change, some composers, notably Gesualdo (whose not otherwise remarkable madrigal 'Moro Lasso' is famous for that reason), were writing highly chromatic music. But without equal temperament tuning of instruments (q.v.), which did not come into use until the 18th century, there were problems and chromaticism remained something of a curiosity for a while. Purcell (late 17th century) often used chromatic ground basses (q.v.), although the main tunes above them were usually less so. Dido's famous lament at the end of *Dido and Aeneas* is an example. After Dido has finished singing and is dying, all the parts are highly chromatic, drooping downwards in sorrow by semitone steps.

Mozart was branded by a disgusted contemporary Italian composer as one 'who divides the octave into twelve semitones', which is quite true, although we are not disgusted by it. In the passage in the Prague Symphony referred to above (p 62), the repeat is decorated chromatically, and this is typical. Mozart's melodies are usually more chromatic than Beethoven's or Schubert's.

Most of Chopin's music is simply a number of tunes, which may or may not of themselves be chromatic. If they are at all slow, they are likely to be progressively more and more encrusted with chromatic ornament. Many of the nocturnes are good examples. It was Wagner who took chromaticism as far as it could go within the key system. Not all the melodies in his most chromatic work, *Tristan and Isolde*, are equally chromatic. The music at the very beginning of the prelude is extremely chromatic, with the melody moving mostly by semitones. It is a series of cadences, each pointing towards a different key, with a silence instead of the expected final chord, so that the music is not even allowed to get properly into a key, let alone stay in it. From the first loud passage, onwards for a while, the music does move into various keys, but each time passes on to another key at once. The melody here is that much less chromatic than before and that much more obviously melodious. The first music is on the brink of 'atonality' or absence of key. As we all know, Schoenberg plunged in, and the effect on melody was colossal. The final, the keynote was gone. Wagner had often withheld it but, as in the incomplete cadences at the start of *Tristan*, we knew what he was withholding, because he was pointing at it. Schoenberg cannot do this, and we must listen to melody with a different set of expectations as to what it is going to do.

In the music of Webern – an even more radical composer – the melody may consist largely of huge leaps of well over an octave, and the instruments playing it may change every two or three notes, thus breaking the melody up into small cell-like fragments. Schoenberg wrote tunes, for example the beginning of his piano concerto, and he even hoped his tunes might some day be whistled by ordinary people, as are those of Schubert. But any two consecutive notes from Webern might exceed the compass of the human whistle (I have about three octaves), which would perhaps justify those who would say, 'It hasn't got a tune'. The sort of melody it *has* – and I personally am very moved by Webern's music – obliges us to think of individual notes on their own, as rhythmically and instrumentally disposed pitches. Melody has been cut down to size as an equal participant with rhythm, timbre and harmony in the process we call music. This is the starting point for composers such as Stockhausen, who have integrated these 'parameters' in diverse and new ways, which are best discussed under the more general heading of form (see p 91).

With voices and traditional instruments the problems of dividing the octave into smaller intervals than semitones, are considerable, involving special techniques and training, and in most cases special instruments. Although some composers have employed microtones fairly extensively, each usually in his own way, the practice has remained something of a backwater. However, where sounds are electronically produced, the whole audible pitch range can be easily divided into any number and size of intervals. Electronic music has not as yet concerned itself very much with precisely pitched sounds, since this approaches too closely to what traditional instruments do so much better. But sounds consisting of bands of frequencies, or groups of frequencies (which will not necessarily sound like chords), or groups of bands of frequencies, will give pitches which can vary in preciseness, as do different percussion instruments. A triangle is fairly high-pitched but imprecise, whereas a glockenspiel is precise. Some drums, for instance, sound definite notes, others do not, but one can still perceive differences in pitch between them. Using bands of frequencies rather than precise pitches produces a new kind of melodic movement. Stockhausen's electronic *Studie II* is a good example.

Melodies sung or played on traditional instruments can be electronically 'processed' in various ways, which can change the pitch, the rhythm, the order of the notes and so on. The result may not still be melody, since pitch can be transformed into something else. On the other hand something else, say the rhythm of the melody, could be transformed into pitch, producing a new melody. The possibilities are considerable.

Western melody has traditionally consisted largely of steady notes. We do, and perhaps should *very* occasionally in performance slide a little up or down to a note or between one note and the next, but nothing is worse than a singer or string player who is continually doing it. We also indulge in vibrato, which involves slight fluctuations in pitch, but the melody itself consists of steady notes. Bartók used sliding notes to great effect here and there, mainly fairly quickly, swooping down or rocketing up, or merely to link up two steady notes. Lately there has been a tendency to use more slowly sliding notes and to explore their changing effect against other sounds, either steady or sliding.

A violin, an oboe, a trumpet, a flute, a horn, a clarinet, a bassoon and many other instruments can all play the same note with the same loudness, duration and so forth, and yet each of them will sound different. This is because their timbre, their tone quality or tone colour is different.

The timbre of an instrument is determined by several factors, but mainly by two. One of these is the disposition and proportion of the overtones, upper partials or harmonics which are – in pitched instruments – the multiples of the frequencies of the note we actually hear. (See p 62.) A brilliant sound like a trumpet has many, a flute comparatively few. A violin and a clarinet have a fair number, but differently disposed. The other important factor is how a note begins. A percussion instrument hit with a hard stick will sound different from one hit with a soft stick, mainly because the sound starts differently. But even instruments which make sustained sounds, like wind instruments and bowed strings, have very individual ways of beginning their sounds. If a tape recording is run backwards, or if the beginnings of the notes are removed by snipping bits out of the tape, it is often difficult to tell what instruments are playing. Early preelectric recordings make a large symphony orchestra sound like an exhausted harmonium, mainly because they could not cope with the high frequencies of the upper partials, and the almost instantaneously changing sounds (transients) at the start of each note.

Our ears are not as naturally sensitive to changes in timbre as to changes in pitch, rhythm and harmony. Schoenberg's idea of *Klangfarbenmelodie* (tone-colour-melody) – a 'melody' of changing instrumental timbres rather than pitches, makes great demands on the listener's perceptive powers. 'Farben' (colours), the third of Schoenberg's *Five Pieces for Orchestra*, is a slow procession of gradually, and subtly changing harmonies, to which we can easily respond as well as to the occasional scraps of melody; but more important is the ever- and often fast-changing instrumentation, which demands tremendous concentration if this marvellous piece is to be fully appreciated.

The instruments of the orchestra are worth knowing, by sight and sound. An average ear can soon distinguish between any of them. No one need be anxious about his ability to hear sufficiently well to enjoy many of the subtleties of tone-colour. But he must practise so as to get the best out of his aural power. Musicians are very keen that all musical training of children in school should be based on ear-training.

Without that, good 'appreciation' is impossible. Sadly many people grow up untrained in this way. Some even go to musical colleges, heavily deficient in the power to distinguish between sounds. More sadly some come away little better. Training in timbre is best done in the concert room. There are gramophone records which demonstrate the instruments of the orchestra, and these are a great help, but even the most efficient stereo set (and I have yet to hear some of the percussion instruments really sounding as they should) is no substitute for actually being there and able to see the instruments as well as hear them. Most television sets reproduce music very badly, though televised orchestral concerts are usually an incessant guided tour of the orchestra which is good for learning about the instruments, even if it leaves only a quarter of an ear for what they are actually playing.

Timbre is a vital element in composition. Every good composer will have his own individual manner of instrumentation. Wagner, for instance, obtains a sonorous, homogeneous, organ-like quality from his orchestra, so that his all-important harmonies can tell. The instrumental timbres must blend into a rich soup without lumps in it. Listen to the prelude to Wagner's *Lohengrin*. Starting extremely high upon violins only, a slow melody gradually spreads downwards, taking in more and more of the orchestra, stirring in new flavours which always blend into one gorgeous sound. The orchestra pit at the opera house Wagner built at Bayreuth in Germany is covered by a great cowl, open only towards the stage, so that the reflected sound of the orchestra and the direct sound of the singers come from as nearly the same place as possible – a spatial blend as well.

Mozart's instrumentation sets off his melodies to perfection. It must not obtrude, and therefore a casual listener may miss its great subtlety and variety. As we have already seen in the previous chapter, Mozart rarely repeats a melody without doing something different to it. The obvious thing is to play it on a different instrument, but it is much more likely that Mozart will add an extra instrument or two to the original instruments; for instance, violins the first time – violins plus a bassoon below or a flute (or two) above, or both, the second time. That is what happens generally in the slow movement of the Prague Symphony, mentioned in the previous chapter (p 62). In the finale of that symphony the general instrumental pattern is more one of alternation between wind and strings, which would tend to emphasize the structure. But both types of instrumentation (and others) occur in both these movements, and any Mozart piece will give many examples of subtle interplay between the available instruments.

Unexpected changes of timbre can break things up. Beethoven, in the middle of the first movement of his Fifth Symphony, effectively isolates two rising notes from the middle of a tune on the strings by interrupting the tune at that point and answering the two rising notes with two rising notes on the wind, and then alternating the two pairs of rising notes on strings and wind, and finally reducing the pairs to single notes, which we still think of as being one note of the original theme.

An obvious example of structural instrumentation is what gave the 'trio' of the minuet and trio its otherwise meaningless name. In the music of the late baroque, that is the late 17th and first half of the 18th century, the instrumentation usually remained fairly constant throughout a movement or section of a movement. The middle dance (dance 2) of the traditional dance 1–dance 2–dance 1 again sandwich, was often given to a trio of wind instruments. The last movement of Bach's First Brandenburg Concerto is a minuet with three trios, which *are* trios. Two of them are for wind, one for strings, while the recurring minuet (which we hear four times and rather tire of as a result) is for the whole band.

Some of the music of the early baroque (c. 1600), especially that of the extremely wealthy and pomp-loving Venetians, was characterized by great opulence of instrumentation. Composers for the first time started designating in the score precisely which instruments were to play what. They also liked to separate the instruments and voices in space, and to 'throw' the music about between them antiphonally, which focuses attention on the contrasting timbres.

The desire for great instrumental wealth reappears in the 19th century. In post-Revolutionary France the *citoyens* were obliged to foregather for massed outdoor performances of revolutionary choral-orchestral works, a practice which continued for some time and no doubt fired the young Hector Berlioz to form his orchestral battalions. In his Requiem (*Grande Messe des Morts*), besides a large chorus and orchestra there are four differently constituted and spatially separated brass bands. But Berlioz was not all massive effects. A highly original composer with great sensitivity to timbre, his music is the delight of conductors (a large part of whose work he has already done for them), and audiences, for the translucency of its textures and the fresh-air quality of its sound. Try the love scene (*Scène d'Amour*) and the 'Queen Mab' scherzo from his 'Romeo and Juliet' Symphony. An interesting comparison can be made between the latter piece and Mendelssohn's 'Midsummer Night's Dream' scherzo, and you can throw in 'Mercury the Winged Messenger' from Holst's *Planets*, which is another ethereal scherzo.

Timbre is a particularly vital element in the impressionistic music of Debussy, since the sheer quality of the sound is so important. Debussy listened to music as sound, and without preconceived notions of what music should or should not be. Thus he was able greatly to admire the music of the Balinese gamelan orchestras and other traditional music of the Far East, at a time when most European musicians would have regarded such music as primitive and quaint if not unpleasant. Gamelan orchestras use a lot of percussion, to the extent that the timbre and the harmony, and to a smaller extent melody, are largely the same thing, or at any rate are inseparable. Any arrangement for different instruments would be a new piece. In Western music timbre usually changes independently of harmony and melody. A tune may be repeated on different instruments with or without the same harmony. Sometimes the harmony may stay the same while the melody changes with or without a corresponding change of instrument. (See *Variation*, p 87.) Debussy tends to line up the three, so that a particular melody and harmony is associated with a particular instrument. In 'Nuages' (Clouds), the first of the three Nocturnes for Orchestra, the second theme one notices is a slow melodic fragment which is on the cor anglais every time it appears. Most of the melodic fragments of the first two movements of *La Mer* stay with the same instruments. The last movement is more formal and overtly repetitious, and consequently less impressionistic. When we remember Debussy's music, it is not just the melody we remember, as we might with Beethoven, but the instrumentation as well.

Of course wherever the instrumentation is striking (and it usually is with Debussy) we remember it: the strange unpigeonholeable start of Stravinsky's *Rite of Spring* with the solo bassoon, a low instrument but playing unfamiliarly right up in the middle of the compass of the much higher oboe, clarinet or flute, and yet sounding like none of these; also from Stravinsky the unique E minor chord, inflexible, authoritarian, in that it recurs when *it* pleases, which starts the Symphony of Psalms.

In Berlioz's Requiem (*Grande Messe des Morts*) there is a high chord on three flutes, sounded together with a low note on eight tenor trombones, with a chasm of four octaves in between, of which Cecil Forsyth, in his book on orchestration says, 'It probably sounds very nasty'.[1] Gordon Jacob, who at least had heard it, quotes Forsyth and vehemently agrees saying, 'It does!'[2] I too have heard it, and say it

[1] C. Forsyth, *Orchestration*, MacMillan & Stainer & Bell. 2nd ed., 1948, p. 135.
[2] G. Jacob, *Orchestral Technique*, O.U.P., 2nd ed., 1940.

does not! But the reader should judge for himself. It is in the 'Hostias' (no. 8) and again in the 'Agnus Dei' (no. 10) – you cannot miss it. What Forsyth and Jacob really meant, is that it does not sound like Wagner or Brahms, and it breaks one of the cardinal rules of 'blend' orchestration which is, 'no chasms'. If Berlioz had wanted the flutes to blend with the trombones in one sound, he would hardly have done what he did. As it was, he was probably depicting the souls in heaven and hell, and what better way? I mention this to show that there is no 'right' and 'wrong' about instrumentation.

Most 20th-century composers have moved well away from the 'blend' orchestration of Wagner. Webern, who rigorously discarded all inessentials, reduced his orchestra often to one only of each instrument, thereby turning it into a chamber ensemble. The more traditionally-minded Schoenberg in general retained the Wagnerian orchestra, but tended to treat it as Mahler had often done, as a number of chamber ensembles. The empirical Stravinsky kept the full symphony orchestra when he needed it (e.g. the Symphony in three Movements of 1945), or modified it when he did not (e.g. the Symphony of Psalms of 1930 which has, besides the chorus, augmented woodwind and trumpets but no violins or violas). Bartók did likewise, and so did other composers – increasingly as time went on. Very few important composers today regularly compose for the standard symphony orchestra, preferring to concentrate on writing for different chamber ensembles. One might imagine that the symphony orchestra, with its eighty or ninety players, has a far wider range of timbres than a chamber ensemble of say, ten or eleven players. But, excluding percussion instruments – and one man can handle quite a large battery of these – there are only about seventeen different instruments in a symphony orchestra, and only ten 'families' of instruments, the individual members of which tend to have somewhat similar timbres, since they are in effect the same instrument constructed in different sizes. So a chamber ensemble of eleven players can have nearly as wide a range of timbres as a large orchestra. It can also, and should, operate in a smaller room (chamber), with greater intimacy and greater detail, nuance etc. communicated to the listener.

The manufacturer of a musical instrument tries to make the timbre as uniform throughout its compass as possible, but the player usually has to help in this. The reason is obvious. There is a famous record of a famous singer, who sings the first line of 'Land of Hope and Glory' in a fruity contralto and then, because the notes are a fraction lower, delivers the next line, 'Mother of the free', in a stentorian bass-baritone. Such inconsistencies of timbre between neighbouring notes are excessive and generally to be deplored, but the timbre of any instrument (or voice) is bound to alter between the extremes of its compass, and a good composer will know the nature of every instrument he composes for, allow for this and indeed make use of it.

Noise

One definition of noise is 'unwanted sound'. We can even call the most sublime music 'noise', if we happen not to want to hear it. Musicians tend to use the word synonymously with 'sound', saying of a certain piece of music that it is a 'nice noise', or that Charlie Snooks makes a 'nice noise' on his fiddle. But we can also mean by noise any *unpitched* sound, that is a sound whose frequencies are not regular, or are 'aperiodic'. All musical instruments make a certain amount of noise. This is obvious in the case of castanets, woodblocks, untuned drums, cymbals etc. But pitched instruments too have their characteristic unpitched noises – the click of a xylophone, which turns into a rattle at speed; the piano making something between a click and a thump, which is easy to hear on the very top notes, where there is more click than note. It is an acoustic fact that any note which starts (or stops) sufficiently suddenly, will do so with an audible click. Every time a string player changes the direction of his bow, it makes a noise. Consequently there is a lot of noise in the rapid bowing of a tremolo, which on a large body of violins can sound almost like a side-drum roll. Even sustained notes have noise in them – the sound like tearing canvas when the brass are 'brassy'; the breathiness of the flute. And if it is thought that noise is a blemish, which pitched instruments are better off without, know that the most expensive electronic organs have a special 'chuff' built into the start of each note to simulate the sound the air makes before the pipe of a pipe organ 'speaks'.

Noise then has always been part of music, which perhaps some people do not realize when they use the phrase 'musical sounds' to mean 'pitched sounds'.

The composer composing for traditional instruments has at his disposal a limited number of well-used and familiar timbres. He may produce new sounds by new and ingenious combinations, but much has been done already, and he is more likely to concentrate his efforts on making his music interesting in other ways. On the other hand a composer of electronic music has at his disposal almost every possible sound, imagined or unimagined. The range of timbres is infinite.

They can also be very precisely controlled. Composing in the traditional way, he has little control over the timbre of say, a clarinet – to obtain a change in timbre he must change the instrument or add other instruments, but with electronic techniques he can modify the structure of the sound itself, as well as make one sound modify or 'modulate' another. Both of these techniques will give rise to new sounds related to the original sounds. The mathematics of it are that whereas the traditional methods can only add and subtract sounds, electronic methods can multiply them by each other as well.

Thus it is in the realm of timbre that electronic music makes its main contribution. Using electronic equipment to make traditional musical sounds is pointless. Traditional pitched sounds and the various sorts of harmony that go along with them are the property of traditional instruments, and in this field electronically produced sounds are just feeble imitations. It was once thought that electronic music could outdo traditional instruments by playing tunes faster, but it was found that the human ear could not hear tunes any faster than human fingers could play them. Not surprising really – rhythm being so physical (see p 51). It is at about this top speed too that the number of notes in a second begins to equal the frequency of vibrations of the lowest notes we can hear, and so we arrive at the frontier between rhythm and pitch. Many composers use traditional instruments and taped electronic sounds together, which is perhaps to date the most effective form of electronic composition. The traditional instruments can take care of the pitched sounds, while electronic sounds (often the same traditional instruments recorded and electronically processed) provide a rich 'counterpoint' of changing and probably related timbres.

4 HARMONY

Discord; concord; interval

Harmony is simply more than one note at a time, the exception being when all the notes so sounded are any number of octaves apart, in which case they sound very much like one note (see p 30). Irrespective of how the word is used outside music, harmony includes discord or dissonance, the opposite of which is concord or consonance. Both are harmony, although they obviously differ in harmonic quality. Anyone with a piano or other instrument capable of playing more than one note at a time, will notice that two neighbouring notes sounded together have the quality of dissonance, but as they move apart this quality decreases and then recurs as they approach the octave, where they will suddenly merge into a single-note sound. Every combination of two notes within this range will have a distinctive quality, depending upon their distance apart, which is called the 'interval' between them. The perspicacious may notice that between the interval of half an octave and a whole octave, something like the qualities already heard will recur in reverse order.

There are some pieces which highlight certain intervals by making pairs of instruments play tunes, always keeping that interval apart. The 'Pastoral Symphony' of Handel's *Messiah* has violins in parallel thirds – that is, keeping three inclusive notes of the scale apart. In Bach's St Matthew Passion in the accompanied recitative (q.v.) which precedes the first aria, 'Buss und Reu', there are two flutes, in either parallel thirds or sixths (which sound rather alike, since a sixth is an octave minus a third and vice versa). The next accompanied recitative (no. 18) has oboes d'amore in thirds and later sixths, and there are plenty of other examples from Bach wherever pairs of obbligato (q.v.) instruments are used.

Thirds and sixths vary between two sizes, major (larger) and minor (smaller) as the instruments play, which gives more variety than other parallel intervals, and is probably one reason why they have been the most common parallel intervals, from the 13th century in England (a little later on the Continent; see p 32) until the 20th. The Romantics loved them, the Viennese adore(d) them. They abound in waltzes and ländlers. Moving slowly with a sprinkling of chromaticism (see below), or swooping about on violins (e.g. the waltz from Richard Strauss's *Der Rosenkavalier*) they are a recipe for sentimentality.

Utterly unsentimental are the different parallel intervals of the 'Game of the Couples', the second movement of Bartók's concerto for orchestra of 1944. The 'couples' are: bassoons in minor sixths, oboes in thirds, clarinets in minor sevenths (a dissonant interval), flutes in fifths and muted trumpets in major seconds (another dissonance).

Chords and chord patterns

Nowadays many people learn to strum chords on a guitar as an accompaniment to their singing perhaps a folk song. And we can, to an extent, say of the chords that they are 'right' or 'wrong'. This is not just a matter of whether the chords are consonant or dissonant with the melody of the song, since chords consonant with it can sound 'wrong' and chords dissonant with it can sound 'right'. It is much more a matter of traditional patterns of successive chords, which we call 'chord progressions', certain aspects of which go back a very long way.

Harmony did not begin with someone trying out chords on a guitar or even on a lyre, since the concept of chords did not exist. It began, probably about a thousand years ago, with two people singing two different tunes simultaneously, who found, among other things, that the most satisfactory way to end was to converge on to a common final. This was the first cadence (see p 43) and the first recurring harmonic pattern. Out of it evolved the 'perfect cadence' (see p 84), the full stop (period) of Western music, the commonest chord 'progression' for about 400 years and still very much with us in popular music. Other traditional chord progressions have arisen in similar ways.

So we can see that harmony has its own grammar, its own syntax, which has arisen out of the simultaneous combining of different melodies, in other words out of counterpoint or polyphony. This syntax, this meaningful way of going on, is not directly related to what an individual chord actually sounds like. A conflict could arise when a composer wants a certain sound which is different from the grammatically necessary chord. Debussy came up against this problem as we shall see.

The basic harmonic principle of polyphony was that the combined melodies should in general make consonant harmony with one another. Dissonance would arise and was tolerated, even welcomed, when it could be heard to be a logical (grammatical) step between two consonances. (At a later period the first consonance could be omitted.) A good example of a strong dissonance arising in such a way occurs in the slow second movement of Bach's first Brandenburg concerto when the melody, which has first been played on an oboe and then high on a violin, is subsequently given to the low instruments of the band. Bach obviously likes the harmonic clash he has produced between this melody in the bass and the simpler melody on the first violins, for he does it again at once, and four more times during the movement. I do not think we can say that Bach liked the clash for its own sake, although that may have been so, but rather that he liked to be able to produce, quite logically according to the rules of counterpoint, a combination of sounds which was not in the book of 18th-century music. Breaking one rule by an uncompromising application of another more important one is often done by great composers. Beethoven was a great one for this. 'Rules', it should be understood, are merely the codification of the practices of composers within a given tradition and period, and as such are 'made to be broken', if music is not to fossilize. It should also be clear by now that harmony is much more than just adding nice noises to a tune.

Discords are not, of course, and never were, nasty noises. You might as well tell a gourmet that a piquant flavour is a nasty taste. The first two loud moments in Schubert's 'Unfinished' Symphony are strong dissonances, and very exciting and full of tension – frightening too, in this first movement which treats its gentle tunes with such violence. The same dissonance is reiterated eight times later on (the first loud passage in the development) with powerful effect, and tremendous 'relief' when the music finally gets away from it. But if this dissonance symbolizes pain, violence, struggle or whatever, its sound is nevertheless magnificent. In Schubert's day a dissonance was still followed by a consonance, although by then many composers would often reiterate a dissonance, as above, or seek other ways of delaying the ensuing consonance.

From early days, discords were used at the cadences. Some styles invariably have a discord→concord cadence formula. This no doubt arose from a tension→relaxation idea, but the cadental dissonances were usually mild, and the practice soon became mere procedural syntax. Thus dissonance had two functions – the expressive one of emotional tension, and the procedural one of aroused expectation.

Inevitably harmonic palates become jaded, and the harmony-conscious composers of the 19th century began to realize that the more complex, mildly dissonant sounds were juicier than the simple consonances or common chords, as we can now disdainfully call them. The dissonance→consonance process became something of an anti-climax. Wagner began to do something about it, but it was really left to Debussy and Schoenberg to take the decisive step and, in Schoenberg's phrase, to 'emancipate' the dissonance. In his atonal, expressionistic, psyche-probing music, it necessarily meant the virtual banishment of the consonance, since even an occasional appearance would suggest key or tonality; and for the same reason he imposed a pretty strict curfew on mild dissonances.

Debussy, in his impressionistic sensualism, was concerned with weaving a rich musical texture out of ear-tickling sounds, and mild dissonances were more his raw material. What he had to do was remove their procedural syntactical function, so that he could use them for their sheer quality as sounds, and at the same time be free to use any chord anywhere. One of his methods is to select a chord of the quality he wants and hold it – half a minute or more is not unusual – while he weaves melodies through it. Another is to make a melody out of the chord itself by moving it up and down *en bloc*. He could do this with concords too, but he had to be careful not to follow any chord with the traditionally expected one. Anything like a perfect cadence, for instance, would make us think of the chords in their traditional role, as links in a chain or words in a sentence, and relatively unimportant as individual sounds. Debussy flirts with atonality in the form of the whole-tone scale (see p 99), using the characteristic harmonies arising from it for his mistier or darker moments. The piano prelude 'Voiles' (Sails) hovers in a mist of such harmonies until suddenly, for a moment in the middle, the harmonic quality completely changes – a ray of sunlight perhaps, or a moment-ary breeze in a dead calm. Words are too specific and narrowing – Debussy puts the titles of his preludes at the end. In his unique opera *Pelléas et Mélisande* the moods and emotional situations are largely underlined by the qualities of the harmonies, usually associated with specific instrumental timbres (see previous chapter). The threatening, stifling darkness of the scene in the dungeons under the castle, has low down whole-tone scale harmonies, and Pelléas's and Golaud's return to the surface and the fresh air is depicted by changing to harmonies not based on the whole-tone scale, along with changes in the instrumentation, such melody as there is (two notes) remaining constant.

There was another, much simpler solution to the problem of the comparatively dull sound of the common chords, which was to use them in the traditional manner, but to ginger them up with added notes – a characteristic of Delius and a number of minor composers. Later on this became standard procedure with certain types of lighter music, an effective example of which was the 'swing' bands of the 1940s. Stravinsky ends his Symphony in three Movements of 1945 with a typical 'swing' band chord. But more than thirty years before that, in the *Rite of Spring* and other works, Stravinsky had extended the Debussy treatment to strong dissonances. At about the same time Schoenberg had come to strong dissonance through extreme chroma-ticism.

Chromaticism was discussed in the chapter on melody (pp 65–66). Chromatic melody need not have chromatic harmony, as we see for instance in the music of Mozart. Conversely a diatonic (non-chromatic) melody can be given chromatic harmony, as in the first strain of Liszt's well-known 'Liebestraum'. The first few variations of Delius's *Brigg Fair* are different chromatic harmonizations of that diatonic folk tune. Bach uses a certain chorale (hymn) tune in five different places in his St Matthew Passion always in different keys and sometimes with different harmonizations. Its final appearance (no. 72) is immediately after the death of Jesus on the Cross, and Bach expresses the poignant emotions of this moment with some highly chromatic harmony. It is well worth comparing this harmonization with any of the others (nos. 21, 23, 53 and 63) which are much less chromatic. The chorale tune itself is always diatonic.

Chromatic harmony *and* melody first appear for a short time in vocal polyphony (madrigals) at the end of the 16th century, usually expressing anguish, sorrow, unrequited love, etc. In the 17th and 18th centuries some composers used it more than others, usually for highly expressive purposes and mainly in slow music. Purcell, for instance, quite a lot – Handel not much. Bach (e.g. *Chromatic Fantasia and Fugue*) and Mozart are two composers who would use it sometimes in faster music as well, where it tends to darken and dramatize the music. Compare the first movement of Mozart's C minor piano concerto (K 491), which has a chromatic main theme, with the first movement of Beethoven's no. 3 which is in the same key, in about the same tempo and possibly modelled on the Mozart, but much less chromatic.

Various 19th-century composers took chromaticism a few steps further; most of Chopin's music is highly chromatic, as is a great deal of another pianist/composer, Liszt. Compare the very beginning of Chopin's third nocturne (B major) and Liszt's A flat piano concerto. The keyboard lends itself comfortably to chromaticism, but it was the almost continuous chromaticism of Wagner's *Tristan and Isolde*, beyond which there was no going without abandoning key or tonality (see p 66) which led to Schoenberg's doing just that. Wagner's harmonies always suggested or pointed towards a key, so that in the end he had to settle somewhere. Schoenberg was obliged to use harmonies in such a way that if they suggested a key (and most, if not all, do), that key had immediately to be contradicted by the next harmony. This almost automatically led him to use all twelve notes of the chromatic scale within a very short space of time, and was pointing towards the ordering of the twelve notes into a row or series, although Schoenberg sailed that course only some years after he had thrown tonality overboard (see p 66). Among possible harmonies, the strong dissonances, the most pungent discords suggest tonality the least, and therefore needed to be used the most in atonal music.

Later on consonances could be used again, but not in their former role.

Important composers who did not abandon tonality usually forged their own harmonic style or styles. Bartók was one, and Stravinsky, who could make the commonest of chords his own personal property by means of a deft and highly original instrumentation and distribution of the notes in the various octaves, enabling him to carry elements of his harmonic style into the ranks of the twelve-note serialist (atonal) composers, which he joined in the 1950s after the death of Schoenberg, without losing his tremendous individuality.

Harmony arose from the simultaneous sounding of different notes of the seven-note diatonic scale. The twelve note chromatic scale added no new intervals and hardly any new chords. Although the 20th century saw much greater use of dissonance, the discords used had virtually all been there before. There were really no new chords to make, except perhaps note-clusters, which are a number of notes clustered very close together (usually four or more simultaneous notes at semitone intervals). They were used in America fairly early in this century by Henry Cowell and Charles Ives, but did not come to be used in Europe until comparatively recently, particularly in the music of Ligeti. Note-clusters do not actually sound much like chords, since our ears have more difficulty in sorting out the different notes, and we tend to hear something between a number of notes and a noise. A great deal depends on the instruments used, and whether the cluster is situated high up, low down or in the middle, how many notes there are in it and so on.

We are now in the strange area of simultaneous different notes not making chords. This sounds rather like 'soapless soap', but in electronic music it becomes necessary to make the distinction between a chord and a 'note mixture'. As we saw in the previous chapter (p 68) a single note on an instrument or voice contains overtones which we do not hear as separate notes (although we can detect some of them if we know what to listen for). This is because they are harmonics, and because they are 'in phase' (their frequencies are in step) and have no independent overtone structure of their own. In other words the ear identifies them as all part of the one sound. Within the sound of a bell we can usually hear several notes – which are not harmonics, although probably of a related frequency – in which case we would expect to hear a chord, but we do not. The reason must be the same, that the ear identifies the different notes as issuing from a single vibrating body. Electronically produced sounds of simultaneous different pitches may well exhibit similar relationships depending on the process which gave rise to them. Also pure tones, that is pitched sounds without any overtones, can easily lose their identity as separate sounds when mixed with others.

Akin to but more subtle than note-clusters is something called 'statistical sound', which might appear to be a definition of dullness. We all know that many violins playing the same note make a quite different (and more exciting) sound than one violin playing slightly louder. This 'chorus effect' as it is called is because of minute differences between the different violins, differences of timbre, phase and pitch, which are changing because of the slightly different rates of unsynchronized vibrato (q.v.). If they differ too much, to the extent of some of them being felt to be out of tune, the effect is not the same at all, as conductors of amateur orchestras know well! Democracy depends upon a reasonable consensus of opinion. With statistical sound however, the intention is not to produce a single note or a chord made up of a number of easily identifiable single notes, but a sound made up of a certain distribution of different pitches between specified upper and lower limits. If it were five different pitches to be evenly distributed over five semitones it would be a note-cluster, but if it were twenty-five different pitches to be distributed over a range of seven semitones with a tendency to favour the average (i.e. a greater concentration of pitches nearer the middle of the range), then the composer has to work out the mathematics of it as well as how best to obtain his effect from the performers. He is not going to ask for (or get) twenty-five precise pitches. Rather he will probably instruct the players to slide about independently within certain (perhaps individually) prescribed limits, which will statistically produce the desired effect. The conservative-minded may ask why? The reason is that many of the most interesting natural sounds are an amalgam of many similar, but not quite identical sounds – the rustling of leaves in the wind, swans in flight, chirping cicadas, 'the humming of innumerable bees', burning sticks, etc. No composer would attempt, of course, to imitate any of these, but to capture their essence. As with Debussy, the intention is to make a music out of an exciting sound texture: harmony and timbre go hand in hand, only more so, in that we can no longer distinguish between the two.

5 FORM

Art of any kind is inconceivable without form. The beauty of structure can be one of the best delights to the music-lover, as it is to the biologist, the anatomist, the painter, the sculptor and the architect.

Music maybe comes nearest to architecture, in the vital part that form or design plays in its life, though it is really unlike any other art; and analogies are misleading.

The simplest elements count in form – the building up of a tiny two- or three-note motive against another motive, of phrase against phrase, sentence on sentence – until a series of these constitutes a section of a short piece. This section will be balanced by a contrasting one, similarly built up in general lines, but with subtle variety in detail; and so a piece grows. The experienced composer can think in long stretches. If we analyse in short ones, we must remember that much of his building may be *subconscious* work. He knows where he wants to go, and that other mind – call it what you like – having been laboriously instructed in his youth, now knows how to get him there, and does not necessarily worry him often about the road and the vehicle. But he may agonize for days over a transition, or shape and re-shape a phrase. Beethoven was a great re-shaper. His notebooks show his processes, and they should make impatient would-be creators humble. Schubert, on the other hand, scarcely ever sketched or altered. Music just poured out of him. Every man to his type. The one is not necessarily better than the other.

But we must be clear about what form is. A symphony has form, but so does a single stroke on a gong, or a single note on a violin. Of the latter two the gong stroke's form is more interesting. We can feel its 'logical' progress from its beginning to its dying-away end. But it is not just a loud clang getting quieter. A good gong (one that goes 'bash' and 'boynngg' at the same time) actually becomes – or appears to become, which is the same thing – louder for a while as the 'sh . . .' part of the bash comes through. The timbre is changing the whole time. A stroke on a good gong is an exciting piece of music in itself. A violinist can make a single note die away, get richer in tone, he can give it more or less vibrato and so on, but what we expect from a violin is a tune, or at any rate more than one note and probably a great many. Conversely nothing is worse than someone endlessly bashing away on a gong, the effectiveness of which tends to vary inversely with its frequency of use.

Form has been put last in the 'elements', not because it is the least of them, far from it, but because it is the means, or rather the process of putting together the others. Rhythm and pitch are put together formally into a melody. The timbre may be incidental or be part of the form as in a concerto, which is essentially a piece of music of contrasting timbres disposed in certain formal ways. In polyphonic music a large part of the form is the putting together of simultaneous melodies, which involves the formal manipulation of harmony. This happens in a simpler way in the chord progressions of a more homophonic style.

Generally speaking, until comparatively recently form has been the manipulation of melody as master, with rhythm (other than that of the melody itself), timbre and harmony as servants. Many aspects of the construction of an extended composition may be found in microcosm in a simple tune.

A–B–A = *ternary form*

The two basic principles of form in music are: repetition with a difference, and repetition *after* a difference. The latter could be represented as A–B–A, often called ternary (three-part) form. In a tune this is likely to be A–A–B–A, since simpler forms tend to have matching pairs of equal-length phrases. The Welsh song, 'All through the Night' is an example, so is 'The British Grenadiers', but when this is played rather than sung – as it usually is – the final A phrase has a few extra notes by way of decoration, so that what was

dum | dum dum dum dum | dum   dum diddle | dum dum diddle diddle | dum

becomes

dum | dum diddle dum diddle | dum diddle dum diddle | dum dum diddle diddle | dum

An element of *variation* has been introduced.

The A–B–A principle obviously operates in the so-called 'minuet and trio', which is really just a sandwich of: *minuet 1 – minuet 2* (called 'trio'. See p 70) – *minuet 1* again, and can be applied to any dance movement. Thus in a baroque suite there might be *gavotte 1 – gavotte 2 – gavotte 1* again. Outside the ballroom the middle dance, the 'trio', need not be a dance of the same type. In Beethoven's 'Pastoral' Symphony, for instance, the scherzo is in the usual three-in-a-bar, but the trio is in two, and he does the same thing in his Ninth Symphony.

A–B–A form is often called 'song form' or 'aria form'. The operatic arias of the late baroque were very often in this form, and are usually called '*da capo*' ('from the beginning') arias, since the direction *da capo* in the score saved any need to write out the A section again. Not that the repeat would be identical to the first part, for the singers would freely embellish the written music when they sang it the second time (rather as in 'The British Grenadiers', only more so). Particularly lavish embellishers were the bumptious *castrati*, who flourished at this time and who had better reason than most artists for feeling that the world owed them more than just a living. Many of Handel's operatic arias take this form, and some of the arias in his oratorios. There are only three *da capo* arias in the *Messiah*, 'He was despised', 'Why do the nations . . .' and 'The trumpet shall sound', though for some reason the middle section of the latter is quite often left out.

A–B–A form is one of the simplest structures, and is very often used in light music, in short pieces and quite often in slow movements, whose structure will tend to be simpler than that of quick movements, since there will be fewer notes in the same length of time.

Half close and full close

Another well-known A–A–B–A tune is 'The old folks at Home' ('Swannee River'). Here the first two As are not quite the same. The first A (A 1) has a few less notes in it latterly, and ends on a higher and less 'final'-sounding note than the second A (A 2).

```
A 1 ... Far—
                    far
                            -way———
                        a-              ←——— ... (keynote)
A 2 ... That's
                where
                            old folks
                    the               stay. ←——— ... (keynote)
```

B is quite different and the last A is A 2, which it must be if the tune is to have an end. A 1 ends with what we can call a half close, a sort of musical comma, whereas A 2 ends (on the keynote or 'final'. See p 42) with a full close, a sort of musical full-stop (period). At this point, if we were harmonizing the tune, we should have a perfect cadence (see p 76). The famous 'Ode to Joy' tune, which is the basis of the choral last movement of Beethoven's Ninth Symphony does the same thing. The two As are identical except for their last three notes.

```
A 1 Freude ... etc.              E- -ly-
                          aus           -si-um
                ... Tochter                   ←——— ... (key-
                                                        note)
A 2 Wir ... etc.              dein
                      -sche    Hei-
            ... Himm-li-             -lig-tum ←——— ... (keynote)
```

These are two examples of just one of the ways in which a melody can 'punctuate' itself. The harmony can do the same, and usually it underlines what the melody is doing, although it can be made to 'wrong foot' the melody and bring it to an unexpected end or, more often, to extend the melody beyond its expected end. All these devices are clearly invaluable to the composer of extended pieces, enabling him to lead us by the hand from one melody to another, rather than just hold them up in turn for our inspection; to interrupt and interpolate, to surprise and even to disappoint, for I am not suggesting that a piece of music has to be a walk through Paradise. The structure of an extended piece can in effect say this: '. . . that's the end of that – but wait . . . here's this gentle, very beautiful melody . . . and here it comes round again, flying higher . . . and round agai- . . . No. Complete change of mood – not gentle at all – and yet now fragments of that gentle melody are being thrown around rather violently. Now the violence has gone and that gentle melody is back but different. It's coming to an end – not just going on round and round as it did before.' That describes the structural procedure of part of the first movement of Schubert's 'Unfinished' Symphony. The passage referred to is quite early on and should not be too difficult to find.

Tonality; binary form
Key or tonality (see pp 42–44) or rather *changing* key can be an important element in form. A composer can have a full close with perfect cadence and all, so that we feel it to be the end of a passage and yet at the same time we know that there is more to come, because the full close is in a key different from the one the music started in. That is precisely what we feel at the place in the slow (second) movement of Haydn's 'Surprise' Symphony (no. 94) where the composer has placed the loud chord that gives the symphony its name. The full close just before the loud chord is not in the initial (the 'home' key), and however loud and big the chord is, we know we are only halfway through the tune even when hearing it for the first time. On a smaller scale in the Christmas hymn 'O come all ye faithful' ('Adeste Fideles') the third line of the first verse ends with the word 'Bethlehem' to the same fragment of melody that ends the refrain to the words 'Christ the Lord'. But 'Bethlehem' is lower down and in an 'away' key, whereas 'Christ the Lord' must be in the home key since it ends the tune.

On a larger scale we can say that concluding the first section of a piece in an 'away' key is a basic formal principle in a huge number of extended pieces – sonatas, symphonies, concertos and so on – from the 17th century to the demise of the key system in the 20th. It is the basis of binary (two-part) form, out of which evolved sonata form (see p 100). Binary form – the 'Surprise' Symphony tune mentioned above is an example – can be represented as A–A–B–B with A finishing in an away key, and B finishing in the home key. But that tells us nothing about the respective natures of A and B. Very often the latter part of B is much more like A than it is like the first part of B, in which case a more faithful representation would be: A1–A1–BA2–BA2. (The Haydn tune is in this category.) In other words most binary-form tunes – and more extended pieces in binary form – will have a considerable ternary (A–B–A) element as well. But there is more repetition than that.

Motives

All the tunes and pieces mentioned in this chapter are fashioned in varying degrees out of a number of motifs or motives. A motive is a tiny scrap of music, just large enough to be recognizable – usually just a few notes and a rhythm, but sometimes just one or the other. A motive will tend to be repeated with a difference. The rhythm may stay the same while the notes change a little. In the A part of the Haydn tune most of the notes come twice (which is a motive in itself), in a rhythm of short-short short-short short-short long – in such a way that we seem to hear two phrases, one 'answering' the other. The nursery-rhyme tune 'Ah vous dirai-je Maman', sung in English to 'Twinkle twinkle little star' has exactly the same rhythmic pattern. The A part of Beethoven's 'Ode to Joy' tune (ternary form) is made out of three motives, two of which are moved up and down. The very short B part appears to be quite different, as it should, but it arises from one of the A motives, altered a little and then decorated, which gives rise to a new motive. And there are other motives seeking to group the notes otherwise than according to the 4-in-a-bar rhythm of the tune. *All* of these things we are aware of – some of them consciously, others subconsciously. These are the things which make the difference between a tune and a mere succession of notes.

Motives are not just the molecules of melody. They play a large part in binding together whole movements and often whole works. Probably the best known of all motives is the four notes which open Beethoven's Fifth Symphony. Not only does this motive pervade the first movement; but as a rhythm it figures largely in all the other movements as well. The opening tune of Mozart's G minor Symphony (no. 40) starts:

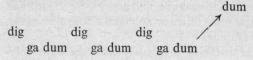

dum

dig   dig   dig
  ga dum   ga dum   ga dum

The three 'digga dums' are identical and are a falling semitone with the lower note repeated. This motive crops up many times, either as part of the tune or on its own, but the falling semitone without the repeated note permeates the whole work. It retains its rhythm to the extent that the accent is always on the first note of the two, which is often drawn out in length, achieving the same effect. But in the main Mozart uses it melodically rather than rhythmically in the symphony as a whole. As does Brahms in his Second Symphony, whose first three notes are a step of a semitone down and back. This motive is not quite so all-pervasive as Mozart's, but it is fairly prominent in all the movements, being the first three notes of the opening tune of the finale, and in the third movement likewise, only upside down (semitone step *up* and back) and with the first note repeated. Sibelius binds together the three-movements-in-one of his Seventh Symphony with a motive of a step down, a step back and a step up; Bach his huge St Matthew Passion with two steps up and one back, Wagner his *Meistersinger* with a jump down of a fourth and a step up, Britten his *Turn of the Screw* with a jump up of a fourth and down a third.

Variation and development

Variation and development are both devices involving repetition with a difference, but they are not the same. Variation takes a tune or theme as a whole and subjects it to certain changes. These changes can be to the tune itself: changing its rhythm, decorating it by adding extra notes, changing it from major to minor and vice versa, even constructing a new tune on the same harmony. Variations by Mozart, Beethoven (probably the greatest composer of variations) and Brahms are usually of this type. Or the changes can be not to the tune itself but to what goes on with it – something Haydn likes to do, for instance in the slow movement of his 'Emperor' string quartet, where his 'Emperor's Hymn' tune remains unchanged throughout, to accompaniments which change with each variation. Sometimes they are just chords (homophonic), sometimes other melodies (polyphonic). In the slow movements of Haydn's symphonies, which are quite often in a fairly free variation form, he usually has a few of the other kinds of variation as well – and occasionally even some development. The 'Surprise' Symphony is a good example, and nos. 53, 55, 92, 101 and 103 (with two themes) are some of the symphonies whose slow movements do the same sort of thing.

In the keeping-the-theme-the-same category come the older polyphonic variation forms of ground bass (*basso ostinato*), chaconne and passacaglia. In these the theme is not so much a tune – since it need not be particularly interesting in itself – as a series of notes, which is repeated again and again usually in the bass (the bottom part), while different melodies are interwoven above. The famous 'Dido's Lament' from Purcell's opera, *Dido and Aeneas*, is a song over a ground bass, and there are many more examples from Purcell both vocal and instrumental (e.g. his Chaconne in G minor for strings), since this form was a favourite of his. Bach has a famous passacaglia for organ in C minor, and Brahms uses one for the finale of his E minor Fourth Symphony. Pieces in these forms are commonly in the minor and in three-time. In a passacaglia the theme can be in any of the parts and can change from one part to another, but in the chaconne, strictly speaking (which musicians usually are not) only in the bass. Both were originally old Spanish dances, presumably in the minor and in three-time. The finale of the 'Eroica' Symphony (in the major and in two-time) is a fascinating mixture of the different types of variation form.

Variation is a form as well as a procedure. Development is a procedure. Variation form is older than the key system; a set of variations can run right through without a change of key, although most 18th- and 19th-century composers will contrive to change key somewhere along the line. Development is a product of the key system and depends very much on changing key. Not surprisingly it is to be found in the development section of a sonata-form movement (see p 102), but quite often elsewhere as well. The English word for this section is not a good one, since 'development' implies growth or improvement, whereas fragmentation and destruction are much more likely to take place. The German word *Durchführung* (literally 'through-leading') is far better, because the purpose of a development section is to *lead* from the away key at the end of the exposition, *through* other keys (i.e. not directly) to the home key for the recapitulation. Commonly a composer will take a fragment of an earlier tune, perhaps just a motive, and play around with it, worry it, while passing through different keys. Schubert is doing that in the first movement of his 'Unfinished' Symphony, when he is rather violently throwing about that gentle melody discussed on page 85 above. This is not the development *section* and to develop a theme here is a little unorthodox (meaning not that a composer should not; only that most pieces do not). Passing a melody or melodic fragment around between the different parts, as Schubert is doing, is a very common polyphonic device. Sonata form is a monodic or non-polyphonic form, but the development provides an opportunity for a composer to show off his polyphonic skill, if any. From Mozart we have many fine polyphonic development sections. Examples are those of the first and last movements of the Prague Symphony (no. 38), the G minor and the 'Jupiter' (nos. 40 and 41), although the finale of the 'Jupiter' is polyphonic everywhere else (another unorthodoxy). There are numerous examples from Haydn too. It was from him that Mozart learned how to use counterpoint (polyphony) in a sonata form movement.

Beethoven could compose polyphonic developments with the best when he chose, but a favourite trick of his is to set up a sort of multiple sandwich of two alternating fragments, one or both of which come from earlier tunes and one of which changes key, so that the other is brought in in a different key each time it appears. (Schubert does this incidentally in the development proper of his 'Unfinished'.) An easy-to-follow example is in the development of the finale of Beethoven's 'Emperor' concerto. The piano plays the first phrase of the main theme of the movement several times, each time in a different key, and each time preceded by a particular key-changing passage from the orchestra (with a tum-ti-tum tum-tum-tum rhythm).

With the abandonment of tonality (key) the distinction between development and variation tends to become blurred. Wagner, as we have seen, spent a lot of time on the move from key to key, giving a feeling of continuous development; though Wagner's music always settles in a key in the end, if not for long. Once key has gone, in a sense there is nothing but development, but we cannot think of atonal music as such, since it is never going to settle in any key. On the other hand Schoenberg's twelve-note system involves one set of twelve notes, which comes in various guises, but recurs *in its entirety* again and again – not unlike a passacaglia, although a fundamental difference is that consecutive notes of the set may also appear simultaneously and thus make the harmony. In other words twelve-note music is a sort of variation form. In the absence of key, development, dependent upon moving from key to key, has no real meaning. But it is possible to have *quasi*-development by indulging in the fragmentation of tunes and other characteristic developmental devices.

Space

Because so much of the music we hear is performed by instrumentalists and singers sitting as near together as they conveniently can, we tend not to notice that music occupies space as well as time. Making music move in space can be done either by having the players move, like a band on the march, or more interestingly by separating the performers and passing the music around among them, in other words by antiphony. In this formal device, probably one of the oldest, one group answers another. If they are playing or singing the same music one after the other, then again we have the basic formal principle of repetition with a difference, in this case a difference of space. Such is an echo. Antiphony has been exploited at various times and places. The music of Giovanni Gabrieli composed in Venice around 1600 frequently needs careful disposition of instrumental and choral forces to achieve its effect. Antiphony, however, does not seem to have been particularly popular in 16th-century England, and Thomas Tallis's forty-part motet, 'Spem in alium', is unusual. Such a large number of parts is quite pointless unless the eight five-part choirs can be well separated *and heard to be so*.

Behind-the-scene effects have been used in music since probably the beginning of opera. Beethoven's off-stage trumpet call in *Leonora* no. 3 (and no. 2) was not an original idea, either in the opera or the overture.

Not really until the 20th century have the full possibilities of spatial deployment been exploited. The intensely geographical (sometimes almost topographical) Charles Ives has several pieces in which the spatial arrangement is vital. In *From the Steeples and Mountains* four sets of tubular bells (chimes) sound from the four corners of the room, and a trumpet and a trombone are played in the middle. For the beautiful *The Unanswered Question* on stage are a trumpet asking, and four flutes trying unsuccessfully to answer while offstage, unseen but all-pervading (since a sound masked from a direct route to the ear will appear to come from everywhere), is a string orchestra with no questions to ask or answer. This is a good example of Ives's Emersonian transcendentalism (see p 49). Nearly fifty years later Stockhausen composed his *Gruppen* (Groups), for three separated orchestras forming a triangle, with the audience as pigs-in-the-middle. *Carré* (Square) of a few years later increases the orchestras to four and adds a choir to each.

It is much easier to deploy four or more loudspeakers than the same number of orchestras, and so taped electronic music lends itself well to such arrangements. Synchronization is no problem, and the number of separate and independent sound sources is only limited by the degree of sophistication of the equipment used. No taped electronic piece will use less than two, as that is the normal stereophonic set-up, but many pieces use more. Stockhausen's 'Gesang der Junglinge' (Song of the Youths) of 1956 used five, and in 1958 the seventy-five-year-old Varèse (who had yearned for electronic facilities back in the 1930s) had some 425 loudspeakers at the Brussels World Fair for his 'Poème Electronique'. But the piece is quite simple and I doubt if visitors to the Philips pavilion would have noticed had the number been halved or even quartered. Which leads us to the important matter of perceptible differences.

Parameters

Serial music began with Schoenberg's twelve-note system bringing both the melody and the harmony under the control of a single, recurring series of twelve notes. The next generation sought to extend the sovereignty of the series over everything else – rhythm, dynamics, attack etc. Composers had now to think more analytically and scientifically about the variables, the different manipulable things, the 'parameters' (a word for these is now needed), which had to be formed into scales; degrees between extremes; degrees of loudness; of duration (note-lengths. See p. 60); of density (number of simultaneous notes); and so on. At first every parameter had twelve degrees to match the twelve degrees of the chromatic scale, irrespective of the ear's (and often of the performers') powers of discrimination. In order to obtain a more precise control over the parameters, some serial composers turned to electronics, which removed the necessity for having twelve notes in the octave – or even for the octave – since electronically we can construct any scale we like (see p 67). However, in electronic music pitch becomes a less important parameter than timbre, which can now be controlled and given a scale of degrees, something impossible to achieve between, say, the timbre of a violin and that of a trombone. These latter are off-the-peg sounds, whereas electronic sounds can be tailor-made. I talk a lot about electronic music, to which some may object, but it is very much with us today. It has affected every branch of music and has played a vital part in the revolution in music that began at the half-century.

Composition of music is the manipulation of the parameters. That is what Bach, Beethoven, Berlioz, Dufay, Debussy, Duke Ellington and Everybody Else were and are doing. In the 1950s everything needed re-thinking, including who should do the manipulating. Not so long ago composers did not tell performers how loud or soft to play. This was a parameter performers could manipulate for themselves and one which, albeit in a somewhat blanket manner, the listener to a broadcast or a recording can now also manipulate. He can choose too *when* he hears a recording. On the old player-pianos the 'operator' could control the tempo as well as the loudness, and we may before long have recordings the speed of which can be changed by the listener without affecting the parameters of pitch and timbre at the same time. I should like to be able to hurry up a Klemperer now and then.

Indeterminacy is the not-very-lovely word given to allowing the performer – or anyone else other than the composer, including Jack Random and Joe Chance – to manipulate some of the parameters. It can range from the minimal 'these pieces may be played in any order', through the freer 'play the notes forwards or backwards in any rhythm' to something like 'play anything on any instrument other than a trombone'. Indeterminacy is itself a parameter with degrees between extremes and is, like many parameters, most interesting in its middle range.

Music theatre

Having given away some of his parameters, the composer can feel justified in taking over someone else's. This is the way to music theatre, in which a composer might direct a group of actors to speak words put together and passed about according to formal musical principles, or he might organize any series of events, which could include someone falling off a ladder (a fairly transient, 'percussive' event), two people playing chess (a more continuous state, perhaps an 'accompaniment'), other people building a structure (a crescendo), etc. The converse to this is the commoner sort of music theatre where dramatic forms are used to organize music. For example, a dancer may activate a reluctant horn player, who awakens a sleeping singer, whose song is the headlines of the evening paper which covered her face while she slept and which is taken from her by the dancer and shown to a rich percussion player with a social conscience . . . etc. . . . .

Random form; 'moment' form

When so many traditional forms require us to remember something which happened five or more minutes ago, it is rather nice to be told we can forget everything we hear because it does not relate to what follows. This we might expect to be the case with music composed by chance operations – throwing dice, using tables of random numbers etc. – as done by John Cage ('My purpose is to eliminate purpose') and others. It is certainly preferable to being unable to perceive the progress forward of a work whose structure has been carefully organized. However there is chance and chance. A coin can only come down one of two ways up, a di(c)e one of six. A piece of music which arranges only three different notes in a random order and rhythm, would soon become too repetitive, although we should tire of the three notes far sooner if their order and/or rhythm had been repetitive too. The random ordering of a fairly small number of possibilities has been present in music for some time. It is the principle underlying the rhythmic structure of sections of Stravinsky's *Rite of Spring* of 1913, and it was not new then. Most of the greatest music ever composed has depended upon our not knowing precisely what *is* coming next, but knowing what *can*.

Stockhausen composed his *Kontakte* ('Contacts') for electronic sounds (on tape) with or without piano and percussion in what he calls 'moment' form. Each 'moment' is autonomous, a complete piece of music in itself, and we are not expected to regard it as a part of something bigger. And yet this long piece (a continuous $34\frac{1}{2}$ minutes) has a great unity brought about by the fact that the electronic sounds have all been constructed in a technically ingenious manner which interrelates their timbre, pitch (if any) and rhythm. At about 24 minutes Stockhausen demonstrates that these parameters, together with that of form, are all part of the same continuum of chopped-up time. A highly timbreful, pitched sound swoops down until it becomes too low to hear as a note, and its vibrations (see p 62) are slow enough to be heard as separate pulses (i.e. a rhythm). The timbre of the original sound (consisting of higher frequency vibrations) becomes a pitch attached to the pulses making them into separate notes, which then slow down further, dropping in pitch as they must. The final pulse becomes a continuous note like a pedal point (or a drone) which is a formal device. There has been a bit of 'cheating' but timbre and melody have appeared to pass continuously through rhythm to form. On the face of it, 'moment' form would appear to be synonymous with non-form, but in *Kontakte* the unity is so great between the other things that the 'what-comes-next' aspect of it may be as free as the composer wishes.

Here we attempt to fill in some of the details. Inevitably there will remain large gaps. There are many books on the rudiments of music for those readers who wish to investigate such matters more thoroughly than there is space for here. On the other hand some readers may not wish to tackle the chapter on the reading of music. Chapters twelve, thirteen and fourteen are interdependent and should be read in that order.

1 SCALES; MODES; KEYS

A piano keyboard looks, as we all know, like this:

Where there is no black note in between two adjacent white notes, the step (the interval) between those white notes is a semitone. Wherever there *is* a black note between two white notes, the step between the white notes is a whole tone (equal to two semitones). We can see that if we take seven steps along the white notes, wherever we start, and whichever way we go, we shall take five whole-tone steps and two semitone steps. These two sizes of step give rise to the word 'diatonic' for this kind of scale. Having taken our seven steps, we have gone up or down an octave and if we go any further, the pattern of whole tones and semitones, whatever it was, will happen again.

If we actually do this on a piano, we find that the set of seven steps from, say, G to G sounds different from that of, say, E to E. Not just higher or lower, but different in quality, in *mood*, because the semitone steps come in different places in relation to where we start and finish. In the G to G going up, the semitones come between the third and fourth notes and the sixth and seventh notes; in the E to E, between the first and second and the fifth and sixth notes. These two scales are in fact two of the old 'modes', the Mixolydian (G to G) and the Phrygian (E to E). All the modes will sound different in this respect, although some will resemble others to a certain extent. For instance D to D (Dorian mode) and A to A (Aeolian mode) both have a semitone between their second and third notes, but differ over the position of the other semitone.

A tune in a mode will not be just a scale (although it could contain one: for example, the folk-song 'I love my Love' which is in the Dorian mode). A scale 'defines' a mode by starting on its lower 'final', and ending on its upper final, and giving all the other notes on the way. The final is the 'homing' note (see pp 29 and 42). Some music shows stronger 'homing' tendencies; for example, a Flamenco singer seems almost irresistably drawn to his final, which happens also to be about his lowest note so that one is reminded of a tethered duck trying to fly. It would be boring just to listen to a Flamenco singer for long (he of course accompanies a dancer) and this is partly because he has no other note demanding special attention.

Take the tune of the Christmas carol 'God rest you merry, gentlemen' (the 'London' tune). This Aeolian mode tune (A to A) starts on its final – something which often happens, but does not by any means have to be the case – then it takes a leap upwards, then comes down the scale step by step and up again step by step:

```
E        you mer-                              -may.      E
D                  -ry,                  dis-              D
C                      gen-              you               C
B                          -tle-     -thing               B
A  God rest                -men,   no-                     A
G                              Let                         G
```

The note (E) which at the beginning the tune leaps up to, is the same one it comes back to after its trip down the scale and up again. So this note is especially prominent. Next comes an exact repeat of that first music to different words, so again that note has prominence which it retains to a smaller degree through the middle section of the tune. At the end its prominence is shared with the final.

```
A                      of                               A
G             -dings                                    G
F         (-i-)                                         F
E     ti-                    co(m)-                     E
D     it's                      (-om-)                  D
C And                              -fort                C
B                                   and                 B
A                                   joy————             A
```

95

The E, which I will now call 'the dominant', is not now as prominent as the final (A) which is at the end of two scales, one going up to the final and the other coming down to it. But the dominant is rather more prominent than it looks. The italicized syllables are those which come on the 'strong' beats, the main pulses of the music (see p 52). Other things being equal, the notes on the strong beats will be more prominent than the others. Over the whole tune, the final and the dominant come out about equal in prominence (the dominant just wins), but both these notes are much more prominent than any of the others. The dominant originated in responsorial singing (see p 40). The solo singer(s) hovered about the dominant (known as the 'reciting note'), then the choir started from that note and finished on the final. Although it was not always so, we can regard the dominant as being the fifth note (up) of the scale, starting on the final. The eighth note up, the octave is the final again. So in going from the dominant to the final we can either go up or down. Looking again at the end of the tune of 'God rest you merry . . .', we can see that it does both those things – *up* four notes (inclusive) from dominant to final on 'tidings of', and *down* five notes (inclusive) from dominant to final on 'comfort and joy'.

A (final)		of			(final)—A
G	-dings				G
F	(-i-)				F
E (dominant)	*ti*	co(*m*)-			(dominant)—E
D			(-om-)		D
C			-fort		C
B			and		B
A (final)			*joy* ——	(final)—A	

The Aeolian mode (A to A) – another tune in it is 'The Wraggle-taggle Gypsies' – and the Dorian mode (D to D) 'What shall we do with the drunken sailor?'; 'Brigg fair' are the commonest 'minor' modes. The other 'minor' mode, the Phrygian (E to E), has an especially pathetic character, since its semitones are immediately above the final and immediately above the dominant. The music will therefore fall on to these important notes by a semitone – a pathetic, cry-like melodic step. The magnificent tune by the 16th-century composer Thomas Tallis, on which Vaughan Williams wrote his fantasia, is in the Phrygian mode. Tallis's tune can also be found in the English Hymnal (no. 92).

Of the 'major' modes, the Lydian (F to F) seems to have existed – before the 20th century – more in name than in fact. The Mixolydian (G to G) is the mode of 'She walked through the Fair' and a lot of American 'country and Western' music ('Old Joe Clark') and 'railroad' songs ('Can'cha line 'em'). The Ionian (C to C) is the commonest of all the modes and is the same as a major key. A minor key is in effect an Aeolian mode (A to A) with borrowings from the Ionian at the cadences (see p 43).

The advantage of keys (the key system) is that the final can be changed without changing the mode. One can construct a scale, major or minor, starting on any note, and have the whole tones and semitones in the same relative places in the scale. A glance at our picture of the piano keyboard at the beginning of this chapter will show that, to do this, we shall have to use black notes as well as white. Both major and minor scales start with a whole tone step up. So if we start, say, on E, we shall have to go straight to a black note, since F is only a semitone up.

In a tune which is in a key, we know which note is the final or keynote, even if the tune has not started on it. This is through experience of other similar tunes, and the narrowing down of the modes to two (see p 43). We have seen that a tune can spend quite a lot of time paying special attention to another note (quite probably the dominant) before returning to the final at the end. The same thing can be done with keys themselves. We can call the key in which a piece of music starts the 'home' key. From there the music can move to another key. This new key is quite likely to be *the key of the dominant*, which means that the note that was the dominant in the home key is now the final in the new key. (We should now use the word 'keynote' instead of 'final', but the two words mean exactly the same thing.) In due course the music will return to the home key before finishing. This is the basic principle of the key system, which was beginning to operate in practice, if not in theory, at the end of the 16th century.

Thomas Morley's lute song, 'Mistress mine well may you fare', published conveniently in 1600, has a four-line verse. The first two lines each have a cadence on the final, and the other two each have a cadence on the dominant, which means that the dominant has temporarily become the new final. But the piece could not end there. A refrain follows, which is repeated and has a cadence back on the original final. I mention this piece out of many because of its utter simplicity, and the fact that every cadence comes twice. It is therefore particularly easy to hear the changes of key.

§ One of the most useful qualities the listener can develop is the power to hear changes of key. Many of a composer's subtle effects are missed if one cannot do this. And form, as we have seen, and shall see in more detail in the next chapter, may depend to a considerable degree on key: the choice of keys, their balance, the nature and amount of key change (modulation), and lots of devices depending on the fact that we can either slide quickly from key to key, or jump with stimulating and exciting effect among them.

Even the tiniest piece of music can show the shaping influence of key.§ An example just mentioned is Thomas Morley's lute song; Schubert's songs are packed with examples, just one of which is the climactic third and last verse of the lovely 'Du bist die Ruh' (You are my peace). The extraordinarily telling effect of some of Bach's harmonizations of the Chorale (Lutheran Hymn) tunes, is because, within the confined space of a single simple tune, he ingeniously leads us through unexpected keys. Changing key, particularly if we do it often, involves chromaticism.

Chromaticism

A chromatic scale is simply a scale consisting entirely of semitones. From the picture of the piano keyboard (p 94), it can be seen that it will take twelve semitone steps to go up or down one octave. Thus on a piano there are twelve different notes before everything starts again in the octave above. Each key therefore uses a particular seven notes out of a possible twelve. (Minor keys have a couple of alternative notes.) If a note is used which is not one of the seven of that particular key, then that note is chromatic. Such a note may well arise as a decoration of one of the notes of a tune, usually an additional note immediately above or below the note to be decorated. The next step up or down the diatonic scale may well be a whole tone, so a note only a semitone up or down will be chromatic. Such chromatic decorations are common, effective and lucid, since it is clear which note is embellishing which – something that might not be so clear with diatonic embellishments. Mozart uses chromatic decorations a great deal, and Chopin more than a great deal in what sometimes amount to ornamented decorations of his embellishments. Chromatic 'passing notes' are another form of the same thing, and simply involve filling in the gap between two consecutive notes of a melody with however many semitones it takes.

In the above cases the harmony will remain diatonic, but once we start introducing chromatic notes into the harmony, the music is likely to change key, even when the melody remains diatonic. With seven notes out of a possible twelve, no two keys will have fewer than two notes in common, and most will have more. To move smoothly from one key to another, a composer will usually employ harmonies common to the two keys. To do it more suddenly and dramatically he may use a chromatic chord, which is a chord belonging to neither key. In the second movement of Schubert's 'Unfinished' Symphony the first phrase of the first tune stays in the home key. The second phrase is exactly the same to start with, but then moves smoothly to another key. However, no sooner has he got there, than Schubert suddenly and dramatically introduces a surprise chromatic chord belonging in neither key, from which chord he neatly steps back into the home key. In the first smooth modulation (key change) Schubert says, 'This is the way we're going', and we go there. In the second, dramatic modulation he blindfolds us with the chromatic chord and says, 'Where are we?', and then with the next two chords simply says 'Back home'. Of course that is far from being all Schubert is saying in that passage.

Other scales
Scales can be constructed out of any pattern of ascending or descending notes. The whole-tone scale (see p 78 and Glossary) is one of consecutive whole tones, and is more of use for establishing a certain atmosphere than anything else. Messiaen has used, to good effect, many scales of his own devising (e.g. alternate whole tones and semitones – two semitones, one whole tone, two semitones etc.) mainly for harmonic purposes, each different scale having its own characteristic set of chords. Most non-European musics divide the octave up in different ways. If we add to that the microtonal scales of some 20th-century Western composers we can see that this is something we cannot go far into here.

Tonic sol-fa
This is the *doh-ray-me-fah-soh-lah-te-doh* business many of us learned at school. It stems (with not much change) from Guido d'Arezzo's 11th-century naming of the notes of the scale for the purpose of teaching singers their notes. The important difference between the Sol-Fa names and C, D, F sharp etc. is that 'doh' is the keynote of whatever major key the music happens to be in. The other notes will always be named in relation to this note, which is the way we *feel* them within a key. 'Soh' will always be the dominant, 'fah' the

fourth note of the scale and so on. 'Doh' itself will be C in the key of C, F sharp in the key of F sharp and so on. Sol-Fa is an ideal way of teaching us to feel the notes of the scale and the intervals between them. It can be (and sometimes is) carried a lot further, but chromaticism with its deliberate key-ambiguity poses problems.

2 SONATA FORM

Sonata form, sometimes called first-movement form, is the form of the first movements, and often of the last movements too, of sonatas, symphonies, concertos, quartets, quintets, trios etc, all the way from Haydn to Brahms and well beyond. That is, from the latter half of the 18th century, right through the 19th and – with many composers – well into the 20th. The reason for its great success and longevity must be mainly that it was an ideal way, within the key system, of getting a variety of musical ideas (tunes; themes) into a single movement.

It grew or – more accurately – crystallized out of binary form which, as we saw on pages 45 and 85, is a form of two sections, each repeated, the first moving out of the key, the other back into it. The earlier (17th and early 18th century) binary-form pieces, which were more polyphonic, tended to go on in the same vein throughout both sections (for example, the well-known and well-loved Air from Bach's third orchestral suite in D). Later binary-form pieces (more monodic) would present a number of different ideas one after another. You find this often happening in the harpsichord sonatas of Domenico Scarlatti, who was born in 1685, the same year as Bach (and Handel), but was a progressive in contrast to Bach's conservatism.

Several different ideas may be presented, say *a*, *b* and *c*, although there could easily be more or possibly less. By the time we get to *b*, we are probably out, or moving out of the home key, and into a new one in which the first section will close. The second section will probably, although not necessarily, run the ideas through in the same order, but the key arrangements will be the reverse, and the return to the home key will usually start at once. The pattern could be represented like this:

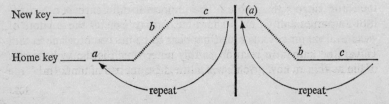

a is in brackets in the second section because here it is going to sound rather different, being on the move back to the home key. Composers liked to draw this bit out, and take in a few more keys on the way back, like this:

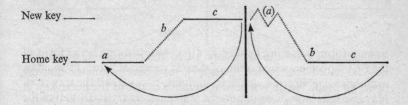

Scarlatti usually did that. *Occasionally* he did this:

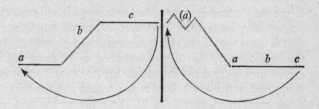

Or this:

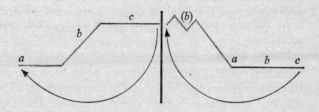

either of which makes the moment of arrival back in the home key coincide with a reappearance of the opening music, *a* in its original form and key, thereby introducing a ternary (A–B–A) element into the form (see p 83). This is in fact sonata form. Scarlatti attached little importance to it but to Haydn, composing fifty years later, it was standard practice. By the time Mozart comes on the scene in the 1770s, the tunes have become slightly longer and there may be more of them. We can now give names to the different bits of the form:

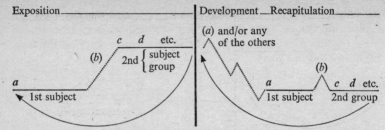

The moving-out-of-the-home-key bit in the exposition, which can now be called the 'bridge' (passage), may have a tune or musical figure to itself. We do not need it to move us out of the home key in the recapitulation, and it can be omitted but composers generally like to have it again, altered, so that the music takes off out of the key again, but then turns round and lands squarely back home. I have already said something (on p 87) about the 'development', which is the new name for the coming-*back*-to-the-home-key bit. Some readers may be surprised at the repeat of the whole second section, that is from the end of the movement right back to the beginning of the development. But this *should* be done (it never is) in six of the eleven sonata-form movements in Mozart's *last* four symphonies, all composed in the late 1780s, which would suggest that then (within a few years of Mozart's death), the practice was still in operation, although going out. . . . The repeat of the *exposition*, however, was still being demanded by Brahms nearly a hundred years later. From Beethoven onwards some pieces require it, others do not. The tendency with performers is to omit it, even if a nonsense is thereby made.

Haydn and Mozart kept their developments comparatively short. Beethoven, in the 'Eroica' Symphony first movement, and in many pieces thereafter, increased the size of the development, so that it became more of a section in its own right. Mozart quite often and Haydn sometimes had, at the end of the movement, a short coda, or tailpiece, a few extra bars to round things off. This too with Beethoven became a section in its own right, partly to 'balance' the larger development, which now required its own 'recapitulation'. Like a development, a coda may well 'worry' a theme or two from the exposition but it must not stray too far for too long from the home key. It is well worth comparing the 'Eroica' first movement's development, which passes through about nineteen keys, with its coda which, after a brief excursion into two away keys, stays firmly at home. The Beethoven pattern, which was good enough for most 19th-century composers is roughly this:

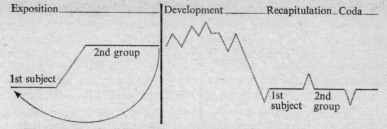

The concerto is different from other instrumental forms in that its most important element is the dialogue between the main protagonists – soloist(s) and orchestra. The first movement of the classical concerto, harking back a little to the baroque 'ritornello' form (see p 46) modifies sonata form by having an orchestral introduction (ritornello) before the soloist plays. It is important that the drama should not really begin until the main character has arrived, and so this introduction generally stays in the home key, giving out a few (rarely all) of the tunes of the exposition proper, which starts when the soloist enters. Balancing the introduction is an orchestral closure of the exposition, coming often at the climax of a steady build-up by the soloist.

The orchestral introduction is not recapitulated as such, but the closure reappears at the end of the recapitulation, and leads to the 'cadenza' (same word as 'cadence'), which is improvised by the performer if he can, unless the composer has provided a composed cadenza. The pattern can be represented like this:

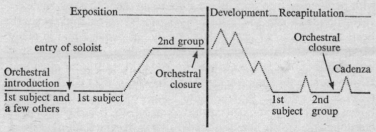

The composer has usually saved up one tune for the orchestra to end the movement. That is the Mozart pattern, although he did, in one or two of his piano concertos, bring the soloist in at the very beginning for just a moment, as Beethoven did in his last two, and as Brahms usually did. But by the time Brahms was writing, other 19th-century composers had dropped the orchestral introduction, although they retained the climactic closure. The cadenza was generally retained,

103

(but no longer improvised) and occasionally 'invaded' by the orchestra.

3 THE REST OF THE CLASSICAL SONATA

Earlier in this book (pp 46–47) we saw how the symphony evolved out of the Italian opera overture (called *sinfonia*) and the French orchestral suite (called overture). I also said a word or two then about the two types of baroque sonata, one of them containing a number of dances and therefore very similar to the suite. By classical times (Haydn and Mozart) symphonies, sonatas, quartets, quintets etc. all had roughly the same standard number and arrangement of movements, with the symphony rather more standard than the others. All are 'sonatas' in fact.

Minuet; scherzo

From the sonata's suite ancestor comes one of the standard four movements, the minuet and trio (see pp 83 and 70), later quickened up (a few of Haydn's and most of Beethoven's) into scherzo and trio. Some 19th-century composers use other dances or other dance-like music, but they keep to three in a bar (waltzes, ländlers). Tchaikovsky has a dot-and-carry-one waltz in his 'Pathétique' Symphony (5 in a bar = 2 + 3). Another unusual, but absolutely right feature of this symphony of despair is that its slow movement is also its last.

Slow movement

The slow movement is usually second in the line-up with the dance movement third, but sometimes these two exchange places, which helps to contrast adjacent movements, if the first movement happens to be a little on the slow side. Quickening up the minuet into a scherzo tended to concentrate the fastest music in the last two movements.

There is no 'standard' form for a slow as there is for a first movement. Slow instrumental music is usually more song-like than quick instrumental music, and slow movements often tend to follow the forms of solo song. Sometimes we get the simple A–B–A song form, as in Beethoven's last and Mozart's last two piano concertos. Probably the commonest slow movement form, though, is what is often called 'abridged sonata form', by which is meant sonata form without a development. This is rather like calling a bicycle an 'engineless motorbike', but it is quite a convenient way of looking at it. The form, which is the one Mozart used for most of his operatic arias, is in fact a binary form without repeats, with its second section starting back in the home key and staying there. In other words the two

104

sections are very much the same, except that the first section moves to an away key about half-way through, and the second section does not. Sometimes there is a short development, in which case the movement is in sonata form, although simpler and closer to the Scarlatti type of sonata form than the sonata form of quick movements. Of Mozart's last three symphonies, the G minor and the 'Jupiter' slow movements have developments, but the E flat (no. 39) has not. Variation form is sometimes used in slow movements. Haydn was fond of this, particularly in the symphonies (see p 87), although he would often mix in something else. Beethoven uses a slightly Haydnesque free variation form in the slow movement of his Fifth Symphony, and the slow movement of his violin concerto is a variation form with interpolations (episodes).

Finale

The traditionally happy ending of nearly all instrumental music demands of the sonata a fastish, gay finale. Sonata form will do for this and very often does. However, the tunes in a sonata-form finale will tend to fall into more clear-cut sections, to be 'squarer', more dance-like in fact than in a first movement. Compare the first and last movements of almost any classical sonata, symphony, quartet etc. Early pre-classical symphonies had jig-like finales. The jig (gigue) was commonly the last dance of the baroque suite. Quite often a finale, especially in a concerto, will be a rondo, which was originally a dance, the *rondeau*. This works on the principle of a recurring refrain (see p 45), which in its basic form can be represented as A–B–A–C–A–D–A etc. The refrain, the *main theme*, being A and the *episodes* B, C, D etc. Classical composers adapted the rondo to sonata form like this. We call it sonata-rondo form:

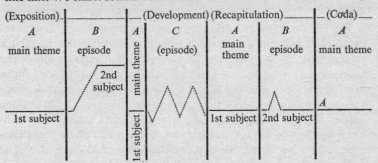

A, the main theme, must be complete in itself and all in the home key, which is why B, the first episode, contains both 'bridge' and second subject. A is cut short on its first reappearance, since this is not the real recapitulation. A's final appearance *can* seem once too many. Mozart has a happy arrangement to avoid this: A B A C *B* A. A and B change places in the recapitulation. He does this in his last two piano concertos (K 537 and 595) as well as in the careering A major (K 488), which must have been the inspiration for the finale of Schumann's piano concerto (in the same key) although in sonata form and not a rondo.

Motives; motto theme; 'cyclic' form

From very early days some composers sought to relate the different movements to each other by having them share some common element. It was done by C. P. E. Bach, J. S. Bach's most illustrious son, who was very much more than just a forerunner of Haydn and Mozart. The usual way is by means of common motives, which I have already discussed on page 86. This was probably of ten unconscious; from Beethoven onwards it became more conscious and in many cases consequently more obvious. A rather crude device, often connected with the literary associations of much 19th-century music, was the 'motto theme' (Berlioz called it the '*idée fixe*'). A theme which will play a part, often of a different character, in all the movements, either as an integral part of a movement, or as an interpolation. The motto theme of Tchaikovsky's Fifth Symphony serves as a sombre introduction to the first movement, as a climactic, terrifying reminder of doom in the otherwise tunefully comfortable slow movement, as an almost casual afterthought at the end of the waltz, and as the main theme of the finale in the character of a majestic tune commanding (sometimes by force) the respect and subjugation of the others. The device is dramatic and literary, and is not a substitute for the motivic relations between the movements which are still there in that symphony.

The phrase 'cyclic form', which strictly means *any* form in several movements such as the symphony or suite, tends to be used for works which employ overt cross-references between movements, even if they are no more than quotations from the other movements in the finale. My objection to this use of the phrase is that it suggests that a relationship between movements exists only in such pieces.

4 THE FUGUE

Equally applicable to voices or instruments, the fugue was a crystallization of imitative polyphony (see p. 41) into its tightest, most succinct form. For this reason fugues are perhaps a little daunting to some listeners, but for the same reason a fugue can be one of the most excitingly satisfying musical experiences, and most fugues are quite short. Try Bach's B minor Mass, which is full of fugues.

We hear, at the start of a fugue, the 'subject', the main theme at first in one of the parts alone, and then successively in the other parts as they start up one by one. Each will give out the subject (which is probably only two or three phrases long) at a different pitch, and having done that, will go on to something else which will make good counterpoint (polyphony) with the subject, which will by then have entered in another part. This (called the 'exposition') goes on until all the parts (commonly four) are in.

Now comes an 'episode', which, like the episodes in a rondo, is simply a passage or section which does not contain the subject. During an episode one or more of the parts will have left off, to enter again with the subject, at the end of the episode. This time the subject may or may not be taken up by some of the other parts. Then follows another episode, and so on to the end of the fugue. The first episode will usually be very short indeed, later episodes a good deal longer.

This sounds very repetitive, but in polyphony a little music goes a long way. The same two (or more) melodies can (and should) be combined in different ways. The one that was on top can later go underneath, or a different third part can go on top or anywhere else. And there are many other devices. All of which gives great variety in the hands of a good composer. In addition the episodes will often change the key, so that the new appearances of the subject will be in different keys. The episodes are not usually all that 'episodic', probably being based on some motive contained in the subject or one of its counterpoints in the exposition.

There are many kinds of fugue: quick, slow, long, short, fugues where the different appearances of the subject keep on coming, so that there are no real episodes (the first fugue of Bach's '48' is one of these). There are fugues on two (or more) subjects, presented either simultaneously or at different times, fugues which depend on the tunefulness of the subject (the opening 'Kyrie' – five parts – of Bach's B minor Mass), fugues which depend on the beauty of the polyphony (the last fugue, 'Dona nobis pacem', in the same work – two subjects treated alternately; no episodes; same music as the 'Gratias agimus').

Fugues tend to start quietly (and end loud) which is probably the main reason they usually are preceded by preludes. The prelude to a fugue will be a non-cerebral piece, probably made out of one idea repeated (e.g. the first two preludes of the '48'), which will wake us up, prepare us and, in the dramatic silence after the prelude, focus our attention on the all-important beginning of the fugue.

Fugues – or more usually just the exposition – can be used within a movement of, say, a sonata or symphony. Beethoven was fond of doing it (in the 'Eroica' finale there are two fugue expositions). Lesser composers often put in a fugue exposition to re-energize a movement which has lost its impetus.

All the examples of whole fugues I have mentioned are from Bach because since him there have been very few great fugues. With him in 1750 died the great polyphonic tradition but, like a fugue, it did not end with a whimper. The fugue is the only musical form known to me that usually ends at its climax, so it is appropriate that in J. S. Bach it reached both its culmination and its demise.

5 PROGRAMME MUSIC

by W. R. Anderson

There is one broad classification of music which forms so pretty a battleground that music-lovers still get endless fun out of it. It is the distinction between what we call 'absolute music' and 'programme music'; that is, instrumental music (music with words is, broadly speaking, ruled out here) which on the one hand has no story behind it, and that which is based on some story or poetic background, or seeks to suggest in any way extra-musical ideas.

First, programme music arises from the natural delight of man in story-telling. Composers early tried it, long before their instruments were suited to it. Even William Byrd, that great master, born over 400 years ago, wrote 'Mr Byrd's Battell' – for a keyboard instrument with a tiny tone! While remembering that programme music is, strictly, music without words, we may note that early madrigalists showed the same liking for description: there is even a vocal Battle (Jannequin's). As you might expect of British composers, the weather as a 'programme' topic, was not forgotten. Some early programme music you can try for yourself if you get one of the sets of Kuhnau's *Bible Pieces* (Peters). They describe such scenes as David slaying Goliath, and many of their strokes are clever as well as naïve.

But broadly speaking, there were not sufficient means for making effective programme music, until the orchestra grew up. From that time a fair proportion of orchestral music has been programmatic, since romanticism in music became self-conscious, round about the late 18th and the early 19th centuries. Think of that period's wonderful efflorescence of romantic poetry and prose, from Percy's *Reliques*, through the 'shudder' school of *The Castle of Otranto*, Mrs Radcliffe, 'Monk' Lewis, up to Scott, Byron, Shelley, Keats and the rest of the great tribe; with Goethe, Schiller, Rousseau, Hugo, Dumas père; with the painter Delacroix, and a score of others. Musically, you will mark it notably through German romanticism in Weber.

There are all kinds of programme music, from delicate mood-suggestion to frankly imitative music. Broadly speaking, the feeling of music-lovers is that music that is largely imitative is seldom worthy. There are highly descriptive moments in such a masterpiece as Richard Strauss's *Till Eulenspiegel's Merry Pranks*, but they matter least: the mastery lies in suggestion, and in the beauties of the music's structure, rather than in the exciting quality of particular strokes. In Beethoven's 'Pastoral' Symphony, we have both painting (a little), and mood-evocation (much): and the latter, not the former, is the source of the music's chief delight.

I cannot see why music written with some literary background in mind need be less valuable than that which arises out of 'purely musical emotion', if such a thing be possible. (It is arguable that it is not: that all art must well up from *some* human experience, however 'purely' – that is, in its own particular terms of shape and form – it seeks expression.) Two things seem worth noting: that it is unfair to expect programme music to be as effective when one does not know its story as when one does; and that, above all, a good story cannot make up for poor music. If these considerations are held well in mind, we may thoroughly enjoy both programme music and absolute music. The former, indeed, may need more attention, since we have to take in the story as well as the music, and also to decide how far the two hang together.

One thing that musicians think important is that if a composer gives no title to a work, one must, in order to appreciate it fully, learn to think of it in *his* terms, not those of some other art: that is, while many people – probably the majority of us – like at times to daydream about absolute music, it is only fair to the composer to realize that when he gives no story, he is thinking of his work in terms of its own life; and it takes time for us to understand what those terms are. That, indeed, is a good part of the process of musical education. Whatever the composer may have been moved by, to cause him to compose, he is not bound to communicate that, except so far as the music itself tells us. Nothing is gained by clapping unauthorized titles or stories upon works, and the music is often obscured thereby. Names need do no harm: some people find them useful in remembering works. Musicians, naturally, remember music by its sound.

It is very difficult in a few lines to plead the seminal importance to the serious music-lover of believing what Sir John McEwen has well stated: 'Whilst language seeks to express a meaning, *music is itself the meaning.*' Whether that meaning can arise without reference to any human feeling, you may doubt; and it is a matter of experience for the listener to train himself to hear music without translating it into the terms of other arts. That is why it is a pretty big adventure to take in a symphony that may last forty or fifty minutes, and tells no story but that of the beauty of form and musical emotion.

In musical aesthetics, sharp definitions are often misleading. We find, for instance, the terms 'Romantic' and 'Classical' used as dividing music into two categories – broadly, the modern (say, since round about 1800) is reckoned 'romantic', and the music of Beethoven, Mozart, Handel, Bach and their predecessors is thought of as 'classical'. This is a pity. Romance is the sap that makes all music live. As in nature, so in music, there are endless forms and shapes, varying satisfactions and degrees of emphasis. 'Classical' music is not merely that which places most emphasis on form, and 'romantic' that which stresses feeling more: that definition is too hard-and-fast. Romance runs through the older music, but it is mostly more restrained; though dramatic and romantic feeling can be readily felt in a great deal of old music – look at the charming romance of Farnaby's music for virginals of three and a half centuries ago, the deep sense of musical drama Bach shows in his great B minor Mass, Handel in the *Messiah*, Mozart in the G minor Symphony – magnificent drama, without any programme. You cannot draw any easy line between 'romantic' and 'classical'. One thing may be noted: that with the strong infusion of poetry, romance became self-conscious, towards the late 18th century; and to mark this development of self-consciousness is about as far as it seems useful to go in dividing music into periods. Those who have the best background of historical understanding will best trace the reasons for changes in musical outlook. We can gather, from reading social history, the way in which musicians, like other artists, were once the servants of princes, and rarely had great culture outside their art; note how this system broke up, and how composers became better educated, more men of the world, more literary-minded (hence the development of 'programme music'), more ready explorers of possible new worlds. The older composers had much to do in foundation-laying and the architectural planning of the world of composition as they saw it opening up. The later comers had more leisure to decorate, and splendidly developing tools and apparatus, in the wealth of instrumental invention and the possibilities of new combinations and permutations, alike of forces and of form.

6 SOME DEFINITIONS AND TECHNICALITIES

by W. R. Anderson

We may as well gather up one or two definitions. When they are so brief, they must necessarily be bald and omit mention of details and exceptions. Sonatas are for one or two players. A symphony is a sonata for the orchestra; a string quartet, quintet, trio, sextet, octet and the like is a sonata for string players.

The 'Concerto Grosso' (roughly Handel and Bach period) uses a small body of soloists (*concertino*) over against the main body (*ripieno*) – fine counterpointing. The later concerto (broadly, from Haydn onwards) throws more limelight (too much, sometimes) on one or two soloists (nearly always one), and assumes modified symphonic shape, with three movements instead of the symphony's normal four. The middle movement is the slow one, the Minuet being omitted. Its 'first movement' form is modified, to give the soloist-protagonist a dramatic life over against the orchestra's; so that besides the drama in the life of the subjects, we get that of these two protagonists. A double concerto is for two soloists and orchestra. Brahms's, for violin and cello, is a noble example.

A few points about the naming and numbering of works may be welcome. 'Opus numbers' (meaning the order-number of the work) are the familiar method of identifying compositions; we speak of Beethoven's op. 12, and so forth. A few works have nicknames, which are handy; but if they were multiplied, who could remember them all? We should get confused. Nicknames are pleasant and friendly, so long as we do not imagine they necessarily have anything to do with the music's 'meaning'. Sometimes (rarely) they were given by the composer; more often, by publishers or music-lovers. The titles of Mendelssohn's *Songs Without Words* are, with one or two exceptions, not his. Handel's famous 'Harmonious Blacksmith' variations had nothing to do with the toil of the smithy: the piece is simply one movement of a suite, without any special significance (it is not even a particularly interesting set of variations; Handel never attempted much in that line). The title was stuck on, many years later, by a publisher who wanted to attract buyers. Legends gather round other works, such as his *Water Music*, which was *not* written to appease an offended monarch.

As to op., note that works consecutively numbered were not always written in that order. Part of the numbering was sometimes done after the composer's death, or he was careless. This may be a nuisance, and even at times a snare if, for example, one expects an op. 125 to be an advance in style on an op. 10. The numeration is more usually that of publication than of composition. Sometimes we find 'op. posth.' – a work published after the composer had died.

Several works (and long ones) may be included in one opus number – as in Beethoven's violin and piano sonatas, op. 12, nos. 1, 2 and 3, and his much-played set of six string quartets comprising op. 18. The numbering system was late in being adopted. For some time systematization was poor. Handel, to judge by it, would appear to have written only about three works! In Haydn's and Mozart's time it was getting into shape. Mozart's music has a special enumeration, which is the most authoritative – Köchel's: so his are known as 'K numbers'. He wrote, for example, several symphonies in the key of D, but the number 'K 181' places one of these with certainty, distinguishing it from all the rest. Mozart's 'K numbers' are chronological, but with other composers who have no opus numbers, any numbers used may well refer to a particular published collection, e.g. the 'Longo' numbers of Domenico Scarlatti's harpsichord sonatas, and not necessarily represent any actual or believed order of composition.

7 INSTRUMENTS

I do not suppose many listeners to a violinist playing are particularly concerned to know precisely how the energy of his bowing arm is converted into the sound they hear. Nevertheless there are a few basic facts about the way instruments work, which it is a help to know. The many ways in which composers have used instruments are dealt with in the later books of this *Companion*.

Anything which makes a sound is a potential musical instrument, and instruments have been constructed to make use of probably every available sound-making method, with special emphasis on pitched sounds.

Strings

Palaeolithic man produced pitched sounds from the stretched strings of his mouth-bow (see p 22), by either hitting it or plucking it which, some 7000 technological years later, is the difference between the piano and the harpsichord respectively. All stringed instruments work on the principle that a stretched string, if pulled (or pushed) out of its at rest straight line state and then let go, will give rise to a sound of a steady pitch – a note. The pitch of this note depends on three things – the weight of the string, its tension, and its length. The weight is decided by the manufacturer, the tension is set before the performance by the process of tuning, and the different notes needed in performance are got by effectively altering the length of the string by 'stopping' off some of it with the fingers, by changing to another, differently tuned string, or (as most instruments do) by both means.

Very nearly all stringed instruments have more than one string, which means that they can play more than one note at a time, though not necessarily that they do. Although often splendid as a solo instrument or tune-player, the plucked string is also ideal as an accompanying instrument, especially to the human voice. This has been its role back to the earliest civilizations. The voice is a comparatively loud, sustained sound, whereas the plucked string is quieter, with a strong (but not violent), clear-cut (therefore rhythmic) attack, the sound thereafter dying away.

Bowed strings are still comparatively quiet, hence the battalions of them in a symphony orchestra. They are equally at home as tune-players or accompanists, since the sound they make is aurally transparent – we can hear other sounds through it. There are many ways of 'bowing'. One stroke of the bow to each note, one stroke to two, more or many notes, lifting the bow off between notes; bouncing it on the strings; heavy, light, fast moving, long bows, short bows, etc. (see Book 2 p 206), each giving different articulation to the music. Some of the subtler bowing techniques will be more applicable to solo and chamber music than to orchestral.

Wind instruments

As a stretched string has a certain natural rate of oscillation which gives rise to a particular note, so has the air in a pipe and, like the string, one of the things the rate of oscillation – and hence the pitch of the note – depends on is the length of the pipe. Many instruments are constructed in 'families', the same instrument in different sizes, and the shorter the pipe, the higher the pitch. Thus the piccolo (short for *flauto piccolo* or 'little flute') is just the baby of the flute family. If we alter the length of the pipe in performance we shall get different notes. The most obvious way this can be seen to be happening is with the slide of the trombone. Another way is by means of the valves (the plungers or keys) on horns, trumpets and tubas which switch in different lengths of extra tube. Woodwind instruments and saxophones do not literally alter the length of their pipe, but they do this in effect by opening up holes in the side of the tube starting from the end furthest from the player's mouth.

The manner of the initial production of the sound varies. In the flute family, recorder family and the 'flue' pipes of an organ, a jet of air is directed on to a fairly sharp edge (as in a whistle). This is probably the 'purest' way of setting the air in the tube oscillating, and it tends to produce a sound without many overtones (see p 68), but with a slight 'breathiness', which is noise (see p 73), particularly as each note starts. The oboe family (which includes the so-called cor anglais) and the bassoon family are double-reed instruments. The player blows between two thin pieces of cane, the squawk so produced being modified into a delicate timbre by the pipe. The clarinet and saxophone families are single-reed instruments, with a single piece of cane covering a slit in the side of the upper end of the pipe. With the brass instruments, horns, trumpets, cornets, trombones and tubas the player's lips are the 'reeds'.

It is possible for the air in a pipe to oscillate in fractions (harmonics) – halves (second harmonic), thirds (third harmonic) and so on. In halves the notes will be an octave higher, in thirds another fifth above that. All wind instruments make use of this. Woodwind instrumentalists, playing up the scale from their lowest notes, uncover so many holes, then cover them all up again and 'overblow'. The 'fingering' starts again from the bottom end, but the notes go on up. Brass instruments make greater use of harmonics. Valve mechanisms for lengthening the tube did not come in until about the second half of the 19th century. Before that, horns, trumpets and tubas could obtain their different notes only by blowing different harmonics, something at which brass instrumentalists are extremely adept, since they can very precisely control the pressure of their lips. But it is only above the eighth harmonic that the notes so produced are close enough together to form a scale. This is why Bach's trumpet music is usually so high up and why Mozart's, lower down, so uninteresting. The horn has a longer tube than one would imagine from the notes one usually hears, because it normally uses these higher harmonics and so, in Mozart's music for instance, plays a more important and tuneful role than the trumpet. Modern brass instruments still play harmonics, using the valves or the slide to fill in the gaps.

All wind instruments have precise and subtle ways of articulating their notes, and therefore the phrasing of their melodies (see p 63). 'Tonguing' with the wind is the equivalent of bowing with the strings – if not with quite the same variety. The tongue can interrupt the airflow for a tiny fraction of time, or more, between the notes, allow it to flow again suddenly or more gradually, thereby producing different degrees of attack and so on. The brass have not quite the delicacy of the woodwind in this respect.

Keyboard instruments

The harpsichord is in effect a mechanical harp. Putting down the keys on the keyboard mechanically plucks the strings. The piano is something of a mechanical cimbalom, the strings being hit by hammers. The piano has the advantage that putting down a key harder hits the string harder, producing a louder note – hence the word 'pianoforte' ('soft-loud'). The only way to make notes louder on a harpsichord is to bring extra strings into play, strings tuned to the same notes or the octaves above or below. This is done by 'couplers', which will add the additional strings to all the notes on the keyboard. Thus, the only way you can play a melody with a quieter accompaniment is to use two keyboards, which most harpsichords have. You cannot make a crescendo or diminuendo, but must get louder or softer in jumps (terraced dynamics). Phrasing (see p 63) is vital. The piano tends to substitute loudness and softness between notes for the true phrasing of the proportion of sound to silence. Obviously the piano has many advantages, but it is in the nature of good musical instruments in the hands of good composers to thrive on their limitations. We miss many of the subtleties of, for instance, a Scarlatti sonata, if we play it on a modern piano, just as we would if we played a Chopin nocturne on a harpsichord. The harpsichord was ubiquitous in baroque music, as the 'continuo' instrument *par excellence*. With its chords it binds together the often heterogeneous sounds of the band. As a plucked stringed instrument it blends perfectly with other instruments, so that it can do its continuo job without obtruding.

The clavichord is somewhat like a piano (with limited soft-loud qualities) in that little metal rods like the ends of screwdrivers hit the strings and stay there, setting the string vibrating and at the same time stopping off a particular length of string. It is a very quiet instrument and at the first hint of violence (i.e. loud playing) it goes straight out of tune.

All keyboard instruments remove the performer from direct contact with the sound-making medium, which is a bad thing, and which is what Beethoven must have meant when, having written the greatest music yet for the piano, he called it an 'unsatisfactory instrument'. The organ is even more indirect, since the player does not even supply the energy. He has consequently to work very hard at the phrasing and such, in order to make the 'king of instruments' get off his throne, take off his crown and dance with the rest of us. An organ has more than one keyboard (manual) for the same reason as a harpsichord. When an organist pulls out a 'stop', he brings into action a 'rank' of pipes (called a 'stop'), one pipe to each note of one of his manuals or of his pedalboard, which is another keyboard for his feet. Some stops will sound octaves above or below other stops. The octave above being the second harmonic, there will probably be stops at the third harmonic (the octave and a fifth above) and possibly others. Each manual – and the pedalboard – has its own set of stops which is called an 'organ'. One of these (sometimes more) will be in a box with openable shutters controlled by a pedal, and this will for obvious reasons be called the 'Swell Organ'.

Stops will differ in timbre, loudness and octave. They will be either flue stops or reed stops. Flue stops (diapasons, flutes) work on the whistle principle (see above p 114). The big metal pipes often seen on the front are like huge penny whistles upside down. They are all a little bit flutey, ranging from flutey-flutey to stringy-flutey. The reeds have a metal reed, a tongue (not unlike the free – i.e. pipeless – reed of a mouth organ, concertina or harmonium) past which the air goes into the pipe. Whereas something of the flute can be heard in all flue stops, something of the toy trumpet (highly refined, though not always) can be heard in the reed stops. Although it can be very exciting for a little while to hear a huge, mammoth organ bellowing forth its stentorian tones, its several horsepower blower-motors running to capacity, it is much more satisfying when just two or three quiet stops are used, and we can hear the subtleties of a fine piece well played.

Electronic instruments

To produce a pitched sound electronically, an electric circuit is made to oscillate in the form of an alternating current or alternating voltage, which is then amplified and fed to a loudspeaker which turns it into sound. Sounds so produced will be very crude in relation to those of conventional instruments. They will have to be made more interesting by either adding overtones to a sound without any, or modifying the existing overtones (see p 68) with filters (tone controls), and by doing something about the beginnings and ends of notes (attack and decay) to stop them sounding 'switched' on and off. Most electronic organs seem to be designed to imitate their piped uncle, who is himself a somewhat synthetic creature. From time to time an electronic instrument has appeared, attracted the attention of a composer or two and then disappeared. Such was the theremin, which was more fascinating to watch being played – it reacts to the *proximity* of the player's hands – than to hear. The ondes martenot has survived largely because Messiaen has composed for it.

Electronic instruments are at their best when well away from what conventional instruments can do so much better, namely play tunes. Pitched sounds can be organized in many non-tune ways – sliding notes, clusters, microtones, imprecise pitch etc. But it is in the huge field of non-pitched sounds (noise) that electronic instruments can really do their cultivating. White noise (see p 136) can be filtered to remove unwanted frequencies, and pitched sounds can be made to interact with one another to produce complex sounds which are neither sounds of a single pitch nor chords.

Synthesizers

Although synthesizers are used quite frequently in musical performances – especially with pop groups – they are not musical instruments in the sense that an electronic organ is. They are instruments for making music in the same sense as an electronic music studio. Indeed a synthesizer is often called a studio, since it is essentially a number of separate electronic devices for the production and treatment of sounds, with facilities for the interconnection of these in a variety of ways. Miniaturization of components has made it possible to get a lot into one box, but there is not and cannot be a standard synthesizer. Given a keyboard – although not necessarily a performer – a synthesizer can play tunes, but it is a colossal waste of facilities if this is all it is made to do.

8 THE READING OF MUSIC

Much of the greatest music was composed for people who were themselves amateur musicians of considerable knowledge and experience.

Much of it was composed simply to the glory of God who, it may be supposed, is a tolerable sight-reader. All the beauties of a Bach prelude and fugue, or a Beethoven string quartet are there to be *heard* but it is very difficult, especially in these days of hurry, to appreciate the greatest composers' phenomenal powers of science in the art of music without being able to read music, or at any rate to follow a score. I personally would find it quite *impossible* to appreciate many of the subtleties of complex polyphony without recourse to the written music.

The best way to learn to read music is to learn to play it, or to sing from the written notes, or preferably both, since the former on its own can be a somewhat mechanical process. This takes time and dogged application. However, I find that many people are surprised at how quickly they can acquire an ability to follow a not too complicated score, once they have a knowledge of the basic elements of music notation. There are many books that set these out, and there is space here for only a few guidelines and tips, though there is still bound to be quite a lot of 'fiddly' detail.

Rhythm; durations

This is the most important aspect of music notation. First we need to know the relative durations (lengths) of notes which, unless otherwise indicated, proceed by a factor of two. Thus each of the following notes has a duration half that of the preceding note.

(British names)	semibreve	minim	crotchet	quaver	semiquaver	demisemiquaver
	o	♩	♩	♪	♪	♪ etc.
(American)	whole note	half note	quarter	eighth	sixteenth	thirtysecond
	1	1/2	1/4	1/8	1/16	1/32

We shall also need to know in due course the signs (not given here) for the equivalent durations of silence (called 'rests') which are subject to the same procedures as the notes. Notes shorter than ♩ can be joined together:

Other proportions of duration will be indicated:

$$\text{♩} = \text{♪} + \text{♪} = \underbrace{\text{♪} + \text{♪} + \text{♪}}_{3} = \overbrace{\text{♪} + \text{♪} + \text{♪} + \text{♪} + \text{♪}}^{5}$$

A dot *after* a note increases its duration by half:

$$\text{𝅗𝅥. = 𝅗𝅥 + ♩} \qquad \text{♩. = ♩ + ♪}$$

A second dot by another quarter (and so on):

$$\text{𝅗𝅥.. = 𝅗𝅥 + ♩ + ♪}$$

An uneven, jerky rhythm is often called a 'dotted' rhythm, because an even rhythm has been made uneven by 'dotting' alternate notes, the extra half duration being taken from each succeeding note, so that:

♫ ♫ ♫ etc. (Tum Tum Tum Tum Tum Tum etc.)

becomes:

♫. ♫. ♫. etc. (Tum ti Tum ti Tum ti etc.)

A pause sign ⌢ over a note 𝄐 increases its duration by an amount not specified and holds up the tempo (see below).

Tempo and time signature

The above durations are relative and have no absolute value until the tempo is known. The most accurate way of indicating the tempo is by a metronome mark, which tells us how many of a particular note should go by in a minute (see Glossary). A much vaguer way, although often preferable, is in words, traditionally Italian (see *Speeds* in Glossary). To interpret these we need to know the 'time signature' – two figures, one above the other. The lower figure, always a power of two, will indicate the note duration – quarter-, half-, eighth-note or whatever – which corresponds to the main pulse of the music, the beat. The upper figure tells how many beats of this note duration go to a bar or measure, each bar being marked off by a vertical line (bar-line).

$$\tfrac{4}{4} = \text{♩ ♩ ♩ ♩ | ♩ ♩ ♩ ♩ | } etc. \quad \tfrac{3}{8} = \text{♫♪ | ♫♪ | } etc. \quad \tfrac{5}{16} = \text{♬♪ | ♬♪ | }_{etc.}$$

These rhythms are not necessarily played, they are the pulses underlying the music. The words *Adagio*, *Allegro*, etc. refer to the rate of these pulses.

At the beginning of the first movement of Beethoven's third piano concerto he writes *Allegro con brio* (*con brio*: 'with verve'). He also puts 'C', which means $\frac{4}{4}$. All this suggests a fairly brisk pace for the four quarter-notes (crochets) in each bar. However, to make it all quite clear, he gives us a metronome mark as well: ♩ = 144. In contrast, the second movement is marked *Largo* and $\frac{3}{8}$. This means that the eighth-notes (quavers) in this movement are going to be a lot slower, and therefore of longer duration than the quarter-notes were in the first movement. In fact Beethoven's metronome mark is ♪ (66), which is very slow indeed. A *sixteenth-note* (semiquaver) is to be more than twice the duration of a quarter-note in the first movement!

Before the 20th century, time signatures generally remained the same throughout a movement. This is more or less true of tempo as well, although some 19th-century pieces do a fair amount of speeding up and slowing down. Counting out the beats in each bar, at first deliberately and consciously and later more or less unconsciously, as musicians do, will be a great help, at first in just keeping up, and later in enabling one to take in more and more of the written music.

Pitch

Anyone who cannot tell whether a tune is going up or down is not likely to be reading this book but for anyone else, following a tune up and down is the easiest part of reading music. It looks like what it is doing. But to know whether a certain written note is going to sound high or low in pitch, we need a little knowledge. The sets of five horizontal lines, called 'staves', on which most music is written, mean nothing until they have a 'clef' on them. The diagram shows the relationship between the two commonest clefs, 'treble' and 'bass', and the 'alto' clef, which the viola plays from. These three clefs are disposed symmetrically about the note, 'middle' C. Notes will lie either on the lines or in the spaces between them.

In a chamber music score there will be as many staves as instruments (two each for piano and harp). In an orchestral score pairs of wind instruments will usually have to share a stave, and the strings will have as many staves as parts (q.v.)

Key signatures

To understand these, one needs to know something about scales and tonality (key: see Part 3, Chapter 1). Key signatures are those bundles of sharps (♯) or flats (♭) after the clef sign at the beginning of each stave. Each sharp or flat in the key signature modifies one of the notes of the scale. A sharp raises it a semitone, a flat lowers it a semitone. But the main concern of the listener following a score is, where is the keynote? Any key signature will indicate one possible major key, and one possible minor key whose keynote will be two notes lower. With a key signature of sharps the keynote will be the note immediately above the last sharp if the key is major, immediately below the last sharp if the key is minor. (We must remember that the keynote recurs in every octave.) With a key signature of flats, the last flat *but one* is on the keynote of the major key. If there is only one flat, the key is F major or D minor. If there are no flats *or* sharps (and the piece is in a key at all) then the key is C major or A minor.

How to tell if it is major or minor? Rule-of-thumb methods are too pernickety to describe here. One should just feel it, but in any case two keys with the same signature are so much in and out of each other's pockets that the difference between them can be slight.

Accidentals

Unfortunately for the would-be score-follower, most music does not stay in the opening key. Composers sometimes change the key signature if the new key is going to be there for some time, but more often they just put the new sharps or flats in front of each note they apply to, in which case they are called 'accidentals'. Accidentals apply to a note up to the next bar-line, and so we need a new sign, a 'natural' (♮), to cancel them out, or to cancel out where necessary any sharp or flat operating in the key signature, which will remain in force until cancelled by another key signature.

The appearance of accidentals in a score need not mean a change of key. They may just be chromatic decorations (see chapter 12, p 98), in which case a particular accidental is unlikely to apply consistently to a particular note, as it will do if the key has changed.

What scores to read

Those who are mainly interested in vocal music will do best, I think, to begin with songs with piano accompaniment and graduate later to oratorio, opera and other choral works. Most people want to be able to read an orchestral score as soon as possible, and the best preparation for this is undoubtedly the string quartet. It has the same layout as the strings of the orchestra. In fact this most important section of the orchestra is really just a big string quartet with double basses (often merely reinforcing the cellos).

Start with Haydn – there are over eighty quartets of his to choose from. Some of the earlier symphonies of Haydn and Mozart have only a few wind instruments in addition to the strings. One can then progress to works with more wind. Chamber music will not necessarily be easier to follow than orchestral music. There will be fewer instruments, but those there are will be busier. In polyphonic music, score reading can open up a new world, but finding one's way through a complex polyphonic choral work is not for the beginner.

9 A GLOSSARY OF SOME MUSICAL TERMS
W. R. Anderson and Roger North

This list is necessarily brief, though it is not confined to the words used in this book. Within the limits of such a section it is obviously necessary to omit many terms. Some foreign pronunciations can scarcely be given without using phonetics. But nowadays few people need go for long without hearing good foreign speech. A little attentive listening to the radio will teach us much. Like most technical vocabularies, that of music is sometimes illogical or dubious: one word, e.g, may stand for several things. One cannot be exhaustive in a line or two: there are reservations about some of the definitions, and other people might define differently. I am trying to combine simplicity, brevity and as much accuracy as possible; and every worker knows how difficult it sometimes is to explain shortly and exactly what the technical terms of his trade mean. As I have remarked elsewhere, those who are sufficiently interested in a subject like to learn its terms. I see no point in elaborate explanatory avoidance of them, which wastes words and is often confusing. I hope no technical term in my part of this volume will remain unclear. I have tried either to explain it when using it, or to catch it and put it in this list. If any slippery fellow has eluded me, I ask pardon. Your nearest musical friend will be glad to explain it.

For those requiring more information, there are several good dictionaries of music. Go first for the shortest and most up-to-date. It is worth bearing in mind that a ten-volume dictionary will give you a lot of information you were not looking for, and may still leave you uncertain. I have omitted words of which anybody knows or can guess the meaning. Nor have I defined again things such as development, or fugue, which are explained in their proper places in other chapters. If one is in doubt about some Italian word not given here, it can not seldom be guessed by thinking what English word is like it. It has been considered out of the scope of this small list (which does not pretend to be a musical dictionary) to give more than one or two German words. A few general notes: *Italian*. Pronounce every letter. The ending '*mente*' equals our 'ly'; *oso* means 'in the manner of'; *issimo*, 'very'; *ino* and *etto* or *etta*, 'a little'; *ato* equals our 'ate' (e.g, *passionato* – 'passionate' or 'impassioned'). Italian vowels: 'ah,' 'eh,' 'ee,' 'o,' 'oo'; 'u' is pronounced 'oo'; 'z' or 'zz' is 'dz'. *German* final 'd' is 't'; final 'ig' is half 'ig' and half 'ih'; 'ie' is 'ee'; 'ei' is 'eye'; 'e' (final) is 'a' (as in 'a thing'); 'u' is 'oo'; 'ä' is nearly 'ay,' (sometimes between that and 'eh'); 'au' is 'ow,' as in 'howl,' or very nearly so.

For all terms indicating speed, see *Speeds*.

For all terms indicating loudness, see *Volume*.

For all names of notes, see *Notes*.

A

 A The orchestra tunes to this (the A a sixth above middle C). The oboe generally gives it. *A* (Italian) means 'in the style of' (e.g, *a cappella*, in church style – meaning, usually, unaccompanied part singing).

ABENDLIED Evening song.

ABSOLUTE MUSIC It has no story behind it: 'the music itself is the meaning'. The opposite is *Programme Music*.

ACCIACCATURA (Ah-chah-ca-too-rah) Crush note, played very quickly before the main note.

ACCIDENTALS Notes not in the key. They are shown by sharps and flats (single or double), and naturals.

AFFETTUOSO Affectionately, tenderly.

ALEATORY Random.

ALLEMANDE An old German dance, used in the suites of Bach and Handel's time. English forms also ALMAN(D) and ALMAIN.

ALTO The vocal part between the treble and the tenor.

AMORE Love. In the form *con* ('with') *amore*, or *amoroso*.

ANTIPHONAL Issuing successively (usually alternately) from two or more performers or groups separated in space.

APPOGGIATURA (Ap-pod-ja-*too*-rah) Grace note on the beat, taking part (commonly half) of the time of the succeeding main note.

ARIA Air. Usually implies a piece within a longer work, opera or oratorio.

ARPEGGIO 'Harp like'. Playing the notes of a chord one after another.

ASSAI (Ass-*sah*-ee) Very.

A TEMPO 'In time (again)': used after some liberty has been taken with it.

ATONAL Not in a key or mode.

B

BAR One of the divisions, of so many beats each, that make up a piece. The word is used indiscriminately for the portion of music thus found between two *bar-lines* (the vertical lines that mark off the bars' length), and for the bar-lines. Note that Americans speak of 'measures' instead of 'bars'.

BASS The lowest part, vocal or instrumental.

BASSO CONTINUO See *Continuo*.

BASSO OSTINATO See *Ground Bass*.

BEAT The unit of time-division. Americans call it 'pulse'.

BEN (It.) Well. Commonly found in phrases such as *ben marcato*, well marked.

BINARY A two-part form: A–B.

BIS Twice (i.e, play a particular bar twice). French people call out '*Bis!*' when they want an encore.

BITONALITY In two keys at once.

BRAVURA With great spirit, dashing, brilliant. Often used of a difficult aria.

BRIO Vivacity, fire. Much the same as *Bravura*.

C

CADENCE The short passage (often only a couple of chords) that brings us to a point of rest, temporary or final.

CADENZA An interpolation by a solo performer at a main cadence at or near the end of a movement or section. Originally extempore, later composed.

CANON A form in which one or more melodies, begun by certain parts, are copied (usually exactly) by others. Hear, e.g, the start of the last movement of Franck's violin sonata, and the fine series in Bach's Goldberg variations. A *Round* is a canon.

CANTABILE (Can-*tah*-bee-leh) In a singing style.

CANTATA A work for one or more soloists and chorus, usually with orchestral accompaniment. Originally, *cantata* was simply a sung work, as differentiated from *sonata*, a 'sounded' (played) one.

CANTILENA A little song.

CANTORIS In church, in antiphonal singing, the part of the choir on the north side.

CANTUS FIRMUS 'Fixed song': the theme (originally Plainsong) on or around which the polyphony of the Middle Ages and Renaissance was embroidered.

CAPELLMEISTER (or spelt with initial K) (Ger.) Master of a body of musicians; formerly, of a choir or orchestra: now used of any conductor.

CATCH A *Round* in which each singer in turn has to catch up the humorous words.

CHACONNE Piece, nearly always in three-time, constructed on a *Ground Bass*. Originally a Spanish dance.

CHAMBER MUSIC 'Room music'. Music for intimate performance: mostly used of music with single performers to each part.

CHORAL, OR CHORALE The Lutheran hymn-tune.

CHORD Notes sounding together.

CHROMATIC 'Coloured'. A chromatic scale moves by semitones. Chromatic notes, chords or intervals are those not belonging to the key in which the music is set. Its opposite is *Diatonic*.

CLASSICAL Broadly, the music of Haydn, Mozart and Beethoven, and their contemporaries before the Romantic spirit became so self-conscious. But it is a poor word, especially when used as the opposite to *Romantic*.

CLAVIER, OR KLAVIER Keyboard.

CLUSTER Chord of notes very close together in pitch.

CODA Tailpiece: that which rounds off a piece, though it can be long.

COLORATURA Showy passage-work: usually used of singing.

COMMON CHORD Consists of a root-note with the third and fifth, in scalic order above it.

COMPASS The pitch-range of a voice or instrument.

CONCERTO A work in several (usually three) movements, for soloist(s) and orchestra.

CONSONANCE; CONCORD Two or more simultaneously sounding notes which, in traditional harmony, do not require the movement of one or more of the notes to achieve a possible point of rest. In practice, a *common chord*.

CONTINUO The harpsichord or other keyboard instrument which, together with a cello or viol-da-gamba, accompanies and leads a baroque ensemble.

COUNTERPOINT Melodies and rhythms woven together. *Polyphony* means the same thing.

COUNTERTENOR In mediaeval polyphony the parts above and below the tenor. Now generally misused to mean a male alto.

CRESCENDO (Creh-*shend*-o) Gradually louder.

CROOKS Different lengths of tubing inserted into horns and trumpets in pre-valve days to set the instrument to play in the right key.

D

DA CAPO From the beginning (head); i.e. repeat.

DAL SEGNO Repeat from the sign: $ (which may be anywhere in the piece).

DECANI (Deck-*ay*-nigh) Over against the *Cantoris*. The south side choir section.

DECISO (Deh-*cheese*-o) Decisive.

DECRESCENDO (Deh-creh-*shend*-o) The opposite of *Crescendo*: gradually softer.

DENSITY A term used in modern music, referring to the number of different notes sounding simultaneously.

DIATONIC Of a scale: one that has tones as well as semitones. Of an interval, note or chord: belonging to the key in which the music stands. Its opposite is *Chromatic*.

DIMINUENDO Diminishing in volume. The same as *Decrescendo*.

DISSONANCE, DISCORD Two or more simultaneously sounding notes so related as to require, in traditional harmony, 'resolution', that is, the movement of one or more of them to form ultimately a consonance or concord.

DIVISI Divided: two notes being written at once for a single part (e.g. the first violin part) the players must divide, half taking the upper and half the lower note. When they come together again, *Unis.* or *Uniti* is written.

DOLCE Softly, sweetly.

DOLENTE Doleful: sadly.

DOTTED RHYTHM Uneven, jerky rhythm, so-called because of the way it may be written down.

DOUBLE FLAT Lowers a note two semitones. In German, *Eses*; It., *bemolle doppia*; Fr., *double bémol*.

DOUBLE SHARP Raises a note two semitones. Ger., *Isis*; It., *diesis doppio*; Fr., *double dièse*.

DRONE Age-old, world-wide accompanimental device of a continuously sounding note. Most familiar to us in the bagpipes.

DUO, DUET Piece for two performers.

E

ECOSSAISE Fr. Scots: a dance form used by some composers, up to Chopin.

ENSEMBLE 'Together': used of chamber-music playing, and of its players – e.g. The 'Melos' Ensemble.

EXTEMPORIZATION Making up music on the spur of the moment. The same as *Improvisation*.

F

FACILE (It., *Fa*-cheel-eh; Fr., Fa-seal) Lit., 'easy'; i.e. it must sound so: hence, fluently.

FALSETTO Lit., 'false'. The high residual boy's voice which the male alto cultivates.

FANTASIA It. (Fan-ta-*zee*-ah. Pronounce in the English way: Fan-*tay*-zee-ah). A piece in free form. The *Fantasy* (*Fancy*) of the 16th to 18th centuries in England was a polyphonic instrumental piece in free *Imitation*.

FERMATA A pause.

FIGURE A short pattern of notes.

FIGURED BASS Bass part only, with figures showing what chords are to be built above it. Used for *Continuo* parts.

FINAL The finishing note of a mode.

FIORITURA An ornament. Applied to florid, decorated singing.

FLAT ♭. Lowers a note a semitone. Ger., *Es*; It., *bemolle*; Fr., *bémol*.

FORZANDO Forceful. *Sforzando* means the same thing, suddenly.

FREQUENCY The rate of vibration on which pitch depends.

FUOCO Fire.

G

GAMELAN The traditional orchestra of South-east Asia, characterized by a large array of tuned percussion instruments.

GAMUT Guido d'Arezzo's notated scale from which modern staff notation developed. From *gamma-ut*, its lowest note.

GAVOTTE Old French dance in four-time, beginning on the third beat.

GEMÜTH Ger. With (*mit*) soul: feelingly.

GIGUE Jig: a dance; the finale of many old suites, such as Bach's.

GIOCOSO Jocosely: sportively.

GLEE An English 18th-century invention: vocal piece for three or more solo voices; secular; usually in several distinct sections of varying emotion.

GLISSANDO Gliding: sliding from note to note.

GREGORIAN CHANT Plainsong. As regulated by Pope Gregory (*c*. AD 600). Still in use.

GROUND BASS Bass subject, repeated throughout a piece, with varied treatments above.

GRUPPETTO Lit., 'group' (of ornamental notes). Formerly, either a trill or turn.

GUSTO Taste.

H

HARMONICA Originally, the musical glasses. Now, a mouth-organ.

HARMONICS (Harmonic Overtones, or Partials.) Higher notes present within a note sounded on an instrument or voice as part of the timbre. The note sounded is called the Prime Tone or Generator or Fundamental. The harmonics are multiples of its frequency. Most instruments can play some of their harmonics. Brass technique depends on this.

HARMONIC SERIES A scale of *harmonics* from the fundamental up.

HARMONY Notes sounding together; and the science of combining them.

HAUTBOIS Fr. form for 'oboe'.

HEMIOLA Lit., 'one and a half'. In effect (although not so written) changing from two bars of three-time to three bars of two-time, or vice versa, the faster pulse-rate being unchanged (see p 55).

HEPTATONIC SCALE Seven-note scale.

HETEROPHONY Singing/playing simultaneously the same basic melody, with individual deviations, usually by way of embellishment.

HOCKET Possibly Lit., 'hiccup'. Fast rhythmic interchange between voices in mediaeval polyphony.

HOMOPHONY 'Block Harmony'. A succession of chords, of which usually the top part comprises a melody.

I

IMITATION One part copying another in melody, or in rhythm, or in both; not necessarily strictly, or for long.

IMPRESSIONISM Like all 'isms', difficult to define. A term borrowed from the 19th-century school of painters who probed effects of light. Though the idea is much older, Debussy may be reckoned its chief exemplifier in music, treating music (especially harmony) as sounds, rather than as a grammatical language (see pp 71 and 77).

IMPROVISATION See *Extemporization*.

INCIDENTAL MUSIC Here-and-there music in a play or film, used where it will heighten the effect of the drama, either during or between the acts.

INDETERMINACY Leaving a certain aspect or aspects of a composition (e.g. the order of movements, the rhythm, which way up the music etc.) to the choice of the performer or to chance.

INTERVAL The distance in pitch between two notes. Count both starting and finishing notes: e.g, C–E is a third.

INTONATION Quality of tone; also, truth or otherwise of pitch; also, the beginning of chanting in *Plainsong*.

INTONING The clergyman's ritual part, chiefly in monotone.

INVERSION Of a melody: upside-down version, notes going up made to go down by the same amount, and vice versa. Of an interval or chord: octave transposition of one or more of the notes resulting in a different one being underneath.

ISORHYTHM Mediaeval polyphonic practice of imposing an unchanging, repeated rhythm on the *cantus firmus*.

J

JIG See *Gigue*.

JOTA Northern Spanish dance, after the waltz style, musically.

JUST INTONATION Tuning by exact mathematical ratios. The opposite is tuning by *Temperament*.

K

KAMMER Ger. Chamber. *Kammermusik*: chamber music. *Kammerorchester*: small orchestra.

KAPELLE See *Capelle*.

KEY A system or mode of tones and semitones. Also used to mean the part of an instrument pressed by the finger.

KEYNOTE The finishing note in a key. Same as the *final* in a mode.

KYRIE Part of the Church service, Roman and Anglican: 'Kyrie eleison' – 'Lord, have mercy upon us.'

L

LANGSAM Ger. Slowly.

LEBHAFT Ger. Lively.

LEGATO Lit., 'bound': notes smoothly succeeding. Opposite of *Staccato*.

LEGER LINE (Ledger) Short bits of line above and below the staff, continuing it, on which notes are placed.

LEGGIERO (Lej-*jay*-ro) Lightly.

LEISE Ger. Equals *piano* – soft.

LEIT-MOTIV (Light-mo-*teef*) Leading theme. A brief, significant theme that stands for some dramatic element – person or idea – in a work.

LIBRETTO The words – poem or prose – which a composer sets as an opera or oratorio.

LIED Song (Pl., Lieder).

L'ISTESSO The same. Common use: *l'istesso tempo* – at the same speed (used where there is a change of note-length).

LUSINGANDO (hard 'g') Coaxingly.

LUSTIG Ger. Pleasurably; joyfully.

M

MADRIGAL See Book V, on Vocal Music.

MAESTOSO Majestically.

MAJOR Major Scale: has tones and semitones, the semitones coming 3–4 and 7–8. Major Interval: A semitone larger than Minor. Not applied to fourths and fifths.

MANUAL An organ or harpsichord keyboard.

MÄSSIG Ger. Moderately.

MAZURKA Polish dance, three-in-a-bar, the second usually accented.

M.D. Abbreviation for 'right hand', in Fr. and It. ('Left hand' is **M.G.** in Fr. and **M.S.** in It.)

MEASURE Bar. So called in America, and sometimes in England.

MESSA DI VOCE (Messa dee *vo*-cheh) Starting a note softly, swelling to loud and diminishing again.

METRE The number of beats in a bar.

METRONOME Time-keeper, to show how many beats per minute. Speed indications are often given in this form: (MM) ♩ = 60, the note unit and number varying. 'MM' (not put in much today) means 'Maelzel's Metronome'. ♩ = 60 means sixty crotchets a minute – one a second.

MEZZA VOCE (Medza *vo*-cheh) Half-voice power.

MICROTONES Notes involving intervals smaller than a semitone.

MINOR There are two forms of Minor Scale. In one, the Harmonic Minor, the tone-and-semitone order is T, S, T, T, S, Tone-and-a-half, S. The Melodic Minor has: Upward, T, S, T, T, T, T, S; Downward (counting from top to bottom), T, T, S, T, T, S, T. A Minor Interval is a semitone smaller than a Major. Not applied to fourths and fifths.

MINUET Dignified French dance-form, in three-time (see p 104).

MODES Usages of the seven notes of the *diatonic* scale, each mode having a different *final* or finishing note, which largely determines the mode's character.

MODULATION Moving from key to key.

MONODY One main melody with accompaniment.

MONOPHONY One melody without accompaniment.

MOTET Lit., 'worded'. Originally a mediaeval polyphonic, polytextual piece, sacred or secular. Later any sacred partsong. See Book V.

MOTIVE, MOTIF A short theme (see p 86).

MOTTO THEME A theme, often having some extra-musical significance, made to occur – sometimes altered – at different points (usually in different movements) of a work. Berlioz called it an *idée fixe*.

MUSIC DRAMA The kind of opera that Wagner developed.

MUSIC THEATRE Either a musical performance organized along dramatic lines, or a dramatic performance organized along musical lines (see p 92).

MUSICA FICTA Lit., 'falsified music'. 16th-century practice of altering the modes at the cadences, which led to the major/minor key system.

MUTA A direction to the player to change his instrument, its tuning, or its crook.

MUTE A damper for stringed or brass instruments. Ger. Dämpfer.

N

NATURAL ♮. The sign that contradicts a sharp or flat. Ger., *Quadrat*; It., *quadro*; Fr., *bécarre*.

NOCTURNE, NOTTURNO Night music, meditative, poetic, sometimes rather melancholy.

NONET Piece for nine performers.

NOTES Sounds; and also the symbols representing them. In U.S.A., for 'sounds', 'tones' is used. British names for the lengths of the various notes, with foreign equivalents – *Semibreve*: Ger., *Taktnote* or *Ganze Note*; It., *semibreve*; Fr., *ronde*; American, Whole Note. *Minim* (in the same order): *Halbe Note, minima, blanche,* Half Note. *Crotchet: Viertel* (Note), *semiminima, noire,* Quarter Note. *Quaver: Achtel, croma, croche,* Eighth Note. *Semiquaver: Sechzehntel, semicroma* (or *biscroma*), *double croche,* Sixteenth Note. *Demisemiquaver: Zweiunddreissigstel, semibiscroma, triple croche,* Thirty-second Note.

For the English note-names C, D, E, F, G, A, B, C, the Germans use the same letters, but H instead of B. (Their B is our B flat.) Italians use the Sol-fa syllables, almost as we know them: Do, Re, Mi, Fa, Sol, La, Si, Do: the only difference in the French use is that they have Ut instead of Do.

O

OBBLIGATO (The German has only one 'b') Indispensable part. Often an instrument or group of instruments especially highlighted in a vocal piece. But the term is sometimes used loosely for a part that *may* be dispensed with – e.g, an additional accompaniment to a song, besides the piano part.

OHNE Ger. Without.

OPERA, ORATORIO See within, Books 4 and 5.

ORGANUM Early polyphony consisting of parts added to Plainsong.

ORNAMENTS Melodic decorations.

OVERTONES See *Harmonics.*

OVERTURE The prelude to an extended work. Concert Overture: a piece of some extent, usually in first movement form, self-contained, and sometimes programmatic.

P

PART(S) The separate strands of melody that go to make up counterpoint and harmony. They can be called 'voices' even in instrumental music.

PARTITA (Par-*tee*-tah) A suite, of the older kind (e.g. Bach's).

PARTITION Fr. (Ger., *Partitur*). Full score.

PASSACAGLIA (Pas-ah-*cal*yah) Originally, an Italian dance in three-time, written on a Ground Bass. A magnificent modern example is the finale of Brahms's Fourth Symphony.

PASSEPIED Fr. (pass-p'yay). A sort of quick *Minuet.*

PAVANE A stately song-and-dance piece in two-time, from the 16th century.

PEDAL POINT Continuously sounding note, usually in the bass, probably deriving from the *drone* and having virtually the same function when the note is the keynote, but when it is the dominant (see p 96), the effect is of a preparation for something important to happen soon.

PENTATONIC SCALE Has five notes. In its commonest form in Western music it is like a major scale without the fourth and seventh notes. 'Auld Lang Syne' is in it.

PIBROCH Bagpipe variations.

PITCH The highness or lowness of a note.

PIZZICATO Plucked (strings).

PLAINSONG, PLAINCHANT Early monophonic worship song of the Christian Church. Still in use.

POCO Little.

POLONAISE Polish processional dance, in three-time. The finest examples in art-music are Chopin's.

POLYPHONY The same as *Counterpoint*.

POLYTONALITY Music in several keys at once.

PORTAMENTO Sliding from note to note, through intermediate notes. Its habitual use proves laziness or inartistry.

PROGRAMME MUSIC Music that illustrates a story, or has some form of literary background. Its opposite is *Absolute Music*.

Q

QUADRUPLET Four notes played in the time of three (or of six).

QUARTER TONE Half a semitone.

QUARTET (Fr., *quatuor*)—A piece for four performers, vocal or instrumental; usually of sonata build. Also, the performers (as, the 'Amadeus' String Quartet).

QUASI As if.

QUINTET (Fr., *quintuor*) As *quartet*, but for five performers.

QUODLIBET 'What you will': a stringing together of tunes to make either verbal or musical fun, or both, often due to incongruity. The Bach family was fond of this diversion.

R

RECITATIVE (It., *recitativo* – reh-chee-ta-*tee*-vo) A free style of declamation, untrammelled by bar-lengths. Much used in opera and oratorio, where it is vocal. Occasionally found in instrumental works. Vocal recitative is known as *recitativo secco* (accompanied by the continuo instruments with a chord here and there), or *recitativo stromentato* (instrumented, i.e. accompanied by other instruments as well, and more fully). The two styles are beautifully illustrated in the four recitatives in Handel's *Messiah*, beginning 'There were shepherds . . .'

REGISTER A definite part of the compass in instrument or voice, having characteristic and distinctive quality. Also used of any organ-stop.

REPRISE A repeat.

REQUIEM Mass for the dead. Also used occasionally for a choral work 'in memoriam'.

RESOLUTION The movement of a discord to a consonance.

RESTS Measured durations of silence. Each of the notes has its appropriate rest. In most languages these take their names from the notes (see *Notes*):

e.g. the German for a semibreve rest is *Taktpause*, for a minim rest, *Halbepause*, and so on. The Italians use *pausa della semibreve, della minima*, or whatever note is in question. The French list is: semibreve rest, *pause*; minim rest, *demi-pause*; crotchet rest, *soupir*; quaver rest, *demi-soupir*; semiquaver rest, *quart de soupir*; demisemiquaver rest, *demi-quart de soupir*. The American system is to speak of 'whole note rest', 'half note rest', and so on.

RESULTANT TONES Extra notes heard when two notes are sounded.

RHAPSODY A declamatory piece, in free form: sometimes based on folk-song (e.g, Vaughan Williams's *Norfolk Rhapsodies*).

RICERCAR Lit., 'search'. 16th-century instrumental form. Later the same as a fugue.

RIGAUDON Fr. (The Eng. is Rigadoon.) Lively French dance, usually in two-time.

RINFORZANDO 'Reinforced': special emphasis on particular notes.

RIPIENO 'Filling up part'. In the old concerto, that portion of the orchestra, over against the soloist-section (concertino).

RITORNELLO A refrain; it also means an instrumental interlude in a vocal work.

ROMANTIC Used, not very wisely, to mark off, broadly, music of the period of the self-conscious romantic revival in literature, in the early part of the 19th century. It is a mistake, however, to make hard-and-fast distinctions between 'classical' and 'romantic' music, for the classics were romantics too.

ROUND A vocal piece in which each voice copies the last, entering at an arranged distance, e.g. 'Sumer is icumen in'.

RUBATO Lit., 'robbed' – which it should not be called, since its essence is the repayment of time borrowed or advanced. In general, swaying the rhythm.

RUHIG Ger. Peaceful.

S

SARABANDE Stately old dance in three-time, accented on the second beat.

SCALE Notes arranged in stepwise ascending or descending order.

SCHERZO 'Jest'. A development (speeding up) of the minuet by Haydn and Beethoven; used in sonatas, symphonies and works of like form.

SCORE Parts for performers. When all are laid out beneath each other, they make a *Full Score*. A *Short Score* condenses more than one on a stave, *Open Score* giving each part its own stave. The *Vocal Score* as its name implies, gives the voice parts in full, with usually a piano accompaniment. The Piano Score condenses the whole work on to two staves.

SCORING Orchestration, Instrumentation. A composer's or arranger's determining of which instruments play what.

SEGNO (*Sain*-yoh) Sign. See above, *Dal Segno*.

SEGUE (*Say*-gweh) Follows.

SEGUIDILLA A Spanish song-dance, in three varieties, from lively to slow.

SEHNSUCHT, MIT Ger. (Zain-zucht) With longing, yearning.

SEMITONE The smallest normal scale interval. On the piano, the pitch-distance from any note (white or black) to that immediately above or below it.

SEPTET (Fr., *Septuor*) Piece for seven performers.

SEQUENCE Repetition of a melodic pattern, higher or lower.

SERENADE 'Evening song'. Usually light music: applied also to Suites.

SERENATA Applied to an 18th-century form of Cantata (Handel's *Acis and Galatea* is a Serenata). May mean the same as 'Serenade'.

SERIES, SET, TONE ROW Applied to the ordered set of twelve notes, which forms the basis of a composition in Schoenberg's twelve-note system. Later serial pieces may use less than the full twelve.

SEXTET (Fr., *sextuor*) A piece for six performers.

SHAKE See *Trill*.

SHARP ♯. Raises a note a semitone. Ger., *Kreuz*; Fr., *dièse*; It., *diesis*.

SICILIANO Italian dance in slowish six-time, virtually the same as the *Pastorale* and beloved of 18th-century composers for slow movements and pastoral songs.

SIGNATURE Written at the beginning of a piece, to show (1) key, and (2) time. Sharps or flats (or their absence) show the former; a fraction, the latter.

SLANCIO (*Slahn*-chee-oh) Dashingly.

SLENTANDO Gradually getting slower.

SMORZANDO (SMORZATO) Quenching the tone; dying away.

SONG FORM A–B–A. One of the simplest forms, with the first music coming back after something different. Used quite often in slow movements.

SORDINO It. Mute. *Senza sordino* means without mute.

SPEEDS The Italian terms are given, in order from slow to fast. A batch of words meaning 'very slow and broad' includes *largo*, *adagio* and *grave*. *Lento* is 'slow', *andante* is 'getting going' (commonly used to mean 'slow', though; and as a general term for the slow movement of a sonata or symphony); *andantino* is a nuisance, because some take it to mean '(only) a little slow', and others, 'a little slower than *andante*'; *allegretto* is clear enough – 'moderately fast'; *allegro* is literally 'cheerful' – hence quick, lively. *Presto* is 'very quick', and *prestissimo*, 'as fast as possible'.

STACCATO Detached. Opposite of *Legato*. Used of notes of chords.

STAFF Set of five lines used in notation.

STRINGENDO (soft 'g') Hastening; implies loudening also.

STRING QUÀRTET Two violins, viola and violoncello.

SUBJECT A theme, especially that of a fugue and those (first and second subjects) in a sonata-form movement.

SUITE Set (of pieces). Formerly built on dance forms. Later, on some common idea, as alternative (e.g. 'Countryside' Suite).

SUSPENSION Holding back one or more notes of a chord, whilst the rest move. Almost always this produces a discord, and then the suspension resolves to make a concord again; a chain of suspensions may thus be formed.

T

TABLATURE Notation for a particular instrument, showing not so much what notes to play, as where to put the fingers.

TEMPERAMENT, EQUAL The modern way of tuning, so that acoustic differences are spread over all keys, and all sound tolerable. See also *Just Intonation.*

TEMPO Time. Commonly means the speed of a movement.

TENOR The higher male voice part, in between alto and bass.

TENUTO Held; sustained.

TESSITURA The main range of a part, the amount of the compass which is covered by the music, excluding occasional very high or low notes.

TETRACHORD The four scale-tones in the interval of a fourth, used in the Greek system of notation.

THEME A tune or motive, which has some significance beyond its own confines. Often that which is varied in variations or developed in developments.

THOROUGH BASS See *Figured Bass.*

TIMBRE Fr. Tone quality; 'colour'.

TOCCATA A brilliant piece to show off the 'touch'.

TONALITY Key.

TONE Two semitones. Can mean a note.

TONE ROW See *Series.*

TOTAL SERIALISM Using a series to determine every aspect (rhythm, loudness etc.), of a composition.

TRANSPOSE Move a whole piece, or section of a piece, up or down in pitch.

TRAURIG Ger. Sad.

TREBLE Highest vocal part. Same as soprano. Also means a boy's voice.

TREMOLO Either the rapid reiteration of one note, or the rapid alternation of two notes more than a whole tone apart. See *trill.*

TRIAD A chord, comprising a note and two others a third and a fifth above it.

TRILL A shake. Rapid alternation of two notes a whole tone or semitone apart.

TRIO Piece for three performers (usually a sonata); or, the performers themselves. It is also used of the middle section of a minuet or a march.

TRIPLET Three notes in the time of two.

TROPPO Too much.

TURN Decoration of a note by alternating it with the notes just above and below it in turn. Written thus: ∿ .

U

UNISON Strictly two or more instruments or voices at the same pitch. Also more loosely (mis)used of the same one or more octaves apart to mean, in effect, no harmony.

V

VAMP Typical accompaniment figure of bass ('oom') and chords ('cha'), e.g. in a waltz: 'oom-cha-cha' etc.

VELOCE (Vel-otch-eh) Rapid.

VIBRATO Fairly rapid, slight wavering of pitch.

VIOLONCELLO Note the spelling (derived from 'violone', the large viol, not from 'violin').

VOCALIZE Singing study, sung to Sol-fa or other syllables.

VOLL Ger. Full.

VOLUME The grading of loudness, beginning at the softest, is: *pianissimo*, *piano* (soft), *mezzo piano* (moderately soft), *mezzo forte* (moderately loud), *forte*, *fortissimo*. The appropriate abbreviations are *pp*, *p*, *mp*, *mf*, *f*, *ff*. More *p*'s or *f*'s can be added at discretion – three or four. Tchaikovsky uses *pppppp* in his 'Pathétique' Symphony.

VORSPIEL Prelude.

W

WELL-TEMPERED Equal-tempered (e.g. Bach's '48').

WHITE NOISE A random agglomeration of sounds from the whole audio-frequency range. An important raw material in electronic music (see p 117).

WHOLE-TONE SCALE Consists of whole tones only. Without the two semitones of the *diatonic* scale, it has no points of rest. Hence its aimless, 'misty' character, and Debussy's use of it.

Z

ZAPATEADO Spanish dance, accompanied by stamping.

ZART Ger. Delicate, tender.

ZINGARESE, ALLA In gipsy style.

Book 2

The Instruments of the Orchestra

by Julius Harrison
revised and expanded by John Gardner
with additional material by Michael Graubart

PART 1 THE RISE OF THE ORCHESTRA

1 INTRODUCTION

The orchestra consists, roughly, of four well-defined sections: the strings, the woodwind, the brass and the percussion. Throughout its 400 years of evolution, composers have created masterpieces for its constantly changing ensemble of instruments. This Book of *The Musical Companion* deals with the development of instrumentation from the early days of culture, but not from the time of the savages or early primitives. The subject has been treated in sections more or less corresponding to those given in the opening sentence of this introduction, the various groups of instruments being briefly traced from their Asiatic or European origin, then on through the dark ages and the Renaissance to the time, early in this century, when the style of the modern orchestra was definitely fixed by the fusion of its various elements. The trend – discernible for more than fifty years with increasing clarity – towards fragmentation and the establishment of variable, smaller, *ad hoc* ensembles for concert, theatre, film and television use is also discussed, as is the effect of the use of electronics.

Civilization, spreading westward through the centuries long years ago and bringing in its train much of the culture of the Orient, was the foster-parent of the modern orchestra. But we must not assume too readily, because of this palpable fact, that ancient Greece, land of the classic lyre, the cythara and similar stringed instruments, contributed the major share towards this record of progress. Far from it. Conservatism was the watchword of the Greeks in music as much as in everything else. Eyes and ears rebelled against the importation of alien instruments coming all the way from Arabia, Egypt, Persia, India and even beyond; instruments that by their very strangeness in both shape and sound constituted a grave menace to the purity of musical style then existing. For the Greeks were not true adventurers in matters of this kind; they had little feeling or use for instruments juxtaposed in brilliant combinations of sounds. And since harmony was then unexplored and Greek music only modal and mainly monodic in character, there could have been few chances for varying the tone-colours of whatever was being performed. So the inevitable happened. Just as Euripides, from his *Medea* onwards, introduced a starker realism destined to divide the house of classical drama against itself, so did the barbarian instruments of the mid-Orient sweep across Europe past the waning culture of the Greeks to add to music those new and richer colours so far either undiscovered or rejected by academic prejudice.

We can easily imagine how these primitive ensembles[1] offended the Greek ear. When Aristoxenus of Tartium, in the fourth century BC, was writing his famous treatise on modes and keys, the foreign invasion had already begun. Instruments were waging their first war for freedom – freedom from bondage to the human voice, to which in Grecian lands it had been allowed to play 'second fiddle' only. The fight was bound to come from without; percussion instruments had hardly any place, and wind instruments little more, in the Greek house of music, though to the 'Barbarians' of the East and South

---

[1] It is perhaps better not to use the word 'orchestra' to denote any musical ensemble until the latter half of the 16th century. The concept of the orchestra, as we today understand the term, is so bound up with the development of western polyphony after the Renaissance that its use in connexion with earlier music, especially such k inds as we are discussing, about which we know only by hearsay, is highly misleading. (J. G.)

they meant variety, tone-colours, massed expression, musical vitality unobtainable from a stringed instrument plucked by a gentle hand in support of voices. Although the barbarian instruments must have been raucous in tone and capable of little delicacy of expression – and the music performed scarcely more than improvisations of questionable merit – yet it must be said that all these efforts undoubtedly marked a step in the direction of progress. In these events we discern the woodwind, brass and percussion instruments striving for alliance with the strings. All the same, many centuries of slow progress were necessary before any real consolidation was possible. It was left to other European nations to put their inventive heads together and give us ultimately what the Hellenic peoples in their conservatism could not or would not recognize to be of any value. And so these alleged barbarians, introducing such instruments as harp, guitar, flute, trumpet, bagpipe and tanboura (an oriental lute), could claim a certain superficial superiority over the cultured race on the other side of the Aegean sea, for such novel combinations must have added many a touch of colour to their primitive music – music performed only in unison or at the octave. Cymbals, drums and other percussive instruments would also act as rhythmical pointers to the melodic phrases, and to produce effects calculated to thrill and to stir the blood of the common people as much as to earn the disdain of the sophists and reactionaries.§

There is a striking parallel in this century to the events described above. The established sounds and forms of Western music have been submitted since the arrival of ragtime some time in the 1890s to a bombardment of exotic styles and sounds, many of which it has defeated by absorption, though always with some modification of its own constitution. Jazz, which is in reality a way of playing any music rather than a special kind of music on its own, is still held at bay, despite the efforts, which cannot be entirely without success, of artists such as the Swingle Singers and Jacques Loussier. Nonetheless the technique and style of its players have influenced all present-day wind-players and many composers (albeit sometimes in an uncomprehending way); whilst its casual, self-sufficient *ad hoc* attitude towards performance, its informality, its stress upon the creative freedom of the executant can be seen to be gradually infiltrating many of the citadels of established attitudes and will, in time, have the effect of transforming them.

In addition and more recently oriental and especially Indian music, which so fascinated Debussy and Ravel when they heard the gamelan bands from Java at the Paris Exhibition early this century, has been increasingly prominent upon our concert platforms, and its techniques influential upon our composers, especially in the matter of time-scale, where its capacity to meditate upon single ideas without subjecting itself to the strait-jacket of classical form with its insistence upon a contrasting section and a recapitulation has fired the imagination of such outstanding figures as Messiaen and Stockhausen.

Through such developments music of the instrumental kind was beginning to mean a great deal to the life of the people of the ancient world; it was becoming more democratic, more interesting and much more exciting in its effect. Small wonder then that the Romans in the heyday of their culture saw great possibilities in all these newer instruments and bent their minds and energies towards improving them. Other types of wind instrument now made their appearance, and it is to the Romans that we actually owe the origins of our modern woodwind and brass instruments. What the lyre and cythara were to the Greeks so were the tibia, buccina, cornu, lituus and tuba to the Romans. From the tibia ('pipe') family of instruments arose the flute, oboe, clarinet and bassoon, while to the buccina and its relations we owe the trumpet, trombone, horn and other brass instruments.

But although we may say, in general terms, that the Greeks favoured strings and wind, the Asiatic and Egyptian peoples the wind and percussion, and the Romans the woodwind and brass instruments, yet all these separate or partly combined efforts did not hasten things to their appointed end for many centuries. The world had changed with the coming of the Christian era, and in many ways for the worse. Religious persecution, the fall of the Roman Empire, the devastation of central Europe by Attila and his hordes, all served to retard the progress made in the previous thousand years. And with the rapid growth of Christianity music turned away very definitely from instrumental to vocal expression. The monks of various orders (almost the sole guardians of learning throughout those long dark ages) left unheeded the many invitations and injunctions contained in the 150th Psalm to praise God 'with the timbrel and dance', with 'stringed instruments and organs', or on the 'high sounding cymbals'. They preferred the expression of the human voice. Instruments were now looked upon as belonging mainly to the secular side of life and, as such, were left to the minstrels, troubadours, jongleurs, Minnesingers and others who made so picturesque the centuries immediately preceding the renaissance of learning among the people at large.

Yet without this lengthy setback the orchestra might never have come into its own, for during the time when everything instrumental was under many a cloud or even banned by the tyrannical edicts of the Church, the monks were busy working out and recording on their parchments the general theory and practice of music. § To such scholars as Franco of Cologne (11th or 12th century) and Walter de Odington of Evesham (13th century) we owe much for our knowledge of mensural notation, i.e. the notation of note-values and rhythm; to an unidentified composer of that time (possibly John Fornsete of Reading Abbey) for that early example of rich polyphony 'Sumer is icumen in'; to the great composer Perotin (1180–1230) of the cathedral church of Notre-Dame of Paris for his reforms of musical notation.

§ But although vocal music was being recorded by hand as early as the year 1200 or thereabouts (Plainsong, Organum, etc.), instrumental music still lagged far behind. Little of the latter kind seems to have been written down until early in the 15th century, being even then quite a rarity. And for this we must blame the Church which, with ruthless power, discouraged or destroyed the cultivation of all instrumental music, leaving to itinerant actors and minstrels the difficult task of preserving what they could from the ruin. Without the enthusiasm of the 11th- to 14th-century trouvères and troubadours of Northern France and Provence – an enthusiasm that eventually won for them the approval not only of the people but also of kings and emperors – all these instruments and the learned skill of the performers thereon would doubtless have perished, to be reborn only after the laborious uphill work of many more centuries. But these minstrels soon began to acquire much skill in the writing of music. Their efforts, however, were vocal-cum-instrumental rather than instrumental alone, for the chief business of the minstrel's art was the composition and performance of fervent love-songs addressed to ladies of high standing or the creation of romances founded on the *Chanson de Roland* or on the chivalry of Charlemagne or even on topical subjects.

Even then, there was little done towards the formation of what we would now term an orchestra. Though the jongleur of the 12th and 13th centuries, attached as he was to the troubadour in the role of interpreter, was a man of many parts, expected to perform with equal facility on the pipe and tabor, citole, symphony (a precursor of the organ), the mandora (much like the oriental tanboura), the seventeen-stringed rote, the manichord, the harp, gigue (from which the dance of that name was derived), the ten-stringed psaltery and so on, yet he and his fellows of equal talent do not seem to have made any attempt to experiment in concerted instrumental music. Perhaps the nature of their calling, paid servants as they often were in some lordly house – for these were pre-guild days – prevented any social intercourse or prolonged exchange of ideas. Life in those times must have been very scattered indeed; occasions for musical arguments few and far between. Yet there is evidence of a Royal Band in the household of Edward III of England. But what the actual instruments were or what music was performed is a matter for speculative thought alone. The instruments known to western and central Europe had by this time become so numerous and varied, thanks to the activities of the minstrels, that we can hazard the guess that no two bands were ever alike or could perform any piece of music in identical manner. Evidence of a possible band is forthcoming in the Minstrels' Gallery sculptures erected in Exeter Cathedral during the reign of Edward III. These carvings illustrate the cittern, bagpipe, clarion, rebec, psaltery, syrinx, sackbut, regals, gittern (guitar), shawn, timbrel and cymbals.§

It is probable that many of the instruments referred to above are not part of the aural and visual experience of the reader though, in fact, they all belong to the three main groups of instruments in use today: strings, wind and percussion (in more homely terms those you scrape or pluck, those you blow down, and those you hit). To these must be added a fourth group which has come into wide use in the past thirty years: electronic instruments, i.e. those which produce their sounds by electronic means.

Stringed instruments are those in which the sounding agent is a stretched string. Some of them are bowed, like the mediaeval rebec, hurdy-gurdy and tromba marina, the viol family and the modern string family of violin, viola, cello and double-bass. All these can also be plucked and, therefore, in a sense are members in part of the other group of plucked stringed instruments, whose long line of ancestry includes the psaltery, gittern, crwth, guitar, lute, mandolin, harp and, though its plectra are actuated mechanically by keys, the harpsichord.

Wind instruments fall into two main categories: brass and wood. The former, though often silver-plated, are correctly so described; the woodwind only partly so, for both metal and plastic are used in their manufacture.

Brass instruments' notes are produced by changes in the lip position of the players (known as 'embouchure') which produce a series of notes known as partials or harmonics (to be explained at length later) modified, in later years, by the use of valves or (as in the case of trombones and sackbuts, their mediaeval forerunners) a slide mechanism. Other members of the brass family include horns, bugles, trumpets, clarions, tubas and sax-horns.

Woodwinds are divided into two chief categories: pipes and reeds. The former are simply blown through (e.g. the recorder, bamboo-pipe and penny whistle) or across (the flute, piccolo and fife); the latter make their sound either by the setting in vibration by the player's breath of a single reed (as in the case of the clarinets and saxophones) or a double reed (as in the case of the oboes and bassoons). There is also a third class of wind instrument whose sound is initially actuated by means of a keyboard. This includes every kind of organ, small or large and, perhaps, the accordion.

Percussion instruments are of two kinds: tuned (glockenspiel, xylophone, marimbaphone, vibraphone, celesta, piano, bells and timpani) and untuned (every kind of drum, tambourine, cymbal, castanet and wooden or metal block – in a word, anything that can be hit or makes its sound by the collision of two or more solid bodies). Percussion-playing, more than any other field of music-making, is open to improvisation and innovation. A recent recording of Mahler's Sixth Symphony, which calls for three hammer blows in its finale, solved the problem of producing this important and essential effect 'by striking in unison (1) a raised piece of platform with a wooden mallet and (2) an extra large bass drum'. Mahler himself had asked for a 'short, powerful, heavy-sounding blow of unmetallic quality (like the stroke of an axe)'.

With such a motley array of instrumental colour as the Middle Ages knew, it may be thought that orchestral music was a highly developed art before the Renaissance. In fact it only became a medium of expressive importance for composers during the baroque period, i.e. after the year 1600. The reason for this must be sought partly in the nature of the human voice which was as mechanically perfect in the Middle Ages as it is today and able, within its range, to sing any note with an infinitely greater variety of controllable tone-quality and dynamic contrast than any instrument. Great composers like Machaut, Dufay and Josquin found a perfect medium for their creative genius in the skilful, well-balanced professional vocal ensembles of the great ecclesiastical establishments. They used instruments to augment and support the vocal ensemble, and no doubt the pieces would sometimes be given on instruments alone. (We do not know, in fact, how the music of the Middle Ages was performed in its day. This gap in our knowledge gives us a very free rein in present-day performances. We do Josquin *a cappella*, on a broken consort, or purely instrumentally with equal justification and varied pleasure.) Certainly the whole style of composition was essentially vocal, whatever medium or mixture of mediums it may have been realized in, and composers thought of all music as a kind of singing whether it was intended to be sung, played or both.

The earliest elaborate instrumental ensemble music was therefore vocal in origin, and it was from the habit of playing rather than singing madrigals and motets that the possibilities of instrumental polyphony were discovered. The word 'canzona' reminds us of this historical fact. Literally it means 'song', but by the 17th century it had acquired the connotation of 'instrumental fugue' and it was in that sense that composers like Frescobaldi and Bach used it in the naming of their keyboard pieces.

Though concerted instrumental music may have sprung from vocal roots it soon began, in the 17th century, to deviate from the previously accepted ideals of vocal music, which could be said to be a careful use of melodic skips, a strict control of dissonance and a harmonious blend of texture. The keyboard music of the 16th century, in the hands of the English virginalists, had already moved away from a vocal basis and could be said therefore to have pointed the way of the future for other instrumental music. Later, vocal music was to be influenced by what had happened in the style of instrumental music, but that is another story which it is not our job to tell.

Before it was possible for an orchestra to develop it was necessary for a well-balanced range of stringed instruments to be evolved, capable of playing satisfactorily and expressively the melodic intricacies of golden-age polyphony. This brings us to the subject of our next chapter.

§ 3 THE STRINGS

The stringed instruments formed a motley collection of all shapes and sizes. Some, such as the rote or crot and the harp, were plucked by the fingers; others, such as the gittern (guitar) and the citole, needed a plectrum; while those requiring the bow (which had found its way into Europe from India and Arabia before the 11th century) were the rebec (under its various names of lyra, geige, gigue, rybybe, etc.), the crowd (cruit or crwth), the monochord (manichord), fidula, fithele (fydele, fiddle or *fithul* as Chaucer has it), all variations of what ultimately became the viol family of instruments.

But drastic elimination of unsuitable and ineffective types was necessary before man's inventive powers could produce a set of stringed instruments capable of expressing the new-fangled music now being written with such skill and over wider ranges of pitch. Treble, alto, tenor and bass voices, often singing in four- or five-part harmony, needed some exact counterpart on instruments; something that would support all voices with a uniform tone and equality of balance. The introduction of the hair bow into Europe gradually solved this problem. But it took a long time to do so, for the majority of the bowed instruments of mediaeval times were small in size, indifferent in tone, and usually possessing no more than three or four strings tuned to a treble or middle pitch. In fact it was some time after the Renaissance that the viol family of instruments displaced the rebec and its variants, and in its turn foreshadowed that now indispensable feature of modern music, the string instruments, known to us all as the violin, viola, violoncello and double-bass.

Quality of tone had been a matter of chance up to the time of the bowed viols, for the best endeavours to sustain the sound at the pleasure of the performer were often nullified by the crude or ineffective instruments themselves. Yet the *ars mensurabilis* of music had been in vogue three or four centuries; the lozenges and diamonds balanced on little poles or with tails attached were all crying out for correctness of interpretation as much from instruments as from voices. The viol family – with all its noble members conforming to one pattern yet of several sizes – brought about this much-to-be-desired end, and for the first time placed the quality of instrumental music somewhere within challengeable distance of vocal. The treble or descant viol, the tenor (*Viola da braccio. Braccio:* 'arm'), the viola d'amore (with seven to fourteen strings vibrating sympathetically beneath the seven 'played' strings), the bass (*Viola da gamba. Gamba:* 'leg'), and the double-bass viol (*Violone*) now offered to the composer a medium for instrumental expression hitherto denied him. Bows were longer and, in shape and quality, not unlike our modern ones. Instruments were shaped to patterns found to produce rich and resonant tone. By the time of Henry VIII a 'Chest of Viols' (as it was called) was the mainstay of an instrumental ensemble, and usually consisted of two treble, two tenor and two bass instruments. In the Royal Band of the year 1539 we find '*viij vyalls*'.§

The days of the viol family were, apparently, numbered. Invented in the 15th century and at the height of their popularity in the 16th – Leonardo da Vinci was reputed to be no mean performer on the viol da gamba – these instruments began to wane in public favour from the 17th century onwards. Their delicate and soft timbre, though allied to the possibility of extremely clear articulation of note and rhythm, did not lend itself to the increasingly 'public' quality of music-making in the baroque period, with its development of opera, ballet and, of course, 'the orchestra', that essentially public medium. Only in this century, after the pioneer demonstrations of Arnold Dolmetsch, has it been realized that, in the performance of their own music (such works, for example, as the fantasies of the Tudor masters and Purcell) the viols are infinitely superior to the violins, violas and cellos which eventually ousted them from their position as standard stringed instruments. What is more, though cumbersome and difficult to tune, they are, in fact, easier to master than their successors. They are the amateur's stringed instrument *par excellence* and, as such, it is interesting to remark their revival in our own era.

§ It was a long time before the stringed instruments that are in normal use today became consolidated into one homogeneous family. We read of violins being introduced into Henry VIII's band in 1547, while the viols were still at the height of their popularity. Many of the older instruments, too, were still very much to the fore, even in the early part of the 17th century. Michael Praetorius, famous composer and theorist at that time, in his *Organographia* describes the String Orchestra known to him as consisting of bandoras, orpharions, citterns, theorboes, lutes and a bass lyra, to which last-named instrument he recommends the addition of a bass viol for the sake of a stronger foundation. § To these instruments were added a keyboard instrument such as the harpsichord, spinet, or (especially in churches) an organ. These double-handed 'harmony' instruments were ideal for supplying a background to the linear texture of the others and, in fact, filled their parts in *extempore* from a single written bass line – the *basso continuo* or thoroughbass. Their inclusion is an inseparable part of the baroque sound which otherwise would tend to consist of one or two strong top lines above a bass and be lacking in middle. The effect of the *continuo* was to bridge this gap and weld the ensemble into one acoustic whole.

§ From the list given above it will be seen that plucked stringed instruments still contended for popular favour with those played by the bow. Not as yet did musicians dare to put aside the seventeen-stringed theorbo-lute (a great favourite with Pepys) or the more plebeian cittern (played with a plectrum) and concentrate on string tone produced by bows alone. Such was the transitional state of music in the 16th and 17th centuries that stringed instruments of a type surviving from the long ago still found themselves cheek by jowl with others that were made but a short time prior to those created by the genius of Antonio Stradivarius.

By the year 1685 the Amatis, Stradivarius, the Guarnerius family and other famous instrument makers living in Cremona had perfected the design and inherent qualities of the violin, viola and violoncello. And so, at long last, the practical and more easily managed four-stringed instruments known as the violin family took complete possession of the field they were never to leave again, ousting their cousins the six-stringed viols in every department of the string orchestra. Only the old violone survived for a while as a foundation tone until the double-bass was firmly established at a somewhat later date. The year 1685 witnessed the births of Bach, Handel and Domenico Scarlatti. By that time the string orchestra so familiar to us 250 years later had come to stay. § Note that it was composed entirely of bowed instruments, though later the harp was to join it as an especial colour effect beloved of 19th- and 20th-century composers, some of whom later introduced the mandolin and the guitar, neither of which, by reason possibly of the tonal limitations of the one and the subtlety of the other, seriously challenged the harp's uniqueness as, the occasional *pizzicato* apart, the orchestra's one plucker.

§ 4 WOODWIND

When the Church, in the Middle Ages, turned against the noisy secular instruments as being obstacles to divine worship, the lyra and cythara alone accompanied the religious service. To these instruments at a later date were added the organistrum and organ and, strangely enough, small 'chime-bells' of the cymbal or gong varieties. But with wind instruments in any shape or form the Church would have nothing to do. These instruments would be kept for public or private merry-makings, royal occasions, fairs, dances and all those sportive events where the spirit of Pan rather than that of Phoebus Apollo predominated. According to the Church, they were born of 'the world, the flesh and the devil' and as such were utterly unworthy of a place in matters spiritual. And so, in a narrow world where the inventive powers of man were crippled by the tyranny of

149

a priesthood continually threatening excommunication and the pains of hell for the smallest deviation from its laws, there was even less chance of progress in this field of music than in that of the stringed instruments.

The ancient Assyrians, the Egyptians, the peoples from Arabia, Phoenicia and further east had known, many centuries before this time, that an ensemble gained greatly in effect if strings and wind were combined judiciously with a discreet admixture of percussive instruments. The Romans knew still more, for their new types of instruments were a great advance on all others previously made. As stated already, they were specialists in the manufacture of many wind instruments, and (like a good north-country-man) loved 'a bit of brass' in particular. Yet all these ancient enthusiasms died out in the later centuries, and for many years strings, woodwind, brass and percussion each ploughed a lonely furrow, caring little whether they acted in any friendly or experimental combinations. We read of Edward I's Troumpour (trumpeter) Roger, and also of Janino his Nakerer (drummer), but there is no evidence that they belonged to some genuine band containing the flower of all the instruments of their day.

No more than a brief survey of the precursors of the modern woodwind family is possible in this article. We must pass over the long vertical flutes of ancient Egypt known as *mam* and *náy*, the Greek *aulos*, and the Roman instruments of the *tibia*[1] family and come to the time when European flutes and recorders (pipes with whistle mouthpiece) tried their best to mingle with schalmeys (shawms) and pommers in sounds that must have been even less pleasant than those of the contemporaneous string families. For they were a mixed lot indeed and, because of their rough designs, incapable of anything like true or tempered intonation. These recorders of the 12th century onwards were actually of the flute family, though played vertically (the German equivalent to recorder is *blockflöte*) and had a compass of some two octaves. Of these instruments there were, according to Praetorius, at least eight varieties extending over a considerable range of pitch. Sometimes as many as twenty-one would be played together, and since their sounds were in agreeable contrast to the crude double-reeded tone of the shawms and pommers, they must assuredly have been the one bright spot in the discordant woodwind family of the Middle Ages and the Renaissance. From them arose the type of flute played crosswise (*flauto traverso*). This instru-

[1] As the name implies, they were originally made from a leg-bone.

ment made its appearance in France as early as the 14th century (*fleuthe traversaine*) and to this day has retained much of its original character. There were various kinds that corresponded to the treble, alto, tenor and bass recorders, but the lower-pitched instruments soon lost their hold (the bass flute excepted), for they were weak in tone and limited in execution. The so-called bass flute is in fact an *alto* flute.

The shawms and pommers (tenor and bass shawms) were played with a double reed like the present-day oboe, cor anglais and bassoon, etc. These instruments, which in all probability found their way across Europe from the East at the time of the early Crusades, were of shrill or raucous quality, almost impossible to combine harmoniously with any other instruments. Their reeds were thick and unskilled in workmanship, as different from those in use today as a piece of cardboard from a wafer, while the instruments themselves, so roughly constructed, must have produced a general out-of-tuneness that would have shocked our ears beyond description could we have heard them. In the 16th century the shawm changed its name to oboe under various spellings worth recording here because of their amusing digression from the original French word meaning 'high wood'. From haulx-bois or haultbois it became hautbois and was then anglicized to hautboy, hoboy, howeboie, hoeboy, howboy and, in German, hoboe. The words shawm, shalm, *shalmele* (Gower in his *Confessio Amantis*, written in 1393), shalmuse and schalmey, etc., gradually fell into disuse, as well they might in face of this new verbal onslaught. To this interesting family Bach owed the oboe, oboe d'amore and oboe di caccia that so often characterized his orchestration, and from these later types used by him are descended our modern and not dissimilar keyed instruments the oboe, cor anglais, bassoon, contra-bassoon, bass oboe, heckelphone, etc., the first four of which have long since become an integral part of the orchestra. And, in concluding this all too brief survey of the main woodwind instruments in vogue during the lifetime of Bach and his great contemporaries, it should not be forgotten that the bassoon was actually derived from the bass shawm or pommer, and *not* from the phagotus invented by Afranio of Ferrara about the year 1540. But, alas, the Italians, uncertain about its actual parentage, gave it the name of *fagotto* and the Germans followed suit with *fagott*. Only the French with *basson* (bas son: 'deep sound') and the English with their own variant of this word kept the instrument away from its mistaken origin, though they, too, gave no clear indication that it was descended from the shawm family and that its forebears had rejoiced in such excellent names as the courtal, bumbarde, waighte (hence our Christmas 'waits') and dulcian.

The story of this group of 12th- to 18th-century wind instruments compared unfavourably with that of the strings. Although there was the same constant endeavour to obtain uniformity of tone and to discover a combination of instruments that would prove acceptable to the ear, the results up to 1685 (which year suggests itself as the most acceptable one for my argument) were indeed disappointing. Actually it was the preponderating coarse tone of the thick-reeded oboes that delayed for so long the balance of effects already achieved by the strings. With their many technical imperfections they simply would not combine with the 'soft complaining' flutes or with the less strident members of their own class, the bassoons. And if these wind instruments in combination formed nothing better than a house divided against itself, there could be little hope of their assisting concerted music by any unconsidered alliance with the strings. By this time recorders had almost vanished. Whereas in Charles I's reign there were six attached to the King's Music, by 1674 only four remained, for as Evelyn wrote five years later – 'the Flute Douce' was now 'much in request'. So the clear and, at times, brilliant pipe effects of the flutes and the few recorders left were now swamped by these unmanageable reeds, with the result that in 1685 the woodwind was far behind the strings in general cohesion of tone-colours. Oboes were now rarely heard in indoor music; their strident tones contended with the trumpets and drums in *al fresco* entertainments where, in numbers equal to those of the clarinets and cornets found in military bands today, they could excite those who, in quantity if not in quality, 'wanted their money's worth'.

And so for many years bands – for I hesitate to use the word *orchestra* – consisted of two kinds, known as the 'whole consort' and the 'broken consort'. The former contained nothing but instruments of one family: it might be a band of recorders or of viols, or perhaps one of lutes and even of shawms. The broken consort would be, as its name suggests, a combination of instruments of different families. But of any advance towards a real union of all available instruments ranking orchestrally there was as yet, despite these occasional broken consorts, hardly a sign. Strings kept to themselves, no doubt afraid of contamination, and, with these few exceptions, so did the wind and brass.§

Especially interesting and characteristic was the use of music in the Shakespearian theatre, the changing colour of different families of instruments, played probably by the same team of players, being suggested variously by such stage directions as Signal, Sennet or March (trumpets and drums); Loud Music (oboes or cornetts[1]); Still Music (recorders); Soft Music (strings); and Solemn Music (organ). This certainly indicates how established was the tradition of thinking in families as far as wind instruments were concerned, and the reasons are not far to seek. Pipe instruments could not match the double-reed instruments' power, an awareness of which fact persisted right into the classical period, for even Mozart used the flute sparingly as part of the wind band, presumably because he knew that, without the bridging tones of the clarinet, it would combine ill with the oboes and bassoons. It was, in fact, the invention of the clarinet about 1690 by Christopher Denner of Nuremberg that helped the formation of a woodwind section in the orchestra as opposed to the addition of one or two wind instruments to the strings, for the clarinet had the ability to match the tone-quality of both flutes and oboes. Though a reed instrument, it does not belong to the shawm family. § Its tube is cylindrical, not conical and, in further contrast to the oboes and bassoon, has only a *single* reed. It was discovered that such an instrument possessed the bright open characteristics of the flute and of the higher-pitched recorders, but with additional power and more roundness of tone that extended over a wide range of pitch. Here at last was an instrument that, for sheer strength, could hold its own against the shawms and, furthermore, was one whose tone brightened the woodwind consort to an unbelievable extent. Yet its progress was slow, possibly due to the imperfections of the early types, and there is no record that it was used orchestrally until after 1750, the year of Bach's death. Although Rameau had made casual use of clarinets in his *Acante et Céphise* (1751) it was not until twenty years later that they sprang into general favour and their special qualities were recognized by Haydn and, more particularly, by Mozart.

And now the composer, ever striving for an ideal combination of instruments that would express his inmost thoughts, soon improved the broken consort of bygone days by reducing the woodwind to something like proper proportions. Two each of flutes, oboes (now

---

[1] The cornett, with accented second syllable, is a wooden, bone or ivory instrument with a cup-shaped mouthpiece, and side holes to adjust the pitch; it was also known by the name of *zinke*. It had a surprisingly gentle tone and was used more than once in his cantatas by J. S. Bach.

reinstated in the concert-room), clarinets and bassoons were found to be adequate for most requirements. In these limited numbers they formed not only a satisfactory blend amongst themselves but also added weight and variety to the foundation-tone strings, and so enabled the composer to think afresh in terms of the most vivid tone-colours.

§ 5 BRASS

But the 'broken consort' was not as yet fully developed, for the call of other instruments seeking admission to its ranks was even more insistent than that of the woodwind. The use of brass and percussion instruments in the Middle Ages and for some time after 'was restricted to royal and noble purposes and the panoply of war'. Yet a time was bound to come when these two classes of instrument would demand entrance to the consort. The drama of music was slowly unfolding. Composers were throwing off one by one the shackles that had bound their art all too closely to the human voice. They sought the expression of worldly as well as of spiritual matters. They sought to portray the incidents and emotions of everyday life; the abstract battle between good and evil; historical scenes; the strife between Greek and Trojan; the thunderstorm; the songs of the birds, and a thousand other phases of life and death that suggested to them many varieties and degrees of sound. All this could not be done with strings and woodwind alone, and the composers knew it. So they experimented, and by degrees added to the orchestra those heavier instruments that nowadays carry the burden of music's greatest climaxes.

The complete story of the brass instruments cannot be told within the limits of this chapter. Reference has already been made to the Romans and to the interest they displayed in the *buccina* and the other brass instruments of their making. From the *buccina* it is not a far step, etymologically, to the bocine, buvsine or buzain of the English and French Middle Ages, nor to the old German word *Buzaun* and the modern one *Posaune*. These names, severally and collectively, indicate very clearly the ancestry of the trombone. But before this instrument was perfected on modern lines it went through a middle period under the name of sackbut. Actually, the buysine was no better than a long straight trumpet (the trombone in chrysalis form!), while its successor, the sackbut, flaunted its slide action as swaggeringly as do the trombones of the present time.

The Roman cavalry instrument, the *lituus*, was the forerunner of our modern trumpet, which also passed through an intermediate stage in the Middle Ages under the name of claro (clarion). However, the word trumpet, under many spellings, also dates back to the time of Chaucer and is one of few survivors from the old English vocabulary of instrumental names.

In the Latin word *cornu* we recognize the origin of the horn. From the Roman instrument of that name arose eventually those circular instruments – circular for the first time in the 14th century – whose tone, mellower in quality but less bright than that of trombone or trumpet, is one of the most romantic sounds in all music. It can almost be said, *inter alia*, that the great classical and modern composers have been more affected by the tone of the French and German horn than by any other instrument, and, in consequence, have poured some of their finest inspirations into this mould, giving to the world so many passages of such wondrous beauty that we who listen are filled with awe and amazement.

Such, then, were the most important members of the brass family that in company with the drums, cymbals, and, maybe, shawms and cornetts, formed by far the noisiest broken consort heard by mediaeval and post-mediaeval ears. To them was allotted all open-air music; they could scarcely be trusted indoors, for their combined tone and sour intonation must have driven many a good man desperate. And when, as time passed, the serpent and the ophicleide (wooden instruments akin to the cornett or zinke family) helped out the bass of the harmony, the cup of misery must have been full to overflowing. 'In the early part of the nineteenth century,' comments Mr Cecil Forsyth on the serpent, in his *Orchestration* (published by Macmillan), 'the instrument's tonal inequalities and its deficiencies of intonation had become more than even the men of Waterloo could stand.' After this trenchant criticism further comment is unnecessary.

Viewing the consort as a whole, we can realize why the frequent importation of instruments not of the brass family was unavoidable. The trumpet and horn were natural (unvalved) instruments in those days; that is, unable to produce any but the notes which accorded to the harmonic series of overtones – with certain exceptions on the horn.[1] And the sackbut or trombone also depended on this principle, though, being furnished with a slide, it had greater facility of execution and could therefore modulate from the key during the progress of the music, an advantage not shared by either trumpet or horn.§

[1] Those who would like a detailed explanation should consult Walter Piston, *Orchestration*, Gollancz, 1955. (J.G.)

The trombones were obviously the most useful and versatile of these three families of brass instruments by reason of their full chromatic compass and the fact that their narrower bell allowed them to be played softly and blendingly with voices and other instruments. Throughout the 16th century they were used widely in ceremonial bands as well as churches. In the sonata 'pian' e forte' of Giovanni Gabrieli (1557–1612) two instrumental choirs – one of cornetts and trombones, the other of violins and trombones – play antiphonally and together in what was the first musical composition to have a specified instrumentation and, therefore, in a sense the first work in the history of orchestration. Later the popularity of trombones waned. There is little use of them in late 17th- and early 18th-century music, though the music Purcell wrote for the funeral of Queen Mary (1695), with its unforgettable use of a trombone quartet, must be mentioned as an exception. Not until the operas of Gluck (1714–87) did the trombone return to the orchestra as a regular member and then only in theatrical scores.

If baroque composers were apparently uninterested for the most part in the trombones, this certainly does not describe their attitude to the trumpet. Purcell, Bach and Handel, to mention only three great masters, wrote trumpet parts that to this day exercise the prowess and stimulate the interest of players more than anything written during the classical era, whose composers confined their trumpets mainly to military rhythms and rarely gave them the tune, largely because the art of playing in the highest register, in which the harmonic series produces a full diatonic scale, had been lost and only the middle register, with its defective scale, tended to be used.

Four passages for horn and trumpet from the baroque and classical periods are given below together with a table of the harmonic series of notes on which they are entirely based. The reader will note that only in the upper register is a full scale of notes possible:

Example 1   'Ode on St. Cecilia's day' Purcell

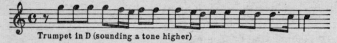

Trumpet in D (sounding a tone higher)

Example 2   Mass in B minor Bach

Horn in D (sounding a minor 7th lower)

Example 3 Symphony no. 3 Beethoven

Trumpets in E♭ (sounding a minor 3rd higher)

Example 4 'Der Freischutz' Weber

Horns in C (sounding 8va lower)

Example 5

Harmonic Series (varying in pitch according to the size of instrument)

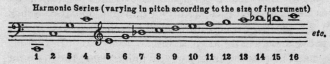

1 2 3 4 5 6 7 8 9 10 11 12 13 14 15 16

§ In the time of Haydn and the Mannheim symphonists the brass often consisted of two horns and two trumpets, a combination which, when added to the timpani, and flutes, oboes and bassoons in pairs, balanced to a nicety the strings of the orchestra. In this modest way did the brass consort, consisting of four instruments only, make its first contribution to that now rapidly expanding instrument, the symphonic orchestra.§ Note that this consort was entirely lacking in bass, a defect that to this day impairs its total sonority. The low-pitched instrument of the cornett family, known from its shape as the serpent, was used in bands regularly (there is a reference to its use in church in Hardy's *Under the Greenwood Tree*) and even graced the orchestral scores of the fastidious Mendelssohn at times (e.g. the oratorio *Paulus*). Neither it nor the brass ophicleide, a near relation of the bugle and described by one wit as 'a chromatic bullock', was satisfactory, however, by reason of its poor, unequal tone-production and its unpredictable intonation. Their use, therefore, was always occasional (the reader may remember that Mendelssohn's 'Midsummer Night's Dream' overture requires an ophicleide, though the part is always played today on a tuba with probably not quite the right effect).

We are perhaps unable to hear the orchestra of the late 18th century without comparing its sound with the better-balanced but quite

157

different orchestra of the late 19th century. It is probable that the lack of bass in the brass section did not worry Haydn or Mozart as much as it does us nowadays with our differently conditioned ears. For one thing the style of playing was probably perfectly adapted to the quality of the ensemble as a whole which was, of course, numerically much smaller than the modern heavyweight symphony orchestra. Brass-playing must have been much lighter and the woodwind, in relation to the strings, much more prominent. Whatever its imperfections may have been, there is no doubt that a definite 'instrument' had been evolved in the classical orchestra: an instrument which differed markedly from the ensembles of the baroque period. Bach used contrast of timbre, but only in terms of complete phrases and sections. Never did he use what is called 'broken work', i.e. the breaking up of a phrase into differently scored fragments. Two quotations will help the reader to identify the two different concepts: one from the second Brandenburg concerto of Bach (Ex. 6), the other from the 'Eroica' Symphony (Ex. 7). If each is studied carefully at least one fact of musical history will be indelibly imprinted on the reader's mind.

Example 6

Example 7

§ 6 PERCUSSION; BALANCE

From all accounts, the desire for sheer noise by congestion of drums, cymbals, tambourine, triangle and other instruments of like character was seldom the way of the ancient peoples of the East, despite their fondness for percussion effects. The Egyptians and early Semites turned these 'instruments of war' into something unusually pacific, using them mainly to give definite rhythmical outlines to whatever was being performed on harp, flute or tanboura. And in their reticence and love of quiet effects, obtainable by contrast of one percussion instrument with another, they showed a degree of skill and aesthetic judgment that glorified rather than debased this important feature of the art. That they used them also in martial style goes without saying, for never did a nation exist that found no occasion for the use of clashing cymbals or the 'double double double beat of the thundering drum' as thrilling incitements to just or unjust warfare. Yet no one, listening nowadays to any oriental, Moorish or Slavonic music on these or similar instruments, would deny that the subtlety of quiet effects therein must have survived from age-old traditions not born of sheer noise or love of barbarism, and that all other effects have been, in the main, the product of a later European civilization given more to the sounds of war than those of peace.

In the differences here implied lies, no doubt, the whole unhappy history of the percussion department of the orchestra. Unhappy is the word, for most of these instruments, lending little or nothing to the definite pitch of sounds in either melody or harmony, have indeed been the playthings of chance ever since they were created by primitive man. Deposed from the high position they occupied in their early oriental days, they became synonymous with everything that was noisy and warlike. They could not develop on lines similar to those that led so successfully in the 18th century to the entente between strings, woodwind and the brass, for their very nature stood in the way. Out of favour with the Church in mediaeval times, equally out of favour with all other instrumental combinations save those functioning out of doors, they led a precarious existence solely dependent on noisy brass, pipe and reed instruments for company.

But since the main percussion instruments have come down to us from the long ago merely as improvements on or variants of ancient oriental types there is no need for me to trace their history except in a general way. Drums have existed ever since primitive man beat on the roughest-made membrane stretched across a wooden frame, and today much the same sounds are made on them in exactly the same way. The same can be said of the tambourine (O. E. timbrel), which has remained true to its character for 2000 years or more. On the other hand, the cymbals, with a much more interesting and picturesque history, have varied in size and shape from the small basin and cup-shaped instruments of the Assyrians, Arabs and Indians to the large circular and hard-clashing types for which Turkey has been famous these many years. Except for the last-named, all these have fallen into disuse, though Berlioz in his 'Romeo and Juliet' Symphony and Debussy in *L'Après-midi d'un Faune* have written parts for the small antique cymbals – parts that are usually transferred, in

159

the absence of the proper instruments, to the glockenspiel (itself, as the name implies, a modern resurrection of the old English 'chime-bells' referred to in Chapter 4, p. 149).

We come to Tudor times and to the introduction into England of the kettledrums, the natural successors to the 14th-century nakers (*nacareh*, in Arabic). These were considered far superior to all other drums yet invented because they could be tuned to a definite pitch. In less than 200 years they were destined to become the most impor-tant percussion feature of the orchestra, acceptable to the ear as much in the concert-room as out of doors. Purcell was the first English composer to employ them in concerted instrumental music (*The Fairy Queen*) and by Bach's and Handel's day they were a recognized and most effective method of giving rhythmical point to the loud *tutti* passages, being always associated with two or three trumpets. At that time a pair of drums was customary but, as will be seen later, others were eventually added to the orchestra to meet the growing requirements of modern music. While all other percussion effects were sadly neglected by composers, the timpani (to give the kettledrums the name in general use today) continued to gain in popularity. Haydn and Mozart used them much more consistently in their later symphonies. Yet we should not forget as a notable exception that the latter dispensed with them in his famous G minor Symphony composed in 1788.

As in the baroque era so in Haydn's and Mozart's orchestral works we often find trumpets and timpani together and even Beethoven, to the very end of his life, still made use of much the same traditional scoring. In addition, this happy union of trumpets and drums solved to some extent the question of balance of tone between the extreme parts of the harmony in all loud passages for, as we have already seen, the disappearance of the trombones from the brass consort had weakened considerably the resonance of that section of the orchestra.

The orchestra now counted among its members representatives from all three families of instruments. True, it was as yet somewhat incomplete in the balance and general blend, but it was indeed an orchestra worthy of the name. It had taken hundreds of years to sort itself out, to get rid of unsuitable instruments of all kinds, to incor-porate new types and then to blend them and the old into something like harmonious cohesion. It was a task of great magnitude, bound up inextricably with the progress of music as an art; made possible only by the ceaseless efforts of the Church and the laity, the monk and minstrel, the theoretician and practician. From the ancient

Egyptian rebab to the first Stradivarius violin is a far cry. Yet from the one to the other we can trace the gradual evolution of a type of stringed instrument recognized by musicians of all centuries as the quintessential feature not only of instrumental music itself but also of vocal music requiring instrumental accompaniment. The woodwind, brass and percussion, less manageable and more assertive than the strings, developed at a slower rate. Not until the days of Monteverdi did it occur to the composer that the general distribution of these instruments, in combination with others less noisy, was unsatisfactory.

And now for the first time the balance of the orchestra, intersectionally, was *considered* in all seriousness. Strings were augmented and other instruments reduced. Even then it took many years to *achieve* anything like a satisfactory balance. The orchestra of Handel's time – a century later than Monteverdi – is to be found still struggling with a devastating number of oboes and bassoons, trumpets and drums, so that we can only conjecture the unhappy and drowned condition of the poor strings in such circumstances. But from the days of Haydn all was plain sailing. The orchestra had found not only its feet, but its sea-legs. It was now fit to weather the many storms that would come its way from the direction of the symphonic and operatic composers. The strings rose from their watery grave to a new and glorious life and became the foundation on which everything else was built. The wind and brass were harnessed at last, mostly in pairs, and took the timpani into their fold. But the degradation of the noisier percussion instruments was now complete. To all intents and purposes they were banished from the new consort. Their eclipse in the classical age of music was to be followed by a revival early in the 19th century, at which time they became the prey of those operatic composers who are now little remembered by their operas but often indeed by the charming but somewhat over-percussioned overtures to those forgotten works.

SIX TYPICAL ORCHESTRAS

1 ASSYRIA. TIME OF ASSUR-BANI-PAL. (6th century BC.)
   (*a*) Harps, trigons (triangular harps), pipes and drums.
   (*b*) *For the dance*. Lyre, harp, tambourine and cymbals.
2 TIME OF QUEEN ELIZABETH I. (16th century.)
   Viol, flute, cittern, pandora (another form of cittern), lute and viol da gamba.
   Note. Only the flute 'breaks' the string consort.

161

3 TIME OF JAMES I. (Early 17th century.)

Pipe and tabor, treble violin, 2 bass violins, 2 sackbuts, mandora (lutina or small lute), and tenor cornett (zinke).

Note. The consort is still further broken by the addition of brass instruments.

4 TIME OF CHARLES II, PEPYS, PURCELL, STRADIVARIUS. (Late 17th century.)

Violins, violas and violoncellos to the number of 39.

3 Bass viols, 2 theorboes, 4 guitars, 4 recorders.

2 Harpsichords, 4 trumpets and kettledrums.

Note. Quite a discreet broken consort that, in an orchestra of 59, would suffer only 8 wind instruments and a pair of drums.

5 TIME OF BACH, HANDEL, A. SCARLATTI, RAMEAU. (Early 18th century.)

Flutes, oboes, oboe d'amore, oboe di caccia, bassoons.

Horns, trumpets, trombones, drums, bells.

Violins, viols, violino piccolo (small violin), viola d'amore, viola pomposa (large-sized viola), viol da gamba, violoncello, violone (double-bass).

Organ.

Harpsichord or clavichord.

Note. All these instruments were used by Bach, but in various small combinations chosen from the above list. The harpsichord or clavichord helped mainly to supplement the middle harmonies, since many of the instruments could not be trusted to perform their parts adequately if left to themselves.

6 TIME OF HAYDN AND MOZART. (Late 18th century.)

2 Flutes, 2 oboes; 2 clarinets (on occasions only, and sometimes displacing the oboes), 2 bassoons.

2 Horns, 2 trumpets; 3 trombones (on occasions only, and never in symphonies).

Timpani (one pair only. Other percussion instruments very seldom).

Violins, divided into 1st and 2nds.

Violas, violoncellos and double-basses.

Note. The personnel of this orchestra was usually about 35 or 40.§

PART 2 THE EXPANSION OF THE ORCHESTRA

§ 1 TROMBONES AND HORNS

Not for long was the orchestra to remain in the state of calm that had produced the shapely Haydn symphonies, for a great dramatic genius was already finding it insufficient for his musical needs. When Mozart was writing his opera *Don Giovanni* in 1787 the trombones had already returned to some favour with composers. Once the numerical balance between strings, wind instruments and percussion had been settled satisfactorily in the main essentials, there seems to have been little hesitation in accepting the trombones (usually three) as rightful additions to the brass section. Gluck, in particular, used them to fine effect in his operas. But no one at that time seemed to want them in the symphony, not even Mozart. Their subsequent elevation to symphonic rank came from Beethoven some twenty years after *Don Giovanni* was written.

Yet it was actually Mozart who rediscovered the trombones in all their splendour of tone. He it was who in the last act of *Don Giovanni* gave them a new and wonderful significance. He it was who, in *The Magic Flute*, four years later, again invested them with an extraordinary duality of character; first, to illustrate the Temple of Wisdom and Light, wherein Masonic rites were performed by the high priest Sarastro and his brethren; and secondly, to depict the final descent of Sarastro's enemy the Queen of Night into her Kingdom of Darkness. If Haydn has been called the 'Father of the Symphony', then assuredly we must rank Mozart as the male parent of modern orchestration. And lest the reader think I am overstating matters, let me recall to his mind the scenes in *Don Giovanni* where, in my submission, the three trombones for the first time foreshadow in the most definite terms the birth of the modern orchestra.

In the churchyard Don Giovanni and his servant Leporello stand before the statue of the dead Commandant who, it will be remembered, had been killed by Giovanni in the first scene of the opera. Suddenly the statue comes to life, warning Giovanni of his impending doom. At this sinister moment and, be it noted, for the first time in the opera, Mozart introduces his three trombones, and by such means gives to the scene a touch of horror the equal of which can scarcely be found in all music. Nor is that all. When, in the banqueting hall, two scenes later, the statue appears unexpectedly, having accepted Giovanni's mocking invitation to supper, the same type of orchestration recurs and continues throughout the terrifying scene until the unrepentant Giovanni is swallowed up in the flames of hell.

Beethoven must have known this opera and *The Magic Flute* in his young impressionable days, and could scarcely have remained unaffected by the masterly orchestration at the points I have mentioned. Here indeed was something new. He would have noted the special use to which the trombones were put: how they were introduced at crucial moments in the drama to give the required effect when all other instruments failed to reach the point of intensity demanded by the composer. And, he might have thought, if this could be done in opera, why not in the symphony? And so it is no mere idle surmise to suggest that the triumphant finale to his immortal Fifth Symphony, in which the three trombones are heard for the first time in *any* symphony, owes its origin to Mozart and his two operas. Since we know of no other music of the period that could have affected Beethoven to a like extent, we must accept this circumstantial evidence and draw the only conclusion possible.

From about this time onwards the orchestra became the centre of feverish activity in all directions. String players were now fairly reliable in technique – witness what Beethoven had the temerity to write – and had greatly increased in numbers. The woodwind too, having adopted the clarinet for permanent inclusion, could now produce something like a true blend of tone-colours, while the brass welcomed the trombones when the music was of the kind demanding their presence and their weight. The age of expansion was now drawing near, for instrumental music was making such rapid headway as a powerful and emotional art that the small *poudré* orchestra of the 18th century was proving totally inadequate for the expression of all the thoughts now surging in the composer's mind. Beethoven, as early as his third symphony (the 'Eroica') already felt the need of some such expansion. When he planned this noble masterpiece as a tribute to Napoleon Bonaparte he found that two horns were insufficient to express all that the music contained, and so a third was added. Never was a decision better made, for almost every bar of the music justifies the third instrument. Without it the symphony could barely exist; through it we inherited such wonderful passages as those in the trio of the scherzo – passages at once the pride of all music-lovers and the despair of nervous horn-players. Yet Beethoven, though such an innovator, did not despise the orchestration of his predecessors. He had the supreme virtue of knowing how to vary his instruments according to the requirements of the music, relying on the Mozartian

164

orchestra for many of his finest compositions and departing there-from only when driven by the daemonic spirit that created such masterpieces as the Fifth and Choral Symphonies.

The following table shows at a glance where Beethoven added certain instruments to his orchestra for specific purposes. The customary strings and timpani are not included here, being common to all the symphonies.

Instrument	Symphonies 1, 2, 4, 7, 8	3 Eroica	5	6 Pastoral	9 Choral
Flute	2	2	2	2	2
Piccolo	–	–	1	1	1
Oboe	2	2	2	2	2
Clarinet	2	2	2	2	2
Bassoon	2	2	2	2	2
Double-Bassoon	–	–	1	–	1
Horn	2	3	2	2	4
Trumpet	2	2	2	2	2
Trombone	–	–	3	2	3
Triangle	–	–	–	–	1
Cymbals	–	–	–	–	1
Bass Drum	–	–	–	–	1

The use of the trombones in the symphony was far from regular, even among Beethoven's great contemporaries and those romantic composers immediately following him. Schubert omits them in his early symphonies, but makes up gloriously in the 'Unfinished' (no. 8 in B minor) and the great C major (no. 9). There is, in fact, no more purposeful or poignant writing for trombones to be found anywhere among the great masters' symphonies than in these two supreme examples. In this connexion I would refer the reader more particular-ly to the slow movements, where there are many quiet passages of surpassing beauty. Schumann included trombones in each of his four symphonies, sometimes with great mastery, often with but a poor sense of blend. Mendelssohn found them unnecessary in his wholly charming and picturesque Scotch and Italian Symphonies (nos. 3 and 4). He omitted them purposely for, of all composers, he knew how to score, using, like Beethoven, no more instruments than seemed necessary to the proper expression of his ideas.

Sufficient has now been written about the trombones to show what an important part they were playing at this period. No less important was the advance of the horns. Between 1841 and 1853 Schumann had used two pairs in three of his four symphonies, an expansion that had already become fashionable in operatic music, noticeably Weber's. All things considered, this expansion was inevitable, and for good reasons. It was still the day of the natural horn and trumpet, when composers had to juggle considerably with their music to make it playable – a difficulty already explained elsewhere. But music, in the hands of romantic composers like Schubert, Schumann, Chopin, Mendelssohn and Weber, had by now travelled far away from the diatonic character that was its chief glory and strength in earlier days. Chromatic harmony was all the rage: quick changes of key the *sine qua non* of this new dramatic art. The old foundations both in instrumental and vocal music were bring sapped one by one by a strong undercurrent destined eventually to sweep away the long-established order of things and bring about a complete revolution in every direction. Once more the composer was ahead of the times, caught between the upper millstone of the chromatic harmonies he had discovered and the nether one of those old-fashioned brass instruments unable to give him what he so ardently desired. Again his ingenuity saved him when he installed a second pair of horns in the orchestra, crooked (that is, tuned) in a different key for the purpose of supplementing the other pair that could only play very intermittently when the music had modulated. Even then everything was more or less a makeshift and remained so until the liberation came about the year 1850. At this time valves were added to the horns and trumpets, a revolutionizing invention that solved for all time most of the technical difficulties confronting both instrumentalist and composer. Chromatic music could now roam at will over any or all of the brass instruments. Crooks gradually fell into disuse, though hesitatingly; no longer was the horn-player compelled to carry about with him all those various tube-lengths that have been so often and unkindly compared to sections of gas-piping. The coming of the valved horns and trumpets marked the end of a period and the creation of a new one.

§ 2 THE ORCHESTRAL REVOLUTION

Revolution was now afoot in all directions. Many of the old classical forms of music were either breaking down or, when they did survive, having a bewildering number of new interpretations put upon them. The prowess of the composer had advanced with such startling rapidity, particularly in orchestral music, that instruments could not keep pace with the general development of the art. From the moment the nucleus of a real symphonic orchestra was formed by Haydn and his contemporaries, musical composition of the instrumental kind was continually ahead, outstripping its own means of expression and demanding more and more instruments as each daring composer came along in all his insurgency.

Naturally it was the group of operatic composers who showed the first signs of dissatisfaction with their lot. They ever do, they ever will. Gone were the Mozartian traditions, lost in an age of vehement romantic music. Now it was well-nigh impossible for the composer to think in terms of the old classical orchestra, to write with the same perfect poise and mastery that had caused Mozart to withhold his trombones from all but two scenes of *Don Giovanni*. To Berlioz, born ten years before Wagner, the orchestra meant more in effects of massed sonority and grandeur than it did otherwise, beautiful as some of his more delicately scored compositions may sound to our ears – witness, for instance, the Queen Mab scherzo from his 'Romeo and Juliet' Symphony. To Wagner, the orchestra, in all the dazzling radiance that could be produced by the addition of many instruments, was the very life-blood of music. In general terms, it was now an age of musical violence, an age caught up in the toils of descriptive programme music: one that demanded much in every direction save the classical. And, as the old proverb says, much wants more. The great school of classical music, wherein the main object and delight of the composer was the creation of works primarily perfect in design, had now been superseded by that of the romanticists and realists whose chief aim was to squeeze the last ounce of sonority from the orchestra.

The orchestra grew apace. New instruments joined forces with those already in use, but not quite so haphazardly as in times past. There was definite order in all the composer put on paper and realized in sound. The age of the old symphonic orchestration had given way to that of the dramatic, and even if this were a musical revolution of the greatest moment, what was done by the composers was done deliberately, with real insight, and yet with respect for the past achievements of the classical masters. Each family of wind instruments was extended and, to balance this extension, the strings were increased in proportion. The percussion department, too, came back into prominence, for the new music was decked out with a large array of drums, cymbals and other instruments of no determinate pitch. And again that was done with some discrimination, which was hardly the case with the lighter operatic composers of the period, such as Auber, Suppé, and even Rossini. There was a genuine revival of interest in all those rhythmic instruments that had fascinated the ancient Assyrians and Egyptians but had in subsequent times been so badly mishandled. Nor should it be forgotten, incidentally, that this revival owed its existence to the fact that a single pair of kettle-drums was found to be quite insufficient, percussively, to support the massed effects now becoming so frequent in music of a restless fevered age.

And so, with all this added wealth of new orchestral timbres at hand, few composers were now inclined to follow slavishly in the path of tradition, though (as Brahms was soon to prove) music of the classical type was by no means played out.

Berlioz, in many ways more revolutionary than Wagner, though less practical, was the leader of this new movement. Nothing was too big for him. His conception of the orchestra was on a scale never approached by Wagner, and much of what he advocated in his *Traité de l'instrumentation* (1843) was entirely outside the realms of 'practical politics'. Here he aimed, theoretically, at the creation of a stupendous orchestra, one that, to perform ideally, must contain no fewer than 242 strings, some thirty grand pianos, an equal number of harps, together with wind and percussion instruments in relatively high proportions. But when it came to scoring his impetuous and intensely vivid music, he was usually content with a far less lavish display of instruments than his theories demanded. In the earlier years of these extravagant theories he soon came to loggerheads with the practical musicians of Paris and so, for true recognition of his undoubted genius, he was compelled to go abroad: to Germany, Austria, and even to England (1851). In these countries his fecund, grandiose ideas, coupled to brilliant orchestration of a kind entirely new, stimulated rather than annoyed his audiences, and he met with increasing success wherever he went. 'I understand,' said the King of Prussia, 'that you are the composer who writes for five hundred musicians.' 'Your Majesty has been misinformed,' answered Berlioz; 'I sometimes write for four hundred and fifty.'

In the overture 'Benvenuto Cellini' Berlioz makes brilliant play with his brass and percussion, which sections, in combination, greatly outnumber the woodwind, as will be seen in the table opposite. And in addition, three notes on the timpani are often sounded simultaneously – a device very dear to the heart of Berlioz. Against these there are pairs of flutes, oboes and clarinets (Haydn used as many) and the extra sonority of four bassoons playing well down in the bass.

The table below, if compared to the list of instruments required

Instrument	Benvenuto Cellini (Berlioz)	Harold in Italy (Berlioz)	The Nibelungs' Ring (Wagner)
Flute	2	2	3 ⎱ four players
Piccolo	1	1	2 ⎰ required
Oboe	2	2	3
Cor Anglais	—	1	1
Clarinet	2	2	3
Bass Clarinet	—	—	1
Bassoon	4	4	3
Double-Bassoon	—	—	—
Horn	4	4	8
Trumpet	4	2	3
Cornet (modern)	2	2	—
Bass Trumpet	—	—	1
Trombone	3	3	3
Contra-Bass Trombone	—	—	1
Tenor Tuba	—	—	2
Bass Tuba	1	1 (or Ophicleide)	2
Contra-Bass Tuba	—	—	1
Timpani	3 (two players)	1 pair	2 pairs
Triangle	1	1	1
Side Drum	—	2 (small)	1
Cymbals	1	1	1
Bass Drum	1	—	—
Glockenspiel	—	—	1
Gong (Tam-tam)	—	—	1
Harp	—	1	6
1st Violin	⎫	15	16
2nd Violin	Number of	15	16
Viola	⎬players not	10 (and solo)	12
Violoncello	specified	12	12
Double-Bass	⎭	9	8

for Beethoven's symphonies, makes interesting reading, more especially as the score of Wagner's *Das Rheingold* (from *The Ring of the Nibelungs*) was completed only thirty-one years after that of the Choral Symphony.

As this chapter concerns the actual growth of the orchestra, consideration of the sounds produced by these new instruments must be deferred until later. But it is well to draw the reader's attention at this point to the enormous expansion of all sections, particularly as required by Wagner. This most practical of all composers, though demanding so much, indulged in none of the freakish tricks that are characteristic of the orchestration of Berlioz. True, he more or less created that new brass family – a family not always at hand when wanted – the 'Wagner Tubas', but that was for specific purposes fully justified in the music. On the other hand, his multiplication of harp parts is now considered fantastic; somewhat failing in the effect intended, and, in short, impracticable. That apart, in all sections of the orchestra, used either singly or in combination, he set a standard of orchestration that, without doubt, has never since been equalled, though imitated by countless composers of all nationalities. Wagner's 64 string players, when compared to Mozart's full orchestra of 35, are eloquent testimony to the richness of sound desired by the composer. Those readers who have been fortunate enough to hear such numbers in any performance of *The Ring of the Nibelungs* can bear witness to the uncanny accuracy of Wagner's calculations in this respect, for never does any one section of the orchestra obtrude on another. With fewer strings the bloom is no longer on the sound; everything becomes discoloured and distorted; the spirit of the composer vanishes into nothingness.

But whether music of the non-operatic kind can live in the luxuriance of all this richly coloured orchestration without palling on the senses sooner or later is a controversial matter into which it would here be unwise to enquire. The post-Wagnerian composers have, on the whole, thought it could; though, while stating this, we must not forget the heroic lone hand played by Brahms in his masterly endeavour to save the world of classical orchestral music from total extinction – an objective that to his mind could only be reached by curbing all desire for brilliant instrumentation for its own sake.§

The fact that Wagner, a methodical and rational craftsman if ever there was one, perceived that triadically based music would be best served orchestrally not by pairs but by trios and quartets of wood-wind instruments and thus, with his accountant's approach to balance and blend, achieved a peerless euphony in his scoring, must not cause us to deny that, in the last analysis, his is just one kind of sound which might not necessarily be the effect that another composer is aiming to achieve in *his* search for self-expression.

Berlioz, on the other hand, created quite a different spectrum of colour, brighter and more clearly contrasted, if less sumptuous and comfortable, and great though Wagner's influence was upon Western music, that of Berlioz was hardly less of a model, even within German-speaking countries. We can trace his example in the clear lines of Mahler and the athletic brilliance of Strauss as well as in the works of his French contemporaries and successors where it is, perhaps, in the brass section that we notice an especial timbre brought about by the use throughout the 19th and well into the 20th century of a pair of cornets as well as a pair of trumpets.

The former, which had valves and therefore a chromatic compass, were shorter-tubed than the latter, a characteristic which gave them greater agility. They are found in such diverse scores as the 'Fantastic' Symphony of Berlioz, the Symphony of César Franck and Debussy's *La Mer*. Anyone who has heard these and other works with the correct instrumentation will testify to the subtle contrast between the tone-quality of the two kinds of brass instrument, awareness of which, of course, guided the composer in the layout of his score. Another well-known French piece which needs but rarely gets cornets is Bizet's opera *Carmen*, throughout which there is real cornet – as opposed to trumpet – music.

There were different kinds of orchestral sound, too, in other streams of musical civilization. In Italy, for instance, Rossini and Verdi aimed at a simpler, more monolithic sound which, though less interesting, perhaps, than that of their French and German contemporaries, had lightness and sparkle when needed as well as the ability to deal devastating hammer-blows (very important in the theatre). Their use of valved rather than slide trombones at times makes for extreme difficulty of clear execution in orchestras which only possess the latter instruments (e.g. in the overture to *The Force of Destiny*), a snag which they later imposed upon themselves, because even in

Italy valved trombones are now almost obsolete, owing to the problems of intonation they have always posed. The slide trombone, together with the stringed instruments is, in fact, the only member of the orchestra capable of playing *perfectly* in tune.

The tendency towards brightness of colour and clarity of texture – two traits not always found in German music – was much stimulated by the belated entrance upon the European musical scene of a school of Russian composers. From Glinka (1804–57) through Stravinsky to Shostakovich, their style and concept of orchestral sound have been a model to many composers of all nationalities. Rimsky-Korsakov's treatise on orchestration sums up in verbal form their prevailing attitude. As in all Russian textbooks the approach is didactic, thorough and very technological – it tells the student exactly how to face every conceivable kind of situation, which was by no means the method of Berlioz's earlier treatise with its fascinating, idiosyncratic and encyclopaedic account of the potential of each orchestral instrument. Especially characteristic is the way Rimsky points out the intrinsic defects (to his ears) in Beethoven's reliance upon double rather than triple woodwind, and especially valuable to the student are his directions for brass chording: a problem Beethoven, in such works as the *Leonora* no. 3 overture, solved by handing over to the conductor and players the almost impossible task of harmonious balancing by means of exhaustive rehearsal.

The Wagnerian–Rimskyan aim of perfect blend at all costs was very much a 19th-century ideal. Bach, in such works as the Ascension oratorio (cantata no. 11) seemed hardly interested in the concept, for there is no way in which the sonorities of flutes, oboes and trumpets can be equated in the final movement of that work. He was, however, writing for players rather than audiences, whereas the 19th-century composer tended to write for audiences rather than players, and thus aimed at the complete audibility of what he had written with the insistence of a playwright upon the clarity of his dialogue.

The zenith of the heavyweight, virtuoso orchestra as the deliverer of an unmistakable musical message to a passive audience was reached, perhaps, in the first quarter of the 20th century. Though standards of execution may have continued to rise since then, composers have certainly shown less and less interest in the dumbfounding powers of the symphony orchestra. It is among *fin de siècle* composers such as Mahler, Strauss, Debussy, Ravel, Schoenberg, Stravinsky, Berg and Elgar that we find the supreme handlers of the new instrument with its fully chromatic brass, its multiple woodwind, its growing percussion and its enormous string band of, say, thirty-two violins, twelve violas, ten cellos and eight basses.

Though most would not regard him as the greatest creator among the names I have listed above, Ravel, perhaps, had the finest instrumental ear of them all. His ability to calculate on paper the effect of a subtle mixture of timbres is peerless; and, if it is said that his talent was often employed upon second-rate musical material, then this merely enables us the more easily to study and admire his supreme prowess as an orchestrator – an opprobrious word, as Stravinsky would, with some justification, have us think.

The ideal of perfect balance still permeates our thinking; an understandable phenomenon if we remember that the bulk of our repertory remains 19th-century. If we look back, however, at the musical history of this century we at once become aware of a tendency for composers to move away from the big orchestra – a medium which reached its climax in such works as the *Gurrelieder* of Schoenberg (1901), the Eighth Symphony of Mahler (1907) and the 'Gothic' Symphony of Havergal Brian (1919) – towards smaller ensembles for a variety of interlinked reasons: social, economic and artistic. Early examples of this trend are the opera *Savitri* of Holst (1908), which uses an accompaniment of twelve solo instruments, and the 'Chamber' Symphony, op. 9 of Schoenberg (1906) which was written for fifteen soloists, though often performed – with the composer's approval and, it could be said, enhanced effectiveness – with multiple strings. Schoenberg got the idea of his chamber orchestra, perhaps, from the *Siegfried Idyll* of Wagner (1870), whose first performance by an orchestra of soloists took place on Christmas Day of that year as a salute to his wife Cosima. (In fact, the *Idyll* cannot be perfectly realized by soloists since both first violins and violas divide at one point. For that reason it is usually performed today by an orchestra with multiple strings.)

In our search for even earlier precursors of the Schoenbergian chamber orchestra we encounter the octet of Schubert (1824); the nonet of Spohr, a masterfully-instrumented work which only occasionally descends to orchestral-type tuttis in which some might feel the lack of added trumpets and drums; and the septet of Beethoven (1800). The two serenades of Brahms (1859) can hardly be classed as chamber music, though the first of them was originally scored for a nonet of almost the same constitution as that of Spohr and both hark back to the divertimenti of Mozart and Haydn, many of which are unequivocally chamber rather than orchestral in style.

In our own century the crucial work is, perhaps, *The Soldier's Tale* of Stravinsky. It must be remembered that in the *Rite of Spring*, Stravinsky had, as it were, both welcomed and banished the heavy-weight orchestra with one gesture. This extraordinary piece, now one of the great 20th-century symphonic 'pops', was a watershed both for us and its composer. The Great War broke out soon after its première in 1913. Both artistically and economically it was a time for a new restraint; therefore, after the Russian Revolution of 1917 Stravinsky found himself in straitened circumstances. Together with author Ramuz and conductor Ansermet he conceived the idea of a little travelling theatre, easy to transport and involving a minimum of histrionic and musical resources. Thus was born *The Soldier's Tale*, a musico-dramatic masterpiece of greater significance for the future of music than even the *Rite of Spring*: one whose small, apparently strangely assorted instrumentation was, together with the earlier example of Schoenberg's *Pierrot Lunaire* (1912), to be a signpost many would follow. Milhaud's *Création du Monde*, Walton's *Façade*, the *Dreigroschenoper* of Weill, the chamber operas of Britten: all these were to be part of a growing stream of reactive works. Though, in a sense, all these pieces are chamber music insofar as they are scored for small groups of solo instruments, they were not conceived as room-music so much as theatrical or concert-hall entertainments.

It will be noted that the musical forces needed for all these works is very much a 'broken consort' of the kind described in a previous chapter on earlier instrumental music. On the whole the 18th and 19th centuries found their ideal in such media as the string quartet and symphony orchestra which were very definitely 'harmonious' consorts, despite the variety of instrumentation found in the latter. The 20th century was to rediscover the interest and effectiveness of non-blend, of the artistic opposition of lines and timbres. Even in symphonic scoring this trend can be found. Berg in *Wozzeck*, for instance, scores the gentle four-part chordal accompaniment for Marie's cradle-song not for four like instruments but for solo fiddle, muted horn, solo viola and bassoon: an effect never to be found in 19th-century music but one which was to recur again and again in the 20th century. His contemporary Webern went even further in the creation of a new style of instrumentation known as *Klangfarbens-melodie*; that is 'melody of tone-colours', in which the traditional concepts of tutti, melody with accompaniment and section-work were almost entirely obliterated by a new spareness and economy which grew out of a fanatical application of the twelve-note method to every aspect of a piece of music. Webern's instrumentation has been of incalculable influence in the three decades which have elapsed since his death. Not all those who have followed his example, however, have possessed his unerring ear which had been educated by years of practice as a conductor of orchestras and choirs and was as finely analytical as Ravel's.

More and more composers were to introduce into their full orchestral works elements of chamber music writing, a practice perceptible long ago in the individual approach of Brahms to the art of orchestration. This is especially noticeable in the music of Britten, in whose War Requiem dramatic use is made of the antiphony of full and chamber orchestras in a way for which there was a precedent in sections of Berg's *Wozzeck* and which, if we pursue the scent long enough, might lead us back to the *Sinfonie Concertanti* of Mozart and Haydn and earlier masters.

It could be said that some of the greatest and most notable innovations in instrumentation are likely to be found on the fringe of established music-making (where, of course, *L'histoire du Soldat* belongs). One reason for this is that, since the symphony orchestra in all countries has been established as a non-commercial, highly subsidized, cultural medium, works written for it tend to use its resources to the full with little amendment or addition. In the world of experimental theatre, television backing, pop recording and other branches of the entertainment industry, where everything costs money and demands stringent justification for its inclusion in the budget, all sorts of new sounds and combinations of sounds are being tried out, some of which have been fed back into the world of established music. One of the first of all electronic instruments, the *ondes martenot*, became established as a versatile creator of mood and atmosphere in the theatre long before it was canonized in the Turangalîla Symphony of Messiaen (1948). The combination of acoustic and electronic instruments is now common, though often held by many to be artistically impossible to condone. Jazz, with its use of electric guitar, electric piano and amplification of certain instruments at certain times, has perhaps helped here. No one wants to hear a jazz singer without a mike (he would either be inaudible or make the wrong sound) nor to forego the delightful singing effect of an amplified piano when it is called for and, though so far symphony orchestras have in the main avoided dalliance with these effects, there can be no doubt that they will enter more and more into our music-making. We must also remember that it is in theatre-music and in jazz that the immense possibilities of players' playing more than one instrument have been most exploited. In the recent show *Cole*, for instance, there was an exemplary small-band score for six players, two of whom played saxophone, flute and clarinet, one trumpet and flugel-horn, and the other three, respectively, drums (and that means a wide variety of instruments in itself), bass and piano. There was an almost limitless spectrum of tone-colour to be enjoyed from such versatility of executive talent.

Most of the 20th-century innovations in the symphony orchestra have been in the field of percussion. Here there is no doubt that jazz and, more recently, oriental music have played the principal role in this evolution of percussion from being, as it were, noises with very little musical significance (except in the case of the timpani) to its present status as a treasury of rich and often exotically colourful and expressive musical sounds. Notable has been the development of what are called 'tuned percussion'. The chromatic timpani have come to stay, whilst the long-established glockenspiel, xylophone and celesta have been joined by an array of related instruments such as the vibraphone (vibes), marimbaphone, xylorimba etc. On the 'untuned' side military instruments like the side-, tenor- and bass-drum have been enriched by such importations from folklore as castanets, maraccas, bongoes, claves, the timbales and an array of different-sized Chinese gongs or tam-tams.

An account of 20th-century orchestral developments is not complete without a mention of the dance-, swing- and jazz-bands, which represent an entirely new stylistic phenomenon belonging only to our age. One of the earliest exemplars was Paul Whiteman's band, though an audition of his records reveals a notable lack of 'swing' despite the inclusion in his band of players like the trumpeter Bix Beiderbecke. Later, with the emergence of bands like those of Fletcher Henderson, Benny Goodman, Glenn Miller, Stan Kenton, Woodie Herman, Count Basie and, above all, Duke Ellington (1902–74), an entirely new style of playing concerted music was evolved which included not only improvised solo and group jazz but also the transmission by a mixture of new-style notation and players' know-how of a simplified jazz style to a whole section or even a whole band. Though for economic reasons in its decline now, the Swing Band has nonetheless developed the capacities of players in quite new directions. It has also brought problems of interpretation to the successful performance of a handful of works; e.g. *An American in Paris* of Gershwin in which the composer has blended swing and straight music with the former style using unequal trochaic note-lengths as the basic realization of its notation (as was often the custom, especially in France, in the 17th and 18th centuries) and the latter equal note-lengths (as we were all taught to play by our first music-mistresses). A few of the best players can play in both manners, though there is still a large residue of older ones who can do only one or the other according to the circumstances of their upbringing. In *An American in Paris* certain passages have to be played 'equally', others 'unequally': a tricky task for those who have been engaged to perform the work. For this reason, therefore, good renderings of the piece are rare.

There is no doubt that the modern orchestra possesses for good or ill a greater virtuosity than its 19th-century forerunner. Composers have realized this by writing not just concertos for the display of a solo instrument accompanied by an orchestra but concertos for the orchestra itself. Perhaps the first of these show-pieces was Hindemith's Philharmonic Concerto of 1932, written for the members of the Berlin Philharmonic and their conductor Furtwängler. Later examples have been the Concertos for Orchestra of Bartók (the most popular display-piece of the whole genre since its première in 1944), Kodály and Lutoslavski (a serious rival to Bartók's though not yet a popular piece).

Such works as these have, in turn, sharpened the edge of players' techniques and made orchestras in themselves under certain conductors star draws, as great singers, pianists and violinists were in the past. It is still, however, impossible to finance a full-time orchestra except by massive subsidy. For instance, in London in 1974, the four independently managed large orchestras were, between them, paid a sum of £482,000 through the Arts Council, from the taxpayers' pockets. Even this was not seen to be enough to guarantee between three or four hundred players a reasonable living in 1975 without overworking them to the pitch when their playing standards might fall. The simple fact remains that, if concert seats are sold at the price the public is willing to pay for them, even a full house will not give the orchestra enough money, after the deduction of overheads, to pay its ninety players their minimum Union wage. So it arranges endless recording sessions to help make up a gap which is finally closed by acceptance of the Arts Council's grant. The Berlin Philharmonic Orchestra, on the other hand, held by many to be the greatest orchestra of them all, does not have to worry about its profitability. Its ample municipal subsidy enables it to rehearse more, concertize less, and still pay its players better fees than its British counterparts.

Both economic and artistic pressures are likely to ensure that the orchestra of the future will be a more versatile instrument than that of today. The great masterpieces of the past must of course be preserved in recurrent performances which themselves must reflect new thinking upon the problems of realizing bygone styles: problems which are for ever changing their constitution as memory fades and research roams farther afield.

The orchestra of the future must also reflect developments in the fields of show-music, jazz and electronics and learn how a satisfactory approach to the classical style can be blended with the ability to play avant-garde music convincingly: a task that some feel involves the attempt to mix incompatible executive techniques, a point of view that should not be unquestioningly accepted. For instance, it is sometimes said that a player, especially upon a brass instrument, who indulges in the broken lines of avant-garde music will lose the capacity to play legato in Wagner, and will develop a tone-quality which is unsuitable in the performance of a classical score. If this really is so, then there is little hope for the orchestra of the future. We must remember, however, that people were saying this sort of thing a hundred years ago about the vocal style of Wagner. Somehow singers were able to adapt themselves to the new demands that were being made upon them and still not forego their Weber, Beethoven and Mozart. It was also said that Schoenberg's violin concerto (1936) required the services of a six-fingered fiddler. Quite a lot of five-fingered ones now play it, if not with ease, without ill effect.

I shall end this chapter by appending a diagram showing the instrumentation of four typical 20th-century works. Two use a very full orchestration; two are written for an ensemble of soloists. Notice the bewildering proliferation of percussion instruments that took place between Mahler's seventh symphony, with its orthodox 19th-century use of 'military' instruments tempered by the less conventional sleigh-bells (a favourite of the composer's), and the Turangalîla Symphony of Messiaen, with its glittering array of exotica. Both the chamber-orchestral pieces are richly-endowed with percussion, too. Notice, however, that the more recent *Marteau* has a more colourful range of instruments than *The Soldier's Tale* which uses standard instruments, albeit in a new manner.

Instrument	Symphony no. 7 (Mahler) (1908)	*Soldier's Tale* (Stravinsky) (1917)	Turangalîla Symphony (Messiaen) (1946)	*Le Marteau sans maître* (Boulez) (1954)
Piccolo	2		1	
Flute	4		2	
Bass Flute				1
Oboe	3		2	
Cor Anglais	1		1	
E flat Clarinet	1			
Clarinet	3	1	2	
Bass Clarinet	1		1	
Bassoon	3	1	3	
Contrabassoon	1			
Horn	4		4	
Trumpet	3		4	
Cornet		1	1	
Trombone	3	1	3	
Tenorhorn¹	1			
Tuba	1		1	
Timpani	4			
Glockenspiel	1		1	
Xylorimba				1
Vibraphone			1	1
Triangle	1	1	1	1
Wood-block			1	
Temple-block				
Turkish Cymbal			1	
Cymbals	1 pair	1 pair	1 pair + 1	5
Chinese Cymbal			1	
Tam-tam (Gong)	1		1	3
Tambourine	1	1	2	
Maraccas			1 pair	1 pair
Tambourin Provençale			1	
Side Drum	1	2	1	
Bass Drum	1	1	1	
Bells	1		8	1
Sleigh-bells	1			
Bongoes				

¹ The Tenorhorn is a kind of tenor tuba or euphonium.

Instrument	Symphony no. 7 (Mahler) (1908)	*Soldier's Tale* (Stravinsky) (1917)	Turangalila Symphony (Messiaen) (1946)	*Le Marteau sans maître* (Boulez) (1954)
Tenor Drum		2		
Claves				
Harp	2			
Mandoline	1			
Guitar	1			1
Piano			1 soloist	
Celesta			1	
Ondes Martenot			1	
Violin I		1	16–20	
Violin II	Number		16	
Viola	of players		14	1
Cello	not		12	
Double-bass	specified	1	10	

N.B. *The Soldier's Tale* requires only one percussionist. *Le Marteau sans maître* requires three altogether: one for the vibes, one for the xylorimba and one for the untuned percussion. Mahler doesn't specify how many he needs for his symphony – probably three or four. Messiaen calls for five players in *Turangalila*. There is, of course, an important part for the contralto voice in *Le Marteau*.

4 A NOTE ON ELECTRONIC MUSIC
by Michael Graubart

The only entirely new way of generating sound that has been invented since living creatures first began to make noises is the electrically-driven loudspeaker. Hitherto, it has always been mechanical energy – whether that of a stream of air, a moving bow or drum-stick or the tension of a string displaced to one side before the plucking finger releases it – that has been converted into the oscillations of the air which affect our ears as sound. Electricity, however, can be controlled much more finely and deliberately, and musicians have experimented almost since the turn of the century with different ways of generating sounds electrically. One can divide the field roughly into three categories, all of which have been exploited on their own, but also in combination with conventional instruments.

Electronic instruments are the oldest, either played conventionally (like the electronic organ) by means of a keyboard, or more unconventionally by moving the hands nearer or further from sensitive parts of the machine, and so on (e.g. the theremin, trautonium and ondes martenot – the last being used spectacularly, for instance, by Messiaen in his Turangalîla Symphony). Into this category, too, come new devices such as those used by Hugh Davies: all sorts of small, everyday objects – springs, egg-slicers, pieces of rubbed sandpaper – which give off fascinating and complex sounds when greatly amplified by means of microphones (air or contact) and amplifiers.

The second category consists of the replaying (in performance) of pre-recorded tape; this began around 1948, some early experiments using disc recordings. At first there was a strict subdivision of this category into *musique concrète*, originating in a surrealist aesthetic, its tapes being made by cutting, splicing, changing the speed and pitch and otherwise modifying and combining recordings of disparate real-life ('concrete') sounds; and pure electronic music, deriving from an ultra-serial approach to musical structure in which it was desired to control every timbre and to arrange timbres in regular scales like pitches, and in which the sounds were laboriously built up out of their constituent sine-tone harmonics. The former approach was originally typified by Henry and Schaeffer in Paris, the latter by Stockhausen and his colleagues in Cologne. Quite soon, however, composers became more interested in the end results than in the provenance of their original materials, and the two ways of making tapes coalesced. Examples of the use of pre-recorded tape combined with conventional instruments are Roberto Gerhard's *Collages* (originally called his third symphony), using a large orchestra; Berio's *Laborintus II* (which uses voices in addition to a large chamber orchestra); and the version of Stockhausen's *Kontakte* (1959) that combines piano and percussion with a purely electronic tape based, nonetheless, on a careful analysis of percussive sounds so that there is continual interplay between the timbres of the instruments and those of the tape. Many works (Thea Musgrave's *From one to another* and – an especially beautiful example – Berio's *Differences* are two chosen at random) have tapes made by modifying recordings of the very instrument or instruments that are to be combined with it in performance.

The third category involves performers on more or less conventional instruments, whose sounds are picked up by contact or ordinary air microphones and amplified (as in the electric guitar) or modified and combined in various ways by electronic devices like filters and ring modulators. A good orchestral example of this is

Stockhausen's *Mixtur*. Some composers (Steve Reich, for example) have experimented with a simple form of transformation consisting of a loop of tape stretched over two tape-recorders, the first one recording sounds played by instruments and the second one replaying them several seconds later, so that a canonic and sometimes cumulative effect is produced, the players continually playing against themselves; whereas ring modulators change not only the timbres but the pitches of notes.

The latest addition to the armoury of the electronically-minded composer is the synthesizer which is, however, in essence no more than a combination of a large number of separate devices into one box, together with means not only of passing signals from one device to another (like a telephone switchboard), but with circuitry (using a principle known as voltage control) allowing one device to control the mode of operation of another. Many pop groups merely use their synthesizers, in conjunction with a keyboard, as a kind of electronic organ. It can, however, be used in any of the ways described above, thus bridging all the categories, and can produce very elaborate, continually changing patterns of sound either live or on to tape; an avant-garde group that uses synthesizers in ambitious and imaginative ways is 'Intermodulation', directed by Roger Smalley.

PART 3 THE ORCHESTRA AS INSTRUMENT

§ 1 ARRANGEMENT OF INSTRUMENTS IN A FULL SCORE

It has long been the practice of composers to write the string parts almost invariably at the foot of the score, for since the time when the violin family superseded the viols, these instruments have been rightly regarded as the foundation tone of the whole orchestra to which all else is subservient and purely incidental, however importantly so. It is only natural, therefore, to find the more delicate woodwind instruments at the top of the score, ranged downwards more or less in order of their pitch – the piccolo is the exception – and resting on their own foundation of bassoons and, less frequently, of double-bassoon. Since the woodwind are entrusted with so much music of the *solo* kind, such, for example, as a flute, oboe or clarinet melody against a string accompaniment, it seems but poetic justice that composers should have accorded this group an outstanding position in the score. Besides which, this arrangement enables the conductor better to see at a glance where often the main melodic interest in the music lies. For the same reason the horns, though not so high-pitched as the trumpets, are usually placed at the head of the brass group. Wagner, however, was a notable exception in this respect, preferring to sandwich the horns between clarinets and bassoons because of their accommodating tone-quality. This quality which, briefly, we can call 'round and mellow', permits this instrument to blend as successfully with the woodwind as with the other members of the brass; in fact with slightly more success, for this very roundness of tone does not always match the open martial ring of trumpets and trombones. Yet, in the hands of a skilful orchestrator, it mingles most successfully with the tone of oboe, clarinet or bassoon. This dual nature of the horn – able to take its place with almost equal success in either woodwind or brass passages – makes the instrument in many ways the most important member of the orchestra after the strings. Listening to a symphony by Brahms, one cannot fail to realize that four horns, shouldering the burden of the middle harmonies in the more sonorous passages, give to the music a sense of cohesion and strength unobtainable otherwise. Whether in combination with woodwind or assisting the brass at moments of climax, they always show up to great advantage; indeed, without their assistance the modern orchestra would be almost invertebrate. § As Tovey so neatly put it: horns were the continuo players of the classical orchestra. By this he meant that their function in the score was often that of filling in the background harmony – of cementing together lines of contrasting timbre that otherwise might lack body.

§ Group	Instruments in order down each page of the score
Woodwind	Flutes, piccolo Oboes, cor anglais Clarinets, bass clarinet Bassoons, double-bassoon
Brass	French horns (German horns and other makes have now largely supplanted these) Trumpets Trombones Bass Tuba
Percussion	Timpani; then smaller instruments such as triangle, tambourine, etc; larger instruments such as cymbals, bass drum, etc; glockenspiel, celeste, piano, bells etc
Harp	Two are frequently employed, but are less frequently available
Strings	1st Violins, 2nd violins, violas, violoncellos, double-basses – all in varying numbers. (14, 12, 10, 8, 8, would fairly indicate the number of strings in a well-equipped modern orchestra.)§

N.B. In the scores of choral and operatic works the voice-parts are normally placed immediately above the strings. Organ parts are usually placed similarly, although they can occasionally (e.g. in Church music) be found at the bottom. In concertos the soloist's part can usually be found immediately above the strings.

Miniature pocket-size full scores of classical and romantic works can be bought nowadays. Modern works, however, usually appear in an intermediate format between pocket- and full-size

§ And since the other brass instruments and the percussion take charge of the heaviest effects, the centre of the page seems a most appropriate position for setting out their share of the music. What is written for them there strikes the eye of the conductor immediately, since in classical works there will be found a large number of pages without reference to these instruments – blank spaces unrelieved by a single note. For it must be remembered that in a well-ordered score the heavy brass and percussion instruments have the least to do. They are reserved mainly (but not altogether) for climaxes, adding their weight to the remainder of the orchestra when the music is most insistent in mood. In Brahms's First Symphony the trombones play only eighty-three bars in a total of 1,262; an instance of restraint completely justified by the wonderful effectiveness of the writing when it does occur.

Such admirable restraint is, unfortunately, none too common a virtue among the minor composers or even with some more accomplished. A crowded full score is as distressing to the ear as a crowded canvas to the eye: there is nothing to choose between them. But the composer of genius, when writing for the orchestra, gathers to himself what I can best describe as certain instinctive formulae for group-combinations. Maybe he will use the strings for nine-tenths of the time, or perhaps longer, treating them separately or in combination with woodwind or horns or both. Then the music may develop in such a way that possibly the strings will be dispensed with for the time being, and woodwind, brass or even percussion, again used either separately, or in combination, will be left to carry on the burden of the music. In due course the strings will return to emphasize the unapproachable beauty of their tone, justifying their claim to be considered the fount of all orchestral inspiration. Or again, a stupendous climax might arise, one clamouring for every instrument in the orchestra. And the passage involved might even be one where harmony was unwanted, where some theme of irresistible forcefulness called for presentation in stark octaves on strings, woodwind and brass alike. Imagine what an effect could then be obtained if such a passage, its power all spent, were followed by the quiet murmur of strings in a muted *pianissimo*, or by fragrant harmonies on the woodwind, perhaps even by chords or arpeggios plucked from a romantic harp. There is no end to the resources of the modern orchestra once the composer's imagination is set in motion, provided that all general rules relating to matters of balance, blend and contrast receive their due observance. Music thus compounded will always look well on paper; a good musician can tell at a glance what is and what is not true orchestration.

Consideration of some of the more frequently used devices in orchestration will be found in other chapters of this book.§

The bewildering complexity of much 20th-century music and the extreme difficulty that even experienced conductors, with a sound knowledge of the traditional repertoire, have in unravelling them and imagining them aurally has led many composers to modify the accepted practice of writing the instrumental parts in a score as the

185

players have to play them. Instead there are often to be found no transposing lines[1] at all in the score in order that the reader may more easily make out the abstruse harmony and counterpoint without the additional burden of transposition. In such cases, of course, the players would play from parts where the appropriate transpositions have been made. Another simplification, introduced probably by Schoenberg and used by him in such scores as the violin concerto and *Moses and Aaron*, is to present the musical elements in the score as coherent wholes and not merely to write each instrumental part one below the other. Thus a chord for woodwind and horns might be presented as a chord on two staves with an indication against each note of what instrument or instruments actually plays it. This practice appears to some to be a hindrance rather than a help to full comprehension of the contents of the score; certainly it can look fearsome to the would-be reader.

§ 2 THE ORCHESTRA ON THE PLATFORM

Since every conductor has his own peculiar idiosyncrasies about the placing of his instruments on what is called the 'concert platform', the reader is asked to accept the diagram on page 188 as being but roughly approximate. Moreover, it must be borne in mind that no two concert-halls are alike, and (more's the pity) that few of these are fitted, either as buildings or acoustically, to house an orchestra without a certain disadvantage to the music performed. There seems, in fact, to be some sort of unwritten conspiracy on the part of architects and those advising them to prevent musicians fully qualified giving practical suggestions as to what is actually required.

However, the general placing of instruments on the platform requires little comment here: it is mostly a matter of common sense, a practical setting-out of what is indicated in the full score, of the music. § In the diagram – which is modelled on traditional platform conditions that are often modified today – it will be observed that the strings are nearest the conductor, their primary importance in the orchestra demanding such a position. It must also be remembered that this concert platform, like most others, has a good 'rake' or tilt upwards away from the auditorium. The first and second violins are shown to the left and right of the conductor respectively, mainly because the antiphonal effects occurring so frequently in baroque and classical music between these instruments are the better heard

[1] For explanation of instrumental transposition see pages 212–213.

and appreciated this way, both by conductor and audience. The famous British conductor Sir Henry Wood, however, felt that in most of the later repertoire first and second violins were used by composers as one great body of instruments and so placed his second violins to his left behind the firsts and put the violas where the second violins had been. He claimed that this much improved the audibility of the viola section, whose sounding boards were thus on the audience side, and made for greater unanimity of violin playing. Nowadays it is usual for the cellos to be immediately right of the conductor and violas to be behind them radiating anti-clockwise towards the second fiddles, thus forming a tenor register link between the cellos' bass and the second violins' alto. It is usual, of course, to place double-basses in the same sector of the orchestra as the cellos. In classical music their parts are normally identical and in most later music extremely closely related. Cohesion of the string parts is, indeed, the conductor's chief care.

§ What has been stated already about the position of the woodwind in the full score explains their more elevated position on the platform. The conductor could scarcely deal satisfactorily with the many solo woodwind passages – passages demanding flexible phrasing, carefully graded expression and, in addition, some artistic licence on the part of the individual players – were these instruments not immediately facing him. He senses their positions just as keenly as the batsman or bowler is aware of his field. He has to turn his head or stance rapidly from strings, brass or percussion towards woodwind, there to caress a melodic phrase or to impart a characteristic touch unaccomplishable were the player placed at too great a distance. It must be recorded here that perfect homogeneity *between* these instruments is also often a matter of chance owing to limitations of room (thanks to non-musical architects); too frequently it is a case of tempering the woodwind to the shorn platform.

The brass are, naturally, further away and at a greater elevation. From their imposing position they enter the music with thrilling effect; there is no mistaking them. But their very position demands great discretion from the conductor. Woe betide the balance of sounds between the various sections of the orchestra if the composer has scored his music too heavily or if the conductor be insensible to the difference between *forte* and *fortissimo*! The domination of the brass can be made a very unlovely thing; from their elevation, three trumpets, even when unsupported by trombones and tuba, have been known to obliterate the rest of the orchestra.

Behind the brass are the percussion instruments, with the timpanist in or near the centre, overtopped by the organ alone (when there happens to be one). Near him are the heavier percussion instruments:

GENERAL DIAGRAM
(Subject to much variation in detail)

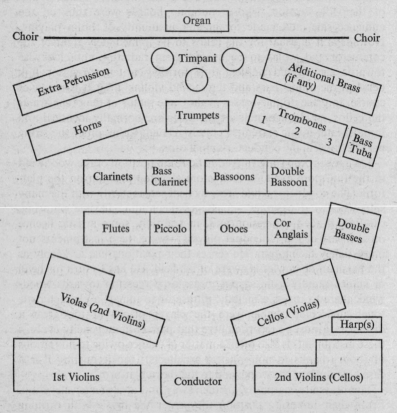

N.B. In a piano concerto the soloist is either placed in front of and slightly to the left of the conductor, or else the piano is placed in as forward a position as possible and the conductor takes up his position *behind* the piano. A certain modification of the strings' positions is, of course, necessary in either case. (J.G.)

cymbals, bass drum, side drum, tambourine, triangle, glockenspiel, xylophone, and so on. And – to conclude this brief survey of the platform – the harp could scarcely occupy any other place than among the violins. On occasions useful, and at all times the most decorative instrument in the orchestra, its rich and romantic tones combine more with strings than with any other instrument. Hence its position.§

A rediscovery in our own century of the three-dimensional qualities of much concerted baroque music has caused conductors and players to experiment with a variety of seating arrangements, some of which have been inspired by new and unconventional concert-giving venues such as churches, courtyards and large buildings originally dedicated to some other purpose, for example the Round House in Camden Town (London).

As long ago as 1664 Schütz, in his foreword to the score of his Christmas oratorio, implied – by his grouping of the protagonists of his drama into differently coloured ensembles of instruments and voices – the necessity of spatial separation, and, before him, his teacher Giovanni Gabrieli (1557–1612) had written works such as the sonata *pian' e forte* which required a similar disposition of performing forces for their full realization. There is no doubt that Monteverdi wrote many of his massive, multi-ensemble pieces with the layout and acoustics of St Mark's, Venice, in mind and many present-day conductors, in awareness of that quality, experiment imaginatively in the use of the available space, in both the horizontal and the vertical planes, so that the work may be brought to life with ever-increasing vividity.

It must not be forgotten also that opera has often made use of the excitement of varying degrees of distance and direction. Offstage fanfares and horncalls, the effect of the singers approaching or departing (very difficult to bring off), hidden choruses: all these effects have been used in the theatre with great skill by many com-posers and stage-directors and occasionally have found their way into the practice of concert-hall music, e.g. the hidden oboe in the 'Scène aux Champs' from the *Symphonie Fantastique* of Berlioz (1829) and the hidden female-voice chorus in the last movement, 'Neptune', of Holst's *Planets* suite (1916) which also includes the effect of a diminuendo caused by the gradual shutting of a door of the room they are singing in – a device which to us in these electronic days may seem somewhat crude.

The auguries are therefore very bright for any composer these days who wishes to bring a spatial element into the performance of his music. After all, except for radio transmissions and monaural gramophone recordings, music does take place in three dimensions and some of its excitement must be due to this aspect of it. The timpanist always sits at the back of the orchestra and one reason we enjoy his contributions is that they come from behind, where they appear to give maximum propulsive power to the music. Were he to be in front, on ground level, or at the side (where sometimes he has to be in amateur performances in which there is no room for him on the stage), he would be reduced to the role of a tiresome interrupter of the others' music-making.

A further development of attitude may well characterize the composer of today. He lives in the aftermath of more than a century of music in which performance on the stage of a great concert-hall seems to be the apex of creative endeavour. Perhaps today he is once more beginning to be aware of the significance of time and place: the association between music and its surroundings. This was very real in the past. The Masses of Palestrina were written for a dimly-seen choir awakening the echoes of a reverberative church and invariably sound less good in a clearly acousticked concert-hall. Similarly the smaller-scale 'orchestral' works of the baroque era come peculiarly alive when performed in surroundings which match the noble but not gigantic rooms for which their composers originally intended them.

These points have impressed themselves more and more upon musicians and audiences during the past fifty or so years, partly as a reaction against the 19th century (which is probably now spent – indeed has been replaced by adulation for Victoriana good and bad), partly because it has been proved that the music sounds even better when given in the right surroundings by the right forces (insofar as the right forces can be obtained these days).

Many composers today therefore write for special layouts of performers in, possibly, uniquely characterized buildings. Stockhausen's *Gruppen* with its four differently constituted 'orchestras' arranged around the audience and relying for its effect partly upon direction as well as timbre, is the outstanding example of three-dimensional creative thinking in our century. Possibly only the economic factor prevents more composers from experimenting in the same way (for only a world-figure can command the capital investment necessary to mount such a work). Tape recorders are, however, a cheap substitute for the real thing and are artistically justified when they produce sounds and effects which are beyond the reach of the live instrumentalist. Stockhausen himself has written for tape-recorder in this way and many others have experimented along these lines. Xenakis's *Bohor* (one of the Knights of the

Round Table) involves electronically the complete circular envelopment of the listener in a deafening continuity of sound, an experience which might be described as listening to the tolling of bells from inside. Its twenty-two minutes of a 'single, evolving musical substance' are derived from the electronically treated sounds of oriental jewellery and a Laotian mouth organ. Audience reaction appears to be sharply contrasted. The composer himself estimated that seventy per cent loved it, thirty per cent hated it.

§ 3 THE CONDUCTOR'S ROLE

Legends about orchestral conductors are many, for their authoritative (even supreme) position, though fully understood by musicians and the musically-minded, is apt to be misinterpreted by that larger and less discerning world which boasts many millions unversed in the art's intricacies.

For the sake of my argument it can be assumed that Beethoven is a household word: a world-figure, like Napoleon or Shakespeare, Julius Caesar or any other leader whose name is on everyone's lips. But whereas there may be millions of the uninitiated who know the pseudo-title if not the music of Beethoven's 'Moonlight' sonata, there are relatively but a few acquainted with all his symphonies and still fewer able to appreciate any sustained argument concerning the merits or demerits of a conductor's *interpretation* of those symphonies.

For the word 'interpretation', as applied to the conductor of an orchestra, conveys to many a meaning so ambiguous as to be almost unintelligible. They find it difficult to appreciate the finer points of an art that in its technique is intimately bound up with some kind of mysterious silence while, on the contrary, the contribution of the players themselves is one of rich and glowing sounds. And so to them the conductor is little more than a 'time-beater'; his bâton but a modern development of that roll of parchment that did rough and ready service in those days of long ago and survived well into the 19th century.

Yet without the silent gestures, the wave of the arm or the quick exchange of glances between conductor and instrumentalist, the art of interpretation as applied to orchestral music would be in sorry plight. The actual time-beating is nothing more than elementary technique, acquired by instinct or study, incorporated in the course of time as an integral part of the conductor's equipment, and then

191

reproduced by him quite automatically. And until he has mastered the technique of the bâton as a directing agency, he will never be able to interpret music with any skill or feeling, for every technical shortcoming is noticed immediately by the instrumentalists supposedly under his control: a feeling of uncertainty will prevail and thereby prevent anything in the nature of stylism or the reproduction of the inner spirit of the music.

The conductor, therefore, learns his technique only to forget it – a palpable truism that applies here as much as it does to all human activities. His sole object is to concentrate on the artistic side of the performance and to re-create in living sounds what the composer has put so inspiredly on paper.

Now it can be stated in Malvolio-like language that some are born conductors, some achieve conducting and others have conductorship thrust upon them. No branch of the art of music is so open to misconception and abuse; charlatanism and insufficiency of knowledge are more in evidence here than anywhere else. Many, indeed, are the conductors who find themselves directing orchestral forces with which they are all too little acquainted. From textbooks they may have picked up a fair amount of theoretical learning which, a dangerous thing in itself, carries them but a short distance along the road of practicalities. A passing acquaintance with one, or maybe two instruments is scarcely adequate for dealing with the thousand and one problems that must be faced during the course of rehearsals, problems cropping up from every corner of the orchestra.

For the work of the conductor falls within two distinct categories: rehearsal and performance. Without the ability to rehearse, the conductor can scarcely hope to give a satisfactory performance, however talented his instrumentalists. The composer, who of necessity must be well acquainted with the peculiarities of all instruments, may write the most intricate passages requiring patient, laborious and detailed rehearsal. If on such occasions the conductor is unable to formulate or communicate to his players any definite ideas as to what is required, it is obvious that any meritorious performance is out of the question. In brief, the conductor must be a man of parts, able at all times to explain the music in terms of the instrumentalist he is addressing. It requires, therefore, but a small stretch of imagination for the reader to realize that the perfect conductor, completely equipped, is about as chimerical as the phoenix, since one lifetime is all too brief a span for any man to acquire a full working knowledge of the manifold intricacies of the orchestra.

Even when a conductor possesses a sound general knowledge of the orchestra – and there are many whose practical experience is quite phenomenal – it does not necessarily follow that his performances will have more than average merit. Other qualities are needed. Magnetism, personality, strong telepathic powers and other marked characteristics are required to set the spirit of the music afire. And this flame of inspiration can only be rekindled through the conductor, whose mind must soar with the composer into the realms of pure fancy. There only can the beauty of the music itself be matched by the beauty of its interpretation. For without the inspiration of the conductor the greatest masterpiece is no better than a heap of dead notes: the composer's temple of sound but a ruin.

And thus it is that the more visible part of the conductor's art can be either eloquent or meaningless. By look and gesture he will convey to the instrumentalists, both individually and collectively, his inner conception of the music. They, on their part, and by some kind of telepathic response, will faithfully reproduce in sound what has been indicated to them in silence.

It follows that the conductor can indulge in many extravagances of style far removed from the original intentions of the composer. By the undiscerning and by the lover of the sensational such extravagances are termed 'individual readings', for which the conductor is far too often belauded to the skies when his treasonable betrayal of the composer should earn him universal condemnation. And, unfortunately, such readings are becoming all too fashionable nowadays, the cult of the bizarre having produced that successor to the old-time prima-donna, the 'virtuoso' conductor. He, having but an eye to personal advancement and avid for any effect that will keep him prominently before 'his' public, upholds with consummate plausibility and with many an extravagant mannerism his own spurious versions of the masterpieces of music.

But the earnest conductor, he who reverences his art, desires no more than the re-creation of the composer in all the expressed detail of the score. He will be sparing of gesture, but such as are used will carry a full significance. Not a single one will occur that is not born of the music itself, for his last thought will be to place himself between the composer and the audience. He will use his right arm, with or without the bâton, mainly to indicate the time of the music; and, where additional stress or strength is required, will occasionally introduce the left arm as an extra rhythmical pointer. But, generally, the left arm and hand will function independently of the right. 'Let not thy left arm know what thy right arm doeth' might well be the motto of many a conductor unskilled in technique. There is nothing so ungainly, so meaningless in interpretation, so irritatingly wind-mill-like in its movements as the left arm and hand (unconvincingly loose-wristed) of a conductor incessantly reproducing what is being indicated on the right. Such actions but flog the music, bringing to it a sense of monotony, both aural and visual, that renders true interpretation impossible.[1] For the left arm and hand should be the phrase and expression makers: delicately poised 'instruments' prompted into action by the conductor's inner feeling for the music and withdrawn when not required. By such means as are here described the heart of the music is sought and found and, under the spell of inspiration, there is established between conductor and orchestra some altogether inexplicable form of telepathy that galvanizes everything into life. The orator's rhetoric is not so remarkable as the conductor's for the latter, with nothing but silent gestures and facial expression at his command, is able to fashion the sounds of the orchestra according to his every whim and fancy. He is no mere time-beater. His knowledge must cover a wider field than that of any other musician while his art, viewed as a whole, un-doubtedly rises superior to all other forms of musical interpretation.§

Only in the past 150 years has the art of the conductor emerged as a credible pastime or vocation. Before that there was little need for his services except as a beat-giver, either visually, or even aurally. Handel directed the première in Dublin of the *Messiah* from the harpsichord, as did Mozart the première in Vienna of *The Magic Flute* from the piano (there is, in fact, *no* piano part in this opera which may throw some light on the nature of late 18th-century performance practice). In Beethoven's day the orchestral leader or concertmaster (i.e. the leading first violinist) usually directed per-formances from his seat in the orchestra, as indeed is sometimes the practice these days with small, expert chamber orchestras such as The Academy of St Martin-in-the-Fields. With Spohr, Berlioz and Wagner, however, a new species of being arose: the man who interpreted music for the performers (and, later, for the audience) by waving his arms about in a manner that, if modest at first, later became both choreographic, histrionic and gymnastic in its efforts to interest the players in the music they were performing. With his rise the art of music changed; or maybe the change in the art of music encouraged him to rise – one cannot say, so intermingled were the

[1] Nikisch, the great German conductor, is said to have tied a pupil's left arm behind his back for a whole term of lessons – a most salutary preventive.

rise of the conductor and the development of virtuoso orchestration which actually needed his services, unlike that of the symphonies of Beethoven, Mozart and Haydn. Certainly the tone-poems of Strauss and the symphonies of Mahler are literally unperformable without a conductor, and it is interesting to note that both these composers were, in fact, great conductors in the sense that their contemporaries Busoni and Rosenthal were great pianists.

In the first half of the 20th century two *maestri* of very different temperament and skill dominated the conducting scene: Toscanini and Furtwängler. If one were to describe the former as Apollo and the latter as Dionysus one suggests the truth without revealing it in full, for neither can be completely identified with either God. Toscanini who, in the words of Giulini, gave a new physiognomy to the orchestra, was a great executant who often missed the inner meaning of the work he was conducting. Furtwängler, on the other hand, was poet, philosopher, knight and – one might add – neurotic. Though his performances could be ragged, they were, at their best, matchless in their insight into what must be accounted a smallish repertoire. Great conductors however, tend to have small repertoires; only hacks try to do everything and do none of it well.

In our own day both Apollonian, Dionysian and hybrid conductors flourish. If asked to pick one figure of supreme accomplishment and significance I would choose Pierre Boulez, who is in the Strauss–Mahler tradition of composer–conductor. A supreme technocrat and possessed of a peerless aural sensibility, he is certainly not Dionysian in his approach to music. Some would say, using rather imprecise terminology, that his approach is mathematical, and there is a grain of truth in that assertion. Certainly his talents are of a kind that few are in a position to imitate, for most conductors are still cast in the old-fashioned mould of fiery, emotional demagogues, whipping their orchestras along with slashes of their bâton (typically Boulez uses no bâton). Conducting is indeed a trade which has always attracted the charlatan because in one sense, the orchestra, provided it is composed of good players, is the easiest of all instruments to master. None would dare to perform the violin in public with as little experience or study as do most conductors essay their debut on the podium. This may be because it is the mistakes of the players one hears, not those of the conductor who has misled them.

In our day, perhaps during the past hundred years or so, the conductor's antics have become the principal visual attraction of concert-going, surpassing that of the well-drilled bows of the string-

Example 8

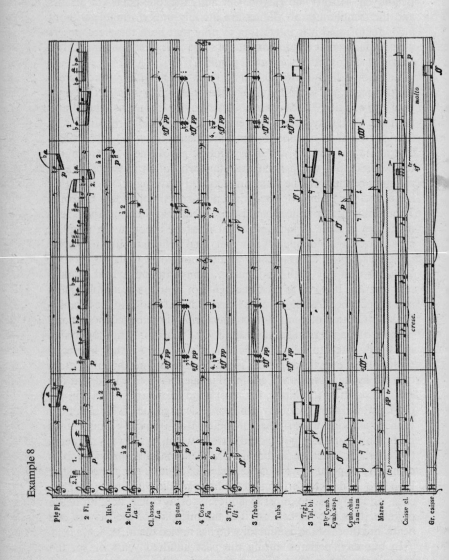

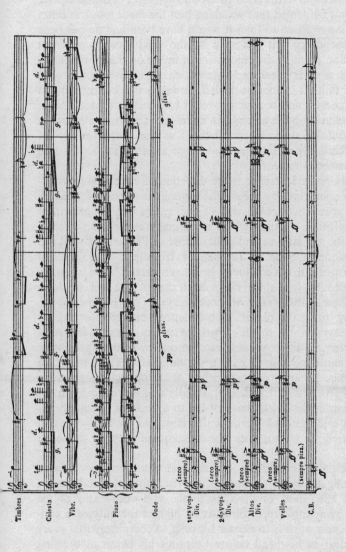

Example 8   Messiaen : Turangalîla Symphony

players, the raised bells of the brass-players, the deft stick-work of the timpanist and the dexterity of the tambourine-player. His movements act as a focus to the collective sound and sight of the orchestra, and it cannot be denied that watching him has made music at times more thrilling to listen to than it would have been had he not been visible. Some decry this elevation of the conductor to principal performer and point to the enjoyment of music on the gramophone or radio as a purer pleasure, from which all bally-hoo has been excluded. I think it cannot be denied, however, that concerts by an invisible orchestra and conductor would be poorly attended and, if that is so, then we have no right to under-rate the visual element in music. Stravinsky, who regarded himself as one of the 'purest' of musicians, certainly maintained that it was as essential to see music being performed as to hear it.

A recently-revived practice is the direction of concertos (particularly piano concertos) by the soloist himself. It is possible that an element of greed (two fees instead of one) enters into the growth of this kind of music-making, which is normally confined to Mozart concertos, though later examples like those of Prokofiev and Ravel have occasionally come in for similar treatment. One point it certainly proves is that a conductor is not as necessary as he is usually considered to be for, since the soloist cannot conduct in those passages where both his arms are occupied in playing his instrument, he can only direct the players in one-handed or purely orchestral passages, leaving them to their own devices in other places. As a rule, however, no difference between the quality of their playing in conducted and unconducted passages is noticeable. There may be a moral in this, though past experience of unconducted orchestras (they were experimented with energetically and idealistically in the Soviet Union in the 1930s) has not led to a spate of conductorless concerts in our own day. Perhaps this is due to the lack of visual focus referred to above, with its concomitant lack of audience appeal.

The task of the conductor in complicated modern scores is so overwhelming that one cannot be surprised that the majority of conductors keep most of the time to the well-worn paths of the traditional symphonic repertoire. At its highest the duty of a conductor of a new work is to master his brief so completely that every sound is clear in his head before he raises his bâton at the first rehearsal. In many kinds of contemporary music, especially those which use aleatory techniques, this is impossible, though a lot of preparatory field-work can be done nonetheless. In those styles, however, where precise notes are still written down, it is theoretically possible for a conductor with a developed inner ear to predict exactly what the sound of the score will be. To those of us who find it difficult to imagine the difference between the chords of C major and C minor this may seem an impossible achievement. Nevertheless we have every reason to believe, despite the fact that absolute proof is difficult to obtain, that there are some conductors who can do this though, recalling Constant Lambert's famous witticism, we must realize that the number of those who can read a modern score is even smaller than those who *say* they can.

As an example of the kind of score a first-class conductor might be expected to imagine completely without first hearing it played we append a page (see pp 196–197) from the Turangalîla Symphony of Messiaen which, though by no means avant-garde, is at first sight frighteningly full of different lines and colours.

§ 4 A GLANCE AT ORCHESTRATION

The art of orchestration is the blending of instrumental sounds of various timbres and is, indeed, analogous to the art of the painter; the composer being concerned with tones in characteristic combinations, the painter with colours. And just as the painter can produce an infinite variety of tone-colours in his pictures, so (it is no exaggeration to state) can the imaginative composer with technique at his finger-tips orchestrate the common chord of C major in a hundred thousand different ways and still proceed similarly *ad infinitum*. In this limitless variety lies the greatness of that modern orchestra we have seen grow in the last part of this Book; from such a combination of instruments have arisen the world's greatest masterpieces in music, masterpieces born of the composer's inspired grasp of the essential qualities of tone-colour. Violin, viola, bassoon, horn, trombone, timpani – to name a few instruments at random – convey the most vivid impressions to the composer's mind and feelings. Maybe he will hear, abstractly, the brilliance, the martial thrill or the solemn pomp of brass instruments. His inventive power then let loose in a flood of inspiration, he is now able to create music whose very life-blood springs from combinations such as these. Or again he hears, similarly, the plaintive quality of the oboe, the rich lyricism of the clarinet or the still richer tones of the violoncello. From his feeling for their special qualities he uses them in solo passages that are set off against a background of accompanying instruments: flowers of melody bejewelled in a meadowland of green. Even the percussion instruments will evoke gems of imagination, as witness the timpani's glorious share of the rhythm in the Scherzo of Beethoven's Choral Symphony, or the triangle's bold usurpation of the *shape* of a melodic phrase in Liszt's piano concerto in E flat. Add to the argument all those important factors in present-day music – (a) a compass of seven octaves over which the composer can roam at will both in melody and harmony; (b) an unlimited range of time-values; (c) a range of expression extending from the scarcely audible *pianissimo* to the most devastating *fortissimo* – and it requires little stretch of imagination for the reader to realize that the resources of the modern orchestra are inexhaustible.

Yet such progress has taken place only within the last 300 years, dating from the time when music began to enrobe itself with those richly coloured garments made possible through the gradual improvement of existing instruments, or through the addition or elimination of other types. Before that time orchestration can scarcely be said to have existed, for all 'orchestral' music written in pre-Monteverdi days was the chance plaything of any ill-assorted collection of instruments ready to hand. But Monteverdi advanced a stage further when in his opera *Orfeo* he laid the foundations of a definite style in orchestration. True, in his choice of instruments he still gravitated somewhat towards the past, despite his incorporation of many of the newer instruments coming into vogue: *gravicembalo* (harpsichord), *violino piccolo* (small violin), *chittarone* (large lute), regal (small reed organ), *cornetto* (zinke), trombone, organ, muted trumpets and so on. His use of the harpsichord in particular must be accounted an early indication of that *continuo* type of orchestration which became the main feature of instrumental music for the next 100 years or more.

Continuo orchestration was, in all likelihood, the outcome of imperfect instruments and equally imperfect instrumentalists – a case, no doubt, of *faute de mieux*. Bach and Handel (both born 118 years after Monteverdi) still had to struggle with many of those problems that had confronted their great predecessor and our own equally great Henry Purcell. And although it was the age of the Amatis, Stradivarius and those other geniuses who perfected the stringed instruments to a degree never since surpassed, most wind and brass instruments, untrue in pitch and sour in tone through faulty construction, could scarcely be trusted except in noisy out-of-doors music where their crudities would be less noticeable. Indifferent instruments produced indifferent players and so, conjointly, succeeded in frightening away the composer from any serious attempts to use them in company with the strings. And since even the string players were suspect, the composer could not altogether trust anyone adequately to perform what was written, the magnificent instruments of the period notwithstanding. Thus it was that *continuo* orchestration became the custom, bolstering up the whole.

This consisted of employing the harpsichord – under its various names or variants such as *gravicembalo, clavicembalo, cembalo, clavecin* (Fr.), *Flügel* (Ger.), etc. – to supplement or displace the string players in passages where the sole use of the latter might be considered unwise or even dangerous. The harpsichord was in the hands of a skilful musician who from a figured bass (as shown below)

Example 9

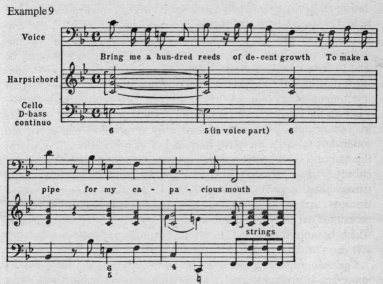

(N.B. The notes shown in brackets were not written out by Handel but were indicated by the figured bass)

could be trusted to fill in the harmonies with judgment, especially the middle-pitched notes.

Composers of the 17th and early 18th centuries found this *continuo* orchestration not unpleasing to the ear and well suited to their general purposes. Those readers familiar with Frederic Austin's version of *The Beggar's Opera* will no doubt recall the many felicitous

201

combinations of harpsichord and strings that give to the work a special colour linking it to its period. Listening to such music nowadays – in an age when every orchestral device and colour seem to have been explored and, often times, exploded – is, in effect, very like the sound of cool mountain water threading its way through an undergrowth of meadow flowers. In fact, it is due to the limitations imposed on composers of this period by the absence of first-rate instrumentalists that we have inherited a school of orchestration unique in certain characteristics. The harpsichord was the universal 'stand-by', relied upon as the most satisfactory and convenient accompaniment to vocal recitative both in opera and oratorio. The strings, as a body, but rarely undertook this task, though the violoncello and double-bass did at times supplement the bass of the harmony owing to the weakness of the harpsichord in its lowest notes. In arias, too, the harpsichord had quite a lion's share of the music, for even here the strings could not be trusted with the more intricate detail, however straightforward the time and rhythm. I well remember my surprise at the fragmentariness of Alessandro Scarlatti's string writing in his opera *Il trionfo del onore* when I happened to look through the score at the British Museum some years ago. Nor was that general distrust of all instruments except the harpsichord overcome until the later days of Bach and Handel. These two composers, though failing to grasp the essential features of a *full* orchestra in the manner achieved by their contemporaries Gluck, Haydn and (in a smaller way) Rameau, yet managed to elevate the stringed instruments to a position of the highest importance. In Bach's six Brandenburg concerti and Handel's many concerti grossi there is string writing of a contrapuntal kind that has probably never been improved upon to this day.

Bach, more intent (and, I dare say, rightly so) on the substance of his music than on any instrumental problems, contributed little to orchestration as we understand the term today. In the Brandenburg concerti, composed in 1721, he wrote for diverse combinations; there was no attempt to blend the sounds in the manner introduced by Haydn with such success in his symphonies less than forty years later. Instead, he strove to invest certain instruments with a definite individuality against a background of strings and harpsichords. In this he was eminently successful. Beyond that he did not go, preferring to express himself in terms of counterpoint of imperishable worth rather than through lavish tone-colours that might detract from the true nature of the music.

The fact remains that concerted instrumental pieces of extended calibre were as yet purely incidental to the bulk of the music being written. The human voice still enchained the hearts and minds of composers more than all else beside; operas, oratorios, arias, motets and anthems were their staple products. And whereas voices had long since passed the experimental stage, instruments were still untrustworthy and little understood in combination. Hence the composer's general avoidance of a medium of expression so little mastered; hence the unconscionable delay before the tone-qualities of instruments were found to be just as amenable to blending as voices. We owe to the efforts of Haydn, Gluck and Mozart this epoch-making discovery. They invested the orchestra with emotion of a new kind. Each instrument now began to speak with a tongue of its own: able to express itself in a thousand different ways, in terms of gaiety, sadness, dignity or impudence according to its kind. The combination of all these qualities brought orchestration at long last to the point when it no longer shambled at the heels of vocal music. It strode abreast and was very soon to forge right ahead.§

It is probably true that in the 19th century baroque 'orchestration' was held in lowest esteem. Since then there has been a steady growth of interest in recreating the sounds of what had become a lost style but which many musicians in this century, notably Arnold Dolmetsch, perceived to be once again realizable given certain conditions of performance: the instruments upon which it was played, the style in which they were played (one which supposed a considerable *extempore* art on the part of the players in the matter of *ad hoc* ornamentation) and an accurate understanding of the implications of their notation, many aspects of which had become totally obscured by the passage of time and the blurring of tradition. Nowadays, certainly, few would talk disparagingly of the sound of the baroque orchestra; many would agree with Stravinsky when he said, 'What incomparable instrumental writing is Bach's! You can smell the resin in his violin parts, taste the reeds in the oboes.' It is significant, perhaps, that he did not use the word 'orchestration', for in a sense, the baroque orchestra was still a chamber ensemble – an assemblage of soloists of equal importance – and there was in writing for it a noticeable lack of using colour for its own sake. Each instrumental part was a character in the drama, not a tint to be applied here and there to bring out some musical beauty or other.

It must be stressed, however, that we cannot recreate the past, only try to recreate the present in the supposed image of the past – a very different task. The performance of music involves a multitude of interdependent factors: the memory and experience of both performers and listeners amongst them. We today, whether playing or listening, have a different background of experience from that of our forefathers on which to build our music-making. It is possible therefore that, as we play or hear a baroque ornament, we may recall the piano-playing of Oscar Peterson; or that, as we hear a chromatic progression in Gesualdo, Wagner's *Tristan* may come to mind. These cross-references between past and present make the interpretation of music, whether as listener or player, a complicated amalgam of reflexes which have been conditioned by a variety of stimuli, some of which have been encountered in the process of training and education and some whilst undergoing musical experience in a state of innocence. The evidence, therefore, certainly suggests that to try to recreate the past is so irrational an aim as to defeat its own object, since we cannot fail to misunderstand the result through unavoidable anachronistic associations. It might be better, in fact, to regard the mere enjoyment of music (in the highest sense of the term) as the truest test of the validity of an interpretation of whatever period in whatever style. This may not be a maxim for musicologists and there are certainly powerful arguments against accepting it. It should not, however, be rejected without thought.

§ 5 SOME STRING DEVICES IN ORCHESTRATION

As no two pieces of music are alike (except those fustian tunes which, to the public amusement, are the subject of copyright actions at law) it follows that in all instrumental music the orchestration, while conforming to certain general principles, will differ in the bulk of its detail. Yet to describe any such detail at length is impossible here for, were the task attempted, the reader's mind could not fail to become entangled in a mass of abstruse technicalities.

But there are certain devices used so frequently that they have become the general stock-in-trade of every composer: 'common denominator' devices on which the main orchestration rests. And of these the majority concern the strings which, of the several groups of instruments, Rimsky-Korsakov, in his admirable treatise on orchestration (*Principles of Orchestration*, published by Dover Books), has aptly described as 'the richest and most expressive of all'. For we must remember that, whereas each woodwind and brass instrument is able to produce only one sound at a time, the strings are capable of playing two, three and sometimes four notes simultaneously, and with a plethora of detail almost endless in scope and variety. Types of bowings, too, are many. The down-bow (⊓) and the up-bow (∨) – marked in the full score and string parts where necessary by all careful modern composers, though not by the classical masters – give variations of style without which orchestral music would be decidedly less interesting and effective. But since lack of space prevents a lengthy description of the many devices found in string music, I have thought it advisable to tabulate, with explanatory notes, the most important features found in all modern scores. In practice, many of the directions given by a composer, even if he be British, are indicated in Italian (music's common tongue), but as there has been a marked tendency by French and German composers in the past hundred years or so to employ their own language, I have added their lingual equivalents only where commonly used. It should be noted that *pizzicato* is the one Italian word consistently favoured by composers throughout the world; any other in its place would be almost un-recognizable. Certainly Monteverdi's direction, *Qui si lascia l'arco, e si strappano le corde con duoi diti* ('Put the bow aside, and pluck the strings with two fingers'), would cause most non-Italian musicians some bewilderment.§

There are also many new devices of string-playing associated with the avant-garde. The energetic stopping of notes on the string by left hand alone without the help of a bow-stroke or *pizzicato* is one. The resultant sound is gently percussive and bears a faint impression of pitch. It is particularly effective in *ad lib.* aleatory passages.

Another device, less favoured by those who treasure their instruments and bows, is the hitting of the body of the instrument with the wood of the bow: a percussive sound which is undeniably exciting, particularly as aleatory, massed effect.

An explanatory table follows, over the page.

§ Table of devices and expressions commonly used in string music
(For explanations consult the notes appended)

Italian	Abbreviated	English	French	German
coll' arco[1]	arco	with the bow	(arco)	Bog. (arco)
pizzicato[2]	pizz.	plucked (pizz.)	(pizz.)	(pizz.)
con sordina }[3]	con sord.	with the mute	avec sourdine	mit Dampfer
senza sordina	senza sord.	without the mute	sans sourdine	ohne Dampfer
col legno (ligno)[4]		with the back of bow	(col legno)	(col legno)
sul (al) ponticello[5]	pontic.	on (at) the bridge	au chevalet	am Steg
sul tasto[6]		on the finger-board	sur la touche	
punta dell' arco[7]		point of the bow		
tallone[7]		heel of the bow	talon	
armonici[8]		harmonics	sons harmoniques: flageolet	Flageolettöne
martellato }[9]		hammered	martelé	
spiccato		clearly detached		
saltando		jumping	sautillé, jeté	
saltato		jumping		
tremolo[10] }[10]	trem.	trembling	(trem.)	(trem.)
tremolando	trem.	trembling	(trem.)	(trem.)
divisi }[11]	div.	divided	(div.)	geteilt (get.)
unisoni	unis.	in unison	(unis.)	zusammen (zus.)
naturale[12]	nat.	in the natural manner	(nat.)	
leggio[13]		desk	pupitre	Pult
corda[14]		string	corde	Saite

Explanatory notes to the above table

1 *Arco* is the word used to indicate the termination of a *pizzicato* passage.

2 *Pizzicato* effects, in single notes, were used by Monteverdi as early as the 17th century, but did not come into general favour for many years after that. I need scarcely add that the effect is obtained by plucking the strings with the index (usually) and second finger (in certain rapid passages) of the right hand and, sometimes, as a 'trick' effect, with the fingers of the left hand. It is one of the modern orchestral composer's most favoured devices and, when not used *ad nauseam*, is amazingly effective both in loud and quiet music, in single notes or in spread chords, in dramatic passages or at moments when an atmosphere of mystery and awe prevails.

3 The mute, clamped on the bridge, deadens the tone, producing effects that can best be described as dreamily romantic. Used with proper discretion, it affords a remarkable and lovely contrast to the natural tone of the strings.

4 Little more than another trick effect, employed very sparingly, and in characteristic music only. The instrumentalist plays with the wood (legno) of the bow instead of with the hair (which comes from the tails of white horses), producing a tone akin to the xylophone, and sounding something like the rattling of bones. In the course of his symphonic poem *Danse Macabre* Saint-Saëns employs this effect most cleverly to represent a skeleton dancing in a churchyard at midnight.

5 This expression directs the instrumentalist to play with the bow near the bridge, the effect being employed only in *tremolo* passages. At certain rare moments, when a touch of the sinister is required, a *sul ponticello* effect stands out remarkably. It is not convincing except in quiet passages, for – as Cecil Forsyth states in his most exhaustive treatise on orchestration, published by Macmillan – 'a painfully glassy and unpleasant quality is produced'. No composer worth his salt would dream of using the effect frequently.

6 Whereas a brittle hardness of tone is produced by playing *sul ponticello*, here the reverse is the case. With the bow on, or (more exactly) very near to, the finger-board a certain veiled quality is obtainable. This effect is perhaps less noticeable than (5) and, consequently, less frequently felt or desired by composers.

7 Finesse of bowing is intimately bound up with these indications. Effects of this kind which are often matters of common sense technique are, in most instances, left by composers to conductors and instrumentalists to work out for themselves.

8 The use of harmonics is an essential part of the string player's technical equipment. They are of two kinds: (a) natural harmonics, where the finger, by lightly touching the string in certain definite places, sets a segment of it vibrating in place of the whole length or 'stopped' (i.e. by the finger) length; (b) artificial harmonics produced by stopping the string with the first finger and touching it lightly with the fourth at the interval of a perfect fourth higher than the stopped note (sometimes at the interval of the perfect fifth above the stopped note). The second kind are unobtainable on the double-bass, because the size of the instrument prevents the stretch of the hand as indicated above. Since harmonics occur so frequently in string music, examples are given below that will enable the reader to recognise the effect in a full score, should he come across it.

Exercise 7.

(a) Natural harmonics (indicated by o)

Exercise 8.

(b) Artificial harmonics (note the method of notation)

9 Types of bowing detail frequently indicated by composers.

10 The *tremolo* is an important and largely used device, consisting of two distinct kinds: (*a*) the *bowed* tremolo which, discovered as a musical effect in Monteverdi's time, was developed by Gluck, to become, eventually, a modern device full of dramatic intensity; (*b*) the *fingered* tremolo, which consists of the rapid alternation of two notes, each group of notes being played *without* change of bow. The effect of either kind, particularly the former, is one of restless vitality. Indeed, it is possible to state that without the *tremolo* such dramatic music as Wagner's 'Ring of the Nibelungs' could scarcely exist, so frequently is the device brought into action. The following examples demonstrate both kinds. Once again the double-basses are precluded, by reason of their size, from performing any effective *fingered* tremolo, and, moreover, the *bowed* kind is comparatively infrequent owing to the 'grunting' quality of the effect produced.

Exercise 9.

11 *Divisi* is the word employed to indicate a sub-division of parts, each part having different notes. *Divisi* effects are usefully employed in decorative music not requiring emphatic utterance; in strenuous passages any elaborate sub-

Exercise 10.

division of parts weakens the total effect of the string tone and is therefore accounted poor orchestration. In Strauss's tone-poem 'Also sprach Zarathustra' there can be found pages where strings are divided into no less than twenty-five parts, the whole being pieced together, jigsaw-puzzle-wise, with infinite care for the smallest details. *Pizzicato* chords and effects with harmonics are here combined with other more normal devices in an array of notes which, dazzling to the eye, fall on the ear in rich profusion and with complete appositeness to the musical context. *Unisoni* is the term employed to denote a cancellation of *divisi*.

12 After *sul ponticello*, *sul tasto* and *col legno*, *naturale* restores the type of tone to the normal.

13 Where the more complex sub-divisions of string parts take place, *leggio* indicates the number of desks required in performance of special passages – e.g. *Leggio 1* or 'Desk 1'; *2 pupitres seulement* (Fr.) or *nur erstes Pult* (Ger.) etc. Here the Italian word is little used; in most instances the composer's own language conveys the necessary meaning.

14 Indicates, in special effects, the string on which the music is to be played: e.g. *IV corda* = 4th string. Sometimes the name of the string is given as an alternative to the foregoing; *sul G*, *sul A*, etc. Incidentally, string instruments are tuned as follows:

The five-stringed double-bass with the low C is occasionally found in orchestras.§

§ 6 WOODWIND DEVICES IN ORCHESTRATION

Of the woodwind and brass there is less to be said for these instruments, by their very nature, are unable to produce the great variety of effects possible on strings. Their contribution is consistently the same, save for such brass effects as are obtainable by the use of mutes.[1] They have their own individual qualities, used either (a) in a solo capacity with (more often than not) string accompaniment as a neutral-toned background, or (b) as a reinforcement of string tone in more strenuous, built-up music. Beyond that, they can no more change their character than the leopard his spots.

In the capacity of soloist, each woodwind instrument – flute, piccolo, oboe, cor anglais, clarinet, bass clarinet and bassoon – is able to produce remarkably beautiful effects. Who with any feeling for musical tone-colours can resist the outstanding effect produced

---

[1] It is also becoming the custom occasionally to mute the oboe, cor anglais or bassoon by the insertion of a soft pad in the bell of the instrument.

by the entry of the flute and bassoon in Beethoven's *Leonora* no. 3 overture?

Example 10

Who can resist the long-drawn-out and lovely oboe melody in Schubert's 'Unfinished' Symphony?

Example 11

Or, again, the exquisite touch of Hiawathian romance on the cor anglais in Dvořák's New World Symphony inspired, so it is said, by a reading of Longfellow's poem?

Example 12

And, did space permit further examples, it would be indeed a labour of love to show how the composer – while admitting that the combined blend of the woodwind lacks something of the homogeneity of the strings – has come to regard these instruments as second to none in their capacity for *individual* expression. Rimsky-Korsakov's descriptions of the woodwind could not be improved upon. 'Artless and gay in the major, pathetic and sad in the minor' is his apt summing up of the oboe. 'Suitable, in the major, to melodies of a joyful or contemplative character, or to outbursts of mirth' describes the clarinet equally well; while, again, no other instrument but the bassoon could possibly suggest 'an atmosphere of senile mockery'.

And so for varied tonal effects of this kind the composer of genius exploits the woodwind with rare understanding. If he requires a cold effect, he knows that low-pitched notes on the flutes can supply the need; if a warm and brilliant one, then high-pitched notes on the same instrument can be used to equal advantage. For sinister touches he may explore the low registers of clarinet and bassoon, often superimposing the one instrument on the other in unison passages of eerie character. Of all orchestrators, no one understood the finesse of these instruments better than did Wagner. He, whom we can call the archpriest of the woodwind, was able by his inspired touches of tone-colour frequently to invest his music with a verisimilitude of greatness completely beguiling the ear of the listener. By such necromantic means, at times little short of black magic (or so it seems to me), he often disguised most successfully the weak thematic basis of much of his music, deluding us into a false estimation of its actual worth. Yet for sheet coloration he is probably unapproached by any other composer. Herein lay his great genius. Listening to the orchestral opening of the second act of *Parsifal*, we sense immediately the sinister magic wielded by the black knight Klingsor, an atmosphere created mainly by clarinets and bassoons used in the manner I have already described above. Elsewhere in the same work Wagner employs the oboe and clarinet in melodic phrases of real beauty to depict the spiritual feeling we associate with Good Friday morning, while a pulsating background of string tone tells us how the sun itself is pouring down its own benison on the day. Or again, what could be more picturesque than the mocking *staccato* woodwind passages in the final scene of *Die Meistersinger*, that illustrate the crowd's rollicking enjoyment of Beckmesser's discomfiture, hoist, as he is, with the petard of his dishonestly-come-by song?

For there is a special kind of technique on these instruments that is all contained in the woodwind player's frequent question to the conductor when in doubt about the proper interpretation of a phrase: 'Do you want it tongued or slurred?' The greater part of good woodwind playing is contained in that simple query. There is no need to delve into the intricacies of a technique which belongs more properly to the text-books but a brief analysis, by example rather than by precept, should show the reader what is meant.

Such details as are contained in (*a*) and (*b*) are the very essence of good woodwind writing; long stretches of music such as at (*c*) are often impracticable, dull in the effect and certainly wearisome to the

Example 13

Example 14

(Clarinets)

5th Symphony Tchaikovsky

Example 15

(Bassoon)

(Any badly-scored composition)

player who, deprived of his natural articulation by 'longs' and 'shorts', can only be compared to a Morse code signaller without dots and dashes. I often think that few composers were better versed in these effects than Schubert. The woodwind writing in his 'Unfinished' and C major (Ninth) Symphonies is sheer inspiration throughout, his use of accents to denote a particular type of stressed 'tonguing' (especially in the slow movement of the latter symphony) certainly more eloquent than can be found anywhere outside his works.§

In the 20th century the technique of woodwind playing has advanced immensely under the dual influence of great players and demanding composers. The device of flutter-tonguing, whereby the player rolls an 'r' into the instrument, used to be confined to flute-writing only; it has now been extended to the clarinet and even the oboe, though some players of the latter instruments find it an elusive accomplishment.

Example 16

Sinfonia da Requiem Britten

Flutes & piccolos
(8ve higher)

Oboes and
clarinets

The clarinet glissando, discovered and established by jazz players, made its way into serious music in the first bars of Gershwin's

Rhapsody in Blue, where the solo clarinet begins the piece with a shake on a low F which turns into an upward scale of B flat which becomes a glissando (i.e. a *portamento* or scoop without any definite notes) that finally comes to rest on the initial high B flat of the opening melody. In 1924 this was certainly innovatory, and at that time few straight players could manage it successfully, for such a technique had not been part of their training. Now they are all expected to learn how to do it.

Oboe technique has advanced recently, especially in the playing of the Swiss virtuoso Heinz Holliger who has extended the effective range of the instrument upwards, overturned some traditional concepts about the instrument's tonal limitations, perfected methods of sounding more than one note at the same time to the point of being able to play chords of three notes in certain circumstances, and generally broadened the attitude of all musicians to his instrument.

There is no doubt that, as the 20th century has advanced, so has the conception of all woodwind playing changed. More and more do they all, including the bassoon, seem to be adopting a timbre which approaches that of a solo human voice, with its inevitable vibrato which at worst becomes a wobble. It is possible that this trend blurs some of the distinction that used to be readily detected, even by inexpert ears, between the tone-colour of the various members of the families. The bassoon in the hands of some of the best living players has begun to resemble the saxophone, best known still because of its immense contribution to jazz, though it originated in 1840 as a military instrument (its inventor Adolphe Sax was, in fact, a bandmaster). Built in many sizes from soprano to bass, the saxophone is a single-reed instrument with a mouth-piece like the clarinet's (indeed most clarinettists can play it without any difficulty), but with a body made entirely of brass. Though undeniably a fascinating instrument and, in the hands of a genius like Charlie Parker, a vehicle for the deepest passions, it has had a raw deal in serious music. Even the tonally-aware Berg wrote a negligible part for it in his violin concerto. It is, of course, quite separate from both the woodwind and brass families and combines especially ill with the former. In the symphony orchestra it is always a soloist unless a member of a section, in which case it will change the timbre of the tutti markedly (e.g. Gershwin's *An American in Paris*). Furthermore its connotations with jazz and light music colour our appreciation of its contribution to serious music. Britten, however, on the few occasions he has used it (e.g. in the *Sinfonia da Requiem* and *Billy*

Budd) has shown a rare appreciation of its capabilities and limitations.

§ The table on page 215 shows, in actual sounds, the compass of the better-known woodwind instruments. But the extreme high notes of all these instruments are rarely used, being squeaky and ineffective, while the lowest notes of the piccolo are too weak to have any value.§

§ 7 BRASS DEVICES IN ORCHESTRATION

One of the main differences between the woodwind and the brass is that between instruments operated by vents and keys and those operated by valves and slides. Compared with the strings and woodwind the mechanism governing the production of sounds from brass instruments is far less mobile technically, and far less suited musically to passages of extreme rapidity. For above all else the noble tone of these instruments suggests dignity, and dignity must not be hustled. The actual production of that tone and, indeed, of the notes themselves, is dependent on the utmost delicacy of lip-adjustment or 'embouchure', as it is usually called.

We have already seen in Chapter 5 of Part 1 and in Chapter 1 of Part 2 how the clumsy crook mechanism of the horn and trumpet was replaced more than 100 years ago by valves (or 'pistons'), a modern device that gives to these instruments a *complete* series of notes throughout their compass instead of the *incomplete* series circumscribed by the natural laws of sound (see Harmonic Series, Example 5). But whatever extra mobility might have accrued to these instruments from this invention, some have questioned whether brass instruments are altogether suited to the expression of rapid chromatic music. Not that the old crook system and the restricted use of trombones was always advantageous to the music. Far from it. Many horn and trumpet parts to be found in Haydn, Mozart and Beethoven are somewhat lacking in melodic content, for they contain little more than stop-gap notes put in as padding wherever the diatonic sounds permitted.

No more significant compromise was ever effected than the one to be found in Rimsky-Korsakov's opera *The May Night* where, amid the many chromatic harmonies so characteristic of this brilliant musician, are to be found *natural* (i.e. unvalved) horn and trumpet parts.

COMPASS OF WOODWIND INSTRUMENTS

§ Example 17

Explanatory notes to the above table

1 Some flutes have an extra key giving the low B. The rarely used bass flute is pitched a fourth lower than the flute. Being what is called a 'transposing instrument', the bass flute has its music written a perfect fourth higher than the actual sounds: *i.e.* the composer will write the middle C when the G below is required to sound.

2 To avoid too many leger-lines the piccolo part is always written an octave lower than the actual sounds.

3 The two extreme notes in brackets are for the virtuoso player only.

4 Another transposing instrument. Cor anglais music is written a perfect fifth higher than it sounds.

5 Clarinets are of many sizes, ranging from the small E♭ to the large bass. With the exception of the C clarinet, now obsolete, all are transposing instruments. The two in constant use are the B♭ and the A. Music for these is written a major second and a minor third, respectively, higher than it sounds.

6 Music for the bass clarinet is usually written a major ninth (i.e. an octave and a major second) above the actual sounds heard, and in the *treble* clef – to conform, no doubt, to the notation of the ordinary clarinets. Wagner's notation is different, however. But I need not confuse the reader's mind by explaining this instance of a composer's waywardness, for the latitude allowed a composer often runs the poet's licence very close.

7 The bassoon is perhaps the most agile of all the woodwind instruments. Able to skip about from treble to bass notes in the twinkling of an eye, it is often looked upon as the low comedian of the orchestra: a reputation by no means deserved. For it is also capable of depicting tragedy in a manner unequalled by any other instrument in the orchestra. A favourite of Tchaikovsky, it is used to fine effect in this composer's last three symphonies, especially in no. 6 (the 'Pathétique'), where its gloomy low notes convey an indelible impression of a man contemplating suicide. The high E♮ at the top of its compass can be found in Wagner's overture to *Tannhäuser*, but I should imagine that few players, whatever their golf handicap, have ever holed out in one, so well bunkered is this note. The low A is also used by Wagner, some German instruments having an extra key.

8 The double-bassoon was greatly admired by Brahms and almost entirely ignored by Wagner, who rarely appreciated its qualities. The former, particularly in his first, third and fourth symphonies and in his St Anthony variations, used it to magnificent purpose, its deep booming notes standing out like a 16-foot foundation stop on an organ. To avoid unnecessary leger-lines, music for the double-bassoon is written an octave higher than it sounds, a system of notation shared with the double-bass. It can also be made to sound fatuously amusing, as, for instance, in the opera *Coq d'or*, where Rimsky-Korsakov employs its low notes to illustrate King Dodon's scatter-brained imbecilities.§

9 Saxophones are alternately in B flat and E flat from top to bottom beginning with the B flat soprano instrument. The two shown in the above table – the alto and the tenor – are the commonest. The former transposes down a major sixth; the latter a major ninth (like the bass clarinet in B flat).

The clarity of the brass writing is, all things considered, quite unique; the 'look' of it on paper little more startling than those older examples quoted as Examples 3 and 4. 'This,' says Rimsky-Korsakov, referring to his method there, 'was purposely done for practice.' For, as he tells us so convincingly in another place in his *Principles of Orchestration*, 'the horn, in spite of valves, has but little mobility and would seem to produce its tone in a languid and lazy manner'. Nor is he convinced that the trombones are any better off, since they are 'rarely required to perform quick passages' – a statement that composers of these later days might contradict with some show of truth. But the trumpet, we must suppose, will always be favoured with brilliant passages now that the addition of pistons has given it such a turn of speed. And perhaps it deserves many a licence by way of compensation, for with certain exceptions it was somewhat neglected in the classical period. Unvalved, untamed, almost unwanted, composers could make little of it in olden days. Music of any distinction would not fit in with its limited number of notes. Its higher notes were of penetrating quality, often obliterating the melodic line of the music through their misapplied power; its lower notes so few as to be almost unserviceable. The notes that were possible on the unvalved trumpet numbered but fifteen, four of which were untrue in pitch (see Example 5, p 157). 'A player on one of these "natural" instruments,' says Cecil Forsyth in his *Orchestration*,[1] 'was like a man continually hopping up and down a ladder, some of whose rungs were so shaky as to be a danger to life and limb.' Below is an example of such trumpet writing, taken from Beethoven's

Example 18

Third ('Eroica') Symphony. The unavoidable 'hops', as marked by the direction lines, constitute a wicked assault on the ears of the sensitive musician. Modern conductors, however, rescued by the valved instruments, substitute on the 2nd trumpet the notes shown in brackets – a wise proceeding that, in many instances of this kind, somewhat restores the balance of sounds.

Now that the brass family is modernized it has infused orchestral music with a far greater intensity than was possible heretofore. Though it is, as has been suggested elsewhere, somewhat wearisome in a long succession of rapid passages wherein the harmonic changes are many, yet, like the woodwind, it has characteristic devices of tonguing and slurring that are more thrilling in their way than anything else heard in the orchestra. The reader with a flair for analysis will note in the few examples of 19th century brass writing quoted below that many of the best effects are obtained (a) by the rapid tonguing of notes that often *remain constant in the pitch*; (b) by sustained chords; and (c) by those melodic phrases that revolve round the notes belonging to the Harmonic Series in some kind of cousinly way. At the same time he must not assume that I am laying down any dogmatic rules covering the whole range of brass writing. The composer of genius, gifted with real feeling for the orchestra, will always be inventing new devices. In fact, there are so many that to quote them in any detail is not possible. From what has been stated already the reader will understand why the following examples are so effective.

We can pass on without describing the mute, that piece of pear-shaped metal – it was made originally of papier-mâché or wood – that from time to time is inserted in the bell of all brass instruments

---

[1] He refers equally to horns and trumpets.

Example 19   Fourth symphony. Tchaikovsky

Example 20   'Capriccio Espagnol'. Rimsky-Korsakov

Example 21   Fifth symphony. Bruckner

Example 22   'Tristan und Isolde'. Wagner

to create a contrast of tone or an effect of distance. It was used by
Beethoven with fine purpose in his Rondino for wind instruments
(where muted horns in the concluding bars gently bear the original
theme almost out of earshot), and by Wagner in *Die Meistersinger*
(where, in the procession of the Trade Guilds, muted trumpets
imitate the toy instrument to perfection). Little employed, in any
true music, on the bass tuba, but rather more on the trombones, it
has long been used with legitimate effect on the horn and trumpet,
especially on the horn. Many beautiful, eerie and amusing passages
have been written with it in mind. For sheer loveliness of effect I
cannot suggest a better example than the eight bars of muted horn
chords immediately preceding the 'Liebestod' in Wagner's *Tristan
und Isolde* or, if the sinister be wanted, the *leit-motif* in the same
composer's *Götterdämmerung* illustrating that mysterious Tarnhelm

218

– which (says Hagen to Siegfried) 'serves, when set on thy head, to transform thee e'en as thou wilt'.

Again, those readers who are well acquainted with the Strauss tone-poems will recall with delight those extraordinary and amusing passages for muted trumpets, horns and violins depicting so vividly the hanging of Till Eulenspiegel, that lovable rogue of the Middle Ages. Everything sounds so strangulated that we can all but feel the rope round our own necks. And, as an example of muted trombones, there is, perhaps, no more beautiful instance than the chords occurring near the end of the slow movement in Elgar's First Symphony.

The horn player can also mute his instrument by inserting his right hand inside the bell. By this means he stops the free egress of the sound from the instrument, completely altering the tone. The notes so produced are actually called 'stopped' notes and play an important part in all modern scores. In fact, some horn players will often manage muted effects by hand-stopping rather than by the use of the metal mute, the effect being practically the same. When blown strongly, these stopped notes are very brassy in quality, or *cuivré* as the French call them – an expression often found in full scores. It is customary to indicate the effect with a small cross (+) over each stopped note. Many examples are to be found in *Tristan und Isolde*.§

It was, perhaps, in the brass sections of swing-bands in the 1920s and '30s that the different colours available by means of different kinds of mutes were first effectively and convincingly exploited. Straight composers on the whole continued to use what were known as straight mutes and so produce the traditional muted effect which is stifled, uncertain of tone and pitch and, though low in decibels, nonetheless implicitly aggressive. Cup-mutes, on the other hand, can cause a trumpet to play as sweetly and unobtrusively as a muted violin: an effect which, for reasons difficult to explain, has scarcely been used by any composer outside the world of entertainment. That fringe composer of genius, George Gershwin, however, directs that the middle-section melody of *An American in Paris* be played with a felt crown. It remains, after nearly fifty years, a perfect example of the often forgotten 20th-century expressive possibilities of solo brass instruments.

§ The bass tuba plays something of a lone hand in the brass family, for it is fat in tone and, owing to its non-combinative quality, scarcely a good bass to the three keen-edged trombones. Yet it justifies its

Example 23

Andante ma con ritmo deciso

Solo trumpet (with felt crown)

mf espr.

incorporation in the orchestra in many of those more forceful modern works where the bass of the harmony constantly needs replenishing with *forte* or *fortissimo* tone. The instrument frequently reminds us that its most characteristic and, possibly, happiest *métier* is the portrayal of such phenomena as Wagner's dragon Fafner, so somnolent are its rich, slowly uncoiling and deeply-caverned notes. Yet, on occasions, it can skip about 'like a two-year-old', and amusingly so into the bargain. Its position in the orchestra is somewhat anomalous, for few composers seem to have given it proper consideration. The bass tuba can mean anything from the legitimate orchestral instruments, the F and E♭, to the rich-toned military 'double B♭', and even – when all else fails – the euphonium. A strange mixture indeed.

Below will be found the various compasses of the more usual brass instruments, together with certain other sounds possible to virtuoso players only. Explanatory notes are appended.

Example 24

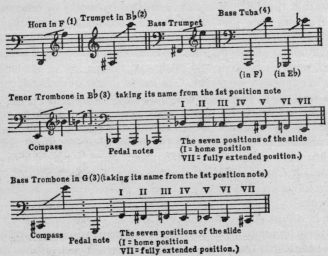

N.B. Many players today in all countries use the so-called tenor-bass trombone. This has a loop of extra tubing which, when added to the main tubing, lowers the pitch of the whole instrument by a perfect fourth and thus converts it into a bass trombone in F. Though the splendour of the G instrument is thereby somewhat missed, the convenience of having a dual-purpose instrument is felt by most to compensate for what is usually admitted to be the loss of sonority. (J.G.)

Explanatory notes to the above table

1 The F horn, by reason of the general excellence of its tone, has become the standard modern instrument. Since all classical and some modern composers have clung to the crook system of notation, despite valves (e.g. horns in G, horns in E, etc.), it is here thought desirable, for the sake of those who find it somewhat difficult to 'sort out' the conflicting details of a full score, to furnish a table of the more usual transpositions.

Horn (crooked in)	Actual pitch of sound below the *written* note
B♭ alto (rare)	major second
A alto	minor third
G	perfect fourth
F	perfect fifth
E	minor sixth
E♭	major sixth
D	minor seventh
C	octave
B basso	minor ninth
B♭ basso	major ninth

(N.B. The compass of the horn varies, *theoretically*, according to the crook of the instrument. But for practical purposes, the reader can accept the compass of the F instrument as conforming to the *general* horn range of sounds. To satisfy the curiosity of those interested enough to ask for the exception to the rule, let me cite the low B♭ on the 2nd horn at the opening of Beethoven's Fourth Symphony – a gloriously rich yet sombrely vibrating sound (when played!); also the famous 4th horn passage in the same composer's Choral Symphony, one demanding an embouchure flexible enough to disconcert many players.)

2 The most favoured trumpets are the B♭, A, F, D and C. The remaining crooks have fallen into disuse. The size of the mouth-piece, so comfortable to the lips, enables the player to indulge in the most daring feats of tonguing. It is interesting to note that double and triple tonguing are controlled technically, as regards articulation, by a recognized system of consonants – *t k* for double, and *t k t* for triple. Hence the amazing brilliance of many trumpet (and cornet) passages on such rhythms as

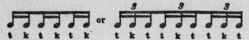

The cornet – actually a kind of short-length trumpet – is broader in tone, but with much the same compass. It is a poor substitute for the trumpet, but in French scores particularly (such as those of Berlioz and Franck) it is often found in pairs supporting the trumpets. The bass trumpet is rarely heard outside Wagner's *Der Ring des Nibelungen*. In the following table it should be noted that some trumpets transpose upwards and some downwards.

Trumpet (crooked in)	Pitch of sound in relation to *written* note
C	sounds as written
B (rare)	sounds minor second lower
B♭	sounds major second lower
A	sounds minor third lower
D	sounds major second higher
E♭	sounds minor third higher
E	sounds major third higher
F	sounds perfect fourth higher

3 In years gone by trombones were more varied in size than they are today. For instance, the soprano *discantus* trombone of Bach's time and the alto trombone in E♭ (pitched a perfect fourth higher than the tenor trombone) are now obsolete, though specimens of the latter are still to be seen. Others are the military in E, the D, and the double-bass trombone, the last-named as found in Wagner's scores. It is a thousand pities that this instrument is not in general use, for it makes a far better bass than the F tuba, and, moreover, can go a semitone lower in pitch. But, as Cecil Forsyth says of it in his *Orchestration*: 'The difficulties of adequate tone-production, to say nothing of execution, are terrific.' Many classical composers have contributed to the repertoire of the alto trombone in their scores, often employing very high-pitched notes indeed (e.g. in the finale of Beethoven's Fifth and Brahms's Second Symphonies). Nowadays the tenor trombone in B♭ and the bass in either G or F are almost the sole survivors of this important family. Two tenor and one bass form the usual orchestral trio. The G trombone, more comfortable to blow than the larger F, is used as the bass instrument in most countries, but in Germany the F is still partly in vogue. More often than not French composers write for three tenor and *no* bass trombone.

Although such details belong more properly to the textbooks, I have purposely shown in Example 24 the seven positions of the trombone from which all the other notes are generated, for there are many misconceptions in regard to this matter. These slide positions act in the same manner as do the three valves (singly or in combination) of the other brass instruments, each position producing a whole series of notes by variation of the lip and breath pressure. Needless to say, each series of notes so produced is but another instance of the functioning of the Harmonic Series. It may surprise some readers to learn that the trombone, unlike the strings or woodwind, can play many passages without moving the slide. The following, all in the first position, is a phrase of my own invention which illustrates the point.

Example 25

Tenor Trombone

1st position only

Pedal note

On the other hand, no composer with any knowledge would dream of writing a rapid passage of this kind:

Example 26

Presto

1st 7th 1st 7th (etc.)

etc.

It would involve the player in a hectic series of travels from one end of the instrument to the other, with no time for anything but a mis-hit at each note, unless he is using a tenor-bass trombone (see above), in which case the passage can be played in the 2nd and 3rd positions – the easiest of shifts.

The pedal notes are the first notes of the Harmonic Series, obtainable by playing with a very loose lip. They are special effects that do not always materialize. Berlioz was very fond of them.

The continental F trombone is pitched one tone lower than the G instrument shown above.§

Certain *glissando* effects are possible on the trombone. Often vulgar, they are sometimes funny but can be expressive. Jazz musicians, to whom all brass players are immensely indebted for their innovations in technique and expression, have evolved a *portamento* (in plain English a smear) style of playing that involves the use of glissandos and requires the highest finesse and artistry on the part of the player if it is not to sound tawdry and offensive. Ravel has set out in his *Bolero*, using notation (jazz players, of course, improvise), some such effects in the trombone solo. They *can* sound good.

4 All composers and conductors would agree that the tuba is the odd man out in the brass section. As a bass instrument he blends best with horns; certainly he blends badly with the trombones, whose scorching tone he cannot match. Bernard Shaw once recalled in a letter to *The Times* how Elgar, in conversation with him, regretted the lack of a real lower bass line in the brass, saying that the problem had never been solved in loud passages. It should be remarked, however, that in softer passages (e.g. the chorale in the finale of Brahms's First Symphony) the contra-bassoon can provide an excellent bass to the heavy brass.

The percussion section is the most nondescript in the orchestra: an odd collection of sounds and 'noises', some of definite, and many others of indefinite, pitch. Those of definite pitch include the timpani, bells, glockenspiel – once the equivalent of the old carillon of small bells, now rarely anything but a set of metal strips struck with wooden beaters: the xylophone – usually made of rosewood, walnut or box strips, also struck with wooden beaters: and the celesta – an instrument of the keyboard kind, the sounds of which are produced by the action of hammers on steel plates. Those of indefinite pitch are numerous and can be said to include any effect that happens to take the composer's fancy. For instance, Wagner wrote for eighteen anvils in *Das Rheingold*, but as Forsyth says: 'In practice the parts are almost invariably "boiled down". Few theatres,' he adds with sly humour, 'can afford eighteen blacksmiths.' Mossolov, the Russian realist, in his *Music of Machines*, finds an appropriate place for the din of metal sheets in a piece representing a factory working at full pressure.

The more usual percussion instruments of no definite pitch are familiar to all and so require little description. However, few modern scores would be considered complete without some reference to the side-, tenor- or bass-drum, the triangle, tambourine, cymbals, and possibly the castanets and gong. There are many beautiful and striking effects to be obtained from this section of the orchestra if the composer be discreet. The thrill of the side-drum in martial music – in the roll (*a*), the flam (*b*), the drag (*c*), or the paradiddle (*d*), heard *pp*, *ff*, *crescendo*, or *diminuendo*

Example 27

are effects without which music would indeed be the poorer. But – to quote from Forsyth's masterly *Orchestration* yet again, in a section on traditional music where the side-drum is under review – 'Like almost all the other Percussion Instruments its principal effect is its entry.'

In that phrase lies the secret of any attractiveness possessed by the percussion instruments, particularly those of indefinite pitch, for novelty of effect constitutes their only right of entry into the orchestra. Once they are heard, however arresting the sound, we are twice shy of any further effect they may attempt; we demand a change of colour, for familiarity with these instruments breeds a certain contempt. The castanets in Carmen's song to Don José in the second act of Bizet's masterpiece are a case in point. When first heard the effect is superb. Yet Bizet, with an unerring instinct for the right touch, knew only too well that the song required something more than castanets as the chief characteristic of the accompaniment. Who, we may inquire, ever spares two thoughts for those castanets once the trumpets (from the barracks outside) intrude upon the song with their dramatic 'retreat'?

The tambourine can be made to sound in three different styles of playing: (a) by shaking the jingles, (b) by striking the stretched parchment with the knuckles, and (c) by rubbing the parchment with the thumb. But of the smaller instruments the triangle is the one most in use. Effective either in single notes or in a roll, it found favour as long ago as the days of Mozart and Beethoven. Thereafter it was subjected to harsh treatment at the hands of those operatic composers who, as stated elsewhere, brought the 'batterie' to such a state of degradation.

Many vital effects, too numerous to mention here, are to be heard on the various drums, on cymbals and gong. One reverberating yet *pianissimo* thud on the bass-drum, such as can be heard in the 'Credo' sung by Iago in Verdi's *Otello*, can suggest to the sensitive mind the most terrifying spectacle of death and decay. Similarly, who can remain unmoved at the dread summons to the unknown contained in that single stroke on the gong near the end of Tchaikovsky's 'Pathétique' Symphony? The cymbals, too, with their various kinds of clashes and that thrilling roll – executed either with timpani sticks or side-drum sticks – have an advanced technique quite their own. The peculiar tone of the side-drum, hard and dry and quite unlike that of the other drums, is the result of the *snares* (lengths of catgut) that are stretched across the lower parchment coming in rapid contact with the parchment itself. This, in its turn, is set in vibration by the action of the drum-sticks on the upper parchment ('batterhead'). By a mechanical device the snares can be loosened so as not to affect the vibrations of the 'snare-head'. This produces that unique muffled sound usually associated with the solemn pomp of royal and military funerals.[1]§

[1] A remarkable instance of the side-drum's powerful effect occurs in the first movement of Carl Nielsen's Fifth Symphony. Here the composer directs the player to improvise his part in a sinister attempt to stop the progress of the music (evil versus good).

Of the timpani something has been written already in this volume. In all large orchestras they are found in three sizes and are these days invariably mechanical: that is, they are tuned not by the manual turning of T-headed screws but by the operation of pedals which automatically tighten the drumhead to whatever pitch is required, even whilst the instrument is being played (an action which produces a *glissando*: an effect beloved of the 20th-century composer).

In the classical orchestra they were used for martial rhythms, for an effect of darkness and menace in soft rolls, and as the climax of a *tutti*, where their explosive power could give an extra push to the general excitement to produce, as it were, a moment of aural orgasm without which the music might seem incomplete and unrealized.

Two mid-20th-century examples of timpani writing follow. The first (Example 28) is taken from Bartók's *Music for strings, percussion and celesta* and shows the effective use of glissandos:

Example 28

The second shows a somewhat virtuosic passage in the setting of Wordsworth's *Prelude* which forms one of the sections of Britten's *Nocturne*, op. 60 (1958):

Example 29

§ There remains but the harp which, in addition to its more normal activities, has two characteristic devices deserving mention here because of their frequency. These are (a) harmonics, and (b) *glissando* passages. The former, of a beautiful evanescent quality, are obtained by lightly touching the string half way down with the part of the hand near the wrist, while the fingers of that hand pluck the string to produce the sound required. In a modern score harp harmonics are indicated by a small circle above or below each note, the sounds heard being an octave higher than those written. The *glissando*, as its name implies, is a very rapid sweep of the fingers over the strings. By various elaborate arrangements of the pedals – a mechanical device far too technical to be explained here – many brilliant effects are obtained. But in recent years the *glissando* has been so over-worked that its appeal is no longer what it was. The wise composer avoids it whenever possible, for he knows that one *glissando* in the right place is worth a hundred in the wrong. The harp is a 'special' instrument and any misuse of its beautiful tones is perhaps the most cloying effect in all music.§

Despite the frequent and effective use of the harp in 19th-century scores it tended to remain a background instrument playing *arpeggio* accompaniments that were picturesque and colourful but in a sense inessential. Only rarely did it convey the thematic burden of the music, unless it were in a solo passage like the Ishmaelite Trio in Berlioz's *Childhood of Christ*. The off-beat Liszt, however, in his symphonic poem *Tasso, Lamento e Trionfo*, writes thematically for harp in the Minuet section in a manner which, in retrospect, seems rather modern and advanced for its day (1849).

The French composers Debussy and Ravel evolved the technique of harp-writing further with their exacting, brilliant but always idiomatically conceived parts in such works as *L'après-midi d'un faune* (1894) and *Daphnis et Chloé* (1912). In these orchestral works, however, the style and function still tended to be accompanimental and it was in chamber works such as Debussy's sonata for flute, viola and harp (1916) and the *Introduction and Allegro* of Ravel for seven instruments (1906) that the harp came to full fruition.

The harp parts of Britten are miracles of aptness and originality and take the instrument far beyond its original function as a delicate, exotic accompaniment. The reader may remember the Harp Variation in *The Young Person's Guide to the Orchestra* with its mixture of showy *arpeggios* and *glissandos* with passages of melodic significance:

Example 30

by Michael Graubart

Actual introductions of new instruments into the orchestra have to all intents and purposes been confined to two areas: percussion and electronics. Influenced, no doubt, by the general movement away from melody and harmony as the only carriers of musical significance, but prompted by their nationalist predecessors to regard not only folk-tunes but their associated 'primitive' instruments as worthy of inclusion in 'sophisticated' concert music, modern composers have brought in percussion instruments from more and more remote and exotic cultures. The Turkish cymbal and 'jingling Johnny' provided an 18th-century precedent; the next general importation was the large Chinese gong or tam-tam, prominent already in Mahler's *Das Lied von der Erde* (1909) with texts based on Chinese originals and the fourth (the funeral march) of Webern's *Six Pieces for Orchestra*, op. 6 (also of 1909). Its use culminated in Stockhausen's *Mikrophonie I* (1964), for a solitary tam-tam played in every conceivable way and with its sounds electronically modified.

Using percussion instruments for their colours instead of merely letting them reinforce the rhythms of the other instruments, composers have extended the 'family' idea to them, too, and they have also increased their independence by using more so-called 'tuned' percussion instruments – that is, instruments that play a definite note or notes. In addition to the traditional timpani (kettle-drums), which today are often equipped with pedals to allow them to change note very quickly and even to play *glissandi*, there are now Javanese gongs (reminding one not only of the general interest in Oriental literature and philosophy, but that Debussy already was greatly impressed by the sound of a Balinese gamelan orchestra which he heard in Paris), the wooden xylophone and its larger and lower relative, the marimba or marimbaphone, and the metal version of the xylophone (introduced via dance and jazz bands), the vibraphone (with its motor-driven vanes that give it a slightly sickly vibrato, but which – as most avant-garde composers have discovered – can be switched off), as well as the higher and sharper-toned but not dissimilar glockenspiel, which has been familiar for much longer.

Amongst untuned percussion instruments, the bass drum and the side-drum have been joined by other, smaller or larger drums of military origin, equipped (like the side-drum) with snares or rattling strings stretched at will across the lower membrane; and various sticks (including the jazz-player's wire brushes) are used. A vast range of new drums, often originally from Africa, and many of them in pairs of high and low or in larger families, has entered the orchestra via South American dance music and jazz: the large tom-toms (with their gay, coloured lacquer), the small bongos, played with the fingers or hand and open at the bottom, the metal timbales, the tall conga drums, and so on. The woodpecker-like wood-block and the sets of pear-shaped, hollow-sounding temple-blocks (nicknamed 'skulls') are of Eastern origin; the claves – two hard wooden sticks held in the hands – come from Central and South America. Perhaps the most characteristic 'avant-garde' sound, though, is that of three or more cymbals, suspended on stands, so that they can be played in a great variety of subtle ways, soft as well as loud, with soft and hard sticks, brushes and so on; these are sometimes joined by similar families of tam-tams varying in size, and by large and small triangles; in all cases, small instruments tend to sound higher than large ones. Even car suspension springs and brake drums have been used, and Mahler's picturesque cow-bells are now struck singly and called metal blocks.

Beautiful examples of the use of suspended cymbals are to be found in the works of Luigi Nono. Pierre Boulez, with his fastidious, Debussy-influenced ear and his teacher, Olivier Messiaen, have used tam-tams in imaginative ways, as well as many other percussion instruments including the vibraphone. But a particular *tour de force* of percussion writing is Edgar Varèse's *Ionisation* (1931), for thirteen percussionists playing thirty-seven instruments – not the only work for percussion alone, but probably the most musically significant and moving.

10 A POSTSCRIPT ON THE 20TH-CENTURY ORCHESTRA
by Michael Graubart

In music, as in painting, there has been one reaction against the priorities of the 19th century which has characterized much of the 20th: the pursuit of colour for its own sake as a factor equal in significance to line, harmony and motivic development. This has had far-reaching consequences. One has only to hear the strained, nasal tone of the unaccompanied bassoon in its highest register at the beginning of Stravinsky's *Rite of Spring* (1912) to realize, for instance, that the criterion for the choice of instrument is no longer that of *appropriateness*. Whereas even as modern a composer as

Mahler strove continually to find instrumental combinations in which the characteristics of the instruments matched those of the tunes they played, and in which the separate lines in a polyphonic texture were as clear as possible, Stravinsky uses the *unexpectedness* of the bassoon's timbre and the inevitable sense of strain in playing such a high melody as a specific expressive means.

If unexpectedness is to become an expressive element, then composers must rely on some things being more *expected* than others. In timbre, as in melody, harmony and rhythm, this is not only a question of what is natural or customary, but also a matter of the building-up of expectations by means of the structure, the pattern and argument, of each particular work. Structures made up of successions of timbres are inevitably more limited than those involving pitch and time, for it is difficult by ear to arrange timbres in scales and to recognize 'thematic' successions of timbres when they are modified by techniques of variation. Yet the third of Schoenberg's *Five Orchestral Pieces*, op. 16 (1909), reduces its motivic and quasi-canonic pattern to a subliminally-perceived background, and the structure as well as the mood of the piece depends primarily on the impression of an almost static, invariant chord continually changing in colour; and the slow second movement of Webern's concerto for nine instruments, op. 24 (1934), consists of a single melodic line (played over a piano accompaniment in one-, two- and three-note motifs) by the eight melody instruments, in which, for example, the opening phrase (one note on the trumpet, two on the viola) is, as it were, 'transposed' and reversed to form the second phrase (two notes on the violin and one on the clarinet, the latter at the same time acting as a link with the succeeding flute notes).

The use of colour as a form-building element reached its climax in some works of the 1950s and '60s. It had always been axiomatic that a different instrumental arrangement of a given set of notes and rhythms (whether in the *ad hoc* instrumentation of works by Monteverdi or Gabrieli as described by Praetorius, or in a piano-duet arrangement of a Beethoven symphony or an orchestration of a Bach organ fugue) did not change the essential identity of a piece, any more than a black-and-white reproduction of a painting made it into a different picture. Now, however, many avant-garde composers (perhaps as a result of the apparent liquidation of 'right' and 'wrong' in matters of notes, and influenced by the chance operations of John Cage and similarly Zen-inspired experimental composers, by the desire to allow the performers some freedom to improvise, and by the ultra-serialists of the Darmstadt school with their replacement of thematic processes by statistical controls over global averages of pitch, duration and so on) began to compose pieces whose identity resided in carefully-specified sequences and combinations of instrumental colours, the actual notes and rhythms that the individual performers played being partly or completely left to chance or the players' own wills. Examples are numerous, and include works by Morton Feldman (such as *In Search of an orchestration*), Cerha, Evangelisti and so on.

The wish to use clearly-differentiated colours as expressive or syntactical elements has led away from the 19th-century German ideal (shared by Wagner and Brahms, whatever else may have separated them) of a homogeneous blend. Most advanced composers nowadays think of an orchestra as a reservoir of individual timbres to be selected. They favour groups in which there is only a single representative of each instrument, even in the case of the strings. Large chamber orchestras with four or five solo strings rather than full string sections are popular, partly for economic reasons: to give a difficult modern work the rehearsal time it requires becomes very expensive when sixty string players have to be paid instead of five. And, perhaps in order to dissociate particular timbres from specific pitch ranges, there is a tendency to use families of high, middle and low instruments of the same kind in the Renaissance or baroque manner. Thus a typical large 20th-century chamber orchestra might consist of flute (doubling piccolo), alto flute; oboe, cor anglais, bassoon; E flat clarinet, clarinet, bass clarinet; horn, trumpet, trombone; harp, celesta; a large percussion section; and single violin, viola, cello and bass. There are examples of works scored for combinations along these lines from Schoenberg, Webern and Dallapiccola to Stockhausen, Nono, Berio and the younger composers of today.

The pointillist use of individual tone-colours has made it difficult to achieve massive effects with the whole orchestra. Some composers, however, and notably Ligeti and Lutoslawski, write music which is built up out of successions of harmonically static blocks of music, each block acquiring an individual texture and inner life or agitation by being given to large numbers of instruments, each playing its own mobile tune, each tune, however, being made up of partly or wholly the same notes as other tunes in the same general pitch region, so that the total number of different notes sounding together in the whole block is not excessive. Whereas Ligeti usually notates the lines in such a way that exact ensemble playing is required, Lutoslawski frequently allows each instrumentalist to play his line (itself exactly notated) at his own tempo, repeating it over and over until the conductor gives the cue for the next 'block' to begin. Good examples of such uses of a large symphony orchestra are Ligeti's *Atmospheres* (1961) and *Lontano* (1967) and Lutoslawski's Symphony no. 2 (also of 1967).

The desire to exploit unusual timbres as an expressive deviation from an expected sound has led many composers to search for unusual ways of playing conventional instruments, and not only by using very high or very low notes. Varèse was one of the first composers to exploit the subtle, half-pitched percussive sounds obtained by clicking the keys of woodwind instruments. After him composers experimented with the harsh sounds of the reeds and mouth-pieces of clarinets or oboes blown without their instruments and with the quiet breath sounds of instruments blown without their mouth-pieces; and Bartolozzi wrote a book describing ways of playing *chords* on single woodwind instruments, and of changing their timbres, which led to a great deal of experimentation – more particularly in solo pieces, of course, but even in ensemble works. Penderecki has made a speciality of using a great variety of unusual bowings on stringed instruments, and composers such as the Korean Isang Yun have carefully specified rates and intensities of vibrato varying from phrase to phrase and from note to note.

Though interest in the large, monolithic symphony orchestra has waned amongst the avant-garde, there is, thus, no shortage of ideas in exploiting the combination of many performers into one kind or another of ensemble or orchestra; and one should not forget even the combination of several *conductors*, each controlling his own group, in works ranging from Charles Ives' Fourth Symphony (1916) to Stockhausen's *Gruppen* (1957) and *Carré* (1960).

Book 3

Orchestral Music

by Julius Harrison
with new material by Robert Layton

PART 1
'ABSOLUTE' MUSIC AND THE SYMPHONISTS

§ 1 INTRODUCTION

The reader, of his charity, will not demand of me here to survey completely the whole field of orchestral music, for that is as impossible as would be the inclusion of every poem in a book on poetry. Already it has been shown that the art (if not the science) of music in this, its supreme manifestation, has developed rapidly only within the past 200 years. To burden ourselves, therefore, with any lengthy historical outlines of the symphony, overture, suite, tone-poem or other forms of orchestral music could only delay unconscionably the argument now being undertaken, since, in previous chapters, we have already witnessed the centuries-old rivalry between the composer and the maker of instruments.

We are now at the point where the living flesh of all this later music concerns us more than the dry bones of mere research into archaic forms. Those who are interested to go into the subject more deeply can read at length in such works as Grove's *Dictionary of Music and Musicians* how the symphony came into being – and that almost apologetically, so small were its dimensions in the initial stages. There they may read not only of Haydn, the 'Father of the Symphony', but of those progenitors before him, such as Abel, Stamitz, Carl Philipp Emanuel and Johann Christian Bach. Yet so absorbingly interesting has this particular form of music become since those early days that many volumes, far too numerous to mention, have been written about and around the symphony. For example, we find the author of the dictionary just named devoting a whole book to the analysis and appreciation of Beethoven's nine symphonies; or, again, some other author supplementing a concert-programme with several pages of explanatory notes in order that the beauty of thought or the structural outlines of some particular piece shall be fully realized.

For obvious reasons such a task cannot be mine here. Rather, in the space at my command, let me follow the advice of the author of *Religio Medici* when he wrote: 'Capital truths are to be narrowly eyed; collateral lapses and circumstantial deliveries not to be too strictly sifted.' The following chapters, therefore, endeavour to show the general structure and internal characteristics of the various forms of orchestral music, beginning with the symphony (as the most important type of orchestral composition), continuing with the suite, the overture and other works of similar kind, and concluding with an account of programme music.

Music is of two kinds: 'absolute' and programmatic. The former, with which we are immediately concerned in the ensuing chapters, speaks solely a tongue of its own, voicing nothing but abstract thoughts and expressing the intangible in moods of gaiety, sadness, comedy or tragedy that cannot be linked with anything more definite. Such music, to the listener, can well bear a thousand different interpretations, their contradictory nature inevitably going to prove the enduring 'absolute' quality of the music itself. Programmatic music, analysed in a later chapter, is equally interesting, even if not on such a high plane as absolute music. But where absolute music ends and the other kind begins, or where the classical loses itself in the non-classical, are matters that have not so far been decided very definitely. We need not worry overmuch on this account as long as we have the music itself.

§ 2 THE SYMPHONY

It is a strange fact that the germ of the symphony originated in Italian opera and was actually the direct offspring of the 17th-century 'Sinfonia avanti l'opera' that, in overture style, preceded the opera itself. And it is equally strange that fifty years later the *sinfonia* detached itself from opera because theatre audiences of those days were unconcerned with purely instrumental music. For those 18th-century operating composers who were endowed with a higher gift than their fellows were often at pains to provide an engaging piece of music that should stimulate the listener into a receptive frame of mind before ever the opera started. But then (as now) he sowed his good seed on stony ground, despite the novel instrumentation of an inventive age that was exploiting the orchestra as never before. The composer, with a pride in his work and encouraged by that minority who took an aesthetic delight in the newly-born orchestra, soon began to transfer some of his interest from the theatre to the concert-room and to those royal and ducal salons where instrumental music was almost a daily necessity.

The impetus thus given to orchestral music of the absolute kind brought about a definite cleavage in the styles of composers, some favouring the opera, others the symphony. Thereafter the true development of music on symphonic lines was only a matter of time.

Whereas the 'Sinfonia avanti l'opera' consisted of one movement only (though it usually included three distinct sections of slow and quick music), the newer *sinfonias* were soon expanded into three and four separate movements, each movement being of distinct type but bearing some relationship to the others.

Yet for many years the symphony (as I shall now call it) remained outwardly stable, once its three and four movements were firmly established. For to a great extent it was 'period' music. One can imagine that the peruked patrons of the symphony would not willingly forgo the stately and popular Minuet which, coming after a long *adagio-allegro* first movement and an equally long *andante* movement of sleep-inducing character, would rekindle the interest and so enliven the mind still further for that final sportive *presto* wherein the quips and pleasantries of the composer made all hearts young again. Therefore it must be presumed that as long as royal and lordly patronage was forthcoming the composer would hardly dare to vary the form of music so acceptable to the age. Instead, he would utilize his genius towards the invention of new themes and instrumental combinations and leave the general form of the symphony more or less where it was. Further, the style of music was often dictated by the exigencies of the moment, for amateur string and wind players flourished in those days. More than that, an amateur of sufficient social importance was able to cajole the composer into writing passages suitable to his skill.

But from this time onwards Europe was plunged into more than a quarter of a century of bloodshed. In the general welter all these pleasant *poudré* vanities disappeared and with them that fashion for the minuet set by Louis XIV more than 100 years previously. In place of the symphony's Minuet (third movement) so favoured by Haydn and Mozart – a minuet which, it should be added, had become considerably 'speeded up' since its stately dance origin – Beethoven introduced a quick one-in-a-bar *Scherzo* that in every respect but the 3-4 time-signature was entirely different from its predecessor.

With this, the symphony came of age. Its links with the suite or overture, and its relationship with the dance, were eroded and then relinquished. True, elements of the dance persist (the waltz movement in the *Symphonie fantastique*) but more often than not in a spiritualized form. Other elements were to intrude: the march in works like Mahler's Fifth Symphony or the scherzo of Tchaikovsky's Sixth. But whatever its diversity in the 19th century, the strength

237

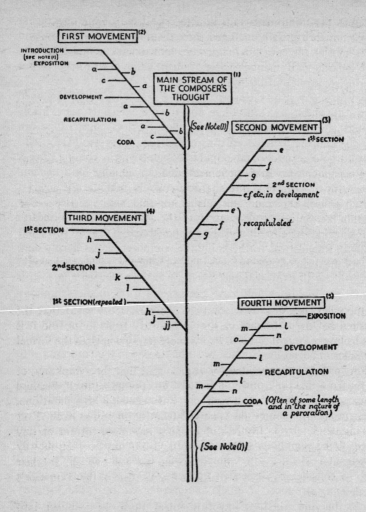

FIRST MOVEMENT (2)

INTRODUCTION (SEE NOTE (1))
EXPOSITION
— a — b
— c — a
MAIN STREAM OF THE COMPOSER'S THOUGHT (1)
DEVELOPMENT
— a — b
RECAPITULATION
— a — b
CODA
— c — b
(See Note (1))

SECOND MOVEMENT (3)
1st SECTION
— e
— f
— g
2nd SECTION
e f etc, in development
— e
— f } recapitulated
— g

THIRD MOVEMENT (4)
1st SECTION
— h
— j
2nd SECTION
— k
— l
1st SECTION (repeated)
— h
— j jj

FOURTH MOVEMENT (5)
EXPOSITION
— m — l
— o — n
DEVELOPMENT
— m — l
RECAPITULATION
— m — l
— n
CODA (Often of some length and in the nature of a peroration)

(See Note (1))

Explanatory notes to the above diagram

1 The underlying mood subsisting throughout the symphony. This can be:
a central idea such as a 'motto' phrase common to some or (occasionally) all movements;
a closely connected scheme of keys governing the four movements;
a cousinly relationship between the main and/or secondary themes of the first movement and other themes heard subsequently;
a scheme of instrumentation which, though containing vivid contrasts, can be said to be always in keeping with the music;
a combination or part combination of the foregoing.

2 Extended sonata form is the basis of most first movements. The Introduction, usually consisting of music in slow time, is frequently omitted. The main theme (*a*) is, in the longer symphonies, followed by other secondary themes (*b*). These act as a bridge passage to the second main theme (*c*), which latter is rounded off with a *codetta* (*d*) that precedes the Development section. The Recapitulation naturally reasserts much of what has been heard in the Exposition, followed by a coda, frequently of big dimensions, to give to the movement a balance of structure and a sense of thematic consolidation.

3 A movement in binary form is shown here with themes and their development indicated by (*e*), (*f*) and (*g*). But, of all the movements in a symphony, this is the one that is most subject to variation and free rhapsodical treatment – a river with many other streams flowing into it from directions most unsuspected.

4 A scherzo or minuet in ternary form is shown here. The first section is divided into two sub-sections (*h*) and (*j*), the latter being usually a lengthy development of the opening theme (*h*). Exactly the same plan is followed in the case of (*k*) and (*l*) in the middle, or 'trio', section. A return is then made to the opening music, with occasionally an elaborate coda (*jj*) to finish.

5 The plan of this movement is, in most modern symphonies, similar to that of the first, and therefore requires no further explanation as to its structure.

of the symphony lies in its organic coherence; the sense that the music arises naturally and inevitably from the basic ideas, and it is this feeling of organic growth that is more important than the formal outline the music traces.

For (to borrow an analogy) it can be said that the symphony, of all forms, is the great river of music. The very name itself, because of its recognized worth and meaning, has become a household one, with connotations often far removed from its original Greek. Ever increasing in volume from some gushing mountain torrent or tiny spring of sound, the main stream of the symphony goes on its way oceanwards, receiving its tributaries one by one, which, in their turn, have been swelled by the brooks and rivulets of the composer's passing fancies.

The diagram opposite – for practical purposes resolved into straight lines – will serve to illustrate my analogy, and at the same time act as a general guide to much of the argument that will follow. It should be understood, however, that this diagram can only *approximate* to the structure of a symphony for, as has been inferred above, each individual work develops its own architectonic form according to the inner life or substance of the music. Many symphonies by Haydn, Mozart and Beethoven have a rondo for last movement. But since the creation of those symphonies wherein

Beethoven showed that such smaller forms as the minuet and rondo were quite inadequate to express all he felt, it has become almost customary for composers to write their final movement in a form more or less corresponding to that of the first. And rightly so. The symphony with a first movement conceived in the grand manner demands a fourth of equal importance.§

3 HAYDN AND MOZART

One of the encouraging features of the post-war scene has been the discovery of Haydn. In the 1930s and '40s, only a handful of Haydn symphonies were in the repertoire (some of the 'London' Symphonies and the 'Farewell'), while in the popular imagination he was revered as the genial 'papa' Haydn. The evolution of his symphonic style could only be studied with success by those who had access to fine libraries: now, thanks to the gramophone and the publication of modern editions of the scores, both made largely possible by the enthusiasm and scholarship of H. C. Robbins Landon, they are all within the grasp of the average music lover. The first symphonies Haydn composed for Prince Esterházy were the three programmatic essays 6–8, *Le matin*, *Le midi* and *Le soir*, all written in 1761, and all retaining elements of the *concerto grosso* style: the orchestra is divided into *concertino* and *ripieno* sections (i.e. a group of soloists, and the whole of the orchestra proper) and formally, they impinge on such diverse genres as concerto, divertimento, suite and symphony. At this time the relics of baroque forms survive in a number of his symphonies: no. 3 has a fugue and so, too, has no. 40 in F, a work misleadingly numbered for it belongs to 1763, and thus precedes the 'Philosopher', no. 22 in E flat (1764), which like its companion, no. 21 in A includes a movement designed in *sonata da chiesa* form. Naturally, Haydn was bound by the resources at his disposal in Esterházy and when in 1763, the orchestra was increased to include four horns, Haydn lost no time in making use of them (in no. 13) though of all these earlier symphonies it is in no. 31 in D and no. 72 in D, another misplaced symphony, that their virtuosity comes into its own.

When in 1766 Gregor Werner died and Haydn assumed full responsibility for the musical life of Prince Esterházy's court, there was a slight falling off in Haydn's symphonic production. True, he composed symphonies without major interruptions for another thirty years but he was also busy in other fields, notably in church music, opera and above all, the string quartet. But the late 1760s produced a greater seriousness and dramatic intensity in the symphonies, and it is from this period that the *Sturm und Drang* symphonies come. The most famous are no. 49 in F minor, *La Passione*, the last of his symphonies to employ the *sonata da chiesa* scheme, the Symphony no. 26 in D minor (*Lamentatione*), based on a Gregorian chant from the Lamentations of Jeremiah (it also turns up in the trio of the 'Farewell' Symphony [no. 45 in F sharp minor] and in Mozart's *Masonic Funeral Music*) as well as the G minor Symphony, no. 39. The latter makes use of four horns (two in G and two in B flat) for technical reasons, and his example was followed by Mozart in the little G minor Symphony, no. 25, K183.[1] These *Sturm und Drang* Symphonies derive their title from the play, *Sturm und Drang* by Friedrich Maximilian von Klinger and mark the heightened dramatic sensibility of the period – of which we are reminded in the work of C. P. E. Bach.

One must say that in the symphonies of the 1770s which include all of the so-called *Sturm und Drang* group (nos. 44–49) except no. 49 itself and the bulk of the symphonies numbered in the fifties, we are offered a variety not only of mood and an inexhaustible fund of melodic invention, but a wide range of formal patterns. The finale of no. 44 (*Trauersymphonie*) is a kind of monothematic sonata form, in no. 42 we encounter a full-scale rondo, in no. 51 we have a divertimento or concerto with difficult solo parts, while in the 'Farewell' itself Haydn offers a sonata movement with an extremely long development and with a second subject that appears only once and then after the double bar! There are, of course, some magnificent symphonies after these years and before the mid-1780s: no. 53 (*L'Impériale*), no. 77 in B flat, no. 70 in D major are among them and we must not forget the splendid festive C major Symphonies that adorn his output in the '70s and '80s (no. 48, *Maria Theresia*, no. 60, *Il distratto* etc.). However, it is true to say – broadly speaking – that after the period 1770–74, Haydn's finest music is to be found elsewhere, and that it is not until the famous 'Paris' Symphonies (nos. 82–87), that we reach another great peak.

If Haydn's isolation at Esterház had forced him inwards on his own spiritual reserves and his inexhaustible inventive resources, his fame had by the 1780s become international. His symphonies were

---

[1] He originally planned to use the same forces in the great G minor Symphony but finally chose two horns, one in G, the other in B flat.

performed in Paris and it was the Loge Olympique and the Comte d'Ogny, for whom Haydn also wrote the Symphonies nos. 90–92, that commissioned the famous 'Paris' set (nos. 82–87). Three of them (nos. 82, 84 and 86) were written in 1786, the year in which Haydn, unbelievably enough, conducted no fewer than seventeen new operas in 125 performances, writing new material for some of them. But the 'Paris' Symphonies, written for a much larger orchestra than their predecessors, embrace a wider emotional range and are more expansive than any of his previous works. There is some particularly rich woodwind writing, no doubt a compliment to the fine accomplishment of the French players. Space does not permit us to dwell on the excellence of these individual symphonies or the two sets of symphonies Haydn composed for his London visits organized by Salomon. The stimulus of the London visits, not to mention the esteem in which he was held, unleashed in him a fount of invention, still greater expressive range, polished craftsmanship, subtlety and depth than anything he had written before. The formal and inventive ingenuity, brilliance and beauty of these symphonies place them at the peak of his achievement.

§ The slow introduction, often in the minor key, that relic of his early days when the 'Sinfonia avanti l'opera' was the fashion, he could rarely forget; with him it never lost its appeal. The 'Clock' Symphony in D major is a good example of this. After an introduction, which,

Example 31

it will be noticed, includes expression marks very dramatic for the age, we are, twenty-four bars later, introduced to a most cheerful *presto* in 6–8 time,

Example 32

with impish little accents that sound like Haydn chuckling with glee over the deceit he has practised on us.

And, for humorous treatment, what could be scored with more effect than the second (*andante*) movement – that movement which gave the symphony its name of the 'Clock'. Bassoons join with *pizzicato* 2nd violins, cellos and basses (the last-named, an octave below the cellos, sounding just like the rusty creak of a pendulum) to give a 'tick-tock' accompaniment to an engaging theme heard on the 1st violins.

Example 33

Space does not permit a complete analysis of the many felicitous touches to be found here. Haydn exploits each instrument in turn with masterly knowledge of effect. At the return of the *maggiore* (major key) section, there is a solo-quartet section scored for flute, oboe, bassoon and 1st violins that is as novel as it is amusing. Even the horns take charge of the tick-tock later on and at a disconcerting altitude; another example of Haydn's humorous appreciation of the lighter points of orchestration.

Had Mozart lived to Haydn's great age the history of the symphony would undoubtedly have been very different. In all probability his output would have been no less, and the symphony would then have been developed on lines far in advance of Beethoven's starting-point.

Passing over the earlier works we come to that amazing period of productiveness that was the culmination of his life's work. From 1786 to 1791 his most famous operas and symphonies almost fought with one another in their efforts to be born, as if afraid that death would claim him before they could be created. The year 1788 witnessed the creation of his three famous and most developed symphonies, nos. 39 in E flat, 40 in G minor and 41 (the 'Jupiter') in C major, all completed within the incredibly brief space of six weeks. A trilogy of happiness, melancholy and strength, they seem to contain between them the quintessential features of symphonic art; perfect models for all time, both architecturally and emotionally.

Mozart largely discarded the slow introduction so beloved by Haydn. His ideas came 'straight from the shoulder'; he would plunge into the main subject of a symphony without preamble or ado (no. 39 is an exception), and once started, the symphony never flagged. For perfect melody, developed contrapuntally with deepest feeling and skill and with the loveliest instrumentation imaginable, let me recommend the reader to a close study of the slow movement of this 39th Symphony, with particular regard to the section commencing

Example 34

(Strings & Horns not shown here)

Again, as an example of bold modulation, it is hardly possible to imagine anything more spontaneous or convincing than the following quotation from the first movement of the G minor Symphony

Example 35

where the composer, concluding the first section in the key of B flat, harks back to G minor for one chord only and then plunges into F sharp minor. It is difficult to explain on paper the actual effect such a quick transition to a remote key has on the mind, for inspiration of this kind defies cold analysis. But we who have known the symphony most of our lives hear in this and similar passages an intensity of expression hitherto unknown: something foreshadowing the music of Beethoven in all its immensity of thought. And, what is indeed extraordinary in this symphony, Mozart was able to achieve this with a small orchestra that consisted of one flute, two oboes (two clarinets were added by him in a later version), two bassoons, two horns and strings.

As a concluding example of Mozart's style, a quotation from the finale of the 'Jupiter' Symphony can scarcely be omitted here, for the movement is one of the most wonderful pieces of music ever written.

Example 36

Practically the whole movement consists of the fugal and imitative treatment of the themes I have numbered in the above quotation. These are treated separately, sometimes by inversion, and then, after the most extraordinary development, are subjected to the ingenious combinations shown above, continuing as shown at the end of the citation. I can only compare this amazing movement to a game of chess in which Mozart saw from the very first every possible move on the board, no matter what combination of pieces might occur.

Of such material many symphonies are not made. Yet each instrument should, as in the 'Jupiter', contribute its logical quota of sound; not in disconnected fragments but in an organized sequence as important to the whole symphony as is the proper flow of words to a language.

Out of that crisis Beethoven emerged, a giant figure, sublime and aloof, with an entirely new conception of the symphony. From his first essay in this direction written in 1799 during that stormy period in history that was destined to change the whole face of Europe, he demonstrated his unique powers. The old-time Minuet, dear to his heart in other directions, was banished, but for one exception. In its place there was substituted that Scherzo, with the invention of which he is often credited, quite erroneously. For the name means a *jest*, and jesting under the name of scherzo was indulged in by J. S. Bach, Telemann, Haydn and others long before Beethoven's time, though it did not appear in the symphony until Beethoven himself introduced it. From that time onwards it has survived. Few symphonies are found without it, for it seems the very embodiment of that kind of musical jesting that can yet hold its head high in the company of still greater music. From the outset Beethoven must have felt the urgent need of this type of music for third movements. Even in his First Symphony (which is somewhat over-credited with the Mozartian manner), the mood of the first movement shows unmistakable signs of the power to come. After the significant introduction, in which there is actually not a trace of Mozart, we are soon taken to a full passage that foreshadows in remarkable style the Fifth Symphony in its most triumphant moments. For the sake of comparison the two themes are quoted here. That from the First Symphony corresponds to theme (*b*) indicated in the diagram of the symphony given on page 238.

Example 37

1st movement Symphony No. 1 in C

Example 38

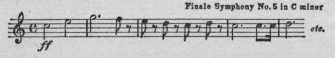

Finale Symphony No. 5 in C minor

Such passages considered, it would be difficult to imagine Beethoven, surrendering to the constrained elegance of the Minuet and Trio complacently in his third movements. The (symphonic) fate of such old-fashioned forms was sealed from the very opening of this symphony, where even the first chord is in the nature of a revolt. In fact, the whole *adagio* introduction is a remarkable piece of music, far in advance of anything similar written up to that time. Beginning with a dissonant chord that most surprisingly favours the key of F, it contrives to delay any full close into the C major key of the symphony until the *allegro* arrives. If, then, in his very first symphony, Beethoven could hear so far ahead that he was able to postpone the actual determination of the key for no less than twelve long bars, we can realize to some extent what developments were in store before the end of his life was reached.

Now such developments imply an all-round expansion of the symphony. Beethoven, before long, found that the usual twenty-five minutes taken up in the performance of such symphonies as the 'Jupiter' were quite insufficient fully to express the logical development of all those magnificent themes and ancillary themes that made up his great movements. The fifty minutes of the Third ('Eroica') and the seventy of the Ninth (Choral) are indeed expansions of musical thought of the utmost significance if compared with the normal length of the First. We can trace this expansion from the introduction of the First Symphony, through the lovely slow movement of the Second, up to that epoch-making masterpiece, the 'Eroica'. Here we find music outpoured from a mind so great that there is not a single movement or theme but would have suffered in beauty of utterance had less time been given to the task. The noble grandeur of the opening movement, with its Napoleonic background (the first real instance of a 'personal note' in the symphony, soon to become such an important factor), the unparalleled poignancy of the funeral march, the Scherzo that is something more than mere boisterous jesting, and that wonderful Finale on an earlier theme, whose profound qualities no man has ever fully grasped, make of it a work truly immortal.

There is by no means such expansion in that strange mixture of seriousness and irresponsible gaiety, the Fourth Symphony, except in the slow movement. Here there is a romantic mood coupled to an especial loveliness of theme that, at the time, might well have represented all that Beethoven felt for the beautiful Theresa von Brunswick. The Scherzo was also lengthened by having its trio section repeated, an innovation that Beethoven re-introduced in the Seventh Symphony. But in spite of its tremendous fun, as enjoyable as any he ever wrote, more than all else I hear deep down in this great symphony that underlying mood of seriousness characterizing the first and second movements. The low B flat on the 2nd horn in the opening bars of the lengthy introduction seems like some black shadow thrown across music that should be nothing but sunny, the depth of which shadow is intensified by those mysterious rolls on the timpani (also on a B flat) darkening the development section of the *allegro* so eerily.

In the entire output of symphonies up to this point, whether by Haydn, Mozart or Beethoven there was little adventure in the choice of keys for the two middle movements. Something of a convention seems to have been established that ignored keys other than the ones most nearly related to the actual key of the symphony. The following table, compiled from symphonies mentioned in the previous chapters, shows this absence of adventure.

| Symphony | Composer | Key of each movement | | | |
		1st	2nd	3rd	4th
La Reine	Haydn	B♭	E♭	B♭	B♭
The 'Clock'	Haydn	D	G	D	D
No. 40	Mozart	G minor	E♭	G minor G major	G minor
The 'Jupiter'	Mozart	C	F	C	C
No. 1	Beethoven	C	F	C	C
No. 2	Beethoven	D	A	D	D
No. 3 ('Eroica')	Beethoven	E♭	C minor C major	E♭	E♭
No. 4	Beethoven	B♭	E♭	B♭	B♭

Now this restricted choice of keys had long stood the classical symphony in good stead, mainly – I should imagine – because the music was always moderate in length and contained rhythmical schemes of great variety to counter-balance any monotony of key that might otherwise be felt. But in the long 'Eroica' Symphony we get a foretaste of what was bound to come. Here, although the actual choice of key for each movement shows no more adventure than is found in no. 40 of Mozart, yet there are many lengthy passages within these movements that explore very remote keys indeed.

In such manner Beethoven's glorious Fifth Symphony in C minor was a new departure in more ways than one. Not only do we hear the music turning from its long and fateful turmoil in the minor key to its eventual apotheosis in the major but, in addition, we recognize those first definite thematic links between movements that have since consolidated the symphonic form more than all else besides.

The first movement, with its powerful suggestion of 'Fate knocking at the door', is nothing short of amazing in its concentrated purpose. Everything grows from its first four notes, even the second theme (Example 40), which, in this instance, concedes little or nothing to a softer mood.

Example 39

Example 40

It all sounds like the breaking loose of elemental forces that have with difficulty lain dormant beneath the surface of the previous symphonies: restless pent-up energy now finding release.

From that relentless mood, 'rugged, terrible in force' (Sir Hubert Parry), to the exquisite beauty of the slow movement is a contrast too well known to need description here. What is more interesting, as the following quotations suggest, is that the first three notes (*a*) seem to have unconsciously prompted Beethoven to the opening phase of the Scherzo (*b*); the marked relationship is felt most strongly.

Example 41

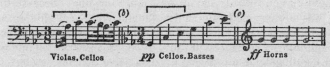

And then, after the tentative start (*b*), we are soon left in little doubt as to the origin of the main theme of the Scherzo (*c*). That it sprang from the opening bars of the symphony itself is indisputable, even though it may have come to Beethoven only through some unconscious functioning of the mind and not by deliberate metamorphosis of idea.

No less remarkable is the triumphant Finale of the symphony, for it is the most inspired and noble climax to all the many moods and thoughts that, one by one, have advanced unfalteringly towards the appointed goal. The Scherzo, in its later stages, becomes but a prelude to it – a prelude fraught with such power and mystery that we almost dread what will befall. Yet from its final bars, compounded of music so hushed and awesome that we instinctively think of the sun's eclipse and of vast penumbral shadows, there arises a mighty song of gladness in the *major* key, one banishing the spectres of darkness. Even if those spectres, in shape of the Scherzo's warning notes (*c*), make a brief return half-way through the Finale, do they not help to remind us that the victory has been hardly won? And, what is again wonderful, the great theme of this Finale (see Example 38) is undoubtedly derived from the three notes of the Scherzo here shown in brackets.

Example 42

Beethoven, in his Sixth Symphony (the 'Pastoral') went to the countryside for inspiration, giving to each movement a sub-title. These are:

1 Awakening of joyful feelings on arrival in the country.
2 By the brook.
3 Village Festival.
4 Thunderstorm.
5 Shepherd's Song. Thanksgiving after the storm.
(The last three movements are written to be played without a break.)

Here again there is an entirely new technique, largely prophetic of that programme-music which was soon to flood all Europe. The whole symphony is one of rare beauty, with effects such as the imitations of nightingale, quail and cuckoo, so naïve that no one but a great genius would have dared to write them. The timpani are reserved for the thunderstorm only – a master-stroke; while the thunderstorm itself – with the raindrops, the uneasy stir of the leaves, the forked lightning, the crashing thunder and, finally, the gradual disappearance of the storm – has never been equalled for sheer and convincing pictorialism. In the 'Pastoral' Symphony the 'speck of blue sky' on the flute that ushers in the Shepherd's Song is inspiration at its finest.

And the older Beethoven grew, the more joy, *mirabile dictu*, crept into his symphonies. The Seventh in A and the Eighth in F are outstanding in this quality, though we must not, at the same time, forget to pay tribute to the noble seriousness of the Seventh's slow movement. The Eighth – with Beethoven's one concession to the older type of symphonic thought, a *tempo di menuetto* movement in place of the usual Scherzo – contains the composer's most boisterous fun, not only in conception but in the highly imaginative and amusing orchestration. The principal theme of the *allegretto* second movement is said to have resulted from a farewell supper given to Maelzel, the inventor of the metronome, at which Beethoven extemporized the melody to the words 'Ta ta ta, lieber Maelzel, lebewohl'. There seems some truth in this story, for the music is most amusingly metronomic.

The Ninth (Choral) Symphony was described by Wagner in most eloquent terms. He compared the first movement to 'a conflict of the soul striving after joy against the weight of that inimical power which places itself between us and happiness', while 'a mad delight takes possession of us with the first rhythm of this second movement; it is a new world into which we enter – a world in which we are carried off in a dizzying and confusing whirl; it is as though, driven by desperation, we were flying before it in order to capture . . . a new and unknown happiness.' The third movement moved him deeply. 'How differently these tones appeal to our hearts. How purely, how soothingly do they resolve the defiance, the wild impulse of the soul . . . into tender and melancholy feelings.' And, to conclude these references to his analysis, he finally wrote: 'With the beginning of the last movement Beethoven's music takes a decided declamatory character. . . . The progress of the musical poem urges a decision – such a decision as can be pronounced only by human speech. Let us admire the manner in which the master prepares the way for the introduction of speech and voice . . . in this thrilling recitative of the bass instruments, which . . . address themselves to the other instruments, urging them to a decision, and finally themselves intone a song-theme which sweeps the other instruments along in its current so full of simple but solemn joy, and thus swells to a mighty intensity. . . . Shouting and exultation fill the air . . .'

Such was the last symphony Beethoven wrote, a work that ended with an 'Ode to Joy', set to words by Schiller. So far had the master travelled along the road of the symphony that now voices must needs be incorporated to express all he felt with such transcendent power. The Choral Symphony is the truest musical conception of humanity ever penned: its message, the triumph of man over every obstacle. It was written in circumstances that beggar description. In 1822 Benedict visited Beethoven at Baden where he found him composing in a room 'in the most appalling disorder – music, money, clothing on the floor, the bed unmade, broken coffee-cups upon the table, the open pianoforte with scarcely any strings left and thickly covered with dust, while he himself was wrapped in a shabby old dressing-gown.'

And about this time there was being written that 'Ode to Joy' in completion of a supreme masterpiece, not a note of which the composer would ever hear (though he was actually present at its first performance), so terrible was his infirmity. How Beethoven turned from the orchestra back to chamber music and found escape from his suffering in those superhuman posthumous string quartets is told elsewhere in this volume.

§ 5 SCHUBERT AND DVOŘÁK

Two outstanding symphonists, Schubert and Dvořák, deserve our special attention, for although their lifetimes were separated by many years they have much in common. On Dvořák's shoulders there fell the mantle of a certain type of spontaneous lyrical melody that was also the very essence of Schubert.§

Dvořák's admiration for him was lifelong: its extent is proclaimed in much of his music and acknowledged in an essay he wrote in America shortly before the centenary of Schubert's birth. Of the first six symphonies, he wrote, as well he might, 'the more I study them, the more I marvel'. The product of Schubert's youth, the First, was written in 1813 when he was only sixteen while the Sixth in C major, D589, is an astonishing achievement for a young man of twenty-one. All six spring from the fertile soil of the Viennese classical masters and yet though Haydn, Mozart and Beethoven were forma-tive influences in shaping the vocabulary, even at this early stage Schubert speaks with distinctive accents. Nothing in the six sym-phonies, however, can be called immature, any more than the op. 18 quartets or Beethoven's First Symphony could be so described. As Maurice J. E. Brown has put it, 'The elementary factors, harmony, counterpoint, dynamic balance and so on, are assured and spontaneous; the melody is often enchanting and key-transitions are bold and original.'[1]

§ Now although it is true that an unchecked flow of melody, however beautiful, will not produce a well-designed symphony, yet there is not a musician alive who would exchange such a symphony for one bristling with superb feats of technique but less inspired in ideas. For, as stated elsewhere, a symphony's character can be such that 'almost every academic law may be broken with impunity and still it will retain the elements of greatness'.§

The First Symphony in D, D82, is predictably enough the least individual: the splendid Minuet is strongly Haydnesque and the slow movement gives little idea of the expressive power Schubert was so rapidly to achieve. Its successor, no. 2 in B flat, D125, shows an advance that is striking not so much in terms of symphonic assurance (the First is not wanting in that) as in sheer personality. No one listening to the B flat Symphony or its delightful successor, no. 3 in D, D200, can be long in doubt of Schubert's identity. Although no. 2 owes not a little to Beethoven, it too proclaims an independent voice and its abundance of ideas and the quality of invention are an unfailing source of delight. There are some thematic correspondences between the young Schubert and Beethoven: much has been made of the resemblance in the second group of the first movement of the First Symphony and the 'Prometheus' theme, and likewise the correspondence in outline between the allegro first theme, of the Fourth Symphony (the 'Tragic') and the second group of the first movement of Beethoven's C minor quartet, op. 18 no. 4. But the melodic spontaneity that informs Schubert does not betoken any want of intellectual power. Schubert's ideas evolve organically though his organic processes are not Beethoven's any more than the latter's use of short pregnant figures as the all-pervasive substance of symphonic thought is the only means of sustaining a symphonic argument: Bruckner is an obvious instance in point. The sheer abundance of ideas in Schubert's symphonic movements and their supreme lyrical character is often in itself so striking that the listener is beguiled into underrating the intellectual power of this master. The spontaneity and effortlessness that so immediately impress us in the Fifth Symphony in B flat, D485, a miraculous work for a nineteen-year-old, can obscure the sheer perfection of design, the mastery of classical proportion that the score evinces. Its stance is

[1] Maurice J. E. Brown: *Schubert Symphonies* (*BBC Music Guides*) London, University of Washington Press, U.S.A. 1970

wholly classical even as far as the scoring is concerned: one flute, two oboes, two bassoons (no clarinets), two horns (no trumpets and drums) and strings, and it surely demonstrates that had Schubert wanted to write conventional sonata-style movements as tautly integrated as Mozart and Beethoven, it was not beyond his powers. Indeed in this connection Maurice J. E. Brown has gone so far as to say, 'As far as Schubert's Fifth Symphony in B flat is concerned, to call this work Mozartian is to pay Mozart a compliment.'

The Sixth is by no means its equal though it is fashioned with fine craftsmanship and high spirits. Its ideas are engaging even if they are wanting in substance by comparison with nos. 4 and 5. Two 'overtures in the Italian style' date from this period and the infectious gaiety of Rossini permeates its first movement and particularly its second theme.

However, it is for the 'Unfinished' and the Great C major that Schubert is really known and on which his symphonic laurels rest. Two attempts precede them: only three months after the Sixth was completed, he began a symphony in D major, D615, twenty-five pages of which survive in piano score, the *andante* of which foreshadows the first movement of the 'Unfinished'. Better known is the Symphony in E major, D729 written a year before the 'Unfinished', the first part of which was fully scored; the remaining sketch was scored by Weingartner. With the 'Unfinished' itself we come to what is one of the most justly famous symphonies in all music. Written in 1822 it inhabits a world far removed from anything he had composed in the medium before: it radiates a tenderness, poetry and a spirituality of the rarest quality while its vein of lyricism has ensured its appeal to the widest and most varied of audiences. The existence of the first two pages of the Scherzo (a second page, fully scored, which came to light several years ago disposes of the theory that the full score was completed but the last two movements lost, as it peters out) and a piano sketch has enabled the Scherzo to be conjecturally completed by various hands and the theory has been advanced by a number of eminent Schubertians that the B minor entr'acte that follows Act 1 of *Rosamunde* may have been the finale at one stage. In the 'Unfinished', Schubert let loose a stream of inspiration so extraordinary that criticism is silenced. The orchestration is of a kind entirely new to the age, rich in colour, daring in its effects and individual in every way.

In this symphony and in the Ninth, Schubert became the master of a new expressiveness in the orchestra. Not only were his melodies

254

scattered about the instruments with deep feeling for their characteristic tone-colours, but the actual range of dynamics was considerably enlarged.

Schubert is also known to have composed a symphony at Gastein during the summer of 1825 though no score of it survives. One of his contemporaries spoke of it as 'his greatest and most beautiful symphony', and many musicians have felt it possible that the Grand Duo in C, D812, might well have been a four-hand transcription of it: the work is strongly symphonic in feeling and Joachim's orchestration gained currency at one time. More recently John Reed has argued persuasively[1] that the 'Gastein' Symphony is in fact none other than the Great C major itself and that the date the autograph bears, March 1828, merely refers to the alterations Schubert made in the finished score. In any event the Great C major baffled the public for many years: it was considered too difficult for the Vienna orchestra of Schubert's own day and Mendelssohn had to withdraw it from his concerts in London, so completely was it misunderstood by the orchestral players. Yet its position now at the summit of his symphonic achievement is unchallenged. It haunted the Romantic sensibility: Schumann spoke of the 'heavenly length' of its *andante* and in describing this famous passage

Andante con moto

he wrote of a horn 'calling as though from a distance, that seems to me to have come from another sphere. Everything else is hushed, as though listening to some heavenly visitant hovering around the orchestra.' The intellectual mastery evinced in this great symphony has been admirably demonstrated by such authorities as Mosco Carner,[2] Harold Truscott,[3] and Maurice J. E. Brown[4] to whose analyses the reader is recommended.

[1] John Reed: *Schubert, The Final Years* Faber, London, 1972 pp 71–79.
[2] Mosco Carner in *Schubert. A Symposium* ed. Gerald Abraham, OUP, London, 1952.
[3] Harold Truscott in *The Symphony* ed. Robert Simpson, Penguin, London, 1966.
[4] Maurice J. E. Brown: *Op cit.*

Schubert's symphonies after no. 6 lend a new dimension to the classical concept of the genre for they embrace a world of feeling that it had hitherto excluded. Both the 'Unfinished' and the Great C major are (to quote Mosco Carner) suffused by lyrical feeling while preserving the essential features of a large-scale symphonic work. 'It is the consummation of Schubert's instrumental lyricism expressed in a medium ... that the classical tradition had nearly always excluded from the expression of personal and strongly emotional accents. It is in the breaking-down of these stylistic barriers that Schubert's revolutionary departure lies.' Certainly one can say that his eloquence touches depths that no master had explored before; his fusion of innocence and experience is of rare spiritual insight.

Like Schubert, Dvořák possessed a seemingly unending flow of melodic invention along with an appealing freshness and spontaneity. It is obvious from his early compositions that Beethoven and Schubert were the composers closest to his heart though by the early 1860s when he was in his twenties, he succumbed to the spell of Wagner whose shadow crosses his Third and Fourth Symphonies as well as some of his later tone poems. Czech folk music and Smetana, under whom he served for a time in the National Opera Orchestra as an orchestral player, were the other formative influences. Until the 1950s only the five symphonies published in Dvořák's lifetime were well established in the repertory but since then his four earlier symphonies have gained ground and Šourek's revised numbering has been widely adopted. Dvořák numbered his five mature symphonies in the order of publication rather than composition: thus, the F major Symphony of 1875 preceded the D major of 1880 but did not appear in print until 1888, three years after the completion of the D minor of 1884–85, and so bore the number 3. Šourek's numbering should perhaps be set down beside the old numbering so as to clarify the position.

Symphony no. 1 in C minor ('The Bells of Zlonice')	1865
Symphony no. 2 in B flat, op. 4	1865
Symphony no. 3 in E flat, op. 10	1873
Symphony no. 4 in D minor op. 13	1874
Symphony no. 5 in F major, op. 76 (originally op. 24)	
formerly known as no. 3	1875
Symphony no. 6 in D major, op. 60	1880
formerly known as no. 1	
Symphony no. 7 in D minor, Op 70	1884–85
formerly known as no. 2	

Symphony no. 8 in G major, op. 88 1889
formerly known as no. 4
Symphony no. 9 in E minor, op. 95 (from the 'New World') 1893
formerly known as no. 5

It is evident from the very opening of the First Symphony, 'The Bells
of Zlonice', the score of which only came to light in the present
century, that Dvořák is flexing genuine symphonic muscle, even if
it is far from fully developed. It has far greater sense of symphonic
momentum and feeling of purposeful movement than is the case in,
say, Tchaikovsky's First Symphony of two years later, though the
Tchaikovsky has the more individual and distinguished musical
ideas. It is as if Dvořák was deliberately curbing his keen lyrical
instinct to serve symphonic ends while Tchaikovsky's melodic genius
was given unfettered rein. In any event the two early symphonies
show Dvořák responding to the symphonic challenge with enthusiasm and, given the fact that he was still in his early twenties, an
astonishing degree of success. In some respects the C minor is a
study symphony: Šourek and others have noted the similarity in key-
scheme between this and Beethoven's C minor Symphony, but its
successor written only a few months later represents a considerable
step along the road to self-discovery. Its slow movement and Scherzo
have something of that luminous glow that radiates from the later
symphonies. Some of this may be attributable to Dvořák's greater
expertise in 1887, when he revised the score, but in the slow movement, for example, what one imagines to be the product of revision
is more often than not the original.

The Third and Fourth Symphonies written in 1873 and '74
respectively can with good reason be regarded as a pair. Both show
the influence of Wagner at its height; both were submitted for the
Austrian State prize which Dvořák won; both were published posthumously before World War I, and with them the tide in Dvořák's
affairs began to turn. The E flat symphony is in three movements
and is Dvořák's only symphony to be so designed: its ideas unfold
far more effortlessly than either of its predecessors and it shows a
far greater organic coherence even if it falls a long way short of the
level of mastery of no. 6 (old no. 1). Its first movement is basically
monothematic and the writing enormously confident. Its slow movement touches on Wagner: its middle (D flat) section recalls the
Valhalla motive from *The Ring* just as in the corresponding movement of no. 4 in D minor, the chorale-like theme which opens it
proclaims its allegiance to *Tannhäuser*. The finale of no. 3 and the

Scherzo of no. 4 are the most characteristic of later Dvořák; their features are clearly defined, the motives are vigorous and spirited and the music has inexhaustible drive and freshness of colouring. The seams in the presentation of ideas are no longer clearly visible, though they have not vanished altogether, and above all his language, though still eclectic, is evolving in both sophistication and independence. With the F major of 1875 he reached out to complete mastery.

What strikes one immediately about this symphony in comparing it with any of its predecessors is the Finale. So far the Finales of all the earlier symphonies, with the exception of the E flat which combined the function of both Finale and Scherzo, had been the weakest of the four movements.

The Finale of no. 5 is highly original in its handling of key, in its pacing, in its dramatic intensity and function within the structure. Indeed, it is more complex and ambitious than *any* other symphonic movement Dvořák had written up to this point. It sets out in A minor and makes a bold showing of sustaining this alien key in the face of constant pressure from the tonic, F major, during the course of which Dvořák pays oblique homage to Schubert: there is a reminiscence of the famous passage from the slow movement of the Great C major where the bell-like tolling of the horns serves as a kind of pedal for undulating string harmonies. By no. 5 Dvořák's orchestration had also acquired the luminous transparency that we associate with the mature composer; the very opening theme on the clarinets supported by horns, violas and cellos, is beautifully calculated and spaced. The idea itself is among the sunniest, freshest and most captivating that Dvořák ever penned. It could hardly be more pastoral in feeling but the countryside it evokes is bathed in colouring that is at one and the same time gentle yet vivid. The movement is compact and masterly.

Apart from the growing concentration and organic integration of his symphonic writing, one of the great differences between the apprentice symphonies of 1865 and their successors can be found in the quality and character of the invention encountered in subsidiary and transitional themes. Certainly the D major symphony of 1880 is one of the very finest symphonies after Beethoven. Its first movement surpasses in breadth and power and in the naturalness with which ideas are unfolded and grow, almost anything composed between the Great C major symphony of Schubert and the D major of Brahms It was Brahms's encouragement and example that inspired Dvořák in the 1870s and in terms of sheer concentration of ideas and their deployment within a coherent musical architecture, this first movement is undoubtedly the first Dvořák worthy to stand alongside him, and in terms of radiance and freshness arguably outstrips him. This is not to say that the symphony *as a whole* is the equal of Brahms's first two symphonies but it is certainly a masterpiece. Although the Brahms D major symphony is pastoral in feeling, the Dvořák reflects a much greater sense of kinship with nature, and assimilates folk elements more readily: the main theme of the first movement derives from the Czech folk-song *Já mám kone* while the Scherzo, a *furiant*, shows the success with which Dvořák had, as it were, spiritualized the folk dance. Its successor, no. 7 in D minor (old no. 2) is by general consent his greatest: Tovey set it alongside the Great C major and the four Brahms symphonies as 'among the greatest and purest examples in this art form'.

Its opening idea is darker in colouring than any of its predecessors. It is a commonplace that lyrical ideas rarely make the stuff of symphonic argument, but the genius of the D minor is that its main idea has all the potential required for sonata development but at the same time preserves the sense of songfulness so characteristic of Dvořák at his most natural. The slow movement is without any shadow of doubt Dvořák's most inspired and its melodic and harmonic invention among his most poignantly expressive. Listening to it and to the Scherzo, a veritable apotheosis of the dance, one is tempted to think that such music composed itself, so natural and infectious is its invention. Yet, as Dr John Clapham has pointed out, Dvořák had considerable trouble with the sketch. As is so often the case, spontaneity is purchased at the price of considerable discipline: being spontaneous is not the same thing as saying the first thing that comes into one's head! Dvořák's melodies were often slow to take shape and it is a measure of his art that the end result sounds so totally fresh and spontaneous.

The Symphony no. 8 in G major (old no. 4) marks a new departure in his symphonic career. Up to this point his energies had been concentrated on mastering traditional sonata practice but in the G major he left no doubt of his intention to write 'a work different from the other symphonies, with individual thoughts worked out in a new way'. Both the outer movements break new ground as far as he is concerned, and the second movement has much more the character of a pastoral mood painting than the slow movements of either of the preceding symphonies. Not that the listener is likely to be much concerned about matters of form or structure, so delightful and abundant is the flow of invention. The first movement opens with a G minor theme which gives way to a first group that is among the most richly stocked and varied in all his music. Given the beauty of the first idea in the second group, it seems extraordinary that Dvořák should not bring it back in the restatement or even refer to it later on. Only a composer of his prodigality of invention can afford this kind of gesture. In the G major, one has the feeling that each of the themes has a life of its own and takes over the course of events. The whole process seems so natural and effortless that the intervention of a composer scarcely seems necessary, and one is reminded of a novel where the characters evolve and develop, and sometimes disappear from the saga, the author acting as a kind of observer of their personal dramas, helpless and unable to intervene.

The slow movement is another highly original piece, as relaxed and luminous as the corresponding movement of no. 7 is intense and searching. The Scherzo is wholly captivating and sweeps one along as irresistibly as do the Scherzi of nos. 6 and 7 while the final theme and variations is characteristically buoyant and attractive. Just as the G major Symphony sealed his triumphant conquest of England, which he had visited no fewer than six times between 1884 and the first performance of the work, his next symphony in E minor was conceived during his stay in America. For most people the 'New World' Symphony is the point of entry into Dvořák's world, just as Beethoven's Fifth or the 'Emperor' concerto is the key to his. Yet it has disappointed many of Dvořák's most devoted champions. Hadow called it 'opportunist'; no doubt he viewed the prospect of the great composer seizing on the folk-music of a people for whom he had undoubted sympathy, but into whose art he could have little real insight, with little enthusiasm. Lambert called it 'fabricated' and Alec Robertson has written: 'It is depressing to contemplate this work from the heights of the D minor and D major symphonies'. He might well have added the G major. Certainly the melodic invention is more variable than is that of the Seventh and Eighth: it ranges from marvellously fresh ideas, the equal of any in his earlier work, to themes that bear the stamp of contrivance; certainly the working-out of some of the material in the Finale is more four-square and routine than in nos. 7 and 8. But for all that, the Ninth Symphony remains a masterpiece: no symphony of his met with greater immediate success than this and none has sustained such a wide following. By any standards the slow movement is inspired and throughout the work whose structure is the most easily followed of all Dvořák's symphonies – a factor that has certainly contributed to its tremendous popularity – there are strokes of unmistakable genius. If it is less elevated in the Dvořákian range than nos. 7 and 8, it still deserves its place in the sun.

The symphony after Dvořák

After Dvořák, only three Czech composers have really established themselves in the international repertoire: his son-in-law, Josef Suk (1874–1935), Janáček, whose contribution lay outside the symphony, and Bohuslav Martinů (1890–1959). Of course, there are others worth mentioning: the Fourth Symphony of Josef Bohuslav Foerster, for example, stems from the tradition of Dvořák, Mahler and Bruckner and has an Elgarian nobility that makes one regret that it is so little known outside Czechoslovakia. But undoubtedly the finest post-Dvořák symphony is the 'Asrael' Symphony of Suk, inspired by Dvořák's death in 1904 and that of his daughter, Otilia, whom Suk married. Into this five-movement work, Suk poured his grief and the work, though it is indebted to Mahler in places, is deeply original and a work of rare vision. It owes a good deal to the 'cyclic' principle that was fashionable at the time but whereas in so many composers the recurrence of thematic material seems a perfunctory gesture, this is not the case here. The 'Asrael' Symphony is a moving human document and undoubtedly the authenticity of its experience sharpens its impact. Although Janáček's *Sinfonietta* must be mentioned in passing, its phrase structure is scarcely organic.

By far the most prolific composer to emerge in Czechoslovakia after the generation of Suk and Novak was Martinů, whose output exceeds in all 300 compositions. He first made a name for himself during the inter-war years when he lived largely in Paris, and was strongly attracted to neo-classical forms. Like many prolific composers his output is uneven but the five symphonies that he wrote during his years of exile in the United States (1942 saw the appearance of the First and the remainder followed at annual intervals) are by general consent among his finest works. A sixth, sub-titled *Fantaisies Symphoniques*, followed in 1953. All six have common features and none of them breaks new ground formally, yet they each establish a world that is radiant and vital, and evince an imaginative power of striking quality. The melodic inspiration is strong and distinguished by syncopation or sprung rhythms that propel the music forward irresistibly. His scoring, particularly in the *Fantaisies Symphoniques* is as distinctive as it is resourceful. Other symphonies

261

from pens such as Pavel Bořkovec, Viktor Kalabis, Václav Dobiáš and Miloslav Kabeláč witness a flourishing symphonic school but none has the originality and power that make Martinů so attractive a personality.

6 THE SYMPHONY AFTER BEETHOVEN

Classical art sets store by perfection of form, balance and proportion; it tends to concentrate on those areas in our experience that unite us with our fellow men. Any work of art is a report on our experience of life but an artist of strong classical instinct will subject his report to objective discipline and scrutiny: certain areas of feeling will lie outside its boundaries or will be carefully seen in their right proportion. The perspective of the romantic artist differs in that he tends to concentrate on what makes his experience unique; he will stress those facets of his sensibility that mark him off from his fellow men and the special characteristics distinguishing his personality will loom larger. Naturally, like all rough-and-ready generalizations, this is not the whole truth: elements of 'romantic' sensibility are to be found in all composers, while an artist abandons the classical virtues at his peril. One can perhaps modify the generalization by saying that for the Renaissance composer from Josquin to Palestrina, his relationship with God was paramount; for the composer of the baroque and classical periods there was a greater awareness of society; and with the 19th century came a discovery of the full extent of one's inner world as a repository of the raw materials of art; there was a greater consciousness of nature and of the complexity of the human sensibility. Small wonder, then, that the vocabulary of music expanded in a variety of ways during the years following the deaths of Beethoven and Schubert. The society for which such artists as Berlioz and Wagner composed was totally different from that of the *ancien régime*; the whole system of patronage had changed; power had passed from an aristocratic élite to the bourgeoisie.

The least experienced listener can immediately discern that the *Symphonie fantastique* of Berlioz is worlds removed from the symphonies of Beethoven and Schubert though it was composed only two years after Schubert's death! Looking at the symphonies of Mendelssohn, however, there is no such contrast: their relationship to tradition is readily and immediately evident. With Berlioz the ordered symmetry of the classical period was undermined and as far as phrase structure was concerned, the horizons of melodic invention broadened. At one extreme we have the long, exquisitely wrought, asymmetrical lines of Berlioz; at the other we find the simple, regularly-balanced and symmetrical miniatures of Mendelssohn or Weber. It was Alfred Einstein who argued that Mendelssohn fell short of unquestionable greatness in the company of Handel and Mozart, because he lacked a capacity for suffering: 'What Mendelssohn lacked for the attainment of true greatness is the courage to say the ultimate – in love or in tragedy.' Certainly he never had to confront the material difficulties that beset Mozart and Schubert, and by comparison with them (and many others) he led a sheltered existence. Mendelssohn's gifts in terms of pure musicianship, i.e. in the facility to give expression to his musical thoughts in the most natural way, were indeed prodigious: the Octet and the 'Midsummer Night's Dream' Overture are little short of miraculous. Even his First Symphony in C minor is an extraordinarily accomplished work for a boy of fifteen, thought its twelve precursors that have entered the repertory in the last decade or so, have less strong claims on our attention. Yet as in the case of other masters, the numbering of his symphonies is misleading: the Second (the 'Hymn of Praise') comes from 1840, the Third ('Scottish') from 1841–42, while the 'Italian', the Fourth, precedes both, dating from 1833, and the 'Reformation' prefaces them all (1830–32), save only the youthful C minor, no. 1 (1824). His critics have spoken of the 'complacency' of his music; certainly works like the 'Hymn of Praise' show him fully attuned with the spirit of his time, but even in the 'Reformation' Symphony, the commonplaces of the first group of the first movement are counterbalanced by the poetic feeling that informs the brief slow movement, a kind of orchestral song-without-words. The 'Italian' Symphony may be wanting the dimensions we encounter in Beethoven or late Schubert; yet it moves with perfect mastery within its well-defined boundaries. It is superbly wrought music, irrepressibly musical, having the kind of perfection that leads one to think that the music must have composed itself.

Mendelssohn does not greatly exceed the vocabulary of the Viennese classics: he certainly did not extend the language in the way that Berlioz did. Nor was he as conscious of the need for formal innovation as was Schumann who seeks all sorts of unifying devices: a motto theme in the 'Spring' Symphony, the close interrelation of ideas in the Fourth Symphony whose first movement, like that of the Piano Concerto, is monothematic.

Much has been made of Schumann's poor scoring. Tovey even went so far as to attribute his failings to his embarrassing experiences as a conductor: these, he suggested, induced him to make 'all entries fool-proof by doubling them', so that if one group of instruments missed their cue, the others would save the day. More recently the view has gained ground that his orchestral miscalculations may possibly have a medical explanation associated perhaps with the functioning of the inner ear, for there are striking variations in the effectiveness of his scoring within one and the same work. Yet Schumann's idiosyncratic orchestration has an authentic-sounding flavour to it: the homespun quality of his sonorities seems to me an integral and lovable part of his musical personality, which is perhaps why attempts to clean up his scoring and sharpen its contours rob the music of some of its warmth and character. Not even Mahler's retouchings have really held the repertory and in comparing Schumann's 1841 version of the D minor Symphony with the less effective and more thickly-scored 1851 definitive edition, it is the latter for all its faults that sounds more authentically Schumann: for in his world, colour is of smaller account than substance.

There is no mistaking Beethoven's shadow in the early G minor Symphony (1832–33), a student work that he subsequently disowned, or in the four symphonies he completed in the decade 1841–51. The melodic substance is closely integrated and particularly in the Second Symphony (1845–46) unfolds naturally and organically. The dignified clarion call proclaims its classical inheritance (this particular figure occurs in Haydn's 'London' Symphony, no. 104, as well as in Mendelssohn's 'Reformation') and its inspired and sublime slow movement ensures the work a very special place in the repertory. Both Schumann and Mendelssohn served as models for countless composers of the mid-19th century from Gade to Sterndale-Bennett. But a parallel development was the 'programme' symphony, a work inspired by a literary scheme and whose form was even dominated by it as in the symphonic poem.

The fact that Berlioz and Liszt both provided elaborate programmatic schemes for their symphonies has often misled discerning musicians into underrating their structural coherence. True, in the 'Romeo and Juliet' Symphony of 1838 there is some genuine confusion of genre, perhaps occasioned by the failure of Berlioz's hopes for *Benvenuto Cellini* at the Paris *Opéra*, and although much of his thinking here can be said to be truly symphonic, the poetic and dramatic elements are every bit as strong. Berlioz's music struck his contemporaries as new and revolutionary (it still sounds astonishingly fresh in our own times), and did so not only because of his orchestration, whose profound brilliance and originality is self-evident but because his melodic style, as Schumann was among the first to point out, is so totally novel. His phrases are long and distinguished by asymmetrical structure: as Schumann put it, 'modern music has never produced a work[1] in which even bars alternate more freely with uneven', and yet as is the case with so many innovatory minds, Berlioz was deeply steeped in tradition but impatient of routine. Just listen to the main theme of 'Romeo seul' to see how astonishingly original is his sense of line with its irregular rhythmic structure and strong chromaticism, yet how classically pure is the overall impression it leaves. In the 'Harold in Italy' Symphony (1834), his second, there is a boldness of vision: a symphonic canvas with the solo viola assuming a narrative rather than a concerto role. Much of the thematic substance comes from the *idée fixe*, though it would be idle to pretend that it undergoes such complex and thoroughgoing transformation as it does in the *Symphonie fantastique*.

The *Symphonie fantastique* is a work of immediately striking originality though the full measure of its achievement was slow in being recognized. Two facts served to obscure the quality of its purely symphonic thought: first, its appealing programmatic origins which are familiar and which have led people to assume that it is these rather than musical considerations that are paramount in Berlioz's musical thinking.

Secondly, its diverse musical origins have prompted attention: the 'Marche au supplice' (The March to the Scaffold) was intended for *Les francs juges*, the dreamy idea heard on muted violins at the very outset of the work comes from a song written when Berlioz was a boy, while the first segment of the *idée fixe* appears in his student cantata, *Herminie*. But this does not mean that the symphony was cobbled together; rather that Berlioz was slow to realize the full implications of his inspiration. No one not knowing its history nor knowing its literary programme would ever question the sheer strength and vision of this symphony. Here is a work that, like Debussy's *La Mer*, seems to step outside the frame of time and place, a feature that distinguishes all *great* works of art. Liszt's 'Faust' and 'Dante' Symphonies, on the other hand, belong very firmly within their period and enshrine many of its ideals. Although some

[1] The *Symphonie fantastique*.

of the ideas for the 'Faust' Symphony were conceived in the 1840s in the Alps, it was written in 1854 but substantially revised in 1861. It was in fact Berlioz who introduced Liszt to Goethe's *Faust* in 1830, sixteen years before the *Damnation of Faust* appeared, the work which probably stimulated Liszt's imagination in the direction of his own symphony. This, incidentally, is dedicated to Berlioz. Its powerful chromaticism and strong sense of atmosphere undoubtedly influenced Wagner who borrowed one of its themes for *Die Walküre*. In 'Faust' we are more firmly in the territory of the programme symphony: each of the three orchestral movements is a character portrait, Faust himself, Gretchen (a marvellous piece and among Liszt's most inspired and enduring utterances) and finally Mephistopheles. A powerfully imagined work, with an eloquent choral finale that Liszt added in 1861, this does not make sense if the listener is unaware of its programme; nor for all its merits does it possess an organic cohesion of the same order as the *Symphonie fantastique*.

7 FRANCE AFTER BERLIOZ

Returning to Berlioz it must be conceded that his influence on the course of the symphony in France was minimal. Indeed none of the really *great* French composers to come after Berlioz (Fauré, Debussy and Ravel) were symphonists: nor in spite of his youthful C major Symphony, was Bizet. It is to classical models that one's mind turns when hearing this perfectly proportioned and miraculously spirited work, which was discovered only in the 1930s by the English scholar, D. C. Parker, who persuaded Weingartner to revive it. Similarly the two slight but delightful Gounod symphonies preserve the classical niceties. Mendelssohn served as a model for the First Symphony of Saint-Saëns and both its successors, no. 2 in A minor and the well-known no. 3 in C minor openly parade their classical banners even if they speak with more facility than depth. But it was to the cyclic example of Schumann's D minor Symphony that César Franck and his disciples gave their most sympathetic response: the opening of the Chausson Symphony in B flat could hardly be more Schumannesque. The popularity of the Franck D minor Symphony (1888) has waned slightly over the past two decades and rarely figures in the concert hall programmes of the 1970s, so that it is no longer so energetically denigrated by critics. Of course, it is four-square, it relies too heavily on sequence, and its structure is far from perfect. But for all that, it creates a distinctive sound world, its slow movement has an eloquence and dignity that are commanding as well as a genuine sense of flow. This movement and much of the first have something noble about them and can be relied upon to survive their detractors.

Franck became a rallying point for French academicism and some important symphonies followed in his wake, all of which make the obligatory cyclic gestures. Vincent d'Indy's Second Symphony in B flat minor is one though its invention is uneven (there is a fine minuet and evidence of delicacy of feeling and an undoubted sense of scale) but the most impressive remains that of Chausson. His debt to Wagner is readily discernible, particularly in the slow movement, and fine though the symphony is, it is in his quieter and reflective vein as in the *Poème* for violin and orchestra and the *Poème de l'amour et de la mer* that his voice is most distinctive, despite the softened Wagnerian lenses that colour his harmonies.

None of the Franckist symphonies match the parallel achievements of Fauré, Debussy and Ravel. Nor do the four symphonies of Alberic Magnard or the five of Guy Ropartz have strong claims on international attention though they are not without their rewards.

France has, however, produced at least one major symphonist in the present century in Albert Roussel. As a pupil of d'Indy he came to music later than most composers, after serving for some years in the French Navy. Subsequently he paid a prolonged visit to Cochin-China and India – a circumstance largely responsible for the exotic style of much of his earlier music. His First Symphony, called *Le poème de la forêt*, dates from 1906. His harmonic language has an impressionist exoticism and a highly evocative atmosphere. The opening chord of his short tone-poem, *Pour une fête du printemps*, originally planned to form part of his Second Symphony (1919–21), has this characteristically picquant flavouring. But it is not so much his exotic textures, alluring though they are, as the motoric rhythms, the sense of momentum and the richly inventive counterpoint that best distinguishes his style. The Third Symphony (1929–30) has a seemingly inexhaustible vitality and, as is the case with his fourth and last symphony (1934), abounds in contrapuntal detail which at times tends to proliferate, thus overloading the texture. Structurally both symphonies are taut (they are much more densely packed than *Le poème de la forêt* and the Second Symphony): indeed in the first movement of no. 3, one almost feels that the second subject has arrived too soon before the material of the first can be fully registered and digested. But the wealth of ideas, the angular on-flowing lines and the unflagging rhythmic vitality and interest of texture makes Roussel an invigorating and original symphonist.

Le groupe des six were bound together more by ties of friendship and a determination not to follow the same path as the Debussyists than any positive common ideals. Poulenc's contribution lay outside the symphony though his sophisticated harmonic palette and refined sense of irony have few parallels in the music of his time. Honegger's pre-war reputation largely rested on his illustrative works such as *Pacific 231* and *Rugby* as well as a handful of dramatic scores, above all *King David*, rather than on his abstract works. After the iconoclastic gestures that he and Darius Milhaud made in the 1920s, the latter with his miniature symphonies, one would hardly have predicted a flowering of interest in this genre. Yet in the 1940s and '50s both composers turned to the symphony. True, Honegger's first essay is earlier: it belongs to the celebrated group of works commissioned by the Boston Symphony Orchestra to mark its 50th anniversary among which Roussel's Third, Prokofiev's Fourth and Stravinsky's *Symphony of Psalms* are to be numbered. The Second, for strings with a trumpet obbligato in the final apotheosis, and the Third, *Symphonie liturgique* are wartime works which reflect something of Honegger's deepening pessimism about the tide of human affairs as well as a growing spiritual awareness. Perhaps the most diverting and (I believe) enduring is the *Deliciae Basiliensis*, no. 4, a work still neglected in the concert hall, and a piece of greater radiance and more substance than the Fifth, *Di tre re*, fine though that is. Roussel's example, albeit fully assimilated, is still to be discerned in the latter's Scherzo, while the bitonality that distinguished Milhaud's early music finds an echo at the very outset. (Indeed it pays homage to Milhaud's Opus Americanum no. 2, *Moses*, written during his wartime years in the United States.) Milhaud's First Symphony dates from 1940 and during the next two decades he produced twelve. Although many of them contain routine Milhaudesque ideas (no. 10, for example) and overladen textures, others offer some inspired music. The Sixth (1954) is a most beautiful symphony: its opening in particular is serene and spacious, while many movements in his other symphonies, the ambling scherzo-like fourth movement of no. 2, for example, have an irresistible, easy-going Mediterranean charm.

Two post-war French symphonists clamour for inclusion: Henri Dutilleux has something of Roussel's exoticism, feeling for texture and organic power, while the most eccentric phenomenon of the post-war scene is the 'Turangalîla' Symphony of Olivier Messiaen (b. 1908).

Not so many years ago the names Bruckner and Mahler were inseparably linked in the popular imagination in much the same way as were Debussy and Ravel, or Bach and Handel. At least the latter share the same year of birth, whereas Bruckner and Mahler are separated by more than three decades, the former being born in 1824, the latter in 1860. True, Bruckner was a late developer, as it were; his First Symphony (1865–66) overlaps Mahler's childhood while Mahler's First (1888) was composed during the last decade of Bruckner's life, at the time when he was poised on the revision of the Eighth Symphony. To be truthful, their names were linked for somewhat primitive reasons: their symphonies were all long and, as far as the Anglo-Saxon world was concerned, rarely played. Time has of course changed all this: Sibelius and Vaughan Williams no longer dominate concert programmes to their exclusion; indeed during the 1960s Mahler became the vogue of the many as opposed to the cult of the few only a decade before. He had always enjoyed greater popularity on the Continent, particularly in Holland, just as Bruckner retained a devoted following in his native Austria. Mahler's influence in 20th-century music has been by far the greater: one has only to think of the examples of Shostakovich and Benjamin Britten. Bruckner's musical antecedents are as different from Mahler's as are his sympathies and his cast of mind. The high emotional temperature and keenly drawn tensions of the one are matched by the purity of language and spirituality of the other.

Bruckner's musical language was late in forming: his distinctive voice does not really make itself heard until the 1860s even though personal touches are to be discerned before this. Even as late as 1855, when he had a number of works behind him, he plunged into an intensive study of counterpoint with Simon Sechter and abstained from original composition for more than six years, between the ages of thirty-one and thirty-seven. He emerged with an enviable mastery of technical resource. His language embraces the naïveté of the folk music of upper Austria, the childlike directness and depth of utterance that we find in Schubert, as well as the block-like structures of Giovanni Gabrieli and the Venetian school. His admiration for Wagner, to whom the Third Symphony is dedicated, undoubtedly coloured his harmonic thinking, although it is true that the latter's precept that the art of composition is the art of transition is one that Bruckner did not emulate.

Indeed Bruckner's art actively eschews smooth transitions in favour of abrupt contrasts, one texture and mood being directly juxtaposed alongside wholly unrelated material. In the Scherzo of the Fifth Symphony, for example, the flint-like stonework of the first theme is immediately contrasted, with only a bar's silence separating them, with an artless, smiling *Ländler* (bar 23). Similarly in the Scherzo of the Sixth Symphony, the trio strikes a note of complete contrast with all that has gone before, so much so that on first hearing it scarcely seems to be related to it at all.

Bruckner's earlier music has an austere beauty far removed from the world of Wagner, though as his personality developed, so did his use of chromaticism. The E minor Mass for voices and wind instruments, which comes from the same year as the First Symphony, shows the extent to which he had assimilated 16th-century polyphony, which he had studied so assiduously with Sechter, as well as the refinement of his contrapuntal artistry. It goes without saying that it also shows the purity and depth of his religious feeling. Bruckner's strong religious instinct remains central to his creative thinking and his faith shines through everything from the three Masses, written in the 1860s, to the unfinished Ninth Symphony whose very dedication proclaims his piety. The simple intensity of this religious fervour together with the want of sophistication that marked his personal behaviour as well as his musical personality, attracted mild derision at one time, but it is the genuineness, the integrity and the spirituality of his art that have conquered. This is not to deny the validity of some criticisms: the Finale of the Fourth Symphony is structurally weak, sequential passages are occasionally obtrusive (the marvellous *adagio* of the Sixth Symphony at bars 45–48), and there are moments when the sheer grandeur of an idea is not enhanced by dint of rhythmic repetition. Yet it is the vision, the profound originality and the awe-inspiring grandeur and innocence that silence criticism.

One problem that puzzles music-lovers is the question of editions. Throughout his life Bruckner was made conscious of shortcomings in the presentation of his material by hostile and well-disposed critics alike and a glance at the accompanying chronological table

		1865	Dvořák Symphony no. 1 ('The Bells of Zlonice') and no. 2 in B flat, op. 4
1866	Bruckner Symphony no. 1 rev. 1868 (Linz version) rev. 1890–91 (Vienna)	1867	Tchaikovsky Symphony no. 1 ('Winter Reveries')

1872	Symphony no. 2 (first draft) rev. 1873, 1877		
1873	Symphony no. 3 (first version) rev. 1874 (second version 1876–77, rev. 1878 (third version 1888–89)	1873	Dvořák Symphony no. 3 in E flat
1874	Symphony no. 4 rev. new scherzo 1878 new finale 1879–80 further revisions 1881, 1886 subsequent revisions by Loewe	1874	Dvořák Symphony no. 4 in D minor
1875–76	Symphony no. 5 in B flat (minor revisions 1877–78)	1875	Dvořák Symphony no. 5 in F major
1879–81	Symphony no. 6 in A	1876	Brahms Symphony no. 1 in C minor
		1877	Tchaikovsky Symphony no. 4 Brahms Symphony no. 2 in D Borodin Symphony no. 2 in B minor
		1880	Dvořák Symphony no. 6 in D
1881–83	Symphony no. 7 in E [1]	1883	Brahms Symphony no. 3 in F
1884–87	Symphony no. 8 in C minor rev. 1889–90	1884–85	Dvořák Symphony no. 7 in D minor
		1885	Brahms Symphony no. 4 in E minor
1888	Mahler Symphony no. 1	1888	Tchaikovsky Symphony no. 5
		1889	Dvořák Symphony no. 8 in G
1891–94	Bruckner Symphony no. 9 (unfinished)	1892	Sibelius *Kullervo* Symphony
		1893	Dvořák Symphony no. 9 in E minor (From the New World') Tchaikovsky Symphony no. 6 (*Pathétique*)
1888–94	Mahler Symphony no. 2 ('Resurrection')		
1895–96	Symphony no. 3 in D minor	1899	Sibelius Symphony no. 1
1899–1900	Mahler Symphony no. 4	1902	Nielsen Symphony no. 2 ('The Four Temperaments') Sibelius Symphony no. 2 in D
1901–02	Symphony no. 5 (rev. 1904)		
1903–04	Symphony no. 6		
1904–05	Symphony no. 7	1904–07	Sibelius Symphony no. 3 in C
1906	Symphony no. 8		
1908	*Das Lied von der Erde*		
1909	Symphony no. 9		
1910	Symphony no. 10 (incomplete)	1911	Sibelius Symphony no. 4 in A minor Nielsen Symphony no. 3 (*Espansiva*)

will show that he struggled with many of his scores over a long period in the search for a definitive version. The fiasco that attended the first performance of the Third Symphony in D minor when Bruckner conducted the score in 1877 struck a resounding blow to his self-confidence: members of the Viennese audience fled at the end of each movement leaving a mere handful in the auditorium at the very end. But the history of this score will serve as an example of the vicissitudes of a Bruckner symphony. The first version of the score was finished in 1873. After the first performance, Bruckner revised it in 1878 and then again in 1888–89, after his labours on the first version of the Eighth Symphony. Thus, there are three different editions in all, the first of which exists in two versions since Bruckner made considerable improvements in 1874. There are two printed versions, one made in 1878 and the other in 1890, both of which differ slightly from Bruckner's autographs. Not all the changes in the 1890 version bear the composer's imprimatur. Bruckner used the 1878 printing as a basis for this revision and in the first and third movements made changes, erasures and added various sheets. The Finale, however, was copied out afresh by Franz Schalk in a shortened version which he made and which Bruckner approved. Two of Schalk's shortened passages were accepted by Bruckner but the third was not and was replaced by a newly-composed passage. Bruckner did not always approve of the changes made on his behalf: Frederick Loewe's changes in the Fourth Symphony are a case in point, but he was all too responsive to well-intentioned advice. When Mahler heard that he was about to embark on a revision of the Third, he pleaded with him against this course, arguing that the 1878 score was in no need of change. It was the seventeen-year-old Mahler who had made a piano-duet arrangement of the work with Rudolf Kryzanowski.

Not all Bruckner's scores underwent so drastic a process of revision as did the Third Symphony and some were edited by other hands in an attempt to make his work more readily palatable to the public. For many years the Fifth Symphony was performed in a version by Franz Schalk that severely truncated its Finale and did so without Bruckner's approval. Insofar as these exercises served to pioneer the composer's cause, they fulfilled a certain historical purpose. However, even when changes were made that do have the composer's imprimatur, it is not always possible to determine which were made against his better judgment and which of two alternative procedures he would prefer. In the case of the First and

Second Symphonies, for example, the mature composer of the Eighth Symphony who re-fashioned some of their detail was a very different artist working from a totally different vantage point than the Bruckner of the 1860s and '70s. Most authorities accept that the so-called Linz version of the Symphony no. 1 and the 1877 edition of no. 2 more truly represent his artistic intentions.

If Dvořák's art represents a rare awareness of man's relationship with man, with his natural environment and with God, Bruckner's art can be said to concentrate – like that of the great masters of the Renaissance – on man's awareness of God and to reveal an intense feeling for the grandeur of nature – particularly the landscape of upper Austria. Only the insensitive music-lover, whatever his feelings about Bruckner in general, could fail to respond to the innocence, purity and awe-inspiring sense of space that informs the opening of the Fourth Symphony: its depth and profound beauty are immediately evident. Many of Bruckner's symphonies begin similarly with what the Germans call an *Urthema*, or 'primordial theme', an idea that is simple, triadic, powerfully tonal, like the opening of the 'Eroica' or Beethoven's Ninth. Obvious characteristics are also *tremolando* strings, long-sustained pedal points, long paragraphs with deeply *espressivo* string writing and climaxes of breathtaking magnificence. What marks them off from any previous symphonies has been trenchantly put by Deryck Cooke:[1] 'They express the most fundamental human impulses, unalloyed by civilized conditioning, with an extraordinary purity and grandeur of expression; and they are on a monumental scale which, despite many internal subtleties and complexities, has a shattering simplicity of outline. These fundamental characteristics are peculiar to Bruckner though the size and grandeur owe something to Beethoven and Wagner.' In terms of scale it is the slow movement of the Eighth Symphony that is boldest and broadest in conception. In terms of sheer duration, it is longer than all four movements of most classical symphonies: it is as long, for example, as Schumann's Fourth Symphony. Yet in the context of a well-conceived performance its proportions emerge as expertly judged and it seems not a bar too long. The same movement can serve as an example of Bruckner's use of key tension: the symphony is in C minor and this movement in D flat major. It is around the chord of D flat which asserts itself, albeit unobtrusively, on four occasions that the whole movement revolves. It is a measure of Bruckner's subtlety in handling classical tonality that D flat has been

[1] *The Symphony* ed. Robert Simpson Vol I. p 287.

eschewed or rather only remotely touched in the two preceding movements and thus sounds new. It still resonates at the very opening of the Finale, a movement of tremendous majesty and power. For all the block-like contrasts that distinguish Bruckner's symphonic thinking, the overall structural conception of his later symphonies shows masterly resource and imagination. The magnificent first movement of no. 8 is a perfect instance in point and the Finale, too, is no less remarkable. It should perhaps be stressed that Bruckner's finales offer a wider variety of types than the scherzos or even the *adagios*: the contrasts embraced by the Finale of no. 8 are striking. Similarly the Finale of the Fifth Symphony, which doffs its cap at the procedures of the Finale of no. 9 and later encompasses one of the mightiest and most respondent displays of contrapuntal ingenuity in 19th-century symphonic literature, is as varied in texture and subtle in procedure. Its world is far removed from those of nos. 6 and 7.[1] The greater chromatic awareness of the last two symphonies, particularly the Ninth, shows a response to the wider harmonic palette Wagner made possible rather than directly to the influence of Wagner himself, for both in the handling of orchestral sonorities and in the treatment of ideas (not to mention the totally different spiritual domain they inhabit) there are few parallels, even if the odd fingerprints can on occasion be discerned.

Unlike Bruckner, Mahler was a great interpreter whose conducting, according to Egon Wellesz, combined the drive and discipline of Toscanini with the warmth of Bruno Walter. Critical opinion in the 1930s, when *The Musical Companion* first appeared, favoured the Mahler of the songs at the expense of the symphonies. Certainly the orchestral songs are, with few exceptions, of the highest order of inspiration and many of them are perfectly proportioned masterpieces. In disputing the view that Mahler's genius was primarily lyrical rather than symphonic, Harold Truscott has argued that although the songs are diverse in range and character, there is the sense that Mahler needs greater space for them to breathe; he needs the larger canvas so that he can develop his thought in a more congenial context. An obvious example is the theme from the *Lieder eines fahrenden Gesellen* that he uses in the first movement of the First Symphony (1888), where it is able to flower at much greater length. Yet the first movement of the Second Symphony (the 'Resurrection') should leave no doubt that in terms of dramatic

[1] Readers will find a thorough examination of Bruckner's musical processes in Robert Simpson's study, *The Essence of Bruckner* London, 1967

contrast and power, his cast of mind could scarcely be more symphonic. Although it is large in scale, it is tautly held together, organic in growth, totally original and shows complete mastery of classical sonata processes. Whether or not the even larger edifices, the fifth movement of the same symphony or the first movement of no. 3 (1895–96), can be so regarded is more open to question; but critics of Mahler the symphonist need ponder no further than the first movement of the Fourth (1899–1900) whose mastery of proportion is self-evident, to see that whatever path Mahler chose sprang from artistic necessity and not inability to handle the sonata design. The much-quoted conversation between Mahler and Sibelius pinpoints a basic divergence in their symphonic philosophies: Sibelius had spoken of his admiration for the logic and severity of the symphony while Mahler countered that for him the symphony must embrace the world. In other words while Sibelius excluded some areas of experience and some kinds of musical material in his pursuit of the organic principle, Mahler took a less classical view. He touches upon areas of emotion that would normally have lain outside the province of symphonic argument and, in looking more deeply into his own psyche for the raw material of his musical thinking and, more importantly, confronting us with it boldly, he can be said to have extended the boundaries of the symphony in his day every bit as radically as had Berlioz.

The ten symphonies – if one includes the torso and the sketches that Deryck Cooke has so brilliantly realized for performance – fall into three major groups: the first four symphonies (1888–1900), the fifth to eighth symphonies (1901–06) and *Das Lied von der Erde*, the ninth and the projected tenth symphonies (1908–11). Apart from no. 1, the Fifth and its two successors, the first of his symphonies to be purely instrumental, no. 5 in C sharp minor, shows the full extent of his contrapuntal mastery. Mahler's melodic style is a compound of numerous ingredients: the frequent recourse to march rhythms is no doubt a relic of his upbringing and they are undoubtedly used to striking effect in, say, the opening of the Sixth Symphony, one of his very greatest works, and to no less impressive ends in the opening of no. 5. The tonal (or perhaps one should say, modal) ambivalences that distinguish some of his ideas contribute greatly to their expressive effect: it is something he inherited from Schubert who frequently exploited the emotional effect of moving unexpectedly from major to minor and back. Mahler exploits this bitter-sweet colouring in a number of melodic contexts (think of the poignancy he achieves in *Der Tamboursg'sell*) or the dramatic effect of the major–minor triads in the Sixth Symphony. His recourse to banal ideas during moments of emotional stress brings a kind of irony new to music: in childhood, at the height of a parental quarrel, he fled into the street to encounter a banal trivial idea being played there, and in later years relieved moments of tension in music by similarly dramatic means.

Although the middle-period symphonies show his mastery of counterpoint, the Ninth finds it serving remarkable ends: its otherworldly first movement shows the extent to which he had transformed the orchestral textures of late romanticism; for example, he elevates the horn to a solo role, assigning it a complex thread in the counterpoint, and liberating it from the continuo-like role it had performed in the 19th-century orchestra. In the finale the traditional harmonic support provided by the wind and horns is removed: in the C sharp minor episode one has a wonderfully spacious and open texture exploring both extremes of the compass. This example was not lost on Shostakovich in the slow movement of his Fifth Symphony. Yet again we find Mahler enriching the expressive spectrum in the volcanic energy, the contrapuntal complexity and angular melodic leaps of the *Rondo-Burleske* of the same symphony. These factors – the angular leaps and intense chromaticism of the lines and the contrapuntal density of the textures – served to lay the foundations for the erosion of classical tonality. For although Mahler's art, and in particular the Ninth Symphony and *Das Lied von der Erde* has, like that of Bruckner, a powerful spiritual dimension, his inward-looking nature, his complex psychology and the high emotional temperature of his art really put him in the vanguard of expressionism. At times the importance he attaches to his own emotion lends him a perspective that is truly romantic: the detail and his investment in it obscures the objective reality. For if he pushed back the boundaries of the symphony enabling it in, say, the Seventh to absorb sentiment scarcely worthy of symphonic attention, he also laid the foundations of its decay.

After Mahler

In Austria, the commanding figure post-Mahler is Franz Schmidt whose four symphonies are venerated in Vienna. The last, dating from the 1930s, has great eloquence and dignity to commend it; Mahler and Strauss are both strong influences but they are fully assimilated into a language that has a powerful coherence. The

Fourth Symphony is a one-movement work whose procedures are deeply organic. Among the composers after Schmidt, mention must be made of Egon Wellesz (1885–1974), Schoenberg's first biographer and a leading musicologist. He became a refugee from the Nazis and settled in Oxford where he wrote nine symphonies, the first of which shows a strong Mahlerian influence.

Hindemith also fled from his native Germany with the advent of Nazism and settled in the United States. His *Mathis der Maler* Symphony and its successor, *Die Harmonie der Welt* falls more into the category of a symphonic suite with material drawn from the opera than into the symphony in its purest manifestation. But there is no doubting the symphonic nature of much of Hindemith's thinking, and his Symphony in E flat and the splendid *Sinfonia Serena* witness the freshness and intellectual power of his art. Further afield, mention must be made of the greatest Polish composer of the 20th century, Karol Szymanowski. His early music showed the influence, not unnaturally, of Chopin while subsequently his musical language was invaded by impressions from Scriabin, Strauss and Debussy. There are four symphonies; the second is Straussian in feeling, the fourth is a *Sinfonia concertante* for piano and orchestra, and the third and finest is an evocative work, full of imaginative colouring and mystical feeling, called 'Song of the Night'. Szymanowski's style is rhapsodic rather than symphonic but his is a powerful and individual voice whose influence can still be discerned in such successors as Lutoslawski and Taduesz Baird.

§9 BRAHMS

Brahms, almost a unique musical figure of the 19th century, is often alluded to as the last of the classical masters. To that proud title he has many claims. Born in Hamburg in 1833, he was brought up on the strictest counterpoint by a famous teacher, Marxsen and, never able to forget his tutelage, continued those contrapuntal exercises to the end of his days. For no composer ever reverenced his art and the great masters more than Johannes Brahms; no composer ever realized as much as he that the creation of true music depended on craftsmanship acquired by years of patient study, study never to be relaxed.

As a young man he fell under the influence of that great romanticist Schumann, and but for his own strict musical upbringing might easily have become such another. But common sense prevailed.

Before he had reached the age of twenty-five he, with an artistic courage remarkable for one of his years, chose the older forms of music as his means of expression, withstanding every temptation to copy the new school of romantic and realistic composition practised so successfully by Schumann, Liszt, Chopin, Berlioz and Wagner. And into those forms he poured his musical soul and gave us many a masterpiece of great individuality and beauty. Once out of his nonage, he spurned the pictorial and the sensational like so much poison, his one desire then being to create absolute music beautiful for its own sake. And in this he succeeded mightily.

For more than twenty years he pondered over his first symphony. Sketches of the great C minor existed in 1856, yet the work was not completed until 1876. But when it did appear its effect was such that Brahms was immediately hailed as the legitimate successor to Beethoven. Thereafter each new work of his was eagerly awaited by an admiring and impatient world of music.

Brahms's art, as exemplified in his four symphonies, is one of the most remarkable manifestations of created music that the world has ever seen. In an age when the orchestra had swollen to an enormous size he wrote for one no larger than that used by Beethoven in his Ninth Symphony. In an age when harmony was running riot with chromaticism he rejected such effects as being a sign of weakness and chose instead the plainer diatonic chords of the classical masters. He would hold no candle to the devil: he remained aloof, untouched by every decadent influence that in the 19th century had afflicted music like a plague. He was, in truth, a great all-seeing genius who pandered to no fashion and stooped to no trickery of orchestral effects. His powers of invention and his orchestration went hand in hand in perfect companionship. But while it cannot be said that he touched the profoundest depths of inspiration as did Beethoven in his finest symphonies, yet he brought to his own a degree of craftsmanship that is unequalled anywhere. His themes have that uplifting quality that links them with Beethoven's. His developments and climaxes are always of immense power, vitally interesting and full of inspired individual touches quite unlike those of every other symphonist.

To him every note mattered. Each instrument had its appointed task. Each key-relationship, either within or between movements, was in perfect accord with an organized scheme. Each theme, too, was related to its context in either a primary or secondary capacity till finally, the whole symphony resolved itself into a work complete in form and detail.

Now such methods might argue dry cerebration and nothing more. But with Brahms that was not so. His intellectual grasp of music was such that he could harness this gift to his inspiration and create symphonies having the fundamental quality of greatness. Beauty and strength of theme were his in noble measure; the architecture of his movements, with few exceptions, perfect models of symphonic structure.

By making a wider choice of keys for his movements he enlarged the general scope of the symphony; the form became more plastic. We have already seen how the classical masters were insensitive to any such variety, being usually content to pitch three movements out of the four in the same key. But Brahms's method was very different, as the following table will show.

Symphony	1st movement	2nd movement	3rd movement	4th movement
no. 1	C minor	E major	A flat major	C minor, then major
no. 2	D	B	G	D
no. 3	F	C	C minor	F minor, then major
no. 4	E minor	E major	C	E minor

In this short article I cannot pretend to analyse the aesthetic reasons for these far-reaching changes. Yet the whole question is a fascinating one, especially if the thematic content of each symphony be considered in relation to the keys chosen. I can only instance the case of the First Symphony and that of the Third. In the former each movement is pitched a major third higher than the one preceding it till the 'wheel comes full circle' and the grim minor-key conflict of the first movement is resolved in the triumphant C major conclusion of the Finale. Absolute music it may be, yet the imaginative listener must surely feel that this noble work somehow represents the struggle of abstract forces contending for the mastery. It may appeal to him as the triumph of good over evil or of the sun over the dark forces of the night. Whichever way, there is no doubt that Brahms's First Symphony is one of the greatest masterpieces of intellectual thought and beauty ever conceived in symphonic form.

The Third Symphony in F major is quite exceptional in the choice of keys. Founded on the motto-phrase F, A, F[1] (in this instance, F,

[1] A device frequently used by this composer.

A *flat*, F), it opens in heroic manner with a magnificent sweep of theme. Yet by the time the third movement is reached the music has become sadly retrospective, even gloomy. And, to follow it, the Finale is in the unexpected key of F *minor*, with dark themes of strange character that recall the austere mood of the First Symphony. This stern mood is retained until near the end, where the motto F A F returns with the major key and the music sinks to a close so beautiful that we are left spellbound.

Brahms planned his material with the utmost care. For instance, in the opening of the first movement of the Second Symphony there are three main themes, used not only separately but in combination.

Example 43

It will be noticed that the first note of each theme combines to produce the triad of D major. Of this Brahms was undoubtedly aware, for each melody is interlaced from time to time with the happiest results and with never a suggestion of artificiality or cleverness for its own sake. This is true symphonic art. Everything is utilized to secure a maximum of effect both contrapuntally and harmonically. In fact, so masterly is the workmanship that it is difficult to say where counterpoint ends and harmony begins. Brahms's intellectual grasp of each detail is so secure that not a point escapes his notice. We are not surprised, therefore, to find that at the very conclusion of this symphony, when our engrossment in the climax has temporarily swept away all recollection of the first movement, a loudly-proclaimed triad of D major is heard on the three trombones.

Example 44

In this epitome, simple as it is, Brahms consolidates the whole symphony. What could be more logical or more symphonic than this ultimate fusion of the thematic material (quoted above in Example 44) into this final triad of D major? Knowing Brahms's methods, it is impossible to believe that all this was merely a matter of chance.

Those who take an especial delight in the structural points of a symphony should study the opening of the Third. After the motto-phrase has been stated in the opening bars it is employed as the basis of the main theme of the movement, cropping up in many unexpected places with a show of technique as natural as it is ingenious.

The Fourth Symphony is perhaps Brahms's finest inspiration. Not even a whole book, let alone an article, could do anything like justice to its remarkable beauty. The general austerity of its mood (save for its ebullient third movement), its other-worldliness and the perfect balance of its orchestration make of it a work before which we can only bow the head in homage. To some musicians it is a closed book, but that is not the fault of the symphony. Others find in it a musical solace scarcely to be found elsewhere; a link with the spirit world, a vision 'seen through a glass darkly', sustaining the soul with the grandeur of its conception. The slow movement, with its solemn opening on the horns and the eerie *pizzicati* that are founded on that phrase,

Example 45

takes us into realms where material things exist no more. The third movement, hardly a scherzo, displays tremendous power in rhythms of great vitality; while the *Passacaglia* that forms the Finale, based on a chromatic version of a ground-bass borrowed from Bach's 150th Church Cantata 'Nach dir, Herr, verlanget mich', is overwhelming not only in its technical achievement but in the music itself. In the E major section the entry of the trombones on those hushed chords quoted below is one of the most inspired moments in all music.

Example 46

(String arpeggios not shown here)

The symphonic Scherzo form did not appeal to Brahms, and he discarded it in all his symphonies. In the first three, a gentle type of *allegretto* movement took its place, acting as a quiet interlude before the powerful Finale. In the Fourth Symphony he roused himself to some purpose, but this wonderful third movement has nothing in common with the Scherzo, either in form or feeling.§

10 RUSSIA

Russian music did not really discover a distinctive voice until the appearance of Glinka, and a genuine symphonic consciousness did not emerge until the 1860s. True, in recent years there has been greater awareness both of the variety and extent of musical activity in Russia before Glinka but in terms of the general repertory, Fomin, Verstovsky, Khandoshkin and Albyayev remain *terra incognita*. The perspective may have deepened a little but no mountain ranges appear in the distance inviting conquest. The kind of indigenous musical tradition that Smetana and Dvořák had behind them has no Russian precedent: 18th-century Russian musical life drew the bulk of its sustenance from imported talent. The Russian symphony clearly drew its inspiration from Western models.

It is often said that the Russian genius for ballet has dominated the greater part of their symphonic thinking. The early symphonies of Tchaikovsky certainly offer evidence of balletic habits of mind: the slow movement of no. 1 ('Winter Reveries') is an obvious instance in point while the main theme of no. 3 (the 'Polish'), and for that matter much else in the same symphony, suggests the dance. In the present century Prokofiev and Stravinsky had the most highly developed balletic instincts that do not fail to surface in the symphonic context. Russian musical thinking in the 1860s and before was deeply affected by folksong with its regular periods and simpler rhythmic structure. And, if much of the melodic inspiration draws nourishment from this source, the difficulties of thinking in large-scale designs and long-breathed paragraphs are all the more apparent.

In his study, *A Hundred Years of Music*,[1] Gerald Abraham has enlarged on the inorganic nature of much Russian music by Tchaikovsky and the Five. 'The Russian,' he says, 'thinks most naturally in episodes and produces his general effects by the accumulation of episodes.' He even goes so far as to add that with the exception of Borodin's symphonies and one or two other works, Russian symphonic music is in general 'patchy and sectional – with the sections badly joined', and cites both Tchaikovsky's music and writings in support: 'All my life I have been much troubled by my inability to grasp and manipulate form in music. I fought hard against this defect and can say with pride that I have achieved some progress, but I shall end my days without having ever written anything that is perfect in form. What I write has always a mountain of padding: an experienced eye can detect the thread in the seams and I can do nothing about it.' Indeed in the case of the First Symphony the seams are visible to the most inexperienced eye yet such is the freshness and generosity of the invention that structural clumsiness seems of small account. Tchaikovsky was, of course, conservatoire-trained while the Five (Balakirev, Borodin, César Cui, Mussorgsky and Rimsky-Korsakov) were all *autodidakt*. If he later blushed for the formal blemishes that afflict the First Symphony he rightly retained an affection for it. It has a naturalness of speech and a spontaneity of feeling that shine through its inadequacies. Looking at the folk melodies that are incorporated into this symphony and its successor, the 'Little Russian', serves to underline the sense of rhythmic uniformity and repetition that characterizes much Russian melodic thinking. Tchaikovsky was blessed with a lyrical gift second only to that of Schubert, seemingly inexhaustible in its riches, and immediately distinctive and characterful. But lyrical ideas are not the ideal stuff of symphonic development and tend to draw the attention of the listener to the beauty of the part rather than the strength of the whole.

The Second Symphony ('Little Russian') of 1872 represents a distinct advance on its youthful precursor. Its proportions are excellently judged, there is greater harmony between the part and the whole, the themes are well balanced in relation to one another and to the symphony as a whole, and the score is totally effective without ever moving outside carefully circumscribed emotional bounds. Much the same might be said of the Third Symphony of 1875 were it not for the fact that the ideas are not so strongly de-

[1] Abraham, *A Hundred Years of Music*, Duckworth 1938, p 148.

lineated and the quality of the thematic substance falls considerably below that of its neighbours without any corresponding gain in organic cohesion. This is not, of course, to deny that the inner movements are wholly delightful but the work is closer to a suite than any of its companions. Its title, the 'Polish', is an English phenomenon as is that of the 'Emperor' concerto, and derives from the *tempo di polacca* marking in the Finale; it was Sir Augustus Manns who fathered this particular nickname.

The year 1877, in which the Fourth Symphony was composed, was a period of appalling crisis in Tchaikovsky's life. It was at this time that he was poised on the threshold of his disastrous marriage which took place in July, and the story of his subsequent attempted suicide and nervous breakdown is well known. It was also the year in which his friendship with Nadezhda von Meck, surely one of the most extraordinary relationships in musical history, began to blossom. He wrote to her of the new symphony: 'Never before have any of my orchestral works cost me so much labour, but then never before have I felt such affection towards any of my compositions. ... Perhaps I am mistaken, but it seems to me that this symphony is an exceptional piece. ... I'm convinced that with regard to its technique and form it represents a step forward in my development which has been proceeding extremely slowly.' Certainly the first movement must be so regarded, and both in terms of organic cohesion and the integration of dramatic contrast the movement must rank among his very finest symphonic achievements. Nowhere in any previous Russian symphony have the contrasts between the leading thematic protagonists been stronger and nowhere have the tonal contrasts been bolder and more subtle; no previous symphony possesses so rich a profusion of ideas. The famous motto theme which Tchaikovsky described as representing 'Fate, the inevitable power that hampers our search for happiness, the power that hangs forever over our heads like some Damoclean sword and cannot be resisted' serves to define the formal demarcations of the movement. It heralds both the development and the restatement. Hans Keller has brilliantly outlined its mastery[1] and the movement surely represents Tchaikovsky's most successful attempt at marrying balletic and symphonic elements, and in the first subject, the most sophisticated integration of the waltz into a sonata context. Neither of the middle movements, though they are less complex structurally and are ternary in lay-out, falls short of the first in ambition. The

[1] *The Symphony* (ed. Robert Simpson), Penguin Books p 345.

Scherzo in terms of contrast of colour and texture, *pizzicato* strings on the one hand and marvellously scored trio on the wind on the other, could hardly be surpassed in brilliance. Generally speaking, as he told Balakirev, Tchaikovsky felt infinitely freer in the sphere of the pure symphony than he did in his programme music, and although he did supply Mme von Meck with a programme, the symphony is totally comprehensible without reference to it.

Much the same can be said of 'Manfred' which comes from the mid-1880s. In 1867 Berlioz had visited Russia and among the works he conducted was his 'Harold in Italy' Symphony, an event that fired the imagination of a number of Russian musicians. Rimsky-Korsakov's 'Antar' was the immediate outcome of this: the motto theme is identified with the hero throughout. It was Balakirev who persuaded Tchaikovsky to embark on this symphonic character-study just as he had in the case of 'Romeo and Juliet', and the result is undeniably one of the greatest programme symphonies of the 19th century. For if Tchaikovsky does not match the ingenuity of Liszt in handling thematic metamorphosis, his invention is vital and alive, the structure powerfully held together and save in the Finale, free of the contrivance that affects the Finale of the 'Polish' Symphony.

With the Fifth Symphony of 1888 we again find the motto, though as Keller puts it, 'march and motto are now rolled into one' and Tchaikovsky's 'symphonization' of the dance or even spiritualization of the dance reaches a perfection matched only by a comparable achievement in the symphonic march that comprises the third movement of the *Pathétique*. As in the slow movement of no. 4 where folk-melody and Tchaikovsky's own speech are inextricably interwoven, the Fifth shows an assimilation of folk material so complete that one barely suspects non-symphonic origins. The main theme of the first movement derives from a fragment of a Polish love-song. The movement itself is an ingenious and masterly sonata structure that can be absorbed in terms of pure music rather than the programme from which Tchaikovsky took his point of departure. Undoubtedly the emotional core of the symphony is its slow movement. It is said that he scribbled over the famous horn melody, the words '*O, que je t'aime! O, mon amie*', but even if he did not the music leaves little doubt of its character, for it speaks with the authenticity of the heart.

The Waltz is one of Tchaikovsky's most perfect and polished symphonic movements: its idea emanates from Florence where Tchaikovsky heard it sung by a street-singer, using the melody in its pristine form in his song 'Pimpinella', op. 38, no. 6. Its spiritual ancestry can also be traced back to the waltz movement, also in A major incidentally, in Berlioz's *Symphonie fantastique*.

Although the Soviet musicologist Semyon Bogatyryev has reconstructed and scored the Symphony in E flat on which Tchaikovsky was engaged in 1892, the first movement of which became the one-movement piano concerto no. 3, the *Pathétique* remains Tchaikovsky's last symphonic testament and in many ways his greatest and most deeply characteristic utterance. The dramatic intensity of the *Symphonie pathétique* exceeds that of any of the earlier symphonies, none of which can be accused of wanting in dramatic flair. Apart from their treatment, the ideas in themselves are so abundant, characterful and varied that this impression is heightened. As Tovey put it, nowhere else has Tchaikovsky 'concentrated so great a variety of music within so effective a scheme'. One might add that the very extremes of dynamics reinforce the dramatic effect: at the end of the famous second group just before the explosive *fortissimo* outburst that begins the development, Tchaikovsky scales down the clarinet to *pppppp*! It would be difficult to find more highly characterized melodic ideas than in the first movement: the first group, derived from the introduction, is capable of enormous impetus and dramatic power while the second, one of Tchaikovsky's (and music's) most famous melodies, has an extraordinary human tenderness and however familiar it may be, never fails to astonish by the sheer quality of its lyrical invention and warmth of feeling. Certainly the development section is the most eventful and powerfully-wrought of any Tchaikovsky sonata movement and its introduction of a quotation from the Orthodox funeral service (*With the Saints*) at bar 201 serves as a reminder of another source of both musical and spiritual inspiration. It is true that the sheer beauty of many of the details leap out of the canvas thus distorting the impression as a whole, in a way that they do not in, say, a symphony by Beethoven or Brahms.

Of course, the formal outlay of the symphony is in itself highly original, a totally legitimate and brilliantly effective solution to the artistic problems posed by the Finale. Mahler in his Third and Ninth Symphonies was to profit by this example. The second movement is by comparison on an even emotional keel but the excitement and brilliance of the march which follows, totally exhilarating though it is at the time, assumes a slightly hollow ring seen with the benefit of hindsight. Whether one takes the view that biographical considerations are of slender moment or the opposite (John Warrack speaks of him acknowledging 'the truth of his condition, the tragedy of a passionate and tender nature doomed to frustration and guilt') the fact remains that the symphony is both a great work of art and a human document of rare truth and power.

If Tchaikovsky's symphonic quest was a long but triumphant quest embracing more than a quarter of a century, his was not the only symphonic voice in Russia even if it is the strongest both in terms of human and musical qualities. Although the composers of The Five were more strongly drawn to programmatic music and to opera, three of them made an important contribution to the Russian symphonic scene. It is an ironic thought that the composition of Balakirev's First Symphony encompasses the whole of Tchaikovsky's symphonic career. It was begun in 1864, immediately after his second Overture on Russian Themes and put aside two years later, before Tchaikovsky's 'Winter Reveries', and not taken up again until the 1890s. Balakirev finished it in 1897, four years after the *Symphonie pathétique*. It retains a remarkable consistency of style considering its extraordinarily protracted genesis. As is the case in Borodin's First Symphony in E flat, the very opening is pregnant with material that seems of little importance in itself but which proves rich enough to fertilize the whole movement. Indeed this monothematic movement shows Balakirev as a symphonic thinker of no mean calibre and it is all the more to be regretted that the remaining movements are not as closely argued or as well proportioned. The Scherzo, not originally intended for this particular symphony, is delightful enough but the quasi-oriental, languorous slow movement which calls to mind Borodin seems by comparison wanting in concentration. The D flat major melody is a beautiful one but it sustains too lengthy an edifice while the Finale, attractive as it undoubtedly is, lacks musical density and in no way matches the organic cohesion of the first. Balakirev's monothematicism in the first movement differs from that, say, of Schumann in the first movements of his Fourth Symphony and the piano concerto, for Balakirev takes this a stage further. He states all the material in his introduction turning the *allegro* section into a kind of commentary on it.

Much the same principle can also be seen at work in the First Symphony of Borodin (1862–67). Both the First Symphony and the Third owe their present form to Rimsky-Korsakov and Glazunov whose unceasing labours in revising and rescoring other Russian music are matched only by Balakirev's eagerness in planning it. For even if he had not been active as a composer, Balakirev played an invaluable role in encouraging and inspiring Tchaikovsky and his colleagues among The Five. Perhaps Borodin's Second (1869–76) is the most compact and organically conceived Russian symphony of the period though this is not to say that it is the greatest. The ideas are strongly characterized but the development serves to underline the factors that bind the two together and finds Borodin fashioning the second theme into the mould of the first. The opening idea is strongly pregnant, the very stuff of which powerful symphonic argument is made. It is said that it has programmatic origins, inspired by the image of a gathering of 11th-century warriors; yet whatever impulse generated it, the result could hardly be more strikingly symphonic, outstanding in its concentration and organic cohesion.

The delightful Third Symphony in A minor survives in a two-movement fragment thanks to the expertise and musicianship of Glazunov. Its colours are more muted and its palette more refined than that of no. 1, but if less dramatic, it is a beautifully paced and proportioned work as far as it goes. The three symphonies of Rimsky-Korsakov, on the other hand, are of relatively minor account: the First, a student work written in the 1860s but revised twenty years later, used Schumann, Glinka and Balakirev as models, but while the Third in C major (1872) has undoubted attractions, only the Second, the programmatic 'Antar' Symphony has retained a hold on the repertory. Like so much of Rimsky-Korsakov, it substitutes repetition, sequence, colour and atmosphere for genuine musical argument. Though ideal ingredients in operatic or ballet music, colour and two- or four-bar phrase structures are not symphonic substance.

Post-nationalist composers

A flourishing school of symphonic composers developed in the wake of the Russian nationalists. Among those born in the 1860s Kalinnikov was too short-lived to develop his precocious symphonic instinct and strong melodic gifts. The seams in his two symphonies are all too visible and their sectional inspiration readily discerned. Yet there are fine passages, such as the marvellously fresh theme which is the second group of the first movement of the Symphony no. 1 in G minor, written in 1895. Kalinnikov reflected the Slavonic romanticism of Tchaikovsky and above all Borodin though it is clear that he was not unaware of the growing influence of Wagner and there are times when one senses overtones of a kind of post-Borodinesque impressionism. His career was cut short in his mid-thirties while Glazunov, born in the previous year, long outlived the fires of his youthful muse.

Glazunov's creative precocity can be seen in the little-played but remarkably vital early symphonies. The First in E flat, written when he was a boy of sixteen, is an astonishing achievement, less highly personal than Shostakovich's First no doubt, but fashioned with impeccable technique and wholly spontaneous in feeling. To judge from some of his later works, Glazunov's very facility proved his undoing; his personality never really deepened and the freshness of his youthful invention gave way to an exhausted pale academicism. But at times one is aware of a deeper vein of feeling, albeit one that never really surfaces but only allows us the briefest glimpse. For example, the cor anglais theme (a few bars before fig. C) in the slow movement of the remarkably accomplished Symphony no. 2 in F sharp minor, written when he was barely twenty-one, is as inspired a passage as any in the Russian music of the period and shot through with a poetic feeling which was slowly stifled in later years. His scherzos are unfailingly inventive and in nearly all the symphonies up to and including no. 6 in C minor, they are the best movements. In the Fifth Symphony in B flat, the abundance of invention, the natural outpouring of melodic ideas is wholly captivating, almost Schubertian in its fecundity. And yet his symphonic odyssey embraces no spiritual progress: his musical vocabulary remains static and though this in itself is of small account, for one can still say deeper things with the same means, the musical ideas seem less felt, less fresh and less deeply experienced. The Symphony no. 8 in E flat and the one movement fragment that survives of a Ninth are tired and disspirited.

The generation born during the 1870s produced two outstanding figures, both masters of keyboard writing as well as master-pianists, Scriabin and Rachmaninov. Scriabin's musical language was at first rooted in Chopin of whom he was a fine interpreter, and like the Polish master he possessed a fastidious harmonic palette. In his half-dozen orchestral works he created a world very much his own, and canvases as highly coloured and exotically textured as *Le poème de l'extase* and 'Prometheus', though they hardly justify their claim to symphonic status, are highly effective displays of *art nouveau* sensibility. Of the two composers, Scriabin was undoubtedly the more outward-looking: Strauss and Debussy enriched his palette just as he in his turn was to influence composers as far removed as Glière, Szymanowski and Messiaen. The early symphonies tend to sprawl and their hot-house exoticism is not to all tastes, though it is in their richness of texture rather than their structure that their main appeal and strength lies. Scriabin's 'mystic chord' (C, F sharp, B flat, E, A, and D) did not open up a new path for others but it lent his own world a distinct and personal colouring.

Rachmaninov, a great keyboard composer as well as a pianist of genius, produced only a small orchestral output, apart from the piano concertos, early orchestral pieces like *The Rock* and the *Capriccio on Gypsy Themes, The Isle of the Dead*, the three symphonies and the *Symphonic Dances* completes the roll-call. Rachmaninov's language does not extend the traditional harmonic vocabulary or even stretch it in any way, yet his art offers greater depth than does that of the 'conservative' Glazunov or the 'radical' Scriabin. The hostile reception of his First Symphony (1897), whose first perform-ance was conducted by Glazunov, resulted in its withdrawal and the composer's nervous collapse. Yet the work came to light in a set of orchestral parts in the 1940s and possesses a symphonic breadth much greater than that of either Glazunov or Scriabin. Its thought processes have genuine continuity and its ideas are both pregnant and well-matched. By the side of the sumptuous lyricism of its successors, its gestures seem restrained and its profile almost austere; it has a highly imaginative slow movement and the work as a whole springs from a natural and deeply-felt response to experience. In the past decades critical opinion has been against Rachmaninov, mistrusting perhaps the ease and generosity of his melodic gift and suspecting that his art, which uses conventional modes of utterance, is perforce second-hand. But his music has something of the same regret at the passing of happiness and the transience of human experience that one finds in Elgar, and relates possibly in much the same way to pre-war St Petersburg as does Elgar to Edwardian England. The Second Symphony in E minor (1907) is more overtly romantic than its predecessor: its splendid tunes and impassioned eloquence have won it belated but well-deserved popularity. Like *The Isle of the Dead* (1909) it has the 'breath' of the symphonist. The Third Symphony in A minor (1936) breathes air so totally at variance with the musical climate of its day that, like no. 1, it met a blank critical response. It prompted Richard Capell's perceptive remark, 'A palace without royalty. Rachmaninov still gives parties on the grand old scale but no guests turn up.' One is tempted to add that the loss was theirs, for even if the second group of the first movement is tired and wanting in spiritual vitality, the ideas of the first group as well as the rest of the work do not show any falling off in quality. It is perhaps the prominence the E major tune enjoys as well as its obviously second-hand quality that encouraged hasty judgments about this colourful work. Much of it may be sectional in structure, but what sections!

With Glière and Miaskovsky we come to the first composers who were to play a part in the musical life of post-revolutionary Russia, the latter as the most influential teacher of his generation as well as the most prolific symphonist. The first two of Glière's symphonies enjoy a certain academic rectitude (Glière was a pupil of Taneyev) and in neither is the thematic material distinctively personal. Like Glazunov, Glière was at his best in the Scherzo and both those of no. 2 in C minor (1907) and the better-known no. 3 in B minor ('Ilya Mourametz') (1911) are compact and inventive. The Third is a vast tapestry, almost eighty minutes in duration, that strikes one as both inflated and discursive though it evinces a robust, instinctive imagination. Its style is close to the fantasy world of Rimsky-Korsakov with its vividly coloured chromatic harmonies, while its slow movement shows Gallic sympathies (though born in Kiev, he was of Belgian descent) and a strong affinity with Scriabin. Throughout the work it is atmosphere and colour that take precedence over symphonic argument but many of the musical ideas are strong enough to resolve the listener's doubts, at least in the last two movements. It is one of the last in the long line of 19th-century programme symphonies.

Few 20th-century composers sound more conservative in idiom than Miaskovsky and were his Symphony no. 27, completed not long before his death in 1950, put alongside 'Ilya Mourametz', few would guess their relative provenance. Indeed Miaskovsky's pre-revolutionary symphonies show a bolder profile. The Third, for example, a two-movement work, dating from 1914 when he was in his early thirties, has a much higher norm of dissonance. Many of his later symphonies make predictable gestures and explore much the same areas of feeling, and such is his facility that he tends at times to fall back on stock-in-trade rhetoric (as, for example, in the Symphony no. 16). But he has the genuine sweep of the symphonist: the slow movement of no. 3 has atmosphere and individuality and the peroration has an imposing dignity and breadth. For a time Mahler fascinated him: the Sixth Symphony is Mahlerian in proportions and its Scherzo has enormous vitality and freshness as well as a trio whose gentle nostalgia is both distinctive and haunting. In his essay on the composer, Stanley Dale Krebs spoke of him as 'a manipulator of form' rather than a master of it and called his polyphony 'laboured'.[1] He is certainly not an artist who can be described as a naturally organic musical thinker any more than he is an innovator. He seeks no new paths and seems to have been born out of his time. But for all the tiredness of idiom, his finest work confounds his critics. The Symphony no. 15 in D minor is strongly held together and his best-known work, the one-movement Symphony no. 21 in F sharp minor (1940) is well proportioned, dignified and in its slow opening section genuinely eloquent. The slow middle section of its successor, no. 22 in B minor, contains some noble polyphony; Miaskovsky is really at his best in slow movements, musing gently on past happiness and its transience. However, judged in a wider perspective Miaskovsky's stature is not in dispute. Along with Prokofiev he was evacuated in 1942 to the Caucasus and his Symphony no. 23 in A minor uses the same folk material as does Prokofiev in his second string quartet; the comparison leaves no doubt as to the enormously greater resource and imagination that Prokofiev commanded.

The impact of the 1917 revolution on music in Russia is well known and the two greatest symphonists to emerge in the Soviet Union, Prokofiev and Shostakovich, afford an illustration of the tensions – by no means all uncreative – that it produced. Few 20th-century composers can rival the sheer fertility of melodic invention that Prokofiev commanded. Even if his melodic ideas tend to fall into easily recognizable patterns with predictably astringent harmonic spicing and unpredictable modulatory sleights of hand, they nearly always have a profile that is distinctive, memorable – infectiously so at times – and full of character. The shape of his ideas does not appear to be indivisibly linked with any particular instrumental timbre: he does not, one suspects, think directly in terms of orchestral sonority as did some of the greatest masters of the orchestra, say, Berlioz or Sibelius. We know, of course, that he kept a notebook in which he jotted down musical ideas as and when they occurred to him and that even his orchestral works were first written out in piano score, a fact that worried him a good deal until he learned that no less an orchestrator than Ravel did the same. One would not suspect

[1] Krebs, *Soviet Composers and the development of Soviet Music*, Allen & Unwin, 1970, p 117.

that much of his composition was keyboard-derived, listening to works like the *Scythian Suite* for the first violin concerto, or the closing bars of the slow movement of the Fifth Symphony, where his musical ideas are transformed into the most magical web of orchestral sonorities.

For a long time the three symphonies Prokofiev wrote during the inter-war years suffered more or less total neglect and Prokofiev's representation in the repertoire was confined to the Fifth (1944), the Sixth (1947) – though to a lesser extent – and the perennially fresh *Classical Symphony* (1917). The latter may have been modelled on Haydn and is perfectly proportioned but its high spirits recall equally well the dance-suite origins of the symphony. Its astonishing mastery of irony and its striking originality should not be taken for granted for it is full of harmonic sleights of hand and tremendous melodic zest. The Second Symphony (1924) consciously strove to compete with the most advanced music of its time. It was written after his departure from the Soviet Union when he had settled in Paris. Prokofiev himself spoke of it as 'a work made of iron and steel' and nowhere, not even in the 'Scythian' Suite, does he surpass its first movement in the sheer volume, complexity and density of the orchestral texture. But if the symphony with its flirtation with the *style mécanique* baffled the Parisian public, Prokofiev's instinct in the last years of his life to salvage the score and refashion it was surely right, for it contains some richly imaginative music. Unfortunately Prokofiev's afterthoughts were by no means always improvements: his revisions of the Fourth Symphony and the cello concerto, the latter becoming the *Sinfonia Concertante* for cello and orchestra, op. 125, tend to pad and inflate.

The Twenties saw a good deal of experimentation in the Soviet Union. Mosolov's 'Symphony of Machines' with its onomatopoeic evocation of a steel foundry enjoyed a certain vogue while Roslavetz made his way along atonal paths. Prokofiev's modernity was tempered to Western fashion and the opening of the Second Symphony with its angular leaps, its massive sonority and the dance-like twists and turns of the melodic line suggests a desire to *épater* Diaghilev. The structure of the symphony is unusual: it is modelled on Beethoven's C minor sonata, op. 111, and is thus in two movements, the second being a set of variations which show Prokofiev at his most resourceful and imaginative. Both the Third Symphony (1928) and its successor, no. 4 in C (1930) derive from stage works, the former from his opera *The Angel of Fire* and the latter from his ballet *The*

Prodigal Son. Prokofiev was always reluctant to waste good ideas and when it became obvious that a production of the opera would not materialize, he determined to rescue some of the material by using it in his new symphony. (Ironically enough, the symphony did not really come into its own until the opera had also entered the repertoire in the 1950s.) Although it began as a symphonic suite and then shaped itself into a four-movement symphony, Prokofiev was at some pains to stress that it was a self-contained work. Yet as is so often the case in Russian music, the programmatic and the symphonic cannot wholly be disentangled and one's understanding of the symphony is undoubtedly deepened by a knowledge of its operatic frame of reference. The symphony has some superbly imaginative music and its second movement in particular has great mystery and magic. Yet as a whole its procedures are closer to the symphonic suite than to the pure symphony and much the same criticism could be levelled at the Fourth.

It is perhaps Prokofiev's very reluctance to waste any ideas that may result in his marrying thematic material that bears little or no organic relationship. Unlike Shostakovich, Prokofiev had little feeling that an idea was essentially symphonic or operatic or pianistic (an exception, perhaps, is the material used in the two violin concertos). One of his well-known piano pieces, the third of the Etudes op. 52 sounds convincingly pianistic: yet it originally appeared in *The Prodigal Son*. Indeed, like many great Russian composers he is more often than not conditioned by balletic habits of mind. This applies far more to Stravinsky, whose interest in the traditional classical forms, as well as his need to think in those terms, is much less.

In matters of form Prokofiev is no iconoclast, and the appearance of being an *enfant terrible* which he presented to some of the more sheltered academics of pre-First World War Russia, among them Glazunov, was deceptive. His modernism, as it then seemed, was in fact confined to a highly-spiced harmonic flavouring and an exotic and extensive vocabulary of orchestral devices. It was the presentation of the material rather than the material itself that posed the problems.

The fourteen years that separate the Fourth and Fifth Symphonies had seen Prokofiev's return to the Soviet Union and they had also seen the liberal artistic policies of the New Economic Plan overtaken by an altogether harsher artistic climate. There has been a good deal of speculation about the effect of Soviet aesthetic thinking on Prokofiev's artistic development. However, the greater simplification in language that distinguishes Prokofiev's music after the Fourth Symphony and which is already in evidence in that work is as natural a development in itself as is that of Bartók in his third piano concerto and the Concerto for Orchestra, and its seeds are clearly discernible before his return. Balletic elements survive in the Fifth Symphony (1944) – the Scherzo is the most obvious instance – but in general terms the thematic substance of the symphony has far greater organic cohesion than any of its predecessors. Prokofiev is rarely less than fluent, but here the outpouring of ideas is matched by a breadth of canvas that encourages lengthier paragraphs. There is greater harmony between means and ends, and a greater rein kept on the sheer profusion of melodic ideas. Indeed the thematic substance is far more closely inter-related here than in the earlier symphonies, which saw the struggle between his richly stocked musical imagination and his sense of symphonic scale resolved in favour of the former. The Sixth (1945–7) also imposes a kind of organic cohesion, but the music itself goes far deeper than any of the others and it is possibly his very finest work in any genre. Its greater emotional range is reflected in its greater complexity. No doubt the suffering of the war years echoes in its pages just as it had in the wartime symphonies of Shostakovich. The astringent and anguished outburst that opens the second movement is at a level of intensity that one rarely encounters elsewhere in his work. Certainly it is nowhere matched in its lightweight successor, the Seventh (1952), composed during the period immediately following the notorious Congress of Soviet Composers presided over by Zhdanov in 1948.

It is true that by the side of Shostakovich, Prokofiev seems reluctant to tackle the deepest issues. His world seems more circumscribed and moves within well-defined emotional boundaries. Yet at the same time Prokofiev's musical equipment, his instinctive and natural melodic gift and his astonishingly assured craftsmanship prevent the worst lapses that disfigure some of Shostakovich's finales. There is a level of realization in Prokofiev, a more thorough exploration of the world that he inhabits than is perhaps the case with the more profound and more uneven Shostakovich. A realized work of art is satisfying because it never excites the listener's expectations beyond its capacity to fulfil them. Only rarely does a composer arise who touches on all dimensions of human experience and it is the achievement of composers of the order of, say, Stravinsky or Ravel that they render seemingly irrelevant such dimensions of experience on which their art does not impinge, so complete is their exploration of their chosen world. In his finest works Prokofiev belongs to this number in a way that Shostakovich does not.

Shostakovich wrote his First Symphony as a youth of nineteen and it immediately established him as the white hope of Soviet music. Unlike Glière, Prokofiev or Miaskovsky, his roots were wholly in the new Russia: he was only eleven at the time of the revolution. No other major figure has shown so consistent and sustained an interest in the symphony as such or has treated it with such freedom. Some of the symphonies (1, 6, 10, 15) are purely abstract and instrumental; others such as the 'Leningrad' (7) or the Eleventh, commemorating the abortive 1905 uprising, are programmatic in content, while some of the later symphonies encroach on oratorio (no. 13) or, in the case of its successor, no. 14, the song-cycle-cum-symphony in the manner of Mahler's *Das Lied von der Erde*. His symphonic corpus spans an even longer period (1925–71) than that of Haydn (1760–95).

In the case of the First Symphony (1925), surely the most remarkable instance of musical precocity in the present century, it is the classical ideal that serves as a model. The symphony is tautly held together, its proportions carefully calculated and its musicianship shows extraordinary accomplishment even allowing for tutorial guidance from Maximilian Steinberg. But most impressive of all is the slow movement which evinces an harmonic awareness and an expressive poignancy of rare maturity. It suggests a dimension that was never to be so fully developed in Prokofiev: a capacity for suffering that betokens a great artist. The triumph of the First Symphony in 1926 was immediate and its very success served to overshadow the achievement of its successors. Neither no. 2 ('Dedication to October') (1927) nor no. 3 ('The First of May') is its equal but they are both remarkable for a composer just in his early twenties. Both are exploratory though in quite different ways: no. 2 has the higher norm of dissonance as well as an original formal lay-out while its successor attempts to keep abreast of modern developments and to come to terms with the aesthetic ideals of the new régime, albeit without unqualified success. Prokofiev, Hindemith, Berg and Stravinsky were all composers with whose thinking Shostakovich was familiar.

It is the Fourth Symphony, still the work of a young man in his twenties, that makes a big leap forward. It takes no special insight to see that the work springs from a profound emotional upheaval and that it is a measure of his maturity that he is able to transmute this experience, to lay bare an inner experience and turn it to artistic advantage. Written at the time of the controversy surrounding the opera, *Lady Macbeth of the Mtsensk District*, the work was withdrawn by Shostakovich when it was in rehearsal late in 1936 and it was not publicly performed until the 1960s. In terms of breadth of canvas the Fourth Symphony is longer than its two predecessors put together and it is not only in terms of its dimensions that it reflects the Mahlerian inheritance. It is prodigal in ideas, and has extraordinary richness of detail, intensity of vision and complexity of feeling; indeed it reflects a higher emotional temperature than any of his other music of this period. The opening, with its combative rhythms, assertive *ostinati* and strident scoring, sets the tone of the whole movement. Comparison of the first movement with the corresponding movement of the Fifth (1937) shows how Shostakovich was to prune detail and discipline his imagination, resisting the impulse to indulge his fantasy in the interest of a greater symphonic coherence. Writing in 1938 one critic argued that without the 'sharp, just, wise, criticism' of *Pravda*, such a work as the Fifth Symphony could never have come into being. Certainly the Fourth Symphony is a harrowing personal document: it is an experience vividly communicated in white heat whereas the Fifth is an experience recollected in tranquillity. The former is more immediately gripping and has the greater capacity to engage the listener's compassion while the latter with its greater harmony between means and ends and greater simplicity of utterance offers the more lasting satisfaction. The Fifth is more classical in feeling and more disciplined, and though the Fourth remains an essential (and fascinating) link in our understanding of Shostakovich, its successor is the more fully realized work of art; the Mahlerian elements are far more thoroughly assimilated. The Fifth brought us the finest slow movement Shostakovich had penned up to this point. Its very simplicity of means enables it to explore a world of feeling ranging from a serene detachment to a direct outpouring of grief. Perhaps it is its very directness of utterance that has served to secure this symphony its widespread popularity.

The Sixth eschews unnecessary complexity but its world is darker and more desolate. Its lay-out is unusual: a long opening slow movement followed by two short quick movements. In the first there are features of the sonata style and it is tempting to think of it as a precursor of the great symphonic *adagios* of nos. 8 and 10, though it is less dynamic in movement than they and more ruminative than dramatic. The first movement of no. 8 even at its most brooding and intense never appears as static as does no. 6, yet closer examination reveals strong motivic integration. Indeed we rarely get far from the thematic substance outlined in the opening paragraphs and the music broods intently on these ideas distilling an atmosphere of the utmost concentration and power. Shostakovich is really at his most deeply characteristic in this movement and in its spiritual relatives in 8 and 10. The darker and more despondent the mood, the more readily he seems to respond to its challenge with music of searing eloquence. Whether the irony and high spirits of the Scherzo and Finale of the Sixth really provide sufficient ballast is a moot point. The wartime trilogy of the 'Leningrad' Symphony (1941), the Eighth (1943) and the lightweight, divertimento-like Ninth in E flat (1945) are no more complex in language. The Seventh is disfigured by the absence in the first movement of any pretence at real development (Shostakovich reiterates a theme depicting the relentless advance of the Nazi armies no less than twelve times) though its *adagio* movement has great seriousness and a genuine spirituality. The wartime symphonies exhibit another disfiguring feature of Shostakovich's symphonic style, the propensity towards meandering recitative over a thin harmonic texture or even the sketchiest of accompaniment. The Eighth is undoubtedly the most uncompromising and intensely-felt of the wartime symphonies and its graphic portrayal of the sufferings and brutality of war did not endear it to the régime. As in the case of no. 6, the long symphonic *adagio*, combining as it does features of the sonata-first-movement and the inward-looking intensity of a slow movement, is matched by two short fast movements, the second of which leads into a *passacaglia* and Finale. This five-movement lay-out seems to have held a strong fascination for Shostakovich at this time (viz. Symphony no. 9, the piano quintet, and the String Quartet no. 3) as indeed did the passacaglia (viz. the piano trio). The Eighth confronts one unremittingly with the appalling sufferings of war-torn humanity; indeed it does for the Russian winter war what Goya did for the Peninsular war more than a century before. Yet just as the Fourth Symphony has almost too close and painful a contact with experience, much the same must be said of the Eighth. In the Tenth the experience has undergone a more thoroughgoing process of symphonic distillation and its argument is every bit as compelling while being far more cogent. The Ninth is a delightfully effective *jeu d'esprit* whose sardonic humour and Haydnesque dimensions, not to mention its refined sense of irony, fluttered the Soviet dovecotes. Not even in 'The Age of Gold' or the concerto for piano, trumpet and strings is his sense of timing more perfect. Both this and the Eighth Symphony were singled out for attack in the notorious 1948 Congress of Soviet Composers presided over by Zhdanov.

With the so-called 'thaw' in the early 1950s after the death of Stalin, we come to a period of particular richness in Shostakovich's output: Symphony no. 10 (1953), the Violin Concerto no. 1 (1954), the fourth and fifth quartets and the Cello Concerto no. 1 (1959). These years enabled him to give rein to greater depth and imaginative vision as well as witnessing a greater mastery and control over his materials. The symphonic processes seem at perfect harmony with the material and the music grows organically right from the opening bars; no episodes are allowed to obtrude and attract the listener's attention away from the overall impact. It is this exercise of what I would like to call the true symphonic discipline that removes the Tenth Symphony from the private world to the universal, from the specific experiences of 1941–45 to the universal sufferings of war true at any age. The finale has always been a problem in Shostakovich, for the normal difficulties it poses have been compounded by an ideological injunction to optimism. The mindless bustle of the finales of Kabalevsky's Second and Fourth Symphonies or Khrennikov's epigonic First, are obvious instances. The Finale of the Tenth is the first Shostakovich movement of its kind to achieve true depth. It meets the traditional classical requirements, its positive outlook is not unmindful of the shadows of reality, and it at no stage compromises the integrity of the symphony as a whole.

The Eleventh Symphony (1956) operates at an altogether lower temperature and at a lower musical density. It is a vast and often impressive tapestry into which material of striking imagination has been woven but it lacks the cohesion and concentration of the Tenth: a detail or an atmosphere register in the memory but not a sense of symphonic fulfilment. During the 1960s Shostakovich's interest appeared to be moving away from the symphony as such to the string quartet. There are no fewer than six quartets (7–12) from this decade and there is a relative hiatus in his symphonic output. The Twelfth Symphony (1961) shows Shostakovich in his least thoughtful vein; the bombast and banality that afflicts the Finale of the Eleventh and that disfigures pages of the two large-scale war symphonies are strongly in evidence and only the 'Razliv' movement and the opening pages seem characteristic of his art. With the

Tenth he put behind him the large-scale symphonic *adagio* that had become the vehicle of his most personal utterance and in its two successors cast himself in the role of composer-laureate of the Soviet regime: the Twelfth Symphony celebrates the 1917 revolution and the Thirteenth (1962), a setting of poems by Yevtushenko including *Babi Yar*, plays its conscience. The Thirteenth is powerful in terms of atmosphere and its rich fund of human compassion but it is closer to oratorio or cantata than to the symphony with its greater density of musical incident and motivic integration.

With the Fourteenth Symphony (1969) we enter an altogether different world, that of the song-cycle symphony. Mahler and Britten are the obvious models: indeed the latter is the dedicatee. Britten's 'Spring' Symphony and 'Nocturne' explore specific themes, and Shostakovich likewise ruminates on one subject: Death. The work has enormous variety and for all its economy (only strings and percussion are employed) remarkable resource in its handling of sonorities. Its vision is as intensely personal as any of the quartets from the 1960s (nos. 10 and 12) and, like that of the first movement of the Tenth Symphony, free from the superfluous gesture. For all its character of song cycle, the work has an organic cohesion and grandeur of conception that justifies the symphonic label. The very familiarity of Shostakovich's idiom is misleading: a few signposts in the landscape deceive one into thinking that one is traversing the same landscape as before. As Peter Heyworth put it, 'all its moods and constituent elements are in one form or another present in earlier works', but are here placed in a new context, and likewise, the Fifteenth Symphony (1971) has familiar landmarks but many disturbing resonances, areas of feeling on which he has not touched before.

Shostakovich has loomed so large on the international scene that he has overshadowed any other Soviet composer. It is almost as if the whole of western Europe and Scandinavia with its rich and diverse musical life were to be represented exclusively by Benjamin Britten. Admittedly Shostakovich's musical personality is so strong that it could be no more disregarded than was Sibelius by the generation immediately following him. His voice certainly eclipsed those of Shebalin, Kabalevsky and Khachaturyan, none of them composers of such substance. His influence is deeply felt in the work of his pupil Georgii Sviridov and in the eleven symphonies of Moïshe Vainberg (b. 1919). The latter's violin concerto (1959) is deeply indebted to Shostakovich's (Violin Concerto no. 1) and his Fourth

Symphony (1961) reflects a common debt to Mahler, Hindemith and other neo-classical models as well as a highly developed sense of craftsmanship and organic continuity. His Sixth Symphony is for boys' voices and orchestra, the Seventh includes a prominent part for harpsichord while the Tenth in A minor, a brilliantly inventive score for strings alone, shows him a composer of considerable range with a developing and searching mind far from closed to contemporary trends, serious in intent and individual in outlook. Among other talents Rhodion Shchedrin (b. 1932) is undoubtedly highly facile and his First Symphony (1958) shows him flexing genuinely symphonic muscle and thinking in broad paragraphs. As befits a pupil of Shaporin, his musical language is traditional (one even thinks of Rachmaninov) but his scoring is unfailingly inventive and full of resource. Judged by the standards of a Shostakovich he has more skill than substance but he is an expert of virtuoso instrumentation. Kara Karayev whose Third Symphony (1962) employs a tone-row, albeit underlining its tonal implications in much the same way as did Berg in his violin concerto, and Boris Tishchenko (b. 1939) are both figures who show a responsiveness to musical developments in Europe, and to their number must be added Alfred Shnitke and Andrei Volkonsky.

11 SCANDINAVIA

The Scandinavian symphony is a 19th-century phenomenon. It is true that in Johan Helmich Roman (1694–1758) Sweden produced a composer who spoke the *lingua franca* of his day with distinctive accents; she also gave sanctuary to Joseph Martin Kraus (1756–92) whose intense and expertly-wrought symphonies were much admired by Haydn. Yet as far as the larger forms were concerned, the Scandinavian countries remained indebted to French, German and Italian models, and only in the climate of a greater national self-consciousness engendered in the first half of the 19th century, do major figures of interest begin to emerge. In Denmark Niels Gade (1817–90) remained a product of the Leipzig school and his musical language was never fully liberated from the shades of Mendelssohn even if the finest of the eight symphonies he composed retain an engaging vitality. Gade became a leading figure in the Danish musical establishment and had Franz Berwald (1796–1868) achieved similar standing in his native Sweden, international recognition of his art might not have been so slow in coming. His neglect during his lifetime was due to two factors: his musical cast of mind was far too original for the highly conservative climate of 19th-century Stockholm and secondly, he absented himself from the Swedish musical scene at crucial moments of his career. He spent many vital years on non-musical projects, running an enterprising and successful orthopaedic institute in Berlin, and later acting as manager of a glass works and a saw-mill in northern Sweden. In this many-sidedness he is, of course, not unique – Borodin held a Chair of chemistry; but Berwald lacked the powerful advocacy that advanced the Russian master's cause, the interest and encouragement of his fellow-composers among The Five. On the contrary, he had to reckon with active hostility and was accorded academic status only in the last year of his life, and that in the teeth of much opposition. Small wonder, then, that of his four symphonies, only one, the *Sérieuse*, was heard during his lifetime, while the most original of them, the *Sinfonie Singulière* was not played until the present century – some sixty years after its composition. All four symphonies date from the 1840s and involved less of his creative energy than the numerous operatic projects by which he set such store. He entered the Stockholm Opera Orchestra as a boy of sixteen and remained there until his early thirties.

His early works baffled critics by the boldness of their modulations and show him responding to the influence of Beethoven, Hummel and Spohr as well as the operatic repertory. The four symphonies do not break new ground in terms of harmonic vocabulary but they immediately establish their own world: here is a voice of great freshness and individuality. The *Singulière*, by general consent the finest, is unlike anything else in the music of its time or indeed any other, and although its language is predominantly diatonic and free from complexity, the work has a refreshing vigour and imaginative vitality that steps well outside the comparatively pale atmosphere of the Scandinavian musical world of its day. Indeed one of the most striking features about Berwald is that his music not only offers resonances of the past but 'reminders' of composers yet to come. He is a keen formal innovator: in the *Singulière* he integrates the Scherzo into the body of the slow movement.[1] He had already done this in the Septet (1828), a practice which has few precedents though C. P. E. Bach adopted it in the C minor concerto (Wq 43, no. 4). In

[1] Most remarkable of all from a formal point of view is the String Quartet in E flat (1849) which carries this a stage further by enclosing the slow movement in which the Scherzo is embedded, in the body of the first movement, whose material thus opens and closes the whole work.

the *Sinfonie Sérieuse* (1842) he recalls the slow movement as a kind of link between Scherzo and Finale, while in the Finale of the Symphony no. 4 in E flat (1845) the first group is replaced at the outset of the restatement in the Finale by entirely new thematic material, there being no subsequent reference to the theme.

Although the formal innovations of Berlioz, Chopin and other contemporaries often centre on this point, the first group being telescoped or the order of the two groups reversed, this particular induction of new and totally fresh material has few if any precedents. Berwald's musical facility and his pure musicianship are not of the same order as those of Mendelssohn or Schumann although his symphonic achievement does not fall far short of theirs. In terms of sheer organic thinking, the first movement of the *Singulière* operates at a level of the first mastery. In the four symphonies Berwald has effectively created a distinctive sound world and like his great contemporary, Mendelssohn, his world moves within a carefully circumscribed emotional orbit whose bounds are never traversed. The epic, the heroic and the dramatic play little or no part in his symphonic make-up but the clarity of his thinking and the warmth of such music as the slow movement of the E flat Symphony and the poetry of the same movement in the *Singulière* ensure him a special place in the development of the symphony post Beethoven.

Berwald's influence in Sweden remained minimal. It can be discerned in the somewhat Schumannesque symphonies of Ludwig Norman (1831–85) and registered in the Symphony in D minor of Oskar Byström (1821–1909). However, it is not a serious force and did not cross the borders of the other Scandinavian countries. In Norway, Grieg's art found its symphonic counterpart in the two symphonies of Johan Severin Svendsen (1840–1911), both of which evince genuine creative vitality and distinct personality. Svendsen's sense of form was a good deal more highly developed than Grieg's as far as extended works are concerned, and even the youthful First Symphony, written when he was twenty-five, shows considerable assurance in its handling of ideas, for all the clearly visible seams and joins in the structure. As is the case with its successor, no. 2 in B flat, Svendsen is at his best in the Scherzo, a fresh and inventive piece with some highly individual writing for the woodwind. He was a skilful orchestrator and a fine conductor; indeed his vocation for the latter proved too strong and deflected him from creative work. He settled in Denmark and conducted the Royal Orchestra in which Carl Nielsen served as a violinist.

The two greatest Scandinavian symphonists were both born in 1865 and their symphonic output embraces the same period: Nielsen's First and Sibelius's *Kullervo* come from 1892, Nielsen's Sixth (*Sinfonia semplice*) dates from 1925, Sibelius's Seventh appeared the preceding year. Nielsen's roots are both Danish and at the same time European: his first two symphonies speak a dialect whose vocabulary and syntax rest on classical foundations and breathe much the same air as Brahms, Dvořák and Svendsen. The musical language is fundamentally diatonic and strongly rooted in tradition. If the First Symphony in G minor with its prodigality of invention and generosity of feeling is a work in which the joins and seams clearly show, it is at the same time so fresh in its impact and direct in utterance that its appeal remains undiminished. It begins in G minor and ends in C major, a bold adventure in mixed tonalities, and one which showed Nielsen's early awareness of key tension in the symphonic context. The Second Symphony (1902) is subtitled 'The Four Temperaments' and shows a much greater concentration and organic cohesion. True, the Brahmsian model is still firmly in sight, much in the same way that Sibelius's Second Symphony of the same year, for all its profound originality, still echoes some of the Tchaikovskian resonances of its predecessor. But its mastery is second to none: it too exhibits the progressive tonality of its predecessor, moving from the B minor of the choleric temperament to the A major of the sanguine. With the Third Symphony, *Sinfonia espansiva* (1911), one finds his spiritual horizons further enlarged and his vision more intense. It represents a striking advance in his ability to sustain longer-breathed, more extended musical paragraphs as well as a heightened awareness of the structural role of key. His sense of confidence and independence are heightened; the sound world he creates is more sharply defined and firmly focused.

It is the Fourth Symphony (*L'Inestinguibile*) (1916) written when Sibelius was wrestling with his Fifth that marks a watershed in Nielsen's art. The gentle, smiling Danish landscape that the slow movement of the *Espansiva* so lyrically portrays is only occasionally glimpsed: the landscape is darker, full of more violent contrasts, and strikes a more northerly note than any of its predecessors. It pits long, singing melodies like the second theme of the first movement alongside violent outbursts, as in the Finale and at the very opening of the whole work. In the third movement there is angular, spare contrapoint with some astonishingly intense string writing beginning majestically, as Nielsen put it, 'like the eagle riding on the wind'.

While there are many assertions of simple major–minor tonality, Nielsen comes closer to an awareness of the threat to the classical key system and its possible disintegration than he has ever done before. It undoubtedly reflects a more highly defined musical personality than its immediate predecessor. From the Fifth Symphony of Sibelius one could not possibly guess that Europe was engulfed in its most terrible and destructive war up to that time, while from Nielsen's symphony one can readily discern its shadows. The title, *L'Inestinguibile* or The 'Inextinguishable' seeks in a single word to hint what only music itself has the power to express fully: the elemental will to Life.

Nielsen possessed a basic optimism, a quasi-Shavian belief in the life force, so that the outbreak of the First World War came as a tremendous psychic shock; the unremitting slaughter, the senseless destruction and suffering haunted Nielsen's imagination. It was evident to him that life could never be the same again, that the war presented the great divide in the affairs of man. His music assumed a new mantle: its contours are harder, its harmonies less rich, its textures darker. The Fifth Symphony, completed in 1922, was his first major work after the holocaust and the prominent role assigned to the side-drum suggests the war experience. While in the Sixth and Seventh Symphonies of Sibelius composed at this time, a sense of nature's power and of communion with nature takes pride of place over human relationships, Nielsen's art seems more affected by the breakdown of values and the subsequent disintegration of musical language that distinguishes the period. The wider vision and greater depth of his music testify to the spiritual growth he underwent. Just as Sibelius's Seventh was unique formally, so the Fifth Symphony of Nielsen is unlike anything else that preceded it.

The Sixth Symphony is less convincing than its predecessor even though its first movement is as searching, powerful and spacious as anything Nielsen ever composed. The slow movement, the eloquent *Proposta seria*, is on an equally elevated plane of feeling and there are inspired passages in the final set of variations. But the work is undeniably flawed by the *Humoreske*, whose sense of direction seems to falter. Nielsen's mastery which rarely fails him does so at this point, for this movement is no foil for its predecessor and an unworthy companion.

Nielsen's art developed along lines which reflect an ever-growing awareness of his own development and that of the world around him. He sprang from soil which had nourished a symphonic tradition and had close links with the great European tradition. Sibelius's art sprang from more hostile terrain. The Finnish capital did not possess a permanent symphony orchestra until 1882 and Finnish musical life was reliant on German talent. Fredrik Pacius (1809–1891) was of German origin; a pupil of Spohr, and Sibelius's teacher, Martin Wegelius studied at Leipzig and was wholly German in outlook. It is astonishing that from this background where the opportunities of hearing orchestral music were so few, and indigenous symphonic activity meagre, an artist of such strong symphonic instinct should emerge.

In his youth Sibelius wrote an enormous amount of chamber music and it was not until his mid-twenties when he studied in Berlin and Vienna (1889–91) that he developed a feeling for the orchestra. His first major venture was the *Kullervo* Symphony, an ambitious five-movement work for two soloists, male chorus and orchestra, more than seventy minutes in length. *Kullervo*, like Robert Kajanus's *Aino* Symphony, which Sibelius heard in Berlin, was the first of many works to draw on the *Kalevala*, the Finnish national mythology, for its inspiration. Considering the fact that his knowledge of the orchestra was of such recent provenance, *Kullervo* shows astonishing assurance, and in style the very opening bars proclaim an independent voice. Whatever its flaws, it leaves no doubt that the composer has an inborn grasp of form and sense of forward movement. The vocal writing in the long centre-piece, 'Kullervo and his Sister', is both highly original and keenly dramatic; indeed it suggests that he could have developed an extremely respectable operatic style had not his encounter with Bayreuth in 1894 proved so crushing to his aspirations.

Sibelius's interest in mythology was lifelong and his identification with nature extraordinarily intense. But it is as a symphonist, not a nature poet or an opera composer, that Sibelius made his unique contribution to music. Sibelius possessed a flair for form rare in the 20th century: his capacity for the organic evolution of his material, for what could be called 'continuous creation', is so highly developed that it has few parallels. It was undoubtedly this that prompted the panegyrics of Cecil Gray and Ernest Newman just as it was perhaps the regional character of his inspiration as well as the pre-occupation with Nordic mythology that prompted a reaction against him in the decade immediately after his death in 1957.

The 1890s saw the formation and then consolidation of a personal language. His early work drew on the Viennese classics, on Grieg and Svendsen, and above all, Tchaikovsky, particularly as far as his harmonic vocabulary is concerned. Tchaikovsky's influence may be said to reach its climax in the slow movements of *Kullervo* and the First Symphony (1899) though Sibelius's growing sense of concentration and organic cohesion is more strongly to be discerned in the latter.

The Second Symphony (1902) inhabits much the same world as its predecessor though it views it through more subtle and refined lenses. As with the First Symphony, it is the first movement that makes the most profound impression not merely in terms of its originality of content but in its harmonious unity of form and content. Its very air of relaxation and effortlessness serves to mask the inner strength that this sunny genial music commands, for each motive seems to evolve naturally from its immediate predecessor. Three of the four movements are in sonata form though it must be conceded that the Finale, though stirring and effective, is the least developed example of sonata thinking in the seven symphonies.

In the Third Symphony (1904–7) Sibelius distilled a language that is much purer and more classical in style, writing in a vein wholly out of sympathy with the times. The language of the Third is all the more potent for being so disciplined, for unlike many of his contemporaries Sibelius chose to develop not denser chromatic textures but rather to exclude the richer colourings of the post-romantic palette. Indeed it is more densely organic than any of his preceding sonata movements with no trace of spare flesh on its frame. Its scoring for double woodwind, four horns, two trumpets, three trombones, timpani and strings contrasts markedly with the luxuries that Strauss and Mahler were permitting themselves just as its harmonic austerity could hardly be further removed from Scriabin, Reger and Debussy.

There is no doubt that the gap Sibelius traversed in the four years that separate the Third from the Fourth Symphony (1911) is incomparably greater than the ground he had covered from *Kullervo* (1892) up to the Third Symphony. The latter, along with such fine works as *Pohjola's Daughter* and *Nightride and Sunrise*, belong to his early forties and reflect an ordered, confident world held in rein by classical discipline: with the Fourth Symphony Sibelius had, as it were, seen into the abyss. The seriousness of the new symphony may (in some measure at least) have been intensified by the fact that in 1908 Sibelius developed a serious illness and underwent a number of operations for suspected cancer of the throat. For a number of years he was forced to abjure alcohol and cigars, and the bleak possibilities that the illness opened up may well serve to contribute to the austerity, concentration and depth of the works that follow in its wake: the symphony, 'The Bard' and *Luonnotar*. In the Fourth Symphony his musical language is more elliptic and in his extensive use of the tritone he comes closer to indeterminate tonality than in any other of his major works. The severity of the work earned it the title, *Barkbröd* Symphony, a reminder of the days of want and starvation in Finland when peasants were forced to eke out the flour for their bread by mixing it with the bark of trees.

The Fifth Symphony in E flat was finished in time for his fiftieth birthday celebrations in 1915 and in its original form, the orchestral parts of which survive, the work was in four movements: the composer linked the first two for a performance in the following year though so far only a double-bass part of this version has come to light. The definitive score took a further three years to complete and reflects none of the concerns we have noted in Nielsen's development at this time. Indeed, the Fifth Symphony (1919) like its two successors stands outside its time. The Sixth in D minor has excited the admiration of connoisseurs of Sibelius (Ralph Wood called it his greatest symphony, 'a dazzling display of a technique so personal and so assured that its very achievements are hidden in its mastery and in its entire synthesis with its subject matter'). It is the most refined in its language and prompted Sibelius's famous remark that while others offered cocktails of various hues, he offered pure cold spring water. No. 6 inhabits a world that is as far removed from the Fifth as that in its turn is from the Fourth. If it lacks the heroic countenance of the Fifth and the stern epic majesty of the Seventh, it possesses a purity of utterance and spirit that have few parallels either in Sibelius or in the music of his time.

The Seventh Symphony illustrates the truth of the assertion that Sibelius never approached the symphonic problem in the same way. If each of the symphonies shows a continuing search for new formal means, it is not because of any conscious commitment to structural innovation but rather a capacity to allow each idea to dictate the flow of the music and establish its own disciplinary logic. The Seventh brings to a summation the 19th-century search for symphonic unity: it is in one continuous movement. Although there are passages that have the character of a scherzo or of a slow section, it is impossible to define exactly where one section ends and another begins, so complete is Sibelius's mastery of transition and control of simultaneous tempi. It comes as the climax of a lifetime's work: one thinks of it as a constantly growing entity in which the thematic metamorphosis works at such a level of sophistication that a listener is barely aware of it.

Viewing the seven symphonies as a whole, one sees that there is no archetypal Sibelius symphony: each is different from its immediate neighbour as well as its companions. In terms of their spiritual progress the journey from no. 1 to no. 7 is greater than that between Brahms's no. 1 and no. 4, even if such predecessors as Brahms, Tchaikovsky and Dvořák may encompass a wider range of human experience and possess other dimensions denied to Sibelius. At the same time the voyage from the climate of Slav romanticism that fostered the First Symphony into the wholly isolated and profoundly original world of nos. 6 and 7 at a time when the general mainstream of music was moving in other directions was one of courageous spiritual discovery. *Tapiola*, his last published utterance, united this symphonic progress with the life-long preoccupation with nature and myth. In it Sibelius exhibits a most subtle mastery of symphonic procedure and achieves a continuity of thought paralleled only in the symphonies. It is unique even in Sibelius's own output: its world is new and unexplored, a world of strange new sounds, a landscape that no other tone poem has painted with such inner conviction and identification. It is to the northern forests what Debussy's *La Mer* is to the sea. An Eighth Symphony was completed by the summer of 1929 but never released for performance; it did not survive the composer's death.

Sibelius is able to establish within a few seconds a sound world that is entirely his own. Like Berlioz, his thematic inspiration and its harmonic clothing were conceived directly in terms of orchestral sound: the substance and the sonority were indivisible, one from the other. Many of the fingerprints of Sibelius's orchestral style are instantly recognizable: the 'cross-hatch' string writing, woodwind instruments in thirds, long-sustained brass chords that open *sforzato subito pianissimo* and then make a slow crescendo, the long-held pedal points and the openness of the textures, show a thorough assimilation of Wagner and Berlioz and its transmutation into a wholly individual expressive technique.

Both Sibelius and Nielsen were figures of international standing: no composer to appear in their wake is of comparable stature. Sweden produced a number of composers such as Alfvén (1872–1960) and Rangström (1884–1947) who ventured into the symphonic lists though their somewhat Straussian gestures and less than sure grasp of structure have inhibited their hold on the international repertory. Kurt Atterberg (1887–1974), the sixth of whose nine symphonies enjoyed much success in the 1930s, is another *petit maître* whose ambitions outstripped his musical material. Wilhelm Stenhammar is another matter. His Second Symphony in G minor is a noble, well-argued work that shows a genuine command of the symphonic process and a distinctive personality. His music has something of the nostalgia and gentleness that distinguish Fauré and Elgar though he is mostly indebted to Brahms, Sibelius and Nielsen. The leading Swedish symphonist of the present century, however, is Hilding Rosenberg (b. 1892) who was likewise quick to respond to the spell of Sibelius and later to continental figures like Schoenberg, Hindemith and *Les six*. His *Sinfonia grave* (no. 2, 1928–36) has the breadth and momentum of the genuine symphonist. One senses a strong feeling for nature and in the slow movement of no. 3 (1939), an atmosphere of gentle melancholy so characteristic of the Swedish sensibility. The symphony shows him in the process of absorbing Hindemith: the preponderance of fourths at the beginning of the Symphony no. 4 ('The Revelation of St John the Divine') (1940) is typical of the period: Hindemith was the pace-setter here as in the dotted rhythms that crop up in no. 3. Rosenberg's achievement was a striking one as far as Sweden was concerned: he opened the doors to Europe, to what was new in music during his lifetime without ever sacrificing his national identity. In the symphonies that followed (there are eight in all) we see a richly-stocked imagination and invention of dignity and nobility. Dag Wirén (b. 1905) has the most spontaneous and natural musical speech: his delightful 'Serenade for Strings' has made him many friends but none of his five symphonies have proved as successful, even the tautly conceived, monothematic Fourth. Wirén's natural mode of speech does not encompass the long-breathed paragraphs that are the stuff of symphonic thinking.

Modern Swedish composers have tended to move away from the symphonic discipline; the post-war generation reacted against the national romanticism of their elders and embraced first Bartók, Webern and the post-serialists, perhaps too eagerly for their own good, although isolated figures like Allan Pettersson (b. 1911) ploughed their own furrows. Pettersson's eleven symphonies are basically tonal; the formative influences are Mahler, Berg and Honegger. Karl-Birger Blomdahl's Third Symphony (1950) is one of the finest post-war examples of its kind: its handling of its material reveals a powerful imagination though his music-making is not as spontaneous and instinctive nor his personality so strongly defined as some of his Scandinavian contemporaries.

Sweden had no major composer of the past in whose shadows they were submerged: the discovery of Berwald was a relatively recent phenomenon. In Finland Sibelius cast long shadows which few have escaped with impunity. Certainly, the Sibelian tutelage weighed heavily on Leevi Madetoja (1887–1947) and it is not until relatively recently that Finland has produced a symphonist who speaks with a distinctive voice and with genuine authority. Joonas Kokkonen (b. 1921) combines independence of outlook and refined craftsmanship with the intellectual power and feeling for pace and momentum that distinguishes the natural symphonist.

Undoubtedly the most commanding figure to appear in the North after Sibelius and Nielsen is the Dane, Vagn Holmboe (b. 1909). Like other Danish composers such as Niels Viggo Bentzon (b. 1919) or Hermann D. Koppell (b. 1908), much of his early music reflects an admiration for Nielsen as well as a pre-occupation with the neo-classical ideals of Hindemith and Stravinsky. In the clarity of his lines we are reminded of Nielsen but the rhythmic vitality that distinguishes the opening of his Fifth Symphony (1944) is Stravin-skian. The luminous quality of his scoring, particularly for wind instruments, is distinctively personal. His Sixth Symphony (1946) is dark and sombre in feeling and its opening pages generate a poly-phony that is both powerful and eloquent. Already the composer makes conscious use of the principle of metamorphosis which both he and his colleague, Niels Viggo Bentzon, championed in the post-war musical climate as 'the form of our time'. In Holmboe's art the subtle shaping of thematic ideas and their organic transformation is an underlying mainspring of his thinking. It governs both the Seventh Symphony (1950) and its successor, by which time Nielsen's language had been fully assimilated into his own personal speech. The same can be said of Bentzon's Fourth Symphony (1948), a highly imaginative score, and his powerful Symphonic Variations (1953). After his Eighth Symphony, Holmboe pursued shorter orchestral designs without ever abandoning the principle of thematic integration and concentrated his attention on his series of twelve string quartets which span these years. His Ninth Symphony (1968) and the Tenth (1972) show an expanding and strongly personal vision that fully testifies to the vitality of the symphony as an expression of the most highly developed musical ideas.

Just as Grieg was happiest in smaller forms, modern Norwegian composers have shown less genius for the symphony than Holmboe and Kokkonen. True, there are fine essays from composers as varied as Bjarne Brustad, Klaus Egge, Ludwig Irgens Jensen and Edvard Fliflet Braein but they have not crossed the borders even into the other Scandinavian countries. Nor for that matter have the five symphonies of Fartein Valen maintained a hold on the repertory: their texture is somewhat unrelieved and they are wanting in concentration. Harald Saeverud is a miniaturist but his symphonies are well worth investigating: the wartime *Sinfonia dolorosa* (no. 6) has genuine breadth even though its dimensions are modest while its successor, subtitled 'Salme', is full of imagination and character. Were he able to sustain his thinking over a larger canvas and were his ideas longer-breathed, he would be a very formidable symphonist indeed.

§ 12 THE SYMPHONY IN BRITAIN

It was Johann Christian Bach, youngest son of Johann Sebastian and his second wife Anna Magdalena, who introduced the symphony to England. Settling in London in 1762 he renewed a friendship with another prolific symphonist, Carl Friedrich Abel, once a pupil of the great Johann Sebastian. Together at their concerts they infused some new life into English music at a time when native composers were few and far between. However, Handel and Mendelssohn were the dominant influences in English music and few native composers failed to succumb to their spell. In the 19th century a whole succession of Principals of the Royal Academy of Music, lone pioneers – Cipriani Potter (Principal from 1832), Charles Lucas (1859), Sterndale-Bennett (1866), and G. A. MacFarren (1875) – wrote between them a number of symphonies; Potter no fewer than nine, one of which Wagner conducted when on a visit to London in 1855. In *Mein Leben* he records: 'I had to play a symphony of his which entertained me by its modest dimensions and its neat development of counterpoint, the more so as the composer, a friendly, elderly recluse, clung to me with almost distressing humility.'

About the time when the Royal College of Music was founded in 1882, Parry – its Director from 1894 to 1918 – had already written two of his five symphonies (the last of which he calls a Fantasy). Stanford, also intimately connected with the College, completed the first of his seven in 1876, and his most popular one, the 'Irish' – still performed with success – in 1887. In his Fifth he sought inspiration in Milton's *L'Allegro ed il Penseroso*. Sullivan, famous in other directions, wrote an 'Irish' Symphony in 1866, and Cowen six symphonies, of which the 'Scandinavian' at one time enjoyed some popularity.

But even so, the symphony in England, moving towards the 20th century, still lagged far behind the Continent.

We see the change coming with a number of other British composers who lived into the 20th century; with Granville Bantock in his 'Hebridean' – founded on folk-music; Hamilton Harty in his racy 'Irish'; and, immensely more important, Elgar in the two symphonies of 1908 and 1910. All were contemporaries.

Elgar was fifty-one when he composed his First Symphony. Here was something entirely new to British symphonic art, in the range of its very personal emotion and the richness of its orchestration. It was conceived on a grand scale in cyclic form (taking fifty minutes in performance), having a motto-theme of striking character designed to frame the whole work in the key of A flat. But, strange to relate, the main movements were pitched in the remote keys (from A flat) of D minor and major and F sharp minor – a development of Brahms's methods of key variation that is indeed remarkable. In this symphony, which has many moments of sheer loveliness, Elgar made use of heroic and romantic melodies in his own highly individual way and consolidated his thematic material with the utmost skill into contrapuntal patterns of great interest. The very elaborate orchestration also shows the hand of a real master of the symphony. Yet to my mind nothing in the whole work is finer than the ingenious way in which he turns the opening semiquavers of the second movement (Scherzo) into the poignant melody that forms the chief subject of the slow movement. For the sake of comparison the two themes are quoted here.

Example 47

Allegro molto (2nd movement)

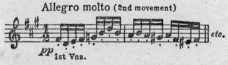

Example 48

Adagio (slow movement)

There is the same elaboration of technical points in his Second Symphony in E flat, to the score of which is appended a line from Shelley: 'Rarely, rarely comest thou, spirit of delight'. Whatever the programme may be, the music is by turns ecstatic, dignified, vivacious, austere and, in the slow movement (a funeral march), deeply moving. The score bears the inscription: 'Dedicated to the Memory of His late Majesty King Edward VII.' A third symphony was in sketch form at the time of the composer's death.

Much of Elgar's orchestral music bears the imprint of Edwardian times. Not inaptly it has often been compared to Kipling's poetry in its more forthright expression. The symphonies are indeed a cornucopia of sounds overflowing with the luxuriance of the age; yet, they remain masterpieces in their own right, music of enduring power.

Holst wrote two symphonies – the early unpublished 'Cotswold' and a Choral Symphony to words by Keats, which is vigorous in style and largely experimental. For, as he once wrote to a friend, he was 'greatly averse to fixed principles in art and I like everything – form, melody, harmony, etc. – to grow out of the original inspiration . . .'. Thus far had the symphony, as a set form, parted company from the 19th century. Equally experimental, Bliss startled the world of music in 1922 with his 'Colour' Symphony (revised 1932), which sought rather bafflingly to unite aural and visual perceptiveness in a series of movements labelled purple, red, blue and green.§

Far more important, both musically and historically, is the Symphony in B flat minor composed by William Walton in 1934–35. So great was the interest in this work that it was first performed in an incomplete form. It is undeniably one of the strongest British symphonies of the present century. In atmosphere it reflects the anxieties of the 1930s but structurally it evolves as organically as a Sibelius symphony. As was the case with Moeran's Symphony in G minor, Sibelius was a dominant influence; but if in Moeran the freshness of the ideas outweighs the weakness of structure that the work exhibits, Walton's First Symphony triumphs on all counts. Its successor, no. 2 (1959) is tautly held together but its substance seems less compelling than any of Walton's music prior to the A minor quartet (1945) and its inner world less freshly experienced.

Undoubtedly the major symphonist of the period is Ralph Vaughan Williams whose output in this genre extends over forty-eight years. § His 'Sea' Symphony – completed in 1910 – is a setting for soprano, baritone, chorus and orchestra of various poems by

Whitman. In every sense it is a symphony of the sea; the first movement 'A Song of all seas, all ships'; the second, a dark, philosophizing nocturne of the seashore where, facing the deep surge of the waters, the singer ruminates on 'the clef of the universe and of the future'; the third movement a riotous scherzo of 'whistling winds' and 'a myriad myriad waves'; the fourth 'The Explorers' culminating in the great choral section 'Bounding O soul thou journeyest forth' – a movement ending *pianissimo* with the words 'O farther sail' and leaving the listener with a picture of vast empty seas. Both ship and soul have sailed beyond the horizon into the Unknown.

The 'London' Symphony (no. 2) came four years later. The city awakens to its busy life. Soon we hear the first two quarters of the Westminster chimes followed by the long first movement, which with all its activity carries its own inner meaning. In the dark moods and impassioned outbursts of the second movement – where, by and large, the 'folkiness' of the main themes is so typical of this great nationally-minded composer – we sense what lies far deeper down than the mere bustle of everyday affairs. Shall we call it the pulse of Time; the history of a thousand years and more? The third movement – a scherzo-nocturne – is a picture of London by night; gay, frivolous and entertaining before the music finally melts away into the silence of a city now drowsy and inactive. The Finale has grandeur and marching pageantry, with borrowings from the first movement. After a most exciting climax the sounds suddenly die away, leaving a distant background of strings through which we hear stealing on the ear *three* quarters of the Westminster chimes. Then as London falls asleep once more an epilogue sums up everything with allusions (in ever decreasing volume) to the music with which the symphony began.

Next came the 'Pastoral' Symphony (no. 3), the strenuous Fourth in F minor and the translucent and beautiful Fifth in D – symphonies composed in 1922, 1935 and 1943 respectively. Spread over twenty-one years they illustrate the range and development of Vaughan Williams's art. The least popular is the 'Pastoral', owing it may be to this restless age in which urban people can so little sit still to enjoy symphonic rural sounds that do not rise to great emotional heights. It is cool music; it does not excite. The Fourth comes as a frightening contrast to the 'Pastoral'. Fierce, untamed, seldom in repose, its strength is undeniable. In the Fifth back we are again with the genial Vaughan Williams: he who can write so eloquently and in such terms of melting beauty when dealing with the more homely aspects of music (cf. the 'Serenade to Music'). Yet classicality is there, for the Finale is a *Passacaglia*. In a few tense moments in the *Romanza* (third movement) we hear certain agitated phrases that foreshadow the opening of the Sixth Symphony.

The material of this Sixth, the most original of all Vaughan Williams's symphonies, dates from 1944 to 1947. In some ways it recalls the spirit of the Fourth; there is a similar turmoil in the first and Scherzo movements and the same inexorable purpose, which finds its expression in countless instances of augmented fourths and diminished fifths flying through the music like chaff scattered by an autumn wind. But while the general mood of the symphony is portentous, yet at the end of the first movement there steals in once again (surprisingly!) a folk-like melody to remind us of the country-side. In the second movement reiterated B flats in metrical anapaests (◡ ◡ –), and coming mainly from trumpets, timpani and muffled side-drum, seem to create that picture of purgatory I have referred to. The impression is further strengthened by the ghostly music of the final movement. This never rises above a *pianissimo* – a fact that makes the movement the strangest and indeed the most original finale ever put into a symphony. Each movement, it should be added, is linked to the next by a held note, the whole work crumbling into a vacuum of unearthly silence – something not unlike what we hear in Sibelius's Fourth, yet still more gaunt and spectral.§

Sinfonia Antarctica is the title of the Seventh, and the music is an extended projection of ideas taken from the incidental music written (1948–49) for the film 'Scott of the Antarctic'. Three of its five movements are headed by quotations from the poets: Shelley, Coleridge and Donne. The Scherzo movement illustrates the 26th verse of Psalm 104: 'There go the ships; and there is that Leviathan whom thou hast made to take his pastime therein.' Effective though much of it is, the 'Antarctica' remains the least symphonic of the nine. Its successor, no. 8 (1956), is a smaller scale work: its Scherzo is for wind only and the slow movement uses only strings. The score uses all the 'phones and the 'spiels known to the composer', but as a whole, the symphony does not quite match its successor, no. 9 in E minor (1957) in terms of substance and depth. The Ninth has been underrated: its thematic inspiration lacks the freshness and character of nos. 5 or 6 but its material is every bit as closely integrated and in some respects the symphonic argument is better sustained.

The seven symphonies of Arnold Bax belong to the years between the two wars: the first was begun in 1921 and the last finished in time for the New York Fair of 1939. Many critics have seen Bax primarily as a rhapsodic composer whose inspiration is more suited to the tone poem than the symphony. However, the very breadth of the symphonic canvas offered scope to his imagination that the tone poem could not wholly encompass. Bax was in his late thirties when he began no. 1 and had many of his finest works such as *The Garden of Fand* and *Tintagel* behind him. Indeed the 1914–18 war saw Bax at the height of his powers and the First Symphony, though it originally began life as a piano sonata, showed no mean grasp of the symphonic canvas as well as a genuine mastery of the orchestra. Admittedly its debt to Russian music is as strongly felt as anything in his pre-war output: the pregnant opening motive recalls the kind of symphonic gesture one encounters in, say, the Second Symphony of Borodin and the first movement has a tautness and cohesion that he did not develop in later symphonies. Rather he chose to develop the brooding, evocative Celtic element that one finds in the slow movement. The Second Symphony (1924–25) has the wildness of imagination and vivid, opulent colours that instantly establish an atmosphere that is as compelling as it is wholly individual. The opening offers a parallel with the beginning of the second sonata and though there are many ideas that are conceived directly in orchestral terms, Bax's imagination was not as idiosyncratic as far as orchestral sonority is concerned as Sibelius whom he revered.

The Third Symphony (1928–29) is more inward-looking than its predecessor though its sense of mystery is no less potent. It was for many years the least neglected (one can hardly say best known) of the seven, and for this very reason some Baxians have tempted to underrate it. It is in many respects more characteristic in its range and variety of mood than is the Fifth or its two successors. Its Epilogue, like that of the Sixth (1934), attains a genuine serenity but not before the music has encompassed a variety of keys, textures and thematic substance.

The Fifth (1932) shows him checking the purely lyrical impulse to which he could give generous vein in favour of a greater degree of motivic integration: it shows him scrutinizing his thematic material far more, rigorously resisting the impulse to luxuriate. The result is deeply impressive and the work has much of the same dark atmosphere and brooding intensity that distinguishes the Sixth (1934) and its noble successor. Some critics of the pre-war years were insular in outlook and their successors overreacted with the result that Bax underwent a long period of neglect. In Vienna a composer like Franz

Schmidt, a decade older than Bax, never fell from grace, a tribute to the level heads of the Viennese. Bax's romanticism was unashamed; however, he survives the test of any composer of worth. His music is immediately recognizable; he created his own world, quite distinctive and unlike that of his contemporaries here or abroad, and he did so with great musical resource and mastery. His output is inevitably uneven: of the symphonies, the Fourth (1930–31) is the weakest and most self-indulgent. Yet at his best his claims on the repertoire are as strong as Schmidt's, even if his sense of structure does not match that of the Austrian master.

Though he is older than Bax but younger than Vaughan Williams, Havergal Brian (1877–1973) is a special case: English music can boast fewer causes lost so long and found so late as his. At last his enormous output is beginning to surface, though its discovery (and some of its composition) has been a post-war phenomenon. He met with some success before the First World War but his *chef d'oeuvre*, the 'Gothic' Symphony (1919) had to wait until the 1960s for its first performance. In fact, although it won the praises of Tovey and Goossens, Brian's music was dramatically and grievously neglected between the wars and it was not until the 1950s that one of his symphonies, no. 8 (1949), was performed. Stylistically what is so interesting is not the affinities his music betrays but its independence. His admiration for Strauss – to whom the 'Gothic' Symphony is dedicated – is evident, Mahler, Bantock, Elgar, Hindemith and all sorts of composers: one is briefly reminded of Busoni at one point in the Eleventh Symphony. There are miscalculations, no doubt: hardly surprising in a composer denied the opportunity to test his inner ear against the reality of performance; so there are for that matter in Ives, another ruggedly independent figure spurned by the establishment of his day, or in the work of the Dane, Rued Langgaard, a contemporary of Nielsen, whose sixteen symphonies chart a course that ranges from visionary inspiration to ineffective banality.

In the Eighth Symphony, despite its slow tempo there is variety of mood and feeling, a striking originality of texture and generosity of feeling. No doubt some of the recent interest is prompted by a natural sympathy and admiration for a composer who has battled against such odds and gone on writing. Yet Brian turned this to advantage: knowing he was writing for himself alone, since no one troubled to perform him, he had no cause to court fashion but merely to pursue his own musical instinct and his own inner vision. The symphonies 8–10 exhibit a community of feeling: they were conceived as a triptych, and even if one feels reservations about this or that detail (a propensity to assert a rhythmic pattern over too long a period or too ungainly an orchestral *tutti*), it is the authenticity and power of the music that is most striking. There is a moment in the Tenth Symphony (1953–54) of visionary stillness that is quite unlike anything else in music. There is a strong sense of purpose and concentration in no. 12, a tautly conceived work with none of the lyrical eloquence of its predecessor. Since no. 12, Brian composed a further twenty symphonies which have yet to stand the test of assimilation into the repertoire. There are pedestrian touches in Brian's music but when he is at his finest, his art has strength and depth and a profile of great character.

While Brian followed his special course, the mainstream of English music was dominated by Holst and Vaughan Williams, though during the late 1950s Vaughan Williams underwent the inevitable period of relative neglect.

The symphonies of Vaughan Williams are firmly established in the repertoire but those of Edmund Rubbra (b. 1901) have earned the admiration of the few and the neglect of the many. Unlike many 20th-century composers Rubbra has remained indifferent to the various changes in the artistic climate of his day and has pursued a solitary path. His sympathy for renaissance polyphony and his naturally contrapuntal cast of mind would seem to equip him more for choral than orchestral music: indeed, one critic has called his symphonies 'motets for orchestra'. Much of his choral music has exceptional depth and eloquence, and so have the finest of his symphonies. At first sight his musical language does not seem to belong to this century: its harmonic vocabulary does not embrace dissonances that his contemporaries regard as stock-in-trade and yet he can suddenly breathe new life into chords as commonplace as the dominant seventh and he uses enharmonic change, making a chord a kind of pivot serving two different functions, in a subtle and individual way. Although his gift for the free movement of musical themes and phrases, linear in intent yet harmonious in their totality, found a natural outlet in his choral music, the breadth of his musical thinking made it inevitable that he should turn to the symphony.

His First Symphony (1936) concentrates on exploring the motivic implications of its material at the expense of their presentation. In terms of orchestral colour there is much that is ineffective both in this and its immediate successor. Yet the quality of Rubbra's ideas in the finest of his symphonies has a simplicity that is astonishingly bold. Take, for example, the opening of the Fourth Symphony, a wartime work, which is little more than an exploration of the changing functions of the chord of the seventh but its nobility and purity of utterance are immediately striking. Rubbra's music often has little surface appeal, however: its textures can seem wanting in transparency; yet there is an inner radiance that is far more compelling and enduring. True, the slow movement of the Sixth Symphony (1954) has both: its texture has ample clarity and openness that serve its directness of utterance while closer acquaintance reveals a tranquillity of spirit rare in the 1950s. The breadth and scale of Rubbra's symphonic thinking emerge in the Seventh Symphony (1956), a work of commanding organic coherence and mastery. Its language is wholly diatonic, vivid testimony to the truth of Schoenberg's assertion that there was a great deal of fine music to be written in C major. By the side of, say, Henze's Fourth Symphony, written at roughly the same time, its sound world appears 'old-fashioned'. Yet its means are wholly attuned to its ends: it is wholly true to its inner dictates and in its totally different way is as uncompromising of truth as any work that bristles with complex stylistic means. Henze's symphony with its refined texture, its powerfully evocative and haunting atmosphere is every bit as truthful and uncompromising, its artistic language responding wholly to the needs of the composer's vision. Since the Seventh Symphony Rubbra has returned to the genre with three powerful new works, all performed in the 1970s, though the Eighth Symphony was composed during the late 1960s. The centrepiece, the Ninth, is choral while the most recent, no. 10 (1974) is a chamber symphony of characteristic depth and integrity.

Michael Tippett (b. 1906) has not concentrated so much of his creative energies in the symphonic arena as has Rubbra, though they share many qualities: a keen spiritual awareness, depth of feeling and a strong relationship with tradition. His study of Tudor music emerges in the madrigalesque rhythms of the second string quartet (1944): his warm human instincts and strong social awareness finds expression in *A Child of our Time* and his operas. There are three symphonies, the first of which appeared in 1945: a strong work structurally, eloquent in its expressive power and the rhythmic freedom and vitality that Tippett learnt from his study of 16th- and 17th-century music. In Symphony no. 2 (1957) he fuses lyrical intensity and rhythmic energy to striking ends though as in the Third (1972), Stravinsky remains a clearly discernible influence, much in the same way that Holst does in Rubbra's Eighth Symphony.

The Third also makes use of a quotation from Beethoven's Ninth Symphony (Beethoven has been a lifelong and at times obsessive enthusiasm) as well as a 'blues' song. The inward-looking slow movements of both these symphonies represent his inspiration at its most deeply characteristic, just as the Scherzo of no. 2 shows him at his most mercurial. At his most ecstatic and visionary, Tippett's ideas clamour for articulation so rapidly that his utterance seems almost tongue-tied in the manner of Lamb's description of a Quaker meeting: yet his halting utterance at such moments is more profound than other people's eloquence.

Like Tippett, Lennox Berkeley (b. 1903) is not first and foremost a symphonist, though it is natural that he should have gravitated to this genre; all three of his symphonies are works of refined craftsmanship and sensibility, qualities that also distinguish Alan Rawsthorne's three symphonies: these are rewarding works that deserve more than the passing mention that space compels. Nor should the eight symphonies of Benjamin Frankel (1906–73) be overlooked. All were composed during the last fourteen years of his creative life, a period overshadowed by ill-health. Frankel's musical technique was formidable indeed and his facility sprang from years of experience as a film composer. His symphonies embrace serial means of organization without abandoning the tonal implications of a series; his sound world is distinctive, his scoring translucent and his textures shining. His sense of his Jewish identity is also strong (Mahler, Schoenberg and Sibelius were all powerful influences) in much the same way that Berkeley's Gallic sympathies and alertness of mind inform his First Symphony.

Composers of the younger generation have tended to move from the long paragraphs and dynamic statement of the symphony and away to the more densely textured and fragmented structures that followed in the wake of Webern. Of the middle generation three names must be mentioned: Humphrey Searle (b. 1915), Peter Racine Fricker (b. 1920) and Robert Simpson (b. 1921). Searle was a leading exponent of the twelve-note school at a time when the English musical climate was hostile to its claims.

Classical tonality provides a series of tensions that perform a structural role in the symphony. In weakening the sense of conflict between key centres, greater stress is thrown on the degree of motivic integration: in the first (1952) of Searle's six symphonies there is a remarkable sense of organic cohesion. Contrasts are strong and powerful in atmosphere and Searle thinks in long paragraphs with that sense of scale that distinguishes the genuine symphonist. Fricker was more drawn to Stravinsky and Hindemith but after the second of his four symphonies presents a less sharply defined profile. In spite of moments of genuine inspiration and craftsmanship of a high order, there is a general-purpose modernity about some of his invention.

Robert Simpson shares with Tippett a veneration for Beethoven and this informs works like his Fourth Symphony (1973) and some of his string quartets. His First Symphony (1951) proclaims his Nordic sympathies (he is the author of a fine study of Nielsen and a penetrating writer on music) and a remarkable command of the organic processes that the symphonist must master. His technical command is completely at his artistic behest: no one not knowing in advance would guess that the beautiful slow movement of his Second Symphony (1956) is a palindrome while his understanding of the vital importance of key tension in works like the Third and Fourth Symphonies shows that even in the present day Beethoven can be a fruitful source of inspiration for a wholly individual and powerful voice.

Not all the composers of the younger generation have turned from the symphony. Richard Rodney Bennett has written two, both fluent and accomplished works while others ranging in style from John McCabe and Ronald Stevenson to Nicholas Maw and Hugh Wood have more than established a capacity for the kind of organic growth and coherence that is the hallmark of symphonic thinking whether or not it bears a symphonic title. The death of the symphony has been often proclaimed but it refuses to lie down.

13 THE UNITED STATES

American music was slow to shake off its European inheritance and discover its own identity. Most of its 19th-century figures reflected those European influences to which they were drawn. Although to those who know Macdowell, Gottschalk and others, this is less than the full truth, as a broad generalization it holds. In fact, art music remained derivative; the more literate and accomplished it became, the more it tended to shun the popular elements which were later to prove so fertile.

Charles Ives was the first to assert a genuinely American style, to challenge effectively the European hegemony, and to follow his own robust, iconoclastic instinct. His First Symphony shows the extent of Dvořák's impact (the Czech master's visit of the 1890s produced more than the 'New World' Symphony), but it is his music from the turn of the century that shows the most vivid fantasy and boldest imagination. No one else had thought to picture the cacophony of two bands approaching each other with such literalness or to such striking effect. The discovery of Ives as the father figure of modern American music has been of relatively recent provenance: in the 1950s when he was still alive, he remained neglected and, as is the case with Havergal Brian in England, had he heard more of his music during his lifetime his development might well have been affected or modified. Its excessive acclaim in recent years is no less extravagant than its earlier neglect was unjust, for in Ives, America produced one of its most remarkable musical phenomena rather than its greatest composer. Many of the devices in his music antedate their use by his European contemporaries (bitonality, atonality and so on), yet his rebellion against tradition was of a different order than that of, say, Schoenberg whose admiration of him is well known. Schoenberg had assimilated and indeed mastered every technical resource of the great tradition and felt the importance of a strong relationship with tradition before embarking on any steps towards a new language. Ives evinced no such mastery and indeed showed scant respect for it: for him Mozart was 'ladyfinger' music, and it was a pragmatism, a lively and inquiring mind and a vivid aural imagination which led him as it were, instinctively. The results are on occasion visionary, lively, inspiring, appalling by turns: they are in fact the raw materials of art rather than the finished work.

America is a continent whose sheer size is barely realized by Europeans. To speak of one composer being typically American is as misleading as describing Vaughan Williams as 'typically European', using the term, moreover, to encompass the area from London to Teheran, or Helsinki to Lisbon. American music, to use Walter Piston's words, is simply 'music by Americans', and varies as widely in character and range as does music in Europe: the wide open spaces of the Middle West are as foreign to a composer of the Eastern Seaboard as is New England to a composer from California. The United States has been a haven to many foreign musicians from the end of the 19th century to the 1940s when the war brought Hindemith, Milhaud, Martinů, Bartók, Krenek, Stravinsky, Schoenberg and a host of others to its shores; moreover, it has produced over the years some of the greatest orchestras in the world, thanks to the large number of immigrant executants and the subsequent growth of magnificent teaching institutions and libraries, the equal if not the superior of their European counterparts. Yet it was not until the late 1920s that art music of any real significance internationally began to emerge. The recent vogue for Ives both in the United States itself and in Europe has served to detract somewhat from the achievement of such masters as Roy Harris, Walter Piston, William Schuman and Roger Sessions, all of them very different and all symphonists of commanding stature. Indeed it is in the 1930s that the American symphony began to flourish in earnest and a whole generation went to Paris to equip themselves with a sound musical training at the hands of Nadia Boulanger, returning to America with a heightened creative awareness and a determination to write genuinely American music.

It was Roy Harris who first captured the public imagination with his Third Symphony, a work that spoke in accents that were as characteristically American as Vaughan Williams is English or Debussy French. In all, Harris has composed eleven symphonies: the first (1928) remains unperformed but thanks to Koussevitsky's championship, its successor, entitled 'Symphony 1933' and the famous Third in one movement, immediately established Harris internationally and hailed the arrival of a genuinely American school.

The work unfolds with an impressive and natural logic from the opening chant-like string threnody to the magisterial peroration: its contrasts are strongly dramatic and yet its evolution could scarcely be more organic in feeling. One senses instantly that one is, as it were, in new country: the textures are open and gleaming and the thematic substance clearly defined and well-characterized. His later symphonies have been charged with self-imitation: Harris, it is said, merely traverses the same ground and there is some truth in this. The Fourth is a choral piece, and neither the Fifth nor the Seventh can in any way be said to extend his language or deepen his insights: nor despite their undoubted merits do they sound as freshly experienced. However, the Seventh (1954) remains an impressive and powerfully constructed one-movement edifice, bold in its harmonic stance and thoroughly effective. Alas, like its successors it remains *terra incognita* outside the United States and even there performances are relatively few.

Easily the best-known of the senior American composers is Aaron Copland (b. 1900), two years younger than Harris, and like him a Boulanger pupil. His musical personality is immediately engaging and has the frank openness and accessibility that one associates with the best in America. Copland turned to indigenous elements in American music and has been much influenced by Stravinsky, particularly as far as texture and rhythmic fertility are concerned. He has absorbed jazz elements in works like the *Music for the Theatre*, the Clarinet Concerto, exotic folk elements in *El Salón Mexico*, and the rhythmic vitality of the 'Dance' Symphony or the Third Symphony, an ambitious work dating from the end of the Second World War, seems inexhaustible. His music wears a distinctive air of freshness and innocence, and it is a pity that in the Third Symphony he absorbs the patriotic 'Fanfare for the Common Man', and brings an otherwise impressive work uncomfortably close to bombast. But unlike Roy Harris who is first and foremost a symphonist, Copland's output has embraced a diverse range of genres: perhaps his finest achievements, like those of Stravinsky, remain in the field of ballet; *Appalachian Spring*, *Rodeo* and *Billy the Kid*, which have great style, flair and inspiration to commend them.

None of Copland's contemporaries enjoys comparable exposure outside the United States yet both Roger Sessions with whom he was closely associated in the late 1920s and Walter Piston are composers of substance. Sessions has been a potent force in American musical life: like Piston he was an influential teacher and unlike many adherents of the serial school, his language is strongly individual. The Second, Third and Eighth Symphonies all reveal a strong sense of purpose and feeling for proportion. Piston's early ballet, *The Incredible Flutist* (1938) shows certain Gallic sympathies but his style evolved a distinctively American flavour in his Second Symphony (1943) with its eloquent and noble slow movement. In a sense he is a musician's musician: his craftsmanship is impeccable and as with Sessions there are no concessions to the groundlings. His language is diatonic while Sessions is highly chromatic but they are both uncompromising. His Third and Fourth Symphonies with their long-breathed lines and deeply-felt eloquence are among the finest examples of the post-war symphony not only in America but anywhere. They unfold with impressive mastery of the organic processes of symphonic thought, and their reticence and discipline enhance their rewards. Of the next generation William Schuman (b. 1910) shows a commanding symphonic talent: like Piston, he thinks in long paragraphs but his harmonic vocabulary is more complex and the textures more densely packed. So far he has nine symphonies to his credit and while Piston expresses a strong feeling for nature and his native New England, Schuman's is very much an urban sensibility and his scoring both more strident and more immediately effective.

Born in the same year as Schuman but totally different in outlook, Samuel Barber achieved early fame with his prodigiously successful Overture to the School for Scandal, a marvellously proportioned piece, and the *adagio* for strings in the slow movement of his string quartet, op. 11. His style is neo-romantic and in terms of vocabulary seems at first sight to belong more to the last century than this. Yet his art has great freshness and in some ways he can be said to possess the most natural musical instinct of any 20th-century American composer. Although the seams in his two symphonies are clearly visible such is the freshness and quality of their invention that they are unlikely to disappear from the repertory. His language is as diatonic as that of David Diamond, another fine symphonist, all too little known in Europe, or Peter Mennin (b. 1923), the third of whose eight symphonies – written when he was only twenty-three – showed an astonishing promise, albeit one which has not been wholly fulfilled. This is one of the few American symphonies of note that reflects English influence (Vaughan Williams and Walton). Its successor was choral but in it as in nos. 5 and 6, Mennin seemed more content to consolidate the personality he had established rather than venture on further spiritual exploration, though an exception must be made for the Canto, the slow movement of his Fifth Symphony.

Bernstein's creative fires burned more brightly during the early stages of his career than they have in the last two decades in which he embarked on his path as a virtuoso conductor. But his early 'Jeremiah' Symphony is a truly considerable achievement and although its two successors, *The Age of Anxiety* and *Kaddisch* impinge on other genres, they contain invention that is strong enough to make one regret that Bernstein has not pursued a symphonic rather than an executant's course. But he, Mennin and Diamond are not the only symphonists working within a primarily diatonic tradition: Robert Ward and Norman Dello Joio are others. While in a more complex chromatic framework and often employing highly imaginative textures are such figures as Andrew Imbrie, a West-coast composer, Perle, the author of a book on twelve-note technique and George Rochberg. Were America not regarded as one unit by outsiders, each of these figures would be much better known. As it is, a composer like Imbrie is not much heard on the Eastern Seaboard.

One of the middle generation to command a wider hearing both in the States and in Europe is Elliot Carter. His muscular rhythms and powerful intellect dominate the piano sonata written immediately after the war but the musical language to emerge in later works from the quartets and the concerto for orchestra shows increasing complexity of means but no less integrity. Gunther Schuller, for many years identified with his advocacy of the third stream and himself an orchestral player, has produced a number of scores, including a symphony, that betray a refined ear, a strong sense of atmosphere and a vivid musical imagination. His use of atonality sounds as natural and unaffected as others who choose to use key centres; it springs from a strong harmonic awareness rather than any pre-determined doctrinaire schematicism. Inspired partly by the venerable Dadaist, John Cage, America has developed a flourishing avant-garde which ranges as widely as its European counterpart and in some cases further. It embraces a wide range of talent: from Lukas Foss whose tonal music, much influenced in the late 1940s and early '50s by Hindemith and Stravinsky, is as distinguished as the improvisatory group he developed in the '60s was unfailingly musical, to such figures as Milton Babbitt, Morton Feldman, George Crumb and Charles Wuorinen. In terms of vitality and openness to new ideas, America is well to the fore and the composers of the '30s and '40s have shown its capacity to forge a new and independent style.

PART 2 ORCHESTRAL MUSIC OF MANY KINDS

§ 1 MAINLY OF SUITES

I have analyzed the symphony at some length, for it is by far the most important branch of orchestral music, a subject not to be dismissed in a few generalizations. By comparison with it the many other forms, though of immense interest in themselves, are less significant. Since the days of the 'Sinfonia avanti l'opera', suites, overtures, rhapsodies, variations, divertimentos, serenades, tone-poems, symphonic poems, dances, impressions, ballets, preludes, fantasias, capriccios, marches, scherzos, idylls, scenes, romances, music for string and wind combinations and many other examples of orchestral art have multiplied to a bewildering extent. To classify them all here is not possible.

In pre-symphonic days the orchestral repertoire was very limited indeed. There were a few suites, overtures, fantasias, ballets and various concertos by Purcell, Lully, Corelli, Bach, Handel and others, but little else. But a great feature of the age was music for strings and continuo, much of which has rightly kept its place in programmes of today. For it is recognized that Handel's Concerti Grossi, and those by Corelli, Vivaldi, Geminiani and other composers of the day, are masterpieces of classical purity: they conform rather rigidly, it may be, to a pattern too little varied, yet containing an inexhaustible and inspired flow of melodic and contrapuntal movement. Nor must Purcell's beautiful string suites, such as *Abdelazar*, *The Gordian Knot Untied* and the one arranged from *The Fairy Queen* music be left without mention.

Bach, in company with Corelli, Handel and others of his time, can be said to have perfected the older suite form. But, if we except those by Bach, the true *orchestral* suite as we now know it was the product of a later age. There was, too, an intermediate post-symphonic stage of the suite when Mozart wrote many under the titles of Divertimento, Serenade, Cassation and the like. These, usually composed for small combinations of instruments or for wind or strings alone, mark an epoch where an old dance form like the minuet was introduced between *allegro* and *andante* movements, which began to reflect the prevailing influence of the sonata and symphonic forms. In other words, they were almost symphonies in miniature, with movements certainly less developed yet planned similarly. And in these 'suites' Mozart gave us some of his most inspired music.

But in more modern days the suite became quite another affair. Commanding the full resources of the orchestra, the modern suite deserted from the classical style just as the symphony had done before it. Actually its more novel developments are of comparatively recent growth; we need scarcely go further back than the days of Bizet and Tchaikovsky to discover the first examples of any importance. Strangely enough, the eminent German and Austrian composers of more recent times have made few important contributions to the form. The finest and most pictorial suites emanate from Russia, France, England, Spain, Norway and Hungary. Brilliant orchestration and sharp contrasts between movements are the main characteristics of these suites. Their movements, being of much shorter duration than those of a symphony, submit themselves more readily to a type of pictorial orchestration that might be considered extravagant in symphonies. And so the many novel effects to be found in the suite have made it an extremely popular form of orchestral music. Often it is nothing more than an effective concert version of incidental music to a theatrical production or of operatic numbers strung together in somewhat loose fashion. But whether written originally for concert purposes only or garnered from the theatre, there is no doubt that the form has stimulated composers of many nationalities to some of their most picturesque efforts.

Among the Russians Tchaikovsky takes a leading place. In addition to his well-known 'Casse-Noisette' Suite, arranged from the ballet of that name, he wrote four other suites, the third of which (in G) has for finale a set of variations that have achieved great popularity. The fourth, called 'Mozartiana', is modelled on Mozart's music. Tchaikovsky's ballets *The Sleeping Beauty* and *Swan Lake* can almost be included among his popular suites. Rimsky-Korsakov in his brilliantly scored *Scheherazade* went to *The Thousand and One Nights* for inspiration. Others are Stravinsky's vivid *L'Oiseau de Feu* (arranged from the ballet), and Prokofiev's *Scythian*, *Egyptian Night* and *Summer Day* suites. Glazunov has written a number of which the best known are *Raymonda* (ballet), 'Chopiniana' and a concert suite *Scènes de Ballet*, that, curiously enough, did not originate in the Terpsichorean art.

Sibelius's *Karelia* is an imaginative suite picturing that Eastern province of Finland, while his other important suites – *Swanwhite*, *King Christian*, *Belshazzar's Feast*, *Pelléas et Mélisande* – are drawn from incidental music to plays by Strindberg, Adolf Paul, Procopé and Maeterlinck, respectively.

Grieg's orchestral pieces also are derived from incidental music or are arranged from his popular piano pieces and songs. The two *Peer Gynt* suites belong to Ibsen's play and the *Sigurd Jorsalfar* to one by Bjørnson. Like them, the *Lyric* and *Holberg* suites – the latter for strings alone – are full of those melting Norwegian melodies and harmonies described so aptly by Debussy as 'pink bonbons stuffed with snow'.

French and Spanish composers have shown themselves equally at home in the suite form. Bizet has given us his *Roma*, the two *L'Arlésienne* (after Daudet's play), his *Jeux d'Enfants* and his *Carmen* suites, all of which bear the stamp of his great genius. The *L'Arlésienne* suites, with their warm southern colouring – for Bizet's music so often touched latitudes far south of his native Paris – never lose their freshness. Of the two by Saint-Saëns, the *Suite Algérienne* is the more frequently performed. Other modern French and Spanish composers, such as Debussy, Ravel, Milhaud and Falla, have given us some very interesting suites indeed. Debussy's *Printemps*, *La Mer* (three symphonic sketches), Ravel's two *Daphnis and Chloë* suites (originally composed as ballet for Diaghilev), *Le Tombeau de Couperin* and Falla's *El Amor Brujo* (adapted from the ballet) are all works of much individuality. Their chief charm lies in the fertility of their orchestral devices; they create an exotic atmosphere that links them with some of the best impressionistic music written in modern times. For delicacy and whimsicality of mood Ravel's *Ma Mère l'Oye* (Mother Goose) is altogether fascinating.

Of lighter texture are the many earlier suites by Massenet, Delibes, Messager, Lacombe and other kindred composers. Massenet's *Scènes Pittoresques* and *Scènes Alsaciennes* and the *Sylvia* and *Coppélia* ballet-suites by Delibes are of particularly striking character, enjoying a great popularity.

Modern Hungarian composers have found the suite form attractive. Dohnányi notably so in his F sharp minor suite, with its first movement a set of variations on a lovely theme; Bartók in four suites, one of them drawn from his ballet *The Miraculous Mandarin*; Kodály in that exciting work so skilfully transcribed from his opera *Háry János*.

With the tardy renaissance of British music in late Victorian and early Edwardian days many suites, of no more than mild interest, came from Parry, Mackenzie, Cowen and others. But the bulk of them and of those that followed, lacking invention and orchestration to fire the imagination, are now discarded in favour of more colourful examples. Such are Elgar's two *Wand of Youth* suites – youthful music, revised in years of maturity from what was written for a children's play as long ago as 1869. These were succeeded many years later by a *Nursery Suite* of equal simplicity and by a *Severn Suite* for brass band. Still more pictorial are Holst's *Beni-Mora* suite – the happy sequel to a holiday in Algeria – and his masterpiece, *The Planets*, in which he set down his own vivid impressions of the earth's nearer neighbours. Frank Bridge's suite *The Sea* is dramatic and highly imaginative in its orchestration – a work of genius, unjustly neglected. Later still we have Walton's two *Façade* suites, music originally written to accompany the recitation of poems by Edith Sitwell. Here with consummate skill and wit Walton parodies Edwardian times and types. His later suite, *The Wise Virgins*, is an adaptation of music by Bach, orchestrated in the most refined taste. Michael Tippett's suite in D owes a good deal to Tudor influences, whereas Britten has gone to Rossini and paraphrased two suites from his music.

Mention should also be made of the many light 'popular' suites written by other British composers. Examples by Foulds, Eric Coates, Haydn Wood, Ketelbey and Fletcher have certain qualities that make them very acceptable to that section of the musical public desiring straightforward tunes coupled to picturesque orchestration. While not for the aesthete with pronounced likes and dislikes, they should not be despised.

§ 2 OVERTURES, VARIATIONS AND RHAPSODIES

In its structure the overture is very like the first movement of a symphony, but less elaborate. It usually consists of two or three well-defined themes that undergo a restricted amount of development and are then recapitulated in brief before a coda that (in most cases) brings the music to a brilliant conclusion. In the 17th and 18th centuries, disguised under the name of *sinfonia* or *toccata*, the overture was, as we have seen earlier, the actual precursor of the symphony. But since the structure of the symphony has already been analysed in detail in this Book, there is perhaps no need further to examine that of the overture.

The overture, originally conceived as an instrumental prelude to an opera, has now lost much of its old identity. Its frequent transference to the concert-room a century and a half ago gave it a new lease of life dependent in no way on any alliance with the opera for which it was written. Being a prime favourite with audiences it soon multiplied exceedingly, and at a later date even developed in non-operatic style into an extended form called the 'concert overture'. This term, being interpreted, means that overtures were written just for their own sake, acting in a preludial or even postludial capacity in programmes of a miscellaneous nature.

But the real operatic overture did not die out until the later days of Wagner and Verdi and so, by comparison, concert overtures are fewer in number and by no means as popular as those many operatic examples written since Gluck and Mozart made them the fashion.

Almost every composer of note, old and new, has written overtures. So formidable is the list that I cannot pretend to enumerate the countless examples by Gluck, Mozart, Beethoven, Schubert, Weber, Mendelssohn, Wagner, Gounod, Smetana, Dvořák, Brahms, Borodin, Auber, Berlioz, Hérold, Bizet, Nicolai, Rossini, Humperdinck, Sullivan, Stanford, Tchaikovsky, Rimsky-Korsakov, Glinka, Suppé, Elgar, Mackenzie, Hindemith and many others. It is far more to the point to note that these overtures fall into four distinct categories. They are:

(*a*) Operatic overtures whose music is not found in the opera itself. Such are Rossini's 'Barber of Seville', Suppé's 'Pique Dame', Mozart's 'Così fan tutte'.

(*b*) Operatic overtures whose music is a *précis* or part *précis* of the main themes in the opera itself. Such are Mozart's 'Don Giovanni', Weber's 'Oberon', Wagner's 'Flying Dutchman', Beethoven's three 'Leonora' overtures written for his opera *Fidelio*, Humperdinck's 'Hänsel und Gretel', Berlioz's 'Le Carnaval Romain'.

(*c*) Overtures that form part of the incidental music to a play. Such are Beethoven's 'Egmont', Mendelssohn's 'Midsummer Night's Dream', Vaughan Williams's 'The Wasps'.

(*d*) Concert overtures of non-operatic type having a pictorial or sometimes a literary basis. Such are Dvořák's 'Carnival', Elgar's 'Froissart' and 'Cockaigne', Mackenzie's 'Britannia', Walton's 'Portsmouth Point' and 'Scapino', and Malcolm Arnold's 'Tam O' Shanter'.

There is little doubt that the finest examples come from the second category, for the composer builds up the most significant themes of his opera in a style that is quite symphonic and highly acceptable to the musical sense of the listener.

Because of the opportunities it affords for real inventiveness, skill in counterpoint and pictorial orchestration, the variation form (as a separate composition) has captured the imagination of many modern composers. Although used extensively by the classical masters from the time of Bach onwards in smaller compositions, it was not taken up by orchestral composers until more recent times. The number of orchestral sets of real importance is therefore small.

Brahms's *Variations on a Theme by Haydn* (St Anton Chorale) undoubtedly take pride of place. On a melody of great dignity and beauty, taken from a *Feldpartita* of Haydn, he has constructed variations that can be said to be the acme of perfection both in classical design and in musical content. The whole work unfolds like an opening flower; there is not an effect, not a note but what seems the logical outcome of all that has gone before, and the unswerving loyalty of the composer throughout the whole work to the five-bar phraseology so characteristic of the theme is an example of intellectual mastery perfect in its control. Strauss's *Don Quixote* variations, of immense cleverness, belong more properly to programme music. Dvořák's *Symphonic Variations*, Tchaikovsky's from his Suite in G, Reger's on a theme by Mozart, German's *Theme and Six Diversions* and Dohnányi's from his Suite in F sharp minor are other sets of outstanding interest.

But among those by British composers the finest are unquestionably Elgar's *Variations on an Original Theme*, the 'Enigma'. Dedicated by the composer 'to my friends pictured within', each of the fourteen variations is intended as a musical portrait, the identity of the friends being but half concealed under initials or a pseudonym heading each variation. Since the first performance of the work under Richter in 1899, it has been hailed everywhere as a great masterpiece. Elgar's happy display of ideas, the inspired treatment and brilliant orchestration have given the 'Enigma' variations a secure place in the world's repertoire. 'Nimrod' has now become a national threnody.

Of the making of rhapsodies there is no end, for the composer can 'gang his ain gait' without much regard for formal design. Surely every composer, no matter what his nationality, has some time or other either written or contemplated writing a rhapsody? While some works of this type, such as the 'Slavonic' Rhapsodies by Dvořák, are thematically original or nearly so, the majority are founded on folk-music. There are Hungarian rhapsodies; Rumanian, Spanish, English, Scottish, Welsh, Norwegian – there is no need to extend the list – and from English composers one for almost every *county*!

In form they are very free. Often beginning with a slow section that contains a quiet type of theme or folk-melody, they wander about at will (yet in most instances quite effectively) until a brilliant section of *vivace* character is reached for finale. Sometimes, as in Vaughan Williams's 'Norfolk' or Holst's 'Somerset' rhapsodies – both of which are based on local folk-songs – the placid mood of the start is recaptured in the concluding bars. This device seems admirable to preserve the bucolic atmosphere of the music: what comes to us in the mist of a May morning disappears in the mellow sunshine of an autumn evening. Delius's *Brigg Fair* – a Lincolnshire rhapsody – answers this description in much the same way. Of all the English rhapsodies it is perhaps the most beautiful. *Mai-dun*, a symphonic rhapsody by John Ireland, deals with the Wessex of Thomas Hardy, while Butterworth's *A Shropshire Lad* is based on melodies from his song-settings of Housman's poems. The latter is a remarkably beautiful work, one that makes us lament the untimely loss of a great English genius in the war of 1914–18.

§ 3 MISCELLANEOUS MUSIC

With the exception of the more important examples of programme music that come under consideration in the next chapter I have now dealt with the chief forms that have occupied the attention of most orchestral composers. To attempt here anything like a complete survey of the many miscellaneous works of smaller calibre (often of a programmatic nature) is as impossible as it seems unnecessary. For these smaller works are mostly *pièces genre*: inspirations that have flashed like lightning through the composers' minds, and which, set down in the ecstasy of the moment, have enriched the goodly store of orchestral music to an untold extent. The idyllic loveliness of Delius's *On Hearing the First Cuckoo in Spring*, the inspired tone-colours of Debussy's *L'Après-midi d'un Faune*, the macabre atmosphere of Sibelius's *Valse Triste* or the stirring patriotism of his *Finlandia*, the brilliance of Svendsen's *Carnival in Paris*, the barbaric splendour of Borodin's Polovtsian dances from *Prince Igor*, the infectious humour and gaiety of Grainger's *Shepherd's Hey*, all and many other pieces like them are needed to give buoyancy, colour and variety to orchestral programmes that might otherwise tend to become too heavy.

Each nation has contributed something. We may hold diverse opinions about the merits of French symphonies; nevertheless

France has given us many other works of great originality and charm. In addition to works by those French composers mentioned in the last chapter but one, there are many pieces by Gounod, Chabrier – his *España* is a *tour de force* – Roussel, Fauré and others – works that are constantly performed with success. Then, for still greater variety, there are the inimitable Hungarian dances arranged by Brahms and those by Kodály and Bartók; Dvořák's Slavonic dances; Grieg's Norwegian; Spanish dances by Moszkowski and Granados; English by Quilter, Malcolm Arnold and others. Nor must we forget works for strings alone. Serenades by Tchaikovsky and Dvořák; many charming arrangements from the classics by various composers, and as a final example Elgar's very beautiful *Introduction and Allegro* for string quartet and string orchestra.

For many years, too, incidental music and entr'actes, transferred from the theatre, have brightened programmes with many delightful tunes. Schubert's 'Rosamunde' and Mendelssohn's 'Midsummer Night's Dream' excerpts spring to mind as perhaps the best examples of this type of music. Then, too, we must not forget Beethoven's classic 'Rondino' for wind instruments; nor yet Wagner's 'Siegfried Idyll' and the many extracts from his operas that still cast their sonorous spell over thousands of music-lovers.

To omit any reference to either Johann Strauss (father and son), Waldteufel, Gung'l, Lanner, Lehar and many other Viennese waltz composers would be doing a grave injustice to a form of light music that has conquered the world by its inspired melodies. Brahms, the great philosopher of music, melted to them. Who of us, too, does not listen entranced to a fine performance of such waltzes as Johann Strauss's 'Tales of the Vienna Forest' or Lehar's 'Gold and Silver'?§

4 PROGRAMME MUSIC

Although programme music is thought of as an essentially 19th-century phenomenon with Liszt and Strauss as its foremost protagonists, the illustrative principle in music is of long standing. Music has been imitative of natural effects or human behaviour throughout its existence and in all cultures. Think of the madrigals of Jannequin, Marenzio and the great English madrigalists, where musical procedures are dictated by illustrative promptings; think of the *Ordres* of Couperin or the onomatopoeic keyboard pieces of Rameau like *La Poule* or *Les Tricotets*, or the countless evocations of hunting that abound in composers as diverse as Blow, in *Venus and Adonis*, and Bach. Vivaldi's concertos abound in picturesque imagery and Telemann's evocation of frogs and crows in his F major Suite for four horns, two oboes and strings could scarcely be more brilliant. In principle Telemann's frogs are not so far removed from Strauss's sheep in *Don Quixote*. But obviously, with the growth and development of the orchestra at the end of the 18th and beginning of the 19th centuries, the richer palette acted as a stimulus to the composer's imagination. The keyboard 'tone-poems' and miniatures of the 18th century were monochrome by comparison with the effects of colour open to composers after Beethoven.

Beethoven dominated the romantic imagination and undoubtedly gave enormous encouragement to its programmatic aspirations in the 'Pastoral' Symphony. However, the illustrative episodes were facets of a symphonic conception and not its substance. As we have seen, from Beethoven arose a great symphonic current that embraced Schubert, Schumann, Brahms and Dvořák, but alongside this tradition runs another in which the programmatic inspiration to which Beethoven had given play in the 'Pastoral' occupies a role of growing importance. In Berlioz, the underlying programme of the *Symphonie fantastique* in no way diminishes its novel architectural strength. Indeed, it is astonishing to think that this extraordinarily original world could have been conceived only three years after the death of Beethoven and the same length of time before the birth of Brahms. Its first movement, subtitled 'Reveries, Passions', yields to none in its richness of invention. Indeed, there are enough ideas in the opening 'Reveries' to nourish a whole sonata movement, and the allegro with its famous *idée fixe* – derived incidentally from an earlier work, his Prix de Rome cantata, *Herminie* – shows Berlioz's *genuine* feeling for form. As Hugh Macdonald has put it, 'Berlioz was more concerned with the working out of a musical idea according to its lights than in forcing the music into formal strait-jackets'. The way in which the musical shape is determined by the character of the ideas has excited the admiration of critics from the time of Schumann onwards. *Harold in Italy* is no less powerful or concentrated; both works show the romantic flair for illustrative detail at its most brilliant. It is true that knowledge of the programmatic scheme of both works adds a vital dimension to our understanding of the composer's intentions, yet both the *Fantastique* and *Harold* have a strength that renders them more than mere symphonic tone-poems. This is not the case with *Lélio*, the sequel to the *Symphonie fantastique*, or the much stronger 'Dramatic Symphony', *Romeo and*

Juliet, which are works unique in genre. Here the musical direction is determined largely by literary rather than exclusively musical considerations. This, it must be said, is the predominant characteristic of the tone poem, developed by Liszt a decade later and perfected at the end of the century by Strauss.

Of the thirteen symphonic poems that Liszt composed, twelve date from his Weimar period (1848–61) and range from *Ce qu'on entend sur la montagne* which he began sketching in 1847 to such familiar pieces as *Nazeppa* (1854) and *Les Préludes*, sketched in 1848 but revised, as was so often Liszt's wont, many times before it assumed its definitive form in 1854. As Humphrey Searle has argued, Liszt could well have written of his symphonic poems that they portray states of feeling rather than illustrative tone painting, in much the same sense as the 'Pastoral' Symphony (. . . *mehr empfindung als malerei*). As is also the case with Liszt's *Faust Symphony* it is the evocation of atmosphere and character that is of primary concern rather than the sophisticated feeling for proportion and balance that distinguishes the classical symphony.

Liszt set great store by the process of thematic metamorphosis as a means of organic unification. Obviously the traditional sonata form mould, for all its dramatic conflict of key and character, was not necessarily suitable for the artistic purposes he had in mind. In a work such as *Les Préludes*, both the thematic substance and the transformation it undergoes are crude, but elsewhere it operates at a more sophisticated level. The invention in many of the tone-poems, particularly a work like the *Heroïde funèbre*, is of an altogether higher level of imagination and whether in this or mood paintings, such as the Gretchen movement from the 'Faust' Symphony or the superbly dark episode from Lenau's *Faust – Der Nächtliche Zug* (*The Nocturnal Procession*), one is wholly convinced by the structure, one cannot fail to acknowledge the high quality of inspiration that informs them.

For the remaining decades of the 19th century, the tone poem fired the imagination of the composer in much the same way as had the sonata principle in the last decade of the 18th. It offered an apparent freedom to the romantic sensibility which the symphony seemed in danger of stifling. It is worth recalling that for every great symphony of Brahms and Dvořák, there were countless academic examples, pale in hue and often wanting in sinew, such as the symphonies of Raff or those of the critic, Felix Draeseke: small wonder that for artists of flair and imagination the tone-poem should seem a vital expressive outlet. In Russia it was to Liszt that Balakirev and his colleagues looked with admiration, and Berlioz's visits had served to stimulate interest in his art. *Thamar* is perhaps Balakirev's greatest single work and shows the extent to which Liszt's art had been assimilated. Tchaikovsky's *Hamlet*, *Romeo and Juliet* and *Francesca da Rimini* show that the 'Mighty Handful' were not alone in their Lisztian sympathies but here, as in Strauss's *Don Juan* or Sibelius's *Pohjola's Daughter*, the invention is shaped in such a way that it satisfies the expectations of both narrative detail and musical design. The symphonic poem became the artistic vehicle of the age: in Bohemia, Smetana in his cycle of six tone-poems, *Ma Vlast* as well as a number of powerful individual tone-poems such as *Richard III* and *Haakan Jarl* found a natural expressive medium, while Dvořák after the completion of his Ninth Symphony turned to the tone-poem, producing works like *The Wood-Dove*, *The Water-Goblin* and *The Golden Spinning-Wheel*, whose mastery and poetry have been much underrated. In France, Saint-Saëns and the Franck circle found the tone-poem no less congenial.

But its greatest master was undoubtedly Richard Strauss, whose essays in this genre encompass the period of the 1880s with *Aus Italien*, *Don Juan* and *Tod und Verklärung* culminating in master-pieces such as *Till Eulenspiegl* (1895), *Don Quixote* (1897) and *Ein Heldenleben* (1898) through to the 'Alpine' Symphony of 1915. As Strauss's mastery of opera grew with *Salome*, *Elektra* and *Der Rosenkavalier*, the stage became the centre of his creative activity and the era of his great tone poems drew to a close. In the greatest of them, *Don Juan*, *Don Quixote*, *Till Eulenspiegl*, one finds a marriage of illustrative detail and formal design that has been rarely matched and never surpassed. As a master of the former, he once joked that he could say knife and fork in music and indeed, as he lay dying, he likened the experience to *Tod und Verklärung*. Yet for all the vividness of his musical imagery, each edifice is soundly constructed, from the superbly wrought set of variations that comprise *Don Quixote* to the vast though more loosely-held-together sonata structures of *Ein Heldenleben* and the *Sinfonia Domestica*. Both scores call for large orchestral forces and their opulence is outstripped in the 'Alpine' Symphony which calls for no fewer than twenty horns. But with the post-war taste for smaller orchestral forces it is natural that the tone-poem should find less favour, though works with illustrative titles still abound. But the richly-scored Strauss tone-poems, and works like Schoenberg's *Verklärte Nacht* and *Pelleas und Melisande* or Elgar's *Falstaff*, signal the high water mark of the post-romantic tone-poem. Sibelius's *Tapiola* signifies its chilling end.

5 KEY DEVELOPMENTS 1900–50

Debussy, Schoenberg, Stravinsky and Bartók

If the development of the symphony shows us the spine of the orchestral repertoire, and the mastery of its form is one of the hallmarks of greatness, there are many masters of the orchestra – and indeed many great composers – who have not found in the symphony a congenial expressive outlet. In France, as we have seen, the symphony found eloquent advocates from Saint-Saëns, Franck and his disciples through to Roussel and Honegger, but the two greatest masters of the orchestra, Debussy and Ravel, did not compose in this genre. The French genius did not reject the sonata challenge (think of Fauré's chamber music or the Ravel string quartet) but the feeling for colour and light made it inevitable that programme music would exert the stronger appeal. It was this heightened awareness of colour and atmosphere that drew them to the Russians, for it was the Russian genius for orchestral colour rather than the symphonies of 'The Five' or Tchaikovsky that attracted them. From Russia Debussy inherited the harmonic palette of Moussorgsky, whose *Sunless* he quotes in *Nuages* (the passage is reborrowed by Stravinsky at the opening of *Le Rossignol*) and indeed, the first appearance of the whole-tone scale itself comes as early as Glinka. Nor should the attraction of oriental music be overlooked. Whatever were the formative influences on Debussy's musical language, be it Massenet or the Russians, it developed accents so totally individual and so completely Gallic that his youthful speech is seen in the light of the strong personality he so rapidly became.

One can argue that this heightened sense of harmonic awareness, the taste for growing complexity of orchestral textures as in Strauss and Scriabin, were manifestations of a society that sensed its own decline. When an art is in decline, the detail assumes greater importance than the whole, the ornamental figure is of greater interest than the structure it adorns, harmonic effects cease to be functional but are used in their own right. Debussy shocked his masters by his harmonic hedonism but in his case orchestral resource and harmonic sophistication was balanced by other classical forces: a finely developed sense of symmetry and awareness of form, albeit one which relied less on motivic development than on balanced phrase structures. It is this finely judged sense of proportion that makes *La Mer* and the Nocturnes so perfect though the former undoubtedly possesses a symphonic dimension, as for that matter does Ravel's *Daphnis et Chloë*. Where the formal sense is weaker, one is left with a mere riot of colour and orchestral effect as in the case of Florent Schmitt's (often evocative) *Tragédie de Salome*.

Ravel's mastery lay in his total command of his sensibility, his superbly polished craftsmanship, the ideal balance struck between exquisitely finished detail and expertly judged proportion, and a complete incapacity to settle for anything less than perfection both of texture and form. 'Open form' or even the controlled aleatorism of a Lutoslawski would have been anathema to him as it would have been for Debussy. In the latter, however, phrase structure is more often additive than the product of organic development: two bars will immediately be echoed or balanced, as they are in *Nuages* for example, but such is the level of artistry that the listener is barely conscious of this, whereas in Janáček he can hardly be unaware of it. With Debussy the degree of identification with experience is so total, the sense of style so highly developed, that the music conveys an authenticity of experience that steps outside time. Although Ravel's art reveals perhaps the most highly sophisticated harmonic sense of any composer of that time, his music worked within the established musical order. The two challenges to the existing order could be summed up as 'impressionism' and 'expressionism', though the latter was by far the more radical. With the whole-note scale came a weakening of classical major–minor tonality and an erosion of the sense of key contrasts. In the whole-tone scale the octave is divided into two tritones thus:

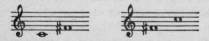

As a result the clearly focused cadential formulae (dominant-tonic, sub-dominant tonic i.e. the perfect and plagal cadences) are removed, just as the clearly focused image in painting had been undermined. With expressionism, the challenge took a more far-reaching form. Here it was less the pleasure principle, a hedonistic enjoyment of sensuous harmonies, and more the increasing expressive load placed on functional harmony. Greater contrapuntal complexity, density of musical incident, a higher norm of dissonance and degree of chromaticism blurred the focus of tonality. Schoenberg's early works grew out of the world of late Romanticism (Wagner, Mahler and Reger) but he and his pupils, Alban Berg and Anton von Webern, soon felt that tonality was no longer capable of bearing the expressive forces that were being unleashed in the early years of the 20th century. Emotions excluded from the world of art in the 18th and 19th centuries were unfettered: it was at this point that Freud was making his discoveries that were to transform our view of the forces at work in the human personality.

Schoenberg saw that the overripe world of *Verklärte Nacht* and *Pelleas und Melisande* held no real future for him and that the path of further harmonic complexity was a *cul de sac*.[1] The dissonances of Strauss's *Elektra* and *Salome*, at first so striking, soon lost their astringency; harmony fades and dissonance loses its power, whereas line and counterpoint retain strength. It was on this premise that his artistic development proceeded. With the increasing chromaticism and angularity of line, classical major-minor tonality was eroded to the point where a key centre was difficult to determine or where no tonal centre of gravity exerted a force. This period of free atonality subsequently gave way to the evolution of the technique of composition with twelve notes all equal in importance. Inevitably the series of twelve notes may be so formed that there may be tonal implications, but in a strictly serial work, a number of factors militated against this. The twelve notes, or the series, could be stated in retrograde form i.e. from back to front, in inverted form, i.e. with the intervals between the notes in the series ascending where they had previously descended and vice versa, and in both retrograde and inverted form. Thus:

Basic series: E flat G A B C sharp (downward leap of minor ninth to) C natural (upward leap of seventh to) B flat (downward leap of a minor sixth to) D natural E F sharp G sharp (downward leap of an eleventh) F natural

[1] According to Wellesz, Schoenberg's musical culture was related more or less exclusively to the Austrian, Germanic and central European tradition and did not extend back much beyond Bach. His attitude towards new music was catholic and outward-looking: the *Vereinung für Musikalisches Privataufhürung*, which he founded, was a forum for all new music of quality. No composer of distinctive voice or profile was excluded; it is interesting to note that one of the most performed composers at these concerts in the first years of the century was Debussy. 'Experimental' music, on the other hand, was for the study, and the insistence on the highest level of craftsmanship and a finished work of art was absolute.

Retrograde series: F natural (upward leap of an eleventh) G sharp F sharp E D (upward leap of a minor sixth) B flat (downward leap of seventh) C (upward leap of minor ninth to) C sharp B natural A G (upward leap of minor sixth) E flat

Inversion of basic series: D sharp (E flat) B natural A G F (upward leap of a minor ninth) G flat (descent of a seventh) G sharp (upward leap of a minor sixth) E D C B flat D flat

Retrograde and inverted: D flat B flat C D E G sharp G flat F G A B E flat

In a serially composed piece, no note can reappear before its eleven companions have been stated. The series also operates vertically, thus encompassing all pitch relationships. Schoenberg's first major work for orchestra that is so organized is the set of Variations, op. 31, but apart from this and the two concertos for violin and piano respectively, his most important serial works are probably the Third and Fourth Quartets and the superb String Trio. In later years Schoenberg, who was as plagued with his disciples and admirers as was Debussy before him, was at pains to stress that there was still a lot of good music to be written in C major, and indeed, a number of works written after he settled in the United States were tonal, among them the Suite in G, and the Chamber Symphony no. 2.

Although the Three Orchestral Pieces, op. 6, and the Violin Concerto of 1935, a work of great poignancy and expressive power, are cornerstones of the repertory, Alban Berg's greatest achievements lie in his two operas, *Wozzeck* and *Lulu*. But it is the greater directness of appeal and overt emotionalism that have secured for Berg a wider popular response than the more densely-packed scores of Schoenberg. Of the three composers comprising the 'second Viennese school', it is Webern who has, at the time of writing, the most precarious hold on the concert repertoire, yet who has exercised the strongest influence on later composers. His combination of keen sensibility and the greatest economy and concentration places exceptional demands on performers and listeners alike but his *pointillisme*, along with that of Debussy, struck powerful resonances in Boulez. Speaking of Schoenberg's imitators, Egon Wellesz once said that the second Viennese school was a response to 'a climate in which we all sensed the breaking up of civilization as we knew it' and the collapse of a musical tradition and its language. To transplant this musical language which was evolved in Vienna to other conditions and environments is 'in a sense, to steal our experience'.

Yet, the example of Schoenberg acted as a powerful force in the first half of the century. To the names of Berg, Webern and Wellesz, a host of others must be added who were drawn into his orbit: Luigi Dallapiccola in Italy, Nikos Skalkottas in Greece, Roberto Gerhard in Spain, Roger Sessions in the United States, Taduesz Baird in Poland, Fartein Valen in Norway, Humphrey Searle and Elisabeth Lutyens in England.

And Schoenberg's example also exercised a powerful fascination outside the ranks of those who embraced free atonality or serialism itself. It invited certain compromises, albeit of a superficial nature, in a number of composers predominantly tonal in outlook. The use of the series as a means of organization occurs in such unlikely figures as Britten (*The Turn of the Screw*), Aaron Copland, whose flirtation was earlier and more serious (Piano Quartet, Piano Fantasy, Statements, etc.), Shostakovich (Fourteenth Symphony, Twelfth Quartet, Violin Sonata, op. 134), Walton (Violin Sonata, Symphony no. 2) and in the Swiss composer, Frank Martin (1890–1974). Martin has evolved a highly personal response to it in works like the *Petite Symphonie Concertante* for harp, harpsichord, piano and double string orchestra where the musical substance of the series is used as a unifying force within a wholly tonal framework. The pale, muted colourings that distinguish the writing of this Swiss master ultimately stem from the world of Debussy and more specifically, *Pelléas et Mélisande*, and it is the great French composer rather than Schoenberg who was the formative influence in his artistic growth. His art is invariably lyrical in feeling and textures are marvellously limpid and luminous. Some music lovers complain of the limited range of expressive devices Martin employs (critics no doubt would attribute this to the compromise with Schoenberg), but at his finest, in the concertos written immediately after the end of the Second World War, his highly personal habits of mind seem totally attuned to his imaginative purposes.

Critics of serialism argue that it is an inhibiting rather than liberating discipline and that to abandon tonality is like dispensing with a sense of gravitational force. The emotional range of a highly chromatic texture is inevitably limited even if the emotional intensity is more highly charged. Critics of Schoenberg argued that his musical language though angular in terms of line and serialized in terms of pitch, merely took over the rhythmic patterns and phrase structures of the old Viennese tradition; hence in the 1950s the doctrine of total serialization was evolved.[1]

If we have followed the erosion of tonality in the first half of the 20th century, we must turn back on our tracks to look at another major figure, whose allegiance to diatonic tonality remained unshaken until the late 1950s, namely, Igor Stravinsky (1882–1971). Stravinsky's genius for the ballet dominated his musical thinking throughout his life, for whatever the expressive outlet he chose, balletic habits of mind were quick to surface. Even the Symphony in Three Movements (1945) proceeds additively rather than organically: movement and the dance were the mainsprings of his imagination. His first ballet, *L'Oiseau de feu* (1910) came into being partly because of Liadov's indolence and Diaghilev's boldness and flair. Liadov had been slow in responding to Diaghilev's original commission and it was transferred to Stravinsky, then a young man in his mid-twenties. He had already scored a success with *Feu d'artifice* ('Fireworks') with its strong resonances of Dukas and Rimsky-Korsakov, with whom Stravinsky had studied in St Petersburg. If 'Firebird' was a marvellously-wrought evocation of the fairy-tale world, it stands as much at the end of one tradition (that of Rimsky-Korsakov's highly colourful but two-dimensional stage works with a harmonic vocabulary derived from Lisztian procedures) as it does at the beginning of a new world. It is full of marvellous inspiration, yet in some ways the most deeply original and characteristic of all his ballets is *Petrushka*, an astonishing work of genius for a composer still in his twenties.

However, it was in *Le Sacre du Printemps* that Stravinsky made his most revolutionary leap forward. The scandal accompanying its first performance in 1913 is well known though it must in fairness be said that the ballet itself, choreographed by Nijinsky, was as much responsible for the uproar as the actual score. Nijinsky's choreography while taking into account the rhythmic implications of each section separately, failed to co-ordinate them into a whole. Such was the uproar that the score was drowned in places, no mean feat when one thinks of the vast apparatus employed; quintuple woodwind, eight horns (two of which are required to switch to tenor tubas), five trumpets, three trombones, two tubas, percussion and strings. He was never to use such outsize forces again. In later life Stravinsky spoke of his love for 'the violent Russian spring that seemed to begin in an hour and was like the whole earth cracking',

[1] See page 351.

an image that would seem to inspire so much of *Le Sacre*. Yet for all its primitive inspiration, Stravinsky did not draw on any folk material, save for the bassoon melody in the opening of *L'adoration de la terre* which he borrowed from a collection of Lithuanian folk tunes but in any event, the innovatory force of this remarkable score resides in its rhythmic and metric originality, which is without precedent in Russian – or any other European music, as well as its highly sophisticated harmonic vocabulary. To chart Stravinsky's subsequent course is of absorbing interest. Making a virtue of necessity, his works composed during the 1914–18 war use the most economic resources, from *Renard* (1916) to *L'Histoire du Soldat* (1918), and the post-war era found him turning his back on the rich orchestral palette of the pre-war years and seeking in pieces like the *Symphonies of wind instruments* (1920) and *Les Noces* (1922) an altogether more austere sound world. Stravinsky's style underwent numerous superficial changes after the 1920s, though his strong and outsize personality impregnates every bar he pens, whether in works like *Pulcinella* (1919) or *Baiser de la Fée* (1930) which have a strong element of pastiche, or in such austere, hieratic works as the Mass (1948) or the serial works composed in his old age. The larger part of his output was written for the ballet or the stage, but almost everything he composed including the Symphony in C (1940), the Symphony in Three movements (1945), the Violin Concerto (1932) could be used as the basis for dance, with the possible exception of the *Symphony of Psalms* (1930). This, *Oedipus Rex* and *Persephone* may be said to represent the apogée of his neo-classicism. If a composer were to be measured solely in terms of originality, Stravinsky would rank among the very greatest composers of all time. His music exhibits razor-keen intelligence, wit and proportion, well-defined and controlled feeling; no note is out of place and no texture miscalculated; he is the supreme stylist. So complete is its mastery that it renders the areas of feeling that it does not encompass seemingly irrelevant, for Stravinsky is essentially an urban composer with little of the feeling for nature that marks Bartók or Janáček.

Another key figure is Paul Hindemith (1895–1963) who pursued a consistently tonal path throughout his creative life. His early work showed the influence of Reger but his strong contrapuntal instinct led him away from atonality and closer to neo-classicism. His fertility of invention and fine craftsmanship made itself evident in the series of *Kleine Kammermusik* that he wrote in the 1920s and for that matter in the first three of his six string quartets. He was, incidentally, an accomplished violist and toured for many years with the Amar Quartet; indeed, he was the soloist in the first performance of Walton's Viola Concerto.

In spite of what struck listeners in the 1920s as a high norm of dissonance, Hindemith's music was never atonal and his thinking always remained key-centred, even though traditional concepts of the major and minor mode were blurred. He based his theories, which he outlined in *Unterweisung im Tonsatz*, on the 'natural laws of sound', discarding the dependence of chords on the diatonic scale and the building up of chords on thirds; he was above all opposed to the arbitrary division of the chromatic scale, systemized by such artists as the Czech composer Alois Hábá who utilized quarter-tones and sixth-tones, and was completely opposed to the twelve-tone technique. Hindemith's musical speech is immediately distinctive, making use, as it does, of regular phrase structures and repeated rhythmic patterns as well as a highly personal harmonic vocabulary and melodic style. His sympathies have lain fairly consistently in neo-baroque directions and he is in many ways North German in feeling and sensibility. His textures are often elaborately contra-puntal and forms such as the passacaglia or the fugue, which were so beloved by baroque composers, have found a sure foothold in his output. The finale of his ballet, *Nobilissima Visione* on the theme of St Francis of Assisi, and the last movement of the *Harmonie der Welt* Symphony are both passacaglias, the former a magnificent one, while the fugue, rarely encountered in Stravinsky (the slow move-ment of the Symphony of Psalms is an exception), was a congenial-texture to his imagination, as his keyboard music and in particular *Ludus Tonalis* demonstrates. Hindemith's regular, carefully-balanced rhythms and periods, his angular lines with their proliferation of fourths and the distinctive cadential formulae he employs lend to his speech a strong identity; so personal is this world and so enorm-ously prolific was he that there are times when his art appears merely self-imitating and its purpose seems to fail. Although there are a number of symphonies, the finest of them is in a sense closer to a suite than a symphony proper. The *Mathis der Maler* Symphony draws its inspiration from the opera of the same name, much in the same way as does the post-war *Harmonie der Welt*, based on the life of the astronomer, Johannes Kepler. One feels a closer kinship to baroque ideals in the series of concertos that Hindemith composed for various instruments than to the practices of the Viennese classics. Be this as it may, Hindemith's musical language exerted a powerful attraction on a host of composers; in Italy, Goffredo Petrassi; in England, Arnold Cooke; in America, Piston, Norman dello Joio, Lukas Foss, Leonard Bernstein and others; in Switzerland, Willy Burkhard, Conrad Beck and Walter Geiser; while in the German-speaking world, Fortner, Blacher, Pepping and Johan Nepomuk David were all in some way responsive to his influence, and in the North, so were Hilding Rosenberg and Niels Viggo Bentzon.

But neo-classicism was not the only path, and the embers of post-nationalism (or in the Americas the fires of an emerging national self-consciousness) were still much alive in the inter-war years. An essential feature of the nationalist composer is a strong relationship with his natural cultural background whether it finds expressive form in identification with folk elements as in Bartók and Kodály in Hungary (or Vaughan Williams, Holst and others in England), or reflects the speech inflections of the country as in Janáček. In the case of Heitor Villa-Lobos, who has almost two thousand works to his credit, or Carlos Chavez it takes the less intense form of absorbing folk elements or themes of folk-inspired character into the lavishly scored, opulently laid-out textures and evocative atmosphere of the post-nationalist tone-poem. But both Bartók and Kodály made intensive studies of the folk music of Hungary and Rumania, and both exploited in their different ways the rich musical legacy their pioneering researches uncovered. Bartók's contribution to the string quartet, his concertos for the piano and for violin are discussed elsewhere in this volume, but his achievement as a master of the orchestra is of a high order. His early *Kossuth* symphony (1903) and his two orchestral suites (op. 3, 1905; op. 4, 1907 rev. 1920 and 1943) are basically Straussian in outlook with some folk-like ingredients, and it was not until the Deux Images, op. 10, and the score to the ballet, *The Wooden Prince* (1914–16) that a strongly individual personality emerges and the influences of Strauss and Debussy are fully digested. Both *The Miraculous Mandarin* (1919) and the *Dance Suite* (1923) offer abundant exotic colour but the most remarkable of his orchestral works is the Music for strings, percussion and celesta (1936), the percussion embodying a variety of instruments, piano, harp, xylophone, timpani and so on. The opening idea ranks among the most highly characterized themes that Bartók ever penned and the first movement is concerned with it to the exclusion of any other material whatever.

The idea, starting on the note A and rising to E flat, consists of four phrases or breaths, some of which are explored later in the work as separate entities. The movement is a fugue, and one of the most remarkably intense and poetic examples of fugal texture in all music. Concentrating single-mindedly on the subject, offering no episodes, no counter-subject or any extended free counterpoint, it has remarkable density, and a refinement of sonority even in Bartók's output. The third movement too deserves special mention, for it belongs to the world of 'night music', that Bartók made so much his own, right from the piano piece, *Out of doors*, down to the Piano Concerto no. 3. Its sonorities are arguably the most poetic, imaginative and exploratory of all his essays in this particular area of feeling: its thematic substance derives from the fugue of the very opening. The smoother contours of the Concerto for orchestra (1943) and its greater popularity should not disguise its mastery and virtuosity. Bartók and Kodály between them lay the setting for a strongly national and flourishing school of composers; Hungary seems particularly rich in talent and figures such as Sandor Veress, Laszlo Lajtha, and among younger figures, Andras Mihaly, György Kurtag and others.

Although he belongs to an older generation – indeed, he was three years older than Elgar and a decade older than Strauss – Janáček's fertility in old age places much of his important output during the war years, when *Taras Bulba* was written, or the 1920s when the *Sinfonietta* and such keys works as the Concertino for piano, the two string quartets and *Mlàdi* came into being. He was a composer with an intense feeling for nature, full of melodic vitality and colour, whose musical thinking proceeded additively rather than organically. In Rumania, Georges Enesco was the commanding national figure though his early style was indebted to Brahms, but in his Third Symphony and above all his highly original opera, *Oedipe*, he evolved a language at once his own and yet highly Rumanian. Perhaps the most interesting 'nationalist' figure between the wars, apart from Bartók and Janáček, is the Polish composer, Karol Szymanowski. His art took as its point of departure the music of Chopin and Scriabin, but he rapidly succumbed to the influence of Debussy and Stravinsky. His early works also show some Straussian sympathies (the Symphony no. 2 is a case in point) but his mature works, the Third Symphony ('Song of the Night'), the two Violin Concertos, the ballet *Harnasie* evince a texture of luminous quality and an atmosphere of ecstatic mysticism. His fastidious taste and refinement of palette can be seen, too, in his keyboard music as well as the touching 'Stabat mater', one of the greatest choral works of the present century.

The existence of a major figure invariably poses difficulties for his successors: Hungarian music lived in the 1950s and '60s very much in the shadow of Bartók, Polish musicians looked to Szymanowski during the same period; in France, Olivier Messiaen dominated, another composer of strong mystical leanings whose contribution to organ music is second to none in the present century. The break in the traditional development occasioned by the Nazi years in Germany resulted in an explosion of activity in the immediate post-war period, when the vacuum, resulting from the absence of Schoenberg, Hindemith and others, was suddenly filled. Karl Amadeus Hartmann, Boris Blacher and Wolfgang Fortner rapidly came to the fore but the youngest stars to emerge, Stockhausen and Hans Werner Henze rapidly assimilated the Schoenbergian experience. Henze in his First Symphony (1947) and Violin Concerto no. 1 produced music of fine craftsmanship and strong atmosphere. Indeed, it is perhaps the sense of atmosphere which is strongest in the fine series of symphonies that punctuate his activity until the 1960s. Henze's art is direct, his ear fastidious, his sensibility acute and the world of feeling he evokes distinctive.

6 WHAT OF THE FUTURE?

During the years since the end of the Second World War in 1945, mankind has, we are told, taken as great a stride forward in terms of scientific discovery and technological change as it has in all previous epochs put together. Modern society is certainly very different from the immediately post-war world, at least in the 'developed' world. Music and its language has been subjected to pressures that are wholly new and that have wrought more far-reaching change than the invention of printing or, one is tempted to say, since modern notation evolved in the West. No great artist from Palestrina, Monteverdi, Schütz through to Bartók has ever evolved without forming a strong relationship with the tradition in which he has been fostered. The existence in the West of musical notation has enabled us to observe the changes in our artistic language that have gone unrecorded in other cultures. In the case of a contemporary of Bach living in northern Germany, his musical background would not have extended for more than a few decades into the past and would largely have been confined to the geographical area in which he lived. Obviously there would be isolated copies of works outside the particular period or geographical entity: Bach himself knew Palestrina's 'Stabat mater', a fair amount of

Vivaldi and a good deal else besides. But in terms of the availability of repertory his horizons were firmly limited as were those of his immediate predecessors. True, composers like Lassus and Schütz travelled but it was not until the advances in communication which opened up Europe and America in the 19th century that travels such as Tchaikovsky's, Berlioz's and Dvořák's became a much easier proposition, and composers' musical horizons correspondingly widened.

The advance of the youthful science of musicology pushed back the frontiers of music in terms of time. But the radio, the gramophone and in particular the long-playing record and its successors changed all that. Within two decades or more, it has made available music on a scale unthinkable in earlier periods. The public, and more to the point, the young composer is confronted not only with the music of his own culture but with that of other countries near and far, not only of his own time but of the Middle Ages and before, not only of Europe but of cultures as dissimilar as those of India, Africa, and the Far East, not only music that is rapidly changing but ethnic music that gives us a glimpse of the musical practices of the remote past. The implications of this cultural explosion are only now beginning to register. It is now often a record of a new work rather than the score which is the more readily available. One shelf, albeit of ample proportions, full of long-playing records represents more than the repertoire available to an active musician of the 18th century throughout the whole of his life. Such is the diversity and quantity of repertoire available now that the composer is almost in the position of a telephone exchange bearing too many incoming calls: he is overwhelmed with information and widely varying musical experience, and it becomes more difficult for him to form as close a relationship with tradition.

The 20th century has seen two appalling world wars and undergone traumatic change: society is far less stable than that of bourgeois 19th-century Europe. Thus, it is hardly surprising that the language of music with its major–minor key system should be strained by the growing complexity of expressive means and density of incident that marked the textures of late Mahler and early Schoenberg. With the erosion of tonality, Schoenberg sought a new order: the tension between key centres that was the lynch-pin of the classical symphony was replaced by the unifying role of the series; composition with twelve notes equal in their importance and functions was the outcome. The series could undergo various permutations: it could be played retrograde, inverted and both retrograde and inverted at the same time. At times, in the Violin Concerto of Alban Berg for example, the series might have tonal implications; at others one would have a quick kaleidoscopic sense of constantly changing tonal references while at others the sense of key centre would disappear altogether. Naturally Schoenberg's was not the only challenge to classical tonality: Debussy's whole-tone scale undermined the dominant-tonic relationship; Sibelius's Fourth Symphony experimented with passages of indeterminate tonality, Milhaud developed polytonality (several keys going at once) while other attempts were made in the inter-war years to divide the octave into more than twelve notes (Hábá, Wyzhnegradsky etc.).

Yet if serialism, which claimed many adherents and even, in his later years, a composer with such strong tonal instincts as Stravinsky, affected pitch relationships, rhythmic organization remained unaltered. Boulez and others felt this to be anomalous: the sense of tonal order was replaced by a new way of organizing pitch relationships while phrase lengths and rhythmic patterns could come from Brahms! Hence, the next step was to apply serial organization to rhythm and then to dynamic markings: in short, total serialism.

From total serialism a reaction was predictable: instead of everything being pre-determined, nothing should be pre-determined. The element of chance entered into the composer's thinking: aleatoric music was born and even as distinguished a composer as the Pole, Witold Lutoslawski embodies such episodes into a work like *Jeux vénitiens*. Not only was this a reaction against total serialization but it was fostered by the 'tyranny' of the gramophone: the unalterable performance which can contain no surprises either of text or nuance. Yet another development given the preoccupation with technology was *musique concrète*, and then subsequently musical sounds produced by electronically generated means which are discussed elsewhere in this volume.[1]

Nor can the art-anti-art movement be passed over without comment though it is a phenomenon rather than a positive development. It derives much of its steam from Dadaism and the work of John Cage. But in extending the banner of art to sound material that is random selected, the artist is of course abrogating his creative and critical function. The two processes are indivisible since creativity presupposes a choice between various courses of action that the artist's imagination opens up and critical judgment is an obviously

[1] See page 180.

vital part of the creative act. It must be noted in passing that the language of music is not the only thing that has been challenged in our decades. Given the example of many 19th-century critics who failed through lack of insight and imagination fully to register the importance of some great artists, criticism has undergone a kind of Beckmesser complex. Like some composers, the critic has abrogated his role: the artist must be right! A great composer may well suffer from the misunderstanding of critics but his art will eventually conquer the public. But in a climate where non-art, indeed artistic phenomena that proclaim themselves non-art, meets a response equal to that of a work of art proper, the effect on a serious composer is infinitely more destructive.

Constant Lambert spoke in *Music Ho!* of 'the appalling popularity of music' but he could scarcely have anticipated the extent of its availability in present-day society, at times in conditions that can only serve to dull and blunt the sensibility. Hence, a public conditioned by its constant availability to listen casually to or even ignore great masterpieces, such as the late Beethoven quartets or the Ninth Symphony, must be shocked into disciplined listening by electronic music or even random sounds parading as art, or so the argument goes.

Much of this reflects the sheer self-consciousness of modern music: in the case of many gifted, serious composers, the concerns are with means rather than ends. Yet, paradoxically enough, the quest for originality, for identity, more often than not produces its opposite. In concentrating on manner rather than matter, in being too responsive and aware of all that is happening in advanced circles, modern composers all too often embrace anonymity. Attending an exhibition of modern painting, art from Finland, New Zealand, the Balkans or South America all looks exactly the same: and much the same holds good for festivals of contemporary music.

The collapse of language, the disintegration of musical syntax makes style impossible. It is only those composers who have maintained a genuine relationship with their language that can use it independently. A work of art is a report on our innermost experiences in a way that can find no other expression: music begins where words leave off. No one can tell what expressive means composers will choose in the future and prediction is fruitless. What one can say with certainty is that any worthwhile art will be subject to the same inner discipline and logic that has been the case in the past.

In 1945 few would have predicted the extent to which Japan would become an important musical centre with a flourishing school of soloists, composers and an abundance of fine orchestras. At that time the musical centre of gravity remained western Europe and the United States. No one can predict where the next flowering of musical culture will be or can be confident of the continued hegemony of Europe.

Book 4

Opera

by Edward J. Dent
with revisions and a section on Modern Opera by
Charles Osborne

PART 1 HOW OPERA AROSE

§ 1 THE OPERATIC CONVENTION

The simplest way of describing what an opera is, is to say that it is a play set to music. In some operas, such as those of Wagner, the music is continuous from the beginning of an act to the end of it; in others, such as the earlier operas of Verdi, the music is continuous, but it is broken up into pieces that we can recognize as songs, and in many theatres the audience applauds them and even encores them. If we listen to an opera by Mozart, we may find that the songs, duets, etc, are separated by what is called *recitative*, a sort of mongrel thing that is neither plain talking nor real singing, accompanied by uninteresting chords on a piano or harpsichord. Readers of Dickens will remember that Mr Skimpole in *Bleak House* had a curious habit (being a gentleman of dangerously artistic tastes) of conducting ordinary domestic conversation in recitative, playing his own pianoforte accompaniment. And there are other operas, generally of a comic type, in which the business of the play is carried on in ordinary speech, but every now and then the characters burst into song.

Children who see an ordinary play for the first time in their lives often suppose that what happens on the stage is 'real' and not pretence. It may take them some little time, perhaps indeed several visits to the theatre, before they can adjust their minds to the convention by which we receive some emotional excitement, whether tragic or comic, from what we are watching on the stage, while the whole time we know perfectly well that it is all mere pretending. Persons who have had a little more experience of theatre-going soon begin to discover that even in an ordinary play of modern life things do not happen exactly as they do in the world of reality; but there is at any rate some illusion of reality, and certain authors, actors and producers take endless pains to be as realistic as they possibly can, just as certain portrait painters try to paint as much like a colour photograph as possible. Some clients prefer it.

The person who demands strict realism in a play or a portrait will be bewildered, annoyed, or possibly amused at what he sees on his first visit to an opera. He is accustomed to the methods of modern comedy, let us suppose; he will find it absurd that people should sing everything that they have to say. People do not sing in ordinary life, except in the bathroom. Let us assume a play-goer who has arrived at enjoying Shakespeare. We can get him to admit that though people

357

do not habitually talk in poetry they may do so in a play the scene of which is remote from our own times; and if he will admit that, it is no great step to admitting that they may sing. Some of Shakespeare's characters do in fact sing, and they are generally those still further removed from our own human environment, a little mad it may be, or spirits from another world such as Ariel. But in Shakespeare, even at his most fantastic moments, the characters behave with some semblance of human reason, whereas in an opera they just stand about waving their arms, singing long soliloquies at the tops of their voices, and sometimes, just when something 'dramatic' ought to happen, standing all together in a row at the footlights and holding up the action by an interminable joint performance. Opera plots are so fatuous; besides, most of them are in Italian. Opera singers never act; if they are not ludicrously corpulent they at any rate never look in the least like the sort of people they are pretending to be. The whole of opera, be it Mozart, Verdi or Wagner, is a mass of absurd conventions, and there can be only one motive that leads people to pretend that they enjoy it – pure snobbery.

Here the serious musician, the frequenter of classical concerts, joins hands with the play-goer and man of letters; for the one the opera spoils the play, for the other it ruins the music. What can be said in its defence?

It is perfectly true that opera is a mass of conventions, but the same is really true of every form of art, musical or visual. The difficulty of understanding and accepting the operatic conventions arises chiefly from the fact that whereas the plays which the average man in this country is likely to see fall roughly into two classes, modern plays and Shakespearean plays, the ordinary operatic repertory includes operas belonging to many more different periods. The play-goer who enjoys Shakespeare and Shaw may well be a little out of his depth when he goes to see a tragedy, or even a comedy, of Dryden; he may easily find Goldoni foolish, and the drama of a hundred years ago ludicrous. There is hardly a play between those of Shakespeare and those of the present century that has not become at the best a 'museum-piece'; but in the operatic world a repertory company – and most opera companies work on the repertory system – will be quite normally presenting musical drama of any period from 1762 to the present day, and it is just as likely to present what musicians would call 'museum-pieces', such as Purcell's operas, as works of the last twenty years.

The hardened opera-goer has in fact accustomed himself, probably without being aware of it, to what would make almost a complete series of illustrations for a lecture on the history of musical drama, and the result is that those readers who are only just beginning their operatic experience must here be treated to the lecture without the illustrations.

§ 2 ORIGINS

The association of music with drama goes back far beyond the beginnings of what we can call the history of music. It is well known that drama originated in the ceremonial dances of primitive peoples, and these dances were naturally accompanied by music – by singing and by such instruments as those peoples possessed. The tragedies of ancient Greece were largely dependent on music for their original presentation, and the theatrical shows of Imperial Rome employed musicians in large numbers. In the Middle Ages the drama passed largely into the hands of the Church, and it is at this point that we may begin to watch the growth of a type of spectacle that contained the principle of opera, although it was not yet known by that name.

For the last 300 years we have drawn a sharp distinction between opera and drama, between plays that are sung and plays that are spoken; but, as we know ourselves, there is even now a border region between the two, and in the Middle Ages it was hardly necessary to make the distinction, because practically no play was ever performed without some kind of music. In the liturgical dramas the words were sung, or at least intoned, throughout. Some very interesting sacred dramas with music were composed by a woman, St Hildegard, abbess of a German nunnery about 1150–60. A drama in plainsong may not sound very operatic to us at the present day; but it must always be borne in mind that throughout the centuries the musical drama has of natural necessity always had to employ whatever kind of music was in use at the time. If we consider the ordinary repertory of today we may find that some operas strike us as more 'dramatic' than others; in some the words seem to be more important than the music, while in others the reverse is the case. But our judgment may very easily be at fault owing to a lack of the historical sense. Two centuries ago, in the days of Handel, operas consisted of a string of songs separated by stretches of recitatives; many modern listeners find such operas unbearable when they are revived as 'museum-pieces', and complain all the more because the songs themselves involve a great deal of repetition, both of music and of words. But to our ancestors who heard those operas for the first time, this was not in the least unnatural: at any rate for those who were musical and understood the language in which the operas were performed. The music was in that particular style and shape because all music of that period was in that style and shape; no other style was conceivable. The same thing applies to the words; sometimes they were written by poets of high distinction. If a modern audience does not understand their merits it is not altogether the fault of the original writers.

If we study the early history of drama we shall notice that changes in dramatic method are paralleled by changes in general social life. Mediaeval drama was religious and popular; it was religious because the Church was the home of all literary and artistic culture, and popular because the Church wanted to use drama as a means of religious instruction for those who could not read or write. It was only comparatively late in the Middle Ages that literary and artistic culture spread from the Church to the upper ranks of society. For many centuries after the fall of Rome the main function of a nobleman was fighting; those of noble birth who had no taste for it took refuge in the monasteries. It was considered disgraceful for a nobleman to be able to read and write, or to take pleasure in things intellectual, unless he was in holy orders; we have the positive testimony of mediaeval writers to this effect. And even as late as about 1500 we can still see traces of this attitude towards the arts; Castiglione, in his famous *Book of the Courtier*, which describes the court of the Duke of Urbino – at that time the most cultivated society of Europe – tells how a certain noble warrior refused to dance or to listen to music and was very properly reproved by his hostess, who told him that he ought to be well oiled and put away in a cupboard along with his own armour until the next war, in order to prevent him from becoming more rusty than he was already.

It is only in the 16th century that any form of cultured drama begins to emerge. The religious drama was in many places organized on a very elaborate scale, and it certainly involved a great deal of music; but the musical records are scanty, and it is clear that the organizers of it had no idea of treating something that should be musically an organic whole, composed by one single musician, like the operas of Verdi or Wagner. Some of the music may have been composed for the occasion, some of it may have been put together from whatever sources were handy; plays with music are still often produced in this country on similar principles.

It was obviously a moment of the greatest importance in the history of drama when permanent theatres began to be built and companies of actors performed in them with some degree of regularity, if not every day. In the Middle Ages all actors, singers, dancers, acrobats and minstrels had been regarded as rogues and vagabonds, unless they were in the regular employ of some prince or nobleman and were classed as his servants. The Church had its mystery plays, but they were got up only for certain festivals, and the humbler drama, performed in inn yards or in the open street, was even more irregular in its appearance. It was not until after the beginning of the great social and intellectual change to which we give the general name of the Renaissance that drama and music, separately or together, could be organized on something like a regular system.

The Renaissance began in Italy, and for the rest of the world it may be said that the Renaissance meant the discovery of Italy as the source of all intellectual and artistic inspiration. It is only natural, therefore, that Italy should have been the original home of opera. Italy created opera, because Italy had no drama, at least, no drama comparable to that of England and Spain. There is nothing in Italian literature corresponding to the plays of our Elizabethan poets or to those of Lope de Vega and Calderon, unless we go back to the 'Sacred Representations', as they were called, which in Spain at any rate had a longer life than in other countries and developed more continuously into normal drama. The Italian religious plays were often of high literary value, but just at the moment when they might have followed the example of their Spanish relatives, they were forbidden to be acted. The only drama that the Italians possessed in the 16th century was either the old Latin drama of Plautus and Terence, translated into Italian, and certain imitations of Latin drama written by court poets, such as Ariosto, for occasional court performances, or else the 'comedy of masks', which was acted by strolling players, wherever they could find a 'pitch', for the amusement of the common people.

The various Italian courts set the example to the rest of Europe in the extravagance of their pageants and masques, as we may call them. There is no need to describe them here, for most readers will have some idea of the masques and other entertainments which were provided on various occasions for Queen Elizabeth I and for James I, we now know that practically all of these were modelled as closely as possible on the entertainments of the courts of Florence and

Mantua in the preceding generation. Music played a large part in them, but it had not yet reached the point of becoming a complete musical setting of a play. None the less, the materials of opera were all ready to hand; the madrigal, which was the main musical form of the century, was gradually leading the way towards musical drama.

It may be well to warn the reader that madrigals (see also Book 5, Chapters 5 and 6) in the 16th century were not invariably sung by a chorus without accompaniment. There is abundant evidence to show that they were very often accompanied by instruments, and that they were also sung as solos for a single voice, the other parts being played by instruments. At court festivities they were often performed by singers and players in some sort of theatrical costume, with the adjunct of scenery. Another thing to note is that even as early as in the days of Castiglione (about 1520) people used to recite poetry to the accompaniment of a viol, though we have no very definite record of how this was done.

In considering the history of opera we can observe three different ways in which music is employed. First, it is the direct expression of emotion. The ordinary man expresses himself in prose; in a more exalted form of drama the characters speak in verse, because poetry is a vehicle of intensified self-expression; and singing is a still further intensification of poetry. The singer in an opera appears in fact to create out of his own emotions the music that he sings, and even today an opera singer cannot really convince his audience unless he acts in such a way as to make them believe that it is his emotions, and not the conductor's beat, that cause the orchestra to play the music written by the composer to express them.

The second use of music in opera is for the purposes of dancing, and under that head we must include not merely set dances, but all movements such as processions, marches, battles, and in fact any kind of dumb show action. Thirdly, music can be used for what we may call 'background' purposes; music that describes natural phenomena such as storms, or that fulfils any other function which might perhaps equally well be performed by visible scenery. We shall see that these three functions of music have been treated in different ways by different composers at different periods.

§ 4 EARLY ITALIAN OPERA: MONTEVERDI

The first attempt at what we can really call an opera was made at Florence in 1597 by a group of musicians and men of letters who were in the habit of meeting to discuss artistic matters at the house of Count Bardi. Their idea was to revive the methods that they believed characteristic of classical Greek tragedy, and their first experiment was a drama on the legend of Apollo and Daphne, written by the poet Ottavio Rinuccini and set to music mainly by Jacopo Peri. The words have survived, but none of the music, except two small fragments composed by Jacopo Corsi. *Dafne* was repeated in 1598 and 1599; in 1600 Rinuccini and Peri produced *Euridice*, an opera on the story of Orpheus and Eurydice. The music of this was printed at the time and has been reprinted in modern form; it is the first opera that has survived complete.

To the same year 1600 belongs what has generally been called the first oratorio, *La Rappresentazione dell' Anima e del Corpo* (The story of the soul and the body); the words were put together from older religious plays and the music was by Emilio de' Cavalieri. The work, however, is not an oratorio as we now understand the term, but an opera, although on a religious subject; it is set to music all the way through, and it was intended to be acted in costume. The *Anima e Corpo* was produced at Rome, but the idea of it was no independent discovery of Cavalieri's; he had been working at Florence for some fifteen years as director of the court entertainments and he was a regular member of the Bardi circle.

Another work that ought to be mentioned here is *L'Amfiparnaso* (1597), composed by Orazio Vecchi, a canon of the cathedral of Modena. It is a series of fourteen madrigals in five parts set to words representing scenes of the comedy of masks. As the printed part-books have little woodcuts representing the characters, many historians have supposed that this work was intended to be acted, perhaps in dumb show, or by puppets, while a chorus sang the madrigals. This is altogether erroneous; the poet (possibly Giulio Cesare Croce of Bologna) says clearly in the prologue that this comedy is to enter by the ear and not by the eye. The *Amfiparnaso* is in no sense an opera; it is merely a musical presentation of the typical comedy of masks, and as such it is both brilliantly amusing and at the same time a most valuable document for the history of the mask plays. It is no more an opera than were the madrigals on street cries written by contemporary English composers.

The creators of these first operas were for the most part men of noble birth. Peri was rather amateurish as a musician; Rinuccini was a poet of real distinction. *Dafne* and *Euridice* were not written for popular audiences, but for the exclusive society of a highly cultivated court. It was only audiences of that calibre who would appreciate the literary quality of these dramas of classical mythology. The next step in the history of opera is the performance of Monteverdi's *Arianna* at Mantua (1607), followed by his *Orfeo* in 1608. Most of the music to *Arianna* has been lost, and the reader must not judge of its quality by the fragment which has been much dressed up for modern concert purposes. Although to the modern temperament *Orfeo* may seem something of a 'museum-piece', it is still a great masterpiece of musical drama. Nowadays it is staged occasionally, not only in order that musicians may see it and learn from it the fundamental principles of dramatic composition, but also because a small but increasing number of music-lovers are rediscovering a taste for the fresh, clear harmonies of pre-classical music. Monteverdi was a much more professional composer than Peri; he had already had considerable experience as a writer of madrigals and of church music. He saw how to utilize simultaneously all the resources available in his day. He collected a large orchestra, and had the imagination to employ different instruments to suit different situations. He has been described as the inventor of very daring harmonies; as a matter of fact most of his devices had been used before, either by himself or by others, but in *Orfeo* he saw how to turn them to account at the appropriate dramatic moments and to do so without destroying the general sense of musical design running all through the opera. *Orfeo* is a great opera, not so much on account of the striking and ingenious effect of detail, as because of its broad sense of musical continuity; considering the date at which it was written, it is a wonderful organic whole, whereas many operas of later times that present singular moments of dramatic power have suffered from the defect of patchiness.

§ 5 STANDARDIZATION

An opera in those days was a large undertaking, such as could only be organized by some great prince for some special festivity; architects of the period who write about the building of theatres take it for granted that a theatre was a purely temporary structure put up for a single occasion. The Barberini family at Rome were great patrons of opera, and it is interesting to note that quite soon after the success of *Orfeo* a comic element began to make its appearance in opera. In 1637 the first public opera-house was opened at Venice by the composer Cavalli, and Venice developed such a passion for opera that within the next half century there was not merely one opera-house but half a dozen or more in that city. Cavalli's forty-two operas were neglected after his death, for nearly 300 years. Recent revivals, however, at Glyndebourne and elsewhere, of *Ormindo* (1644) and *Calisto* (1651) have served to confirm his status as a leading figure of 17th-century Venetian opera, second only to Monteverdi.

As soon as opera was thrown open to the general public on payment it necessarily became standardized. The orchestra was standardized, and it is at this date that the quartet of strings becomes its regular normal basis. Plots were standardized too; Venetian audiences did not want stories from ancient mythology, in which the main interest lay in the beauty of the poetry, but stories about human beings, though they did at least want their human beings to be heroes. The history of ancient Rome, and still more of the later Roman Empire, was the favourite material of the operatic poets; but a love interest was required too, and gradually a sort of standard form was evolved in which we generally find four princes and three princesses whose love affairs resemble more or less a game of musical chairs. The comic element became more and more prominent; here we see the influence of the comedy of masks. Still more important was the scenery; it was a great age of engineering, and the transformations and other spectacular effects, if they really answered to the stage directions and the designs that have come down to us, must have been far beyond anything that our most ingenious and ostentatious producers can show us today.

Venice was a city of great wealth and a great international centre of trade; the only places which could attempt to follow its example were Hamburg and London. But the opera spread from Venice to various other cities in Italy and also to Vienna and other German courts. We must cast a brief glance at the beginnings of opera outside Italy.

§ 6 VIENNA AND PARIS: LULLY

The Imperial court at Vienna was in those days the most magnificent in Europe, and it was always closely in touch with Italy, especially with Venice. Italian operas, chiefly by Cavalli and another Venetian, Cesti, were produced at Vienna on the most sumptuous scale; the designs for scenery by Burnacini, who worked chiefly at Vienna, are among the most beautiful that have ever been made for the stage. Munich, Stuttgart and other small German courts followed the example of Vienna as lavishly as they were able.

In Paris there had been various performances of a spectacular kind, and some of them served as models for the English masques; the most famous was the *Ballet comique de la Reine*, organized by Balthazar de Beaujoyeulx (who was really an Italian) in 1581. It was more like a masque than an opera, and the music was put together by various composers. From 1643 onwards Cardinal Mazarin made continuous attempts to establish Italian opera in Paris, perhaps more from political than from artistic motives, but it was a long time before he had any success. Madame de Motteville was on duty as a lady-in-waiting at an Italian opera in February 1644, and wrote in her memoirs that there were only about twenty people in the room, 'and we all thought we should have died of cold and boredom'. In 1655 Michel de la Guerre produced an opera to French words, but the French composers achieved nothing of real importance. Cavalli himself was brought over by Mazarin in 1660 and his *Serse* (Xerxes) was given with magnificent scenery by the great Italian engineer Torelli, but there were endless intrigues among the Italians themselves as well as the intrigues of the French musicians, who were always bitterly jealous of the Italians, and Cavalli finally left Paris in disgust. French audiences did not really care for Italian music; they found it too noisy and violent. It is difficult for us who are accustomed to Verdi and Puccini to find passion and violence in the Italian operas of the 17th century, but there is definite evidence to prove that the French regarded them as almost an outrage on good taste.

Jean-Baptiste Lully (originally Giovanni Battista Lulli), born of humble parents at Florence in 1632, was discovered by the Chevalier de Guise on his way from Malta to Paris in 1646 and taken by him to France, where he was soon handed over to Mademoiselle de Montpensier as a sort of page boy. His natural gift for singing and dancing attracted attention to him, and so did his talent for making scurrilous songs. He eventually became a companion to the boy King Louis XIV and danced with the king himself in the court ballets. After various collaborations with Molière in plays with ballets, he astutely managed to secure a patent from the king giving him the sole right to produce operas in Paris, and produced the first really notable French opera, *Les Fêtes de l'Amour et de Bacchus*, in 1672.

If ever opera was a court function, it was in the days of Louis XIV. Every opera of Lully had to begin with a prologue of gods and goddesses in praise of the king, and the whole opera was carried out in a style that reflected the stiffness of court etiquette. To our ears

Lully's music sounds dry and conventional; how much of it was actually Lully's is very uncertain, for he employed several assistants. But the conception of the whole was his, as was the characteristic style of the recitative, entirely different from that of the Italians, although as a matter of fact Lully never learned to speak French correctly himself. The declamation is said to have been modelled on the great French actors of the day. To French ears the declamation of verse was more interesting than the singing of airs, and both ballet and chorus played a much larger part than in the Italian operas. Lully's music has little of the inward beauty that we find in his contemporaries Purcell and Scarlatti, but he had a genius for construction on the grand scale, and there are few to equal him for grandeur and stateliness.

§ 7 ENGLAND : PURCELL. GERMANY

England, as one might expect, treated opera as a field for amateurish experiments. Just at the moment when opera might have had a chance of establishing itself, the Civil War put an end to theatrical enterprise. But the Puritans were at any rate lovers of music, and Sir Wiliam D'Avenant, who had been the last writer of masques under Charles I, saw that it might be possible to get opera accepted when plays were forbidden. What he really wanted to do was to produce his own heroic dramas in verse; in 1656 he got his play *The Siege of Rhodes* set to music by various composers in collaboration, and produced it on a diminutive stage such as one might find in a village hall of today. But it excited interest, and more operas were given, the music of which was chiefly by Matthew Locke. These English operas were quite unlike the Italian or French ones in subject and style, for they were conceived as plays with incidental music. After the Restoration the theatres were re-opened, and D'Avenant's operas were succeeded by adaptations of Shakespeare, such as *The Tempest*, in which large quantities of music to words by D'Avenant were introduced. The best of these so-called operas on a large scale was *King Arthur* (1691), by Dryden and Purcell; but it is not an opera in the modern understanding of the term, for most of the principal characters do not sing at all.

The music of *The Siege of Rhodes* is lost, but we possess that of *Psyche* (1674), a very curious opera by Shadwell and Matthew Locke, imitated (but not adapted) from the French *Psyché* of Molière and Lully. It could only be revived now as a 'museum-piece', if at all, but it is interesting as showing the English feeling for picturesqueness in preference to formality. Blow's *Venus and Adonis* (1685), though called a masque, probably because it was performed quite privately at court, is a true opera, for it is set to music all through; it was revived in 1920 by Rutland Boughton at Glastonbury. *Venus and Adonis* served as the model for Purcell's *Dido and Aeneas*, the earliest opera that, in Britain at any rate, we can call almost a repertory work and not a mere museum-piece.

Dido and Aeneas was composed in 1689 for performance at a school for young ladies in Chelsea. The reader will note that neither of these two genuine English operas was intended for the public stage; the English public of those days would probably have refused to tolerate them. Both of them are isolated and exceptional works; one may say that they had neither ancestors nor progeny. They are both chamber works; they stand to the public theatre as a string quartet of Mozart does to the great symphonies, and are too delicate and intimate for anything but a small theatre. But *Dido and Aeneas* is none the less one of the great masterpieces of early opera. 'It lasted only an hour,' said a modern opera-goer once, 'but I felt as if I had been through all the emotions of *Götterdämmerung*!' It is fairly often performed nowadays, and deserves to be one of the standard works in the professional repertory.

In Germany native opera took much longer to establish than in England and France. The first attempt was made by Heinrich Schütz, a famous composer of Protestant church music. Schütz had been a pupil of Gabrieli at Venice, and in 1627 he got Rinuccini's *Dafne* translated into German by Martin Opitz, a poet of some distinction. It was performed at Torgau, a small town in Saxony, to celebrate the marriage of a princess of the Electoral house. The music is lost, and we cannot even be certain whether Schütz composed new music to the play himself, or whether, as is more probable, he arranged the original music of Peri. But the Thirty Years' War (1618–48) was as disastrous to German opera as the Civil War was to English opera. The great German music of the 17th century is mostly sacred, and such attempts at German opera as were made in Nuremberg, Leipzig and Hamburg were mainly on biblical subjects. The first permanent opera in Germany was started at Hamburg in 1678.

Hamburg was the Venice of the north in those days, and in some ways the life of Hamburg was very like that of Restoration London. Jeremy Collier's denunciations of the London stage were a mere trifle compared to those of the Hamburg clergy, and although Hamburg had begun with a sort of religious opera in 1678, the public soon preferred those of Reinhold Keiser, whose first opera at Hamburg in 1701 dealt with the crimes of a notorious local highwayman. The Hamburg opera must have been a very rough-and-tumble affair, depending largely on amateur performers. Keiser was a man of wildly dissipated life, but there was a spark of genius in him, and he exercised a powerful influence on the young Handel, who came to Hamburg in 1703.

§ 8 SURVEY OF THE 17TH CENTURY

If we take a general survey of operatic history in the 17th century we see at once that the main line of its development lay in Italy, though we must not neglect the very important branch of French opera. French opera was the creation of an Italian, but we shall see that France in the following century had very notable contributions to make to the musical drama. In Italy we see opera initiated by a small coterie of aristocratic intellectuals at Florence. It gradually becomes more professional in style, but for a long time it remains associated with the courts of princes, except at Venice. Even at Venice it can hardly have been a popular entertainment; it must always have been supported by the wealthy classes, and we know that the Venetian theatres were built mostly by the great noble families such as the Grimani. At Bologna it was the Formagliari family who did most to establish opera; at Naples, where opera began with the visit of a Venetian company in 1671, it was dependent on the court of the Spanish viceroys, or of the Austrian viceroys during the years in which Naples belonged to Austria.

Looking at the music of the operas by itself, we see a gradual transformation of style and method. At all periods composers of opera have had to employ the musical language and the musical forms of their own day. (For the history of those forms the reader must be referred to other parts of this volume.) We have at all times to take into account the interaction between the theatre and the concert-room. The concert-room standardizes the regular forms of song, dance, fugue, etc, because they are in constant demand there. We ought perhaps to warn the reader that we are using the word 'concert-room' not in its modern sense, but simply as a collective term for all the occasions, not being church or stage, where music is performed and listened to for its own sake.

But the theatre, as soon as it was definitely established, gradually became the supply centre of musical expression, as opposed to musical formalism. Musical form is not the contradiction of musical expression, as some amateurs imagine; it is the shaping of a series of sounds in order to make them expressive. Take any simple piece of music that you feel to be expressive, an ordinary hymn tune or even a chant; the expressiveness is due not merely to the particular note that excites emotion, but to the particular place in which it occurs; if it was put in a different place, it would lose its significance. But expression becomes conventionalized with repetition and loses its emotional force, and it is then that we need the influence of the theatre to stimulate a keener expression of emotion, which in its turn gets transferred to the concert-room and again becomes standardized.

And it often becomes standardized in the theatre too; when that happens we have a period of operatic decadence. But in listening to old operas, and especially to museum-pieces, we must try to put ourselves back into their own period, and learn to adjust our minds to their methods of expression; and it is in these cases that the value of emotional expression is settled not by its violence, but by its being placed exactly in the right situation.

The whole tendency of opera in the 17th century was to become more musical and less like an ordinary play in verse; that means that the emotion, instead of being distributed more or less evenly throughout the opera (and therefore never covering a very wide range) became concentrated in the songs, while the recitative (which was necessary to carry on the story) became more and more conventional and dull. We notice this all the more in the Italian operas, because the Italian theatre made hardly any use of 'background music'. A palace may fall to ruins, or a dragon rise from the sea, but the music takes no notice of it whatever. Music had not yet discovered the technique for that sort of thing, and if it had, it would probably have been impossible to synchronize it with the stage effects – we know how difficult it is to achieve this even nowadays in an opera of Wagner.

We notice more and more the over-elaboration of scenic effects and spectacle; if it were possible to reproduce exactly a 17th-century performance of an opera by Cavalli today, we should probably think that the music was negligible in relation to the scenery. This passion for 'machines' was characteristic of the age; it affected the French and English theatres no less than the Italian. It was a worship of mechanism at which we moderns have no right to scoff, for we worship mechanism just as foolishly, and with considerably less sense of beauty.

The 17th century at any rate realized that opera must deal with subjects remote from common life. Shakespeare, though he never adopted an operatic attitude to music itself on the stage, had something of the Italian operatic view of drama, in that he separated the lofty style of his tragic and serious parts from the low comedy of his clowns. The opera never attempted comedy of manners, and such a thing did not exist in Italy, even in the spoken drama. An Italian opera by the end of the century bore a considerable resemblance to a Victorian melodrama, with its chivalrous hero, its villain, its persecuted heroine, often in disguise, and its comic servants, male and female. The reason is that our English melodramas are actually descended from the opera, just as our Victorian pantomimes were descended from the so-called operas of Purcell. The word melodrama means music-drama, and *melodramma* was for most of the 17th century the regular name for an opera; we meet it constantly in the word-books, though sometimes the work is called *dramma per musica*. The name *opera* appears to have been a colloquial expression, and it penetrated to French and English fairly early in the century. Evelyn's diary speaks of an 'Opera (for so they call shews of that kind)' at Rome in 1644; D'Avenant uses the word in 1656. The word *opera*, it need hardly be said, simply means 'a work'.

PART 2 THE EIGHTEENTH CENTURY

§ 1 ITALIAN INFLUENCE: SCARLATTI

Purcell died in 1695 and it so happened that there was no English composer living who was equal to carrying on his work for the theatre. Early in the following century an attempt was made to introduce Italian opera in London, and, though the first efforts were not in themselves very successful, Italian opera soon became so firmly established that it is with us still. There was nothing surprising about this. Paris was the only great city which supported an opera of its own in its own language. The German courts all had their Italian operas, and Hamburg was becoming gradually Italianized; Keiser's operas were often sung in a mixture of Italian and German. Madrid and Lisbon set up their Italian operas in the course of the century; Copenhagen and St Petersburg did the same. All over Europe Italian was the language of music, except in France, and even France had eventually to yield to the Italian invasion, though it did so by the process of swallowing the Italian composers, as it did Lully, and doing its best to make Frenchmen of them.

When we say that Italian was the language of music, we do not mean that all musicians habitually talked Italian, or even that they always set Italian words to music; though even in the matter of spoken language Italian was certainly the one in which musicians of different nationalities would most probably converse with each other. When Dr Burney travelled over most of Europe in 1770–72 in search of materials for his *History of Music*, he seems to have found Italian the most useful language, as he had very little knowledge of German. Germany was overrun with Italian musicians, and German musicians had to Italianize their musical style if they wanted to be anything more distinguished than mere church organists. Ever since about 1600 German musicians, if they could possibly manage it, had gone to Italy to learn composition, and even German church music in the 17th century shows the ever increasing influence of Italy. Most of the great palaces and churches of the period were not only designed by Italian architects (or at least by pupils of Italians) but actually built by Italian stonemasons, who travelled everywhere, for no country could produce their equals in skill. Readers who knew Dresden before 1939 may remember a restaurant on the river near the opera-house, called the *Italienisches Dörfchen* (Italian village); it derived its name from the fact that there actually was an Italian village there in the 18th century, inhabited by the descendants of the masons who came to build the court church.

When Handel went to Italy in 1706 as a young man of twenty-one, the greatest composer living was Alessandro Scarlatti, who divided his career between Rome and Naples. Most of his operas were written for Naples, and he is the creator of what was then the standard Italian opera form and style. Today his operas are not even museum-pieces, and the only songs from them that are familiar to the ordinary concert-goer, such as 'O cessate di piagarmi', belong to his very early works and are not typical of his maturity. The favourite opera songs of Handel will give the general reader a sufficiently adequate idea of his riper style.

Scarlatti's operas show a gradual reform of operatic method, though those reforms led to conventions that a modern musician finds very hard to appreciate. In the first place, the chaotic libretti of the Venetians were simplified and made more dignified in style; the poets were in all probability influenced by the plays of Racine. We see the comic characters being kept in order and put in their proper place; they gradually sink like a sediment to the ends of the acts – in the third act entering just before the final *dénouement*, which is really an untying of knots. A little later on the two comic characters drop out of the opera altogether, and their scenes become *intermezzi* which could without trouble be transferred from one opera to another.

In the second place, Scarlatti is responsible for the standardization of the *aria* in the *da capo* form that is the horror of musicians nowadays. His own audiences would never have felt that there was anything odd about it; it was much clearer and more concise, capable too of more intense expression, than the forms it superseded. It could be adapted to any emotion – joy, sorrow, rage, despair. Scarlatti also invented the accompanied recitative, as it is called. Most recitative – the dull parts which had to get on with the story of the play – were accompanied only by the harpsichord in what is called *recitativo secco*, dry recitative, as many writers have with obvious facetiousness observed. To bring in the stringed instruments to accompany recitative created a new emotional atmosphere. Most readers will remember the way in which Bach, in the St Matthew Passion, always brings in the string quartet to accompany the words of Jesus. We have been taught to notice this effect in Bach but we are apt to neglect it in the oratorios of Handel, for few singers and conductors realize that the entry of the strings means a change of mood and a new emotional atmsophere in the character who is singing.

A third and a very important invention of Scarlatti was the 'ensemble of perplexity' which is still characteristic of opera and a valuable means of effect that cannot be obtained in a spoken play. A situation arises, affecting perhaps four characters on the stage, each in a different way; they express their feelings simultaneously in a quartet. Sullivan parodied the device in *The Mikado* – 'Here's a howde-do!' Old Scarlatti had parodied himself nearly two centuries before.

§ 2 MORE ABOUT CONVENTIONS

It is appropriate at this point to discuss some of the conventions of opera which are apt to irritate unmusical people and those who expect absolute realism in opera. Even in the 18th century, as we shall see, some people objected to the action being held up in order that a singer might show off his voice. But the cause for objection lay not in the musical form but in the music with which second-rate composers filled it. Nobody ever complained of the ensembles in *Carmen* or *Meistersinger* for holding up the action, simply because the music is so enthralling that we only wish it would go on longer.

Supposing that in some play a messenger comes on and says 'The queen is dead'. This is a mere piece of information; it must be made as clear as possible, so that nobody can miss it. In an opera, therefore, it must be stated in recitative. But the queen's death will certainly produce various emotional states in the characters on the stage, possibly in the messenger himself. Any actor knows how difficult it is to express these emotions if he has no words to say. A poet can give him words, though they are not the words he would use in private life; the musician must give him music to sing, and the shape of that music will depend partly on the quality of the emotion and partly on the normal musical style of the period. Handel will have to do it one way, Wagner another; their styles will differ just as Shakespeare's will from a modern poet's. The musician, especially in Handel's day, will hold up the action longer than the poet; but it is a curious property of music that it can destroy our sense of time, as long as it really holds our interest. An 'ensemble of perplexity', if it were spoken, would probably be unimpressive and possibly ridiculous; even if a great poet achieved it, the actors would find it curiously difficult to speak, for it would have to be timed accurately and very carefully rehearsed, so that the different speeches dovetailed into one another like a piece of music. Like a piece of music – music does this for the singers without their having to think about the technique of it.

§ 3 THE CASTRATI

Handel's operas are mentioned here in preference to Scarlatti's because most English readers are more or less familiar with the Handelian style of music; moreover since 1920 there has been a great revival of Handel's operas in Germany and elsewhere, and performances of several of them are nowadays not infrequent. Between 1711 and 1741 Handel produced nearly forty operas on the London stage. Scarlatti's last opera came out in 1721, and Handel, whose real genius belonged to the theatre, carried the Scarlattian type of opera to its climax; but by force of external circumstances Handel's operatic career was on the whole a failure.

Italian opera now began to be a profitable business, and Italy's chief export. What made the success of Italian opera was not so much the music as the singers, and here we must speak of that curious phenomenon, the Italian artificial soprano. It had been discovered more than 100 years before that a boy's treble voice would be preserved by castration, and it was further discovered that in favourable cases such voices could be immensely strengthened in the course of years. This horrible practice did not begin in the theatre, but in the church, owing to the difficulty of obtaining good choirboys in Italy; it was officially condemned but connived at in practice, and singers of this type were singing in the Papal choir at Rome almost up to the end of the 19th century. As far as can be ascertained, the practice was confined exclusively to Italy, with the exception of a small number of Germans; male sopranos, or *castrati*, dominated the operatic stage in all countries except France, but the singers themselves were Italian. Dr Burney made great efforts to find out where the operation was generally performed, but there was not unnaturally some mystery about it; he came however to the conclusion that Naples was the chief source of supply.

The first Italian *castrato* heard in England was Siface, who came over at the desire of Mary of Modena, wife of James II, in about 1687; he had previously been a member of the Pope's chapel. The last who appeared on the English stage was Velluti, who sang in London in 1825; he died in 1861. For practically two centuries all the hero parts in Italian opera were sung by sopranos (or sometimes contraltos) of this kind; at certain periods women were forbidden altogether to sing on the stage in Rome, and *castrati* had to take female parts as well. In the early days of Italian opera in London, on the other hand, the *castrati* parts were sometimes sung by women. Nicolini, whose acting was highly praised by Addison, was the first to make a success on the London stage. Out of the thousands who submitted to the operation, only comparatively few attained eminence, but the most famous of them obtained gigantic salaries, especially in London.

The great difficulty of reviving Handelian or even later Italian opera nowadays lies in the fact that the chief male parts were always written for *castrati*. If they are sung by women, they lose their dramatic character; we find it difficult today to tolerate even a female Siebel in Gounod's *Faust*, though we still accept Mozart's Cherubino. (Part of the reason may be that Siebel is a serious character and Cherubino a comic one.) If we transpose the music for tenors, the music suffers, especially as hardly any modern tenors can sing the florid passages. The singers of the 18th century, and especially the *castrati*, cultivated an extraordinary agility in florid passages; audiences of those days delighted in a type of *coloratura* that would have horrified even the age of Patti. The only opera songs approaching that style which are heard now are those of Mozart, and even the songs of Constanze in *Die Entführung aus dem Serail* (The Abduction from the Harem) and of the Queen of Night in *Die Zauberflöte* (The Magic Flute) are simple compared with the flourishes every singer was expected to throw off in the days of Handel.

§ 4 METASTASIO. THE FRENCH SCHOOL : RAMEAU

Opera had indeed become no more than a concert in costume, though there were a few composers who maintained a fairly high standard. The curious thing is that just at this very moment there arose the strange case of a librettist who was a real poet – Metastasio. His first drama for music was *Didone*, set to music by Vinci in 1724. Metastasio devoted his life to writing libretti for operas; they have great dramatic force, within their peculiar convention, and they belong to the great things of Italian literature – on this point all Italian critics are agreed. The result was that every composer in Italy, and many outside, set Metastasio's dramas to music over and over again; there are even cases of composers setting the same play twice, to entirely different music. Audiences of those days must have known the plays by heart, and this tended even more to turn operas into a sort of singing competition.

All this time France remained severely apart. Lully died in 1687 and his tradition was continued by Campra and Destouches; in 1739 Rameau, then no longer a young man, started on his career as an opera composer. Rameau's operas, for some of which Voltaire furnished the words, have all the stiff ceremonial of Lully's, but Rameau was a really great musician and his operas have in this century been revived in Paris with no less success than those of Handel in Germany. Rameau's music, with the exception of a few of his harpsichord pieces, is not widely known in England; unfortunately the performance of one of his operas would entail enormous labour and expense if it was to be at all adequate. His subjects, like those of Lully, are chiefly classical, but treated in the manner of Racine, one may say; the declamatory recitative, of which Rameau was a consummate master, was a great attraction for his own audiences. The songs, exquisite as they are, seldom have the passion or grandeur of Handel's; on the other hand, the choruses and ballets are magnificent. The art of Rameau was essentially French, and intimately associated with the French language. To most English-speaking people, even to those who know French pretty well, French poetry is singularly difficult to appreciate; but if our ears are open to music Rameau's operas will do much to explain to us its beauty.

§ 5 COMIC OPERA IN ITALY AND FRANCE

Practically all the operas we have so far considered were composed for court theatres and for audiences of highly cultivated people with a dignified taste both in literature and in music. The modern reader may think it shocking that in those days culture was the privilege of an aristocracy, but it was culture carried to a very high degree, and we shall see later on how the destruction of that aristocratic culture imperilled the future of opera.

We must now turn to an altogether different type of musical drama, which from the 18th century onwards has acquired increasing importance – comic opera.

Quite early in the 17th century there had been attempts at comic opera, especially at Rome, and one or two composers produced some very amusing scenes of popular life, but there was no continuous tradition of comic opera as a *genre* by itself until 1709, when a little theatre at Naples was opened for operas in the local dialect dealing with everyday characters instead of classical heroes. Even the great Scarlatti himself wrote a comic opera for this theatre in 1718, when he was nearly sixty, and seems to have thoroughly enjoyed making fun of his own grand manner. Pergolesi's *La Serva Padrona* (The Maid as Mistress) (1733) gives some idea of their musical style, but this charming little work is not a real comic opera of its period; it is only a set of comic *intermezzi* intended for performance between the acts of a serious opera. The comic operas were generally in three acts and sometimes even had their own comic *intermezzi*. They were generally performed by people who regarded themselves as actors; the *castrati* never sang in them, although the custom was kept up of giving the chief male parts to high voices, sung by women in male costume. We see here the origin of the 'principal boy' of a Victorian pantomime or musical comedy.

A Neapolitan comic opera company came to London in 1740 and performed *La Serva Padrona* with fair success, but its great reputation was made in 1752, when an Italian company acted it in Paris. The visit of this company was the cause of the famous *guerre des bouffons*, the war of the musicians (and still more of the journalists) over the relative merits of French and Italian music. The ultimate victory was with Italy; French audiences were becoming tired of the grand academic manner of Rameau, and could hardly resist the natural spontaneous humour of the Italians and their lively tunefulness. Here it may be mentioned that in those days French opera was unbearable to anyone who was not a Frenchman; both English and Italian travellers give the most ludicrous accounts of it – to their ears it simply was not music at all.

Pergolesi was by no means a great composer; his grand operas are often dull and carelessly written, and Martini, the learned theorist who taught Mozart as a boy, quite rightly said that his famous Stabat Mater was in the style of a musical comedy. But he is an historic figure, and he had a certain sentimental charm so attractive that it conquered the whole of musical Europe. In another section of this work there is an account of the complete change of musical language that took place at this time in German instrumental music, the change from the suites and concertos of J. S. Bach to the sonatas of his son Emanuel and the symphonies of the men who just preceded Haydn and Mozart. The new style of melody was not their invention; it came from Naples, from the trivial comic operas which everybody wanted to hear. People in provincial towns north of the Alps, who could not go to see an Italian opera, wanted to play the music at home on their own violins and harpsichords; the composers provided them with suitable sonatas. Electors and Prince-Bishops wanted Italian musical comedy tunes played during dinner; as their chapel-masters could not obtain the originals (for they were never printed), they composed something that sounded much the same. And they wrote sonatas and symphonies, not because they thought there was anything particularly noble or uplifting about that particular form, but simply because it was the ordinary musical form of the opera songs, whether serious or frivolous.

More Italian comic operas came to Paris; Naples was always the chief source of supply, but Venice contributed a good many. A composer from Parma, Egidio Romoaldo Duni, settled in Paris, followed the example of Lully in writing his name as Duny, and created a prolific school of French comic opera, in which he was followed by Monsigny, Dalayrac and others. The main difference between the French and Italian comic operas was that the French preferred the connecting dialogue spoken, whereas the Italians always stuck to recitative.

§ 6 ENGLISH COMIC OPERA. THE EUROPEAN POSITION

In England there was a similar wave of comic opera; but it had begun much earlier, with a more or less native product. In 1728 there came out *The Beggar's Opera*, a brilliant social and political satire by John Gay; it also satirized the Italian opera in its form, as it contained a large number of amusing songs which Dr Pepusch, a learned German musical antiquary, adapted to the popular tunes of the day. People sometimes talk of *The Beggar's Opera* as if it was all made up of English folk-songs, but many of them were of French or Italian origin, and there were bits of Purcell and Handel as well. Gay's amusing sequel to this opera, *Polly*, was forbidden performance by the censorship of the government; the enormous crop of English 'ballad operas' which delighted popular audiences up to the end of the century gradually drifted more and more into mere namby-pamby sentimentality. Italian influence made itself felt in London, as in Paris; Galuppi of Venice enjoyed an enormous vogue, and his comic operas contributed a good deal towards the formation of the characteristic English style.

England being always closely in touch with Hamburg, the first English ballad operas made their way to Germany, and, just as the German theatre owed its rise to the visit of the English actors in the days of Shakespeare, so German comic opera derived its origin from English music. J. A. Hiller and Dittersdorf were the most successful composers in this line. German comic opera, however, was also influenced by the Italians; Galuppi had been fortunate enough to have librettos written for him by the famous playwright Goldoni, and Goldoni's librettos were often adapted by the German composers.

Let us pause for a moment and review the general operatic situation of Europe as it was about 1760. We saw opera start in Florence as the experiment of a few intellectuals. It is taken up as a diversion for princes. Venice commercializes it and to some extent vulgarizes it, but at the same time gives it an impetus that causes it to spread beyond the Alps. Wherever it goes, it requires the patronage of a cultivated court; if it fails to find that soil, it degenerates either artistically, as at Hamburg, or financially, as in London. The small Italian courts lose their political importance, and in the 18th century their place (as far as opera is concerned) is taken by Paris and the German courts that are trying to follow the model set up by Louis XIV. In Paris opera is French, but everywhere else it is Italian. Italy makes the operas and exports them, along with composers, singers, players and scene-painters. For Italy, at any rate, it is a huge commercial business, and as soon as opera becomes commercial, it becomes degraded. French grand opera survived up to the end of Rameau's days only because it was purely French.

Comic opera, as a work of art (for we can regard the Neapolitan comedies as artistic), could only come into being after serious opera had established a routine technique of composition. It was a welcome reaction against the over-conventionalized form of the grand opera which it often satirized; but comic opera became commercialized even faster than serious opera, because it was cheaper to produce and more lucrative to undertake. When the last performance of Rameau's *Dardanus* took place in 1760 there was not a single composer in Europe whose operas had the least claim to distinction, except Hasse at Dresden and Jommelli at Stuttgart, the last survivors of the dignified Neapolitan style.

§ 7 GLUCK

The moment was right for the historic reforms of Gluck. Gluck was born on the borders of Germany and Bohemia; he had been sent to Italy to learn composition and had written several operas of a conventional Italian type. In 1745 he was in London, where his opera *La Caduta dei Giganti* (The Fall of the Giants) composed to celebrate the battle of Culloden was a complete failure. But he met Handel in

London, and is pretty certain to have heard some of Handel's oratorios; he went on to Paris, where he heard operas by Rameau and met some of the leaders of French musical criticism. For some years he continued writing Italian operas, and French comic operas too, for Vienna, until in 1762 he produced his *Orfeo* in Italian. How far Gluck himself was the originator of the theories attributed to him is a matter of some uncertainty; it is probable that he was a good deal directed by his librettist, Calzabigi, and by the influence of Algarotti, a diplomat and man of letters, who had written a severe criticism of Italian opera in general a few years before.

Orfeo is still in the European and American repertory and is the oldest opera that is not revived merely as a museum-piece. The version now generally performed is not that of 1762, nor even the revised French version of 1774, but a rearrangement of the latter made by Berlioz in 1859, for Madame Viardot-Garcia, the great contralto, and it is mainly due to her superb interpretation that the opera has remained as a classical display-piece for contraltos.

Orfeo in its Italian shape is quite unlike any Italian opera of the period. It could only have been produced at the court of Vienna, where the imperial family were all accomplished musicians and sometimes themselves performed musical entertainments for which Gluck composed music. It is almost a chamber opera in style, and its libretto suggests a deliberate reversion to the ideals of Rinuccini's *Euridice*. It is French in its use of the chorus, French in its ballet-music and its little instrumental interludes for stage ceremony, French in its systematic use of accompanied recitative to the total exclusion of *recitativo secco*, although vocally its musical style is Italian. The fact that it has only three characters, instead of the six or seven princes, princesses, confidants and confidantes traditionally required in Handelian opera, suggests that it was composed for an intimate audience of connoisseurs. The same applies even more to Gluck's later and less known opera *Paride ed Elena* (1770), which also has three characters only, and a large quantity of ballet. Both these operas are far more lyrical than dramatic in the ordinary sense of the word; very little happens on the stage, and all along we know exactly what is going to happen. The interest lies in the beauty of the treatment and in the subtle presentation of delicate grades of emotion. Much of *Orfeo* is terribly dull unless one understands the words and can follow every sentence; they do not give us much positive information of importance, but they take us through a series of emotional experiences.

The audience thought *Orfeo* depressing, for it began with a funeral, and there were no showy florid songs. There is one in the modern version, but it was put in for the French performance of 1774; it is taken from one of Gluck's earlier Italian operas. *Alceste* (1767) was considered to be a funeral from beginning to end. It is more dramatic than *Orfeo* and is notable for the overture, which was deliberately designed to prepare the audience for the tragic atmosphere of the opera and leads into it in a strikingly effective way.

Gluck enjoyed the favour of the court, but the public was decidedly hostile to his reforms, as may be imagined. In 1774 he succeeded in getting his *Iphigénie en Aulide* produced in Paris, mainly through the patronage of Marie Antoinette, who had been his pupil in Vienna. *Orphée* (the French version) followed in the same year, and a French version of *Alceste* in 1776. In 1777 he composed *Armide*; although it is the most beautiful of his operas and technically the most finished, it has had few revivals. His last work was *Iphigénie en Tauride* (1779).

The war of words over the *bouffons* was nothing to the war of the Gluckists and Piccinists. Gluck was a German and under the protection of Marie Antoinette; that set both the old French party – the admirers of Rameau – and the pro-Italian party against him. Piccini, a Neapolitan composer who had written some very successful comic operas, was brought into the field against him, very much against his own wish, it is said. Piccini was defeated, and no wonder, for he was not really at home in grand opera; but the Italians really won the battle, for, after Gluck went back to Vienna to die, Paris once more capitulated to the fascinations of Sacchini, Paisiello and Paër, writers chiefly of sentimental opera, a new type that had come into being in response to the general craze for sentimental novels and *comédie larmoyante*.

Handel said of Gluck that he knew no more of counterpoint than his own cook did; and the weakness of Gluck lay in his clumsiness of musical technique. The ordinary listener perhaps does not notice this; one certainly hopes that he does not, but the conductor and the other people who have to study the operas and prepare them for performance soon discover those awkward places that it requires so much forethought and ingenuity to cover up. What charms a modern audience in Gluck is the illusion of classical dignity; they are ideal museum-pieces, for they give the modern listener the impression of a purely imaginary ancient Greece populated not by human beings but by statues of white marble. We enjoy a strange and wonderful sense of calm beauty remote from all human passion, like the happy spirits in Gluck's Elysian fields; but it may be doubted whether that was altogether what Gluck intended.

§ 8 MOZART

We reach the moment at which Vienna becomes the centre of the musical world – the age of Haydn and Mozart. A new factor has arisen in musical life, the classical orchestra, with its concertos, its *divertimenti* and its symphonies; it has learned its new skill because the players, both strings and wind, have been trying for a generation to imitate the airs and graces of the Italian opera singers. They have acquired a new elegance of phrasing, a new tenderness of expression; the orchestra is the new toy of the moment, and enterprising music-publishers in Vienna and Paris are turning out sets of symphony parts by the hundred. The classical orchestra has become standardized, and so has the symphony. This is the background of Mozart's youth; circumstances, if not natural inclination, made him a symphonist, an instrumental composer, before he had the chance of writing an opera, apart from his efforts as a child prodigy.

But it was the opera that had created the symphony and the opera created the concerto too, for it was a deliberate adaptation of the grand operatic *aria*. Mozart's greatest works, the works in which he is most intensely himself, are his operas, and also his concertos. He could never have composed those concertos unless he had had a genius for opera, and one of his great achievements in opera was the utilization of the symphonic technique – not just what people call orchestration, but the building up of a stage scene on the lines of an orchestral work.

Mozart was still a child when he wrote his first operas, and one should not expect to find in them either the maturity and depth of feeling of his adult years or the astonishing ability to characterize in music which was to lift him, as a musical dramatist, above Haydn. But that there is much pleasure to be derived from the purely musical invention and the grace and charm of these early works is proved by the fact that such operas as *Bastien und Bastienne*, *Lucio Silla* and *La finta giardiniera* (The False Gardener's Maid) are nowadays occasionally staged.

In the whole history of music there are few operas that achieve the incomparable grandeur of the one with which Mozart opened his real dramatic career at the age of twenty-five – *Idomeneo*. Although it was not staged in Britain until 1934, and in the United States was first given in concert form at the Berkshire Festival in 1947, it is now considered an integral part of our operatic repertory. It belongs to the age of Gluck and Jommelli with its classical story and its soprano hero, but it achieves their ideals with a far higher mastery of craftsmanship, for it has all the Italian serenity of Jommelli and all the dramatic sincerity of Gluck, together with a new sensitiveness to the expressive power not only of the orchestra but also of what was at that time modern harmony. To present *Idomeneo* adequately it has to be given with a superb cast of singers and on a vast stage with every magnificence of spectacle, for it belongs to an age when time, labour or expense did not enter into the considerations of the illustrious patrons of the musical drama.

Mozart's next opera, written in 1782, was the comic opera in German, *Die Entführung aus dem Serail*, which used to be known in England as *The Seraglio*. Only a few years earlier he had scorned the idea of writing a German opera; German opera in those days meant a trivial affair for the common herd. *Die Entführung* is the first German comic opera by a great composer and for that reason it is historically epoch-making. It is full of delightful things, but in style it is a jumble; Constanze's famous song might have come out of *Idomeneo*, Pedrillo's 'Im Mohrenland' is Neapolitan comic opera, some of the other airs are purely German, and the finale is in the French style. The opera holds the stage now by the irresistible charm of the music, whatever its style may be, and by the humorous characterization of the comic bass, Osmin.

Die Entführung, for all its success, could not keep the German company alive, and the court preferred its comic opera in Italian. After *Der Schauspieldirektor* (The Impresario), a one-act comedy written for performance at the Court Theatre in the palace of Schönbrunn (1786), Mozart's next three operas were all in Italian and all comic. For all three, *Le Nozze di Figaro* (The Marriage of Figaro) (1786), *Don Giovanni* (1788) and *Così fan tutte* (All Women are Like That) (1790), Mozart had the inestimable advantage of collaborating with Lorenzo da Ponte, one of the wittiest and most skilful librettists in operatic history. It is no wonder that two such accomplished technicians produced undying masterpieces. Owing to the stupidity of 19th-century audiences and critics, especially in Germany, *Così fan tutte* remained for about a hundred years under a cloud; we owe it to Richard Strauss that it was interpreted afresh in its true character, and it at present enjoys an extraordinary popularity.

Figaro and *Don Giovanni* are the foundations of all subsequent comic opera, Italian, French, German or English. But we must not forget that Mozart had his predecessors too, and that much of what people now think characteristically Mozartian is merely the conventional small-talk of dozens of minor Italian opera-manufacturers. The chief technical achievement in operatic construction that Mozart found ready to his hand was the comic *ensemble* and the comic *finale*. In the Scarlattian opera all interest was centred on the *aria* for a single character; it summed up the emotion of its particular scene, and after singing an aria that character invariably left the stage. Duets were rare, and any larger ensemble most exceptional. When Scarlatti first introduced a formal ensemble he called it an *aria a quattro*, a song for four people, and it conformed exactly to the conventional shape of an aria, including the *da capo*. It was only the comic characters who could be allowed to sing bustling duets, generally expressing some sort of altercation. Out of these there gradually grew up the bustling finale, which became bigger and longer as years went on. The finales of Leo and Pergolesi suggest that no curtain fell at the end of an act, for the characters come on gradually, and go off gradually too. (In the English Restoration theatre the curtain never fell till the end of the play, and it was not until about 1760 that it was let down after each act. Opera had its own habits in stage practice, and not much is known about its details, but Rameau's method of ending an act with a short recitative after a long ballet and chorus suggests that the Paris opera followed the same rule.) Later Italian comic operas developed the well-known comic device, a scene of confusion in which all the characters are singing at once and no one in the audience can realize exactly what is happening; on a scene of this kind it is evident that the curtain must fall in order to bring it to an end.

It is probably to the operatic finale that the symphonists owed their conventional habit of ending a movement or a section of a movement with a good deal of empty repetition of the dominant and tonic chords; it always sounds as if the composer and orchestra were applauding their own music, and in Mozart's case we gladly grant him the right to do so. In the theatre it is obvious that applause was wanted, and the example of the orchestra might well stimulate the audience. Mozart and Da Ponte accepted the convention; we have Da Ponte's very amusing corroboration of this in his autobiography. Mozart, with his long experience of symphonic writing, built up his finales on a larger scale than his predecessors, with the result that in each of them there are several pages in which all are singing together at the top of their voices and it is a matter of complete indifference what the words are; the singers for the moment have become an orchestra. We accept this in Mozart; he compels us to believe that whatever he does is always right. But in the course of later generations we shall begin to find this symphonic finale something of a nuisance.

Mozart's operas bring the 18th century to an end. Beaumarchais's *Mariage de Figaro* was the prologue to the French Revolution, and one can imagine how Mozart remembered the days when he too was a mere servant and was kicked out of the presence of his archbishop. Don Giovanni, last remnant of the old nobility, is taken down to Hell, and his servant and peasants only laugh at his disappearance. In *Così fan tutte* Comedy in the person of Despina the chambermaid makes fun of everybody and everything.

In the last year of his life, 1791, Mozart composed two operas almost simultaneously. Though *La Clemenza di Tito* (The Clemency of Titus) reverts to the style of the old *opera seria*, nevertheless in it Mozart produced a work which modern performances have revealed as one of great musical beauty and a certain dramatic power. *Die Zauberflöte* (The Magic Flute), on the other hand, opens the mysterious door to a new age. It is the first great work of music – perhaps it was the only one – that was composed for the humbler classes of society.

PART 3 FROM MOZART TO WAGNER

§ 1 CHERUBINI. BEETHOVEN

The French Revolution and the Napoleonic Empire affected the course of opera no less than that of European life in general. The spirit of the Revolution gave a serious and ethical turn to what was officially called comic opera. What the French designated as *opéra comique* was opera with spoken dialogue, and the adjective lost its original meaning so completely that in later years the French had to invent a new category, *opéra bouffe* (from the Italian word *buffo*, comic) to signify operas the main function of which was to stimulate laughter.

We find this serious turn in the operas of Méhul, whose *Joseph*, composed during the Revolution, is still occasionally performed in France and Germany; it deals in a style of great dignity with the biblical story of Joseph and his brethren. The most important composer of this period is Cherubini, an Italian who spent most of his life in Paris. Cherubini was associated with the musicians of the Conservatoire founded by the Republic in 1795, and was never on good terms with Napoleon, who disliked his independence of spirit and preferred Paisiello. Cherubini is remembered now only by *Médée* (1797) and *Les Deux Journées* (1800) – known in England as *The Water-Carrier* – for which Beethoven had a profound admiration. Another Italian composer favoured by Napoleon was Spontini, whose *La Vestale* (The Vestal Virgin) came out in Paris in 1807. *La Vestale* is thoroughly typical of the Empire; it has all the frigid stateliness of Empire architecture and furniture. Like Mozart's *Idomeneo*, it achieves with greater technical skill what Gluck set out to do, but it lacks Mozart's warmth and sensuous beauty; its dignity is too deliberately 'antique', at any rate to modern audiences. It is still revived occasionally in France and Italy, and it deserves revival, as a museum-piece on the grand scale.

The one opera of this period that still remains intensely alive for all of us is Beethoven's *Fidelio* (first version 1805; final version 1814). It has often been said that Beethoven had no understanding of the stage, but he undoubtedly had a keen ambition towards it; at the same time, his ethical idealism made him unwilling to write what was merely attractive and amusing, and even led him so far as to condemn the subjects of *Figaro* and *Don Giovanni* for their immorality. His models in opera were *The Magic Flute* and *The Water-Carrier*.

Schikaneder, the theatrical manager who commissioned Mozart to write *The Magic Flute*, was a character who might have been invented, name and all, by some German Dickens as a German equivalent of Mr Crummles. Giesecke, who actually wrote most of the libretto, was a young intellectual passing through a momentary phase of bohemianism at the time. The opera was intended to be no more than a fairy pantomime, but in the course of composition it became a Masonic allegory with a profound mystical symbolism. Beethoven was not himself a Freemason, but he had associated with those who were. German Freemasonry in the 18th century had stood for the principles of English libertarianism, which were naturally regarded with horror by continental autocrats and by the Catholic Church. Masonry had done much to bring about the French Revolution, and *The Magic Flute* is full of the spirit of enlightenment.

It was for this reason that the opera sank so deeply into Beethoven's creative mind. But he did not wish to write another fairy pantomime; for the libretto of his opera he turned to a French model. Serious *opéra comique*, like Cherubini's, appealed to the new revolutionary public, whereas spectacular grand opera on the lines of *La Vestale* was the glorification of the autocratic state.

Beethoven has been so much monumentalized in the course of a century and a half's reverence that his modern devotees fail to understand the true significance of *Fidelio*. In Germany, after the Revolution of 1918, *Fidelio* was often played as a drama of revolution; the characters, described in the libretto as being of the 16th century, were transferred to the end of the 18th, and the final release of the prisoners was supposed to be brought about not by royal clemency but by a rising of the people. Such treatment of the opera did less injustice to Beethoven than the attempt to exaggerate the moral grandeur of the music itself. The monumental treatment is futile, for the only characters that can be monumentalized are Leonora and the chorus, so that the net result is for *Fidelio* to become a *prima donna's* opera, a producer's opera and, what is worst of all, a conductor's opera. The other characters simply will not stand exaggeration, as experience has shown over and over again. The only way to interpret *Fidelio* is to accept the limitations of its form and style. It requires an intimate theatre, and an intimate style of singing, and the conductor must realize that his function is to accompany an *opéra comique* and not to turn it into a symphony concert. *Fidelio* begins quite naturally as a comic opera; it passes gradually through a phase of sentiment to a climax of anxiety. Like *Don Giovanni*, it reaches, as if accidentally, a moment in which anxiety is deepened into tragic terror; it is a 'rescue opera', like *The Water-Carrier*, in which a poor peasant risks his own life to save that of a political prisoner, and, as in *The Water-Carrier*, its dramatic form is balanced by a happy end. The secret truth is that the happy end has to be monumentalized in order to disguise the conventionality of it; Mozart's use of the symphonic finale tempted Beethoven, the greatest of symphonists, to forget the exigencies of the theatre and to prolong his ending to an inordinate length.

Operas of a later period have caused audiences to find *Fidelio* conventional, because it is written in the musical language of a long past age. It is not 'realistic', but it is intensely real and human; Florestan and Leonora are not intended to be eternal symbols, like Wagner's gods and goddesses, nor even heroes of antiquity like Gluck's and Spontini's; they are human beings, and (allowing for the necessary artificialities of all stage plays) they go through experiences such as did happen to real people during the Reign of Terror. Bouilly, the author of the original French libretto (music by Gaveaux, Paris, 1798), said that it was a true story and that he had known the facts himself.

§ 2 CIMAROSA. ROSSINI

Fidelio stands isolated in the history of opera; it represents a 'dead end', for it has no musical descendants. The main line of operatic history still derives its inspiration from Italy. In the days of Mozart one of the most popular Italian composers had been Domenico Cimarosa; some of his contemporaries thought him to be the greatest living master of serious opera, but his serious operas are utterly forgotten and he is remembered now only by a single comic opera, *Il Matrimonio Segreto* (The Secret Marriage) (1792), first produced at Vienna, where the Emperor was so delighted with it that after the curtain fell on the first performance he commanded supper for the entire company and then ordered them to perform the whole opera again.

Il Matrimonio Segreto has often been revived in England and elsewhere and is a good example of the comic operas which Vienna preferred to those of Mozart. Cimarosa's music has an irresistible verve and sparkle, though looked at closely it is seen to be very thin stuff. Mozart took over all his conventions – his breathless back-chat in recitative, his charming tunes, his patter songs for the comic bass, his chattering ensembles – and added to them his own warmth and

389

harmony and ingenuity of orchestration. Mozart's audiences thought that he had given them too much; they were quite content with Cimarosa's elementary accompaniments, and probably they talked freely during the long and rather vapid instrumental introductions to his songs.

Cimarosa belongs musically to the 18th century – to a century when an Emperor could encore a whole opera; but humanly he belonged to the new age, for in 1799 he took the side of the French republican army which marched into Naples and was imprisoned and condemned to death. His sentence was eventually commuted into one of banishment, but before he could take refuge in Russia he died from the effects of his imprisonment.

The operas of Cimarosa served as the chief models for those of Gioacchino Rossini. Many people would share Beethoven's opinion that comic opera was the form in which Rossini was supreme, and at the present day *Il Barbiere di Siviglia* (The Barber of Seville) (Rome, 1816) is the Rossini opera most familiar to the general public. But the work which made Rossini famous throughout Europe was the serious opera *Tancredi* (1813). In 1822 Rossini visited Vienna, where his operas had the most extravagant success. The Viennese musicians were naturally infuriated, but not even they could resist the extraordinary vitality and excitement of his music. They may have hated Rossini for his success, but his melodies went to their heads and stuck there; Weber and Schubert show the influence of Rossini very conspicuously, and even Beethoven, deaf as he was, managed to pick up something from him and use it in the most unexpected situation.

Rossini learned a good deal from Austria and Germany too. He had long ago earned the nickname of 'the little German' because of his devotion to Haydn and Mozart, and in Vienna he heard Beethoven's 'Eroica' Symphony and Weber's *Freischütz*. But German music taught him nothing new in the way of melody, for he must have known better than anyone how much the great German composers owed to Italy; what he learned from Germany was the use of the orchestra and probably the art of building up movements in the symphonic style. *The Barber* may owe something to Mozart, but it owes far more to Cimarosa, and so does *La Cenerentola* (1817); and it is interesting to note that in a letter of about this date he speaks of the German composers, Beethoven especially, as having brought the art of music to utter ruin. He probably changed his mind after his visit to Vienna in 1822.

Rossini's latest operas were produced in Paris; *Semiramide* (Venice, 1823) was the last that came out in Italy. *Semiramide* and *Moïse* (Paris, 1827) show great dignity and solidity of style, and are still quite frequently performed in Italy. *William Tell* (Paris, 1829) also remains in the repertory of the greater opera-houses, though its appearances are not frequent, as it demands singers of exceptional powers. After *William Tell*, Rossini, mainly for reasons of ill-health, retired into private life and wrote no more for the stage.

§ 3 BELLINI. DONIZETTI. AUBER

After the Napoleonic period Paris became the centre of musical life; the hegemony of Vienna ended with the death of Schubert in 1828. Opera had by now become part of the normal routine of life, one may say, but it had always to be subsidized by princes if it was to have any solid foundation. Paris passed through various revolutions, but it did not matter whether France had a republic, an emperor or a king; the government supported the opera as a national duty. Paris was not only the centre of musical life, but of all artistic and intellectual activities; it was an international city and it supported an Italian opera as well as a French one. Italian opera still went on in Italy itself, but even at Milan and Naples performances were often very rough, except from individual singers of outstanding merit. In London also the opera band was regarded by contemporary critics as 'a torture to the ear'. In Germany there was a perpetual struggle between the Germans and the Italians, and it was a long time before the Italians were finally turned out.

The history of opera at this point becomes complicated, because Italy, France and Germany develop on distinct lines of their own which are constantly crossing. The Italian line is the clearest, and will therefore be treated first. Rossini at the end of his operatic career deserted the Italian theatre for the French, but the Italian line was still continued by a number of composers now forgotten, and also by three who are remembered – Bellini, Donizetti and Verdi.

Bellini has little in common with Rossini; he was gifted neither with comedy nor with the grand manner. But he had a vein of pure and rather elegiac melody which can still appeal to us. Bellini's operas are the source from which Chopin drew many of his most moving themes, and there are constant reminiscences of them in Liszt, quite apart from the actual transcriptions that he made from the operas. Bellini's influence extends even to the days of Tchaikovsky, who had a great affection for his music. Although for a time Bellini's operas lost their popularity, they are now frequently encountered in opera-houses all over the world. Whether this revival of interest in the *bel canto* operas is due to the emergence of a new generation of singers with the style and technique to do them justice, or vice versa, is a moot point. *Norma* is undoubtedly Bellini's masterpiece, but the tuneful *Puritani* and the gentle, pastoral *Sonnambula* are almost its equal.

Of Donizetti's more than sixty operas, many of the tragedies and histories have in recent years been re-staged and re-appraised. *Maria Stuarda*, *Anna Bolena* and, of course, *Lucia di Lammermoor* are among the most popular. Several of the other tragedies, however, contain more than their fair share of empty rhetoric and cliché. Donizetti's comic operas, *Don Pasquale*, *L'Elisir d'amore* (The Elixir of Love) and *La Fille du Régiment* (The Daughter of the Regiment) are delightful works, full of charm as well as opportunities for vocal display. Apart from these works, comic opera almost ceased to exist in Italy; it degenerated into utter triviality, and a later generation preferred to import its trivialities from France and England.

Italian opera had again become commercialized. Italy itself could hardly be said to support opera; it produced it, and the verdict of an audience that was growing steadily more and more democratic decided its success or failure. If an opera made a success in Italy, the composer might hope to make more money out of his work in Paris or London. Italian audiences were supposed to be critical, and they are even said to be so now, but their criticism of music is that of complete ignorance. They can enjoy an obvious tune, and they are accustomed to a high standard of vocalization; the gallery speaks its mind without hesitation or restraint – that is all that their critical faculty amounts to.

Verdi accepted the situation and wrote frankly for commercial purposes, at any rate for the earlier part of his career. He achieved popularity all over the world by his extraordinary concentration on *l'effetto*, a word that constantly recurs in his letters; but instead of resting content with popular success he managed to go on educating himself – stimulated in later life by the influence of his intimate friend and librettist Arrigo Boito, a poet of profound intellectual culture, and something of a composer himself. The result was that he ended his long career not as a tired survivor from the past but as a pioneer and prophet of the future.

In France the early 19th century gave birth to what we might call 'political opera', as the natural outcome of the grand manner of Spontini. Rossini's *Moïse* was followed at once by Auber's *La Muette de Portici* (The Dumb Girl of Portici) (1828), better known in England under its Italian title of *Masaniello*. There were many reasons for the immense popularity of *Masaniello* – its catchy tunes, its Neapolitan atmosphere and the curious vagary which made the heroine congenitally dumb (though not deaf!), so that the part was acted not by a singer but by a star of the ballet; the plot deals with the rising of the Neapolitan people against the Spanish rulers in 1647, and it was a performance of the opera at Brussels in 1830 that started the rising of the Belgians against the Dutch king. Rossini's *William Tell* (1829) was another opera glorifying the revolt of an oppressed people against a foreign tyrant.

Auber's slender talent was not equal to opera on the grand scale, and 'political opera' was carried on by Meyerbeer and Halévy. French grand opera of this period is a plutocratic modernization of the grand operas of Lully and Rameau. Every resource was utilized, chorus, ballet, machinery and orchestra, on the largest scale and on a standard conventional design. The opera-house at Paris (erected 1861–75) might have been designed as a monument to Meyerbeer, for it shows the same mastery of construction and the same oppressive wealth of ornament.

The French genius for neat craftsmanship saved comic opera from the decay into which it fell in Italy. Here again Auber took Rossini as his model; *Fra Diavolo* (1830) is an admirable example of French comic opera. But, like the grand opera, it became stereotyped and commercialized; out of the hundreds that were produced in the course of the century, hardly one is remembered now, though a few may still be seen in France, especially in the provinces.

§ 4 ROMANTICISM AND WEBER

Neither French nor Italian opera was seriously affected by the Romantic movement, in spite of the fact that Paris was one of its leading centres in literature and the other arts. In Germany romanticism expressed itself more characteristically in music than in any other form, and most intensely in the opera. Romanticism, in the exploitation of the supernatural and the macabre, had indeed made a momentary appearance in Mozart's *Don Giovanni*, though ghost scenes had been a common feature of opera as far back as the 17th century. The distinguishing feature of the romantic treatment of the supernatural, however, is the prominence of the satanic element, the heroic treatment of the power of evil. Meyerbeer's *Robert le Diable* (Robert the Devil) (1831) is the last word in neo-Gothic romanticism as far as subject is concerned, but in his musical technique Meyerbeer remains for the most part classical. It was only in Germany that romanticism changed the whole outlook of composers on musical form.

The great pioneer of romanticism in German opera was Carl Maria von Weber, whose *Der Freischütz* (The Freeshooter) (1821) is a landmark in the history of German music. Weber's musical style is found to be a mixture of very heterogeneous elements, if we take the trouble to analyse it. A great deal comes from Rossini, and sounds like scraps remembered and played on the pianoforte by ear after coming home from the opera-house; much is derived from the popular German music of the day, the triviality of which many writers seek to excuse or glorify by calling it 'folk-music'. And there is too the whole background of German symphonic music, including the works of Beethoven's middle period. Weber's works for the concert room show that he was no great symphonist; they are showy and rhetorical rather than intellectual or deeply emotional. Brought up in the theatre, he had a vivid sense of stage effect, but his operas, and his choice of librettos, show that he had very little sense of drama as a whole. His opera songs start often with a fascinating melodic phrase, generally more instrumental than vocal, and curiously difficult to sing owing to the awkwardness of the words; after that the music only too often collapses and is bolstered up by symphonic conventionalities that again are instrumental in style and utterly unvocal. As to his 'unfailing sense of the stage', those who have to work out the details of stage management know that Weber presents the most uncomfortable problems in every one of his operas; his greatest opera, *Euryanthe* (1823), is by common consent practically impossible to put on the stage.

Despite all these things Weber – especially in *Der Freischütz* – has an extraordinary power of thrilling an audience, even today. His music has a rapturous impetus that carries us off our feet; in the middle of some movement that may by now have become commonplace and tedious we are suddenly struck by some masterstroke of emotional expression, and behind everything there is the picturesqueness of what we recognize as the modern orchestra. Weber had a marvellous genius for 'background music', as we have called it. Previous centuries had hardly attempted it, though we may find something of it even in Lully, and more in Rameau and Gluck, but the scene of the Wolf's Glen in *Der Freischütz* was something entirely new, and it is the foundation of all the descriptive music, operatic or otherwise, of the 19th century.

Euryanthe, a story of mediaeval chivalry, contains much beautiful music, but it is so badly constructed that it has always been a failure. In 1826 Weber was invited to compose an opera for London, and Planché, a hack playwright with a great knowledge of heraldry and other antiquarian lore, provided him with a libretto planned on the lines of Purcell's *King Arthur* and borrowing copiously from *A Midsummer Night's Dream* and *The Tempest*. Absurd as it was, it provided Weber with exactly the right opportunities for his genius, and *Oberon* ought certainly to be revived in England, for it exhibits Weber's characteristic style at its very best.

The Romantic movement, in which the revival of Shakespeare played a notable part, broke down the exact distinction between grand opera and comic opera. *Der Freischütz* is technically a comic opera with spoken dialogue, and the romantic operas of Marschner, once enormously popular in London, continue the mixture of the comic and the macabre. Pure comic opera in Germany is represented by Lortzing, who is still popular in his own country. In France and Italy, comic opera soon became commercialized and degenerated into operetta.

From the days of Weber onwards the orchestra plays an increasingly important part in German opera. A German music critic pointed out that the orchestra was the only medium for representing these supernatural powers with which the romantic heroes and heroines found themselves in conflict. The singers of these parts soon became acutely conscious of the conflict. Mozart was accused in his day of making the orchestra more important than the singers, and the same accusation has been brought against practically every German composer up to the present day, though history shows us that whatever the balance of power between singers and orchestra may be, audiences gradually accustom themselves to the standard of the generation before their own, and regard that as right and proper. The Germans have always been more interested in instrumental music than in singing, and the development of the orchestra, and consequently of pure orchestral music, has been mainly a German achievement.

The danger of this to opera has lain not so much in the amount of noise that the orchestra produces (for in these days we all know that the largest orchestra can be kept under adequate control if the composer has written for it with proper skill) as in the tendency of German composers to regard the orchestra as the chief medium for the expression of their thought. Many operas of recent times, not only by German composers, have failed to convince an audience simply because the main interest of the music was in the orchestra and not on the stage. The only thing that a character in an opera can do to convince the audience that he is a real person in whom they are compelled to take an interest is to sing, and the amount of interest they take in him (as a character in a drama, be it understood, not as Mr So-and-so, the famous tenor) will be proportionate to the interest of the music the composer has put into his mouth. He may drop into recitative when it is necessary to give us some definite information about facts in order to carry on the play, but otherwise the moment he ceases to hold our emotions by music he fades out of existence. We may easily cease to be conscious of his bodily presence on the stage altogether. The Italians have never lost sight of this fundamental principle of opera. One could listen to an opera of Verdi, such as *Il trovatore* (The Troubadour) sung without any accompaniment at all, and still obtain some dramatic satisfaction from it, but an opera of Wagner would be meaningless without the orchestra, and indeed we could get a considerable idea of it from that alone without the singers.

§ 5 WAGNER

The wars of the *Bouffons* and of the *Gluckists* were insignificant compared with the perpetual war of controversy that surrounded Wagner. The Wagnerian war was a war of journalists too, with Wagner himself as journalist in chief, but it was a war of musicians as well, to a greater extent than the operatic wars of Paris a century before. At the present day, when Wagner sits safely enshrined among the classics of the past, there is little need for any except historical researchers to trouble their heads much about Wagner's theoretical writings. Wagner's position in the history of music is due simply to his genius as a musician. His constructive theories about opera as a *Gesamtkunstwerk*, a joint work of art produced by the union of poetry, drama, music and all the subsidiary arts of the theatre, were nothing in the least original; their fundamental principles were laid down by the early Florentine group and were reaffirmed in the 18th century by Algarotti and Gluck. Wagner felt compelled to assert them once more, because in his day, as in Algarotti's, commercial opera had become standardized, and the average opera, now utterly forgotten, was of negligible musical value. Wagner stood for 'music-drama' as against 'opera', and many of his later admirers have clung to this distinction as if it were a dogma of religious faith, but it really means nothing. The old Italians called their operas *dramma per musica* too; if *Idomeneo* is an 'opera' rather than a 'music-drama' it is only because its convention belongs to its own age. We must not forget, however, that Wagner has taught us moderns to try to produce all operas, however 'operatic', in a Wagnerian spirit, that is, with proper attention to the interaction of all artistic factors, and to listen to them in a Wagnerian spirit, that is, without interrupting the course of an act by applause after each song. The question whether the music of an opera should be continuous or divided into separate movements is purely a question of musical technique, which varies according to the general musical style of the age. It is true that most operas have been saddled with bad librettos, but with the examples of Rinuccini, Metastasio and Da Ponte before us, we cannot lay the blame on the operatic form itself. Wagner probably judged opera librettos by the current German translations of Mozart's and by the standard of Weber's collaboratress Helmine von Chezy, whose nonsense has made her immortal; some critics have even dared to suggest that Wagner himself was more of a musician than a poet.

Wagner's first important opera, *Rienzi* (1842), continues the style of Meyerbeer; *Der fliegende Holländer* (The Flying Dutchman) (1843), reverts to Weber and Marschner. *Tannhäuser* (1845), combines Weber with the construction of Meyerbeer while *Lohengrin* (1850) derives so much from *Euryanthe* as to make it fortunate that Weber's opera is hardly ever performed. But with all their faults (and the present age is beginning to be uncomfortably conscious of them) these romantic operas of Wagner have a strength that Weber could never achieve. Wagner in his own day was abused by the adherents of 'absolute music', but although he wrote next to nothing in that line he was himself a genuine symphonist; he could conceive of a whole act, indeed of a whole opera, as one organic piece of music. The second act of *Der Freischütz* – the Wolf's Glen – attempts that, and Mozart certainly visualized his operas as organic wholes, although the technique of his day did not permit of their being continuous and unbroken.

Wagner had the benefit of coming after Beethoven; he assimilated the constructive technique of his later symphonies and the *Missa*

Solemnis, and he gradually absorbed that of Liszt and Berlioz too. The Wagnerian method of composing is based on the development sections of Beethoven's symphonies, and this was further assisted by Wagner's employment of the *leit-motiv* (guiding theme): that is of musical themes associated with particular characters or ideas. Later composers sometimes tried to imitate this practice, about which Wagner's enemies said that each of his characters presented his visiting-card; and in the music of later composers the 'guiding-themes' are indeed no more than labels. The value of Wagner's themes lay not so much in their repetition and development as in the fact that they were singularly arresting and musically significant in themselves. Whether they 'represent' or 'depict' the ideas associated with them is a matter of opinion, but they serve their purpose; the entry of an important theme at a critical moment always impresses us by its musical value, even if we have forgotten its particular name in the directory.

The *leit-motiv* occurs in the early operas, but it does not become a systematic method until after Wagner's flight from Dresden in 1849, followed by his close association with Liszt and his careful study of Liszt's symphonic poems. If the early operas seem now to be a little old-fashioned – and considering that they were composed well over 100 years ago it is not surprising – this is due mainly to their rhythmical monotony. We are not much troubled by the fact that *Lohengrin* is almost entirely in common time, and most of it *andante*, but we do become wearied of the perpetual alternation of feminine and masculine verse-endings, and the favourite metre of Wagner's verses – 11, 10, 11, 10 – as well as of his characteristic Meyerbeerian way of accenting it.

The complete change of literary style and metrical method which Wagner adopted for *The Ring* and *Tristan* contributed very greatly to the formation of his new personal style in the music itself.

With these operas we are in an entirely new world. Removed by the circumstances of banishment from Germany from the daily contact with standardized opera inevitable to a working conductor, Wagner had the leisure and the mental freedom to construct for himself an ideal opera and to plan the construction of an ideal theatre to house it. It is advisable here to give the dates of composition of

Wagner's later works: the libretto of *The Ring* was not written in the order of the operas, but in the reverse order, beginning with *Götterdämmerung* (The Twilight of the Gods) and ending with *Das Rheingold* (1852). The music of *Rheingold* was composed 1853–54 and *Die Walküre* (The Valkyrie) in 1854–56. *Siegfried* was begun in 1857, but laid aside for *Tristan und Isolde* (1857–59) and *Die Meistersinger von Nürnberg* (The Mastersingers of Nuremberg), begun 1862; *Die Meistersinger* was interrupted by the resumption of *Siegfried* in 1865, and finished in 1867, *Siegfried* not reaching completion till 1871. *Götterdämmerung* was partly sketched in 1848, then left until 1870 and finished in 1874. The complete *Ring* was first performed at Bayreuth in 1876; *Parsifal* was first sketched in 1857, but mainly composed between 1877 and 1882, in which year it was first performed.

§ 6 WAGNERIANISM

A great deal of nonsense has been written – some indeed by Wagner himself – about the philosophical and moral significance of his operas. To us at the present day they are simply masterpieces of what has now become classical music; we see them and listen to them in the same spirit as we do those of Gluck or Mozart. Wagner's ideas of 'redemption through love' and so forth could be applied to any opera or any play that was ever written; it is obviously quite impossible to translate philosophical ideas of this sort into musical notes, and those who try to translate musical notes into words are by no means certain to agree in their interpretations. All that is now necessary to the enjoyment of a Wagner opera is an unprejudiced mind and, if possible, a previous reading of the libretto.

There is, however, one aspect of Wagner's philosophy which we must take seriously. His ideal of creating a truly German art is a matter of purely local interest, and it may be observed that Wagner was extremely pleased to find his works appreciated in other countries. But Wagner's view of opera as a festival drama, to be approached in what for want of a better word we must call a religious spirit, was fundamental to his philosophy. Here again the idea was not Wagner's own, as he knew perfectly well; all he wished to do was to insist on its importance at a period when it had been forgotten. Wagner's own age was already tending to approach music – such music as the Ninth Symphony of Beethoven – in this spirit, and English audiences of today are quite ready to hope that attendance at the Albert Hall on a Beethoven night will be reckoned up by the recording angel as equivalent to attendance at church. But except at Bayreuth and on a few other occasions when a Bayreuth atmosphere is carefully staged, few people even now can bring themselves to regard an opera as an opportunity for mystical experience.

It is difficult to write of these things, for as soon as we begin to think about them we are confronted with ultimate problems of life, art and religion, which everyone has to work out for himself as best he may. Mozart offered us initiation into these mysteries in *The Magic Flute*; Beethoven exalted our conception of humanity in *Fidelio*. But if we have in these days learned to approach opera, or even to wish to approach such operas as are worthy of it, in the spirit of *Fidelio* and *The Magic Flute*, it is Wagner, more than any other musician of the theatre, who has pointed our minds in that direction.

§ 7 OPERETTA

It has been said that the real history of music is not the lives of the great masters but the history of bad music – the history of the kind of commercial popular music, secular or sacred, that at all periods has formed the general background against which the men of genius stand out. They do not always stand out from it very clearly; they too were influenced to some extent by the popular music of their day, and it is often impossible to arrive at an intimate understanding of the great men without some knowledge of the ephemeral music that they could never escape hearing. For this reason it is necessary to say a few words here about the more trivial forms of dramatic music, more especially as they were a very characteristic product of the second half of the 19th century.

All music tends to become classical as time goes on, and we have witnessed in recent years a great revival of what we may call classical rubbish. This has been due partly to modern movements in music, which have apparently widened the gulf that always existed between serious and popular music. Operas or operettas that in their own day would never have been allowed mention within the walls of a state-supported theatre are now revived there as classical works; age has conferred respectability on them, but managers hope that it has not lessened their powers of attraction.

Many of the comic operas of the 18th century must in their own day have appealed mainly to what we should now call a 'musical comedy audience'; that type of audience became much more numer-rous in the days of Louis Philippe and young Queen Victoria. The title *opérette* was first used by the French composer Florimond Ronger, known as Hervé, and the music he wrote in these little works was appropriately described as *musiquette*. Hervé's career began in 1848, but it was in the 1860s that he achieved his greatest popularity, both in Paris and in London, with *Chilpéric* and *Le petit Faust*. He became naturalized as an Englishman in 1874.

Hervé's successes, however, were eclipsed (at any rate until 1880) by those of Jacques Offenbach, whose real name was Jakob Eberst, born at Cologne. He came to Paris as an eccentric violoncellist, but in 1855 he began producing operettas at a small theatre which from that time came to be known as the Bouffes-Parisiens. Before his death in 1880 he had composed some ninety operettas, as well as the unfinished score of *Tales of Hoffmann* which was completed by Guiraud and produced in 1881. Offenbach's operettas, of which the best known are *Orphée aux Enfers* (Orpheus in the Underworld) (1858), *La Belle Hélène* (1864), *La Vie Parisienne* (1866), *La Grande Duchesse de Gérolstein* (1867) and *Madame Favart* (1879), enjoyed an enormous popularity all over Europe, and indeed they deserved it for the inimitable gaiety and spirit of their music, which has hardly even yet lost its exhilarating vitality, although the topical wit of their librettos has to a large extent evaporated.

Needless to say, Offenbach during his lifetime found imitators in other countries. Johann Strauss, the composer of the 'Blue Danube' waltz, supplied Vienna with a succession of operettas, beginning with *Indigo* in 1871. Several of these are still popular, among them *Die Fledermaus* (1874), *Eine Nacht in Venedig* (A Night in Venice) (1883), and *Der Zigeunerbaron* (The Gypsy Baron) (1885), but their eternal waltz tunes can sound cloying to non-Viennese ears, and Strauss's sentimental Austrian temperament could never quite achieve the reckless drollery of Offenbach. A little later England produced a native rival to Offenbach in Arthur Sullivan, who in the earlier part of his career had made his name as a composer of oratorios and church music. 'Onward, Christian Soldiers' dates from 1872, and 'The Lost Chord' from 1877. But as early as 1867 he had written music for *Cox and Box*, adapted by F. C. Burnand from Maddison Morton's well-known farce, and in 1871 he collaborated for the first time with W. S. Gilbert in *Thespis, or The Gods Grown Old*. During the 1870s Offenbach's operettas were very popular in London, and in 1875 Sullivan and Gilbert produced, for an Offenbach season, a so-called 'dramatic cantata', *Trial by Jury*, the success of which led to a long collaboration between librettist and composer. The first of their operettas was *The Sorcerer* (1877); it was followed by *H.M.S. Pinafore* (1878), *The Pirates of Penzance* (1880), and many others, the names of which it is not necessary to set out here in full.

The aim of the collaborators was to create a type of entertainment that should compete successfully with those of Offenbach and also attract a class of theatre-goer who regarded Offenbach as 'rather too French'. Gilbert's librettos were considered exceedingly witty in their day, but for the present generation they must contain many allusions now quite incomprehensible without historical footnotes. These operettas were enormously successful in America, and *The Mikado*, a satire on the Japanese Village exhibited in 1885 at Knightsbridge, had some success in Germany, but otherwise they never achieved the international fame of those by Strauss and Offenbach. Probably Gilbert's librettos were too local, and often too much concerned with purely English political satire, for foreigners to understand; Sullivan's music, despite its charm, had not quite the light-footedness of Offenbach or Strauss. Sullivan could never completely shake off the character of the church organist, and it is perhaps that very quality of respectability which has endeared him to generations of English listeners.

To chronicle the lesser lights of operetta is impossible. The French composers have always kept up the highest standards of elegance and finish, as exemplified by the operettas of Audran and Messager. Vienna had Suppé and Millöcker in the days of Strauss; their operettas are occasionally revived, but they are held to be unpresentable without considerable modernization. This rewriting of old operettas is a convenient way of securing a new copyright in a work that has long been public property. The 20th-century Viennese school, including Lehár with his *Die Lustige Witwe* (The Merry Widow), Kálmán and Stolz, exploited the waltz for all it was worth, and apparently the public are not yet tired of it. Towards the end of the last century England produced a yet more trivial type of operetta which was given the name of 'musical comedy'; some of these even enjoyed a certain popularity abroad, notably *The Geisha* (1892), by Sidney Jones. Their foreign popularity was due not so much to stage performances as to the fact that the favourite tunes were much played by bands in places of entertainment. *The Geisha* has a certain historic importance owing to its obvious influence on Puccini's *Madame Butterfly*.

PART 4 FROM VERDI TO THE PRESENT DAY

§ 1 VERDI

Time tends to make all music 'classical', and the early operas of Verdi, which contemporary criticism found tawdry and brutal, have in recent years been revived in a Wagnerian spirit of devotion as a reaction against those of Wagner himself. The passage of years, assisted by the ingenuity of modern conductors, has reduced their 'brutality' to 'dramatic intensity', and the barrel-organ tunes that excited our ancestors to disgust or laughter have acquired the sentimental associations of a picturesque period. Popular audiences have always adored Verdi's operas; critical opinion in England adopted a snobbish and puritanical attitude to them for many years, but has long since capitulated. *Nabucco* (1842) and *Macbeth* (1847) are now almost favourite repertory pieces, as the three masterpieces of Verdi's middle period – *Rigoletto* (1851), *Il Trovatore* (1853) and *La Traviata* (1853) – have always been. Most recently, a number of the other early works have come in for reappraisal, and have been found to be extremely effective in the theatre. The youthful energy and directness of purpose of, for instance, *I masnadieri* (The Robbers) (1847) or *Attila* (1846) are qualities as greatly appreciated by present-day audiences as the mature mastery of *Un ballo in maschera* (A Masked Ball) (1859). *Don Carlos* (1867) and the final three great works, *Aida* (1871), *Otello* (1887) and *Falstaff* (1893).

Verdi in his youth was a frankly commercial composer, but his inborn musicianship was too strong for him. This is clear from the way in which he continuously educated himself up to the end of his life, and even in these earlier works what mark him off from Bellini and Donizetti are the thoroughness of his workmanship, his firm yet daring sense of harmony and his sensitive and ingenious orchestration. *Rigoletto* is remarkable for a new kind of music that hovers between recitative and aria; the character of the title-part is a marvellous psychological study, and this new medium was evolved from the necessity of this characterization. *Il Trovatore*, the plot of which has become the classical example of unintelligibility, lives by virtue of its intense dramatic concentration; even when many people in the audience have not the remotest idea what is happening, the relentless crescendo of emotional excitement carries them along with the force of a torrent. To old-fashioned opera-goers *La Traviata* was no more than a display-piece for a *prima donna*'s voice, Paris gowns and diamonds, while the rest of the cast appeared in costumes of the 17th or 18th century, because no audience could stand opera in the dresses of its own period. That period has now passed into the era of the picturesque, and recent productions have made *La Traviata* into a chamber opera of singularly touching delicacy.

Aida marks a new stage in Verdi's development. As it was composed to celebrate the opening of the Suez Canal at Cairo. the subject was taken from ancient Egypt, and the opera was made as spectacular as possible; it is still the best spectacular opera in the repertory, both as opera and as spectacle. After *Aida* Verdi's operas appeared at longer intervals; he had ceased to be a commercial composer and was beginning to write for himself, now that his position was assured. In those days Verdi and Wagner were continually placed in opposition by journalists who wanted to enjoy a controversy, and Verdi was sometimes accused of having submitted to Wagner's influence, but he always indignantly repudiated the charge. After Wagner's death in 1883 Verdi was the only great opera composer living, so that his *Otello*, produced in 1887, was awaited with considerable excitement. Verdi's technique had by now matured beyond all expectations, and *Otello* was found to be considerably in advance of its time, at any rate for Italy. A still more astonishing achievement was *Falstaff*, especially as Verdi was then in his eightieth year. For many years neither of these operas obtained real popularity in Italy: they were more appreciated in Germany, but even there their progress was slow.

Needless to say, Verdi was still further accused of imitating Wagner; but his attitude to opera remained fundamentally different. The change of style represented by *Otello* and *Falstaff* was due in large part to the new type of libretto provided for him by Boito, whose adaptations of Shakespeare are the work of a real poet, and partly to the gradual change that was going on in all musical technique, which made it possible for Verdi to acquire a looser and more supple texture than he had been able to employ even in *Aida*. The example of Wagner no doubt stimulated him, or rather encouraged him, for he did not need the stimulus to take opera seriously as a work of art rather than as mere commercial entertainment. But for Wagnerian ideas of 'music-drama' Verdi had not the slightest sympathy. In Wagner's later works the characters recede further and further away from us; we see them only through the haze of the orchestra. It is the orchestra, with its perpetual development of *leit-motiv* – a development that only the orchestra could carry out – that expresses the inward mind of the composer. With Verdi the orchestra, however exquisitely treated, is no more than an accompaniment to the voices; the characters seem to stand in front of it, and Verdi's aim is not to use them as the vehicles for his philosophy but to make them intensely real and alive. German conductors, accustomed to regard the orchestra as the most important thing, often misunderstand *Falstaff* completely; its vocal line is complex and broken up, at least on paper, but it is the vocal ensemble that carries the real thought of the composer and the voices must always bear that burden and consciously take the lead.

Arrigo Boito was not only a poet, but a composer as well. His opera *Mefistofele* (produced 1868, revised 1875) was the attempt of a pure idealist to summarize in one musical drama the whole of Goethe's two Faust dramas. His technique is in many respects amateurish, but his work is profoundly thoughtful with a singular beauty of its own; during this century it has almost achieved popularity in Italy. *Nerone* (1924), on which Boito worked for forty years, was not brought out until after his death; it is distinguished in style, but too much overloaded with archaeological learning to be effective on the stage.

§ 2 FRENCH OPERA

France during the latter half of the 19th century contributed little to the history of opera, but it produced a small number of works destined to attain popularity all over the world. The first of these is Gounod's *Faust* (1859). Gounod's other operas, fairly often performed up to the end of the century, seem now to have lost their attraction, though *Philémon et Baucis* (1860), *Mireille* (1864) and *Roméo et Juliette* (1867) contain many delightful numbers. The charm of Gounod's music lay in its delicate sensuousness; the colossal manner of Meyerbeer was unsuited to him, and he professed to take Mozart as his model. Ambroise Thomas survives only by *Mignon* (1866). We see in both *Faust* and *Mignon* a type intermediate between grand opera and *opéra comique*; its emergence is due to the gradual change taking place in opera audiences. Opera was no longer the exclusive property of a highly cultured aristocracy; it had (especially in France) to make its appeal to a bourgeoisie whose culture was steadily improving, but had not yet reached a very elevated standard.

That public could hardly be expected to enter into the spirit of Berlioz's few attempts at opera. *Benvenuto Cellini* (1838) has been revived recently, and with success; *Béatrice et Bénédict* (1862) receives occasional performances as a respected classic. *Les Troyens* (The Trojans), Berlioz's double masterpiece – it consists of two opera's – *La Prise de Troie* (The Capture of Troy) and *Les Troyens à Carthage* (The Trojans at Carthage) – completed in 1858, was never performed in its entirety until Mottl, the great Wagnerian conductor, produced it at Karlsruhe in 1897. It has had occasional performances in recent years, most notably at Covent Garden in London and at the Metropolitan Opera in New York.

Bizet's *Carmen* (1875) took some years to become popular; it is now perhaps the most popular of all operas in the repertory of the world. The most unsophisticated listener who walks into an opera-house for the first time in his life is fascinated by it, and the most jaded of learned musicians is never tired of it. It owes its obvious attraction to its powerful story and to the opportunities it gives to the singer of the title-part, especially if she considers herself to be a highly temperamental actress and a woman of irresistible charm. More knowledgable listeners will appreciate the picturesque Spanish colour of the music, and the way in which Bizet combines a wealth of ravishing melody with harmonic devices of great ingenuity and originality.

Carmen is also of historical importance, for it is the foundation of what in later years was called *verismo*, the operatic treatment of sordid and brutal subjects with every emphasis on these characteristics. We shall revert to this later on.

The voluptuous manner of Gounod was further developed by Massenet, whose *Hérodiade* (1881) attempted to combine it with something of the Wagnerian method. *Hérodiade* (on the story of St John the Baptist and Salome) is still popular in France, especially in the provinces, but its allure has now become decidedly elderly. *Manon* (1884) retains a certain 'Dresden china' charm, and *Werther* (1892) is a really masterly study in sentimentality. Massenet has a ttuly French standard of delicate craftsmanship, and it was this that made *Le Jongleur de Nôtre-Dame* (The Juggler of Nôtre-Dame) (1902) an exquisite musical illustration of the well-known story by Anatole France.

Of the various operas by Saint-Saëns, only *Samson et Dalila* (1877) has remained in the repertory; it is strange to think that its merits were first recognized by Liszt, who brought it out at Weimar, and that its first French production took place at Rouen in 1890. It has often been described as being more of an oratorio than an opera; perhaps that is why (ever since the Lord Chamberlain was persuaded – it is said by a very illustrious personage – to license it) it became, for a time, a great favourite in England. Its solidity of workmanship commands the respect of all musicians.

Two more French composers must be mentioned here, though their operas have almost disappeared from the stage. Alfred Bruneau created some stir with a series of operas for which he utilized librettos in prose, taken from the works of Emile Zola. Bruneau, with his prose librettos, had an influence on Gustave Charpentier, who created a new type of opera with *Louise* (1900), the story of a humble dressmaker and her artist lover in the slums of Paris. Charpentier was seriously interested in the musical education of the working classes, and *Louise* had a genuine social idealism behind it. Musically it is not very original, but it is well put together and attractive, so that it enjoyed great popularity for many years; not so its sequel *Julien*.

§ 3 MASCAGNI. LEONCAVALLO. PUCCINI

In 1890 the musical world was startled by the sudden appearance of *Cavalleria Rusticana* (Rustic Chivalry), an opera that had won a prize offered by a publisher, and the composer, Pietro Mascagni, leapt into a fame he was never afterwards able to sustain. The success of *Cavalleria* was due to its crude realism and brutality, enhanced by melodies of no great distinction that immediately fixed themselves in the ear of the public. It was followed at once by Leoncavallo's *Pagliacci* (Clowns), an obvious imitation of *Cavalleria*, and though the subsequent imitations by Giordano and others had only a short-lived success, *Cavalleria* and *Pagliacci* have become inseparable twins indispensable to the repertory of every opera-house in the world. The realistic opera of low life is derived, as has already been said, from *Carmen*; it made its appearance at a time when opera was becoming still more democratized. It was easy to write, for it needed only a sordid libretto and a rough-and-ready acquaintance with the coarser aspects of Verdi's technique; but the public gradually became tired of *verismo*, although its example continued to affect certain types of opera, both in Italy and outside, for several years.

Mascagni's later operas have never had any real success, but he deserves credit for honesty and sincerity in his *Iris* (1898). *Iris* must have been written to satisfy some inner craving of the composer, for it makes not the slightest effect to please the average audience; it is a grim story of Japanese life, treated in a quasi-mystical manner, with obvious reminiscences of Wagner. It was the first opera in which a Japanese subject had been employed and treated with ruthless seriousness; this ought to be remembered in view of subsequent (and earlier) operas and operettas in Japanese costume.

'Real and permanent success,' wrote Hugo von Hofmannsthal to Richard Strauss in 1909, 'depends on a combined appeal to both the coarser and the more refined sections of the public, for the latter create the prestige without which one is lost just as much as one is without popular appeal.' This was thoroughly well realized by Giacomo Puccini the most uniformly and universally successful composer of operas since Verdi. Most of Verdi's operas had dealt with what one may class as heroic subjects; *La Traviata* is one of the few treating of emotions that any ordinary person might experience. Verdi's heroine is the ancestress of the various misguided females whom we meet in the operas of Puccini – Manon, Mimi, Tosca, Butterfly and Liù. It is significant that when Puccini planned his last opera *Turandot*, an entirely new character, Liù, had to be added to the original play; and Liù became Puccini's real heroine.

Puccini's technical craftsmanship was in every way far ahead of that of Mascagni; whether one likes his music or not, one is forced to admire its skilful orchestration, and the supple way in which it adapts itself to the exigencies of the stage. His languishing melodies are admirably suited to the voice, especially to the voices of those Italian singers who have no shame about exploiting an erotic appeal that would have horrified the audiences of Handel and Rossini, probably those of Verdi too; lest the humblest member of the audience should fail to catch them, the tunes are generally played by the bass of the supporting harmony, as well as by the treble. Any demarcation between grand opera and *opéra comique* of the sentimental order has entirely disappeared; with one exception Puccini's operas are all 'tragic', in that they come to an unhappy end, but of tragedy in the classical sense there is not the slightest trace – they are all *comédies larmoyantes* in everything but the concluding death-scene. Puccini seems to have taken a curious delight in the musical representation of physical torture.

Apart from certain conspicuous mannerisms, which make the music of Puccini recognizable to everyone, his musical texture is always eclectic; he owed much to his contemporaries in France and even in England, though his English borrowings came from the lower grades of theatrical entertainment. It was only natural, as we shall shortly see, that his world-wide popularity should cause composers in other countries to borrow from him, and his very eclecticism made this all the easier, for reminiscences of Puccini could be made to fit into any style.

Since the death of Puccini, Italy has produced no operas of equal popularity; those that attempted to continue his manner need not be mentioned here, though Mascagni's played-out talent continued to produce operas until the mid-1930s.

§ 4 FROM WAGNER TO STRAUSS

Let us now pick up the thread of German opera after the death of Wagner. Even during his lifetime German opera has little to interest us; along with Lortzing's there are the equally provincial comic operas of Flotow and Nicolai.

A little later there appeared three comic operas that have never attained popularity despite frequent revivals, although they have always commanded the respect of serious musicians – Cornelius's *Barber of Baghdad* (1858), Goetz's *Taming of the Shrew* (1874) and Hugo Wolf's *Der Corregidor* (The Magistrate) (1896). None of these can be called Wagnerian in manner, although Cornelius in many ways anticipated the style of *Die Meistersinger*.

The only outstanding opera of the generation which followed Wagner is *Hänsel und Gretel* (1893), by Humperdinck, who was one of Wagner's most intimate assistants during the preparations of *Parsifal* in 1880–81. *Hänsel und Gretel*, which ever since its first production has been the delight of all opera-goers from the youngest to the oldest, may be described as Wagner for the nursery. *Königskinder* (The King's Children) (produced as a play with music 1896, revised as a complete opera 1910), by the same composer, treated fairy-tale in a more tragic form, and never became popular; but it certainly exercised a strong influence on Hans Pfitzner.

Various attempts were made to imitate the grandiose heroic manner of Wagner, but all of them have disappeared into oblivion, even in the country of their origin. The only hope lay in comic opera. Humperdinck's success led to a small output of one-act comic operas, of which D'Albert's *Die Abreise* (The Departure) (1898) was about the best. Unfortunately D'Albert turned his attention to melodramatic opera in the 'veristic' style, and after his *Tiefland* (1903) had achieved unparalleled popularity in Germany, owing to its adroit combination of *Carmen*, Puccini and Wagner, he pursued a very successful financial career with works over which it is better to draw a veil. *Die Abreise*, however, which is fresh, witty and clever, would be well worth reviving.

Richard Strauss was already famous as a composer of symphonic poems for the concert-room before he made his first operatic hit with *Feuersnot* (1901), a comic opera in which his librettist, Hans von Wolzogen, more or less openly proclaimed him the successor of Wagner. *Feuersnot*, despite all its cleverness, did not become a serious rival to *Die Meistersinger*.

Strauss from the first adopted the fundamental principle of Wagnerian 'music-drama' as opposed to 'opera'. Every one of his operas, including the one for which he was his own librettist, has a libretto of high literary quality. The basis of his system was that the orchestra should carry on the main fabric of the opera without letting it be broken up into separate 'numbers', while the characters on the stage declaimed, as forcibly as possible, the words of the play. Thus in *Salome* he set Oscar Wilde's drama (in a German translation) practically unaltered, and he did the same with the *Elektra* of Hugo von Hofmannsthal, which had already appeared as a spoken play.

In *Salome* (1906) and *Elektra* (1909) Strauss laid the foundations of modern German music; but, after shocking public opinion both morally and musically with these two operas (which still remain his greatest works for the stage), he reverted to a more popular style in *Der Rosenkavalier* (1911).

The libretto of *Der Rosenkavalier* had been written for him by Hofmannsthal, and he continued to collaborate with Hofmannsthal until the poet's death in 1929. They were in some ways a very ill-assorted pair – the poet an ultra-Viennese aristocrat (though partly Jewish) widely read in several languages, inclined to be decadent in taste. the composer a Bavarian *bourgeois*, robust and full-blooded, ultra-professional as a musician and with an innate tendency to vulgarity – but the partnership worked and set a new example in operatic collaboration. What they had in common was a sense of humour and incomparable skill, the one in words, the other in notes.

Der Rosenkavalier was a story of aristocratic and decadent Vienna n the days of Maria Theresa; *Arabella* (1933) presented the same Vienna as it was in 1860: both comedies were really too delicate to stand the inevitable exaggeration of a grand-operatic setting, but they achieved enormous success, due largely to Strauss's copious flow of melody and also the poet's cleverness in keeping the stage always on the move. Their operas on classical subjects were more static and overloaded with scholarship: *Ariadne* survives most confidently by

410

its luxuriant melodic sensuousness. *Der Rosenkavalier* was conceived by Hofmannsthal as a modern version of *The Marriage of Figaro*; *Die Frau ohne Schatten* (The Woman without a Shadow) was meant to do the same for *The Magic Flute*. It is a complicated oriental fairy-tale, suggested probably by the fairy plays of Carlo Gozzi (about 1765), requiring elaborate scenic effects; Strauss provided lusciously tuneful music which, at its best, has great emotive power.

At one time, it was considered that the operas Strauss composed in the 1920s and '30s showed a decline in his creative ability, but, with repeated hearings of these late works, this view has now been proved to have been a superficial one. *Intermezzo*, which Strauss wrote to his own libretto, using his wife and himself as models for the leading characters, is a charming domestic comedy with a bite. First staged in Dresden in 1924, it reached Glyndebourne in 1974, having had its American première in New York in 1963 in a concert version. *Die aegyptische Helena* and *Die Liebe der Danae*, together with *Daphne*, all of them treating of classical subjects in one way or another, are still generally confined in performance to the German-speaking countries, but *Arabella* has, in recent years, bid fair to become second only to *Der Rosenkavalier* in popularity elsewhere.

Strauss's last opera, *Capriccio* (1942), composed to a libretto written by the conductor Clemens Krauss, is a fascinating 'conversation-piece', of which it is necessary to understand and follow every word, for there is hardly any action, and it is entirely a discussion on the relative merits of music and poetry.

Strauss was hailed in his early days as the inaugurator of a new era in music; after his death at the age of eighty-five he was the last survivor of a dying tradition. The post-Wagnerians, like Wotan's offspring, may be classed in various families. Hans Pfitzner, of whom more later, descends from *Parsifal*; Strauss throughout his career, could never forget that he was firmly rooted in the stock of *Rheingold*.

§ 5 THE RUSSIANS

There is yet another aspect of 19th-century opera that must be considered before we pass to the moderns. One result of the Napoleonic upheaval was the emergence of nationalism, and opera was an obvious field for its expression. We have already noted this in Weber's *Der Freischütz*; a still more aggressive example is Glinka's *A Life for the Tsar* (1836). We are told that the Russian aristocracy of the time called it 'the music of coachmen' and that Glinka replied

'What does it matter, since the men are better than their masters?' The answer was equally characteristic of its age. The libretto belongs to the category of 'rescue operas', like Cherubini's *Water-Carrier*, but the historic enmity of the Russians and the Poles forms a strongly nationalistic background to it. The music makes copious use of folk-tunes, both Russian and Polish, and to Western ears this exotic colouring may well be singularly attractive. It may be observed here that, since German folk-song was absorbed into German artistic music at a very early date, musicians outside Germany have hardly ever discovered in it the peculiar fascination they have derived from the folk-music of remoter nations. For some three centuries Germany's chief contribution to music in general has been the intellec-tualization of the art, and consequently we who have learned to revere and love German music for the spirit that created Bach's Mass in B minor and Beethoven's Mass in D are inclined not unnaturally to hold the romantic reversion to simple folk-song (except perhaps in so childlike a composer as Humperdinck) a descent into trivial commonplace.

Glinka's opera is picturesque, but his dramatic technique was feeble, and his music collapses into conventionalities just where it needs to be most forcible. Much the same might be said of the Polish national opera, Moniuszko's *Halka* (1850), though the dramatic parts are certainly better managed than in Glinka's work. The most successful specimen of folk-song opera of this generation was Sme-tana's *The Bartered Bride* (1870), in which the peasant comedy of the libretto provides the folk-song of the music with its natural happy environment, with the result that this opera has not only become the national opera of the Czechs, but has won unstinted popularity in other countries.

Smetana, the musical spokesman of Czech nationalism, composed a number of more overtly national, patriotic operas, such as *The Brandenburgers in Bohemia*, *Dalibor* and *Libuše*, as well as gentler, more personal works (*The Two Widows*, *The Kiss*). His last completed opera, *The Devil's Wall*, suffers from a particularly confused and confusing libretto, but musically it reveals Smetana at his peak. All of these operas have remained in the Czech national repertoire, and several have proved successful abroad, though none so decisively as *The Bartered Bride*.

Folk-song has been prominent in most of the operas of the later Russian composers. Tchaikovsky's *Eugene Onegin* (1879) uses it merely as a background to the main drama, which is based on a novel in verse by Pushkin. *Eugene Onegin* belongs to the same category as *La Traviata*; it is intimate opera and requires a theatre small enough to secure this character in its interpretation. It has the lyric charm of Tchaikovsky's songs rather than the vehemence of his orchestral works, and its sensitive handling of intense feeling, always restrained within the limits of a high-bred delicacy, makes it one of the most touching operas ever put on the stage. Of Tchaikovsky's eleven operas, the only other one frequently performed outside Russia is *The Queen of Spades*, which also has its source in Pushkin.

Nationalism elevated to an almost epic grandeur is to be seen in Mussorgsky's *Boris Godunov* (1874) and *Khovanstchina* (left unfinished at the composer's death in 1881, completed by Rimsky-Korsakov and first performed in 1886). Both of these works have a religious background difficult for the Western listener to enter into, but they have a singular impressiveness that lifts them into a plane far above the usual type of opera, even of heroic opera.

Rimsky-Korsakov, whose editing of Mussorgsky's operas has been the subject of much controversy, into which it is not possible to enter here, is a link between the music of the 19th century and that of our own day. He was at his best in legend and fairy-tale, as *The Snow-Maiden* (1882) admirably shows. Others of the same type were *Tsar Saltan* (1900), *Kitesh* (1910) and *The Golden Cockerel* (1910). After the 'battle, murder and sudden death' of the majority of 19th-century operas, these provide a contrast that at first is enthrallingly attractive, especially as the composer had an unfailing vein of characteristic Russian melody and a masterly command of the orchestra; but after frequent hearing they become monotonous and cloying, for there is a certain sameness about their music and one soon foresees what is coming. *Kitesh* has a religious background that, as in *Khovanstchina*, is difficult for Western hearers to appreciate. *The Golden Cockerel* is satirical, and perhaps for that reason has made a peculiar appeal to English audiences.

§6 A NOTE ON SOME ENGLISH OPERAS

The popularity of Weber and Marschner in London from 1824 onwards encouraged English composers to develop a romantic opera of their own. *The Mountain Sylph*, by J. F. Barnett, a cousin of Meyerbeer, had a notable success in 1834 and was followed by a long series of similar works that enjoyed considerable popularity in the reign of Queen Victoria. Three of them survived well into the present century: *The Bohemian Girl* by Balfe (1843), *Maritana* by Wallace (1845) and *The Lily of Killarney* by Julius Benedict, a pupil of Weber (1862), especially in provincial theatres. The foundation of the Carl Rosa company in 1873 led to the production of more native operas, though most of them are now forgotten, and to the introduction of many foreign operas sung in English; the fashionable opera seasons at Her Majesty's and Covent Garden were exclusively Italian. Heroic efforts in the cause of national opera were made by Stanford (*Shamus O'Brien*, 1896, *Much Ado About Nothing*, 1901, and *The Travelling Companion*, first performed in 1925, a year after the composer's death); all these works might well achieve popularity if they were given often enough to become familiar. Other outstanding English operas were Rutland Boughton's *The Immortal Hour* (1914) and Ethel Smyth's amusing comedy *The Bo'sun's Mate* (1916).

Towards the end of the 19th century there was a great revival of interest in folk-song, stimulated by the example of Brahms and Dvořák; it was manifested in other continental countries, and in the British Isles it attained an almost religious fervour throughout a whole generation or longer. The three last-named operas were strongly influenced by it, and it inspired almost the whole output of Ralph Vaughan Williams, whose *Hugh the Drover* (1924) was designed as a popular national English opera analogous to *The Bartered Bride* of Smetana.§

PART 5 MODERN OPERA

1 FRANCE

We are now firmly in the 20th century. 20th-century opera, however, is not necessarily modern opera. Among the 20th-century works we have already mentioned are several by the last two great masters of 19th-century opera, Puccini and Richard Strauss. The former produced his last opera, *Turandot* in the '20s of this century, and the latter his, *Capriccio*, in the '40s. Both these are, therefore, indisputably 20th-century operas: neither, however, could fairly be described as a 'modern' opera.

What is still thought of as 'modern music' begins with Debussy. His *Pelléas et Mélisande* (1902), written in reaction against Wagner, now seems to us to owe a great deal to *Tristan und Isolde*. It differs in that Debussy has returned to an ideal to which Wagner paid but lip-service: that, in music drama, the music should be the servant of the text. The music of *Pelléas et Mélisande* sensitively accompanies the text of Maeterlinck's play, without which it would sound exquisite but meandering. To some ears, even with the text to give it substance, it still sounds poetic but enervating, and it cannot be said to have spawned important offspring. The other major French composers reacted to or against the all-pervading influence of Wagner in their various individual ways. Paul Dukas's one opera, *Ariane et Barbe-Bleue* (1907) could be said to combine Wagnerian and Debussian influences, and it too is a setting of Maeterlinck, livelier and more dramatic than Debussy's. Albert Roussel wrote several works for the stage, though none can be described as pure opera. His opera-ballet *Pâdmâvatî* (1923) is far superior to the average exercise in Oriental orchestral colouring.

The genius of Maurice Ravel would have been ideally suited to opera, and it is a pity that he left only two one-act pieces. *L'Heure Espagnole* (The Spanish Hour), a cynically witty reaction against musical and theatrical romanticism, is a brilliant *tour de force*. The composer's mastery of orchestration and rhythm combines with his unfailing sense of timing and pace in a comedy that is sheer delight. His *L'Enfant et les sortilèges* (The Bewitched Child) (1925), to a libretto by the novelist Colette, is equally attractive, warm and tender-hearted, in contrast to the earlier work's icy glitter. Making use of pastiche, jazz, a general eclecticism, this charming fantasy of a naughty child and the toys which come alive to torment him is difficult to stage convincingly. It would make a splendid cartoon film.

Three of the six composers who comprised the group known as *Les Six* made notable contributions to French opera: Darius Milhaud, Francis Poulenc and the Swiss, Arthur Honegger. Milhaud's prodigious talent took in influences from a variety of sources, and this fact is reflected in the somewhat bewildering diversity of form of his operas, ranging from *Les Malheurs d'Orfée* (The Misfortunes of Orpheus) (1926), through *Le Pauvre Matelot* (The Poor Sailor) to a libretto by Cocteau (1927) and the *Trois Opéras-Minutes* (1927) which are indeed minute, as they last about ten minutes each, to Milhaud's most important opera, *Christophe Colomb* (1928) with its libretto by Paul Claudel. *Christophe Colomb*, in twenty-seven scenes, contains elements of Greek drama, mystery play, expressionism and such modern techniques as the use of film. Milhaud continued to write operas, but his later works are distinctly weaker than those of the '20s.

The talent of Francis Poulenc displayed two distinct facets, both of them quintessentially Gallic: wit and religiosity. The former is displayed in the engaging and popular *Les Mamelles de Tirésias* (The Breasts of Tiresias) (1947), in Apollinaire's text as much as in Poulenc's music, and the latter found its finest flowering in the composer's conservative and sentimental *Dialogues des Carmélites*, about a group of Carmelite nuns martyred during the French Revolution. Though hardly persuasive in dramatic terms, the opera possesses a lyrical charm which has ensured it a number of performances beyond France. Poulenc's most successful opera, however, is probably the one-act *La voix humaine* (The human voice) (1959), based on Cocteau's monologue. Scored for solo soprano and orchestra, *La voix humaine* is as effective in concert performance as on the stage, given a singing-actress of some calibre.

Like his colleagues, Arthur Honegger tended to create works for the stage which do not lend themselves to easy classification. The earliest of his stage works, *Le Roi David* (King David), described by its composer as a dramatic psalm, is as much oratorio as opera; closer to the operatic tradition is his other biblical drama, *Judith*, produced at Monte Carlo in 1926. The two which have made the greatest impression and seem most likely to retain a place in the international repertoire are *Jeanne d'Arc au bûcher* (Joan of Arc at the Stake) (1938), its text by Claudel and its leading role written not for a singer but an actress, and the three-act opera *Antigone*, staged in Brussels in 1927. *Antigone*, its libretto by Cocteau, is a work of individuality and power, highly expressive, its music sharply dissonant, sparse in texture and to the point.

2 ITALY

Having led the world in opera in the 19th century, Italy has in the 20th relinquished her position of supremacy. A number of elderly *verismo* composers continued to produce operas in the style of the turn of the century almost until the Second World War – one thinks not only of Mascagni, already mentioned, but also of Leoncavallo, Giordano, Zandonai, Alfano and others – but the younger composers, unwilling to continue writing in the played-out language of *verismo*, yet unable wholeheartedly to accept the lead given by the second Viennese school of Schoenberg and Berg, tended to lapse into a bewildered and bewildering eclecticism. There have, of course, been honourable exceptions to this state of affairs, but they have been few and, as far as one can judge immediately, not especially successful.

Doyen of Italian modern composers, Ildebrando Pizzetti produced a number of operas during the course of a long life. One of the earliest of them, *Fedra*, to a libretto by D'Annunzio, produced at La Scala in 1915, was at the time highly regarded but appears not to have survived. For the majority of his later operas, Pizzetti wrote his own librettos. Musically, these works are carefully constructed and impeccably scored, but they exhibit no signs of a strong creative individuality. *Fra Gherardo* (1928) is generally thought to be the best of them, while *L'Assassinio nella cattedrale* (1958), based on an Italian translation of T. S. Eliot's play *Murder in the Cathedral* about the martyrdom of Thomas à Becket, has at any rate been performed frequently outside Italy since its première in 1958. Pizzetti was in his late seventies when he wrote it, and his score possesses something of the calmness and inaction of old age, if not its serene warmth.

Virtually a contemporary of Pizzetti, Gian Francesco Malipiero wrote several operas in a variety of styles. The most unusual, certainly the most complex, is *L'Orfeide*, a huge trilogy which was first staged in German translation in Düsseldorf in 1925. Melodically more inventive and gifted with a wider-ranging creative imagination than Pizzetti, Malipiero has, in a sense, been the victim of his own restless fertility: a gifted musician, hindered by his own awareness of the break in tradition. Another gifted Italian composer, Alfredo

Casella elected to place his gifts at the service of Mussolini's fascist régime. His neo-classical *La donna serpente* (The serpent woman) (1932) was followed by a glorification of the Italian invasion of Abyssinia, *Il deserto tentato* (The attempt on the desert) (1937), a one-act piece which was highly praised when first performed at the Florence Maggio Musicale, but which, understandably, has since sunk without trace.

More likely to survive are the operas of Italy's leading dodecaphonist composer, Luigi Dallapiccola, who has in some measure succeeded in effecting a marriage between the requirements of his compositional technique and the basically lyrical style still necessary in writing for the human voice. *Volo di notte* (1940), a one-act opera based on the novel *Night Flight* by Saint-Exupéry, is one of the most strikingly individual works for the stage composed in Italy this century, and *Il prigioniero* (The Prisoner) (1950), also in one act, is really contemporary both in musical technique and subject matter. A moving comment on the ingenuities of man's inhumanity to man.

Italian state-subsidized opera-houses are required to perform a certain quota of new works, so there is no danger that the supply of Italian operas will dry up. Unfortunately, there appears also to be no danger at present that any new composer of genius is about to burst upon those stages.

3 GERMANY AND AUSTRIA

It is in Germany and Austria that more interesting developments and exciting achievements have occurred during the present century. The operas of Ferruccio Busoni, for instance, are among the most remarkable of modern times. Busoni was half Italian, but his childhood was spent chiefly at Trieste, then part of Austro-Hungary, and in various other places in Austria. He studied composition in Graz, and his four operas were composed to German texts adapted by the composer himself from other sources. *Die Brautwahl* (1912), on a libretto taken from E. T. A. Hoffmann, was not very successful, but *Arlecchino* (1917), a brilliant satire on various aspects of human nature, especially on militarism, continues to be produced. *Turandot*, first performed as a companion-piece to *Arlecchino*, has been eclipsed by Puccini's opera of the same title. Busoni's last and greatest work, left unfinished at his death and completed by Philipp Jarnach, is *Doktor Faust* (1925), on a deeply poetical libretto by Busoni himself (in German). It treats the Faust legend in a way that is entirely different from the *Faust* of Goethe. Busoni in his later years was a violent anti-Wagnerian, and his own style was developed mainly from Verdi's *Falstaff*; his extreme intellectualism was the product of his German training at an earlier period of his life, but his attitude to opera and to the human voice remained consistently Italian. *Doktor Faust* may never become a repertory opera, but its grave dignity and tragic intensity make it a work for occasional performance.

Hans Pfitzner is another composer who stands somewhat aloof from his public. By date he belongs to the generation of Richard Strauss, and in some ways to an earlier one, for his musical style, consciously and intensely German, traces its origins to the late wōrks of Schumann and to *Parsifal*. He also owes a good deal to the example of Humperdinck's *Königskinder*. His early operas, unknown outside Germany, deal with romantic subjects with a painful insistence on emotions of moral anguish; his Wagnerian ancestor is Amfortas. For nationalist reasons he came at one time into considerable prominence in Germany, although his intense Germanism is purely poetical and in no sense political. His *Palestrina* (1917) is a very free treatment of the legend that grew up around the famous 16th-century composer of Roman church music, but Pfitzner's hero is really a portrait of himself. It is a long and on the whole tedious opera, but commands sincere respect for its lofty idealism and also for moments of striking beauty. Pfitzner's last opera, *Das Herz* (1931), owes a great deal to Busoni's *Doktor Faust*, although Pfitzner attacked Busoni very acrimoniously in his critical writings during Busoni's lifetime. *Das Herz* has a symbolical and rather incomprehensible story; painful emotions are again prominent, but it must be admitted that Pfitzner never leaves a certain high plane of spiritual fervour.

Paul Hindemith, romantic, neo-classicist and exponent of a concept of *Gebrauchsmusik*, or music for everyday use, wrote therefore in a variety of styles. His first full-length opera, *Cardillac* (1926), goes back to Handel for its formality of structure, but is musically dry and dramatically static. The composer revised it many years later, but when the revised version was staged in 1952, it was thought to be no improvement upon the original. Considerably more successful, certainly more entertaining, is *Neues vom Tage* (News of the Day), the day being 1929 and the news including a scene in which the heroine, lying in her bath, sings the praises of electric heating. A gas company in Breslau applied for and obtained an injunction against a local performance, claiming that this song was damaging to its trade. *Gebrauchsoper* is no empty concept!

The one-act *Hin und Züruck* (There and back), produced in 1927, was a clever and amusing sketch. Hindemith's more serious though not necessarily more worthy operas are *Mathis der Maler* (Mathis the Painter) (1938) and *Die Harmonie der Welt* (The Harmony of the World) (1957), both flawed by their lack of melody and dramatic action. Hindemith's smaller, workaday pieces are his real contribution to modern opera. The same could be said of Kurt Weill, a pupil of Busoni who achieved immense popularity with *Die Dreigroschen-Oper* (The Threepenny Opera) (1921), based on an adaptation and modernization by the German poet and playwright Bertolt Brecht, of Gay's original book of *The Beggar's Opera*, the scene being laid in a very imaginary modern London. The music employed a jazz-band as orchestra, and for the vocal numbers the English term *song* was adopted as an up-to-date substitute for *lied* or *aria*. The opera is extremely amusing and original, while at the same time the venomous bitterness of its satire is the sincere expression of a deeply felt sympathy for the sufferings of the starving and destitute. The same sense of horror too grim for pity was apparent in Weill's *Die Bürg-schaft* (The Surety) (1931), a serious allegory of modern social and economic conditions, which in its stage technique derived much from Milhaud's *Christophe Colomb*; an oratorio chorus seated above the orchestra by the proscenium commented on the moral signific-ance of the action. *Die Bürgschaft* contains much genuinely fine music, and the teaching of Busoni bore evident fruit, both in tech-nical detail and in moral idealism.

The quintessential Weill is to be found in his *Aufstieg und Fall der Stadt Mahagonny* (Rise and Fall of the City of Mahagonny), in which, in collaboration with Brecht, he united operatic form with catchy, popular melody in order to depict and comment upon modern capitalist society. After the rise of the Nazis, Weill emigrated to the United States of America, where, a refugee from decadent Europe, he revitalized the popular musical theatre of the New World, the Broadway musical, with such 'serious' musicals as *Street Scene* and *Lost in the Stars*.

In Nazi Germany, Carl Orff composed a number of popular works for the stage such as *Carmina Burana* and *Catulli Carmina*, though whether these pieces, simple and repetitive in rhythm, indeed almost brutal, can properly be described as operas is doubtful. Musically inventive though lacking in drama are the operas of Werner Egk, which include *Columbus* (1942) and *Irisch Legende* (1955). Egk's comic opera, *Der Revisor* (1957), based on Gogol's *The*

Inspector General is more successful. The distinguished composer Boris Blacher experimented in opera, though his main interests lay in purely instrumental music. His sparse, dissonant, quite distinctive style is displayed to most advantage in *Preussisches Märchen* (Prussian Fairy-tale), and *Abstract Opera No. 1*, both produced in the early '50s. Rolf Liebermann, though recently too busy as an opera administrator to devote much time to composition, has written at least three works for the stage which are charming, inventive and thoroughly professional: *Leonore 40/45*, which tells of a German soldier's love for a French girl in war-time Paris; *Penelope*, first performed at the Salzburg Festival in 1954; and *Die Schule der Frauen*, based on Molière's *L'Ecole des Femmes*.

The leading German opera composer today is undoubtedly Hans Werner Henze, whose first opera, *Boulevard Solitude* (1952), is a modern re-working of the story of Manon Lescaut. His later operas include *König Hirsch* (King Stag), staged in Berlin in 1956, *Der Prinz von Homburg* (1960), and two works written to English libretti by W. H. Auden and Chester Kallman. These are *Elegy for Young Lovers* of which the composer himself has said that his aim in it was to 'penetrate fully into the world and imagination of Auden', and *The Bassarids*.

Several of the German composers mentioned above were influenced by the Viennese New School, and in particular by the theories of Schoenberg, and the music of Schoenberg and Alban Berg. One of the masterpieces of 20th-century opera is Berg's *Wozzeck* (1922), based on a play by Georg Büchner, a dramatist of a century ago. Arnold Schoenberg, of whom Berg was a pupil, had already made some very curious experiments in opera, notably in *Erwartung* (composed 1909, first performed 1924), a one-act opera with only one character, a woman who walks through a wood to meet her lover and at the end finds his corpse. The technical system of Schoenberg's music and that of his disciples is mentioned elsewhere in this volume. Berg's music to *Wozzeck* is in theory based on various conventional forms – fugue, variations, passacaglia, etc. – but in the theatre one is not conscious of this. The play, a peculiarly grim and sordid story of humble life, is acted in recitative that rarely gives way to lyrical song, and the orchestra underlines every emotion with a poignancy that is almost unbearable. Much of the music of *Wozzeck*, considered by itself, is to most concert-goers completely incomprehensible; in the theatre its emotional force is so intense that few people can hear it for the first time without being profoundly overcome by it. Before 1933, *Wozzeck* had been performed at a large number of German theatres, including many quite small ones; after the National Socialist revolution of that year it was under a cloud, but it had already won appreciation outside Germany and its return to the stage was a mere matter of time and took place soon after the war. Berg's second opera, *Lulu*, though not quite finished, is an almost equally effective work in the theatre, though it lacks the compactness and humanity of *Wozzeck*. Schoenberg's *Moses und Aron*, though only two of its projected three acts were completed, is a work of arresting power and originality, austere and less immediately accessible than his pupil Berg's operas, but undeniably gripping in its impact. It was first performed in 1954 and has gradually made its way into the international repertoire.

The operas of the Austrian Franz Schreker deserve a passing mention here, even if they seem at present to have been consigned to utter oblivion, for they were a strange example of unbridled eroticism and sensationalism, although Schreker, to do him justice, was inwardly far more of an idealist than a commercial composer. He voraciously absorbed every modern technique of his day, but he was not gifted with genuine musical invention, and it was the fundamental musical weakness of his work, even more than the schoolboy crudity of the librettos, which he wrote for himself, that prevented his operas from maintaining their momentary popularity. His first opera, *Der ferne Klang* (The distant sound) (1912) attracted great attention; his second, *Die Gezeichneten* (The Stigmata) called for an orchestra of more than 100 players. A later work, *Der Schatzgräber* (The Treasure Seeker, 1920) is musically perhaps the most interesting of them.

The Viennese Ernst Křenek has written a number of operas of distinction, among them the once notorious jazz opera, *Jonny spielt auf* (Johnny strikes up), first performed in 1927. Its jazz elements are used to characterize the negro violinist, Jonny, and the opera ends in an expressionist vision of Europe being conquered by the jazz rhythms of the New World. Among the most frequently staged of Křenek's later operas are *Karl V* (1933), written in the twelve-tone method, and *Pallas Athene weint* (Pallas Athene weeps), staged in 1956, still predominantly atonal, and a highly dramatic and exciting piece.

The son of a famous Viennese music critic, Erich Korngold had immense success in his home town with a number of operas written in the language of Richard Strauss. One of them, *Die tote Stadt*, is still occasionally performed in Vienna, though rarely elsewhere. It was given its American première by the New York City Opera in 1974. Korngold made his way to America in the '30s, where he became a popular composer of music for films.

After Křenek, the most important Austrian composer of opera today is Gottfried von Einem, several of whose works, conservative in idiom, yet none the less enjoyable for that, are in the repertoire of the Vienna Opera, and are not infrequently staged abroad. They include *Dantons Tod* (Danton's Death) (1947), *Der Prozess* (based on Kafka's *The Trial*) (1953) and *Der Besuch der alten Dame* (The Old Lady's Visit, based on Dürrenmatt's play) (1966).

4 RUSSIA

One of the giants of 20th-century music, Igor Stravinsky ranged well beyond the confines of Russian music. Yet, though most of his music was written outside Russia, he is, despite his cosmopolitanism, deeply Russian. Originally a pupil of Rimsky-Korsakov, he began by composing in the style of that master, but by the time of his first opera, *The Nightingale*, he had already begun to develop the first of his own many styles. The first act of *The Nightingale* is still reminiscent of Rimsky-Korsakov, but the later two acts are pure Stravinsky, albeit a Stravinsky of richer harmonies than are to be found in his middle and late periods.

Stravinsky experimented as much with forms and genres as with musical styles. Although his second opera, *Mavra*, is a conventional enough piece, in which the beginnings of his flirtation with neo-classicism can be traced, it shared the bill at its Paris première with the hybrid *Renard*, described as 'a burlesque story about the fox, the cock, the cat and the goat, to be sung and played on the stage'. The roles are mimed by actors or dancers, the voices being provided by singers placed among the orchestra. Stravinsky's other part-operas are *Les Noces* (The Wedding), first performed as a ballet with songs and choruses, and *Oedipus Rex*, an opera-oratorio whose libretto is by Jean Cocteau. *Oedipus Rex* can be performed as oratorio or as opera. As an opera, though static, it is undeniably dramatic, even moving.

Stravinsky's operatic masterpiece is the formally conventional, neo-classical *Rake's Progress* (1951) composed to an English text provided by W. H. Auden and Chester Kallman. Making no concessions to modernity, this old-fashioned opera of arias and recitatives, choruses and ensembles, is almost Mozartian in manner and in stature, though not in musical style, for its dryness and wit are those of Handel rather than Mozart. The final scene in Bedlam is beautiful, affecting and one of the finest achievements of 20th-century opera.

Serge Prokofiev, less experimental by nature than Stravinsky, was blessed with a rare lyric gift. He wrote his first opera, *The Giant*, at the age of nine, and throughout his life continued to produce works for the stage, both operas and ballets. His achievement is uneven, but at its best is remarkable. *The Gambler* (1916), based on Dostoevsky's novella, is effective on the stage, though musically disappointing. His most famous opera, *The Love of Three Oranges* (1919) is a delightful, highly colourful fairy tale, rhythmically exuberant, melodically generous and wittily satirical. Completely different is *The Fiery Angel*, a study in religious obsession and hysteria set in the 16th century. This drama of extraordinary power had to wait thirty years for its first production in Venice in 1955, but it has since then rapidly established itself in the international repertoire.

Prokofiev's Soviet operas are fascinating, ranging from the small-scale comedy *Betrothal in a Nunnery* to the patriotic resistance-drama, *Simeon Kotko* (rarely seen outside Russia, but extremely effective on the stage, as demonstrated to the present writer by a Bolshoi Moscow production), and the vast *War and Peace*, an operatic *Gone with the Wind* rather than a musical equivalent of Tolstoy.

The Soviet Union's most distinguished recent composer, Dmitri Shostakovich, composed two operas. *The Nose*, written in the '20s, is an expressionistic comedy based on Gogol's story about the nose which takes on a life of its own. *Katerina Ismailova*, a grimly realistic tale based on a novel written in the manner of Dostoevsky, began life as *The Lady Macbeth of Mtsensk* in 1934, but fell foul of Soviet censorship. Rehabilitated under its new title in recent years, it proved to be an uneven work, scenes of dramatic strength alternating with sentimental banalities. There is little opportunity in the West to assess the operas of other modern Soviet composers, as they are hardly ever staged outside Russia. Shaporin's *The Decembrists* is a melodious and well-constructed work dealing with the revolutionary uprising in 1825. The operas of Kabalevsky, including *Colas Breugnon*, are highly regarded in the Soviet Union, as is the Shakespeare opera, *The Taming of the Shrew* by Shebalin. This writer was present at its première in Moscow in 1957, and found it not unpleasant but decidedly unoriginal, and lacking individuality and form.

It can hardly be claimed that Switzerland has contributed its own national type of opera to the European repertoire, though a Swiss composer, Heinrich Sutermeister, has successfully specialized in the writing of operas. Not really contemporary either in language or temperament, Sutermeister has been influenced by both late Verdi, as regards style, and Carl Orff, from whom he has learned the virtue of simplicity. His most successful opera, and one which has been widely staged, is *Romeo and Julia* (1940). Its libretto, after Shakespeare, is by the composer. A second Shakespeare opera, *Die Zauberinsel*, based on *The Tempest* is musically of less substance than the earlier work.

Sweden, with its flourishing opera company, has given the world some fine singers. It has exported fewer operas, though Karl-Birger Blomdahl's so-called space-age opera *Aniara* (1959), whose action takes place in a spaceship, created much interest: more on account of its unusual libretto than its music with echoes of Bartók and Stravinsky. Another Swedish composer, perhaps the most notable one, is Lars Johan Werle, whose eclectic style renders his music easily accessible to international audiences. His opera, *Tintomara* (1973), starts at the point where Verdi's *Un ballo in maschera* ends: the assassination of Gustav III in 1792.

Hungarian opera is represented in the 20th century by no more than two works of international stature and interest. Kodály, who with Bartók was responsible for the reawakening of interest in the ethnic roots of Hungarian music, contributed an earthily enjoyable ballad opera to the repertoire in *Háry János* (1926), while Bartók, in his only opera *Duke Bluebeard's Castle* (1918), a one-act version of the Bluebeard legend, produced a work of sombre power, magnificent orchestration, and thrilling dramatic effect. It is, surely, only its awkward length that has militated against its greater success abroad. Hungary's neighbour, Czechoslovakia, has been more fortunate in that its leading composer of the late 19th-early 20th century, Leoš Janáček composed a large number of operas, all of which have over the years come to be recognized as adding up to an important oeuvre. His strongly individual style, admitting to influences from Russia and specifically Mussorgsky, is closely allied to the rhythms of Moravian speech. Thus, despite his warmth of feeling, much of his music for the stage sounds less effective when sung in translation. This, however, has not seriously hindered productions of most of the operas abroad, particularly in Germany and England. *Jenúfa* (1904), *Katya Kabanova* (1921), *The Cunning Little Vixen* (1924), *The Makropoulos Affair* (1926) and *From the House of the Dead* (posthumously produced in 1930) have all been produced by English and American opera companies in recent years. Other Czech composers of opera include Jaromir Weinberger, whose *Schwanda the Bagpipe Player* (1927) was a great popular success until the Nazi invasion when its composer's Jewishness put an end to further performance. It has failed to re-establish itself, though it has at least given a well-known polka and fugue to the international orchestral repertoire. Bohuslav Martinů composed ten operas, of which *Julietta* (1938) is the most highly regarded. The standard of the others, as of Martinů's music in general, is said to be variable.

The only Polish opera widely known outside Poland is *The Devils*, by Krzystof Penderecki. Based both on Aldous Huxley's *The Devils of Loudun* and on John Whiting's play which was derived from it, the opera was first produced in Hamburg in 1969 and has since been seen in many operatic centres throughout the world. The music is powerful, skilful, atmospheric, rather in the manner of superior mid-20th-century background music for film or theatre: the success of the work, therefore, can only be explained by our age's obsessive and guilt-ridden interest in sado-masochistic violence and torture. The libretto, by the composer himself, is laid out with masterly theatrical insight, and there is no denying the opera's dramatic effectiveness in a really strong production, such as that staged in England by the English National Opera. The operas of Szymanowski are not widely known. *King Roger*, however, produced in Warsaw in 1926, is an exciting and spectacular work of great emotional power.

Modern Spanish opera stems mainly from the *zarzuelas* or operettas of the 19th century. But, although most Spanish composers attempt to write operas, very few seem to make their way into the international repertoire. Albéniz, for instance, composed not only *zarzuelas* but a number of grand operas with libretti by the English banker Coutts (for which he was well paid by Coutts, later Baron Latimer). Most were still-born, and none has survived. *Goyescas*, an opera by Granados based on ideas suggested by the paintings of Goya, did at least achieve performance outside Spain – it had its première at the New York Metropolitan Opera in 1916 – but it has fallen into desuetude. More successful was Manuel de Falla, two of whose three operas, folkish in idiom but with the advantage of the composer's rich sense of orchestral colour, have helped to popularize the Spanish idiom abroad. *La Vida breve* (Life is short) (1913) whose folk basis is overlaid by sophisticated borrowings from early Stravinsky is really a ballet-opera, whose ballet element is perhaps even more important than its vocal passages. *El Retablo de Maese Pedro* (Master Peter's Puppet Show) (1923) is unusual in being written for both puppets and live singers, while de Falla's third opera, said to be based on themes from Chopin, has never been performed.

If Spanish opera has failed to establish itself as a distinct entity, opera in Spanish and Latin America has fared little better. The Mexican composer Carlos Chávez had a certain success with *Panfilo and Lauretta* which was first staged in New York in 1957, its libretto by the American poet Chester Kallman. There is, however, nothing particularly Mexican about its musical language. Argentina is represented by Alberto Ginastera whose lurid melodramas set to fragmented atonal music are noted for their theatrical effectiveness. The most recent, and reputedly the best, is *Beatrix Cenci* (1971). The Brazilian, Heitor Villa-Lobos is more widely known, and indeed much of his music for orchestra, piano or chamber ensembles is popular in many countries. But he is uneven: at his best tuneful and spontaneous, too often he reveals the reverse side of that particular coin by producing work that is merely trivial and meretricious. His operas reveal the same variability of standard. *Izaht*, composed in 1913 but not performed until 1940 and then only in concert form, was followed by three other operas, performances of which are extremely rare.

6 THE ENGLISH LANGUAGE

Vaughan Williams's *Hugh the Drover*, mentioned earlier, was virtually the last English opera of any stature to derive essentially from the folk-song movement, though the composer went on to write further works for the stage, including his Falstaff opera, *Sir John in Love* (1929), *Riders to the Sea* (1937) which is a one-act setting of the play by J. M. Synge, and the static *Pilgrim's Progress* (1951) which, though designed for the stage, seems more suitable for concert performance. Mention must be made here of Alan Bush whose simple, old-fashioned style derives from, or at least is adhered to because of, his Marxist political stance. It is hardly surprising that Bush's operas have been staged mainly in East Germany, or that they have been neglected in England, though one of them, *Wat Tyler* (1950) finally achieved London production in 1974. The operas of Delius have been similarly neglected, though there are signs that they may now be coming into favour. In recent years there have been productions of *Koanga*, composed in the mid-1890s, and *A Village Romeo and Juliet* (1901). Neither work can be said to advance the art-form of opera in any way, and their appeal is to the lover of Delius's palette of tone colours rather than to the opera enthusiast who is more likely to find them rambling and undramatic. Gustav Holst composed a number of operas, only three of which achieved production. *Sāvitri* (1908) and *The Perfect Fool* (1921) are melodically generous, but lack dramatic impetus.

The lack of a living operatic tradition in Great Britain militated against the viability of English opera until immediately after the 1939–45 war, though Arthur Benjamin, Australian by birth, wrote two one-act operas in London in the early '30s. It was, however, not until 1953, when his full-length opera *A Tale of Two Cities*, was broadcast (and four years later was produced by Sadler's Wells Opera), that it became clear his talent was basically operatic. By this time, the post-war English operatic revival had been got under way with the huge success of Benjamin Britten's *Peter Grimes* at Sadler's Wells Theatre in 1945. Since then, the story of English opera has become virtually the story of Benjamin Britten. Indeed, Britten is arguably the finest 20th-century composer of opera. His musical language, deriving from both the Viennese tradition, from Haydn to Mahler, and the 17th-century English world of Purcell, is personal, highly recognizable and immediately accessible. His genius for characterization and his unerring dramatic sense was displayed in a remarkable series of works; some written for large forces such as *Peter Grimes*, *Billy Budd* (1951) and *Gloriana* (1953); some for smaller ensembles, specifically for the English Opera Group which he helped to found, including *The Rape of Lucretia* (1946), *Albert Herring* (1947), *The Turn of the Screw* (1954), *A Midsummer Night's Dream* (1960) and *Death in Venice* (1973); some, called parables for church performance in one act, written for even smaller forces and first produced in Orford Church in Suffolk (*Curlew River*, 1964; *The Burning Fiery Furnace*, 1966; *The Prodigal Son*, 1968). *Owen Wingrave* was written for and first performed on television (1971), and was later successfully transferred to the stage. Britten's versatile and compassionate genius was responsible for the revitalization of the English operatic scene, and was an enormous encouragement to younger composers.

It was also, presumably, an encouragement to two slightly older composers, William Walton and Michael Tippett. Walton came late to opera with his *Troilus and Cressida* (1954) whose weak late-romantic lyricism made little impression; much more interesting was

Tippett's *A Midsummer Marriage* (1955), music of depth and resonance allied to a libretto (by the composer) of pretentious obscurity, its Jungian ideas ill-digested. In *King Priam* (1962), Tippett appeared to be marking time, but *The Knot Garden* (1970) was an intriguing piece of musical theatre, perhaps made to seem more substantial than it really was by Peter Hall's imaginative production.

In recent years, a number of younger composers have had operas produced by one or other of the leading British opera companies. One of the most prolific, and most popular, is Malcolm Williamson whose fluent technique and amiable musical personality have been apparent in several operas which are engaging if not especially memorable. Of these other composers who have had one or more operas produced, the most talented are Richard Rodney Bennett, Peter Maxwell Davies and Nicholas Maw. Nicholas Maw's *The Rising of the Moon*, commissioned by Glyndebourne Opera and staged at Glyndebourne in 1970, is the most enjoyable operatic comedy since Britten's *Albert Herring*.

Operatic composition in the commonwealth countries has not yet produced works of more than local interest, though the names of Peter Sculthorpe and Larry Sitsky in Australia and Harry Somers in Canada may be worth noting.

In the United States of America, a lively operatic tradition goes back to the mid-19th century. No early American operas have survived in the international or even national repertoire; in the 1920s and '30s the Metropolitan Opera attempted to encourage native composers by commissioning and staging a number of works, but none of these have been revived in post-war years. The American composer and music critic Deems Taylor had his first opera, *The King's Henchman*, staged at the Met. in 1927, and his second, *Peter Ibbetson*, in 1931. Both were enthusiastically, even hysterically received at the time, but Taylor's fluent eclecticism lacked the breath of creative, created life, and neither these nor a third opera has been revived or produced elsewhere. A more interesting and original dramatic talent was discerned by critics in the Russian-born Louis Gruenberg, whose opera *The Emperor Jones*, based on Eugene O'Neill's play, was produced at the Met. in 1933. Distinctly less good was the Metropolitan's 1934 choice, *Merry Mount* by Howard Hanson. It became clear that the instant success of all four of these operas had been due in large part to the remarkable talent of the American baritone Lawrence Tibbett in their leading roles. Tibbett starred in these and other American operas of the '30s, to immense effect, but was unable to keep any of them alive beyond their opening seasons. A more durable career in operatic composition was launched in 1937, when the twenty-five-year-old Gian-Carlo Menotti had his one-act *Amelia al ballo* (Amelia at the Ball) produced in Philadelphia. Menotti, Italian by birth, went on to compose a series of light operas, some comic, some dramatic, Puccinian in idiom if not in power and melodic generosity. *The Telephone* (1947), *The Old Maid and the Thief* (1939) and especially *The Medium* (1946) and *The Consul* (1950) are all successful pieces of musical and theatrical journalism, while *The Saint of Bleecker Street* (1954) could well be described as a throw-back to turn of the century *verismo*. Menotti's more recent work has been less successful even on his own terms, which are finally theatrical rather than operatic.

Samuel Barber's two operas have both achieved a *succès d'estime* at the Metropolitan. *Vanessa* (1958) was staged at the old house, and *Antony and Cleopatra* (1966) opened the new opera-house in Lincoln Centre. In neither work, however, does Barber reveal any creative individuality, though he writes music which falls agreeably, undramatically, on the ear. Two distinguished American composers who have ventured into the field of opera with some success are Virgil Thomson and Aaron Copland. Thomson's amusing surrealist *Four Saints in Three Acts*, 'an opera to be sung' to a Gertrude Stein libretto (1934), unpretentious, unashamedly trivial, and undeniably entertaining, has had several revivals, while his second opera, *The Mother of Us All* (1947) again succeeds precisely because it aims unerringly at its audience, in other words not too high. Aaron Copland's *The Tender Land* (1954) is more conventional, but contains some of its composer's finest music. American opera, however, has yet to find itself a central figure around whom it can focus itself, and against whom it can react, as England has found Benjamin Britten. The most vital American opera is still Gershwin's *Porgy and Bess* (1935), composed for a Negro cast. It has plenty of flaws, but it has also numbers which, eminently singable, have virtually passed into the realm of American folk-music. At one time it seemed as if Leonard Bernstein, with his extraordinarily eclectic talents as composer and man of the theatre, might be the figure America was seeking; but his *Trouble in Tahiti* (1952) has not been followed up, and he is likely to be remembered as the composer of such first-rate Broadway musicals as *On the Town* (1944) and *West Side Story* (1957). Perhaps the Broadway musical, with its ability to attract talents of the calibre of Bernstein, Weill, Richard Rodgers and Frederick Loewe, is the American equivalent of European opera.

PART 6 A RETROSPECT AND A PROSPECT

§ In these pages we have not been able to offer more than the merest outline of operatic history, and many works of interest have of necessity been omitted altogether. Our aim has been not to compile a work of reference, but rather to suggest to ordinary opera-goers points of interest in the operas they are reasonably likely to have some chance of seeing on the stage, and to show how in the course of centuries opera has developed into an art-form with conventions of its own that are constantly changing as time goes on, in accordance with the changes that have affected all music.

We have drawn attention systematically to the social history of opera, because the social background has always had a very noticeable influence on operatic development. The social aspect of opera is now of urgent importance, for political and economic changes during the last forty years or more have practically destroyed the social class that for some three centuries was the chief mainstay of the musical drama. Opera, if it is to live, has now got to rely on state patronage to a great extent. The history of music, however, shows us that most of the music now acknowledged to have been of epoch-making importance was in fact originally composed for a small and exclusive circle of initiates – it matters not whether at various times they were princes and dukes, cardinals and bishops, or poets and intellectuals. The great masterpieces of music do not reach a popular audience until they have attained a respectable age. But however profoundly we may venerate the great masterpieces we cannot, if we are artistically alive, rest content with the art of the past alone. The artist must still create and it is our duty to find him an audience.

Under modern conditions of life the appreciation of serious opera (to consider only this branch of music) has spread to wide circles; but generally speaking, the majority of music-lovers call for the operas of fifty or 100 years ago, rather than those of today. It so happens that most of the operas of that period were written for social conditions very different from our own and demand for their adequate performance a financial outlay that the present generation appears unable to face. They could be made economically practicable by performances in vast auditoriums, as is demonstrated by performances in the Roman amphitheatre at Verona, which holds some 30,000 spectators; but even for Italy the amphitheatre of Verona is an exceptional building, and, questions of aesthetics aside, open-air opera would not work in the English climate.

431

The intolerable expense of opera production is due not so much to scenic requirements, as many people might imagine, but to the cost of large orchestras and the necessary rehearsals; we cannot lower this cost without sacrificing artistic efficiency and the players' right to an honourable wage. The reader of these pages will already have learned who were to blame for the fact that modern audiences, especially the more sophisticated ones, have come to regard a large orchestra as an indispensable requirement of opera. Modern composers may have reacted against Wagner's theories and against his musical technique, but, until comparatively recently, they have been even more extravagant in their orchestral demands.

World War II reduced most European countries to the verge of ruin; the increased cost of living changed the structure of society and it might have been expected that opera would eventually come to an end altogether, all the more so since many theatres had been laid in physical ruins. Yet Germany, which had suffered the worst damage, set to work to rebuild her opera-houses and to carry on opera in whatever buildings were available, often before many of the other amenities of life were put into order again, and after less than ten years had passed opera throughout Europe was as flourishing as it had been before. The revolutions that had followed World War I had put an end to princely patronage, but governments were almost everywhere ready to provide the subsidies, without which opera cannot be carried on, subsidies, too, that were surprisingly generous in view of the general impoverishment. New audiences were created, and on a general view they seem to have become much more ready to appreciate new movements in the art of music itself. How far this new approach to modern music has been stimulated by new developments in broadcasting and cinematography it is difficult to estimate, and it would be out of place to attempt a discussion of it here.

In England the position of opera has always lagged a long way behind that in continental countries, and neither the Crown nor the government has ever shown the slightest practical interest in opera. Even among musicians there was a general tendency to regard opera as an inferior form of musical art; it was a common thing to hear it said – and generally with a self-satisfied puritanical smugness – 'We are not an operatic country; our national art is oratorio.' At the present moment, however, opera seems nationally very much alive, and oratorio, unless put on the stage, slowly dying out. The operatic revival in England owes much to the enthusiasm and perseverance of a number of private individuals, and most of all to the foresight of the late Lord Keynes, who initiated and created what is now known as the Arts Council of Great Britain, which has made it possible for innumerable artistic institutions to carry on their work, although the government subsidies it controls and distributes are lamentably exiguous compared with those of some other countries.

Since 1945 much has been done to build up new audiences for a national opera in which we can take pride, giving honourable performances of the standard repertory in English with singers of our own, besides encouraging the production of new operas by our own composers.§

The development of Britain's two leading opera companies into the Royal Opera at Covent Garden, and the English National Opera at the Coliseum, as well as the small-scale tours of the Arts Council's 'Opera for All' groups and the establishment of strong regional companies based in Scotland and Wales but doing much of their touring (in the case of the Welsh company, most of it) in England, has done much to revitalize operatic life in this country. Many problems remained to be solved, and there are some which will never be permanently solved: for instance, the difficulty of finding intelligent administrators and imaginative and knowledgeable artistic directors. Nevertheless, the encouragement given to British composers in recent years by the emergence of so many showcases for their work has been enormous. There has been a parallel broadening of the historical repertory thanks to the many music festivals, especially London's Camden (formerly St Pancras) Festival, where many rare 18th- and 19th-century operas have been revived. The engaging anachronism of Glyndebourne continues, performing for a few weeks in the summer to audiences largely, though not entirely, comprising the musically ignorant: even here the repertoire has been intelligently widened, and Glyndebourne productions now tour with the aid of Arts Council funds. Opera has also been an important feature of the Edinburgh and Aldeburgh Festivals, and the *raison d'être* of the Wexford Festival.

These developments will continue, not only with regard to large-scale opera, but also on a smaller, more flexible scale. The lead given by Britten in his church parables has been taken up by such younger composers as Maxwell Davies and Birtwistle, and new audiences are coming to opera through the works written for various 'music theatre' ensembles, works which can be staged or semi-staged under conditions which would not be suitable for larger, more conventional works. Now that the principle of state subsidy has been accepted by

433

all political parties and shades of opinion, the future of opera in Great Britain is assured. Currently, it is in a transitional stage: the prospects are exciting.

In the United States, the operatic scene is no longer dominated by the Metropolitan Opera of New York, as for years it used to be. In New York itself, the Met. now faces the strong competition of the City Opera, with its livelier repertoire, and greater sense of ensemble in productions. Furthermore, throughout the country there is now much more operatic activity, much of it encouraged by the National Endowment for the Arts, a government agency empowered to offer subsidies. The flourishing opera companies of Chicago, Boston, Dallas, Santa Fe, San Francisco are among the many which are reaching wider and newer audiences. Here, as in Europe, it is the *stagione* system which is favoured, rather than the old repertory methods of the past. In other words, fewer operas are mounted in any given period, but each is given a run of performances and a reasonable amount of rehearsal-time. The social patterns of opera-going are changing, and the new audiences demand a higher standard of staging than their fathers and grandfathers did. This means that, perhaps for the first time, the art form of opera is being seen and heard to its best advantage. For it is, after all, the highest, most widely ranging form of theatre art, the nearest modern equivalent to the ancient Greek drama, amalgamating as it does music, drama, poetry and visual design into one total theatrical experience.

Book 5

The Human Voice

by Alan Blyth
incorporating material by
Francis Toye and Dyneley Hussey

All of European vocal music may be said to have developed from the Gregorian Chant. The kind of music indissolubly linked with the name of the great Pope Gregory was not an invention; it was rather a compilation, a standardization of current tunes that existed for centuries before Gregory. They were used in churches; St Ambrose of Milan had even made a hymn book of them. Nobody knows very much about their origin. To some extent they may have been a direct legacy from the music of Greece and Rome; they were almost certainly influenced by the old Jewish ritual music practised in the synagogues. What Gregory did was above all to remove excesses of ornamentation, so that the words were clear, to eliminate the tunes he thought unsuitable for ecclesiastical purposes and to codify the rest, as well as the various liturgies to which they were sung in different European centres. This happened about the year 600, and, thanks largely to the devotion and enthusiasm of the Benedictine order, his standardization gradually became accepted by all civilized Europe.§

The fundamental characteristics of the Gregorian Chant can still be heard on Sundays in Roman Catholic cathedrals and churches, though the embellishments were far more ornate and some think that the rhythm was far freer than what we usually hear today. During the 16th and 17th centuries under the guise of 'reform' new editions of Plainsong, as it is called, were issued which did violence to its very nature but made it easier to accompany on the organ.

§ Plainsong was written in what are known as modes. As explained in Book 1 (Part B, Chapter 12) the modes can be understood if the reader will imagine the scale of C major and then build scales on each of the notes without any accidentals. Thus, the mode which we suppose built on the note D would have semitonal intervals between the second and third, and the sixth and seventh notes; the mode supposedly built on F would have a semitonal interval between the fourth and fifth and between the seventh and eighth notes; and so on. These modes had Greek names: Dorian, Phrygian, Lydian, Mixolydian, presumably because they came to the Roman via the Byzantine Church, which in its turn inherited both them and their names from the Ancient Greeks. The old names, in fact, were quite wrongly used, but the principles underlying both the Greek and the mediaeval modes were the same, especially the very important principle that each mode had a definite aesthetic, even a moral, character of its own. Except to point out that this may have been the reason underlying, during many centuries, the Church's severe attitude towards tampering with the modes, and that from them eventually sprang our minor and major scales, nothing more need be said about modes, though this does not imply that they are not of the greatest importance. Apart from the fact that they are in current ecclesiastical use today, several composers have made great use of them in their music. Nobody can truly understand vocal music without knowing at least what they were.

By about the end of the 6th century the characteristics of Plainsong may be said to have been definitely fixed. To this music were sung not only the various parts of the Mass but various Latin hymns. They were usually sung unaccompanied, one group of monks answering another antiphonally, which is indeed the origin of the chanting of the verses of the psalms in Anglican churches, first by one half of the choir and then by the other. At the culmination of its development, when its characteristics had been standardized, the use of Plainsong was extended to other purposes than the Mass and hymns; whole mystery- and Passion-dramas were written in Plainsong style, such as the Plays of Daniel and Herod, which have been revived in recent times. Thus Plainsong remains a link between the past and the present civilization of Europe. To anyone initiated in the convention, it remains even today highly expressive, a form which, when practised by singers of talent and imagination, covers a considerable range and is capable of much variety.

Exactly how or why men developed the desire to sing in two parts instead of one, we do not know. Anybody who listens to a modern crowd singing knows that there are certain individuals who seem naturally inclined to sing below the tune, usually at the interval of a fifth. This, however, may be an inherited habit rather than a primitive instinct. In the first instance, as we have seen, Gregorian music consisted of only one vocal line, but by the 10th century, if not the 9th, we find the practice established of placing a note at the interval of a fourth or a fifth above or below each original note of the Plainsong. This particular technique was known as the art of organum or organizing. It was extremely simple. As the Plainsong moved in one direction or another the second part slavishly followed it, note by note, the mediaeval theorists regarding these intervals of a fourth or a fifth as the normal concord corresponding, let us say, to our major third. Gradually, however, musicians began to discover that it was at least as agreeable, if not more so, to have the two parts moving in contrary, instead of similar, motion. This extremely important dis-

438

covery once made, the way was open for further and comparatively rapid progress. Some time in the 12th century there appears what is known as descant, which consisted of a vocal line, in definitely measured rhythm, above the Plainsong. In the first instance this rhythm was always in triple time, apparently for the typically mediaeval reason that the personages of the Holy Trinity numbered three, and that, therefore, anything in threes was preferable to anything else. Duple time did not make its appearance till more than 100 years later.§

Musica enchiradis, a 10th-century treatise of disputed authorship, is the earliest work to deal with polyphony (called *symphonia*) and contains examples of parallel organum in which the melody is doubled at the fourth or fifth. This and later manuscripts found in France show that the drawn-out plainchant melody has a richly melismatic upper part. By the time of Guido d'Arezzo in the 11th century, a Benedictine monk who helped advance notation, contrary motion was permitted as the cadence was approached, another technical advance. These laid the foundation for the Notre Dame School. Gradually the voices became more important, and the third, so long considered a discord, came into use.

Léonin and Pérotin were the great masters of early polyphony. Léonin's *Liber Magnus* was the first important collection of polyphonic music. It used the principle of organum for very florid and ornate vocal music, very soloistic in character. Pérotin's style, with its three- and four-part organa, seems to have been grander, more 'gothic'. With the idea of a slow-moving tenor part, the beginnings of canon and motet can be perceived. During the 13th century, the worldliness and unpopularity of the Church led composers away from church music, and the more important developments of the next century were in the realm of secular music.

2 MINSTRELS AND TROUBADOURS

The origins of secular music are more obscure than those of church music because, while church music was written down and carefully preserved, secular music began by being an oral tradition. It seems to have developed at all levels of society. There were the court minstrels, probably the first professional musicians. Next came the goliards, the wandering scholars who preceded the development of universities. Thirdly there were the jongleurs (literally, jugglers) who combined music with acrobatics. However, it is not until we reach the troubadours, poet-musicians, that secular song can be said to have risen to an important position in the world.

The troubadour movement developed in Provence. We even know the name of the first of them, Guilhem VII, Count of Poitiers and Duke of Aquitaine, who lived between 1071 and 1127. They were partly the outcome of the social circumstances of the time, which allowed prosperous princes time to spend on the arts. Essentially, though, this was a literary movement, and far more poems survive than their musical settings. The basis of the poems and the music was *amour courtois* (courtly love); they were written in the Provençal tongue, which came to be considered the ideal language for the poetry of love, in which the poet usually idealized a woman of a higher class than himself. The ethic of *amour courtois* was essentially adulterous; in the days of arranged marriage, true love often existed only outside marriage. Intrigue and secrecy were other elements.

The daughter of Guilhem, or Guillaume, was Eleanor of Aquitaine who married Louis XII, and so moved north, spreading the movement to northern France where the troubadours were called trouvères. It was at her court that Bernart de Ventadour rose to prominence.

The songs fell mostly into two basic forms: the long narrative poems, such as *lai* and *chanson de geste* (*Tristan and Yseult* among them); and the repetitive type, the *forme fixe*, represented by the *rondeau*, *virelai* and *ballade*. These forms became the standard ones for the French composers of the following centuries.

Meanwhile the movement spread to Germany when Frederick Barbarossa married Beatrix of Burgundy. There, the troubadours were called Minnesinger, and they adapted French ideas to their own needs. Walther von der Vogelweide, who flourished in the 14th century, was the link between them and the Meistersinger, who eventually supplanted them. Incidentally, it is by no means certain that the Meistersinger who, as everybody familiar with Wagner's opera knows, were artisans, registered an improvement. It has been said that their style was definitely less refined, and their influence, which lasted until the 17th century, may have retarded the development of vocal music in Germany compared with that of other European countries.

However, as a whole, the troubadours' music, in its eventual evolution, is the basis of all modern European secular song. In that the modes were used, it remained definitely akin to the music of ecclesiastical hymns although, in the end, there is an undoubted feeling for our modern major scale in some of the songs.

The term *ars nova* derives from the writings of the French composer-poet Philippe de Vitry (1291–1361). His treatise outlined his technical innovations, involving improved notation such as accidentals and duple and triple subdivisions of rhythm. This was opposed by the Church, specifically in a decree promulgated by John XXII, one of the Avignon popes ('certain disciples of the new school, much occupying themselves with the measured dividing of time, display their methods in notes that are new to us, preferring to devise ways of their own rather than to continue singing in the old manner . . .'). Similar ideas were being developed in Italy; the polyphonic songs that were cultivated in Florence and its environs from the 1320s onwards were new enough in conception, as was their notation.

One of the manuscripts of the period, the *Roman de Fauvel*, is a compendium of the music popular in the early part of the century. The *roman* itself is a biting attack on the vices of the time, Fauvel being a horse personifying the sins represented by the letters of his name: Flattery, Avarice, Usury, Villainy, Envy and Lowness. The next important documents are the manuscripts of Guillaume de Machaut (c. 1300–77), the first great mediaeval composer, an all-rounder who wrote a Mass Ordinary and sacred motets but whose main work was secular. As David Munrow has commented: 'His poetic ingenuity at writing a pair of delicately balanced texts, his musical ability at setting one against the other, the agility and expressiveness of the vocal writing and his skilful use of diminution in the isorhythmic tenor parts towards the end of a piece all make Machaut's motets one of the high points of medieval art.' Vigour and tenderness are here marvellously served by technical expertise. His secular songs, ranging from austere to joyful, are solos with instrumental accompaniment, and he wrote but one piece of purely instrumental music, the Hocket. Machaut's successors at the Papal Court of Avignon continued to develop the intricacies of musical notation and dissonant harmonies.

The most notable exponents of the parallel development in Italy (typically rather more volatile and florid in technique) were Jacopo da Bologna, Giovanni da Firenze, and especially the blind organist and lutenist Francesco Landini (c. 1325–97). Imitation and canon were popular with these Italians, and are most notably represented by the *caccia* (literally chase), in which the poetic conceit was that of hunting, often as a fairly obvious symbol for the pursuit of love. These composers also wrote madrigals, two or three stanzas and a refrain (not to be confused with the 16th-century form). The home of these was Florence where Landini worked. In the church of San Lorenzo in Florence, his tomb shows him seated at his small organ, although none of his organ works survive. Like the madrigal, the ballata was basically a literary form; here the first section is repeated at the end. Landini is again the chief composer here, and his pieces in this form are notable for their freshness and vivacity. Niccolo da Perugia is another important figure in this field, writing mostly two-part works. Italian pieces of the time, as compared with French ones, are notable for their sensual rather than their intellectual qualities, a difference, it has been said, between the southern and northern 'New Art'.

4 ENGLAND AND FLANDERS

In discussing the beginnings of English music the six-part round, 'Sumer is icumen in', has always been given an almost undue prominence. It is a secular piece found in the records of Reading Abbey, in the hand of a monk called John of Forsete and thought to have been written about 1250. Its interest lies in the extraordinary six-part sonority unique for its time and place, and apparently conceived in isolation unless it is the sole surviving specimen of a school of which we know nothing. At any rate the rest of British mediaeval music is certainly more primitive in conception. The earliest form of polyphony in England was to be found in the gymel, a two-part composition in which the voices move primarily in thirds and sixths; it is secular and its origin may be from folk-song or from Celtic influence.

This polyphony developed considerably in the 14th century. Bury St Edmunds, in the east and so influenced by France, was one centre, Winchester and Worcester others. In some of the surviving music, quite advanced Ars Nova methods are to be observed. In the secular field there was the burden, a link with the French *virelai* and the Italian *ballata*. Then there was the carol, which developed out of the Latin non-liturgical but religious song, such as the 'Angelus ad virginem' mentioned in Chaucer. Although originally single-part, the carol with its mixed Latin and English text became polyphonic in texture, and the so-called Agincourt Song, celebrating Henry V's victory, is of this kind. These are mostly written in the English discant form of thirds and sixths.

About this time the Household Chapel, or Chapel Royal, of Henry IV and V came to the fore. This was not an institution but a group of musicians moving whither the court moved. A collection of 15th-century Chapel Royal music, mostly settings of the Ordinary of the Mass, is to be found in the so-called Old Hall Manuscript (named after the hall, near Ware, where it was long placed). Among the composers represented, the most important is probably Leonel Power, who brought to his setting of the Mass ('Alma redemptoris') the unifying device borrowed from Plainsong, of a single theme in the tenor section, the *cantus firmus*, or fixed song. Generally Power, and his greater contemporary John Dunstable, liberated their music from the shackles of rigid mediaeval practice through the freer use of Plainsong and the isorhythmic techniques of repetition.

Dunstable was strongly influenced by the Continent, where he was also held in greater esteem than in his homeland. Dunstable's enterprise can be discerned by comparing his work with that of his contemporaries at the Royal Chapel. They ventured no further than to make a rare and rudimentary use of canon. In such a work as his motet 'Veni, Sancte Spiritus', there is a big advance towards a more melodic and individual treatment of the individual parts. He also ornaments a given chant melody freely. His religious music was highly regarded in France and Flanders; in his secular pieces, the influence was the other way, as can be heard in 'Puisque m'amour' and 'O rosa bella'.

§ In addition to his contribution to the formation of a true polyphonic style, Dunstable must be credited with great learning and ingenuity. He is described in a contemporary epitaph as 'an astrologian, a mathematician, a musitian and what not'. The mathematical side of his mind was not allowed to subdue his musicianship. He was the true Renaissance humanist, a man of all-round taste and erudition. Sometimes he indulged in the intellectual puzzles that were fashionable, but such exercises served as the whetstone of his technique. They were not carried to the absurd lengths adopted by the Flemish composers of the next generation.

The epitaph preserved by Stow and restored in St Stephen's Church, Walbrook, proves that Dunstable was not without honour in his own country, but it was on the Continent that he was held in the greatest esteem and it was there that his influence was most deeply felt.§

The leadership now passed to the Burgundian School whose first masters were Guillaume Dufay and Gilles Binchois. Dufay, in fact, drew on many styles to form his own, in both his sacred and his secular works. In the former, he developed a new expressive style for his Masses and motets. They were written with a greater sense of the equality of the voices, and developed the unified setting of the Mass, coming to full fruition in the Latin hymns, the Magnificats and the five late Masses. Parody enters in such works as 'Se la face ay pale', based on his own chanson. In listening to these works, one seems to hear the music that Memlinc's angels sang; it is so pure and sweet.

In Dufay's secular music, we have the final flowering of the mediaeval *chanson*, in which he adhered to old forms. They must have been an adornment to the court of Philip the Good (1419–62), these attractive *chansons* and *rondeaux* showing off Dufay's fruitful melodic gift and challenging his lyrical inspiration. Gilles Binchois, Dufay's colleague at the Burgundian court, rivalled his contemporary in melancholy and expressive love songs. These pieces are in three parts with the tune on top and the other two used in imitative fashion.

Where Dufay and Binchois were obviously influenced by the English – a contemporary French poet meant it as a compliment when he said they followed *la contenance anglaise* – the masters of the next generation, Jan Okeghem and Jacob Obrecht, to a certain extent followed their Burgundian predecessors. Okeghem, like Dufay, wrote a Mass on *l'homme armé*, and several others on similar secular tunes. Okeghem's methods were often complex. Although there is less evidence of imitation in his work than is sometimes claimed, his Masses and motets do evince a well developed canonic and contrapuntal technique. In his relentless pursuit of technical difficulties, he has been likened, quite justly, to Schoenberg.

Okeghem served three kings of France as court composer. Jacob Obrecht worked at the ducal court of Ferrara. His significance and stature are just as great. He helped to move the composition of the Mass along freer lines, full of rhythmic energy and expressive harmony. He also developed the four-part *chanson*, the instrumental *canzona* and wrote songs in Flemish, one of the few Franco-Flemish composers to do so.

§ Josquin Desprez made full artistic use of the new technical mastery. Josquin combined the learning of his master, Okeghem, with an artistic genius that turns even his most recondite exercises into beautiful music. Not only is his music incomparably richer in texture than that of the older masters, but it is capable of reflecting the character of the words in a way that was inconceivable in the days of Dunstable and Dufay. The change that had come over music might be compared with that which the researches of the Florentine painters into the problems of perspective and of pigments wrought during this same century upon their art. There is a new depth, a richer colour, a greater mastery of form and a more subtle expressiveness. Sometimes, indeed, his melody seems extraordinarily modern. We even find him anticipating in his four-part motet, *Ave Coelorum Domina*, the first strain of Schubert's 'Du bist die Ruh'. This coincidence, in itself of no importance, shows how far music had by this time gone along the road towards diatonic harmony, a journey begun by Dufay.

Josquin's music is more varied than that of any of the composers so far mentioned. It ranges from a light and satirical humour, which is not always excluded from his sacred works, to the most profoundly moving expression of grief. Nothing could be more poignant than his famous setting of David's lament for Absalom or the elegy which he composed on the death of Okeghem. Josquin usually lavished on his motets the whole resources of his technical skill, and his recondite artifices have sometimes been criticized. He was, however, only glorifying the central rite of the Church, after the manner of the architects who adorned the choir more elaborately than the rest of a cathedral. As he developed, he did, indeed, simplify his style in the direction of a purer musical expressiveness, and in his later Masses and the motets this side of his great genius is most clearly displayed.§

Further points of Josquin's style: word-painting (contrasts of tessitura, poignant discords and so on) is consistently used in his motets and in his chansons, both of which are tremendously expressive; he expanded the vocal range of his voices (as Okeghem had already done, he made his basses sing lower, below the stave in fact, and his sopranos higher); his motets and his chansons, but not his Masses, are in five or six parts. To sum up, Josquin is the first composer to base his music fully upon the principle of harmonic propriety, so that his phrases become intelligible musical sentences, quite apart from their expressiveness as renderings of the text.

The fame of Clément Jannequin, a French composer, rests mainly upon his secular music. He specialized in the composition of four-part *chansons*, in which the songs of birds, the sounds of hunting, the street-cries of Paris, and the noise of battle are imitated. These descriptive pieces, whose titles remind us of the instrumental music of his 17th-century compatriot, Couperin, are full of a naïve charm.

It should be noted here that there has been, during recent years, an immense revival of interest in mediaeval music. Arguments continue about how the music should actually be performed, but that is just one of many indications that it is alive and not just part of the

445

history of music, able to communicate to late 20th-century audiences with quite the force of classical and romantic music, and with a good deal more than much of the music of today.

5 FLANDERS AND ITALY: LASSUS, PALESTRINA AND VICTORIA

For 100 years, the Flemish composers dominated European music. Their influence spread through Germany, where Heinrich Finck and Heinrich Isaac, a widely-travelled Fleming, established a solid tradition. Isaac was one of the greatest of Josquin's contemporaries. He did most to set up the new school of German-speaking composers and based much of his music, for example his 'Missa Carminum', on popular tunes of the time. He was employed at the court of the Habsburg Emperor Maximilian I at Augsburg and Vienna.

§ In the next generation, that is to say in the first half of the 16th century, we find Flemish composers permanently settled in Italy, chief among them Adrian Willaert, a Netherlander, in Venice, and Jacob Arcadelt, a native of Roulers in Flanders, at Florence. Italy now began to take the leading position in European music, which she was to occupy for more than two centuries, and it was in Italy that polyphonic music reached its highest point of development. One of the first signs of Italian influence at this time is the rapid growth of secular music, which soon became an independent form of art equal in importance to the music of the Church. This was a natural enough development, since in every other art the adventurous minds of the Renaissance were turning more and more from an exclusive preoccupation with sacred subjects.

The chief form taken by secular music in Italy was that of the madrigal, in style far more complex and subtle than the French and Flemish *chansons*. The term had been applied centuries before to songs of a pastoral nature, but for our purposes the history of the madrigal begins about 1530. Most of the early madrigals are homophonic, that is to say, the melodic interest is concentrated in one of the four parts in which they were usually written, and it appears likely that they were sung as solos with instrumental accompaniments as well as by voices with or without accompaniment. The madrigal was in fact a wedding of Flemish contrapuntal technique with the Italian *frottola*, which was a form of song popular in Northern Italy. The words of the *frottole* were either comic or sentimental, though they were not without wit in the one direction or poetry in the other. It was the sentimental element in these songs that the madrigal composers developed most freely, though there are also many examples of madrigals that are frivolous and gross. The Italian madrigal is a typical product of aristocratic culture, and its chief characteristic is a refined voluptuousness, the erotic double meanings of the poems being delicately underlined by the music.

At first the chief exponents of the madrigal were the Italianized Flemings, Arcadelt, Willaert and Philippe Verdelot. Arcadelt was a composer of considerable distinction and charm. His madrigals, notably the beautiful 'Il bianco e dolce cigno' on the favourite theme of the swan's last song, are typical examples of the genre at its best. Willaert adopted a more massive style, which has a true Venetian grandeur, and he is the first of these composers to give us the impression of thinking vertically in chords, rather than horizontally in separate parts whose harmonic effect is fortuitous and subsidiary to the interweaving of the voices. His chief pupil, Ciprian de Rore, another Fleming who came to Venice at an early age and succeeded his master as organist of St Mark's, followed his example, and by his experiments in chromaticism carried a stage further the trend towards a more harmonic conception of music. He seems to have been responsible for increasing the number of voices from three or four to five or more.

Ciprian's considerable fame as a composer rests upon his more conservative compositions, but these chromatic madrigals opened the way for the more daring experiments of Gesualdo, Prince of Venosa, and of Luco Marenzio at the end of the century, and soon madrigals written frankly in the diatonic keys are to be found.

All the composers we have just mentioned also wrote church music, in which as yet the effect of the new madrigal style hardly appears, and in the next generation we come to the great triumvirate who brought the music of the Roman Church to the highest point of perfection. Roland de Lassus or Orlando di Lasso, to give his name its more common Italianized form, was the last and greatest of the Flemish School, but like his contemporaries, Giovanni Pierluigi da Palestrina, the Roman, and Tomás Luis da Victoria, the Spaniard, he transcends the boundaries of school and nationality. Of the three, Lassus was the most versatile, the most profound. There is no form of vocal composition, sacred or profane, no depth of emotion, grave or gay, that he did not touch. We find him at one moment setting the words 'rore tegens' to chromatic harmonies by way of punning reference to Ciprian, at another creating in his *Seven Penitential Psalms of David* a profoundly moving masterpiece, published in 1584 but composed twenty years earlier. It is significant that in spite of his love of puns and other frivolities, Lassus's finest achievements should be in this tragic vein, for at Munich, where he spent the last thirty-four years of his life as musical director to the Bavarian ducal chapel, he died insane of melancholia.§

Giovanni Pierluigi was born in 1524 or 1525 at Palestrina and, like so many other early composers, took his name from his birthplace. On his coffin he was dubbed 'Prince of Music' and he was buried in the old church of St Peter's, Rome, where he was choirmaster from 1551 until his death in 1594. If his position in the Renaissance hierarchy is not so high today as it once was and his music is regarded as conservative, that is perhaps because we now know so much more about his contemporaries. As Jerome Roche, one of his recent biographers, has put it: '. . . we can now view him as one among equals, and appreciate with greater discrimination the particular character of his music, the stature of individual works, and the greatness of his achievement as a whole.'

§ The essential quality of Palestrina's music is its absolute purity. It seems almost to come from another world, divorced from the common emotions of humanity. In their place is a religious devotion whose intensity saves it from frigidity. Such perfection could only be achieved within a narrow scope, and Palestrina had neither the versatility of Lassus nor his grace and charm. His madrigals, lovely though they are, show few marks of a secular style to differentiate them from his sacred music. But it is sufficient that in his Masses, notably the famous *Missa Papae Marcelli* and the not less beautiful *Missa Assumpta est Maria*, he should have set up once and for all a pattern for the Roman Liturgy. Perhaps the most striking quality of his best music, from the modern point of view, is its agelessness. So great was his mastery of his material that he avoided the common-places of idiom that stamp the music of lesser men and fix for the listener its date in time.

Palestrina's music has not the sumptuousness that marks the more worldly school of Venice, best represented in the works of the Gabrieli family and comparable with the rich compositions of their fellow-citizens, Veronese and Tintoretto. He has often been likened to Raphael, and his music has the same kind of spiritual beauty free from insipidity as that painter's best work; on the technical side his complete mastery produces an effect of shapeliness and balance, of depth and roundness, that accords with Raphael's complete solution of the problem of representing a solid body upon a flat surface. The aloofness of his Masses is in the very spirit of the Catholic Church, whose central rite is regarded as a sacred mystery not to be approached too closely by the uninitiated. But in his motets he comes nearer to the common mind of humanity, without tainting the purity of his style.

If Palestrina sums up the past, Victoria, his Spanish contemporary, looks towards the future. He is the true representative of the Counter-Reformation, which had its centre in Spain and the Inquisition as its instrument. Although trained in the Roman School he remained a true Spaniard, and his music breathes the exalted mysticism of his race, which in painting finds its extreme expression through the work of El Greco. His mastery of the resources of his time is equal to that of his great contemporaries and, though his mysticism leads him sometimes into an almost morbid sensualism, and even into sensational effects of ecstasy, at their best his raptures are constrained by a noble and dignified bearing. In some works such as the *Missa Salve Regina*, he seems to be using musical themes to forge meaningful links between different parts of the work. If there were any doubt of Victoria's claim to stand as a master in his own right and not, like Anerio and others with whom he used to be classed, as a mere satellite of Palestrina, it is only necessary to set beside the Roman master's Good Friday Antiphon Victoria's *Tenebrae factae sunt*. In the one the emotions of the text are fused into a single, sublime musical idea, perfect in its shapeliness and tranquil beauty; in the other there is an exaltation and a dramatic force undreamt of by Palestrina. Each emotion – the gloom of the darkened skies, the despairing cry of Jesus in the hour of death and the tender sorrowfulness of His last emission of breath – passes in turn across the texture of this magnificently tragic piece.

Palestrina's death in 1594 marked the end of a musical era. Already Luca Marenzio had brought the Italian madrigal to its highest point of development and expressiveness in reflecting the mood of the text (especially in the exploitation of chromatic harmony). The next decade was to see the revolution destined, under the leadership of Monteverdi, to alter the whole course of musical history. The immediate cause of this revolution was the desire to find a more dramatic means of expression in music than was possible within the smooth texture of polyphony. A deeper cause was the unconscious feeling that the rich mine of polyphony had been worked out, that all that could be said in that way had been said, and that new country must be explored. That the path actually taken was that of diatonic harmony may have been natural, but it was not inevitable. Nor did it bring progress in the sense of immediate improvement. Music, having sacrificed the technical resources accumulated during two centuries of effort in favour of a more naturalistic and forceful dramatic expression, had to go to school again. It is more than a century before we find composers of choral music worthy to rank with Lassus, Victoria and Palestrina.

§ 6 ENGLAND: TUDOR ERA AND PURCELL

We have seen how the tide of polyphony flowed southward from England through Flanders and France to Italy. It ebbed again towards the north, passing by the French, who have always been more impervious to foreign artistic influences than any other nation. The final triumphs of polyphonic music were achieved in England. Ever since the time of Dunstable an unbroken musical tradition had persisted in England, submerged at times by the dynastic wars that preceded the establishment of the Tudors. It was a sturdy, individual tradition, little affected by the developments taking place on the Continent. During the more settled time of Henry VII's reign there is a prolific school of composers, the chief among them being Robert Fayrfax and William Cornyshe. It is not, however, until the following century that we find, under the favourable influence of Henry VIII (himself an amateur composer), any English composers of a distinction comparable with those of Flanders and Italy. The leading composers of this reign are John Taverner, Christopher Tye, Robert Whyte and Thomas Tallis, who, surviving into his eightieth year, became with William Byrd one of the founders of post-Reformation Church music.

The influence of the Flemish composers begins to appear in the music of Taverner and Tye, not only in matters of polyphonic technique, but in the use of popular melodies as the basis of sacred compositions. As Josquin Desprez wrote Masses on *l'homme armé* and *Una masque de Biscaia*, so Taverner and Tye each composed one upon the folk-song 'Western Wind'. Neither Taverner, in spite of his bold rhythms and the grand scale of his work, nor Tye broke entirely free from the rigidity of the conservative English style. Even Tye's six-part Mass *Euge bone*, usually considered his masterpiece, is not free from stiffness, in spite of its fresh melodiousness and masterly construction.§

The music of Tallis and Whyte is free from the antique stiffness of

450

the older men. Tallis, probably born in 1505, held the post of organist to the Chapel Royal jointly with William Byrd, about forty years Tallis's junior. Although he wrote for virginals and for the organ, his fame rests on his vocal music to both Latin and English texts (the change in church practice over language took place during his lifetime because of the Reformation). His most famous work is the forty-part motet *Spem in Alium* calling for eight five-part choirs. Apart from showing Tallis's extraordinary technical facility, the work has a majestic flow almost unique in vocal music. The *Lamentations of Jeremiah*, in five parts, is another masterly example of ease of writing, its grave beauty extremely telling in a fine performance, and it is fit to be ranked with Lassus's *Penitential Psalms*.

With the gradual changeover to English in services came the specifically English form of the anthem to which Tallis contributed various masterpieces, of which 'If ye love me' is a noble example. His large number of Latin motets include the moving 'O sacrum convivium' and 'Audivi media nocte'.

Robert Whyte also wrote for Latin and English worship. His setting of the *Lamentations of Jeremiah* is nearly on a par with that of Tallis, and he wrote many other rewarding and rather neglected church pieces.

§ The simplification of church music, decreed by the Reformers and summed up in Archbishop Cranmer's dictum 'One syllable, one note', was incidental and was not, in fact, carried out to the letter. With characteristic complacency, English composers quietly worked out a compromise that satisfied both the ecclesiastical authorities and their own artistic consciences. In fact Cranmer's ideal was precisely the same as that of the Council of Trent, which was simultaneously engaged in an investigation of the abuses in Roman Church music and ended likewise in compromise by accepting Palestrina. It is interesting to compare with events in England what happened north of the border, where John Knox ruthlessly swept away everything except psalm-singing in unison.

One rather surprising fact is the tolerance that was shown to heretical composers on both sides during the Reformation and the Counter-Reformation in the reign of Mary. John Merbecke, who hastily provided an admirable setting for the English services in the First Prayer Book of Edward VI, was permitted to retain his post at St George's Chapel, Windsor, through the Marian reaction, while William Byrd, steadfast Catholic to the end, remained unmolested through Elizabeth's reign. Taverner seems to have been the only composer who lost his artistic soul as the result of these events (the modern British composer Peter Maxwell Davies has written an absorbing opera, *Taverner*, on the change that came over his 16th-century predecessor). Repenting of his 'Popish ditties', he sought in a fanatical Protestantism his possibly less important personal salvation.

This tolerance was fortunate for English music, since Byrd, one of its greatest ornaments, was born too late to have achieved his masterpieces under the Catholic regime. Tolerance, indeed, is too negative a word to describe the attitude of the Elizabethan authorities, since Byrd and Tallis were granted a patent, amounting to a monopoly, for the printing and selling of music and music-paper, English and foreign. In his turn Byrd showed compliance with the conditions of his time by supplying the English Church with the first great settings of its services. But it is in his Masses and Latin motets that his genius is not unnaturally seen at its finest. He himself indicated the mystical attitude of his approach to the Roman rite in the preface to the *Gradualia* (1605), where he speaks of 'a certain hidden power in the words themselves, so that as one meditates upon the sacred words and constantly and seriously considers them, the right notes, in some inexplicable fashion, suggest themselves quite spontaneously'. It is hardly surprising that a temperament so essentially religious should have found difficulty in adjusting itself to the lighter style of the madrigal. Like Palestrina's, Byrd's secular music has a gravity not always wholly consonant with the texts. There are, indeed, one or two madrigals, of which 'Though Amaryllis dance in green' is the most familiar, wherein he exhibits a gayer manner, but these are rare exceptions to the rule.

The introduction of the vernacular in the Church Service turned the attention of English musicians to their own language, and the importation from Italy of madrigals by Marenzio and others gave them an example of the way to put the rich resources of the English literary genius to musical use. England is the only country in which the madrigal became entirely naturalized and took on a distinctive character of its own. Compared with the hot-house sensuality of the Italian madrigals, the English have a fresh and vigorous air.§

The English madrigal tends to follow the sense of a poem with many onomatopoeic effects. Each voice has equality with the others and musical phrases are tossed in imitation between them, and, as Thomas Morley (see below) pointed out, 'You must not make a full close till the full sense of the words be perfect'.§ Whether they were celebrating the glories of Elizabeth or writing light love-songs or setting graver semi-philosophical poems, the composers were able to draw upon an inexhaustible fund of melody and, while not lacking in science, their music is, at its best, spontaneous and free from artificiality. There is no pedantry in Byrd's elaborate cross-rhythms and his bold harmonic style, which led him to warn singers against the hasty emendation of supposed misprints, is as striking as the consistent tunefulness of all the parts in his music.

Morley is the most characteristically English of the madrigal-composers. His taste lay in the direction of cheerful subjects, which he treated with an exquisitely light touch. He was especially happy in using the ballet-form, which he himself describes as 'a slight kind of music and as I take it devised to be danced to music'. The ballet was of Italian origin and is distinguished from the madrigal by its quick dancing rhythm and fa-la-la refrain. Morley completely anglicized the form, and his ballets are among the most delightful things in the music of this period. His madrigals and canzonets, with their more elaborately contrapuntal style, however, contain Morley's finest music, and it should not be forgotten that he also composed some church music, including the noble anthem 'Out of the deep', and a Burial Service, which is a serene and powerful work. Altogether Morley, with his variety of achievement, his great rhythmical invention and his almost complete emancipation from modal influences, must be reckoned as one of the most accomplished composers of his time. Morley was responsible for bringing together twenty-five other composers to contribute pieces to *The Triumphs of Oriana* (1601), that compendium of all that is best in the English madrigal school.

Thomas Weelkes presents a contrast to Morley. His music is far closer to the Italian models, and his fondness for bold contrasts of mood expressed by means of chromatic progressions gives his music the same kind of passionate expressiveness that characterizes the madrigals of Marenzio and Gesualdo. At the same time there is a certain antique quaintness in his style and, in spite of his harmonic inventiveness, he adheres more closely than most of his contemporaries to the modes.

John Wilbye combines the expressiveness of Weelkes with a smoother workmanship. He is equally successful in the light vein of such things as 'Flora gave me fairest flowers' and 'Lady, when I behold', in which he rivals the delicacy of Morley, and in the tender gravity of his more serious pieces, which need not fear comparison with the madrigals of Byrd himself.

There remains one great figure, belonging to the next century and to the reign of James I, Orlando Gibbons, whose genius brings the long line of polyphonic composers to a glorious close. For, although polyphonic music still continued to be written, the main stream of music began to flow into a different channel at the beginning of the 17th century. Even in the music of Gibbons himself there is already a change, not of method but of underlying mood. The best of his church music is contained in the anthems, where there is more scope for personal expression than in the setting of the ritual words of the Services. 'Hosanna to the Son of David', 'O clap your hands' and 'Lift up your heads'. to name three of the most famous examples, are texts suggestive both of physical movement and strong human emotion, and Gibbons set them to music that is essentially direct. These joyful anthems are not, however, as characteristic of the composer as 'Behold, thou hast made my days as it were a span', for he was of a melancholy, introspective temperament. The poems he chose for his madrigals – Raleigh's *What is our life?* is typical – are without exception pessimistic, and the only humour that relieves them is the bitter one of satire. It is only necessary to compare Arcadelt's most famous madrigal, 'Il bianco e dolce cigno', with Gibbons's 'The Silver Swan', likewise the most familiar of his compositions, to see how far he had moved both in words and music away from the voluptuousness of the Italian madrigal and towards a more philosophical standpoint.§

Gibbons was also one of the composers who wrote fantasies bringing together the 'Cries of London', for a consort of viols, and viols were now being used to accompany voices.§ Although it is quite clear that both sacred and secular music had for a long time been accompanied by instruments of various kinds, these accompaniments were in no way independent. They merely supported the voices and may be described, in modern terminology, as being *ad libitum*. Towards the end of the 16th century we find an increasing tendency to use viols to support the voices in madrigal-singing, and it is quite clear that madrigals were sometimes sung by a solo voice accompanied by viols, which played the remaining parts.

It is not surprising, therefore, to find developing concurrently with the madrigal in England what we must call, in default of a better name, the art-song. Solo songs – folk-songs, ballads and so on – had, of course, been in existence all along and had, as we have had occasion to observe, supplied composers with material for Masses as well as for madrigals. By the reign of Henry VIII we find arrangements of three-part songs for solo voice and lute, the instrument taking over two of the parts. The practice was probably introduced by foreign musicians in the King's employment. Later in the century madrigals, for example those by Morley, begin to appear in alternative versions for voice and lute in which the instrumental part often betrays its vocal origin. The first genuine solo-songs appeared in 1597, though their composition may well have antedated their appearance by some years, in John Dowland's first *Book of Ayres*. These are songs for tenor voice with lute and bass viol. Reversing the procedure of the madrigalists, Dowland also provided an alternative version for voices in four parts, so that the songs could be performed by a group of amateur singers.

John Dowland, 'whose heavenly touch upon the lute doth ravish human sense', was one of the great virtuosi. He travelled about Europe singing his songs at the courts of kings and princes. In England he seems to have been without fame or honour, for he himself contrasts his 'kingly entertainment in a forraine climate' with his inability to 'attaine to any place at home'. Dowland had been anticipated by Byrd in the composition of solo-songs with instrumental accompaniment, such as the well-known 'My sweet little darling' for voice and viols, but he was the first composer to specialize in this form. Dowland's best songs – his early ones are somewhat square-cut in spite of their melodic charm – set at once the standard of agreement between 'music and sweet poetry' which has been one of the chief virtues of English vocal music ever since. Dowland and his fellows – Morley, for example, in his settings of Shakespeare's songs – were solving in a characteristically English way the very problems which in Italy were consciously exercising the minds of Monteverdi and the other theorists. Dowland's songs have this in common with the madrigal, that they are free in rhythm. Nothing is more remarkable than the ingenuity with which, like all great artists, he surmounts the limitations of his medium and indeed turns them to account. His songs are for the most part love-songs and his mood is usually sad.

Thurston Dart has remarked on the dance-like character of Dowland's early songs, which often appear transcribed as 'Galliards' or 'Pavans' in early 17th-century collections of instrumental music. In his later books Dowland's vocal melody acquires a greater suppleness and grace, and his writing for the lute becomes increasingly idiomatic and free. Sometimes he anticipates the practice of a later age, concentrating the musical interest for several bars at a time in the accompaniment. In his last songs, for example 'From silent night' and the poignant 'In darkness let me dwell', the harmony is often daringly original and the voice-part is given greater expressive power under the influence of the new declamatory style.

Dowland's example was copied by other composers, among whom Thomas Campian, the poet, was the most prolific. His songs are simpler than Dowland's and less elaborate in their accompaniments. Yet the best of his songs, among which 'Follow your Saint' is one of the most familiar, are marked by the aptness of their settings and their poetic imagination. Philip Rosseter, Robert Jones, John Danyel and Thomas Ford, whose 'Since first I saw your face' is among the most popular of Elizabethan songs, are other composers who can here have no more notice than mention of their names.

Unhappily neither Henry Lawes, the subject of a eulogy by Milton, nor his contemporaries maintained the standard of excellence achieved by the song-writers of the previous generation. The most fashionable form of musical entertainment became the masque, which had already taken its place, in a small way, in the last of Shakespeare's plays, *The Tempest*. The Jacobean and Caroline masques involved a large number of singers, dancers and instrumentalists, most of whom were amateurs. It will be readily understood that, in order to keep the singing and dancing in time with the orchestra, which was apparently not so closely in touch with the performers on the stage as it is in a modern theatre, a more regularly rhythmic music than the free madrigalian style, where accents fell at uneven intervals according to the sense of the words, was absolutely necessary. It was inevitable, therefore, that the music of the masques should be in square-cut rhythms derived largely from dance-music, which is by nature regularly accented. The bar-line, hitherto used in vocal music only to aid the eye of the performer, becomes henceforth an important factor in the structure of all music. Added to this influence of practical conditions is the fact that diatonic melodies, which had by now almost completely supplanted the modes, seem to predicate a regular rhythmic pulse.

That Henry Lawes is the most distinguished composer of the Caroline and Cromwellian periods is a measure rather of the decline in musical standards than of his greatness. His music is dullest when he is most concerned with the fitting of 'just note and accent', which meant that he was attempting to translate into music the rhythm of a poet's reading of his verse. When he forgets about the problems of declamation, his music is often charming. These two aspects are exemplified in the music for Milton's *Comus*, which is the most familiar of his compositions.

The rule of the Puritans had important reactions upon music. In the churches the organs were silenced and the choirs banished. Yet in spite of this severity and the disapproval of dancing, music was given an unexpected stimulus under the Commonwealth. Cromwell and some of the other leading men were fond of music, and when the theatres were closed an exception was made in favour of performances with music. In consequence of this dispensation, the enterprising Poet Laureate, William D'Avenant, offered to the public, starved of recreation, an *Entertainment by Declamations and Musick*, which was introduced by a prologue beginning:

Think this your passage, and the narrow way
To our Elysian field, the Opera.

From this cautious beginning of 'declamations and music', D'Avenant succeeded in developing a genuine English opera.

With the restoration of the monarchy, music returned to the Church. Old part-books were brought out and new choristers were trained. But the tradition of church music had been broken and, though it might have been restored, tastes had changed. King Charles II set the fashion for the new French style of music, in which violins, hitherto unknown in England and, in the opinion of John Evelyn, more suited to the tavern than the church, played an important part. What Charles liked was a good jigging rhythm to which he could beat time, and this was provided in the instrumental *ritornelli* that were introduced between the sections of the anthems. These passages were completely secular in style and rarely bore any relation to the musical or to the literary material of the composition as a whole. They may be likened to the cherubs, growing every year more and more like Cupids, with which the interiors of churches were being decorated at this time. After the anxieties of the Civil War and the repression of the Commonwealth, England wanted to be amused, not edified, and readily fell in with the tastes of the 'merry' king.§

It was into this unpromising world that Henry Purcell was born. Purcell probably had as much natural, instinctive musicianship as Bach or Mozart. He was the greatest British composer in the baroque era. For example, in the magnificent Coronation Anthem 'My Heart is inditing' is embodied all the dignity of a great ceremonial occasion.

His teachers were John Blow and the unjustly neglected, short-lived Pelham Humfrey, composer of the fine solo piece 'Hymn to God the Father', a setting of the John Donne text. From them and from his contemporary Matthew Locke, he learned his distinctive declamatory style, evident in 'Saul and the Witch of Endor', for soprano, alto and bass soloists with continuo. The 'alto' is the male voice known as counter-tenor. In recent times Alfred Deller, and his successors in that kind of voice, have proved how expressive it can be.

Purcell's dramatic music is dealt with in another part of this volume. Of his sacred music, the most famous examples, beside the Coronation Anthem already mentioned, are 'Rejoice in the Lord' (the so-called Bell Anthem), the setting of the Psalm 'Jehovah, quam multi sunt hostes' and the *Te Deum and Jubilate* in D. In addition to these, there are the 'Evening Hymn' and 'Now that the Sun', whose sheer beauty have ensured their popularity, along with 'Dido's Lament' and the above-mentioned dramatic setting of the scene between Saul and the Witch of Endor, which is a miniature oratorio. His secular choral works include a number of 'Welcome' Odes, which celebrate the return to town of the several sovereigns whom he served. More distinguished still are the *Odes for St Cecilia's Day*; the sincerity and beauty of these hymns in praise of his art lift them above the comparative flatness of the adulatory texts. Of these the finest is 'Hail bright Cecilia', written in 1692. The songs for one or more voices, which range from dramatic scenas, like 'Mad Bess', to rounds and catches, are innumerable, and testify to Purcell's unlimited fund of melodic invention, in which he is rivalled only by Schubert, and his exact sense of the setting to music of English words, which has served as a model to our composers, with one or two notable exceptions, ever since.

If the claim for Purcell's potential greatness in a later age seems exaggerated, let it be remembered that he, almost first of composers, shows an instinctive sense of key-relationship, which is the basis of sonata-form, that his feeling for dramatic expression in music was equal to that of the greatest operatic composers, and that his fertility and variety of invention were unfailing.

7 ITALIAN AND GERMAN BAROQUE

Baroque for years had basically a connotation in art rather than music. Today it applies equally to music composed between c. 1600 and 1750, from Monteverdi to Bach and Handel. One of the main distinguishing features of the new style was the increasing importance given to instruments *vis-à-vis* the voice, and in particular to the violin, partly through the growing ascendancy of violin-makers. The orchestra as it is known today came into being (but for its development see the part of this volume devoted to it). In connection with voices, baroque often meant the new *concertato* (literally, concerted) style, in which the instruments had parts independent from the voices.

Monteverdi was the first to use this style with real imagination, and both for that and for his extraordinary use of harmony as an expressive means, his work is of outstanding importance. Even more adventurous is the dissonance to be found in the music of Gesualdo already mentioned. Monteverdi's most famous ecclesiastical composition is the *Vespers* of 1610, combining soloists, chorus and orchestra in an ornate splendour that is typical of the Venetian School at its greatest. Other church pieces by Monteverdi that reveal his special skill and audacity are the motets 'Beatus vir' and 'Laudate Dominum', and his four-part Mass settings. In the secular field, besides the nine books of madrigals, with their enormous diversity of feeling and style, there are the delightful *Scherzi musicali* of 1607, charming trios, and the *Scherzi musicali* of 1632, a set of airy solo songs.

Monteverdi was, of course, as famous as an opera composer (Book 4, Part 1, Chapter 4), but he did not write in the new form of oratorio, developing concurrently in Rome. Throughout the 14th and 15th centuries there were frequently performed musical settings of incidents from the Old and New Testaments, deriving in all probability from the old mystery plays. But it was St Philip Neri, the 'Apostle of Rome', who first laid special stress on the advantages of such pieces for instructional and devotional purposes, introducing them before or after the sermon in the Oratory of his own church in Rome. Hence the title that became attached to them. These performances proved so popular that they were not discontinued after his death in 1595. On the contrary, his successor, Emilio De'Cavalieri, developed them with enthusiasm, for his performances seem to have been more elaborate in every way than St Philip's. The most famous of his works, an allegorical piece called *La Rappresentazione di Anima e di Corpo*, has solos, choruses, dances and instrumental numbers, all linked by recitative. In the Salzburg Festival performances in the Kollegienkirche during the early 1970s, it proved as relevant today as it was of old.

This first kind of oratorio was a near relative of opera. Oratorio as we know it was 'invented' in the middle of the 17th century, in such works as Carissimi's *Jephtha* – action as such being replaced by a narrator. Alessandro Scarlatti practised both forms with equal success, and wrote oratorios that are practically indistinguishable from operas; but he also wrote with success for the new cantata form, usually a series of two or three operas, separated by recitative, on a mythological or historical subject. He wrote no less than 500 chamber cantatas of various kinds, and they represent, if not better work than is to be found in his operas, work superior to anything that he wrote for the Church or for instruments alone.

The Italian baroque style soon spread to Germany, carried there principally by Italian musicians and by the visit of foreign musicians to Italy. Heinrich Schütz, the most famous German composer of this period and style, studied in Venice with Giovanni Gabrieli (and later came under Monteverdi's influence). His first published work was a series of five-part Italian madrigals. Then he began to write in the baroque vein in the vernacular: *The Psalms of David* (1619), followed by the *Symphoniae Sacrae*, to both Latin and German texts. Schütz also wrote the first German opera, *Daphne* (now lost). He introduced to his country the Italian declamatory style and to the concertato, instrumental writing; but probably his greatest achievement, looking at it in a historical perspective, was his dramatic religious works. He wrote with a devout intensity bringing to life the scriptural texts by closely allying his urgent music to the words. His three settings of the Passion story – Matthew, Luke and John – paved the way for Bach's even more remarkable works in that genre. Two contemporaries of Schütz, Johann Hermann Schein and Samuel Scheidt, were also important figures in German Reformation music.

Mention should also be made here of sadly neglected Spanish baroque, of which Cabanilles is the leading figure. He was the main exponent of the devotional *villancico*, a form based on the popular refrain-song. By his time, that had developed into a profuse variety of solo songs, duets and trios to polychoral works, using many baroque devices in creating florid writing of deep passion.

§ 8 BACH AND HANDEL

A tendency to institute comparisons between Bach and Handel is perhaps inevitable because of the accident that they lived at the same time. It is none the less regrettable because, alike in their music and their lives, no two men could have been more dissimilar. Religion was the mainspring of Bach's every important musical activity; Handel, pious and upright though he was, was essentially a man of the world. Bach approached music through the organ-loft, Handel, generally speaking, through the theatre. Bach, despite an undoubted interest in certain works by his foreign contemporaries, remained in essence wholly German; Handel was the very embodiment of cosmopolitanism. The only real connection between the two lies in the fact that they were both supreme masters of two different facets of the art of music. The assignment of superiority to one rather than the other is probably more a matter of musical fashion and the idiosyncrasies of personal taste than anything else.

Bach, like Handel, wrote oratorios, it is true, but they were always oratorios of a reflective, not of a dramatic, nature. The best known of these is the Christmas oratorio, in reality rather a collection of cantata-numbers than an oratorio in the narrow sense of the word. Indeed, Bach here definitely made use of four numbers of an early cantata called *A Musical Drama in Honour of the Queen*, and six others from another cantata called *The Choice of Hercules*. This fact is of importance and interest because it illustrates to perfection, first, the essentially craftsmanlike attitude of the early 18th-century composer, who would never willingly sacrifice any material that could usefully be saved; second, the then shadowy line of that distinction between sacred and profane music which used, at any rate, to be so popular in England. How many music lovers would have known that some of this apparently devout music was originally written to illustrate the dilemma of a Greek demi-god or to celebrate the glories of a queen of a German kingdom? In this case, as in so many others, the matter is merely one of verbal association, the character of the music itself being hardly, if at all, affected. On the other hand, it is only fair to state that Spitta, Bach's great biographer, is of opinion that all Bach's music, however secular the words it sets, remains essentially religious, partly because of the nature of the man himself, partly because, fundamentally, he always thought in terms of the organ.§

The majority of Bach's vocal output consists, in fact, of church cantatas. He probably wrote nearly 300, though only some 200 now survive.

The principal difference between Bach's cantatas and their Italian prototypes, apart from any question of personal characteristics, is in the important part played by the chorales which were, of course, typically German and Protestant institutions. The cantatas from his Leipzig appointment (1723) forward were integrated into the services. They usually consisted of a chorale, recitatives, several extended arias, sometimes duets, and a concluding chorale in which the congregation joined. There are some 200 of these works, one for every appropriate occasion in the ecclesiastical calendar, and they contain a wealth of hidden treasure (hidden because they are so seldom performed today, although many are available on record).

The St John and St Matthew Passions extend the procedures adopted in the cantatas and project them on a grand scale. An Evangelist tells the New Testament story in vivid recitative; the chorus takes the part of the crowd; soloists ponder in arias and duets on the meaning of the Gospel; and Jesus's words are given to a bass soloist.

The John is the more direct, dramatic work, and has come to the fore in recent years as a composition of equal inspiration to that of the Matthew, but the latter probably still holds a higher place in public esteem. In it, every suggestion in the text that can possibly be illustrated by a musical equivalent is so illustrated. The old Pharasaic Law, for instance, is represented by strict musical forms; Christ's sayings are given noble *arioso* life; and the arias truly reflect the New Testament's compassionate message. Technically the work is a marvel; expressively it is eloquent.

§ Although in a sense hardly so personal as the Matthew Passion, the Mass in B minor represents to perfection, as music pure and simple, Bach's peculiar attributes in their most striking form. It may seem curious that so convinced a Protestant as Bach should have set the Catholic Mass to music at all. Doubtless, in the first instance, the composition and the despatch of the original two numbers, the 'Kyrie' and 'Gloria', to the Roman Catholic Elector of Saxony were due to strictly practical motives. Doubtless the Mass was never even intended to be performed as a whole in a Catholic church, as were some of the small previous Masses written by the composer. But the fact remains that in the gradual completion of the work, whether by fresh composition or by the adaptation of numbers already written, Bach achieved a universality of outlook rare, if not unique. Bach, we know, took a definite interest in theology, and he may well have desired to emphasize his claim to be regarded as a Christian belonging to the Church Catholic in the widest sense of the term. To this he devoted all his unparalleled resources of polyphony and expressiveness, so that the Mass, alike in its choruses and its solos, remains perhaps the most impressive statement of religious faith in existence.§

Telemann, Bach's lesser contemporary, wrote several attractive solo cantatas and oratorios of which *Der Tag des Gerichts* is probably the best known. Meanwhile in France the court of Louis XIV was graced by the music of Lully and Lalande. The former wrote clear, noble choral works to the glory of *le roi soleil*; the latter, particularly in his motet *De Profundis*, touched perhaps a more emotional vein. More attractive still, and unaccountably neglected, is the vocal music of François Couperin, particularly the *Leçons de Ténèbres*, in which the texts from the Lamentations of Jeremiah are interspersed and contrasted with Hebrew ritual phrases, using elaborate vocal and instrumental combinations to glorious effect. His motet in praise of St Susanna is also of great beauty, and has a smooth lyricism typical of this school of French music. Marc-Antoine Charpentier wrote in a grander, less personal style, but his choral writing has an impressive sonority that banishes criticism. In Italy, the oratorio tradition was carried on after Carissimi by Vivaldi in his secular work *Judith Triumphans*; while Pergolesi deserves a mention if only for the continued popularity of his Stabat Mater (1736), a euphonious setting for two high solo voices, originally *castrati*, nowadays female soprano and mezzo. Domenico Scarlatti, Alessandro's son, also wrote in this vein, notably in his ten-voice Stabat Mater.

§ The one figure bestriding both the Italian and German baroque fields is that of Handel. Not even Mozart, who possessed two musical nationalities, was so cosmopolitan as Handel, who possessed three. Needless to say, he owed much to Germany: his original bent of mind and the solidity of his workmanship; but he owed almost as much to Italy, where he learned the value of clarity and the secret of writing mellifluously for the human voice. In all probability he owed more to England than is usually supposed. He certainly must have heard Purcell's music at the very outset of his English career; there is a typical English freshness about *L'Allegro*, while the oratorios he wrote towards the end of his life show that his long practice at setting English words to music was beginning to have its effect.§

When he first came from Italy (where he wrote his setting of *Dixit Dominus*, a work of youthful exuberance and daring hardly surpassed in any of his other works) to England he came primarily as a composer of Italian opera. And it was as a composer of Italian opera that he was known for many years. When, living in the service of the Duke of Chandos at Cannons, he wrote the music to a masque by Pope entitled *Haman and Mordecai* he never dreamed that twelve years later, under the title of *Esther*, this would become the first English oratorio, because of the refusal of the Bishop of London to allow a biblical subject to be produced on the stage with scenery, costumes and action. Yet so it was, and nothing could better illustrate the dramatic origin of a style of composition that was to prove itself particularly dear to the English temperament.

§ Handel's English oratorios and similar works were direct descendants of the original Italian model, though with considerable adaptations to suit the changed environment, especially in respect of the greater importance attached to the chorus. Indeed, one of the first of them, the pastoral serenade *Acis and Galatea*, which is now regarded more as a work for the stage, was a new treatment of a subject that he had already handled in his Italian days. Moreover, what may be called the epic tradition, characteristic of Carissimi's oratorios, rather than the purely dramatic tradition, was perpetuated in Handel. The fact that in recent years the *Messiah* has become much the best known and is the most frequently performed of all his works has tended to make people forget that it is unique among his oratorios in being of a specifically reflective nature.§

The range covered by Handel's oratorios is so immense that little more can be done than give a general indication of them. The *Messiah* is so familiar that it is perhaps unnecessary to write anything about it. It is first and foremost a work of art, characterized by all the poetry and vivid imagination of a work of art. It has little or nothing in common with the Lutheran piety of Bach's religious music; it is full of colour and studies in intentional contrasts ranging round the central mystery of Redemption. Happily today the anachronistic large-scale performances are becoming a rarity, and due attention is being paid not only to the size of forces employed but to the vocal ornamentation common in Handel's own time.

§ When we come to the other oratorios, it is very difficult to know where to begin, a selection from their many-faceted beauties being so much a matter of individual taste. As choral writing there is the unparalleled finale of *Israel in Egypt*, the great double chorus at the end of *Solomon*, 'Then round about the starry throne' in *Samson*, or in as lightly different vein, 'How dark, O Lord, are Thy decrees' in *Jephtha*, not to mention the overwhelming effect of works like the coronation anthem *Zadok the Priest*. It was of music such as this that Mozart was thinking when he wrote of Handel, 'When he so wills, he strikes like a thunderbolt'. To these should be added the graphic quality of 'He saw the lovely youth' in *Theodora*, which Handel himself thought the best of all his choruses, the voluptuous bridal choruses in *Solomon*, and the sheer rusticity depicted in 'Mirth, admit me to thy crew' in *L'Allegro*.

At the same time, no man ever wrote more exquisite or more diverse music for the solo voice. Indeed, it is extraordinary that one mind should have evolved conceptions so utterly varied yet all so perfect as 'As when the dove' (*Acis*), 'He shall feed his flock', 'The people that walked in darkness' (*Messiah*), 'Oh Sleep why dost thou leave me' (*Semele*), 'With thee, the unsheltered moor I'd tread' (*Solomon*). 'Deeper and deeper still' (*Jephtha*), to mention only a few of the more familiar. In all these and many more again the voice is written for with a plasticity, an expressiveness and an imagination such as no composer has ever surpassed. Above all the mood and particular psychology of the situation are established immediately, almost in the first phrase, showing that in dramatic insight Handel was no whit inferior to the great masters of opera: Mozart, Wagner and Verdi. His immense dramatic range is to be marvelled at: the perfection of conventional pastoralism in *Acis and Galatea*; the love of and feeling for nature in *L'Allegro*; the splendour and lusciousness of *Solomon*, which is like a series of great frescoes by Michelangelo; the psychological subtlety of *Hercules*; the tragedy and despair of *Samson* and *Jephtha*; the daring of *Saul*. It is an extraordinary catalogue of variety, which those who love Handel claim to be unmatchable in all the annals of music.§

9 THE CLASSICAL TRADITION

However secular in concept and execution choral music may have become in England under Handel's influence, in Germany and Austria it remained firmly in the Church's province. In Vienna, certainly, there were few public performances of choral music until Haydn gave *The Creation* and *The Seasons* about 1800. Canons – Mozart, Haydn, Beethoven and Cherubini all wrote some – might be sung in the home, and the Freemasons' influence caused Mozart to contribute to their enlightenment. Otherwise it was the Mass that predominated. In their settings the great Viennese composers were less influenced by Bach and Handel than by the Italians, particularly by Alessandro Scarlatti and Pergolesi.

For long Haydn was considered primarily as an instrumental composer. *The Creation* apart, his choral music, not to mention his operas, was largely neglected. In fact much of his church music, and the late Masses in particular, are complementary to his symphonic and chamber music output. His comparatively early *Applausus*, *Il ritorno di Tobia* and Stabat Mater (although this last contains fine music) need not detain us in a general study, but the Masses, even the *St Cecilia* of the early 1770s, are all appreciable works, and the last six are masterpieces. These latter come directly after the 'London' Symphonies and show Haydn's formal and expressive mastery at their greatest. They were mostly written to celebrate occasions, grave or cheerful, and reflect one or the other feeling. The *Missa in Tempore Belli* (1796), written when Napoleon was threatening Vienna, suggests its time in the trumpets and drums of the 'Dona nobis pacem'. The *Missa in Angustiis*, better known as the 'Nelson Mass' (1798), was written at the time Nelson's victory at Aboukir was announced and tells as much in the striking outburst of trumpets at the climax of the 'Benedictus'. It is perhaps the supreme offering of Haydn in this genre. However, the *Theresienmesse* of 1799 is not far behind in invention or originality. It is named after Empress Maria Theresa, wife of Francis II, who later sang the soprano solos in *The Seasons*. The *Schöpfungmesse* (1801) is so named because it quotes from *The Creation*. It is probably the weakest of the last six, but to show that Haydn's powers were in no measure waning, the *Harmoniemesse*, with its prominent wind band, crowns the group. As Rosemary Hughes says in her biography of the composer: 'Written at the age of seventy, this is his last large-scale work, and no isolated quotation can do justice to its breadth of design. . . .' As a whole these Masses are remarkable for their daring counterpoint displayed in masterly fugal movements, their clever adaptation of the sonata form created in the instrumental works to choral purposes (particularly in the *Kyries*), and the subtle mixing of solo voices with the choir.

The Seven Last Words from the Cross (1785) arose out of instrumental versions (orchestra and quartet) of the same work. Solo voices are carefully contrasted with the chorus throughout seven slow movements, with the exception of the earthquake representation, which is entirely choral. This fine piece is unjustly neglected. Not so *The Creation* of 1798. Haydn, having been in London, had at last felt the influence of Handel, as can be heard in the majesty of the choral writing: 'The Heavens are telling' is worthy to stand beside Handel's best pages. What Miss Hughes calls this 'magnificent flight of imagination' (referring to the whole work) starts with an orchestral 'Representation of Chaos' of extraordinary harmonic originality matched by control of design. It is succeeded by movement after movement of choral and solo inspiration both in the depiction of the naïve realism of the Book of Genesis and in commentary upon it. Points are made directly and economically, often with a simplicity that is the very opposite of the academic. It is a work at once profound and inspired.

The work's sequel, *The Seasons*, may suffer a little by comparison with its great predecessor, but it does not deserve its comparative neglect. Again the freshness of concept and invention, and its idealization of simple rusticity is, in a way, unique in musical literature. For all its delights in things pastoral and countrified, it has movements of moving nobility, such as the chorus 'God of light' that brings 'Spring' to a close; and the final numbers of 'Winter', where man's and the year's end are correlated, are touching as the composer's last vocal testament.

If Mozart did not contribute to the choral repertory on the scale of Haydn, his Masses deserve more attention than they usually get. Of those written for Salzburg, several show intermittently the composer's quality. The *Coronation* (1779) is more consistent, with several ravishing movements. Of the other early works, the *Litaniae de Venerabili Altaris Sacramento* (1776) is worth investigating, but it is only when we reach the sadly uncompleted C minor Mass, K 427, that we have a work of consistent greatness, with choruses, the 'Qui tollis' in particular, of stern power and solos of operatic brilliance, including the very difficult soprano aria 'Et incarnatus est'. Also unfinished is the Requiem Mass, later completed by friends, a work of great intensity and even tragedy. The brief 'Ave verum corpus' is a microcosm of Mozartian sensibility.

Schubert also contributed substantially to the choral tradition with his many Masses, of which the mature works in A flat, the better work, and in E flat are most notable. §But beyond question the most important work which may, generally speaking, be regarded as a product of this school is Beethoven's great *Missa Solemnis* (although his earlier Mass in C should not be ignored). This, a product of Beethoven's complete maturity, is one of the great choral masterpieces of the world, containing as it does some of the most expressive and intensely felt music, for soloists and chorus alike, ever written in the history of music. As a work of art it is superior in every way to the choral movement of the Ninth Symphony, which may have attempted more but scarcely can be said to have achieved as much in the way of expression.

The very essence of Beethoven's music is an expression of personality, and it is from this essentially personal expression that most of the great choral works of the 19th century derived. Apart from Cherubini's Masses, which retain a certain classical objectivity, very attractive in its way, all the great choral music of the 19th century was definitely subjective.

It has sometimes been claimed that Mendelssohn turned his attention to the oratorio form as a result of his well-known enthusiasm and propaganda work for Bach's music. This, however, is not wholly true because, during his lifetime, Mendelssohn not only continually performed Handel's oratorios but actually rescored certain works. Moreover, the dramatic effects in the first part of *St Paul*, the 'Watchman Scene' in *The Hymn of Praise*, the conflict between the priests of Baal and the Prophet, and the coming of the rain in *Elijah* remind one more of Handel than of Bach, though it is scarcely necessary to add that none of Mendelssohn's oratorios can be classed with the works of those two supreme masters.

Mendelssohn's genius should not be belittled, but it is hardly to be found at its best in the oratorios. The charm of Mendelssohn is to be sought mainly in his lyricism, his admirable sense of orchestral colour. Traces of these qualities, of course, can be found in the oratorios, especially in *Elijah*, in which many of the choruses are admirably and most expressively written; but Mendelssohn did not possess either the religious depth of Bach or the dramatic sense of Handel. His piety, entirely genuine though it was, was too apt to degenerate into a kind of smugness, and the dramatic qualities of *Elijah* consist in reality of the picturesque and the effective rather than of the genuinely dramatic. There is no denying, however, their complete success within their own confines.§

As against Mendelssohn, the works of Spohr do not rate very high, but Schumann's *Paradies und die Peri* (1843) and, more importantly, the 'Scenes from Goethe's *Faust*' (1844–53), the latter somewhere between oratorio and opera, contain much beautiful music even though they lack formal and dramatic unity. Liszt's *The Legend of St Elisabeth* (1865) and his *Via Crucis* (1879) are choral mirrors of his later symphonic style. They show him attempting to put his strange mysticism into practical form in his music. In *Via Crucis* he fulfils his aim to a considerable extent by allying his new harmonic technique to old liturgical forms. The result is deeply moving. *Christus*, a late oratorio, shows his reaction to the Bible story, a very individual reaction expressed again in a strange amalgamation of Gregorian Plainchant and romantic orchestral colouring. The once popular sacred works of Gounod and César Franck have fallen almost entirely from favour; so have those of Stanford and Parry. The oratorio tradition has gone into a severe decline.

10 MOSTLY OF REQUIEMS (1835–1900)

During the 19th century composers tended to concentrate on secular music – symphonic, operatic, chamber and concerto. Their religious works usually conformed in style to their secular ones. Thus Rossini in his Stabat Mater (1842) and his *Petite Messe Solennelle* (1863), a 'joke' title as it is not particularly small and certainly anything but solemn, built on his previously successful but now defunct operatic style, for that was the only honest way he could work. For all that, neither work is any less devout than if he had attempted something more 'serious', while both are filled with music of vitality and character.

At the other extreme to these basically undemonstrative works comes Berlioz's Requiem (*Grande Messe des Morts*, 1837). This involves huge forces, encompassing strange and impressive sonorities peculiar to the composer, but also includes passages of the utmost refinement. Berlioz is bold in his mixture of styles and textures, but everything borrowed has been brought securely under his own individual umbrella and he imposes a certain unity on the mainly disparate sections. It is understandable that Berlioz averred that he would, if granted the choice, permit this work to be saved from destruction above all his others. Among those, his *Te Deum* is another powerful choral outpouring, and *L'enfance du Christ* is a sensitive, often arrestingly beautiful creation (especially in the 'Shepherds' Chorus' and tenor's description of the 'Repos de Jésus'). The dramatic legend, *La Damnation de Faust*, is another original, and in this case inspiriting work, alive to the inner meaning of its inspiration in Goethe and full of keen incident. Although it does not lend itself to, and was not intended for, stage representation, it might well be suited to imaginative film or television treatment. Other works by Berlioz require choral forces, but fall more easily into discussion of his orchestral music.

Verdi's Requiem (1873) which has become the most popular work in the choral repertory after the *Messiah*, and a certain sell-out whoever the performers, is quite as overwhelming an experience in a great rendering as Berlioz's and less ambitious as far as requisite forces are concerned. Again a composer is true to his nature in a religious work – Verdi was, in any case, an agnostic – and the piece represents with as great a sincerity as success the fundamental characteristics of his mentality, a utilization by a master of drama of the words of the liturgy to express his profound emotions. Similarly with Brahms's *Ein Deutsches Requiem* (1868), although this is not strictly a Requiem at all but a setting of certain passages from the Bible. If its consolation today can sometimes seem a little obvious and comfortable, the expression comes from the depth of Brahms's being, and its polyphonic excellence in the choruses is self-evident. It has rightly overshadowed his other choral works of which *Schicksalslied* (The Song of Destiny) (1871) is possibly the most successful. The *Alto*

Rhapsody (1870) as its name suggests, is more solo than choral; it, too, is a piece of profound sentiments cogently expressed. Verdi's last major work, the *Four Sacred Pieces*, is a moving summation of his life's achievement.

Unlike Verdi and Brahms, Bruckner was constantly and consistently true to his faith and addressed his series of Masses to the greater glory of God. In style not dissimilar to his symphonies, they are products of a mind that becomes more singular and impressive the more you investigate it, and was almost certainly grossly underrated until the latter half of this century. His Masses were mostly written in the early part of his career while he was an organist at Linz. Of these, the ones in D minor, E minor and F minor have every right to be in the mainstream of choral writing and performance for their structural unity and glorious manner. The first and last are big, symphonic pieces requiring a large orchestra. They are in the direct line from Beethoven and Schubert, while at the same time owing a debt in his own time to his beloved Wagner. The Mass in E minor explores, as do the composer's ethereal motets, the link between old modes and mid-19th-century tonality. It is written for eight-part choir with wind accompaniment. After moving to Vienna, Bruckner wrote two further choral works of distinction, the Te Deum and a setting of Psalm 150, both massive in their greater glorification of God.

Dvořák, although not chiefly admired for his sacred music, wrote several religious works displaying his deeply-held conviction in music of sincerity and beauty. The suffering of the Stabat Mater (1880) inspired him to a suitably profound setting and his Requiem (written for Birmingham in 1891) does not deserve the neglect into which it has fallen. There are passages of conventional 19th-century sentimentality in all his sacred works but many more of surpassing beauty. The same could be said of *St Ludmila*, a big-scale oratorio in which Dvořák makes subtle use of representative themes. His setting of Psalm 149 for male-voice choir and orchestra is a magnificent paeon of praise in C major aptly reflecting the general sense rather than the detail of the text.

In France the religiosity of Gounod and César Franck was quite absent from Fauré's restrained treatment of a familiar text in his Requiem (1888). False dramatic gestures and puffed-up choral writing, which harm so much 19th-century choral writing, are here quite absent. Faith is expressed in simple, unadorned terms by a soprano and baritone soloist, chorus, organ and orchestra. Divine contemplation is all.

§ *The British Isles*

The term 'folk-song' connotes the melodies sung as a spontaneous expression of the musical feeling of the people. The tunes are anonymous, often indigenous, and traditional, and in any region there will be found groups of songs conforming to a pattern as well as variants of individual melodies, since the songs have been preserved by oral tradition, not fixed by publication. Yet such is the strength of oral tradition among an illiterate people and a naturally conservative class that Cecil Sharp found songs and dances in the Appalachian Mountains of America differing hardly at all from those persisting in England, despite the lapse of several centuries since the ancestors of the present inhabitants left England. Indeed, according to Sharp, the traditions had been preserved more strictly in those remote places than in their native land, where contacts with modern developments were more easy. Although it was possible seventy years ago to find in England villages where some of the inhabitants had never been in a train nor gone further afield than their own feet or a horse could take them, mass travel abolished such isolation, and the ubiquitous radio and records brought symphony and pop song without discrimination into every home. Folk-music, spontaneously created, is, at any rate in England, a thing of the past, superseded by pop music, usually written according to stereotyped patterns. Even its spontaneous performance is rare. It belongs now to the specialists – a thing to be revived by societies, and by singers practising the art as a commercial proposition.

Some of the songs that have survived are of great antiquity, as is evident both from the modal character of the music and from the words, which have often become so corrupt as to lose their meaning. The numerical songs, constructed on the 'House that Jack built' principle, seem to have been educational, designed to inculcate the elements of theology and so on. 'I will sing you one, oh!' and 'The partridge in a pear-tree' are familiar examples of these cumulative songs, in which the words have so far been corrupted by oral transmission, the child imitating incorrectly the sounds made by his father, that only expert philologists can hope to unravel their meaning with the aid of versions existing in other countries.

English folk-song has generally been characterized by directness and simplicity, healthy jollity and contented humour. The music is free from excessive ornament and eccentricities of rhythm. The subjects of the songs are usually the homely ones of the countryside – hunting, poaching, the employments of agriculture and, of course, love-making, which is expressed with tenderness rather than passion. Other songs deal with the pathetic subjects of youth cut off in its flower and of maidens deserted by false lovers. In these songs there is often a peculiar eeriness that may be accounted among the most remarkable characteristics of English folk-song. In form the majority of these songs conform to the A–A–B–A design – a statement repeated twice, a contrasting phrase and a return to the original theme. Even before the revival of interest in folk-song created by modern enthusiasts, a great many traditional melodies had been preserved in collections like the *Fitzwilliam Virginal Book*, and Playford's *Dancing Master* and in *The Beggar's Opera*.

The folk-songs of Scotland, Ireland and Wales have each a distinctive character, though they are related to one another by their common Celtic origin. In contrast with the songs of England, those of the Scottish Highlands are wild and irregular in rhythm. The older specimens are rhapsodical recitatives rather than songs and show little or no attempt at rhythm or formal shape. Of the Lowland music there is no record before the 17th century, though it is probable that some of the melodies then written down are of a much earlier date. A few of them are written in the pentatonic scale; others are modal, the Dorian and Aeolian being prevalent. It may be mentioned that the 'Scotch Snap', which consists of a semiquaver followed by a dotted quaver, is not a general characteristic of Scottish music, but is confined to certain dance-rhythms, such as the Strathspey Reel, though it appears occasionally in songs based upon these dance-tunes, e.g. 'Green grow the rushes, O'. The snap was incorporated in the common musical language of Europe by Italian composers of the 18th century, and was much used by Mozart, Beethoven and Mendelssohn.

The music of Ireland is more melodious than that of Scotland and either more plaintive or more light-hearted than that of England. Few countries can boast anything more beautiful than the long melody known as 'The Londonderry Air' and sometimes called 'Emer's Farewell to Cuchullain'. For the preservation of a vast quantity of Irish music we have to thank Thomas Moore, who collaborated in the publication of seven volumes of songs for which he wrote the words, as Robert Burns did for many melodies of Scotland.

In view of the long tradition of music in Wales and the natural beauty of Welsh voices, we should expect to find there an exceptionally rich treasure of folk-music. But Welsh music is on the whole disappointing. There are a few fine melodies, but they are exceptions, and artistically the Welsh songs are less interesting than those of other parts of the British Isles. The popular 'March of the Men of Harlech' is quite characteristic of Welsh melody, both in its lack of subtlety and in the stirring effect of the tune as a whole. This tune contains in its final phrase an example of the 'Scotch snap'.

§ *Europe and America*

When we cross the Channel to France we find a folk-music with more artifice in it. The graceful and charming *chansons* have wit and polish. There are, of course, other styles, as is only to be expected of a nation containing peoples so diverse as the Provençals, the Bretons and the Gascons. There are serene songs like the beautiful 'Angelus' collected by M. Bourgault-Ducoudray in Brittany, which might be the musical counterpart of Millet's famous picture, and there are tougher, more racy songs from Auvergne. There are, too, simple, unaffected songs from Normandy and delightful children's songs and lullabies from the South. Cumulative and enumerative songs also occur, and the existence of 'La Perdriole' on the North Coast suggests a French origin for our 'Partridge in a pear-tree'.

The Italians, too, show much variety in their folk-songs, ranging from the barcarolles of the Venetian gondoliers, and the street-songs of Naples, which have furnished the models for a hundred popular operatic airs, to the music of Sicily, where there are still to be found traces of the old Hellenic civilization, besides the influences of other races that have from time to time established themselves in that much occupied island. The folk-songs of modern Greece seem to have no connection with the ancient culture, but are of Byzantine and liturgical origin.

In Spain the influence of foreign culture is even more obvious. The *Cante hondo* of Andalusia, with its narrow compass and reiterations of short phrases, is clearly a relic of the Moorish occupation, though its Oriental character lies rather in the manner of its performance than in the melodic material. As a whole the folk-music of Spain, in contradistinction to that of Italy, is instrumental and rhythmical rather than vocal. It is essentially music to be danced to, and singing plays a subsidiary part. A false notion of Spanish music has been widely disseminated through the use of a few well-worn clichés by European composers in search of exotic ornaments with which to

473

deck out their trite ideas. But this notion was corrected by the music of men like de Falla, Granados and Albéniz, who showed, especially the first-named, that Spanish music is not a pretty affair of a high comb and a shawl to be donned at will, but something harsh, cruel and passionate.

Russia is enormously rich in folk-music, and, because of the peculiarly backward condition of her musical culture in the 19th century, her composers were able to turn that wealth to good account in a way that could not be achieved (though it has been attempted) in a more advanced country like our own. One characteristic of Russian folk-song is its fondness for reiterated phrases, which it shares with Spanish folk-song. Another is its frequent use of uneven measures (five beats in the bar), a feature conditioned by the peculiarities of the language, which inevitably has an enormous influence upon the folk-songs of any country. The popular vogue of Russian music seventy-five years ago was due, like the similar vogue of Spanish music, to its strange and exotic character, but it was not long before the short phrases repeated again and again, and the halting rhythms, at first so exciting, began to pall upon our ears, and made us once more realize that there was, after all, some merit in continuity and shapeliness.

The music of Czechoslovakia and of Hungary has attractions and limitations similar to that of Russia, though each, and especially the Hungarian, has a very distinctive character of its own. Hungarian music, which is not to be confused with the gypsy-music that has so often passed for it, is, indeed, as distinct from other European music as the Magyar language is philologically unrelated to any others except those of Finland and Turkey. Bartók and Kodály, both in their educational and research work in this field, and in their practical example, acknowledged the significance of their country's folk heritage. It is strongly rhythmical and, like the Spanish, essentially dance-music. The characteristics of Czech folk-music can be found in familiar works by Dvořák and Smetana, but with the warning that while Bohemia joined in the Western development of culture, Southern Moravia and Slovakia remained in contact with the East. Two different trends are therefore observable in Czech and Slovak music.

German folk-songs are of an intimate and homely kind. They are sentimental but vigorous, and, in spite of their simplicity, highly organized and compact. It is, indeed, but a step from the folk-song to the art-song or *Lied* of the great composers. It is quite impossible, for instance, to detect, except by external evidence, which of Brahms's strophic songs are based upon traditional melodies and which are entirely his own invention. Indeed, the whole of German music from Bach down to Mahler is intimately based upon the idioms of national melody. Haydn, consciously or not, made frequent use of Croatian folk-melodies in his compositions.§

American folk-song falls into two kinds, that of European and that of African origin. During the early part of the 20th century much field work was done in collecting and collating in the various localities of the US where groups of immigrants from one area had been established. Another tradition is that of the ballad, stemming originally from England and developing or declining into the hill-billy. Many solo singers in more recent times, such as Bob Dylan, have carried on from there to create a kind of neo-folk music of their own. Out of the suffering of the blacks in the 19th century emerged the spiritual, often but tenuously derived from African originals. Indeed the Negro music was often infiltrated by European influences.

§ *Carols*

Akin to folk-songs are carols, which are religious folk-songs celebrating the chief festivals of the Church, and not necessarily connected with the season of Christmas. Many of the finest English examples, indeed, are not Christmas carols, even though some of them have in recent times become associated with that season. The sentimental words of 'Good King Wenceslas' were fitted by a worthy clergyman of the last century to the beautiful melody of the spring *cantio* 'Adest tempus floridum' ('Now the time of flowers is here'), which is at least 350 years old. And among the finest is the lovely 'Corpus Christi Carol', which attains a mystical beauty and an eeriness unsurpassed in any other music. Another carol connected with the same festival is the 'Coventry Carol', which was sung at the Coventry Nativity Play on Corpus Christi Day. Many so-called Christmas carols celebrate the secular side of the festival, such as 'The Boar's Head Carol' and the Wassail-songs, which date from pre-Christian days.

The mediaeval carol was made up of uniform stanzas and provided with a burden which began the piece and was repeated after each stanza. The carols were processional dance-songs, usually performed, as nowadays, during a house-to-house collection (*quète*) of money or food and drink. The dance element is obvious in such carols as 'The Holly and the Ivy'. The words were either in the vernacular or in mediaeval Latin, and sometimes macaronic – that is, a mixture of the two. For instance, 'Orientis partibus', which was sung at Sens and Beauvais in the 13th century, has a refrain in the vernacular.

Among other nations the French are most rich in carols or 'Noëls'. Many of these have what were originally secular melodies, and we need not be shocked at the discovery that the tune of the rollicking Drinking Song in *The Beggar's Opera* belongs to a 'Noël', for Pepusch was only putting the tune to its original purpose. A far less suitable adaptation is that of the joyous Christmas hymn 'Freuet euch ihr Christen alle' to the doleful Lenten 'Forty days and forty nights'. English hymnody has, indeed, borrowed freely from the carols and Christmas chorales of Germany, whose church music is rich in noble melodies suitable for congregational singing. From Germany, too, come many beautiful cradle-songs, associated with the Nativity.

12 EUROPEAN SONG IN THE 19TH CENTURY

§ *Introduction*

Songs of all countries already showed during the 18th, if not the 17th, century the main outlines of the characteristics that were subsequently to distinguish them. Mainly, of course, the basis of song in all nations is folk-music. The extent of the influence of the folk-music, however, varies in each country. It was very strong in Germany and Russia; less strong in France and Italy, and comparatively slight in England. In England, for instance, there has on various occasions been a struggle between the vocal models imported from abroad (in the main from Italy and Germany) and folk or national songs. The success of the ballad operas in general, and of *The Beggar's Opera* in particular, was perhaps the most noteworthy instance of a reaction against vocal forms of an origin foreign to England. 18th-century composers, such as Dibdin and Arne, not to mention many of those who provided songs for the entertainments at the famous Vauxhall Gardens, may at least claim credit for having preserved in their music a genuine English flavour, subsequently lost in the perhaps more scholarly but less attractive vocal compositions of the latter part of the 19th century.

In Italy folk-song has always been kept alive in the various provinces but with little effect, so far as one can see, on what would nowadays be termed 'serious' music. Indeed, the history of Italian song, glorious as it is, is identified in practice with the history of the opera, so that it mostly lies outside the scope of this part of *The Musical Companion*. Certain songs written by Rossini after his retirement, such as 'La Regata Veneziana' and the wonderful tarantella known as 'La Danza', should, however, perhaps be mentioned as exceptional.

The characteristics of French song in the 17th and 18th century up to the time of the Revolution are well known. The French have always had a special gift and affection for the art of the *chansonnier*, apparent at the very outset. The 19th-century composer and editor Jean-Baptiste Weckerlin made a collection of songs of this period. They show all the typical characteristics of French chansons – malicious, tender, usually gallant, sometimes definitely lascivious, always elegant. With the advent of the Revolution these attributes vanished, giving place to political songs that emphasized the civic virtues and the glories of democracy. Nevertheless, in their very reaction, these revolutionary *chansons* were the lineal descendants of the songs of the monarchical age, serving, together with them, to fix the characteristics of French song as a whole.

Though the outstanding features of French song preserved many of the typical features of French folk-music, the two were rarely so inextricably intertwined as in Germany. At the beginning of the 17th century, when solo songs first seem to have made their appearance there, it is often difficult to tell exactly where folk-song ends and art song begins. Italian operatic influences may at times have made themselves felt, but the exceptionally intimate connection between the *Lied* and the folk-song persisted, not only in the compositions of rather shadowy figures such as Kirnberger and Sperontes (who have been hailed as the real begetters of the *Lied* in that they first set different verses differently and varied the accompaniments), but in the songs of the comparatively late 18th-century composers, of whom Hiller and Schulz may be regarded as the patriarchs. As a matter of fact the influence of folk-song remained exceptionally strong in all the masters of the German *Lied* up to, and including, Brahms and Mahler; apart from any question of general feeling and sentiment, this is shown by the diatonic character of much of the music and the almost aggressive prevalence of four-square rhythm.§

German song

For most people the German *Lied* begins with Schubert. There were, however, songs of the first importance written before his day, particularly by Haydn, whose classical simplicity of form often hid deeper emotions. Of his twelve English canzonets, 'She never told her love', a setting to words from *Twelfth Night*, is particularly eloquent.

Mozart wrote at least two masterpieces in pure song form, 'Abend-empfindung' and 'Das Veilchen'; Beethoven wrote several very fine songs, notably 'Wonne der Wehmut' and 'Vom Tode', apart from that song cycle in embryo, *An die ferne Geliebte*. Still, the fact remains that both these composers rose to far greater heights in other fields, whereas Schubert is immortal as much for his songs as for any other part of his marvellous music.

§ Of all the musicians who ever lived Schubert excelled the most in grasping, as it were, in the twinkling of an eye, the salient character-istics of a poem and wedding them, almost as he read, to music ideally adapted to the human voice. As a rule the fundamental im-pulse was lyrical; but by no means always. There are songs that are definitely dramatic, even to the extent of employing recitative; there are songs that are pictorial, descriptive, even philosophical; but in all of them, whatever their character, it is generally true to say that the process of manufacture was not so much intellectual as instinctive, almost unconscious, if you will. Doubtless Schubert's lack of purely technical training has been exaggerated, but two things about him cannot be exaggerated: his natural facility and his inaptitude for what, for lack of a better term, may be defined as self-criticism. In their combination these characteristics sum up his countless merits and few defects as a song-composer.

Examples that prove his facility and instinctiveness are so numer-ous that we cannot even begin to cite them. The mere number of his songs (of which he wrote in his short life nearly 600, representative of every kind of mood: grave, gay, passionate, tender, simple and com-plicated) provides the most striking evidence of them. He could and did write songs as easily as the average person writes a letter and, like Rossini, he would have found no difficulty in setting anything, even a laundry bill, to music.

The song, 'Gretchen am Spinnrade', alone suffices to illustrate to perfection Schubert's extraordinary natural gifts. It is difficult to understand how any boy of seventeen, even a Mendelssohn or a Mozart, could have written such a song, but it is impossible to offer any rational explanation as to how a raw, inexperienced youth like Schubert produced a masterpiece of this kind. Nor does this parti-cular song stand alone, for in the following year, when he was only eighteen, he wrote no less than 100 songs of which such masterpieces as 'Erlkönig', 'Rastlose Liebe', 'Meeresstille', and 'Wanderers Nachtlied' remain outstanding examples. Still, 'Gretchen am Spinn-rade' came first in point of date and may usefully be cited as typical of Schubert's earlier production. To begin with, by his accompaniment to this song Schubert may be said to have revolutionized the whole of German *Lied*. Never before had a German song-writer achieved such expressive and, it may be added, such difficult writing for the piano. That in itself is remarkable enough, but in reality, perhaps, the capacity shown to enter into the subtle feelings of Goethe's heroine was more remarkable still. Indeed, it is doubtful if such an emotional achievement on the part of a youth in his teens can be paralleled in the whole history of music.

Now there can be no question that this miracle – for a miracle it remains – was a miracle of instinct. During the subsequent years Schubert somewhat developed his technical resources, but he can scarcely be said ever to have produced a song more satisfactory as an entity. Or, if this statement be considered too strong, let us say that he never produced a song that was better except in degree – 'Der Atlas', for instance, or 'Der Leiermann' or 'Der Doppelgänger'.

Another point also is worth noting. It was in his earliest years that Schubert chiefly set to music the words of Goethe, needless to say by far the best words that ever came his way. In later life his choice of words became less, not more, satisfactory. Apart from isolated instances too numerous to mention, take his two famous song-cycles, *Die schöne Müllerin* and *Winterreise*, both collections of poems by Wilhelm Müller. If these words are examined with an unprejudiced eye they will be seen as what they are: the self-pitying sentiments of a second-rate poet. Yet, in fact, the inferior quality of these words seems to have made little difference to Schubert's inspiration, for some of his greatest masterpieces are to be found precisely in these two song-cycles. Words as words must have meant very little to Schubert; he often set them with a callous disregard of stress and accent. All that he demanded was that a poet should provide, as it were, the spark to light his musical imagination. Whether that spark was a Müller or a Goethe remained practically immaterial; we cannot even be certain that he was conscious of any qualitative difference between the two. The unerring instinct of his genius, however, was such that he in fact interpreted the general sense of a poem, with an insight difficult to parallel among song-writers. Sometimes, as for instance in 'An Schwager Kronos' and 'Geheimes', he achieved almost by accident a perfect unison between the music and the individual words as such. Generally speaking, however, it is as the interpreter of a mood, an emotion or a situation that Schubert remains the supreme master.

With the reservations indicated above, Schubert is undoubtedly the greatest of song-writers. To those who regard melody pure and simple as the most important factor, outweighing all others, he is undoubtedly the greatest song-writer without any reservation whatever. The spontaneity, the variety and the originality of Schubert's melodic gift cannot be exaggerated, but his inspiration was not exclusively confined to the vocal line. The importance of the piano part in 'Gretchen am Spinnrade' has already been emphasized, but only because it provided the first outstanding example of his methods in this respect. There are countless other instances. For instance, the accompaniment in 'Die Forelle' typifies the play of a fish in a brook, the triplets in 'Erlkönig' convey the breathless horror of the poem's atmosphere. His harmony, too, is as happy as are his figures, being almost always perfectly adapted to the mood and the sentiment he wishes to convey, particularly in his arresting use of modulation. Small wonder, then, that Schubert's influence can be traced in the works of every song-writer who came after him. Sometimes it is more, sometimes less, marked; but it is always there. He set a standard. He is the very foundation and embodiment of the German *Lied* as we know it.

Mendelssohn's songs are marred by a certain weakness that has been, not unjustly, dubbed effeminacy. Nevertheless, some half dozen of them are wholly charming: the graceful 'Der Blumenkranz', for instance, and 'Suleika', not to mention the familiar 'Auf Flügeln des Gesanges'. The duets for female voices, despite their hackneyed associations, show Mendelssohn at his best as a vocal writer. 'Gruss' and 'Ich wollt' Meine Liebe' may be sentimental, but they are very pretty; 'Abschiedslied der Zugvögel' is a model of delicacy, and the once so familiar 'Maiglöckchen und die Blümelein' is almost worthy to rank with the *Midsummer Night's Dream* music.§

Franz is a composer of lighter calibre, almost entirely neglected nowadays, but the sincerity and the lyrical charm of his simple songs, which are largely in strophic form, deserve a better fate. In a sense Loewe is the most important of the minor song-writers, because he created the German dramatic ballad. His setting of 'Erlkönig' does not suffer entirely in comparison with Schubert's, and his interpretation of the text is in many ways effective. Others that deserve attention are 'Edward' and the grand-scale 'Odins Meerestritt'. He was also quite capable of writing light-hearted humorous pieces, such as 'Die Wandelnde Glocke', and the ingenious 'Hinkende Jamben'.

§ Nevertheless Robert Schumann must be regarded the legitimate successor to Schubert. His career as a song-writer was very curious in that it was practically confined to the year 1840, when he suddenly wrote more than 130 vocal pieces, having up to that time, as he himself admitted, rather despised song-writing than otherwise. There is an intimate charm, an elegiac tenderness about Schumann's best songs that cannot be surpassed even in the glorious annals of the *Lied*. One has only to think of the most familiar numbers of the song-cycle, *Dichterliebe*, the exquisite 'Frühlingsnacht', 'Mondnacht', and 'Schöne Fremde' from the op. 39 *Liederkreis*. On the other hand, there is something self-conscious in his deliberate essays in the folk-song manner, which sometimes seem almost a parody of themselves; the settings of Burns appear to an Englishman, at any rate, very artificial, and some of the *Frauenliebe und Leben* cycle is rather sentimental, chiefly because of the weak verse, though the sad, final song is eloquent indeed. There are one or two things that Schumann achieved as a song-writer more successfully than any of his predecessors or contemporaries. His sense of literary values, to begin with, is decidedly more intimate. More striking still, perhaps, is his capacity to intertwine the vocal line and its accompaniment on the piano so as to construct a perfect unity of expression. Two songs, very different from one another, both show this characteristic to perfection: 'Der Nussbaum', which everybody knows, and another, 'Hidalgo', which is not so well known as it should be. Altogether Schumann's handling of his accompaniments must be regarded as even more successful than his handling of melody. This is scarcely a matter of surprise in a composer who wrote so much and so successfully for the piano. The paradox remains that a little gem like the piano-epilogue to the *Dichterliebe*, so satisfying, so exactly right, remains, perhaps, the most striking attribute of Schumann's as a song-writer!

Brahms is the next great exponent of the German *Lied*. His vocal compositions in lyrical form, not counting his arrangements of folk-songs, constitute approximately one-third of his total output, and they are part of his mastery as a miniaturist, also to be found in his piano pieces, especially the late ones. Brahms's music, like that of Schubert, possesses a natural affinity with German folk-song. There is nothing self-conscious in his approach to it; it was a part of his being. Even when, as in 'Vergebliches Ständchen', the piano accompaniment to a folk-song theme is comparatively elaborate, it is just the right kind of elaboration; the spirit remains exactly akin to the original. It was doubtless this love of folk-song that prompted

Brahms, despite the elaboration of most of his songs, to declare that in his heart he preferred the simplicity of the strophic form. Lastly, he shared with Schubert a tendency to look at words primarily from the musical point of view, rather than with any great appreciation of their literary value as such. His superior education saved him from Schubert's worst lapses in this respect, but his treatment of stress and accent is sometimes equally cavalier. However, in what may be called the alliance of literature and music, Brahms is not the equal of Schumann.

One of the outstanding characteristics of Brahms's vocal output is its wide range, but the range is one, as has been well said, rather of musical than of emotional material. Many people must have felt conscious of the fact that Brahms's music reflects the limited emotional experience of his life, so that passion seems almost a closed book to him, though he comes near to it in some of the *Magelonelieder*. Generally speaking, however, the theme of his best love-songs may be defined as being rather placid or introspective; 'Nicht mehr zu dir zu gehen' and 'Sapphische Ode' are examples of such songs at their best.

In many instances the addition of melodic inspiration to Brahms's excellent workmanship has endeared the songs to professionals and amateurs alike. 'Wie bist du, meine Königin', 'Feldeinsamkeit', 'Ständchen', 'Immer leiser wird mein Schlummer', 'Botschaft', are instances selected at random that show his all-round appeal. The fact is that nowhere, perhaps, more strikingly than in his best songs did Brahms display his personal melodic gift to greater advantage.§

Brahms reached the pinnacle of his accomplishments as a song-writer in the *Vier ernste Gesänge*, four beautiful songs that constitute an essay in philosophic resignation akin to the mood of the *Requiem*. Lastly, there are the delightful *Liebesliederwalzer*, written for four solo voices and piano duet accompaniment, and *Zigeunerlieder*. The former are a wholly admirable embodiment of the Viennese waltz that sprang from the *Ländler* of Schubert and his contemporaries; the latter reproduce to perfection the ardour and the flaunting colours of 'Hungarian' gypsy music.

§ Hugo Wolf was practically contemporary with Brahms, a composer whom he, as an ardent disciple of Wagner, cordially disliked. Of all his predecessors Wolf owes most, perhaps, to Schumann, though it would be unwise to exclude altogether the influence of Liszt, who is of far greater importance as a song-writer than is usually realized, having achieved half a dozen first-rate compositions in the form.

In a sense, however, Wolf is akin to no other German writer of *Lieder*, even his purely musical treatment being often associated with the new *leitmotiv* procedure of Wagner's music-dramas and Liszt's symphonic poems, and he succeeded in attaining a perfect parity of interest between the vocal and the instrumental parts of his songs. As we have seen, many of the German song-writers, notably Schumann, attached great importance to the piano, but none of them carried the principle so far as Wolf. The piano parts of his songs are not only as important as the vocal ones, but often seem to be almost complete in themselves. At the same time the vocal parts, though rarely lyrical in the Brahms–Schubert manner, are delightful to sing for anyone able to grasp the principles of their wonderfully plastic line.

Wolf was fastidious in his choice of poems, and notable for the skill, unrivalled before or since, with which he handled words. There is no question here of a worthless poem being chosen as a kind of peg on which to hang the music. It is the poem itself that fixes the style and the contours of the music. No composer has ever equalled Wolf in his psychological penetration of literary meaning. Alike in the fifty-three songs by Mörike, the forty-seven by Goethe and the twenty by Eichendorff that he set to music, his grasp of the implications of a poem is almost uncanny; just as in the thirty-four songs of the *Spanisches Liederbuch* and, even more, in the forty-four songs of the *Italienisches Liederbuch* his grasp of the fleeting colours and moods of the words is almost uncanny. No kind of style or subject seems alien to him. Moreover, he is able to suggest an atmosphere or depict a situation with the economy of means that comes from the highest possible degree of concentration.

As we might expect in a musician of such literary perspicacity, his actual handling of the words was invariably conscientious in the highest degree. It is difficult to find in any of his songs a stress that is unjustified or an accent that is misplaced. Of none of his predecessors, not even of Schumann, can this be said, so that this new respect for words as such should be singled out as Wolf's most important contribution to musical development.

From the technical point of view so many of Wolf's songs are perfect that it seems futile to single out even half a dozen of them as masterpieces. In the case of such a composer, so skilled, so completely a master of his medium, the final appraisal of the song depends on the extent to which the musical ideas themselves seem more or less felicitous because, in every analyzable attribute, Wolf's work is almost invariably beyond criticism. The musical value of a phrase, however, remains in the last resort, unanalyzable. In the hands of Wolf's successors and imitators his methods have often been successfully copied, but their ultimate musical value has very rarely been the same. Those who love and admire Wolf's songs claim that at their best they are the greatest of all. Inevitably among his output there are inequalities; sometimes the treatment is laboured; sometimes the means seem disproportionate to the end. As a collection, however, Wolf's songs strike a balance between idea and treatment as perfect as that achieved by any other master.§

Strauss's contribution to the song repertory comes third to his work in the operatic and orchestral fields. He shows craftsmanship and insight into the poems he has set, though the quality of his songs varies with that of his texts, and he writes gratefully for the voice. No one can deny the sensuous beauty of such songs as 'Traum durch die Dämmerung', 'Morgen', 'Freundliche Vision' and 'Ich trage meine Minne'. The charm of their melodies and the picturesque aptness of their accompaniments make them a valuable addition to the corpus of German lyrics. In his old age he summed up his affection for the soprano voice in the *Four Last Songs* with orchestra, an outpouring of pure lyricism, deeply moving in its expressiveness, that proved him to be no 'extinct volcano'. Strauss had also shown that he could outballad the ballad-mongers with 'Zueignung', which is everything that a popular sentimental song should be.

Those who find Mahler's symphonies too much of a good thing usually have a kind word for his songs, the argument being that when restricted by the limits of poetic form he was less able to indulge his penchant for sprawling construction. Be that as it may, his contribution to the genre is both consistent and appreciable, right from the early and neglected (until recent years) *Das klagende Lied* (1880) for soprano, alto and tenor soloists, chorus and orchestra, which shows his style already well on the way to its mature state, down to *Das Lied von der Erde* (1908), a work that would place him high in the Valhalla of composers even if he had written nothing else.

The earliest of his regularly heard song groups for soloist and orchestra is *Lieder eines fahrenden Gesellen*, in which the brilliance and range of his vocal and instrumental characterization is already evident as well as his extraordinary gift for creating mood. His next settings were of the old German folk poetry of *Des Knaben Wunderhorn* (1888), for two soloists and orchestra, which range from the grotesque and fantastic to the ingenuous and charming. The *Kindertotenlieder*, for low voice and orchestra, is a moving cycle to poems

484

by Rückert depicting the emotions of a parent on the loss of his children, subjective expression at its most sublime.

Das Lied von der Erde is, however, Mahler's crowning achievement in this field. It is a setting for tenor, contralto (or baritone) and orchestra of six German translations of ancient Chinese poems, which Mahler transmutes into a work of symphonic proportions and raises, emotionally, into his farewell to life and beauty (he did not live to hear the work performed). The orchestral colouring is as elaborate as that in any of his symphonies, yet – except possibly in the first song – the writing is mostly fastidious, and often very delicate. By its side, the setting of the Latin hymn, 'Veni, Creator Spiritus' and of sections of Goethe's *Faust* for eight soloists and a huge chorus and orchestra in the Eighth Symphony (1907) sound overblown.

French song

After German *Lieder*, the French *mélodies* was the most important category of song composition during the 19th century. The genre did not, however, derive from its German counterpart, but stemmed from the 'romance' that had developed in France from the middle of the previous century and profoundly influenced the earlier work of Berlioz and Gounod. Berlioz was, in fact, the first to use the word *mélodie* as a title for a composition for one voice and piano; it is always used to designate a 'serious' song from then on, *chanson* being the word for a simpler, more popular, usually folk-inspired piece.

In speaking of his contribution to song-writing in France, Berlioz commented that his pieces 'have nothing of the form or style of Schubert'. They owe much more to the influence of theatre music of the early part of the 19th century. His most important contribution to this field is undoubtedly the *Nuits d'été*, six settings of the poet Théophile Gautier, first published with piano accompaniment in 1841 and later orchestrated (most eloquently). Although often sung by a single type of voice, Berlioz ideally intended them to be divided between soprano, mezzo, tenor and bass. They are typical examples of Berlioz's sensuous, sinuous writing for the voice, and the four central songs are profoundly romantic in flavour, pensive and elegiac too. Earlier, Berlioz had written the superbly dramatic lyric scene, *La Mort de Cléopatre* (1829), as his entry for the *Prix de Rome*; it proved far too revolutionary in harmony and general outline for the conservative judges. Other isolated songs, such as 'Sara la Baigneuse' (for chorus), 'La Captive' (soprano) and 'Zaïde' (soprano) are worth investigating for Berlioz's atmospheric matching of music to imaginative texts.

Gounod rather than Berlioz is the true begetter of the *mélodie* and among more than 200 songs, many deserve to be preserved, among them 'Venise', the beautifully contoured 'Sérénade' and 'Au Rossignol'. Those who would belittle Massenet should think of the grace and clarity of songs like 'Crépuscule', 'Les Oiselets', and, best of all, 'Si tu veux, mignonne'. Needless to say, the songs of both these composers are comparatively simple, being, often – especially in the case of Gounod – in pure strophic form, and delving but little into the more subtle implications of the poetry. They remain, in fact, exclusively lyrical.

§ Had Gounod and Massenet been in themselves of less importance then they were, they would be noteworthy for the influence they exercised on their successors. The most original of French composers, Debussy, never attempted to conceal his early debt to Massenet, while the earliest songs of Fauré, one of the greatest of French song-writers, bear evident traces of the influence of Gounod.

As a collection, the three volumes that contain Fauré's sixty separate songs, and the nine settings from Verlaine's poems grouped together under the title of *La Bonne Chanson*, are on a par with the vocal achievements of any other French song-writer. This may seem a bold statement in view of the pre-eminence rightly accorded to Debussy as a composer, but Debussy's songs are, perhaps, the least important feature of his work. He showed in them, as ever, an amazing sense of colour and great imagination in setting words to music but, generally speaking, the vocal line seems definitely subordinate in interest to the piano part, remaining more or less a study in free declamation. This is not true of his best songs such as 'Mandoline', 'Fantoches', 'La Chevelure' or 'Green', this last, incidentally, providing almost the only example among the many settings made by Debussy and Fauré of the same poems where the superiority may undoubtedly be assigned to Debussy. Nevertheless, his songs as a whole must be judged, despite their admirable and highly poetical qualities, somewhat deficient in true melodic inspiration.

As a song-writer pure and simple Reynaldo Hahn possesses great merit. Indeed, he has achieved the distinction, in his setting of Verlaine's beautiful poem, 'D'une Prison', of having produced a song more satisfactory than that written by Fauré to the same words. Still, his output as a whole is of too slight a calibre, too facile, if you will, despite its elegance and charm, to be compared with Fauré's achievement. Henri Duparc is a composer of far more serious import. Many people consider that his best songs, 'L'Invitation au Voyage', 'Phidylé' and half a dozen others, register the high-water mark of French vocal composition. The faultless quality of their workmanship has certainly not been surpassed, while their strength of utterance and intensity have, perhaps, not been equalled by any other French song-writer. Duparc, it is well known, himself destroyed most of his compositions, leaving only the sixteen songs by which the world now knows him.

Fauré, in his songs, can be said to have explored the whole avenue of intimate emotions, and to this extent the designation of him as the 'French Schumann' is not inept. He resembled Schumann, moreover, in his 'sweetest melancholy', though the care and discrimination with which he handled words was more akin to that of Wolf. Further, though Fauré's songs are full of sentiment, they are rarely sentimental, much less naïve. Nothing could be more French, alike in their grace, their clarity or their delicious sensibility.

From the purely musical point of view Fauré is remarkable for two things, notably the continuous evolution of his style. It is not till one becomes impregnated with the flavour of his musical personality that one can trace any connection between the first volume of his songs and the last collection called *La Chanson d'Eve*; his output between these two reflects the whole development of French music. Then there is the amazing suppleness of his modulation. It would be impossible to take any particular chord and say 'This is typical Fauré', but the manner in which he treats the sequence of harmonies remains entirely his own. 'Après un Rêve', 'Nell', 'Claire de Lune' are fine examples of the beauty of his melodic line; so are the less familiar 'C'est l'Extase' and 'En Sourdine' which, when their comparative complication has been mastered, can be seen to be equally remarkable, alike for their beauty of melody and for the subtle suggestion in the piano accompaniment. However, Fauré's masterpiece is *La Bonne Chanson*, wherein he showed an insight into the mind of Verlaine equal to Wolf's penetration into the meaning of Goethe and Mörike. These songs, too, apart from their exquisite workmanship, show a vitality, and what can only be described as a luminous quality rarely met with in the rest of his vocal compositions. Compared with the great German masters, Fauré's characteristics remain essentially feminine, one is almost tempted to describe his Muse, so distinguished, so refined, so subtly perfumed, as 'The Great Lady of European Song'. Of Fauré's contemporaries, Chabrier, Chausson and Roussel all contributed significantly and quite individually to the genre.§

Ravel's contribution to *mélodies* of just thirty-eight songs shows his usual fastidiousness, and they are all apt examples of his genius. The three poems with orchestra that comprise *Shéhérazade* are delicate evocations of the East. *Histoires Naturelles* are wonderful character studies of the animals depicted in Jules Renard's verse, subtle and appropriate in both colour and expression, while the arrangements of Greek, Spanish and Hebrew songs underline the style of the originals by their deft harmonization. *Don Quichotte à Dulcinée*, Ravel's last work, written in 1932, was originally intended for a film of Cervantes's classic with Chaliapin in the main role, but other songs were eventually used; a pity, because Ravel's marvellously mirror the old man's noble yet exasperating character.

Francis Poulenc virtually brought the history of *mélodies* to a close, and his finest songs are object lessons in the marriage between the French declamatory style and pure melodic gifts. As he himself wrote: 'The musical setting of a poem should be an act of love, never a marriage of convenience,' and he kept his word throughout more than 140 songs. If *C*, to words of Louis Aragon describing French people in 1940 fleeing their homeland before the invader, is his most moving piece, his settings of Guillaume Apollinaire and Paul Eluard, in their reflection of the poetry's humour and melancholy, are not far behind.

Other nations

The Russian School is remarkable not only for quantity but also for quality. Glinka and Dargomizhsky were the founding fathers, although earlier writers, such as Teplov, had composed rudimentary art songs at an earlier date and Alabiev was the instigator of the realistic vein in Russian song. Most of Glinka's successful pieces date from 1837–40, when he was resolved to 'write music in Russian' and did so in songs such as 'Midnight Review', 'Wedding Song' and four songs to Pushkin texts. More conventional, but utterly beautiful are some of his love lyrics. Although Tchaikovsky described Dargomizhsky as 'the supreme example of the dilettante in music', his songs – particularly the later ones – point the way to Mussorgsky's subordination of the music to the text.

Their successors were the so-called 'Mighty Handful': Balakirev, Cui, Borodin, Rimsky-Korsakov and the now-forgotten Lodizhensky. Influenced by Schumann and Liszt, this group of composers gave more emphasis to the piano's role, and they are apt to have instrumental melodies. Still, the best songs of Balakirev, who was probably closest to Glinka, and of Cui, who followed Dargomizhsky's manner in his detailed treatment of the text, deserve more attention than they usually receive, and Borodin's gifts of subtle figuration and soaring melody are often heard at their best in his songs.

§ Mussorgsky's art was much more rough-hewn than that of his contemporaries. Though he did, in fact, write some songs in purely lyrical form, his vocal art as a whole is characterized by a declamatory setting of words, the music serving primarily to throw the various points of the poem into the strongest possible relief. In this respect Mussorgsky showed genius of the highest order. Whether he is dealing with scenes from peasant life, as in so many of his songs, or with children, as in the *Nursery* cycle, or indulging in pure satire, as in *The Classicist*, he succeeds in painting a musical picture that for sheer vividness of colour and directness of expression can scarcely be matched in the whole range of vocal writing. Mussorgsky's songs possess a flavour all their own, and it has been claimed with some justice that in them may be found his most valuable attributes as a composer, in that it was in the imaginative setting of words that he particularly excelled. Certainly nowhere else, not even in *Boris Godunov*, does his music interpret with such uncanny genius the various characteristics of the Russian people that he delighted to portray. From the purely musical point of view, moreover, his very fidelity to the text served to correct a shapelessness often noticeable in his instrumental compositions.§

Tchaikovsky's songs are at the opposite pole to Mussorgsky's. He left more than 100, mostly lyrical outpourings of elegiac beauty, such as 'At the Ball', 'Cradle Song', and 'Do not leave me'. As Gerald Abraham has put it: 'He was a singer himself . . . and he refused to subordinate his music to the poem.' But Tchaikovsky chose good verse to set, and he was always faithful to the general mood of a poem. He himself wrote: 'The essential in vocal music is truthful reproduction of feeling and state of mind.'

Rachmaninov was a worthy successor to the mantle of Tchaikovsky. His songs again reflect a mood of Russian melancholy – and he too could capture the essence of a text, like all good song-writers – through his subtle writing for voice and piano, although the latter does tend to dominate the former, as one might expect from a virtuoso pianist-composer. Medtner, now almost forgotten, also wrote well for the voice, showing a refined style.

Both before and after the Revolution, Prokofiev wrote significant songs, particularly in his settings of Pushkin and Anna Akhmatova, and Shostakovich composed two or three poignant cycles, although song is not a major part of his output.

§ Grieg's songs form a very remarkable collection. Like Schubert, Grieg suffered from the defects of his qualities, and in far too many of his songs there is an abuse of the strophic form. Those, however, who think of him only as the composer of the popular 'I love thee', or 'Solvejg's Song', will be surprised at the variety and the range of his vocal compositions as a whole. Even if we discount the more exclusively Norwegian songs, which are not often met with in this country, but in fact contain some of the finest examples of his talent, there remain in the five volumes of his collected songs more than sufficient to attest his great gifts as a song-writer. A few of them, such as 'From Monte Pincio', are masterpieces, but many are wholly charming. The fact is that the best of Grieg, even more than the best of Mussorgsky, is to be found in his songs; for here are seen to the greatest advantage the national flavour of his idiom, the piquant colouring of his harmony and the freshness of his melodic inspiration. The very simplicity by which he achieves his effects has perhaps tended to lead many people to overlook their originality.§

Sibelius's songs often suggest Grieg's in manner, but they tend to spread themselves on a broader canvas, often following the brooding, rather mysterious mood of his other music. Of other Scandinavians around the turn of the century, his fellow Finn, Yrjö Kilpinen is probably the most significant. His songs show great sensitivity to texts (often German ones) and a kinship to Wolf in their verbal declamation.

Following a marked flowering of classical songs during the 17th century, many of them accompanied by guitar, Spain had little individual to offer in the genre until the early part of the 20th century when writers such as Granados, particularly in his *Tonadillas* (evoking the *majas* and *majos* of Goya) and de Falla, above all with his *Seven Spanish Popular Songs*, brought back a truly native character into Spanish song-writing. They were followed by Turina, Mompou and Montsalvatge who all set Catalan and Spanish texts with a distinctive flavour to them.

13 CHANGE IN THE AIR

After the early years of the century the two most important figures in vocal music as in much other were Schoenberg and Stravinsky.

Schoenberg followed the ultra-Romantic, large-scale *Gurrelieder*, for soloists, chorus and orchestra with the song cycle, *Das Buch der hängenden Garten* and the expressionistic monodrama *Erwartung*, both of which point towards a new harmonic language and are definitely without a main tonal base. As Schoenberg himself remarked at that time: 'Now that I have finally embarked upon this path I am conscious that I have broken all barriers of a past aesthetic.' More startling (at the time) from a vocal point of view was *Pierrot Lunaire* (1912) where the voice part is written throughout in *Sprechgesang*, literally Speech-song, in which the singer is concerned with rhythm and interval but not with exactitude of pitch. These macabre expressions of a tortured mind are perfectly mirrored in the angular vocal line and revolutionary treatment of harmony. After *Pierrot*, most of Schoenberg's major works were operatic or instrumental but the unfinished oratorio *Die Jacobsleiter* and the late piece, *A Survivor from Warsaw*, for speaker, chorus and orchestra, ought to be mentioned. The harsh dramatic force of the latter, describing a heroic episode in the fight of Polish Jews against the exterminating Nazis, is emphasized by the twelve-note technique Schoenberg had by then perfected, a technique that he described as denying the supremacy of a tonal centre in the use of the twelve notes of the scale. The system, even sixty years and more after its invention, has not endeared itself to the ordinary listener although its influence on the composers that have succeeded Schoenberg is undeniable.

Berg, one of Schoenberg's chief disciples, also began his musical life writing in a romantic vein and his fine *Seven Early Songs* stem from the same tradition as Mahler's and Wolf's. His other important non-operatic vocal work, *Der Wein* (1929), a concert aria with orchestra, setting poems by Baudelaire, and extolling the properties of wine, is strictly twelve-note in composition, but vocally very grateful to a wide-ranging soprano or tenor. Webern also employed the technique in several sets of cantatas and songs; they are also fine examples of his spare, almost disembodied style. Songs by Zemlinsky, Schrecker and Křenek, among Schoenberg's contemporaries and after, are not deserving of their current neglect. Hindemith, in more eclectic style, also contributed positively to the song repertory, particularly with *Das Marienleben*. Hindemith adhered basically to tonality, and the vocal line in this cycle is predominantly traditional.

Stravinsky's chief influence was in fields other than vocal, but *Les Noces* ('The Wedding', 1923), a translation of a primitive rite into modern terms for a ballet of that name, is important as one of the first works to go to primitive music for its inspiration. Quite different is the *Symphony of Psalms* (1930), a choral work that is no less fervent for being austere in its expressive means. Then *Perséphone* (1934), a melodrama for reciter, tenor, chorus and orchestra is a more relaxed, appealing score. These works, like those for instruments alone, show Stravinsky's fundamentally eclectic mind, taking ideas from a wide range of sources and then making them peculiarly his own. The same is even more true of his later vocal works. Thus the severe *Mass* (1948) shows him incorporating what had inspired him in pre-classical music and his *Cantata* (1952), his first use of serial technique. His first twelve-note works, and again one must note how wonderfully he absorbed them into his own style, were *Canticum sacrum* (1955) and *Threni* (1958). Only in *Requeim Canticles* (1966) did the well of composition begin to run dry.

Bartók, that other key figure of the century, did not write many purely vocal works but of course part of his importance lies in his discovery and use of folk-song already mentioned; he made several arrangements of Slav folk-songs as well as incorporating them in his *Village Scenes* (1926) for female voices and chamber orchestra. Kodály worked with Bartók on collecting folk-music and it influenced his music even more than that of his contemporary, as can be heard in the patriotic *Psalmus Hungaricus* for tenor, chorus and orchestra written for the fiftieth anniversary of the union of Buda and Pest in 1923. The *Cantata Profana* of 1930 was written in lieu of another possible work for the stage. It is an effective and colourful setting, in translation, of a Romanian ballad for tenor, baritone, double chorus and orchestra. Its sub-title is 'The Giant Stags' and it is a simple legend with the universal theme of freedom.

Nationalism in the music of Janáček took the form of adapting his vocal line to his native Czech language, most notably in the *Diary of One who Disappeared* (1919), which describes in vivid, subjective terms a young man's seduction by a gypsy girl. The youth is sung by a high tenor, and the alliance of the music to verbal intonation is startlingly acute. In the ninth, tenth and eleventh songs Zefka, the gypsy, is sung by a contralto. The composer intended the work for semi-dramatic performance on a half-darkened stage but it is hardly ever performed thus, which is a pity. Later in his career he composed his 'Glagolitic' Mass (1927) – 'Glagolitic' refers to an old Slavonic alphabet – a deeply felt expression of a simple faith using the composer's partially discordant idiom and displaying his flair for orchestral colour.

Apart from the vocal music in Szymanowski's Third Symphony, the Polish composer wrote several appreciable works for voices, showing his importance at a much wider than merely national level. Two of the most significant are late pieces – the Stabat Mater and Veni Creator, both dating from the mid-1920s. The Stabat Mater, a setting of Polish words, uses idioms of its time, but remains a simple, even austere expression of human suffering. Many of his songs do not deserve their current neglect.

§ 14 REVIVAL OF ENGLISH SONG

The revival in English choral music at the end of the 19th century owes much to Parry and Stanford, but its true flowering came in the music of Elgar. A Roman Catholic, Elgar achieved fame in the Anglican cathedrals of the Three Choirs Festivals without abating his own faith, though not always without offence to stricter Protestant susceptibilities. Having no professional training of any kind, he developed a sound technical craftsmanship and became the acknowledged leader of music in England, reaping every official honour open to his profession.

Of Elgar's early vocal works little need be said, for their good qualities are those that are also to be found in his mature work, while the obvious weaknesses are the faults of a mind finding its own way slowly towards the technical means and methods of expression best suited to it. In the same year (1899) as the *Enigma Variations* Elgar produced the *Sea Pictures*. In these songs, written for Clara Butt to sing at the Norwich Festival, the qualities and defects of his vocal writing are clearly displayed. Like Strauss, Elgar could go straight to the heart of his text and produce music expressive of all that is essential to it. Yet for an assiduous reader of poetry and for an English composer, he was curiously insensitive to the niceties of poetic rhythm and even to the more simple problems of accentuation.

No such reservations need be made about Elgar's choral works in which, whether he is writing a part-song, or a large-scale oratorio, his technical mastery is absolute. This is not, of course, to say that his musical inspiration was always on the same high level. Even in *The Dream of Gerontius* (1901), which is the most consistent of his oratorios, there are lapses of imagination, especially in the second part. The first part of this work, which portrays the death of Gerontius and the setting forth of his soul into eternity, is of so fine a character, of so great an originality, that it never fails to entrance the ear and astonish the mind of the hearer. That the composer should not have risen so successfully to the ineffable heights of the angelic choruses in the second part, is perhaps only to say that he did not achieve the impossible.

Gerontius was followed by an even more ambitious project, a trilogy of oratorios, of which the first part, *The Apostles*, was produced at Birmingham in 1903 and the second, *The Kingdom*, in 1906. The third part was never completed, and thereafter Elgar concentrated on symphonic works, producing no choral work on a large scale nor indeed anything of importance in that medium, with the exception of the setting of Binyon's poem, *For the Fallen*, a poignant elegy for those who fell in the War of 1914–18. Neither *The Apostles* nor *The Kingdom* has achieved the popularity of *Gerontius*, and, although both the later works contain noble music and at times show an even greater mastery in the handling of the material and a more subtle expressiveness, popular opinion is probably, as it usually is in the long run, right.

Elgar's most important contemporary in England was Delius, whose main contributions to music were, however, orchestral. Even the treatment of the voices in his choral works is often deliberately instrumental, and his imagination is displayed at its finest in such things as the wordless chorus which enters to form the climax of *The Song of the High Hills*. Delius had even less than Elgar's regard for the niceties of accentuation in the setting of English poetry, a failing that was as much due to his own temperament as to his foreign parentage and domicile. A dreamer of dreams, he cared as little for the rules of prosody as for the technique of fugue and symphonic form. They were things inessential to the expression of his musical ideas. The best of his vocal music is contained in the profoundly expressive *Sea-Drift* for baritone, chorus and orchestra, in such miniatures as the wordless *Songs to be sung on a summer night on the water*, in the more tranquil passages of his uneven masterpiece, *A Mass of Life*,§ and in the recently revived, defiantly anti-religious *Requiem*, rightly described by Andrew Porter as 'a score fired by manly joy, in which rapture never becomes self-indulgence, and in which the discoveries, harmonic and textural, of that extraordinary mind and ear are set out in concise, masterly and inspired form'.

§ In the next generation the outstanding figures in England are Vaughan Williams and Holst, both, like Elgar, natives of the Western Midlands. Both came under the influence of the folk-song revival, but neither remained enslaved by it. Vaughan Williams, in particular, so absorbed the spirit of English folk-music into his system that it be-

494

came an integral part of his own intellectual process. An even more important influence on these composers was the revival of interest in the Tudor composers. In the music of Byrd and Tallis, of Weelkes and Morley, Holst and Vaughan Williams found a starting-point for explorations into a new harmonic world.

Holst expressed himself with a directness that left no doubt about his absolute sincerity, even though one might suspect that, especially in his later music, he had not really put down all he meant to say. In the 'Choral' Symphony he seems to play upon his hearers the trick practised on the Wizard in *The Perfect Fool*, substituting clear spring water for the magic potion. His finest choral works are *The Ode to Death* and *The Hymn of Jesus*, in which his peculiar susceptibility to nuances of timbre, his exact knowledge of the effect produced by any given combination of voices and instruments, and his bold, yet never perverse, handling of the modal material are fully exploited. The curious combination of ecstasy and austerity, of ice and fire, in the *Hymn* is characteristic of Holst's best music, and goes hand in hand with the compound of simplicity and recondite mysticism in the texts he usually chose.

Vaughan Williams's vigorous choral Sea Symphony, the best of his early works, exemplifies both his strength – the bold, swinging melodies, the delight in the picturesque details of the sea and ships and the characteristic and essential transformation of the sea-faring into a mystical adventure of the human soul – and his inability at that stage to make smooth and convincing transitions or to work his material into a really coherent form, independent of conventional formulas.

From the Sea Symphony to the Mass in G minor, *Sancta Civitas* and the *Tudor Portraits* is an enormous step, measure of the composer's advancing mastery. In the Mass the composer takes up the traditions of the great Tudor polyphonists, and yet it is in no sense a pastiche. While conforming to the conventions of a different age, it bears indelibly the stamp of the composer's personality. In *Flos Campi*, a work based upon texts from the Song of Solomon, the chorus is used orchestrally, as Holst had used it in the 'Neptune' movement of *The Planets* and Delius in *The Song of the High Hills*. No work of Vaughan Williams's is so bewildering as this mixture of naïve exoticism and native mysticism that yet provides a record of sensuous experiences. *Sancta Civitas*, a cantata with a text drawn mainly from the Apocalypse, is undoubtedly one of Vaughan Williams's masterpieces, and it is astonishing that a work so consistently beautiful should have fallen into neglect.

The *Five Tudor Portraits* are a racy realization in music of the poetry of Skelton, with a contrasting slow movement which is one of the composer's most charming pieces. Notable among his later works are *Dona Nobis Pacem* and a Christmas oratorio, *Hodie*, which is as fresh and delightful as anything in his oeuvre. Of his smaller vocal pieces, 'Silent Noon', 'Linden Lea' and the cycle *On Wenlock Edge* represent Vaughan Williams's gift as a song-writer.§

In the next generation Constant Lambert followed up the success of his effective *Rio Grande* with a major work, *Summer's Last Will and Testament*, a choral symphony to words by Thomas Nashe. Walton, after an even earlier revelation of cleverness and wit, best represented in *Façade*, in which a reciter reads Edith Sitwell's poems over peculiarly apt accompaniments for a chamber group, startled the musical world in 1931 with one of the most powerful choral works ever written, *Belshazzar's Feast*. Though based upon a biblical text, it is entirely secular in spirit. Nothing could better exemplify the difference in spirit between this work and a 'sacred' oratorio than a comparison of the bloodthirsty exultation of Walton's setting of the words 'Babylon is fallen', and the music provided for the same words in Vaughan Williams's *Sancta Civitas*. Amid this atmosphere of hatred and pagan splendour, there shine out several passages of remarkable beauty, such as the setting of 'By the Waters of Babylon' and the unaccompanied chorus, 'The trumpeters and pipers are silent'. Throughout the work, from the grinding dissonances of the mournful opening to the ecstatic Alleluias of the close, Walton shows a complete mastery of his material and of every device of choral effect. His most important songs are contained in the cycle *A Song for the Lord Mayor's Table* (1962), celebrating London in poems (chosen by Christopher Hassall) grave and gay.

The tradition of these composers has been carried on successfully to a degree by such composers as Herbert Howells (*Hymnus Paradisi*), Bernard Naylor and Anthony Milner, but two composers, Britten and Tippett, in their own ways, created a new and different tradition, Britten more especially in the field of song-writing, although his *War Requiem* (1962) could be considered the most vital and arresting choral work since *Belshazzar's Feast* by virtue of its original and powerful setting of poems by Wilfrid Owen for soprano, tenor and baritone intermingled with the traditional Latin texts. In his 'Spring' Symphony, really a cantata for solo voices, chorus and orchestra, he set an anthology of poems about spring. The score includes lively parts for boys' voices, for which Britten has always composed with special sympathy, as in the delightful *Ceremony of Carols*, the *St Nicholas* cantata, *The Golden Vanity* and *Children's Crusade*.

In his songs, he evolved a style of writing for the solo voice that is extremely flexible and capable of taking any text in its stride, and his choice of poetry has at all times been fastidious. Most of his output in this field has been written with the tenor Peter Pears very much in mind. From the refinement of *Les Illuminations*, through the highly imaginative *Serenade* for tenor, horn and strings, to a setting of the sonnets of John Donne, his early works in this field created their own special atmosphere and style. So did the evocative *Nocturne*, the four canticles, modelled on Purcell's dramatic scenas, and *Winter Words*, where Hardy's poetry is marvellously illumined in both the voice and piano parts. The *Songs and Proverbs of William Blake*, written for Fischer-Dieskau in 1965, are tougher propositions, but their more concentrated mood only reflects again the feeling of the texts. His folk-song arrangements are remarkable for their clever but never too sophisticated support of simple tunes.

§ Lennox Berkeley's vocal music is at once deeply felt and beautifully fashioned. His setting of Stabat Mater for six solo voices and chamber orchestra exemplifies his lyrical style and his command of a complex yet translucent texture as well as his invention of ornamental detail, which here embraces almost rococo floridities. The four songs to poems of St Teresa of Avila, for contralto and strings, reveal a more mature and serious side of the composer in their passionate ecstatic utterance, and *Autumn's Legacy* and *Four Poems of Ronsard* (1965) are song-cycles of distinction.§

Tippett really established himself with his oratorio *A Child of Our Time* (1941), fashioned on the model of the Bach Passions, with solo arias, excited crowd choruses and meditative chorales for which Tippett borrowed the melodies of spirituals. His next major choral work came twenty-five years later with what the composer called the 'complex yet luminous' setting of *The Vision of St Augustine* for baritone, chorus and orchestra. Tippett's early, lyrical vein is well represented by the cycles *Boyhood's End* and *The Heart's Assurance* his later, more eclectic and severe style by *Songs for Dov*, a 'spin-off' from the opera *The Knot Garden*, and his Third Symphony (1973) contains a solo soprano part.

The utterly individual Priaulx Rainier deserves a mention for her beautifully wrought *Requiem* and arresting *Cycle for Declamation*, for unaccompanied solo voice. Fricker has also contributed significantly to the choral repertory with his *Vision of Judgment*.

Sprechgesang seemed a strange and outlandish form of musical expression to our fathers, but today the expansion in the possible language of the voice, like that for instruments, has gone far beyond the ideas of Schoenberg and his school. Indeed the voice, in many vocal works, has been used as just another instrument. Singers interested in modern music have to be prepared to extend their techniques to encompass modern coloratura writing that will take the voice in a very short space from one extreme of its register to another. They must tackle new kinds of notation, cope with aleatoric suggestions, and sometimes 'act' on the concert platform. These new demands on the singer's resources derive in part from the breakdown, in most advanced scores, not only of traditional notation but also of traditional forms. Vocal music can no longer be neatly categorized into choral music and song. Voices are used, as already suggested, as extra instruments in what are predominantly instrumental works. In other pieces, such as Boulez's setting of Mallarmé in *Pli selon Pli*, the poem is only the starting-point for the work's structure. Indeed the composer has stated that: 'In my transposition or transmutation of Mallarmé, I take it for granted that the direct sense of the poem has been acquired by reading it'. In a further category, voices become more like sound effects as in Stockhausen's *Carré* and *Stimmung*. Some of these experimental pieces, such as Milton Babbitt's *Philomel*, incorporate synthesized tape, and other electronic devices. In others, a singer will have to tackle a vocal line against another of his own, pre-recorded on tape.

Certain key figures have led this revolution – for it is no less – in the history of vocal writing. In France the leading influence has been Olivier Messiaen, whose *Poèmes pour Mi* (1936) and *Harawi* (1945) extended the vocal boundaries in the use of words and colouristic effects. He did more than any other composer to link the 'advanced' composers of the pre-war period with those of the post-war. Meanwhile in Italy Dallapiccola, while adhering fairly strictly to twelve-note principles, also widened the frontier of vocal music in some of his pieces, some for chorus, others for solo voices and chamber groups. Roberto Gerhard (a Spaniard exiled in England), especially in his big oratorio *The Plague*, a setting of Albert Camus's book of that name, for narrator, chorus and orchestra, Křenek, Fortner (particularly in his cantata *The Creation*), and Blacher are other composers who kept a foot in the serialist camp while attempting to come to terms with more recent techniques.

Carl Orff, in Germany, was meanwhile developing along different lines. His *Carmina Burana* (1937), a setting of mediaeval German and Latin songs of pleasure, employs insistent rhythms, plain harmony and percussive orchestral sounds. Its appeal is direct and it can claim, with *Belshazzar's Feast*, to be one of the most popular choral works of recent times. Yet it has had heaps of critical scorn poured on it, including the comment that Orff had replaced twelve-note music with one-note music. Certainly the composer has not had commensurate success with his later offerings, and he has not encouraged any successors.

The Polish modern school probably had its founding father in Szymanowski, who wrote a great number of songs worthy of more than local interest and not deserving current neglect. After beginning as a late romantic, he later absorbed the influences of Stravinsky and Schoenberg which fertilized without overwhelming his own fastidious style. Lutoslawski carried on and developed the new-found and individual voice of Polish music, while bridging the way between Bartókian ideas and the more recent and radical of Western ideas. In vocal music this can be heard most gratefully in *Paroles tissées*, written for Pears and the Aldeburgh Festival (1965). His younger contemporary Penderecki, in his Stabat Mater and St Luke Passion, although sometimes employing advanced methods of notation, wrote music that was readily comprehensible to the layman and concerned as much with feeling as technique.

American music began to find its feet and its own path as the century developed, although the major developments were not perhaps in the field of vocal music. MacDowell, at the end of the 19th century, wrote several songs in which the fundamental concern is for the declamation in the vocal line. After the locally important work of Sidney Homer, we come to Charles Ives whose numerous songs are bold in detail and individual in general accent, even when they quote specifically from ballads, war songs and hymns. They are written in a supremely eclectic style, employing tonality, atonalism, broad polyphony, and all together. Virgil Thomson, Copland, Barber (particularly in *Knoxville* for soprano and orchestra [1947]) and Carter have contributed substantially to the growing body of American song. Copland's *Twelve Poems of Emily Dickinson* (1950) has gained a hold in the song repertory, as has his folk-opera, *The Tender Land*. And of more than merely ephemeral interest are the popular songs of Jerome Kern and Cole Porter.

None of these, however, stepped nearly as far beyond traditional methods as the younger generation of Americans, although they may have been inspired by Ives to experiment. Milton Babbitt, although born as early in the century as 1916, and at first a strict twelve-note composer, adhered to the strictly mathematical school of writing. Voice, a soprano, was combined with tape-synthesized electronic music in his Dylan Thomas setting, *Vision and Prayer* and in *Philomel*. George Crumb, among the younger generation, has written several exotic works for voice, the most significant of which is *Ancient Voices of Children*, a setting of Lorca. It is typical of many avant-garde pieces in its complex layout and special effects such as fantastic vocalizes and pseudo-Japanese cries sung into the amplified piano. Despite its trendy requirements, the work undoubtedly exerts a powerful spell over its twenty-five-minute length.

Spatial movement, another new development, has often turned the concert-hall into a theatre, particularly in the works of Berio (one of the two leading Italian avant-garde composers – Nono is the other) such as *Circles* (1960) and *Epifanie* (1965), written for his former wife Cathy Berberian, who also 'composed' her own unaccompanied vocal montage of strange noises called *Stripsody* (1968). Nono, in *Il Canto sospeso* (1956), with a text declaimed against an electronic sound, has contributed notably in a vocal way to the extension of concert-hall experience.

British composers have been no laggards in this field, but before mentioning those who have made most impression among the younger generation it is as well to remember the pioneering work done by Elisabeth Lutyens at a time when the musical establishment did not want to know what was happening as regards Schoenberg and his disciples. Much of her best work has been done in the vocal field both in imaginative choral pieces such as the *Wittgenstein Motet* (1954). In this she takes a seemingly intractable text from the philosophical writings of Wittgenstein and allows its formal, abstract nature to free her from literally interpreting the text. Instead the music has its own logic and inevitability. Her many works for solo voice and chamber groups, such as *Quincunx* and *And Suddenly it's Evening*, show the refinement of her style, her sensitivity to words and her grateful writing for the voice.

Among a younger generation working in a basically orthodox style, Nicholas Maw has written with outstanding facility and some romantic ardour for the voice in his *Scenes and Arias*; so has Malcolm Williamson in his song-cycle *Celebration of Divine Love*, and his Symphony for Voices. Gordon Crosse, in his *Changes* for soprano, baritone, children's choir, chorus and orchestra shows an eclectic taste carefully assimilating various influences into an individual style; as does his *World Within* (1977), for speaker, soprano and instrumental group, based on the poetry, diary and fantasies of Emily Brontë.

The work of Peter Maxwell Davies and Harrison Birtwistle has been more experimental. Maxwell Davies has been ingenious in fertilizing his own ideas with those from mediaeval and jazz sources in such works as *O magnum mysterium*, written for Cirencester School (where he taught), *L'Homme aimé*, and *Revelation and Fall*, a kind of *Sprechgesang* montage for soloist and instrumental group. In *Eight Songs for a Mad King*, a monologue for George III, in costume – an arresting piece for a vocally acrobatic soloist, flute, clarinet, and cello, written with the composer's own group, Fires of London, in mind – there are many historical and musical allusions, but in spite of its complexity, it is a readily understandable work. It is typical of one kind of composition in the 1970s in being tailored to a specific group of musicians and in expressing a dramatic idea within an economical frame.

John Tavener's muse is altogether more florid and baroque as in his dramatic cantata, *The Whale*, for speaker, soloists, organ and orchestra, drawn from the biblical story of Jonah, his *Celtic Requiem*, and his semi-staged, spatially daring *Ultimos Ritos*. Whatever strictures may be made of these ambitious, sometimes grandiose, works, they form a welcome antidote to some of the more insipid, etiolated sounds of his contemporaries.

Meanwhile in Germany Henze, under the influence of a political conversion to the Left, moved away from the lyrical style of his early years to something altogether tougher and more aggressive in his *Raft of the Frigate 'Medusa'*, dramatizing the struggle of the oppressed in a single event and employing narration, singing and a huge orchestra. *El Cimarron* and *The Tedious Way to the place of Natascha Ungeheuer* follow a similar path on a smaller scale.

Even more advanced experiments than those already adumbrated have been undertaken by composers such as Ligeti, Pousseur, Cardew and Cage, to mention only four prominent names at random. They may – or may not – be leading towards an entirely fresh employment of the voice. More likely, the new techniques of tape, amplification, analysing of vowel sounds, shouts and murmurs will 'develop' alongside the more conventional uses of the solo singer and chorus. The human voice is something much too beautiful and delicate to be constantly exploited in the cause of *le dernier cri*.

Book 6

Chamber Music

by Hugo Cole
incorporating material by Edwin Evans

PART 1 BEFORE BEETHOVEN

§ 1 EARLY BEGINNINGS IN ENGLAND AND ABROAD

The most admirable definition of the term 'chamber music' is that which describes it as the music of friends. Though much of it is now performed in public, it is essentially the music of those who come together to make music for themselves, as distinct from those who gather at concerts to have music made for them. Soloists rarely play or sing to themselves, except for study or practice, and even an amateur orchestra comes together with the view of eventually performing to an audience, but the true devotees of chamber music have no need of an audience for the enjoyment of their pursuit. They find it in the interplay of individualities, in the dovetailing of their individual contributions to the whole. They meet as friends and admit a few friends to their intimacy. That is the real spirit of chamber music, by this it was animated during a great part of its history, and this still inspires countless private societies in which it is cultivated for the sheer joy of performing it.

The public concert is a comparatively modern institution. In Italy, where the term *musica de camera* originated at the time of the Renaissance, it was used to indicate the music provided at princely houses, as distinct from that intended for the Church or, in later times, for the stage. Though the hospitality of such houses might extend to a multitude of guests, the performances were, in their essence, private, as distinct from public performances given elsewhere. When the practice extended to Germany the distinction was further narrowed. A reigning house – and they were many in those days – might distinguish between *Hofmusik* (Court music) and *Kammermusik* (chamber music), the latter being for the delectation of the princely household, the former for the enlivening of court functions. Germany becoming eventually the scene of the greatest expansion of chamber music, it is from this, rather than from the Italian precedent, that the term acquired its present connotation. During the later part of the 18th century and nearly the whole of the 19th the cultivation of chamber music in this modern sense spread quickly among the middle classes, and as the German classics began to become known in other countries, so did the cultivation of chamber music.

It would, however, be a mistake to begin our survey of chamber music from the rise of the German classics, for, although it took a new form then, it really had a much longer history, and existed for generations before the term came into general use. Chamber music is in fact as old as concerted vocal music. As has been pointed out elsewhere in this volume already, it is quite wrong to imagine the music of the polyphonic period as consisting entirely of unaccompanied motets and madrigals. Instruments were in use for purposes of accompaniment and for entertainment, and as the resources of vocal counterpoint were developed it was natural for instrumental performers to avail themselves of them. But vocal music had a long start, and instrumental music was at first slow to follow. It should, however, be borne in mind that the madrigal enshrined the same ideal as chamber music in being the music of friends. The part-books would be handed round in the same spirit, and no doubt if any present could play an instrument he was invited to join in. Thus originated in Italy 'madrigali per sonare e cantare', and in England madrigals 'apt for voices and instruments'.§

2 CHAMBER MUSIC OF THE 16TH AND 17TH CENTURIES

Fifty years ago, performances of pre-classical music on the instruments for which it was written were almost unknown. Early music was a subject for antiquarians, and those who studied it in libraries had little opportunity to find out how it would have sounded, played with understanding and on the appropriate instruments; not so long before, when Arnold Dolmetsch wished to revive the recorder, he could find only two in playable order in the country. Today, we are luckier. Much long-inaccessible music is available, in published scores and often in performing editions; it is possible to buy a recorder, a lute, a viol, or a crumhorn almost as easily as a violin or flute (in the case of the recorder, much more easily). We should not be too hard on Parry for writing of the 'cumbrous and coarse-sounding viols', or André Mangeot for adding 20th-century bowing and phrasing to Purcell's Fantasias; since we can do what they could never do – hear the music of the past played by specialist performers on the instruments for which it was written, and decide for ourselves on its value and interest. For the listener, early music offers new timbres and new types of ensemble; for the performer, the stimulus of new techniques to be mastered (and for the amateur, there is the attraction of simplicity: recorder, crumhorn, and even viol are not so hard to master up to the point of reasonable fluency); for the musicologist, there are endless problems to be solved as to authentic manner of performance. But for all, the greatest attraction lies in the quality of the music itself – the riches, still largely unexplored, of 16th and 17th centuries, with the possibility, as time goes on, of fresh discoveries in the music of even earlier times.

We have only a sketchy knowledge of instrumental ensemble music, and of the ways in which it was performed, up to the middle of the 16th century. Even when the music was written down, the notation often did no more than provide an outline for decoration and embellishment or serve as a mnemonic for those who were trained in a particular tradition. A great variety of instruments was in use; an inventory made at Henry VIII's death in 1547 lists hundreds of instruments belonging to the king, including lutes, viols, shawms, recorders, flutes, cornetts, guitars, and horns. A concert given at a Florentine christening party in 1565 was made up of madrigals, each one accompanied by a different group of instruments. In most cases, instrumentation depended on the instruments available and was not specified in the score; naturally enough, very few ensemble pieces seem to have been written in idioms specific to any one sort of instrument. Henry VIII's own simple three-part dances may or may not have been intended for viols, and can as well be played on wind instruments. The song- and dance-collections of the French publisher Attaiwgnant and the Antwerp publisher Susato are straightforward arrangements in four parts with a little contrapuntal interest, suitable to be sung or played by all comers.

It was, all the same, these collections, and others like them, that provided one of the two chief starting-points for the chamber music of the latter half of the 16th century; music written for the pleasure of performers and of a few listeners rather than for practical purposes (to dance to, or for use on liturgical or ceremonial occasions). Collections of French chansons became popular in Italy, and provided models for the light and lively *canzoni da sonar*, in which dance rhythms and song-like tunes were given freer and more sophisticated treatment, sometimes with exact instrumentation specified; though more commonly, alternatives were suggested. (Well into the 17th century, we find instrumental music published for viols, cornetts, recorders, viols or violins, or, in a few cases, with no indication of instrumentation of any sort.)

From the early years of the 16th century, composers had also been writing instrumental music of another sort. The *ricercar* was an instrumental motet composed in the manner of the polyphonic choral motet: many-voiced, generally learned in style, often built round a slow-moving cantus firmus derived from Plainchant. Some were no more than transcriptions of vocal music; some were exercises in scholarly skills rather than live musical works (Apel refers to a piece by Buus 'in which one single theme is made the basis of a monotonous contrapuntal texture of nearly 300 measures'). But others are written in true instrumental style. No clear distinction can be made between the *ricercar* and the fantasia, another class of polyphonic pieces founded on vocal models.

One of the most notable collections is Willaert's *Fantasie e Ricercari* 'sonare d'ogni sorte di stromenti' published at Venice in 1559. In England, the favourite form was the *In nomine*; a fantasia based on a particular phrase from a Mass by Taverner; there are also many Fantasies and Fancies, freer in form, inspired by Italian models. Even in the early *In nomines* of Christopher Tye, we find some development of specifically instrumental traits, such as quick repeated-note motives combined with wide leaps.

Learned, contrapuntal *ricercari* and *In nomines*, and light, mainly homophonic dance suites continued to appear in Italy and England well into the 17th century. But at the same time, a new way of writing that combined light and learned styles was coming into use. In many sorts of music written for diversion or for practical use: in suites and transcriptions for keyboard or lute; in songs with instrumental accompaniment; and in madrigals. The amount of instrumental ensemble music, however, is small compared with the great volume of keyboard and vocal music in the new style.

By 1600, yet another change was on the way. Polyphony was passing out of fashion, and a simpler, more dramatic sort of music was taking its place, in which harmonic effects were for the first time exploited for their own sake. Giovanni Gabrieli's grand instrumental motets, with their clearly-marked contrasting sections and use of broad dramatic effects, are the first true orchestral works. The brilliant, expressive, violin was coming increasingly into use, and with it, a new sort of music suited to the instrument and the virtuosi who performed on it. From the beginning of the 17th century we can date the use of expressive dynamics, double-stopping, many types of articulation and bowing, a great upward extension of range, and non-polyphonic figurations characteristic of Italian violin style. In England the viol maintained its supremacy, and it was in England that the most interesting ensemble music of the 17th century appeared.

English viol music

The violin was well known in England by the beginning of the 17th century (Holborne's Dances of 1599 and Dowland's 'Lachrymae' of 1605 both have parts for viols *or* violins); but the viol retained its position as the chamber-music instrument *par excellence* for another fifty years. Many English viol players held positions in German courts; English collections were reprinted in Germany; Mersenne, in his treatise of 1636, published in Paris, illustrated the use of viols with an English six-part fantasy; André Maugars, a leading French viol player, visited the English court twice to learn from English masters. Viol music continued to follow old polyphonic models; the English were proud of their traditions: 'In the Fantasia may more art be shown than in other music', wrote Thomas Morley, who warned composers against admitting foreign influences. Christopher Simpson, writing at the end of the Golden Age, in 1667, declares that no nation is equal to the English for 'their various and numerous Consorts of 3, 4, 5, and 6 Parts made properly for the Instruments'.

In the early years of the century, music for whole consorts of viols was less popular than that for broken consorts. Morley's *First Booke of Consort Lessons* of 1611, for example, is for treble lute, pandora, citterne, bass viol, flute (recorder) and treble viol. Only three sets of viol music were published between 1597 and 1638, as against thirteen for mixed collections of instruments. Even so, over 1,000 *In nomines*, fantasias, and sets of dances for viols exist in manuscript in English libraries, about a tenth of which have been published since the last war.

In spite of Morley's warnings, English consort-music composers were a good deal influenced by French and Italian models. The names of English dances often reflect their origins: kickshaw (*quelque chose*); tucket (toccata); round O (rondeau) and so on. Many composers were influenced by the expressive uses of harmony, including chromatic harmony, in Italian madrigals and instrumental music. But the most important developments came from within the tradition, and through persistence in following their own path. Leading characteristics of the old polyphonic motets were retained; English composers were still writing *In nomines* in the 1650s, though their treatment of cantus firmus motives was often of a new sort; in the fantasias of Alfonso Ferrabosco II, themes (including the *In nomine*) are treated with an almost Lisztian boldness and freedom.

English consort music was written in from two to six parts, the fewer-parted pieces tending to be livelier and lighter in mood than the great six-part fantasias. The make-up of the ensemble was variable; thus, the three fantasias by Thomas Lupo to be found in Musica Britannica's *Jacobean Consort Music* are respectively for (treble, treble, bass); (treble, treble, tenor); (bass, bass, bass). Where there are two trebles, in general neither leads. When concertante elements appear, as in some fantasias by Lupo, Alfonso Ferrabosco II, and Robert Whyte, it is one or both bass viols that often come to the fore, with brilliant decorative passages that seem to foreshadow Boccherini's virtuoso cello parts. But more often, except in the latest consort music, we find a polyphony of equal voices; even in the trios in the Italian manner, of Gibbons, Lupo and Coperario (born John Cooper) the style is far more contrapuntal than that of the original models.

In the course of fifty years, consort music developed many new characteristics and forms. The earlier fantasias of Morley show little differentiation of texture, tempo, or contrasting themes; the contrast with William Lawes, John Jenkins, or Matthew Locke is very great. Lawes, perhaps the greatest, certainly the strangest of the English composers of viol music, was one of Coperario's pupils and a member of the Chapel Royal; he died at the siege of Chester in 1645. Lawes wrote every sort of music, including trio-sonatas for the new violins with organ continuo, music for bass viols in the virtuoso manner that the experts of the day demanded, and fantasias for viols that introduced new sorts of melodic and harmonic expressiveness into the vocabulary. His themes are sometimes almost without apparent tonality; wide-ranging, chromatic, almost extravagantly expressive, suggesting new, but not unrealistic, views of the instruments' characters. In his many dance movements, he will write in a clear, diatonic style that would never have shocked Morley. Jenkins too composed in every genre, and left many beautifully-worked polyphonic pieces; Locke, equally versatile, was also a daringly progressive composer, whose chromatic harmonies, abrupt modulations, and far-fetched motivic developments, place him at the furthest point from Morley of all the composers mentioned.

Formally, the fantasias show every sort of variation. While Byrd and Gibbons generally divide their fantasias into short separate sections (some contrapuntal, some dance-like), others, including Bull, Alfonso Ferrabosco II, and Jenkins write in single, sustained contrapuntal movements. Gibbons and Alfonso Ferrabosco II sometimes make use of themes that recur, in altered forms, in different sections. The common feature found in all is the polyphonic style – so well suited to viols with their clear, thin tone, generally so inappropriate for the brighter, stronger violins. To play the closely-interwoven six-part fantasias of the great viol composers on violins is just as unsatisfactory as it would be to play the emphatic, close-blending opening chords of Beethoven's quartet op. 127 on viols. As Thomas Mace wrote, in his *Musick's Monument* of 1676: 'And *These Things* were *Performed*, upon so many *Equal, and Truly-Sciz'd Viols*; and so *Exactly Strung, Tun'd, and Play'd upon*, as no one *Part* was any *Impediment* to the *Other*. . . .' But when Mace wrote, the violinists and virtuoso bass viol players were already in the ascendant; the basso continuo, which provided a scaffolding on which brilliant scales, arpeggios and decorative figurations could be improvised, had arrived, and the great age of viol music was all but over. Only Purcell's three-, four-, and five-part fantasias, written in a deliberately archaic style in 1680, when the composer was twenty-one, were still to come; magnificent music – but no more characteristic of their period than Grieg's Holberg Suite or Prokofiev's Classical Symphony were of theirs.

Ensemble music of other countries

We know as much about performing practice and types of music played in Spain, France and Germany in the 16th century from instruction books written for practical musicians as from scores and parts. Much information on repertoire and on the technique of viols and recorders is to be found in the treatises of Agricola, Gerle, Ganassi, Ortiz, Praetorius and Mersenne (named here in chronological order).

Early French viol music includes a set of Basse Dances for viols of 1530 and the Danceries of 1547 (both published originally by Attaignant). There are Dances for viols written by Claude Gervais (1555); and many later pieces influenced by English viol music, including music by Lejeune and Caurroy from around 1600, two-part teaching pieces by Metru, fantasias by Dumont and Louis Couperin from the middle of the 17th century. Antoine Forqueray and Marin Marais belong to a later tradition (related to that of Christopher Simpson in England) in which ornamentation, improvisation, and a precise and mannered style of interpretation are essential factors. The large amount of music for from one to three bass viols (with continuo) belongs to this tradition, and to virtuoso rather than to chamber music.

Most 16th-century German and Flemish ensemble music that has survived is written for mixed consorts; though Gerle's *Musica Teusch* (1532) contains examples of viol and rebec ensemble music. Schein's *Banchetto Musicale* (1617) contains twenty dance suites, probably for viols, as well as a pavane for four crumhorns and an intrada for cornett, violin, and recorder. There is much mid-17th-century German wind music, written for municipal and state occasions, for waits and town musicians, which has been unearthed in recent years for the benefit of those who today play it for recreation and entertainment, and which we can perhaps classify as *second-degree* chamber music. It seems probable that much more 16th- and 17th-century ensemble music will be revived and republished to meet the increasing demand for a repertoire for recorders, crumhorns, cornetts, and other instruments now once more available to early-music enthusiasts.

§ 3 THE COMING OF THE VIOLIN

Nearly all the music so far mentioned was composed for viols. Some of it has appeared in modern garb for the instruments of the violin family, but it must not be assumed that the effect is that intended by the composer. The violin has superseded the viol by virtue of its greater brilliance. A cynic has said somewhere that in the evolution of musical instruments the law is the survival of the loudest.

The first stage was represented by the succession of Italian violinist–composers who developed the manner of writing for the instrument. The outstanding names are those of Maurizio Cazzati and his pupil Giovanni Battista Vitali, Giovanni Legrenzi, Giuseppe Torelli, Giovanni Battista Bassani, and finally Arcangelo Corelli. They were not specialists in chamber music. In fact their greatest achievement, the concerto grosso, created by Corelli, lies outside the scope of this Book as it represents an early stage of orchestral music. But all of them wrote works that come under the description of chamber music. This phase reached its culmination in the five sets of sonatas by Corelli, some of which are *Sonate da chiesa* and some *Sonate da camera*. Not only are they of great musical interest in themselves, but they represent the standard form taken by a vast quantity of early chamber music, that of the sonata for two violins and a figured bass which was played plainly on the cello (or viola da gamba) with the figuration on a keyboard instrument, organ or cembalo according to circumstances. The annals of the period show a superabundance of such sonatas in all European countries. Such were for instance the sonatas of Henry Purcell. The type continued long afterwards. William Boyce published a set of twelve in 1747. A set by Pergolesi was published in England about 1780, almost a generation after Haydn had written his first string quartets.

This figured bass, or continuo accompaniment, is in fact the hallmark of an entire classical epoch of chamber music, which Professor Tovey described as characterized by 'a scheme of instrumental music in which the main parts are left completely free to execute polyphonic designs, while the task of supporting these designs with a coherent mass of harmony is relegated to a continuo player extemporizing on a suitable keyboard instrument from a figured bass'. The continuo thus represented a kind of impersonal background before which the real characters of the tone-play disported themselves. Philipp Emanuel Bach declares it to be necessary even when not distinctly heard, as in larger instrumental bodies.§

The appropriate way to realize a continuo, however, varies greatly with the style and period of the music. Between 1600 and 1750, a more elaborate style of realization developed, involving discreet imitation of figures and themes in the instrumental parts, and suggestions of polyphony. In music of all periods, elaborately-worked contrapuntal realizations are generally out of place, as are the plain block-harmony realizations of many recent *Urtext* editions of later trio sonatas.

§ When no keyboard instrument was available, the playing of the bare notes of the continuo on a cello or bass was considered a mere makeshift. In some scores provision was made for both being available, in which case the cello would be provided with an ornate version of the bass part whilst the continuo player would improvise on its bare notes. It is of importance to understand the actual function of the continuo for its passing out of current usage marks two revolutionary changes in the essential character of chamber music. The first consists in the tendency to make the instrumental parts cohere without its support – an ideal that was to be realized in the string quartet. The second consists in the promotion of the keyboard instrument, when included in the combination, from the mere ancillary position of a harmonic background to a valued and sometimes even predominant collaborator.

The influence of the Italian violinists was widespread. They travelled to all musical countries and set a fashion, not only in playing, but in composition. In each country they had their imitators. In Germany there were many, few of whom achieved any noteworthy success. Although Bach himself was attracted, as is evidenced by the many Italian works he arranged, the robust art of North Germany was too firmly entrenched to 'go down' before the invader. To that art is sometimes ascribed the first music for string quartet composed in Germany. The reference is to the *Hortus Musicus* of Johann Adam Reinken, the Hamburg organist whom Bach as a young man tramped many miles afoot to hear. It would, however, be stretching a point to regard this work, published in 1704 and consisting of six suites, as a prototype of the string quartet. It is laid out for two violins, viola da gamba, and figured bass, and is rarely in more than three independent parts. The position of Bach is better defined. A considerable portion of his music comes under the wider application of the term 'chamber music', but the circumstance that it consists largely of solo and duo-sonatas excludes most of it from our purview here. In the narrower sense his chamber music consists of a trio for two violins and continuo, one for two flutes and continuo, and two for violin, flute and continuo, the second of which forms part of the *Musikalisches Opfer* that he wrote for Frederick the Great in 1747 on a theme supplied by the King himself. As the continuo part has been worked out by Bach's pupil, Kirnberger, his version presents the nearest approach to chamber music in the modern sense to be found in his works.§

Bach's contemporary Telemann was also a prolific composer of chamber music. Each of the five sets of *Tafelmusik* contains a trio and a quartet, for various instrumental combinations; Telemann himself prized highly the twelve quartets for flute, violin, gamba and cello (with continuo) written when he visited Paris in 1737. His music delighted players and listeners in his own day; smoothly flowing, inventive within its own narrow limits, and admirably written for instruments, it can still give much pleasure in our own time.

§ 4 THE NEW ART IS BORN

Its birthplace can almost definitely be stated to have been Mannheim, where Johann Wenzel Stamitz, the founder of the Mannheim school of violinists, began giving chamber concerts in 1743. Among his pupils were his two sons, Carl, who remained at Mannheim, and Anton, who went to Paris, as well as Cannabich who succeeded him as conductor. Others associated with the Mannheim group were

Franz Xaver Richter, Anton Filtz, and Carlo Toeschi. Meanwhile Jan Zach, a Czech like Stamitz, Georg Matthias Monn, and Georg Christoph Wagenseil were producing chamber music in Vienna, and Placidus von Camerloher was doing the same at Munich. Most of these wrote quartets and more than one of them has been put forward as having done so before Haydn, but a whole army of precursors in the form would not detract from his merit in having endowed it with substance as none did before him. There is therefore no interest in investigating the claims of composers none of whom, save Stamitz who seems to have the best title, produced music of sufficiently outstanding merit to endure.

Curiously enough Haydn himself would almost appear to have unconsciously stumbled upon the form. In his young days he acquired a reputation for writing cassations, divertimenti, serenades and the like for any instruments that happened to be available, often to be played in the open air. On the strength of that reputation he was invited in 1755 to a country house at Weinzierl, near Melk, whose owner, von Fürnberg, was accustomed to have such music played. Haydn wrote a number of these compositions and at first made so little distinction between them that what was undoubtedly his first symphony has somehow got among his quartets, where it figures as op. 1, no. 5. The idea of the string quartet as a form seems to have emerged gradually at some stage after the writing of the first two sets of six, op. 1 and 2, which, except for the one that is a symphony in disguise, have five movements apiece.

§ 5 A PAUSE FOR DEFINITION

Having now reached the threshold of chamber music as it is understood by the modern world, it behoves us perhaps to pause and take stock of what it comprises. Strictly speaking it includes all concerted music for any number of performers from two upwards to the point at which the orchestra begins. That point is commonly understood to be the one at which individual instrumental parts are duplicated, as is the practice in orchestral music. But there is an intermediate point at which a combination, without duplicated parts, is called a chamber orchestra, and that really transcends the ordinary limits of chamber music. Although, for instance, Schoenberg's Chamber Symphony really conforms to the definition, few people would be disposed to regard it as chamber music, because the number of players is too large for the intimacy that is the true characteristic of the 'music of friends'. We will therefore begin by defining chamber music as consisting, for our purposes, of works performed by not fewer than three players and, except in very rare cases, not more than nine.

Much of this music is for strings. The string quartet was for long regarded as the most perfect, concise, and self-contained combination in all music, consisting as it does of four instruments of similar hue, whose collective range is comprehensive in the sense that they can reach every part of the scale except the extreme bass, which is not required with so small a volume of tone, and that they are sufficient for four-part harmony. Almost all composers – even opera-writers like Rossini, Auber, or Verdi – have experienced the desire at some time to write for this ideal combination. But it is a treacherous field. Precisely because it is so self-contained it demands scrupulous musicianship. In the turmoil of the orchestra a composer can get away with workmanship that would be mercilessly exposed in a string quartet. That is why so many composers have either preferred to keep out of this field until comparatively late in life, or have abandoned it, temporarily or permanently, after an early venture that brought them little satisfaction.

Works for fewer strings than four are less common. Most of those for two violins and cello are a legacy of the continuo period, but from Mozart and Beethoven to modern writers, such as Hindemith, composers have gradually furnished an attractive selection of trios for violin, viola and cello, to which others, such as Kodály, have added trios for two violins and cello or viola. In fact if any member of a quartet party disappoints there is no reason why, with an adequate library at hand, the other three should not console themselves for his absence. For upwards of four players there exists ample material: quintets, some with two violas, some with two cellos, sextets, and octets, which are generally double quartets. The double bass makes only occasional appearances in chamber music of classical and romantic periods.

The instrument most frequently associated with the strings in chamber music is of course the piano. We have seen how the keyboard instrument entrusted with the continuo performed purely ancillary functions but, with the advent of chamber music as we understand it, it was not long before the keyboard was reinstated in a more honourable position. The process was begun by Haydn in his trios, but more than any one work it was Mozart's G minor quartet that established the piano in its new functions as a partner, later to become sometimes a predominant partner. Musical purists occasionally demur at the blend of piano and strings as not perfectly harmonious. It is a fact that whereas string players use natural intonation in enharmonics, the 'well-tempered' piano substitutes a compromise, but only the most sensitive ear can be incommoded by the difference. On the other hand it may be admitted that the percussive quality of the piano gives it an advantage which is foreign to the real freemasonry of chamber music and that, especially in late romantic works, the pianist is readily tempted to regard himself as playing a concerto with stringed accompaniment. There are, in fact, many modern chamber works weighted with piano parts that make as heavy demands on virtuosity as any concerto. On the whole the combinations with piano have not the same purity as those of strings only, but in practice that has not deterred the greatest composers from writing splendid chamber music in which the piano is prominent. It consists in the main of trios for piano, violin and cello, quartets for piano, violin, viola and cello, and quintets for piano and string quartet. For convenience these are commonly referred to as piano trios, piano quartets and piano quintets. Piano sextets are relatively uncommon.§

Until the 1950s, almost the only works involving wind instruments which appeared regularly in chamber music performances were the Mozart quartets and quintets for solo wind and strings, the Brahms clarinet quintet and horn trio, Beethoven's septet and Schubert's octet and, occasionally, the piano and wind quintets of Mozart and Beethoven. Today, with the great increase in the number of expert professional wind players, and with so many enthusiastic amateurs in search of performance-material, many long-forgotten works are resurrected and many new ones composed. We have discovered that the wind ensemble can be brought in from the open air, and that wind quintets (generally flute, oboe, clarinet, bassoon and horn) and even brass quintets (generally two trumpets, horn, trombone and tuba) can be heard with pleasure even in small halls, if the players are musicians of skill and discretion.

Since Schoenberg wrote his second quartet, op. 10, with soprano solo, many composers have written chamber works involving solo singers. Earlier works in this genre were generally songs with instrumental accompaniment; but with the evolution of new techniques of vocal and instrumental writing, in which voices may be used instrumentally, strings and wind vocally (or even percussively), the old divisions between vocal and instrumental musics have become

517

blurred. And in the music of many advanced composers, even the louder percussion instruments are often used (very effectively) in chamber music contexts.

§ 6 CHAMBER MUSIC AND SONATA FORM

By far the greatest bulk of chamber music, particularly in classical and romantic times, is composed in sonata-form. At the end of the 18th century there were divertimenti, and occasionally in the 19th some composer would venture to write a suite, but for practically the whole of that century the string quartet was so closely associated with sonata-form that to mention one was to imply the other. The devotees of chamber music were so imbued with this tradition that it was difficult for them to take seriously any work not in sonata-form. Friedrich Kiel must have been a very venturesome fellow indeed to write two sets of waltzes for string quartet and when, later, the Russians began to write agreeable sets of pieces for that sacrosanct combination, it was taken almost as a mark of self-confessed inferiority to German standards. This priggish attitude has done chamber music an incredible amount of harm. It was peculiar to the 19th century. The 18th liked its music crisp, clear and on occasion gay, the earlier 20th liked it pungent, concise, and on occasion ironic. But it is the 19th that has contributed the bulk of the repertoire, and that is the reason why to the man in the street, the term chamber music was for a long time commonly accepted as indicating lengthy, erudite works for the consumption of the few.

If the Mannheim school is most probably to be given the credit for launching upon the world in its definitive form the institution we know as the string quartet, the shape of the music written for it was determined by the new symphonic form, the introduction of which is generally attributed to Carl Philipp Emanuel Bach. He it was who gave sonata-form its new direction, and though Haydn does not appear to have been associated with him at any time, there can be little doubt that in his search for the ideal form he was influenced by the elder master. C. P. E. Bach wrote a quantity of chamber music as did also two of Johann Sebastian's younger sons, Johann Christoph and Johann Christian, the latter known as the English Bach, from his long residence in England. These younger Bachs were, however, Haydn's contemporaries, not his precursors.

Haydn's large output of chamber music is conveniently divided into two periods by an interval of ten years between two consecutive sets of quartets, op. 20, composed in 1771, and op. 33, composed in 1781. Of the latter he has himself said, in a letter, that they are in an 'entirely new style'. This interval also corresponds with a period of great activity in Mozart's career, from his fifteenth to his twenty-fifth year. Haydn was destined to outlive Mozart by many years, and if the younger composer benefited at first from the elder's example, there can be no doubt that the debt was amply repaid in the end, Haydn's later works, such as the well-known Salomon Symphonies, being distinctly influenced by Mozart. Although this influence is not conspicuous in the first quartets that followed the ten-years' interval, it asserted itself also in these before the last of them was penned. This gives an added significance to the subdivision of Haydn's chamber music. The earlier period was one not so much of experiment, for which Haydn had little need after the experience gained in the first dozen quartets, as of quest – search for the most congenial mode of expression. As Professor Tovey has said: 'If Haydn's career had ended there (after op. 20) nobody would have guessed which of some half-dozen different lines he would have followed up', and he proceeds to enumerate them, but begins the next paragraph with: 'Something different happened.'§

The quartets of op. 1, 2, and 3 show so few signs of Haydn's later chamber music style, or of his own character as a composer, that it hardly comes as a surprise to learn that nine of the eighteen are now known to be orchestral in origin, or to have been written by another composer. The orchestral nature of op. 1 no. 5 has been mentioned already. Op. 2 nos. 3 and 5 are simply the string parts of divertimenti (with horns); the work discovered in an Amsterdam edition of the quartets by Marion Scott, for some time accepted as 'Haydn's first quartet' is under suspicion, and is now degraded to a divertimento, while all six op. 3 quartets (including the third one, which contains the famous 'Serenade') are almost certainly by Hofstetter, a Benedictine monk whose works were issued by the unscrupulous publisher Bailleux under Haydn's more illustrious name. (Bailleux repeated the process with a spurious set of op. 28 quartets.)

The development of a true chamber music style in the op. 9 quartets followed Haydn's appointment in 1761 as second Kapellmeister at the Court of Esterház. There, he came into contact with players of great technical skill, and an audience which was ready to listen to works more subtle and extended than the earlier divertimento-like pieces. Haydn's new techniques were developed and extended in the 126 trios he wrote for baryton, viola and cello, almost certainly for the use of Prince Nicholas Esterházy. The baryton is a gamba-like instrument with sympathetic strings behind the finger-board that can also be plucked to provide a bass; limited in range, and confined almost entirely to major keys. (Modern reconstructions have lately appeared, so that Haydn's trios can be heard again on the concert platform.) Haydn's trios show the evolution of a free instrumental style, in which the roles of the instruments are not rigidly fixed, and where any instrument may take the lead, or supply a middle or bass part. The trios are mostly modest in scale, but contain much delightful and characteristic music.

In the op. 9 quartets, the independence of individual parts, in any of which extended and elaborate solos may appear, is even more striking. Thereafter, the main features of Haydn's mature style are all present; sometimes only in embryo, sometimes already well developed; there are many early minuets and sets of variations which could equally well appear in quite late works without any obvious dislocation of style. Development and variation of material may begin from the start of the first movement exposition (as in the second phrase of op. 17 no. 4). Finales, hardly more than concluding flourishes in the earliest quartets, now have each a distinct character, though they are still brief and light in tone. Development sections become longer, and here Haydn increasingly allows his imagination and invention free play (the first movement of op. 17 no. 5 provides a shining example). In the fugal finales of op. 20 nos. 5 and 6, we find for the first time that blending of the learned and the light which is a characteristic of so many later quartets, and which so greatly influenced Mozart. In minuets and slow movements, we find less change of technique or manner – Haydn knew what to preserve as well as what to discard.

§ Whilst Haydn gave the continuo its quietus so far as the quartet was concerned, he was at the same time paving the way for the modern use of the keyboard instrument in chamber music. The majority of his numerous piano trios belong to this early period and though not all of them approach the quartets in musical value, there is a special interest in the manner of their progress. At first the cello part is almost limited to duplicating the essential notes of the bass already present in the piano part. Such trios form the connecting link with the continuo period. Nor can it be said that subsequent emancipation proceeds very far, but it proceeds far enough to afford an inkling of the role the keyboard is to fill in later chamber music. It was left for Mozart to give a clear indication, but not until he had won his spurs in quartet writing.§

8 MOZART

Mozart's fifteen early quartets were all written before he was eighteen, and have been so completely overshadowed by the later works that they are rarely played today. The first (K 80) is a tuneful and quite elaborate essay in the style of Sammartini (the rondo added later is more individual in manner); the next three are symphonic in style, only needing added oboes and horns to make convincing symphonies (the first, K 136, deserves to be as well known as any of the early symphonies). In the six quartets, K 155–160, written in 1772, Mozart began to evolve his own chamber music style. Already in the early quartets, among much that is conventional and perfunctory, we can discover striking and characteristic passages: a development section unexpectedly dominated by a newly-arrived rhythmic figure in the first movement of K 156; a striking thirteen-bar theme in the slow movement of K 157 that provides welcome relief from the symmetry prevailing elsewhere; a slow movement in K 158 as rich and varied in texture as anything in the mature works. The next group of six, K 168–173, written in 1773, show many traces of the influence of Haydn's op. 17 and op. 20 quartets. There is much contrapuntal working and imitation; some use of short motives to build up extended sections (as in the first movement of K 169). The gay, robust opening themes of the finales of K 169 and K 170 could come from Haydn; but the two final fugues are stiff and unconvincing compared with those of Haydn's op. 20 quartets. There is little that is personal or memorable in these quartets, even though the manner is unexceptionable. Themes belong to the common stock; Mozart is still writing, in the spirit of the divertimento, time-passing music in which any display of deep feeling would be almost an impertinence, and in which interest and invention are often spread as thinly as decency allows.

Mozart wrote no more quartets till 1783, when he began work on the great series of six quartets dedicated to Haydn. 'Essi sono, é vero, il frutto di una lunga e laboriosa fatica' he wrote; but the wearisome labour is never apparent in these expressive and profoundly human utterances. For variety of thematic matter, concentration of musical thought combined with ease of manner, emotional range and sensuous appeal, the six quartets must be ranked among the most perfect chamber works ever composed. They were also *ideal* works in a special sense, being among the very few which Mozart wrote, not to commission, but for his own satisfaction; probably for this reason treating the instruments more freely than in any earlier quartets, as technical equals of one another. There are direct references to Haydn's op. 33 quartets in the opening of the D minor K 421 and the minuet of the E flat K 428; the handling of short motives (such as the changing-note figure in the slow movement of the C major K 465) also derives directly from Haydn; but the music itself is entirely Mozartian. The range covered is wide. From the sunny G major K 387, with its richly decorative slow movement and brilliant and energetic finale which uses fugal elements in quite new ways, Mozart moves to another world in the sombre D minor, in which even the extended minuet has tragic significance and weight. And so on through the series; each asserts (always within established conventions) its own types of melody, harmony and texture, and its own emotional climate. Mozart achieves the highest degree of concentration, not by overloading the texture – though it is as well to remember that listeners did once find these works (and not only the atonal opening of the C major) alarmingly full of unexpected notes – but by ensuring that every motive, harmony, and musical consequence was, structurally and emotionally, of total relevance.

The four later quartets, including the three dedicated to King Friedrich Wilhelm of Prussia, with their important cello parts, are rather less personal in tone, but of equal mastery and perfection, the contrapuntal ingenuity being perhaps even greater. The G minor and C major string quintets are deservedly famous. The addition of an extra member to the ensemble leads Mozart into new musico-dramatic situations; first violin and first viola have elaborate operatic duets; second viola supports first viola in thirds and sixths, but has its own personality too. The essence of second-viola character is contained in those short comments on the C string in the slow movement of the G minor quintet, K 516; while the introduction to the finale of this quintet is surely one of the more profound and mysterious of all Mozart's utterances. The divertimento trio for strings in E flat K 563 is another sort of masterwork, expansive and richly decorative, often in concertante style, yet true chamber music nevertheless. The chamber works with piano are not all at the same high level of invention or expressiveness; but the G minor piano quartet, and the quintet in E flat for piano and wind K 452 are incomparable works, in the first of which Mozart anticipates Beethoven in his use of a powerful and striking opening motive which functions almost as a motto theme throughout the first movement.

In the works with wind instruments, as in the string quintets and trios, the requirements of a new situation produce in each case a rather different Mozart, of whom otherwise we might know nothing. For the flute, of which he had the poorest opinion as an instrument, he wrote two quartets in the lightest style, raising the clichés of the salon to an other-worldly level. In the horn quintet, all the instruments are a little infected by the horn's rusticity and inability to discourse except on its own terms. In the oboe quartet and the two chamber works involving clarinet, he leads us in each case into a new musical landscape. The clarinet itself shows a different side to its character in company with viola and piano in the trio (K 498) and in the quintet with strings (K 581). Last of all, there are the many divertimenti and serenades for wind instruments: staple diet of most of today's wind ensembles; from the cheerful, open-air music of the earlier sextets to the C minor Serenade for octet (K 388) (as dramatic, and often as sombre and passionate, as any of the other great C minor works); and the great Serenade for thirteen wind instruments (K 361) in which Mozart creates yet another unique sound-world, and which, if no other works for the instrument existed, would justify the resurrection in our own time of the bassethorn.

§ 9 HAYDN: SECOND PERIOD

Haydn's op. 33, which seems to have had such a stimulating effect on Mozart, and with which he resumed the series of his quartets, consists of six works, variously known as the 'Russian', from their dedication to the Grand Duke Paul of Russia, 'Gli Scherzi', from the fact that their minuets are thus designated by Haydn, and 'Jungfernquartette'. Their central point is the well-known quartet in C, nicknamed the 'Bird', from the duet which serves as trio to its scherzo. The whole set stands very high among Haydn's works, both for the rich quality of the first movements and for the lightheartedness of the finales, which breathe the spirit of serene comedy. They are followed by an isolated and somewhat short quartet in D minor, op. 42. The next set of six, op. 50 was, like the last three of Mozart, dedicated to King Friedrich Wilhelm II of Prussia. The best known of them are the last three, respectively in F sharp minor, F and D. The two last are of those known among enthusiasts by their nicknames. The one in F, a particularly lovely one, is called 'Le Rêve', from its slow movement, and the one in D is known as 'The Frog', from the leaping character of its finale.

In 1785 Haydn composed *The Seven Last Words* in response to a request received from the chapter of the Cathedral of Cadiz for instrumental music appropriate for performance on Good Friday. It was also produced in London as a 'Passion Instrumentale' and afterwards enlarged by the addition of vocal parts. From this music seven movements were arranged as string quartets under the same title. They have, of course, nothing to do with Haydn's other works in this form, but in some editions they are inserted here, on chronological grounds, as nos. 50–56, whilst in others they are added as a kind of supplement to the seventy-six quartets proper, numbered 77–83. The next two sets, op. 54 and 55, comprise only three quartets each, in which are included some of the finest examples.

Of the next set, op. 64, the fifth, in D, is the best known by the entry of the first violin, from which it derives its nickname of 'The Lark', and the short rapid movement with which it concludes, but the sixth runs it close in popularity, and the third and fourth are often played. Then follow once more two sets of three each, op. 71 and 74, the latter including another famous one in G minor, known as 'The Rider' from the jog-trot rhythm of its opening movement, but especially admired for its largo. Then follow the six quartets, op. 76, of which the third contains the famous 'Variations on the Emperor's Hymn' from which it takes its name, and the fourth is known as 'The Sunrise'. With the two quartets, op. 77, Haydn's last completed works in this form, and in the opinion of many his greatest, and an unfinished fragment in B flat we complete the list.§

Haydn's reference to the 'entirely new and special manner' of his op. 33 quartets has been variously interpreted. It may have been no more than sales-talk designed to whet subscribers' curiosity; or an allusion to the increased degree of independence of all four parts; or to the ways in which short motives are detached from their context to serve further uses; or to the greater length and significance of first-movement development sections. These last three characteristics do distinguish the later quartets from the rest; other features singled out for admiration in our own age are the free use of asymetrical phrases and irregularly-structured paragraphs, and a whole group of processes loosely lumped together under the heading *monothematicism*; used to describe the way in which Haydn will allow one leading theme to dominate a movement (as in the opening *Allegro moderato* of op. 74, no. 1); or the way in which short basic motives reappear transformed in contrasted themes (as in the first movement of op. 71 no. 3); or in which some single idea (sometimes only a rhythm) is woven into the texture of a whole movement, sometimes in the foreground, sometimes in the back (as in the first movement of op. 50 no. 4, where the figure ♪ ♫♫ | ♩ is omnipresent, as in Beethoven's Fifth Symphony). But to list such features is only to make a beginning. Much well-composed and dull music has been written exhibiting democratic distribution of parts, irregular phrase lengths, economical use of thematic material, and so on. The infinite superiority of Haydn's quartets to those of his contemporaries is also connected with the unexpectedness of his inventions, with his refusal to fall into routine (every first movement follows its own laws) and with his ability to be serious and profound while maintaining the easy, friendly approach of the provider of entertainment.

At all stages of his career, Haydn wrote quartet movements of high simplicity; there are passages in the op. 74, 76 and 77 quartets where the first violin sings for long stretches against the plainest repeated quaver or semiquaver accompaniments, just as it did in the op. 20s. Tovey acutely remarked that the inner parts of Cherubini and Spohr quartets are often more interesting and just as idiomatically written as Haydn's. Yet no second violinist or violist will object to their long successions of repeated quavers if the musical interest is still maintained; and so too, in the piano trios, the most accomplished cellist will delight in his subsidiary part if he keeps his ears open. In the same way, quite distinguished actors will play Osric or the Second Gravedigger with pleasure – to take part in *Hamlet* at any level is a sort of privilege.

10 BOCCHERINI

Luigi Boccherini, virtuoso cellist and composer of more than 100 string quartets and 113 quintets for two violins, viola and two cellos, was born in Lucca, travelled widely in Europe during his early years and spent much of his later life in Spain, first as composer and cellist in the household of the Infante Don Luis; after the Infante's death, he was still patronized by Charles III, by the King of Prussia, and (towards the end of his life) by Lucien Bonaparte, who became in 1799 Ambassador of the French Republic at Madrid. At the court of Don Luis, Boccherini came into contact with a family of remarkable musicians, named Font, who formed the resident quartet, Boccherini himself often playing second cello in his own quintets. The precise manner of playing required in Boccherini's later chamber works was even in his own time not generally understood; when the famous French violinist Boucher arrived in Madrid in 1799 and attempted the first violin part of a Boccherini quintet, he made so little impression that Boccherini begged him to stop at the twelfth bar; it is hardly surprising that 170 years later the necessary style and technique should have been almost lost, and that only very lately have a few ensembles begun to give convincing performances of music best thought of as an isolated offshoot from the main 18th-century stem, to be appreciated by those who are prepared to forget the standards and expectations associated with the chamber music of Haydn and Mozart. Boccherini's quintets (the quartets are still hardly known today) tend at first to sound rather alike, and to exemplify shortcomings we have been taught to deplore, in their square, symmetrical phrasing and often primitive harmonic substructure. Interest lies in the ornate, sensuous, and sometimes passionate tunes; intricately-worked textures; and in opportunities offered to highly skilled and sensitive performers to introduce often unnotated refinements and subtleties into the music. Spanish influence is often strong; we hear echoes of dance-rhythms, snatches of folk-song, guitar imitations, as well as the twittering of the birds which lived in Don Luis's great aviary. Much of Boccherini's music is now available on record; the more we hear, the easier it is for us to understand why his reputation stood so high, and why he was so much esteemed by the Infante that his salary was larger than those of Don Luis's confessor, physician, librarian, and the nobly-born chief officer of the wardrobe.

PART 2 FROM BEETHOVEN TO BRAHMS

§ 1 BEETHOVEN: FIRST PERIOD

Much has been said of the division of Beethoven's creative career into three periods, which was first suggested by Fétis, then worked out by Wilhelm von Lenz, and has since been adopted by practically every writer on music. For the major works it is a well-proved classification. Beethoven's masterpieces do indicate three distinct styles or modes of expression, which Vincent d'Indy has defined as periods of imitation, of externalization and of reflection. The first is that in which the young artist continues the art-production of his time after the manner of his predecessors, or of his favourites among his contemporaries. The second is that in which he begins to walk alone and to reach self-expression. The third is that in which he retires within himself to create in pure joy and sorrow, without external preoccupation. Obviously that is also the period in which from the ripeness of his experience he enlarges the confines of his art. But if this classification can safely be followed, for instance, with Beethoven's string quartets, it is unwise to trust it implicitly. Such phases of a composer's work are not sharply marked off one from another. There is no ascertainable date at which they move forward from one to the next. If, therefore, we adopt this classification here, it is with the reservation that it is to be regarded simply as a matter of convenience and not as dogma.

Beethoven's earliest chamber music consists of three piano quartets composed in 1785, when he was fifteen, but not published until 1832, five years after his death, a sure guide to his opinion of them. His practice with the works of his youth appears to have been to revise such as he thought to have been of any value and to ignore the others. His next chamber work, a piano trio in E flat, slightly later, also remained unpublished until after his death. In 1791–92, however, he began to compose music for which he subsequently had a higher regard. He then wrote an octet for wind instruments, of which the original version did not appear until 1834, though he made a revised version of it for string quintet, which he published, in 1797 as op. 4, and in later years another for piano trio, op. 63. It was about the same time that he wrote the rondino for wind instruments, and the first version of the trio for violin, viola and cello which was eventually published as op. 3. With two other works mentioned below, this completes what has survived from the Bonn

527

period. Late in 1792 the composer settled in Vienna and was for a time immersed in study. The earliest chamber work of this period is a trio for two oboes and cor anglais, said to have been composed in 1794 but not published until 1806 when it appeared as op. 87. We now reach the stage at which the composer felt himself ripe to produce his op. 1. This consists of three piano trios composed early in 1795 and published by subscription. The following year produced the quintet for piano and wind instruments, op. 16, and two revisions of early works, one a serenade trio for violin, viola and cello, op. 8, and the other a sextet for string quartet with two horns, which was to reach its final form in 1809 as op. 81b. The three string trios, op. 9, were probably also begun that year and completed in 1797. They were published 21 July 1798. To that year belongs the trio for piano, clarinet and cello, op. 11, the variations in which are on a theme taken from an opera by Joseph Weigl, *L'Amor marinaro*, produced on 18 October 1797. This finale was the occasion of the encounter with Steibelt that caused Beethoven to dislike it ever afterwards.

Many of the above works still hold their own in the chamber repertoire, but they pale in significance beside the two with which Beethoven's first period reaches its conclusion: the first six string quartets, op. 18, and the septet, op. 20. Both were completed in 1800, but there is evidence that some of the quartets had been begun some years earlier and probably the septet had been in preparation at least a year. Beethoven was now thirty. He had produced many well-known works, such as the Pathétique Sonata for piano. As long ago as 1795 Count Apponyi had commissioned a string quartet from him. That he delayed so long may perhaps be taken as an indication of how acutely he felt the responsibility. Be that as it may, it was only now that he embarked upon the series of quartets which, to chamber music enthusiasts, are the most important works ever conceived in this form.

The first of the six op. 18 quartets to be composed was the one which, in order of publication, appears as no. 3 in D. It was followed by that in F which now opens the series. The next were the second, in G, and the fifth in A, the fourth and sixth being the last completed.

The septet for violin, viola, cello, double bass, clarinet, bassoon and horn is one of Beethoven's most popular works. It was first heard at a private party given by Prince Schwarzenberg, and then performed in public at the Court Theatre on 2 April 1800. The theme of the variations forming the fourth of its six movements is a folk-song from the lower Rhine, which Beethoven probably heard as a boy at Bonn, and the Minuet is a different version of that belonging to the little piano sonata in G, op. 49, no. 2, composed in 1796. The septet was an immediate success, and soon appeared in numerous arrangements, which caused Beethoven afterwards to hold it in light esteem, although one of them, for piano, clarinet (or violin) and cello, was from his own pen and published as op. 38.§

Though a sense of historical perspective is an admirable thing, it may, in Beethoven's case, lead us to undervalue early works which contain few premonitions of later developments. It is a measure of his youthful genius that he could write music that was individual, forceful, and attention-compelling without having to flout the conventions in any spectacular way. The op. 1 trios are no more 'immature' than the late quartets – they are the mature fruit of a different season; containing the seeds of later developments, it is true, but to be appreciated for what they are rather than for what they were to give rise to.

The op. 1 piano trios, the op. 18 quartets and the septet are well known and much written about. But several less familiar works are worth a few words, both for their own sake and because they often introduce us to a less familiar Beethoven. The string trios, it is true, contain premonitions of the quartets. The richly modulating coda of the Serenade op. 8 makes one think of the equally striking coda of the variations in op. 18 no. 5; the first movement of the stormy op. 9 no. 3, one of Beethoven's most impassioned C minor utterances, of op. 18 no. 4; while its finale shares a first theme with the finale of op. 18 no. 1. Many other movements have no successors. In the Serenade, the impudent opening march and the brilliant scherzo with its mournful, almost rhapsodic slow tune sandwiched in the middle and reappearing at the end are highly uncharacteristic of Beethoven as we generally think of him, while the ornate final *Allegretto alla Polacca* looks back to Boccherini and forward only to the finale of the triple concerto. In the trio for flute, violin and viola, op. 25, Beethoven appears as composer of *galanteries,* with the lightest of touches – only the finale, with its grotesque principal theme and dramatic displaced accents suggests that he soon tired of this particular game. The quintet for piano and wind, op. 16, modelled on Mozart's work for the same instruments, does not equal its model in subtlety of construction or instrumental psychology, but in its expansive first movement and romantic slow movement creates its own individual atmosphere. The quintet for strings, op. 29, has a symphonic breadth of utterance in its first movement, a fine slow movement with one of the most beautifully-worked transitional passages in all chamber music, and a finale that contains one of Beethoven's most notable surprises in the form of a march-like theme that emerges unexpectedly from the stormy, measured-tremolo development.

§ 2 BEETHOVEN: SECOND AND THIRD PERIODS

The string quintet just described could equally well be considered as belonging to Beethoven's first or second periods; but a very different story has to be told concerning the three string quartets, op. 59, begun on 26 May 1806, and dedicated to Count Rasumovsky, by whose name they are familiarly known in musical circles. Count Rasumovsky probably became acquainted with Beethoven through his brother-in-law, Prince Lichnovsky, who was one of the composer's patrons. He was a highly cultured man and a good musician, playing the second violin in a quartet party comprising Schuppanzigh, leader, Weiss, viola, and Lincke, cello. Presumably out of compliment to his nationality Beethoven included two Russian folk-tunes in the quartets. The first is a simple little song which furnishes the theme of the finale of the quartet in F, op. 59, no. 1, and the second is the well-known 'Slava' used by Mussorgsky for the Coronation Chorus in *Boris Godunov*. Here it forms the trio in the scherzo of the quartet in E minor, op. 59, no. 2.

Though the severest critics deny to these quartets the formal perfection of those still to follow, their judgment savours of the academic and does not reflect the attitude of those whose knowledge of them is derived from the intimacy of performance. Among devotees of chamber music the Rasumovsky quartets rank with the best appreciated works of their kind and not a few prefer them to the posthumous quartets as being more accessible and less of a tax upon musical understanding. They were followed, before the end of 1808, by the two piano trios, op. 70, in D and E flat, the first Beethoven had written in this form since his op. 1. They naturally show a tremendous advance, but are in turn overshadowed by one that was to follow, and have perhaps met with less than their due appreciation. Then followed another string quartet, op. 74 in E flat, composed in 1809 and published the following year with a dedication to Prince Lobkowitz. It is famous for its beautiful slow movement in A flat, one of those which foreshadow the Beethoven of the third period. Yet another quartet, op. 95 in F minor, was composed in 1810. It has two features calling for special notice. The first is the remote key, D major, chosen for the second movement. The second is the evidence afforded in the finale of the composer's desire, as in the sonatas, to emancipate himself from the convention of the final rondo, to which he returns only once in the later quartets, in op. 132. It was followed in 1811 by another of those works that have been held in general affection by generations of players for upwards of a century without showing any signs of becoming staled by familiarity. This is the Archduke trio in B flat, op. 97, so called because it is dedicated to the composer's great friend, pupil and patron, the Archduke Rudolph of Austria. The variations and finale of this work belong to the greatest movements to be found in Beethoven's chamber music.

Between the chamber works of second and third periods there is a clear break, and there can be no doubt at all that the third period begins with the E flat quartet, op. 127, the last to be published during his lifetime, composed in 1824, performed for the first time on 6 March 1825, and issued in parts in March 1826. It had been commissioned by Prince Galitzin in 1822, but Beethoven was then deeply immersed in his Ninth ('Choral') Symphony. D'Indy calls this quartet the last of his pastoral symphonies, for it was written in the country and breathes the love of nature that was so characteristic of the composer. It contains yet another great slow movement, an adagio with variations.

The posthumous quartets stand alone. They were not composed in the order in which they are numbered, the first being the A minor, op. 132, which dates from the illness the composer suffered in the summer of 1825, to which he refers in the inscription that heads the third of its five movements: 'Song of Thanksgiving in the Lydian mode, offered to the Divinity by a Convalescent'. Then followed the B flat, op. 130 in six movements, which was begun in 1825 and finished in the summer of 1826, the finale then consisting of a 'Grande Fugue tantôt libre, tantôt recherchée', but the composer's friends were so intimidated by its vast dimensions that they prevailed upon him to substitute the present finale, which was composed in November 1826. It is in this, the substituted finale, that will be found the theme which instigated, rather than inspired, Borodin's quartet in A major. The fugue, one of Beethoven's most colossal conceptions, is now known as a separate work, op. 133. Op. 131, in C sharp minor, and op. 135, in F major, were both composed in 1826, the latter being dated 26 October. Another fragment that dates from

November of that year is the Andante maestoso in C major from the sketches of a projected string quintet commissioned by Diabelli, and published by him about 1840 in arrangements for piano solo and piano duet under the title 'Beethoven's Last Musical Thought'. He died on 26 March 1827.

The posthumous quartets made their way in the world but slowly. For many years after Beethoven's death they were regarded as, to say the least, enigmatic. Even today, when their glorious achievement has long been acknowledged and understood, there are still some who pause before them as before some temple to which initiation is necessary. This is the less surprising in that Beethoven's immediate successors for the most part misunderstood his teaching, both as regards cyclic form, and as revealed in the Beethoven variation. When Liszt and Wagner initiated so-called metamorphosis of themes they were thought to have diverged from the classic line, represented by Brahms, whereas in reality they were carrying out the indications of the Beethoven variation. As for cyclic form – the development of a cyclic sonata from thematic cells – there exists scarcely a sign of it between Beethoven's posthumous quartets and the mature works of César Franck.§

The volume and complexity of Beethoven criticism has increased at a frightening rate since Edwin Evans wrote these chapters. Computers have been brought in to deal with questions of stylistic and harmonic analysis; new terms and semi-mathematical concepts have appeared, making the new criticism a matter for specialists only. At the same time, the music itself has grown easier to listen to, partly because we can all become familiar with it through radio and recording, but also because of the general raising of standards of performance. In the past, the late quartets sounded *difficult* because they were indeed difficult for the performers; *obscure* because players found it hard to get through the technical difficulties to the musical thought that lay behind. Today, even the terrible difficulties of the *Grosse Fuge* are occasionally mastered, so that playing and listening are no longer the ordeals they once were. 'Beethoven, why are you so bad-tempered – especially in your second period?' Busoni once wrote. But today, the face no longer wears the old portentous frown. The mystery of the late works is as great as ever; they have lost none of their power to convey deep emotion; but we are better placed now to appreciate their exuberance, sensuous use of the medium, light-hearted and light-handed humour, rather different from the deliberated jokes of early- and middle-period works. Beethoven was at one time thought (on the strength of a few remarks made to careless players in moments of exasperation) to have resented the physical limitations imposed by instruments and performers, and to have written for the ideal instruments of his imagination. Yet there are hardly any quartets (except those of Bartók) which grow in like manner from the nature and technique of the instruments.

§ 3 THE ROMANTIC DAWN

Before proceeding with Beethoven's contemporaries in his own part of Europe it is appropriate that we should turn aside in favour of one who was not only his senior by ten years but with whom there was an exchange of influences, recalling that between Haydn and Mozart. Beethoven had the highest regard for Cherubini, whom he esteemed above all living writers for the stage. He even declared that if ever he wrote a Requiem, he would borrow from Cherubini's. On the other hand Cherubini was profoundly impressed with Beethoven's quartets, of which eleven had appeared before he, the older man, wrote his first, in E flat. This was in 1814. Cherubini's second quartet, in G, is merely an adaptation of the Symphony composed in 1815 for the Philharmonic Society of London, with a new adagio added in 1829. His best quartets were yet to come. The third, in D minor, was completed on 31 July 1834, the fourth 12 February 1835, the fifth 28 June 1835, and the sixth 22 July 1837, after which he wrote a string quintet which was completed on 28 October 1837. Beethoven had then been dead ten years, and Cherubini was advanced in his seventies. He had absorbed all that Beethoven had written and, like him, had reached a stage of inward reflection, composing without external preoccupation. A further analogy is that Cherubini's last three quartets were published posthumously. He was a great musician. He could scarcely have been otherwise and earned Beethoven's warmly expressed admiration. The worst that can be said of him is that his great skill is sometimes too apparent. But by the 1830s the Romantic Movement had set in and he was too austerely classical to find favour at such a time. Nevertheless, his quartets held their place in the repertoire until comparatively recent times.

In the compositions of Hummel there is much that is still of interest today. His best-known work is the septet for piano, flute, oboe, viola, cello, double bass and horn, op. 74, which is still occasionally heard, but there is greater merit in the piano quintet, op. 87 (with double bass), which is his best chamber work. He also wrote seven piano trios, three string quartets, and a 'Military' septet, op. 114, so called because of the inclusion of the trumpet, the other instruments being piano, flute, violin, clarinet, cello and double bass.

Weber is the first of the great Romantics we encounter in the field of chamber music, but it was not congenial to his flamboyant temperament and his contribution amounts to no more than three works, the composition of which was spread over many years. Thus the adagio of the piano quartet, op. 18, was composed at Karlsruhe, on 15 October 1806, but the work was not completed until 25 September 1809. This is the best known of the three. The clarinet quintet was begun in 1811, on the composer's becoming acquainted with Heinrich Joseph Baermann, a virtuoso of that instrument, with whom he travelled, but it was not completed until 24 August 1815. Strictly speaking, it is a solo work for clarinet with string accompaniment, and in no way to be compared with that of Mozart. The slow movement, bearing the title 'Shepherd's Lament', of the trio for piano, flute and cello, op. 63, originated in October 1813, the rest of the work in 1818 and 1819. It was not so much a case of sketching and revising as of piecing together movements that were not part of a self-contained musical conception.§

There has been a revival of interest over the last decade in the works of Anton Reicha, a Czech composer who spent his working life in Austria, Germany and Paris, and who had been an intimate friend of Beethoven's when he was attached to the court orchestra at Bonn. His wind quintets have remained in the repertory partly because of the shortage of wind ensemble music for the growing number of wind chamber music enthusiasts. But they are worth playing for their own sake, as the music of a cultivated composer, evidently familiar with the chamber music of Haydn and Mozart, whose twenty-five quintets are expertly written for the instruments, in true chamber music style.

The Spanish composer Arriaga y Balzola wrote three quartets while he was still a student at the Paris Conservatoire. Their high quality was at once recognized, and they were published in Paris in 1824, two years before his tragically early death at the age of nineteen. In the quartets, Arriaga sometimes falls into the common student fault of allowing too little light and air into the music; but their freshness and easy eloquence are delightful qualities. Developments are resourceful, the treatment of instruments apt, interest well distributed between parts; most important of all, the tone of voice is Arriaga's own. His small but individual contribution to the chamber music repertoire has a value out of proportion to its size; Arriaga remains the only composer who is remembered today primarily for his quartets.

§ 4 SCHUBERT

It is rather to Schubert that we turn as the pioneer of the Romantic Movement in chamber music, to which he was inured from boyhood. His was a musical family, and quartet meetings were frequent; at them two of his elder brothers played violin, he the viola, and his father the cello. When he grew older the meetings took place elsewhere, but all his life he was an active participant in chamber music, and it is therefore not remarkable that it should represent a substantial proportion of his creative output. It was many years, however before any of this music became known beyond the circle of his friends, and it took even longer to persuade publishers that it had any value. In all probability what has survived is only a part, for Schubert wrote with such ease that he often forgot all about his compositions and many of them went astray. He wrote fifteen string quartets, besides one for flute, guitar, viola and cello. Although even the earliest of them, dating from 1812, show individual movements in which the essentials of his style are present, it is not surprising that this boy of fourteen, gifted as he was, took a little longer to gain complete technical clarity and assurance. The eleventh quartet, composed in 1816, is in this respect a landmark. Other works belonging to this early period are, in order of composition, a sonata-movement for piano trio (1812), 'Eine kleine Trauermusik', and the minuet and finale of an octet, both for wind instruments (1813), the guitar quartet (1814), an Adagio and Rondo for piano quartet and string trio in one movement (1816), and a string trio in B flat (1817). Although Schubert was not yet twenty, such was the experience gained that this may be said to close the youthful period of his productivity.

The next phase opens with the 'Trout' Quintet, op. 114, for piano, violin, viola, cello and double bass, so called because it includes variations on the composer's song of that name, composed at the request of Paumgartner, a friend of Vogl the singer, with whom he was travelling at the time in Upper Austria. It dates from 1819, a period when otherwise Schubert was not much concerned with chamber music, his 'home team' having meanwhile grown into a small orchestra requiring symphonies for its provender. It was in 1820 that he returned to the string quartet and wrote the single movement in C minor which ranks as twelfth in the series. This remarkable movement, in no way comparable to the youthful quartets, shows Schubert in his early maturity. It is followed by a break lasting four years.

In 1824 Schubert wrote the octet, op. 166, for strings and wind instruments, and two string quartets in A minor and D minor respectively, thirteenth and fourteenth in the series, the latter known as 'Death and the Maiden', from the variations on the song of that name. These, however, were not composed to comply with any suggestion from without. The spirit of the song, composed seven years earlier, permeates the greater part of the whole work, which is one of Schubert's most moving compositions. Another string quartet, the fifteenth and last, in G major, followed in 1826, a work which seems to indicate a new departure in method, of which, alas, we were not destined to see the further outcome. Then, in 1827, he wrote his two finest piano trios, op. 99 and 100, respectively in B flat and E flat. These are the two works which Schumann described as one 'passive, feminine, lyrical', the other 'active, masculine, dramatic'. Not only did Schubert hear these performed in public, but the second of them was actually bought by a publisher for the munificent sum of 20 florins, 60 kronen, equivalent to something less than a pound English money! Another publisher was found to pay him 30 florins for the great C major string quintet, op. 163, which he composed in 1828, within a few months of his death. In the opinion of many, it ranks among the finest of all chamber music works.

In his concerted chamber music, Schubert, whilst producing half a dozen works that retain their hold upon our affections, did not develop to any extent the forms used by his contemporaries. On the contrary, as the first of the Romantics in this field, he may be said to have sown the seed which, many generations later, was to lead to formal disintegration. The looseness of his form, and the fluid, freely modulating tonality, which is so characteristic of him and in which he had such remarkable skill, were the first signs of that general departure from classic coherence and conciseness destined to mark the last stages of the Romantic Movement.§

Ludwig Spohr, in youth a friend of Beethoven and a great admirer of the op. 18 quartets in particular (which he led at their first performances in Leipzig and Vienna) lived to champion the works of Wagner at Cassel, where for long he held the post of Hofkapellmeister. As violinist and composer, he was for many years one of the most admired and influential musicians of his age; like Schubert, bridging the gap between classical and romantic styles. His chamber works range from violin duos (of genuine musical as well as technical interest, like the duos of Bartók) to double quartets for strings and the nonet for wind and strings which is today probably even better known than the once famous violin concertos. As a virtuoso player, Spohr wrote for strings with particular – perhaps too intimate – understanding; individual parts are always interesting to play, lying well under bow and fingers. His works display many of the most valued qualities we look for in classical chamber music – to quote a contemporary critic: 'lovely fluent song, surprising modulations, many bold canonic imitations, novel, charming and ingenious instrumentation.'

Sometimes, Spohr's gift of fluency leads him to develop and expand material in ways too easily forecastable, and to go on after our interest is exhausted (the same could be said of Mendelssohn's less inspired chamber works). Even in the first movement of the nonet, we may feel that the changing-note figure is developed too persistently; the 'eternal mastication of the theme in all voices and in all positions' noted by one hostile critic becomes wearisome, and the smoothness of manner begins to pall. But the better works are above such criticism. The octet for clarinet, two horns, violin, two violas, cello and bass (which includes a set of variations on the 'Harmonious Blacksmith' theme) does not suffer by comparison with the Beethoven sextet for strings and two horns, which it in some ways resembles. The nonet is the most charming and urbane of latter-day divertimentos, full of witty inventions. Spohr is conventionally censured for the 'cloying chromaticism' of his music, but in his best works, chromaticism is used as skilfully and discreetly as in Mozart's later works. Of Spohr's quartets, the E flat, op. 15 no. 1 stands out as a work of high quality and individuality, worthy to appear in company with the best quartets of Mendelssohn and all but the greatest of Schubert.

§ With Mendelssohn we approach the main phase of the Romantic

Movement. It will therefore be expedient if we digress to explain that Movement in relation to chamber music. An important school of aesthetics describes the history of any art movement as divisible into three chapters: primitive, classic, and decadent. In the first the artist fashions the idiom, in the second he finds it ready to his hand and exploits it, and in the third he is driven to expedients to eke it out, which he does either by emotional exhibitionism or by calling to his aid elements with which it is not immediately concerned. From that point of view romanticism (as distinct from romance, which exists always) indicates the phase which, after the classics, heralds the decadence, and its hallmarks are the free rein given to subjective emotion, and the tendency to choose themes from outside the art – in the case of music, literary or pictorial themes. Though the term 'programme music' is usually applied to that originating from the latter procedure, in reality it applies to both, for subjective emotion is itself a 'programme'. Chamber music is, however, by its very nature, not well suited to excesses in either direction. The outpouring of great passion demands more violent means, and the representation of literary or pictorial themes more colour, than lie within its scope. Hence, when we speak of the Romantic Movement in chamber music, we are speaking of its mildest manifestation. There has been scarcely any avowed 'programme' chamber music, nor has there been much that was highly charged with emotion except in a purely lyrical sense. Thus during the later decades of the 19th century chamber music was mercifully preserved from the Byzantinism that overtook the orchestra. The string quartet was never acutely threatened with the excesses that at one time appeared likely to bring the symphony to destruction.

Mendelssohn was a romantic, but his aristocratic fastidiousness made him averse to excesses, even when writing for the orchestra. For a time it became the fashion to decry him on account of the gentle romanticism that to later generations appeared as mere sentimentality, but in the revaluation of the past that has resulted from the reaction against later excesses, he is gradually becoming rehabilitated on the ground, not of his romanticism, but of his almost classic formal elegance. It is now realized, probably more vividly than when he was at the height of his fame, that, whatever may have been his weaknesses, his sense of form was well-nigh impeccable. His initiation into chamber music took the form of three piano quartets, op. 1, 2 and 3, composed 1822–25, the first in his fourteenth year. Of these the third is the most interesting, even though the piano part is made more prominent than accords with the nature of chamber music. About the same time, he also wrote a piano sextet in D, posthumously published as op. 110. But the most important work of this early period is the famous octet, which is an astonishing composition to have been produced by a lad of sixteen. It is still delightful to hear, and the scherzo, said to have been suggested by a passage from the Walpurgis-Nacht of Goethe's *Faust*, is the equal of any that he wrote in adult years. It is sometimes heard in an orchestral arrangement. The six string quartets were not composed in their numerical sequence, the order being 2, 1, 4, 5, 3, 6. The one in E flat, op. 12, contains a charming canzonetta, which is one of Mendelssohn's 'best-sellers'; but the best of them are the three comprising op. 44, and composed in 1837–38. The sixth, in F minor, op. 80, is generally believed to have been inspired by the death of his beloved sister Fanny, which would explain its elegiac feeling. He contemplated writing another quartet, but only the two middle movements came into existence and these were posthumously published with a capriccio and fugue of earlier date. Mendelssohn also wrote two string quintets, in 1826 and 1845. But next to the octet the works most frequently heard are the two piano trios in D minor and C minor, op. 49 and 66, composed respectively in 1839 and 1845. Of the first Schumann wrote: 'This is the master-trio of our time', but the second, which he had not then heard, has a more profound significance. Its mysteriously dramatic opening is typical of the early maturity of the Romantic Movement.

Though Schumann outlived Mendelssohn by nine years, he was only one year that composer's junior. It is mainly Mendelssohn's precociousness and Schumann's tardiness to approach any form of composition except that for piano which makes them appear as if separated by a longer interval of time. As is well known, having kept to piano music for nearly ten years, he plunged headlong into other kinds of music in turn. Thus 1840 is commonly called the 'song year' and 1841 the 'symphony year', there being in both cases ample reason. Then, at the beginning of 1842, he took a headlong plunge into chamber music. In the spring of that year he and Clara had been studying together the Haydn and Mozart quartets. By the end of June he had composed the three string quartets, op. 41. In September and October he added to them the magnificent piano quintet op. 44, at the first performance of which Mendelssohn played the piano part at sight. In November and December he wrote the piano quartet, op. 47, and the *Fantasiestücke* for piano trio, op. 88. Well

539

may 1842 be known as Schumann's 'chamber music year'. He did not return to this field until five years later, when he wrote the two piano trios, op. 63 and 80, in D minor and F major. A third trio followed in 1851, op. 110 in G and a set of *Märchenerzählungen* for piano, clarinet and viola in 1853, the last year of Schumann's creative life. Despite the excellent and strikingly personal quality of the string quartets, Schumann's triumph in this sphere is represented by the two great piano works, the quintet, which held the field unchallenged as the finest work of its kind until Brahms supplied a worthy pendant to it in 1864, and the quartet, which may perhaps be a little less effective in the spectacular sense, but is almost equally full of musical interest. The best of the piano trios is the first in D minor. The string quartets are attractive as exhibiting the many facets of Schumann's musical imagination, but on a lower plane of achievement. Even so, the feat he performed in that one year has not ceased to impress lovers of chamber music.

We have now reached a period which might almost be described as one of mass-production in German chamber music – a period when every German city had its group of highly respected composers, each one of whom considered himself more or less under a moral obligation to supply the countless chamber music organizations, amateur and professional, with a succession of works. Curiously enough, these rarely fell below a certain acceptable level of competence. Though not epoch-making, they were pleasant to play; they overtaxed neither the executive proficiency nor the musical understanding, as may hardly be said of much music composed today. But the bulk of this music is as dead today as any music can be. It has proved far easier in the present state of musical taste to revive Boccherini than Raff. Whether the reason is the same as the one that makes feminine fashions of a few years back appear frumpish, whereas those of half a century ago have become picturesque, is difficult to say. It may be that in the twenty-first century musicians will delve as industriously among neglected music of the 19th as those of the 20th delve in the 18th. But it would serve no useful purpose to crowd this survey with such annals, and until modern times are reached it will be well to be more sparing in the citing of names.

§ 6 BRAHMS

Thus we reach Brahms, the outstanding figure in 19th-century chamber music, to whom is due, more than to any other composer of his time, the extraordinary cult of which that music became the object in its later decades. Excluding duet-sonatas his contribution is represented by seventeen works; among them there is not one in which it could be said that 'Homer nodded'. There was one – the first piano trio, op. 8 – but the composer substituted an entirely new version. That was his first surviving chamber work, composed originally in 1854, the first version of which was certainly somewhat undisciplined, but so attractive that habitual players were, for a time, reluctant to transfer their allegiance to the 1891 edition. The next work, the strong sextet in B flat, op. 18, shows a pronounced reaction towards classical form, as if already he were conscious of the imperfection of op. 8. The slow movement comprises a splendid set of variations. Next followed the two vast piano quartets, op. 25 in G minor and op. 26 in A major, in which the form attains to that personal compromise between classical and romantic which is Brahms's characteristic achievement. Of this we see the immediate effect in the magnificent piano quintet in F minor, op. 34, which had been a string quintet and a two-piano sonata before reaching its final form. It has often been said that Brahms's works followed each other in pairs which were not similar but contrasted. This is commonly applied to the symphonies, but in the chamber music there are similar instances. Thus the G minor piano quartet, the piano quintet, and the G major string sextet which followed as op. 36, have for their pendants in the other mood, the A major piano quartet and the two string quartets, in A minor and C minor, which appeared in 1873 as op. 51. These were his first published string quartets, but he had discarded many earlier works before producing one to his satisfaction. He was to write only one more, in B flat, op. 67, and this, the lightest-hearted of the three, followed as a complete contrast to the piano quartet in C minor, op. 60, which had meanwhile appeared, and which opens with one of his most tragic movements. An interval of six years separates op. 67 from the next concerted chamber work, which is the piano trio in C, op. 87. Neither this, nor the work immediately following, the string quintet in F, op. 88, can be reckoned among general favourites. Once again they form a contrasted pair, the former being introspective, whilst Specht compares the latter to 'the meadows at Ischl in the sunshine'. Its first movement is said to have been a message of congratulation to Ignaz Brüll on his betrothal. Yet another dissimilar pair of works followed: the piano trio in C minor, op. 101, and the second string quintet, in G, op. 111, the former passionately tragic though with moments of tenderness, the latter irrepressibly high-spirited. The playing of Richard Mühlfeld, the great clarinettist, furnished the incentive to the two works which conclude the list, the clarinet trio, op. 114, and the clarinet quintet, op. 115, both published in 1892.§

In the clarinet quintet and the trio for violin, horn and piano, op. 40 (last of the great chamber works to be written for the old valveless instrument) Brahms responded to the nature of the solo instruments by writing his most lyrical, romantic, chamber music, in which subtle art and apparent spontaneity are combined with complete success.

§ With so much ground to cover it is impossible to give these seventeen works individually the consideration they deserve. Whilst nobody nowadays contests the greatness of Brahms, not all are agreed as to its nature. In the first place he added little or nothing to the wealth of musical resources that came to him from the classics. Almost alone among the great masters, he was not an inventor, he did not expand the means of his art. Then there are still many who regard him as at his best in the art of the miniature, who extol the best of his songs and look upon the last twenty piano pieces, op. 116–119, as the most ideally perfect addition to the literature of the instrument between Chopin and Debussy. His own greatest admirers unconsciously did him a disservice in fostering the legend that comprehension of his works was the mark of a superior musical intelligence, or of high caste, whereas in reality any difficulty of apprehension there may have been was due, not to the profundity of his thought, but to one of his weaknesses which can be colloquially described as the urge to pour a quart into a pint-pot. It is because of that urge that his best chamber works are those which include the piano and those which employ a large number of strings, such as the sextet in G. That is also probably the reason why he wrote only three string quartets. Good as these are, the effort to subdue his luxuriance to the sonorous possibilities of four stringed instruments would not seem to have been congenial to him. He needed more elbow room. He was the exact opposite of a Latin artist on whom limitation of means acts as a tonic. He was essentially a great German lyricist who served and enriched his art with deep devotion.§

7 GERMANY AND AUSTRIA AFTER BRAHMS

As already stated, the impetus given to chamber music by the works of the early Romanticists precipitated such a plethora of works that it would be hopeless to attempt to deal systematically with them. The works of few of Brahms's contemporaries or immediate successors are remembered today, though the names of Rheinberger, Goetz, Thuille, Reinecke and Paul Juon still appear occasionally in radio programmes or on recordings.

Meanwhile, composers who looked to Wagner rather than Brahms for leadership wrote little chamber music. Bruckner's substantial and dignified string quintet is well enough written for the medium, but lacks conversational ease and any sense that the interplay of parts may be as much a part of the music as the overall effect. In Hugo Wolf's delightful Italian Serenade for string quartet (1887), however, there is much sparkling conversational interplay. His earlier quartet in D minor, much influenced by late Beethoven, is densely textured and full of complex and elaborately worked out detail; its $\frac{6}{8}$ finale has something of the lightness and wit of the Italian Serenade. The whole work, though difficult to bring off in performance, deserves to be played much more often than it is.

Max Reger, like Brahms, was a natural lyricist who was also an immensely skilled and fluent contrapuntist. When he died in 1916, aged forty-three, he had already reached his op. 147; when we take into account the complexity and note-density of most of his works and consider that many of the opus numbers cover whole sets of works, we may marvel at and also be terrified by the industry that made it possible to produce so many extended, and manifestly *serious*, works as easily as if he was an 18th-century composer of serenades and divertimentos. In many of Reger's chamber works, the academic and the traditionalist overrule the poet. But towards the end of his life he achieved a real clarification and lightening of touch in the Serenade Trio for strings, op. 141a, and the quintet for clarinet and strings, op. 146, in which contrapuntal expertise is never paraded, and in which subsidiary parts, intricate as they are, are never obtrusive. Reger's developing feeling for colour and timbre suggests that he might have developed into a composer of striking originality if he had been less well-versed in traditional techniques and less full of reverence for 19th-century German masters. The time had come for a break with the past; the future of German music lay with Schoenberg and Hindemith, who seemed, in the first decades of the century, to be violently rejecting both the traditions and the limiting expressive vocabulary of the late Romantics. Their works, and their influence on those who followed them, can more aptly be discussed in a later chapter.

PART 3 NATIONAL SCHOOLS

§ 1 NATIONALISM AND CHAMBER MUSIC

The gradual assertion of musical nationality in the course of the 19th century is due to two causes. One is the subjective tendency inherent in the Romantic Movement. Once the composer stood committed to the subjective expression of things not necessarily connected with music – literary themes, pictorial impressions, his own emotions and so on – it was only to be expected that he would take themes from the literature with which he was most familiar, record impressions of the scenery of his native country, employ a national melodic idiom and, consciously or unconsciously, express that side of himself characteristic of the nationality to which he belonged. The other incentive to nationalism was the stifling effect of the German predominance. The influence of the German classics had become so universal that practically all music except that of French and Italian opera was perforce conceived in a German melodic idiom; as Germans naturally handled that idiom better than all others, it was almost impossible for a non-German composer to excel in his art. This seems a strong assertion, but subsequent history justifies it. Take as an example Britain, whose musical renaissance dates from the time when British composers ceased to take their musical instruction from Leipzig.

As we observed when dealing with the Romantic Movement, the nature of chamber music rendered it all but immune from the excesses of programme music, and as nationalism in music has in itself something of the nature of programme, it follows that chamber music was correspondingly slower to show the outward symptoms of nationalism, whatever changes might be taking place in its inner substance. There is very little in chamber music corresponding to Smetana's *Vltava*, Glazunov's *Stenka Razin* or Vaughan Williams's *Norfolk Rhapsody*; and what little there is is mostly of quite recent date. In chamber music nationalism began quietly, almost surreptitiously. There is no sign of it in the chamber works of Sterndale Bennett – English nationalism was as yet unborn – and there is but the faintest suggestion of it in those of his Danish contemporary, Niels W. Gade.

Apart from the rather mild suggestions of Gade, the first country to raise the flag of musical independence was Bohemia, where a national school was created by Smetana, followed by Dvořák and Fibich. Smetana wrote chiefly operas and orchestral music, the latter of 'programme' type. His chamber music also is definitely programme music and autobiographical at that. The trio (1855), which concludes with a funeral march, records the death of his eldest daughter, who at the tender age of four had shown signs of musical talent. The first of his two string quartets (1876 and 1882) is aptly described 'From my life'. It depicts in turn his early romanticism, the days of his youth when he wrote dance music (in this case a polka), his love and marriage, and his discovery 'how to treat the national material in music', and hints at his oncoming deafness in a persistent high note in the finale. The second, an incoherent work with moments of beauty, takes up the story after this catastrophe. 'It expresses the whirlwind of music in the head of one who has lost his hearing. Nobody has a notion how musical ideas fly about in the brain of a deaf man.'

Antonin Dvořák, the second of the pioneers of Czech music, was a copious contributor to all forms. Apart from seven unpublished works of his youth (five string quartets, a string and a piano quintet) he has bequeathed to us twenty-one concerted works for more than two instruments, thirteen for strings alone, and eight with piano. The interest in these works seems to grow in the degree in which the national character asserts itself, culminating in the fine quartet in E flat. This work was commissioned by the Florentine Quartet with the condition that it should be in the composer's 'Slavonic' style. It is amusing to note that the writer of a work on chamber music published in 1904 finds it necessary even at that date to say of Dvořák: 'True, the Slav idiom pervades a number of his works, but this is, as it were, a mere accident of his nationality, and in no way detracts from the splendour of his achievements.' The implication that it might have been expected to do so is evidence of the pertinacity of the general belief that music, to be good, must sound German. Of the E flat quartet in particular the same writer says: 'The melodic substance of the work is chiefly Slavonic in character, but the genius of the composer has transformed and ennobled that which otherwise would have remained as the rough material of a mere musical dialect,' as if that were not precisely what the German classics did in their day with the rough material of the German musical dialect! The national feeling also pervades the charming little pieces grouped as the Bagatelles.

The next string quartet, in C major, op. 61, composed in 1881, is less characteristic of its composer. It is as if, having begun to write under the influence of Schubert's romanticism and passed thence to nationalism, he now felt the need of Beethovenish classicism. It was followed in 1883 by the fine trio in F minor, op. 65, a work of sombre splendour. Three years passed without producing any more chamber music and then, in 1887, two works made their appearance. The first was a miniature, a trifle, written for three amateur friends for two violins and viola, a charming intimate composition which, out of place in the concert-room, has endeared itself to many for enjoyment in private. The other was the great piano quintet in A major, op. 81, which was for many years considered to be the third panel in the triptych of which the two first were represented by the piano quintets of Schumann and Brahms. Almost of equal rank is the piano quartet in E flat, op. 87, which followed in 1889. A highly characteristic work is the Dumky Trio, op. 90, for piano, violin and cello, composed in 1891. The word 'Dumka', which has been freely translated as 'Elegy', describes a movement of which the chief feature is an alternation of yearning melancholy with unrestrained gaiety. Dvořák frequently uses the form for slow movements, or scherzi, sometimes making the rapid section, usually a 'Furiant', into a separate movement. Here he has taken six Dumky, of which, however, the first three are linked together, whilst the others correspond to slow movement, scherzo and finale. Of course the style does not make for the coherence of a cyclic work in sonata form, but its folk-tune character and charming simplicity have long since established the Dumky Trio as a firm favourite.

The following year Dvořák accepted the American engagement, the memory of which was to be perpetuated in the symphony 'From the New World', and in the quartet in F major, op. 96, of 1893. The composer had paid a visit to a colony of his countrymen who had emigrated and settled at Spillville. He was charmed with his surroundings and pleased to find such peace after his hectic experience of New York. Though the 'Negro' melodies have attracted more attention there is very nearly as much of lyrical, nostalgic feeling expressed in the work. In the middle of the finale there is even a suggestion of the organ in the Spillville Church, upon which Dvořák was invited to play during his visit. The same year also produced a string quintet in E flat, op. 97, in which American suggestions are equally plentiful. Its scherzo is said to have been prompted by an Indian dance. But even in this work the Slavonic Dvořák is not long silent. On his return he wrote the string quartets in G major, op. 106, and A flat, op. 105, in that order. Apart from a glimpse of America in the former, these two fine works reveal the composer back in his own country. The rest of his life was spent upon operas, and upon symphonic poems on subjects derived from the national folk-lore. In these two quartets, among the most beautiful he wrote, he bade a last farewell to chamber music.

Zděnek Fibich, the third of this trio of pioneers, was not the equal of the other two, but an active participant in the rise of Czech music. Moreover, it was he who, in an unpublished quartet, composed in 1874, introduced for the first time into a chamber work the national dance of Bohemia, the polka, said to have been invented by a country waitress in 1830, and brought to Prague by some students. Smetana introduced one two years later in his first quartet. Fibich's published works comprise a string quartet, and a trio, quartet and quintet, each with piano.§

Leoš Janáček came to chamber music late in life, and followed Smetana in writing two quartets based on emotional rather than formal programmes. The first, based on Tolstoy's *Kreutzer Sonata*, reflects the agony and misery of the murderer and his victim in the original story (there is no connection with Beethoven's music); the second more lyrical quartet 'Intimate Pages' was inspired by a passionate attachment which Janáček formed during the last decade of his life. While composers who follow the central Western tradition have so often occupied themselves with the maintenance of melodic continuity and the extension of thematic material, Janáček (and particularly in the first quartet) builds mosaic-like structures out of the smallest melodic units. Both quartets make use of folk-song-like material; through their use of sometimes obsessive repetition, declamatory gesture, unpredictable and abrupt changes of mood and texture, they suggest strongly the spontaneous ebb and flow of human emotions; no other quartets produce quite the same sort of psychological effect on the listener. Janáček also wrote a light-hearted concertino for piano, two violins, viola, clarinet, bassoon, and horn, and a suite for wind quintet with added bass clarinet, *Mládí*, in the same individual and fragmented manner.

Bohuslav Martinů, who spent the middle years of his life in Paris (where he studied with Roussel) is best known today, in chamber music, for the unrepresentative *La Revue de Cuisine* for clarinet, bassoon, trumpet, violin, cello and piano; an arrangement of movements from a ballet score. He was influenced by Stravinsky and by jazz, and most of all by the forms and textures of the 18th-century Concerto Grosso, the influence of which can be seen in the sometimes over-busy contrapuntal textures of his chamber works, of which he wrote more than fifty. Later in life, he turned increasingly to the string quartet ('I feel at home here, intimate and at ease') and to thematic material drawn from the folk-music of his own land. In the last four of his seven quartets, there are many reminders of his kinship with Dvořák. His ready melodic invention and his ability to write music that appeals to players as well as to listeners supports the comparison.

3 SCANDINAVIA

Sweden has a long tradition of chamber music composition. The well-written but not very individual quartets of Johan Wilkmanson were seen and approved by Haydn. Franz Berwald, a composer of bolder imagination of the early romantic era wrote three quartets and two piano quintets, which might be better known if it were not for the clumsiness of the piano writing.

But the first Scandinavian composer to write music with a distinctively national flavour was Edvard Grieg, whose string quartet contains much delightfully picturesque music and can be enjoyed by anyone who does not insist on every chamber work conforming to classical patterns or treating of deep and serious matters. The Dane Carl Nielsen is best known in England for his symphonies; but the fourth of his four early quartets is a vigorous and tuneful work with many characteristic Nielsen touches. The later wind quintet is by far his most original and successful chamber work; an inventive and often witty piece, in which the characters of the original players, as well as the characters of their instruments, are written into the music of the final variations.

Sibelius's one quartet, *Voces Intimae*, broad and masterful in design and serious in import, is one of the finest of his non-symphonic works. Only the title could be criticized; since the tone of voice is never intimate, and the manner of writing for the instruments, effective though it is, has little of the subtlety of nuance or suggestion of close interaction between players that distinguished most quartet writing from Haydn's day to Bartók's.

Vagn Holmboe is the most considerable Swedish chamber music composer of recent years. He owes as much to external as to national influence, having studied with Ernst Toch in Berlin, and spent some time in his youth collecting folk-songs in Rumania. The influence of Bartók is sometimes apparent in his ten quartets, written between 1946 and 1969; most of all, in the concentrated use of short, narrow-intervalled motives. Holmboe often makes use of tone-rows, not necessarily of twelve notes, and of orthodox serial procedures of inversion, retrogression, and octave transposition, but without losing touch with the rhythms and melodies of his own country. The tone of voice is not always easy for Western ears to catch; but Holmboe's musical character, as revealed in the quartets, is interesting and complex, and well worth exploring.

§ 4 RUSSIA

In the fields of the opera and of symphonic music Russia has furnished the classic example of the rise and full fruition of a nationalist movement followed by a return to eclecticism once its object of emancipation had been attained. From our specific stand-point, however, the example is less complete, because chamber music does not provide any early illustrations of it and because, even in its prime, chamber music remained the section least affected by it. The founder of Russian musical nationalism was Glinka, whose operas *A Life for the Tsar* and *Russlan and Ludmilla* inaugurated the movement. But his chamber works, comprising a Trio Pathétique, two string quartets, a string sextet, and a septet, are earlier and reflect his striving for mastery of form rather than any desire to be Russian. In texture they show a grounding in the German classics, in style a leaning towards Latin elegance and refinement, but they do not aspire to any great achievement in either direction, and even in Russia they are seldom played. His immediate successors, such as Dargomizhsky and Serov, did not write chamber music, and contemporary eclectics like Afanasiev, Bachmetiev or Asanchevsky, who did, produced works worthy of respect, but little more. It was Anton Rubinstein who added most to the repertoire of Russian chamber music, and though he occasionally made use of a Russian theme, as Beethoven had done before him, his whole musical personality was so saturated with German tradition, German ideals, and German methods that there remains little ground for regarding him as a Russian composer.

It is characteristic of Tchaikovsky's position in musical history that, whilst non-Russians are almost unanimous in regarding him as eclectic, with or without Teutonic bias, Russians have become almost equally unanimous in regarding him as a national hero, now that the bitter controversies concerning nationalism are forgotten. And it is of interest to note that, whereas the avowed nationalists were less uncompromising in their chamber music than in opera or symphony, Tchaikovsky allows more of the Russian idiom to come to the surface in his chamber music than in his dramatic or symphonic works. He wrote three string quartets, in D, F, and E flat minor, completed respectively in 1871, 1874, and 1875, a piano trio in memory of Nicholas Rubinstein (1882), and a string sextet, *Souvenir de Florence* (1890). The first string quartet is famous for an andante cantabile based on a folk-tune communicated to the composer by a carpenter of the government of Kaluga in Great Russia. It is an exquisite movement and deservedly ranks with the most popular of Tchaikovsky's many 'household words'. There is also a typically Russian movement in the second quartet, but this time it is the scherzo, which is in a characteristic septuple rhythm. The third quartet is dedicated to the memory of Laub, the violinist who had led the Moscow String Quartet in performances of its two predecessors and was a close friend of the composer. It includes what has been described as the saddest movement in all chamber music, a very beautiful *Andante funebre e doloroso*, after which the brisk little Russian tunes of the finale come as a welcome relief. The trio, consisting of an Elegy in sonata-form followed by a monumental set of variations, is one of Tchaikovsky's greatest works. The theme of the second part is one that Tchaikovsky, Nicholas Rubinstein, and some of their colleagues from the Moscow Conservatoire had had performed to them by some peasants during a country walk. It appealed to the composer as peculiarly suited to enshrine the memory of his friend. The trio is a profoundly impressive work.

Meanwhile the banner of nationalism had been raised at St Petersburg by the 'Kuchka' or Big Five: Balakirev, Cui, Borodin, Mussorgsky and Rimsky-Korsakov. Of these, it was Borodin, the composer of *Prince Igor*, who not only made Russia prominent in this field, but also exercised considerable influence in other countries, notably in France. He remains the arch-type of the amateur possessed of genius, for he never abandoned his original scientific profession, but his fame lives on as one of the most important nationalist composers. He was devoted to chamber music and played the cello in a quartet of friends. His youthful works have remained unpublished, and at least one, a string sextet, is irretrievably lost. His reputation as a writer of chamber music rests thus mainly upon two very beautiful string quartets completed respectively in 1879 and 1885. The first of these is described as prompted by a theme of Beethoven from the finale of the B flat quartet, op. 130, but this relates specifically to the first subject of Borodin's first movement. No other use is made of the theme, and both quartets are written in a manner that diverges completely from the German tradition. The themes have a more sensuous and plastic quality and the treatment of the instruments is of the kind which, whatever may be the case now, a conscientious German critic of the time would have condemned as too orchestral for chamber music. Its brilliance is now universally recognized and players of chamber music have long since accustomed themselves to a certain measure of quasi-orchestral effect in quartet-writing. The two Borodin quartets rapidly made their way to Paris, where they so charmed the musical world that two of the best-known French quartets, those of Debussy and Ravel, are said to owe their incentive to a desire to emulate Borodin's example.§

Rimsky-Korsakov wrote little chamber music; his early wind quintet has picturesque charm, his later more academic works are today of little interest. Taneiev, a pupil of Tchaikovsky, and author of a famous textbook on counterpoint, produced several chamber works with piano, and six quartets, idiomatically written and individual in tone of voice. Arensky, first a pupil of Rimsky-Korsakov, then of Tchaikovsky, is better known today for his sombre Piano Trio in D minor and the beautiful variations on a theme of Tchaikovsky in his quartet, op. 35, for violin, viola, and two cellos (there is a second version for string orchestra).

The composer who at first seemed most likely to carry on the Nationalist tradition was Alexander Glazunov christened by Balakirev 'the little Glinka'. The story of Glazunov's career embraces the heyday and decline of nationalism. A fluent and prolific composer, he broke new ground with his *Five Novelettes*, op. 15, charming and picturesque genre pictures in Spanish, Oriental, Viennese and Hungarian idioms, with a central 'old-world' episode. He continued to write occasional movements in his chamber works of lighter and less formal character; but from the time of his fourth quartet, written just before the turn of the century, his chamber works became increasingly smooth; formally correct, displaying classical perfection without the vitality or immediacy of their models.

The tradition of light-hearted chamber music which gave rise to some of Glazunov's best work owed much to the publisher M. P. Belaiev, whose Friday evening chamber music parties were attended by many composers who came prepared with occasional pieces. Many of these were collected and published as *Les Vendredis*; the collections including movements by Sokolov, Glazunov and Liadov in collaboration, and Borodin, whose scherzo was later amplified to become part of his unfinished Third Symphony. Though Belaiev befriended and encouraged so many Russian composers, none of his protégés made a lasting name for himself, nor was the atmosphere of post-revolutionary Russia favourable to chamber music.

The best-known chamber music composer of the inter-war years was Prokofiev, whose two quartets (the first written in America in 1930, the second after his return to Russia in 1941) are tuneful, arresting in texture and fascinating in detail but, like so much of his non-dramatic music, revealing little of the man behind the conjuror's mask. The second makes use of Caucasian folk-material, but the spirit of the work is characteristically Prokofievan. The earlier *Overture on Hebrew Themes* (1919) and quintet for oboe, clarinet, violin, viola and double-bass (1924) are engaging entertainment pieces in Prokofiev's more astringent Parisian manner. It was not until the 1940s, when Shostakovich embarked on his series of quartets (to be considered later) that Russia produced another major chamber music composer whose quartets are central to an understanding of his musical character.

§ 5 FRANCE

The renaissance of 'absolute music' – symphonic and chamber music – in France is, despite its strong national character, not comparable to the nationalist movements we have hitherto described. France did not need to emancipate her music from foreign influences or to rediscover in the domain of folk-lore the sources of a national idiom. At most did she need a renewal of contact with her musical past. But in France music had become consistently an art of the theatre. No composer could hope to win fame except by writing for the stage and, in the striving for popular success which is the incentive in the theatre, French music had lost sight of its ideals. It is the recovery of these, rather than any assertion of nationality, that is the achievement of the French renaissance, and it is significant that, although it had set in earlier in the century, it began to gather momentum after the chastening experiences of 1870. It would seem as if these had induced a mood of *recueillement* and that, precisely, is the mood in which the noblest music thrives.

Although Gossec, one of the earliest writers of string quartets, outlived the French Revolution and the First Empire, and Grétry had somehow found time, between his innumerable operas, to write half a dozen of them, one does not imagine those disturbed times to have been conducive to indulgence in chamber music. Nor are the serious works of Cherubini, who was both a predecessor and a successor to Beethoven, likely to have found much favour in the Philistine days of the Restoration. The 19th century was well on its way to middle age before signs of a revival of interest became apparent. If then performers sought a repertoire abroad, it is no occasion for surprise, as the native repertoire was at its lowest. Small wonder that typical programmes displayed an anti-national bias resembling that evident in Britain, then and later.

When in 1840 César Franck, then a student at the Paris Conservatoire, wrote his three trios for piano, violin and cello, followed two years later by a fourth, few can have had any conception either of the status the young composer was to attain in the musical world or of the influence he was to exert on others. Long before Franck came to write the later works on which his fame now rests, and before his pupils began to make their way in the world, two other composers simultaneously entered the field of chamber music, Edouard Lalo and Saint-Saëns. The former, whose *Symphonie Espagnole* is so well known, wrote three piano trios and a string quartet which, although not ranked with his best works, are characterized by the sense of colour and rhythm one associates with him. Saint-Saëns's output in this sphere was more copious and more important. It began in 1855 with a piano quintet, op. 14, and continued almost to the end of his life. He was a superb craftsman and a master of the classic style, but whilst producing brilliantly polished work, he contributed to it little that was new.§ Such stylish and brilliant, if heartless, works as the septet for piano, trumpet and strings, help us to see the point of Busoni's judgment: 'He was a man of this world; but he was at least a *grand seigneur* in the kingdom of music.'

It is not easy to identify any particular tone of voice or to guess at the depth of feeling behind the music of Saint-Saëns. Gabriel Fauré, his near-contemporary, was a less versatile composer; but his intimate, subdued chamber works have remained in the repertory, their particular flavour being unlike that of any other chamber music. The manner is restrained; rhythmic interest is not great; the smoothly-flowing tunes move mainly by step; harmonies are as personal to the composer as those of Tchaikovsky. The lyrical first and the more impassioned second piano quartets are Fauré's master-works in this field; the two piano quintets contain much beautiful music; but in the smaller ensemble, with its lighter textures, he seems to have found the ideal medium for what he has to say. All the chamber works, except for the late and rather uninteresting *Quatuor pour instruments à cordes sans piano* are piano-centred; but Fauré's piano is the gentlest and most cultivated of instruments, fit to consort with quieter, non-percussive strings.

§ In 1878 César Franck began the composition of his piano quintet, his first chamber work after an interval of thirty-six years, during which he had attained to mature mastery. It is scarcely necessary to dilate upon the quality of this work which for many years held its place beside the great quintets of Schumann, Brahms and Dvořák. In a truer sense than any of these, Franck shows himself in this work, and perhaps even more in the string quartet of 1889, a close follower of Beethoven, carrying out what might be termed the latter's testamentary dispositions as indicated in the posthumous quartets. It is not, however, only in his works that César Franck lives, but in his disciples.§

Vincent d'Indy is remembered today as the founder of the *Schola Cantorum* rather than for his compositions, which included two string quartets and a string sextet, and several works with piano. In these he developed further Franck's principles of cyclic form and variation, suppressing his genuinely poetic imagination in the process. Ernest Chausson (another pupil of Franck) wrote a *Chanson perpétuelle* for soprano and piano quintet and a concerto for piano, violin and string quartet; delicately woven, mournful and sensuous works which occupy a middle-ground between Massenet and Debussy. Guillaume Lekeu and Alberic Magnard left a few chamber works of real individuality which deserve to be better known outside France.

§ It seems strange that only four years should separate the string quartets of César Franck and Debussy, but one was the fruit of a mature mind of classical build, the other the utterance of a young composer whose entrance into the musical world had about it something of the dramatic. Scarcely known at first beyond the limits of a small côterie, Debussy created on the general public the impression of being that rare phenomenon, a genius without precursors. We know now where his antecedents were to be found. As for his string quartet, two influences presided at its birth. Debussy had attended Franck's organ class at the Conservatoire, and although he never studied composition with him, it is unlikely that he left without knowing something of cyclic form as understood by the master who was so devoted to it. The concerts of Russian music organized by M. Belaiev in connection with the Paris Exhibition of 1889 had precipitated a great vogue in Paris musical circles for the members of the 'Kuchka'. Borodin's string quartets suddenly became famous. They had the qualities of formal elegance that appeal to Latin taste, and more than one French composer found in them an ideal to emulate. Thus Debussy's quartet recalls in its substance Borodin and in its form César Franck. It is not strictly cyclic, but one theme is common to three of its four movements and the other has a remote affinity to certain movements of Borodin. At the same time its harmonic texture is intensely characteristic of Debussy himself, of the course his development was to take. His only other piece of concerted chamber music was a sonata for flute, viola and harp, written in 1916 as one of an intended set of six various sonatas (of which only three were completed).

A decade separates Debussy's quartet from that of Maurice Ravel, a pupil of Fauré, who was beginning to attract attention by the originality of his harmonic ideas. He, too, is said to have been prompted by the example of Borodin. He is also said to have been influenced by Debussy, but that is scarcely borne out by a comparison of contemporary works by each. Ravel's whole outlook was more formal, more precise, and more pointed than Debussy's. He had an 18th-century passion for clarity, and was temperamentally averse to the 'atmospheric' effects that played so important a part in the art of Debussy. His string quartet, which is dedicated to his master, Fauré, is transparently clear, despite an apparent complexity of construction. § Ravel's next chamber work was an Introduction and Allegro for harp, flute, clarinet and string quartet, a refined, yet sensuous work, in which Ravel discovered a new character for the harp, avoiding the usual clichés and mannerisms associated with the instrument, and using the unconventional ensemble with Mozartian precision and imagination. He was equally successful in discovering new textures and relationships between instruments in the much-exploited medium of the piano trio; his magnificent trio, finished in 1914, is one of his most powerful, sustained, and closely-integrated works, with an emotional depth that is possibly connected with his use of themes and rhythms from his native Basque country.

Albert Roussel, one of the most distinguished of d'Indy's pupils, shows few affinities with his teacher or with any of his contemporaries. His liking for bright, harsh textures, strong and often dissonant harmony, energetic *détaché* rather than smooth legato, and clear formal design, separates him from the impressionists; but his works have none of the conscious detachment of the Parisian entertainers of the inter-war years. His most characteristic chamber works involve wind instruments; and include a delightful divertissement for piano and wind quintet, a serenade for flute, harp and strings, and a trio for flute, harp and cello.

The years after the First War brought a reaction against the high seriousness of Franck and d'Indy. The misty harmonies and vague forms of the pre-war impressionists gave way to neo-classicism and the light, brittle entertainment pieces of 'Les Six' and of the distinguished emigré composers who had made Paris their home – including Martinů, Prokofiev, and Stravinsky, whose wind octet could almost be called the best and most typically French chamber work of the period. Poulenc's witty and tuneful sextet for wind and piano and trios for oboe, bassoon and piano, and for trumpet, horn and trombone, are among the best examples of light music for sophisticated listeners. But the frivolity of two other members of 'Les Six' was only skin-deep. Honegger was a fundamentally serious composer whose three string quartets, highly contrapuntal abstract works, belong to no national tradition (which may partly be accounted for by his Swiss origins). Milhaud, in his eighteen string quartets, showed a Haydn-like ability to be serious and light-hearted almost in the same breath. He followed 19th-century traditions in regarding the quartet as the most rewarding and exacting form of composition, 'at once an intellectual discipline and the crucible of the most intense emotion'. The emotional and technical range is very wide, the mixture of styles and techniques sometimes disconcerting. Naïve diatonic tunes are submitted to every sort of polytonal and polyrhythmic treatment. Milhaud learnt much from both Stravinsky and Schoenberg; there are echoes of folk-music of many lands, of jazz, and even of the Haydn quartets Milhaud used to play in his youth. There are movements of great contrapuntal complexity and ingenuity, as in the 14th and 15th quartets, which can be played separately or simultaneously, but also simple, lyrical movements of charm and easy sentiment. Milhaud sometimes seems to be too ready to accept any idea that comes into his head as material for prolonged discussion; but there is much fine music in the quartets to give us insight into his attractive musical character; buoyant, energetic, and perpetually enquiring.

Jean Françaix has written several very light yet individual works, including a string trio and a short quartet for saxophones. Messiaen, the most distinguished of the older generation of French composers, has written only one chamber work: the *Quatuor pour la fin du temps*, composed while he was a prisoner of war in the 1940s; a work of immense length and variety, in which sensuous organ-loft harmony, pentatonic tunes suggesting Eastern origins, echoes of bird song (and of César Franck) all meet. The whole is brilliantly written for virtuoso performers, and has the strong, unmistakable atmosphere and the appearance of existing outside normal musical time that are so characteristic of this composer's best works.

§ 6 BRITAIN: EARLY BEGINNINGS

The British renaissance stands on a different footing from that of any other of the nationalist movements that originated in the 19th century. Its task was the heaviest, for surely never was any musical nation so completely subject to alien influences as England a century ago, never did a musical nation break so completely with its own past tradition as England did with that bequeathed by the Tudor classics, and never did a group of composers have to face so stubborn an anti-national prejudice as that which confronted the pioneers of that movement. If the battle has been won, credit must be given not only to these pioneers, but even to those precursors who, though they did not yet produce music that we recognize as English, did at least show such audiences as were prepared to listen to them that English birth was no insuperable impediment to the writing of music on classical models. And in each generation there has been some one composer who did this with so much credit as to pave the way for the renaissance that was to set in later. In that sense the story goes back to Mendelssohn's contemporary, Sterndale Bennett. His piano trio is a rather frail plant, and even his piano sextet is not very sturdy, but how pleasant both are in comparison with the works of his contemporary G. A. Macfarren! Then came the age of the great precursors Parry, Stanford and Mackenzie. Of these the last-named produced an early piano trio, string quartet and piano quartet, Parry wrote numerous early concerted works, and Stanford, with very little encouragement, continued writing them most of his life. Despite the Scottish strain in Mackenzie, and the Irish in Stanford, the influence of early German studies weighs so heavily upon all this music that it is difficult to realize its bearing upon later developments; but one must admire the persistent hammering upon the door of British prejudice, against which was being waged a war of attrition, the results of which were to show later.

There were three reasons why, in the early years of the 19th century, the situation looked brighter for the British chamber music composer than at any previous time. First, during the whole of the 19th century, as far as can be ascertained, not a single string quartet by a British composer had been published in England. The very few that had found their way into print appeared in foreign catalogues. When in 1903 Novello's published McEwen's fourth string quartet, they took a step which augured well for the 20th century, in the course of which this reproach has been largely removed.

Second, a little later, in 1905, Walter Willson Cobbett, who throughout his long life (1847–1937) was one of the keenest amateur chamber music players in the country, instituted a series of competitions for works in a form that was intended to be a modern equivalent of the 'Fancy' – short instrumental compositions that were common in the Golden Age of English music from Tudor times to the Restoration. It then enjoyed comparative freedom from formal rules, but modern practice, with its devotion to sonata form, interpreted the Phantasy as a kind of condensation of the usual three or four movements, in which sections equivalent to a slow movement and scherzo were interpolated between exposition and recapitulation. Even so, considerable freedom remained in the choice of thematic material, which might be related or contrasted, and in the general method of construction. The first competition was for a string quartet and the prize went to W. Y. Hurlstone, a young composer of great promise whose career was unfortunately cut short at thirty years of age. A second competition followed, for a Phantasy trio, in which the three prizes went to Frank Bridge, John Ireland and James Friskin. Yet others followed, and by 1915 the repertoire had been enriched by no fewer than twenty-four works in this form. A few more competitions were held, in addition to which numerous works were commissioned from composers of established repute. Mr Cobbett also instituted free libraries, prizes at the Royal College of Music and a Cobbett medal for services to chamber music, and compiled and published, in 1929, a monumental *Cyclopedic Survey of Chamber Music* (a supplement, edited by Colin Mason, was added in 1963). There are very few English composers of chamber music whose works do not include at least one due to his initiative, and this applies to many whom we shall not have space to mention.§

The third reason why composers of chamber music (in London at any rate) could feel encouraged, was that at last there existed in London a regular weekly series of chamber concerts, running for six months of the year. At the South Place concerts, organized by another enthusiastic amateur violinist, A. J. Clements, many British works were included in the programmes, and a yearly prize was given for a chamber music work. At these concerts (which, in 1977, still continue at Conway Hall) a regular audience was built up; the best instrumentalists in London came, often without fee, to play for Mr Clements; composers were sure of a sympathetic and discriminating audience. For the first time, chamber music came to be regarded as a necessary part of the London scene.

7 BRITAIN: FROM ELGAR TO BRITTEN

If a composer is really interesting to us, we will be interested in everything about him – his love-life, his laundry lists, and his chamber music; even when he has no particular bent in that direction. In the case of Vaughan Williams and Elgar (and, later, of Walton and Britten) the chamber music is peripheral to their output, and throws little fresh light on the composers' personalities. Elgar's piano quintet and string quartet, both first performed in 1919, are postludes to his main work, in which Elgar reverts to the emotional moods and techniques of earlier days. Thus, in the quartet, the first movement seems to look back to the optimistic first movement and scherzo of the Second Symphony, the second could almost be mistaken for an intermezzo from the *Wand of Youth* (but Elgar feels bound to draw it out beyond intermezzo-length); the third, a vigorous bustling movement, is as clearly destined from the beginning to be a finale as the last movement of the Enigma variations. Interest is predominantly in the top line; it is hard not to feel that much of the music would sound better in Elgar's orchestration; while the type of string virtuosity that is so thrilling in, say, the *Introduction and Allegro* becomes almost tame on solo strings. Yet the work has so many beauties and characteristic Elgarian happenings that we should be the poorer without it. The same could be said of the piano quintet; though here, Elgar's failure to find inspiration in any particular aspect of the piano's nature is bound to deter potential performers.

For Vaughan Williams there was rarely any temptation to overindulge in instrumental virtuosity. The themes of both quartets can be sung almost as well as they can be played; the predominant texture is one of smooth, song-like counterpoint. It is difficult today to understand how the G minor quartet (written in 1908 and revised in 1921) could ever have puzzled critics, as it did in 1909. It is a graceful, easy-going work of perhaps self-conscious simplicity and neatness, strongly indebted to Ravel's quartet in its tunes and textures (Vaughan Williams studied with Ravel during the time of its composition). Well-made and inventive, it stands in the same relationship to later works as, say, Bizet's youthful symphony stands in relationship to his; and tells us as much about the composer's later character.

The second quartet, written in 1944, and dedicated to the violist Jean Stewart, has a leading part for viola. Here, Vaughan Williams speaks in the language which he had made his own, and which his audiences had learned to recognize and to respond to. The work covers a wider emotional range; yet, perhaps because it does embody a Vaughan Williams we already know very well from other works, the quartet seems to establish itself in the memory as an independent musical entity less clearly than the not so characteristic early work.

Parry and Stanford had proved that composition could be a respectable and responsible profession; Elgar, Vaughan Williams and Holst had, by the 1920s, almost convinced the British public that it was possible for an Englishman to write music that could be compared favourably with products from abroad. The 1920s was a period of high hope and much activity in British music, and also one of relative isolation from outside influences. Composers were not anxious to submit themselves again to continental domination and were beginning to believe in their ability to work out their own salvation. Fired by unaccustomed feelings of group solidarity, English composers began to act on their beliefs – that music was, in essence, song; that natural inspiration rather than intellectual discipline was the best guide for the young composer; that extreme measures, and violent breaks with tradition, were neither desirable nor necessary, and that the English composer must discover his destiny without reference to the strange happenings in Central Europe.

Much of the chamber music of the period, with its rhapsodies, pastorals, jocund $\frac{6}{8}$ finales inspired by folk-music, is limited in vocabulary, casual in structure and over-reliant on inspiration which may have been genuine but was not necessarily, for that reason, of high or durable quality. Yesterday's music, moreover, is never as attractive as the music of the day-before-yesterday; and so, Bax,

Moeran, Ireland, and a whole crowd of lesser composers of their time are today almost forgotten, while Rachmaninov and Elgar are back in favour. The few who enthusiastically kept up with European traditions have survived little better. The chamber music of Cyril Scott, influenced by Debussy and Scriabin, is today forgotten; the complex works of Busoni's friend and pupil, Bernard van Dieren, and of Eugene Goossens, whose chamber music is full of dashing modernisms of French and Central European cut, have also sunk almost without trace. Frank Bridge, who was little influenced in later life either by British or continental contemporaries, is better remembered. Bridge was himself a professional viola player and a member of a leading quartet. His early works have a lyrical freedom and ease which is still very attractive; the piano trio of 1907 (one of the best works to win a Cobbett prize) is conventionally neo-romantic in idiom, but already bears the marks of a distinct and interesting musical personality. Bridge, who composed much light music of outstanding sensibility and dexterity, perhaps accepted too readily the unstated propositions that the opposite of light was *serious*, and that opposites never meet. His quartets do indeed reveal more of the dark and turbulent side of his character than the more innocent early works; but the seriousness of his self-imposed task and pre-occupations with questions of style and idiom seem to have inhibited his powers of free communication, so that the powerful third and fourth quartets have something of the nature of partly-solved cross-word puzzles. Too many clues are missing for us to guess what, if the times had been different, Bridge might have done.

Arthur Bliss, an avant-gardist in the 1920s, when his early chamber works found their natural habitat at the International Society for Contemporary Music Festivals, matured into the fervent, neo-romantic composer of two powerful quartets, an oboe quintet and a clarinet quintet. Bliss's style of musical oratory seems at times just too grandiose for the medium – the vehement and impressive opening of the first quartet would lose little and gain much if it were played by a large string orchestra. But this quartet and the clarinet quintet (admirably written for the instrument) are still two of his best works, written when he was at the height of his powers, and are full of striking musical invention. Rawsthorne's chamber works are by comparison subdued in tone, economical in use of thematic material or of florid melodic arabesques or decorative subsidiary parts (characteristic features of Bliss's chamber music). In three string quartets, a piano trio, a quintet for piano and wind, and several other works, he showed a Haydn-like skill in the close working of short motives and in holding just balance between harmonic and contrapuntal interest.

Tippett's three quartets are all contrapuntal in texture, and seem, like the chamber works of Vaughan Williams, to derive from vocal rather than instrumental origins. The second quartet is best known, perhaps because it is the most varied in style and content. The first movement makes use of madrigal techniques, with imitative points running freely against the basic metre, or creating several simultaneous metres. The slow movement is a fugue; the third, a scherzo, largely homophonic, in irregular metre, with Stravinskian skipped and added beats; the finale skilfully combines busy contrapuntal activity with serene melody; and here, after three movements in which themes have confined themselves to movement by step or in small intervals, we at last encounter a wide-ranging tune characterized by leaps of a ninth.

Tippett runs certain risks in relying so much on contrapuntal techniques – nothing becomes so soon monotonous as the *moto perpetuo* of never-resting imitative parts treading on each other's heels – but the ease and freedom of his mainly diatonic music, with its long-breathed melodies, has special attraction in a restless and anxious age, and the best music in the quartets seems to have sprung from deep levels of consciousness. Walton's one quartet and Britten's first two seem, in contrast, to be the works of craftsmen; pleased to be exercising their skills (with genuine mastery) in a new field, but driven by no inner compulsion. Britten's second quartet, immensely resourceful in its use of every sort of idiomatic string-technique, is one of the most effective and entertaining works in the modern repertory. The last movement is something more. Written in the form of the chacony (the work commemorated Purcell's 250th anniversary) it consists of a set of twenty-one variations (six harmonic, six rhythmic, six melodic, with three by way of coda) which build up into an extended and imposing structure. The late third quartet, first performed after the composer's death in 1976, is a quiet, inward-turned work, with a slow movement of visionary beauty.

8 THE UNITED STATES

In America, emancipation from conservative European (chiefly German) influence came even later than in England. The music of

MacDowell, Parker, and Chadwick was competent, founded on the best Germanic models, and was held to represent the best in American 'serious' music. The independents who are acclaimed today (including Ives, Griffes and Sousa) were not considered worthy of serious attention. Charles Ives, now hailed as the founding father of American music, has described the prevailing tone of professional and public opinion in the early years of the century, and his many encounters with academic musicians who believed that 'music had crawled into Brahms's coffin and died'. Ives himself was not drawn to the refined and polished sort of performance that conventional musicians aim at in chamber music. His second quartet was written partly in protest at the 'weak, trite, and effeminate' playing of a well-known professional quartet, which affected him as though he was 'resting his ears on a perfumed sofa-cushion'. In this work, each instrument represents a single character (the second violin that of a particularly conservative music critic). Conversation in the first movement is succeeded in the second by argument and fighting; finally they 'shake hands, shut up – then walk up the mountain-side to view the firmament'. The argument is illustrated by some of Ives' most complex and disruptive music; the second violin's attempts at sentimental cadenzas being forcibly suppressed by the other players. The first quartet, 'A Revival Service', is consonant and straightforward by comparison, though it too makes use of poly-tonality and polyrhythm. Hymn-tunes, popular songs, and dance music provide much of the material in both quartets.

Even before the First War, many younger American composers went to Paris rather than to Germany for their training: but it was not until the 1920s that the first distinguished and distinguishably American composers appeared on the scene, and that American contemporary music began to be heard in the concert-halls. Aaron Copland has described the formation of the International Com-posers' Guild in 1922 (by a Frenchman, Edgar Varèse) and the violent reactions of established conductors and performers to the New Music. Copland himself studied in Paris with Nadia Boulanger, and several other young Americans followed his example. Copland wrote two major chamber works in the inter-war years. The sextet for clarinet and strings, later re-written as the Short Symphony, is characteristic of his work at this period; sparing of notes, sternly economical in its use of thematic material, concerned with rhythmic rather than melodic development. Copland's liking for clean tex-tures, strongly athletic movement, plain functional developments in which every note works for its living, seemed at one time characteristically American, and comparisons of his music with skyscrapers and the wide open spaces of the prairies were common. Today, the strength of his own individuality and the aptness of the musical means to the subject-matter appear more significant than national characteristics. The piano quartet, a later and more easy-going work, uses two eleven-note tone-rows to motivate the action in a similarly thorough-going manner. Relationship between piano and strings is particularly happy in a work in which (to quote Copland's own comment on Liszt's music) the music was 'born in the piano ... could never have been written at a table'. The instruments used in the nonet of 1960 (three violins, three violas, three cellos) give a clue to its nature and scope. As in Bach's third Brandenburg concerto, the main point of the work lies in the nine-cornered interplay of voices. Themes themselves are relatively impersonal and restrained in character, so that the conversational arts themselves become the theme of the music.

Roy Harris, who was also for a short time a pupil of Nadia Boulanger, wrote in the 1930s much chamber music of strong individuality, including three string quartets and a piano quintet. Harris's music is generally, and justly, described as 'rugged', dealing as it does in broad and powerful musical statements and generally eschewing delicate and subtle shades of meaning. Harris's idiom owes something to American hymnology and popular music; long melodies grow from small motivic cells; the language is basically diatonic and highly contrapuntal. The third quartet consists of four preludes and four fugues (as Copland said of his music of this period: 'No Harris piece is complete without a passacaglia or fugue somewhere during its course, preferably a double or triple fugue for good measure'). Roger Sessions and Walter Piston developed from neo-classical beginnings into fluent and resourceful chamber music composers, international rather than national; unless the strong rhythmic drive of their music can be regarded as specifically American. Lastly, two powerful individualists who advanced very far on the narrowest of fronts may, on an instrument-count, be considered as chamber music composers. Edgar Varèse (founder of the International Composers' Guild which, in the words of one of his friends, 'shook the musical world into an awareness of new music and created an atmosphere tolerable for serious composers'), wrote his *Octandre* for seven wind instruments and double bass; Carl Ruggles, his *Angels* for six muted trumpets – two works which inhabit separate

564

sound-worlds of their own and lie well off the mainstream of American music. If, indeed, there is a mainstream? The days when Copland and Harris seemed to be the precursors of a new generation of national composers are past. If America had been left in musical isolation, perhaps things would have been otherwise. But the movement towards internationalism was inevitable, and was hastened by the arrival in America, before or during the last war, of the most eminent European reformers and revolutionaries of the age – Schoenberg, Stravinsky, Hindemith and Bartók.

9 NATIONALISTS OF OTHER COUNTRIES

The spirit of Italian nationalism and of the *risorgimento* expressed itself in opera, but not in chamber music. For earlier Italian composers, the writing of chamber music was regarded as a school exercise, or else as a diversion from the serious business of music. Donizetti's eighteen quartets and Rossini's five quartets and wind quintet were all written in their composers' student days, and Verdi attached so little importance to his one string quartet that he refused to publish it. Today, Rossini's quartets seem to have lost little of their youthful freshness and verve, and still have the power to delight and amuse us. Verdi's quartet is a work of no great emotional depth; but his admirers still feel a certain affection for it, perhaps because it contains so many characteristic turns of phrase and harmony. The scherzo and finale have a lightness and dexterity which must appeal to all who love *Falstaff*.

Towards the end of the 19th century, a few Italian composers appeared who were prepared to take chamber music seriously. The Sicilian Antonio Scontrino studied in Germany with Max Bruch and came home to write four quartets, which are discussed in Cobbett's Encyclopedia of Chamber Music in a twelve-page article with sixty-three examples. The complete oblivion that has descended on his works reminds us how short is the life-expectation of much conscientiously-composed and no doubt genuinely inspired music. The same fate seems likely to overtake the eight quartets of Malipiero, fluent melodious works, excellently composed in a contrapuntal idiom which avoids the clichés and vulgarities of Italian popular opera but seems to have found no attention-compelling substitute to replace them. The most influential composer of his day was Alfredo Casella, an articulate and active internationalist who was associated with many of the New Music movements of the 1920s, who similarly reacted against the crudities of *verismo*, 'the so-called passionate style', and who wrote much lively and entertaining chamber music, generally eclectic and neo-classical in idiom. The piano trio and the Serenade for clarinet, bassoon, trumpet, violin and cello are good examples of his up-to-date divertimenti aimed at the élite audiences of the inter-war years. The more pretentious chamber works of Respighi and the serious but rather colourless quartets of Pizzetti have worn less well. In the post-war years, Dallapiccola and Petrassi have written chamber works of distinction and individuality, the former having been particularly successful in adapting serial techniques to his own ends.

Poland produced only one distinguished composer of chamber music before the Second World War – Szymanowski, whose fine second quartet owes a great deal to Ravel's influence, very little to national inspiration. In Spain too, French influence has been dominant since the time of Arriaga. Of the nationalists who followed Pedrell, the first truly Spanish composer of recent times, only Joaquin Turina, who had been a pupil of d'Indy at the Schola Cantorum, evolved a convincing chamber music idiom. *Escena Andaluza* for piano, viola, and string quartet and *La Oracion del Torero* for string quartet, both based on traditional material, are attractive and picturesque works. Falla's concerto for harpsichord and six instruments is equally indebted to French and Spanish influences; it is a brilliant and characteristic work, in which neo-classical procedures are made to serve highly personal ends. Carlos Chavez and Heitor Villa-Lobos, of Mexico and Brazil, can also be mentioned here; since they have more in common with the Franco-Spanish than with German or North American composers of their time. Both have written much chamber music, but their natural exuberance and love of brilliant colour has not won them many friends among the generally staid chamber music lovers of Europe.

Hungary, for long under Austrian domination, produced no composers of chamber music of any note until late in the 19th century. Dohnányi, who studied in Budapest under the German Hans Koessler (himself a prolific chamber music composer) wrote three quartets and two piano quintets, strongly influenced by Brahms but not without a character of their own; and a serenade for string trio, op. 10 which is one of the liveliest and best-written of all works in this genre, and which avoids the prolixity and occasional over-elaboration of the larger chamber works. Zoltán Kodály's two quartets and his trio for two violins and piano are pleasant, tuneful pieces, but are not to be compared with his far more interesting and characteristic works for voices or orchestra. (Bartók's chamber works will be discussed later.)

Hungary, in common with almost every other European country and many non-European countries, including Israel, has produced in the last half-century many skilled and prolific composers of chamber music; but few of their works have been heard outside their native countries, except in rare concerts given by visiting ensembles or in 'exchange' radio programmes. Nationalist traits are still to be found in the works of many East European composers; but in the West, the upheavals of the inter-war years led to the emergence of some composers who had no national ties but who could still hardly be thought of as international; since their music fell into no Schoen-bergian, Hindemithian, Stravinskian, or other recognizably 'inter-national' category. We have assigned Milhaud to France, Martinů a little doubtfully to Czechoslovakia; but Ernest Bloch cannot be thought of as either Swiss or American, though three of his four quartets and the fine piano quintet were written after he had settled in America. His extended chamber works, written in an individual tonal idiom, have intellectual vigour and a strong emotional content. Bloch was himself a string player; the powerfully expressive style and technique of the late-Romantic solo string-player who deals in public rather than intimate utterances is implicit in the quartets – deeply-felt works that are always effective in performance, for which some niche in musical history should surely be found.

But we have by now over-passed the end of the period in which composers can sensibly be divided up nation by nation. Though there are today many systems and dialects, ideologies and credos, the divisions between composers of different persuasions pass across national frontiers. The world of the contemporary composer is becoming increasingly an international one, in which Shostakovich, Britten, Elliott Carter, Messiaen, Stockhausen or Cage may be the chief influence on any young composer in almost any country. For the time being at least, the force of nationalism, expressed through music that speaks in the native accents of a single country, seems to be spent.

PART 4 INTERNATIONALISTS, CONTEMPORARY AND AVANT-GARDE

1 SCHOENBERG TO STRAVINSKY

The great revolutionary composers of the first decades of the present century were all confirmed chamber music writers, who early in their careers abandoned the use of the vast orchestras developed by Wagner, Mahler and Strauss. The reasons for this change of direction are many. First and most obviously, that composers were tired of the super-saturated sound of the conventional symphony orchestra, which had also become associated with the expressive clichés of music against which they were reacting. Next, that the very complex and subtle music of Schoenberg and his pupils demanded dedicated specialist performers rather than all-purpose orchestral musicians. Third, that composers were drawn positively to experiment with new and strange timbres and sound-combinations (in this, Mahler's example had strong influence). Lastly, that in times of economic stress the number of composers whose orchestral works regularly reach performance is very small indeed.

Schoenberg's *Pierrot Lunaire* is the father of many of the works for chamber ensemble of his own and succeeding generations; heard and appreciated by Stravinsky, Debussy, Milhaud, Hindemith, and even Puccini, and known today by countless listeners who would never switch on the radio to hear one of the abstract chamber works – which are still very little played today, in spite of Schoenberg's high standing in the world of music and of the many appreciative and analytical articles that regularly appear in the musical journals. Therein lies part of the trouble; Schoenberg has become for us too much of an interesting historical figure, so that we approach the music with reverence and furrowed brows, ashamed of our inability to hum the tone-rows, or listening for the discords that made history and missing the music itself in the process.

In fact, the 'unclassifiable discord' which caused *Verklärte Nacht* to be rejected by one Viennese concert society at the end of the 19th century cannot inflict the smallest shock on today's listeners, hardened by exposure to so many picturesque, non-functional discords in more recent music (as Hans Keller has pointed out, our inability to be upset is not pure gain: 'while the work's first audiences were too much taken aback to understand, we aren't taken aback far enough'). The difficulties of Schoenberg's music still exist, but they lie in other directions: lack of reinforcing repetitions; far-fetched processes of thematic development; lack of clear-cut contrasts of textures and tempo; the often uncomfortable emotional message of the music, in which the deepest subconscious experiences seem to be exposed. The music, moreover, is literally 'difficult' for performers; its complex and dense counterpoints cannot be heard at all, in any meaningful sense, in indifferent performance.

In *Verklärte Nacht* there are no serious problems; Schoenberg's string sextet, composed in 1899, is founded on a poem by Richard Dehmel, which describes a passionate meeting of strangers in a bare, cold wood. The music is closely related to that of other late-romantics, and most obviously to that of Wagner and Strauss. The motives are much-exposed, and are developed in conventional ways which the listener can easily follow. The sensuous harmony and the rich and complex polyphony combine to make *Verklärte Nacht* one of the most fervent and eloquent of all chamber works.

In the first and second quartets, both written before Schoenberg evolved the twelve-tone system, we witness a progressive move towards atonality (or at any rate away from fixed tonality) and a growing concentration of musical thought. Today, we hear them as belonging to the same tradition as the quartets of Brahms and Reger, and recognize them as masterworks of their kind; though we may well be put off by the sustained richness and elaboration of texture, by feelings of inferiority brought on by works which demand the almost-impossible of the listener (only initiates can hope to follow a quarter of what is going on in performance) and by their particular emotional flavour.

The works written after Schoenberg had evolved his method of 'composition with twelve tones related only to one another' are generally less ebullient in style, more symmetrically structured and characterized by the use of simpler classical forms. The wind quintet of 1924 is one of his least approachable works; dense in texture, built around themes that are curiously unmemorable, and which do not seem to be conceived in terms of the instruments involved. Here the working-out of thematic processes seems to take precedence over all else. The Serenade for clarinet, bass clarinet, mandoline, guitar and string trio (with bass solo in one movement) and the Suite for three clarinets and piano quartet are among the lighter-hearted, though still complex and highly-organized, chamber works, in which there is a Mahlerian vein of parody. Simple elements of march, dance, and even a diatonic folk-song (in the variations of the Suite) are involved in sophisticated compositional processes. Something of the spirit of neo-classicism here enters Schoenberg's work, and the third and fourth quartets, while still highly polyphonic, are also very clear in form; less richly ornate and also less inventive than the more expressive early chamber works. The string trio of 1946 (which, as Schoenberg told Thomas Mann, embodies the experiences of a serious illness and recovery) marks a return to a freer, more fluid style, and is one of the most imaginative and inventive of his later works.

Alban Berg wrote only one chamber work, the Lyric Quartet, a complex and deeply expressive piece, in which the finest shades of expressive nuance have to be observed and the most precise balance achieved if the composer's intentions are to be fully realized. Berg's twelve-tone music maintains connections with tonality, and the strength of the lyrical and poetical impulse helps the listener to forget the complexity and extreme sophistication of the compositional methods employed. Anton Webern's early *Five pieces for quartet*, op. 5 and the *Six Bagatelles*, op. 8 are carefully-worked essays in an expressionist idiom, in which textures and types of movement vary often from bar to bar. The quartet op. 28 and string trio op. 20 are characteristic of his mature style; music which foregoes all expressive gestures and all matter which is not strictly thematic; in which no instrument is ever responsible for more than two or three consecutive notes in any motif or note-row, and in which normal sorts of continuity are further disrupted by wide leaps; dynamics are generally at the lowest levels. Webern's chamber music pieces are the most delicate organisms, no better fitted than viol music for survival under normal concert conditions; but they have introduced into music new sorts of sound-experience (and silence-experience). Though Webern's technical procedures have stimulated later composers, the works themselves have had no significant successors, except the late chamber works of Stravinsky and (by remote derivation) the refined, almost inaudible pieces of Morton Feldman.

Hindemith, like so many other chamber music composers including Mozart, Dvořák and Frank Bridge, was a viola player; he was also a member of the Amar Quartet, which gave the first performances of three of his four early quartets. He was in youth a militant anti-romantic, rejecting any idea that the prime object of music might be to express subjective emotion. He reacted against the smooth, well-turned music of the previous generation of German composers by writing works of high dissonance level, in which conventional key-relationship schemes were ignored or contradicted; with angular, often grotesque themes, sometimes drawn from popular music. His scores, with their rare dynamic marks and utilitarian phrasing, seem to protest against the minutely marked works of Schoenberg, Berg, and Webern, who were so much concerned with subtle nuances. The second, third, and fourth quartets are remarkable for their clean textures, exhilarating energy and rhythmic drive, and for the ruthlessness with which Hindemith seizes every opportunity to develop and extend material by imitation, canon, fuguing, augmentation and diminution. Hindemith's works for children and amateurs, in which well-known tunes are sometimes ingeniously submitted to every sort of bizarre contrapuntal treatment, are of the same high quality as his concert works (though not always suited to their purpose; the first-position pieces for strings could never be played even approximately in tune by any but the most experienced amateurs). Hindemith much disliked being labelled as the composer of *gebrauchsmusik* – workaday music; but the label has some appropriateness for one who composed so easily and whose music has a sort of impersonality that keeps the listener at a distance. The *Kleine Kammermusik* op. 24 no. 2 for wind quintet (written in 1922) is, however, a masterwork, perhaps the only one in this genre; full of remarkable thematic inventions, perfectly written for the instruments (and recognizing their characters and idiosyncracies as Schoenberg's quintet does not). It is also concise to the point of epigram; an unusual virtue in Hindemith – as a wholly practical composer he perhaps recognized (and benefited from) the wind instruments' limited powers of endurance. The many later chamber works are smoother and blander in tone; as skilfully composed, but mostly lacking the character and interest of the earlier music.

Stravinsky, who had heard and been impressed by *Pierrot Lunaire* in 1912, began to write for chamber ensemble in Switzerland during the First World War, when opportunities for large-scale performance were few. The three short *Pieces for String Quartet* of 1914 are slight but ingenious essays in unconventional uses of the medium, in which mostly primitive material is treated in sophisticated ways. In *Histoire du Soldat* and *Renard* he evolved his own entirely original uses of the chamber ensemble, the first being much influenced by jazz, the second centred round the sounds and techniques of the cymbalom. Stravinsky's role at this time, and in post-war Paris, seemed to be to shock and entertain audiences with every new work. In 1923, he surpassed expectations with the *Octet for Wind*, the prototype of so many neo-classical works, in which classical forms, contrapuntal techniques, 19th-century formulae so long discarded as 'empty' were brought together in a work of outstanding individuality, humour and vitality. The octet (for flute, clarinet, two each of bassoons, trumpets and trombones) contains more than an element of caricature; but the work, entertaining as it is, has a Mozartian power to stimulate and hold attention by means of ever new and unpredictable developments. In the contrapuntal septet of 1953 (for clarinet, bassoon, horn, string trio and piano) Stravinsky arranges a meeting between classical and serial techniques and idioms. The tone of voice is less personal, the discussion more abstract than in the octet, as though he was already moving towards the beautiful but austere, and inward-turned, works of his last years – the *Double Canon* for quartet (a tribute to Raoul Dufy) and the brief *Epitaphium* for flute, clarinet and harp; purely contrapuntal works from which all trace of virtuosity and musical showmanship has vanished.

2 BARTÓK AND SHOSTAKOVICH

Bartók and Shostakovich may be historically less influential figures than Schoenberg and Stravinsky, but they have much greater importance for chamber music enthusiasts. They are the only 20th-century composers to have written a substantial number of quartets which have entered the international repertory and seem likely to remain there; they could well turn out to be the last composers of stature to have explored their own characters in depth through the quartet, developing in the process highly personal idioms which belong specifically to the medium.

Béla Bartók was as inflexible as Schoenberg in refusing to compromise or accept easy solutions, and equally indifferent to public opinion. Even today, the high dissonance level of the later quartets and the strangeness of the musical idiom and the thought-processes behind ensure that performers and audiences still regard them with a certain awe. The six quartets, written between 1909 and 1939, reflect the crucial stages of Bartók's development. In the first, external influences have not been fully assimilated. The grave opening fugue owes much to the example of Beethoven's op. 131; the leading theme of the allegretto is expressive in a familiar and romantic way, and is often harmonized in smooth Brahmsian thirds and sixths. The final *allegro vivace*, with its strong motor rhythms and insistent repeated-note figures, is the most characteristic of the later Bartók. The second is the most easily approachable of the quartets. There are no disruptive elements in the first movement, with its extended lyrical themes (which have no successors in later quartets) that lead the listener so easily on. The scherzo, in Bartók's most brilliant 'barbaric' vein is also straightforward; only the strange, desolate, mainly pianissimo final lento has the enigmatic stillness of suppressed emotion.

An interval of ten years separates the second from the later quartets, which are characterized by increasing use of short motives, generally compact and covering a small pitch range; by close and complex contrapuntal working (intricate canons are a recurring feature); by the use of polyrhythms; and by the novelty and ingenuity of their structural plans. Though the bar-by-bar processes of extension and development are never hard to follow, the larger repetitions, variations and recapitulations are often so elliptical as to be almost imperceptible to the listener (two separate commentators have been driven to describe the recapitulation of the first section of the third quartet as psychological rather than physical). The third, fourth and fifth quartets still present a forbidding aspect to listeners with their high dissonance levels. Bartók's use of dissonance is peculiar to himself; in contrapuntal writing, he inclines, like Schoenberg, to treat all intervals impartially as far as dissonance-value goes; he will also use dissonance picturesquely, to colour a melodic line with parallel dissonant chords; or, more traditionally, to underline the effect of a strident climax by raising the dissonance level. Many characteristic features derive directly or indirectly from folk-music. In the slow movement of the fourth quartet, the improvisatory and highly decorative melodic line has a distinctly Hungarian inflection; the scherzo of the fifth is cast in a number of irregular additive metres such as $(4 + 2 + 3)$ and $(3 + 2 + 2 + 3)$. Many of the themes contain reminiscences of folk-music scales, particularly in their use of the sharpened fourth. In the fifth and sixth quartets, there is some lowering of tension; more playful elements appear, and the listener is less aware of the sense of strain that comes from total concentration on a few key-issues. The curious episode in the finale of no. 5 where the theme of the first episode arrives back over banal tonic-dominant harmonies may be heard as parody (like the parallel passage in the slow movement of the Concerto for Orchestra where a Shostakovich tune is derisively quoted), but it also provides a moment of light relief and relaxation. The sixth quartet, in which all four movements are linked by a recurring motto theme, is also one of the most varied in mood. The ferocious 'Marcia' (in which we again catch distant echoes of Beethoven's op. 127) is set off against a playful 'Burletta' and a quiet and expressive last movement from which all strain has vanished (commentators differ as to whether Bartók has attained peace, or only the quiet of desperation).

Bartók's later quartets, which presuppose an ensemble of virtuosi, extend the technical vocabulary of the quartet in many ways – by use of quarter tones, glissandi, multiple stopping (sometimes used with percussive effect) and by special effects such as snap pizzicato, in which the string is plucked so that it strikes sharply against the finger-board. They tax the players to the utmost, but are written with so much understanding of the instruments' characters, limitations, and potentialities that they continue to fascinate, rather than scare off, prospective performers.

When Bartók finished his last quartet in 1939, only the first of Shostakovich's long series of fifteen had been written (the last appeared in 1975). Yet the later works seem to belong to another and earlier age. Shostakovich's harmonic and melodic idioms are only marginally influenced by the innovations of Debussy, Schoenberg, or Stravinsky. He grew up in another world of music, and his own development, which was to take him far from his starting point, followed an independent course. While Bartók's quartets are concentrated, economical in use of material, conceived in a language every phrase of which bears the mark of its creator's individuality, Shostakovich's idiom is more often than not plain and straightforward. He shows none of the Western composer's dread of falling into commonplace or cliché, and admits into the quartets movements of no great intellectual weight or concentration; according to the Russian viewpoint, chamber music is an all-embracing medium, in which a composer can be discursive or passionate, and in which there is room for other things as well as the civilized contrapuntal conversations of the great chamber music composers of the main Western tradition. Characteristic of Shostakovich are long, flowing contrapuntal movements, wandering and almost improvisatory in nature, such as the first movements of his eighth and ninth quartets; barbaric scherzos, related to those of Bartók, brilliantly written and demanding a forceful and virtuosic style of playing that does not belong to classical chamber music, (a style that Westerners have sometimes mistakenly condemned as 'orchestral'); or closely-organized contrapuntal variation-movements, such as the passacaglia of no. 9. But Shostakovich's quartets conform to no set pattern, and often he will surprise us by doing just the opposite of what we have predicted – as when, in the eleventh quartet, a solemn hymn-like theme that seems to have been made for solemn fuguing is invested with spiky, dissentient counterpoints. Shostakovich shares with Britten a happy gift for saving themes from commonplace by means of a single happily-conceived harmony or turn of phrase. Like Tchaikovsky, he is never afraid of repetition or of driving home the obvious point. Sometimes, he will take his ease, content to wait for a striking idea, like a good conversationalist who knows that sooner or later he will hit on a good line that will lead him in the right direction. Yet in spite of apparently casual methods of construction, his sense of direction is sure, and the plans of his works as ultimately revealed are generally clear and satisfying.

In later works, textures are generally more contrapuntal, and Shostakovich often concentrates on the working of a very few key-motives; a development that has been noted with approval by Western commentators. Sometimes, key motives are rather transparently made for use in many contexts; or obsession with thematic economy seems to impoverish the music; in the autobiographical eighth quartet (which quotes from earlier works, including the excellent piano quintet) the DSCH motive (S = Es, or E flat; H = B natural) is much over-exposed. The main strengths of the quartets lie rather in Shostakovich's power to invent every sort of motive, from short, trenchant key-phrases to long and cunningly-articulated tunes; to sustain and develop musical action over long periods; and to make music the vehicle for every sort of dramatic or personal statement, giving us deep insights into the character of a complicated, and immensely resourceful, composer.

3 THE SIXTIES AND SEVENTIES

The American composer Lukas Foss suggested hopefully a few years back that all composers could be thought of as workers on one great cathedral. To the observer in the midst of things, no such grand overall plan appears; the scene rather resembles a developing suburb in the 1930s, with independent builders running up houses in every conceivable style to please actual or prospective clients – traditional red-brick, Stockbroker's Tudor with or without stained glass porches, aggressively contemporary chrome-finished and round-cornered dwellings influenced equally by the traditions of Bauhaus and Odeon. It may be that some over-all pattern will emerge in the future; at present, we are bewildered by the proliferation of idioms and compositional methods; by the greatly increased vocabulary of sounds that are accepted, by certain people in certain places, as musically valid; by the lapsing of the established master–servant relationship between composers and performers (so that we are never too sure, in listening to unconventionally-notated works, how much of the credit should go to composer and how much to performer); by the number of different listening-attitudes required of the listener who is trying to respond to Boulez, Tippett, Cage, or Steve Reich.

For the chamber music lover, there are three developments of special interest and significance:

(*1*) The chamber ensemble of variable constitution has almost superseded the string quartet (and, to a lesser extent, the conventional symphony orchestra) as the favoured medium for composers wishing to make extended and well-considered musical statements.

(*2*) While the flow of works in 'serious–contemporary' idioms, fully and precisely notated, demanding some intellectual effort of the listener, has hardly fallen off, today such works co-exist with others (often indeterminate) in which traditional relationships between composer and performer, and composer and listener, are no longer apparent. For all three, the rules of the game have changed so far that the critic may be as much out of his depth if he tries to assess performances of 'serious–contemporary' and 'avant-garde' works by the same standards, as the sportswriter who comments on a golf tournament under the impression that he is reporting a croquet match.

(*3*) The audience for almost all sorts of chamber music has increased; while with the new variety of types of ensemble, of composition and of required attitudes, chamber music has ceased to be an élitist and has become, almost, a popular art-form.

In the short survey which follows, the works for conventionally-formed ensembles are discussed first; thereafter, traditionally-notated works for chamber ensembles of various types, moving gradually through the spectrum towards the freely-notated experimental works of the extreme avant-garde.

Quartets

Many composers with an overriding interest in processes of construction, development and formal inter-relationship in abstract music have continued to write string quartets since Schoenberg's death. Two of his most distinguished pupils, Egon Wellesz and Roberto Gerhard, became naturalized Englishmen. Wellesz's nine quartets and Gerhard's two owe much to Schoenberg's influence; Gerhard, like Milton Babbitt in America, extending and modifying the original principles of twelve-tone composition to apply to time-values as well as note-pitches, and regarding the basic rows not so much as a source of motives as of configurations (harmonic, rhythmic, or melodic) which can be very freely varied while maintaining a basic identity. Gerhard suggests a parallel with the identity of the triad of conventional harmony with its inversions. In the second quartet of 1960–62, attention is focussed on the patterning of textures and many effects are introduced (such as playing between bridge and tailpiece, tapping the belly of the instrument, tapping on tailpiece with the wood of the bow) which anticipate the devices of later avant-garde composers.

Mátyás Seiber, who lived in England from the time he was thirty, also adapted Schoenberg's techniques to his own ends. His third quartet, the *Quartetto Lirico*, is a particularly successful work, its textures owing something to Bartók, though the particular brand of lyrical romanticism is Seiber's exclusive property. Apart from Elizabeth Maconchy, whose fine series of eleven quartets, written between 1933 and 1977, is central to her output, very few younger or middle-generation British composers have written more than one quartet after their student days. Alexander Goehr and Hugh Wood have composed substantial and serious works, owing a good deal to Schoenberg's influence; Nicholas Maw's one quartet is eloquent and romantic in manner, highly elaborate but never turgid.

One of the few composers who continues to write quartets which make a deep impression on all who hear them is the American Elliott Carter. His immensely difficult and complex first quartet was written during 1950–51, 'largely for my own satisfaction and out of an effort to understand myself'. In the first movement, four strongly-contrasted themes appear in every sort of contrapuntal combination, the processes paralleling, according to the composer, the interlocked presentation of ideas in the works of Joyce and others, as well as introducing characteristic devices involving grammatical ambiguities, punctuation, and direct quotation from other composers. In the second movement, the soft contemplative music of the two violins is answered by the rough and impassioned recitative of viola and cello; in the final variations, different themes are repeated faster at each recurrence, 'some reaching their speed vanishing-point sooner than others'. In the second quartet, there is little thematic repetition or development, but the instruments are often type-cast, first violin playing in rhapsodic *bravura* style, second in regularly marked rhythms, viola lyrically and *espressivo*, cello in progressively fluctuating tempi. The combination of variable and fixed tempi leads to notational situations of great complexity, and there are often no common points of reference in phrasing and metre. The richness of thematic material and the passionate intensity of utterance in Carter's quartets make up to the listener for the frequent moments of confusion when the melodic strands become, in performance, inextricably tangled. The third quartet is organized as two duos (one of violin and cello, the other of violin and viola) which discourse separately and in dialogue. Here too, the metres of the two dialogues, though precisely notated, are very rarely heard to coincide on the first beat of any bar.

Milton Babbitt, whose logical and often mathematical extensions of serial techniques have taken him forward into 'total' serialization (of pitch, rhythm, timbres, and dynamics) at one time favoured the quartet as the ideal 'abstract' medium, but today is more concerned with electronic realization of his sound-theorems. Ross Lee Finney is a composer of considerable vigour and range of expression who has been liberated by serialism from the more staid conventions of his earlier works, and whose later quartets have real individuality and aptness to the medium. Many younger American composers have been stimulated to write quartets by the existence of the magnificent Composers' Quartet (attached to the New England Conservatory of Music in Boston). The quartet devote themselves largely to the new-music repertory, and have, in conjunction with the Conservatory, established prize competitions to select works for performance, providing a stimulus to potential quartet-composers that is lacking in England.

Most of the avant-garde composers who have written quartets have studiously avoided traditional lines of approach. Krystof Penderecki's two quartets are interesting compendiums of special effects, in which there is no continuing linear development and little polyphony. Witold Lutoslawski's quartet, described as 'a sequence of mobiles to be played one after the other', specifies normal playing techniques and notates them, in the parts, in normal ways; but there is often no strict co-ordination between parts: 'each particular player is supposed not to know what the others are doing, or at least to perform his part as if he knew nothing of what the others are doing.' John Cage's one quartet, also conventionally notated in the parts, avoids all polyphonic textures, the whole being conceived as a single, elaborated melodic line. In George Crumb's *Black Angels* for electric quartet, the sounds are electronically amplified and modified, while the players also whisper and shout, play tam-tam and glass harmonica, and trill with tiny cymbals attached to the finger-tips. Notwithstanding such extravagances, *Black Angels* is a powerfully expressive work, and many of the effects called for seem to belong by right to the medium. In England, Barry Guy, who is also a bass player, is one of the few to have adapted avant-garde techniques successfully to the conventional medium of the string quartet. In his three quartets (the third with solo soprano) he makes effective use of such experimental playing-techniques as bowing on top, or on the wrong side of, the bridge, or inserting the bow-nut vertically between two strings, beating rapidly from side to side. Surprisingly (to orthodox musicians) he has still written works that are of great musical interest, and can be recognized as real string music.

Chamber ensemble

The flow of new works for the once-loved medium of the piano trio has today almost dried up. In England, Alexander Goehr is one of the few composers of distinction to have written a trio in recent years; a work which reverses the usual order of things in focussing attention on violin and cello, whose microstructured, intricately organized and fragmented parts are deployed against a piano part which confines itself to providing essential support (there are no octave doublings, chords of more than three notes are rare, and the *acciaccatura*, the quickly-played note or cluster of auxiliary notes just before a structural note, is the only pianistic device appearing in the part). The notation, exacting as to detail and requiring that the finest discriminations of dynamics and articulation should be observed, is an extreme example of the authoritarian directives developed by composers from Schoenberg to Stockhausen, now largely abandoned by advanced composers. Lennox Berkeley and Don Banks have followed Brahms in writing trios for violin, horn and piano, in which the instruments play their traditional roles, the horn appearing both as romantic singer and in rousing athletic outbursts. Shostakovich's magnificent piano quintet of 1940 seems to have been the last major work of its kind; Copland's, the last piano quartet to have established itself in the repertory.

Such pioneer works as Schoenberg's *Pierrot Lunaire*, Stravinsky's *Histoire du Soldat* and *Octet for Wind*, Boulez's *Le Marteau sans Maître* and Berio's *Circles* have inspired younger composers to write for chamber ensemble; while the virtuosity and musical sophistication of a new generation of wind-players and percussionists have also encouraged them to include instruments previously shunned as coarse-toned and lacking in musical finesse in their chamber works. Virtuosity has in its turn been stimulated by the flow of exacting new works, while the enhanced skill and status of the instrumentalist has encouraged composers to hand back to the performers some responsibility for the end-product. The appearance of indeterminate works reflects the view that the composer is not necessarily the best and only judge of the way in which the music should go, at a particular time and place.

With the increased use of mixed chamber ensembles, chamber music has become a less austere and abstract art. In Ligeti's static, atmospheric music, Cage's pieces for prepared pianos, or Partch's for ensembles of exotic or newly-invented percussion instruments, pleasure comes as much from savouring delectable and unusual timbres and textures as from following through thematic developments in the old way. Many composers, like Ives, Nielsen and Elliott Carter, have introduced a new interest into chamber works by treating instruments like characters in a play. Roberto Gerhard, in his *Concert for Eight* (1962) concentrated interest on the interplay of timbres and rhythm: 'the eight instruments are introduced somewhat in the manner of *dramatis personae*, but the play itself consists of purely musical events, and must not be taken as evoking or illustrating any extra-musical parallels whatever.' In Richard Rodney Bennett's series of four *Commedia*, each instrument has its character which is maintained throughout. Thus, in *Commedia I*, flute represents Columbine, alto saxophone Harlequin, bass clarinet Pantaloon, trumpet Pulcinello, cello Pierrot. There are soli, duets, and ensembles in which each behaves true to type; as when an impassioned love duet for saxophone and flute is followed by a sad aria for the deserted flute – Columbine. Chamber works may also become semi-theatrical events, as, for instance, Maxwell Davies's *Eight Songs for a Mad King*, which involves the crushing of a violin, or in Kagel's

Two-Man-Orchestra, in which two players at the centre of a complex of wires, strings, treadles, and strangely-adapted keyboards play, directly or indirectly, on their 250 'construction elements'. Visual action may be used less spectacularly to clarify musical action, as in Thea Musgrave's third chamber concerto (a work which uses both precise and free-running notations) and her *Space-Play*, in which players stand in turn to lead the ensemble, sometimes vying for the leadership. (The Gerhard, Bennett, and Musgrave works mentioned have been chosen as examples because they are particularly fine works of three leading British chamber music composers).

Before going on to discuss some of the more experimental chamber music of recent years, room must be found for the many composers who carry on the tradition of the Russian and French composers who wrote so much civilized chamber music for the recreation and entertainment of performers and particularly amateurs. In England, Malcolm Arnold, Malcolm Williamson, John McCabe, and Franz Reizenstein have been among the most distinguished composers to have composed works that are approachable by non-specialist audiences, and that are often playable by the skilled amateurs who today form a vital part of the musical community. Arnold's brass quintet and Williamson's *Concerto for Wind Quintet and Two Pianos* deserve special mention as works of real individuality and invention, which deserve to outlive many of the more pretentious 'serious' or experimental works of our time. It is curious that, while the brass-band players have an immense repertory of brass quartet music (most of it of doubtful quality, judged by the standards of straight musicians) very little chamber music has been written for the orchestral-brass ensemble until very recently. Elliott Carter's brass quintet (1974) is the first work by a composer of international stature for the medium; though excellent works have also been written by Gunther Schuller in America, and by John Gardner and Justin Connolly in England.

Stockhausen's *Zeitmasse* for wind quintet (1957) was the fore-runner of many works in which metrical passages alternate with passages in which there is no exact synchronization of contrapuntal parts as in the Musgrave chamber concerto referred to above. Many composers who have abandoned metrical forms and strict synchronization of parts have adopted proportionate (graphical) notations, in which durations are represented on a horizontal time-axis; a procedure which, in spite of its apparent exactitude, is inevitably associated with tempo-freedom in performance. The score may also allow freedom in matters of pitch and even in choice of instruments; a straggling line may indicate approximate pitch-levels, or pitch notation may be reduced to a graph indicating only 'high', 'medium' and 'low', as in Morton Feldman's earlier works. In other works, exact pitches will be given, but in the form of note-heads enclosed in a box (as in Berio's *Circles*) which can be used as a basis for *ad lib* extemporization using the pitches indicated. In some cases, the composer will provide no more than the rules for collective improvization or for musical games in which each player's course may be determined by the sounds and actions of his colleagues (as is Christian Wolff's *Duet II* for horn and piano). Performers (their instruments unspecified) in Stockhausen's inspirational works are given no more guidance than a short written text to which they respond according to their intuition; thus, in his *Across the Boundary* (1974) they are invited to 'imagine they are higher beings proving to their co-players that their instruments are humorous Master Interpreters'.

In such works, the quality of the end-result will be decided largely by the unwritten traditions that govern the performance of a particular group. or by the lucky or unlucky chances of the occasion (in the same way, the value of a football match to the spectators cannot be forecast as accurately as the value of an all-in wrestling match, in which every move has been pre-rehearsed). Generally, the performances supervised by the composers themselves or their near associates make the greatest impression. Stockhausen's intuitive pieces are most effective when presented by his own improvising group; Maxwell Davies's recent chamber works have received their definitive performances from the Fires of London group which he directs. Berio, Ligeti, and Kagel are others whose presence seems to be almost essential for wholly convincing performances of their ensemble works – most of which, even though they are written for a few skilled instrumentalists, fit into no recognized chamber music category. Such pieces as Stockhausen's *Mikrophonie I*, in which the sounds made by two players tapping, stroking, or scraping a huge gong with a number of implements are electronically modified into a strange sort of sound-tapestry that cannot be related to its origins, belong to a new world of music. Many other works which employ louder percussion or electronic aids are really 'public' works in the sense that they break the bounds of expressive moderation established by the older chamber music composers, and are to be compared rather with the works of pop groups, whose four or five players may produce a physical effect as overwhelming as that of the largest Wagnerian orchestra, and who can communicate their message to live audiences of many thousands. A few avant-garde composers continue to write music that carries on some of the traditions of the past. Feldman's very quiet, very slow pieces for small ensembles deal in subtle reactions and are best heard in small halls by select gatherings of sympathetic initiates. Steve Reich's long pieces for percussion ensemble, based on slowly-changing ostinati, which are often played at low dynamic levels, return to an austerer view of music as pure pattern-making. Even the recreations, musical and non-musical, organized by members of Cornelius Cardew's Scratch Orchestra and known as *scratch activities* had a chamber music quality to them, being undertaken by music-lovers who enjoyed getting together in some sort of pre-planned ensemble. Certain sorts of jazz, refined and intellectual, and no longer strictly functional, are really chamber music in all but name; though it takes a specialist to criticize or evaluate the major works in this genre.

4 CHAMBER MUSIC IN A CHANGING WORLD

Stockhausen declares himself to be an electric composer; Boulez announces the death of opera and the string quartet; Cage and Cardew deplore the undemocratic processes of pre-planned music in which the composer dictates to the performer a precise course of action; many sincere music-lovers, appalled by the casual use of music as a background to living, forecast the end of attentive, intelligent listening. In spite of everything, enthusiastic interest and active interest in the chamber music of past and present times, far from falling off, has increased greatly over the last fifty years. Fears that radio and recording would turn us from a race of active participants (which, even in the golden 17th century, we never were) into a race of half-listeners have not been justified. There has probably been some falling-off in the amount of domestic music-making (though this is hard to assess) but any decrease has been more than offset by greatly increased activity at universities, polytechnics, evening classes, summer schools and camps. It is true that we listen casually to music as we have not in the past; music accompanies us as we eat, travel, work, shop, converse. In the day of the transistor, the spread of casual listening is inevitable, but it need not be deplorable. Great music is robust enough to withstand every sort of treatment, including mistreatment by half-listening.

Through radio and recordings, many listeners come to an intimate knowledge of great works of a sort that 100 years ago would only have been possible for performers or dedicated score-readers. For every one who had even heard of the quartets of Dittersdorf, Reger or Nielsen fifty years ago, there must today be scores of people who are familiar with the music through the electronic media. Because of its limited dynamic range and number of separate voices, because the tone of voice is conversational, and because its natural habitat is the medium-sized living room, chamber music is the best sort of music for diffusion by radio or record.

The position of composers and performers has improved greatly over the last fifty years. Universities and benevolent foundations support composers and performing groups, so that those who follow their natural bent in writing or playing chamber works may even earn modest sums in the process. Composers do not dominate the scene as they did fifty years ago – today, the performers rather than the composers are often the real stars of an avant-garde occasion. Concerts of modern chamber works are no longer the formal occasions they once were; while the freer sorts of co-ordination allowed for in indeterminate scores leads to the formation of close-knit performing groups working together in intimate understanding. The music of such groups can be more reasonably described as the 'music of friends' than the polished and expert performances of some illustrious ensembles who may have spent years perfecting their interpretations of a few masterpieces. Often, today, it is the listener at an avant-garde concert who is left out in the cold while the players are absorbed in some new musical game – and here too, there is a parallel with 18th-century domestic music-making. But such parallels must not be pushed too far. The music of the present day is *sui generis*, belonging to the present day and to no other. The chamber music enthusiast has not, perhaps, greatly changed his nature; but he has access to a greater quantity and variety of music than at any previous time in history. The risks of disorientation and musical indigestion are certainly great – but as the possibilities of intellectual and spiritual enlargement are correspondingly just as great, it may be said that the prospects for the future are bright.

Book 7

The Solo Instrument

by John McCabe
with an opening section on Keyboard Instruments by
F. Bonavia

KEYBOARD INSTRUMENTS

§ INTRODUCTORY

The history of musical art, as exemplified by the solo instrument, is germane to the history of the development and growth of the instruments themselves. As composers grew more exacting in their demands, devoted craftsmen sought to meet their requirements during the centuries that preceded the modern era (which, for our present purpose, may be taken to begin with Beethoven), when all essential progress in the development of the two chief musical instruments, the violin and the pianoforte, was an accomplished fact. No better violins have been made than those built by Stradivari and although the pianoforte of today is a better instrument than that which served Beethoven, the music Beethoven wrote for his instrument makes full use of every improvement the ingenuity of present-day makers has been able to devise.

The demand of the composer came first; technical developments followed. When the maker attempted to anticipate the composer, his experiments were not so successful; take, for instance, the saxophone, which, in spite of Berlioz's eulogy, has not found a permanent place in the orchestra. The great period of violin making, remarks Parry, nearly coincides with the early period of music for string instruments and he goes on to say that the highest point in violin making was reached when string music took definite and permanent shape in the works of the great school of Italian violinists and composers. This statement is perfectly accurate historically; but it ignores the force of the impulse given to instrumental as well as to vocal music by the *musiche nuove* of the Florentine school. Monteverdi's *Orfeo* was performed and published before Stradivari was born and the violinists who took part in those performances must have been acutely conscious of the poverty of their instruments. The dashing passages typical of the true instrumental style, the *tremolando* that Monteverdi was the first to use, must have lost much of their effect when played on the instruments of the period and thus called the makers' attention to the possibility of improvement.

For the pianoforte the evidence proving how the maker followed the composer is more definite still. The earliest example of a 'sonata' we possess is that of Giovanni Gabrieli, which was published in 1597, the year when Dr John Bull delivered his inaugural address as first Gresham professor of music at Oxford. Gabrieli calls his first sonata

'Pian e Forte' the name which, slightly modified, the instrument still bears. It is true that the Gabrieli Pian e Forte sonata was not written for a solo instrument but for cornet, violin and trombones. It must be remembered, however, that vocal and not instrumental music was then the main concern of the composer and that any new departure in the instrumental field would at once attract the attention of all instrumental musicians. Like Monteverdi, if in a lesser degree, Gabrieli had the genius of the instrumental composer. That is to say, he realized that if in dissociating instrumental from vocal music, in setting the sonata ('a piece played') against the cantata ('a piece sung') there was bound to be a loss, there could also be some compensations and he found them in the contrast between extreme loudness and extreme softness, a sharper contrast on instruments than in voices.

The invention of the piano is attributed to Cristofori who in 1711 made the first instrument known to us and called not by its present modified name but, as in Gabrieli's sonata, Pian e Forte. But there is reliable evidence to show that instruments known as Pian e Forte were being made only a very short time after the publication of Gabrieli's sonata. It is then not improbable that Gabrieli's venture started the quest for dynamic contrast, especially in the case of the only instrument that could reproduce the full harmonic range of Gabrieli's chamber orchestra.

1 VIRGINAL AND HARPSICHORD

§ (a) *The English school*

The foundations of an instrumental style were well and truly laid by the English composers of the Tudor era. It is poetic justice that the glory of opening up the path which led to the music of the 19th century should belong to an age that, more than any other, honoured and understood the art. There was then no misconception; the Tudor age did not believe in the Greek fallacy of music as a science – the fallacy which, inherited by later generations, caused music to be linked, in the Quadrivium, with astronomy, arithmetic and geography. But it was given an honourable place by the side of science and philosophy.

Just as it was customary for philosophers to meet at the University or in the house of a great nobleman and dispute on a given theme, so musicians gathered together to play and sing. There is a vivid account of the journey through Elizabethan London by an Italian philosopher on his way to the house of Fulke Greville where a debate was held.

We know in the same way of the 'vertuous contention in love' between William Byrd and Ferrabosco when they improvised forty ways 'showing most rare and intricate skill . . . upon the playne songe "Miserere"'.

The final achievements of the Tudor composers in vocal art have led the historian to give less attention than is due to their instrumental compositions. String music was, at first, intended as a support for the voices and was certainly not practised to the same extent as in the later Jacobean times. But the virginal was in favour with old and young. Both Elizabeth and her sister were able musicians, and the 'prodigy' was also known, for it is said that the daughter of Castlenau, Maria, aged six, could handle musical instruments so well 'that you cannot tell if she is of bodily or incorporeal substance'.

The greatest collection of instrumental music of the time is the Fitzwilliam Virginal Book in the Fitzwilliam Museum at Cambridge. Other valuable collections are the virginal books of Benjamin Cosyn and Will Forster; Lady Nevill's book, which contains forty-two pieces by William Byrd, and *Parthenia*, the first book of music to be printed in England; it appeared in 1612 and contained twenty-one pieces by Byrd, John Bull and Orlando Gibbons.

A glance at the titles of their pieces is sufficient to show how wide the sources were from which the Elizabethan composer drew his inspiration. William Byrd's battle piece ('Mr Bird's battaile' of Lady Nevill's collection) may not stand higher amongst his compositions than the Battle of Vittoria does in Beethoven's; it provides a link in the chain of not particularly successful battle pictures in music, extending from the early 15th-century examples to the modern essays of Tchaikovsky, Strauss and Bartók.

The Elizabethan composer, however, addressed himself to all sorts and conditions of men and provided music for every occasion. He wrote dances for the nobleman's palace and, for the village green, corantos and jigs; he paid tribute to the church with psalm-tunes and compositions which, written upon a Plainsong melody, were entitled *In nomine*; the songs of the common people with their attractive names – 'John come kiss me now', and 'Bonny sweet Robin' – inspired him; merrymaking at the tavern was celebrated in 'Watkin's Ale' and 'Malt's come down'.

These songs provided the theme of elaborate variations wherein the skill of the musician could shine. A florid style, the natural outcome, penetrated even religious music and led to a protest by Cranmer who objected to music 'full of notes'. What was ill-becoming to religious music was eminently adapted to the instrument. Trills and ornaments were of practical value to the player on the virginal, for he had no other means of sustaining sound. Moreover while the bulk of the music remained rare and unpublished it was impossible to think even of altering a theme. The notion of modifying a set melody could never occur to the Tudor composer, since in improvising it was obviously important that the subject of the improvisation should remain untouched, the solid basis on which graceful fantasies and embellishments could be elaborated. It is difficult for us to realize exactly how far the musicianship of the Elizabethans went, for, like the Italians, they placed highest the art of improvisation which leaves nothing behind but a tradition when the improviser dies. It is said of one so well remembered as Frescobaldi that the full extent of his abilities could only be grasped by those who heard his improvisations. But we know that they were executants of consummate skill, for only an exceptionally gifted performer on the harpsichord could undertake to play elaborate passages with ease so long before it occurred to anyone to make use of the thumb. We have it on the authority of Daniel Speer that in the 17th century the scale was played with two fingers – 3, 4, 3, 4, 3, 4, 3.

Evidence of an instinct for form and novelty is not lacking. In his admirable study of Byrd, Dr Fellowes comments upon the way in which in the variations on 'O Mistress mine' Byrd quite simply re-states the theme in the last variation and notes that the device has since been employed with great effect by other composers, including Schubert, who made use of it in the *Death and the Maiden* variations of the string quartet in D minor. Another historian is struck by the way in which in 'The Carman's Whistle' Byrd dallies for a short while in the key of D minor before returning to the tonic, C major, and sees in this a promise of a wider harmonic scope. John Bull's 'The King's Hunting Jigg' appears even more significant when looked at from a purely aesthetic point of view. This remarkable composition conveys an excellent idea of the excitement and the joy of pursuit; but it has also an imaginative quality not often found in the music of the period; it does not only imitate, but also gives the impression of one who knew what magic there is in the sound of hunting horns in the woodland.

After the Elizabethans, the greatest figure in the world of music in England is Purcell, whose genius cannot fully be appraised from those of his instrumental works falling within the limits of this chapter. These, however, are by no means negligible. The minuet which takes the place of the traditional jig in the G major suite, the gavotte of the suite in C major, have some of the freshness and charm that endear his more important compositions. If his harmonic range is not here particularly daring and striking, there is no error of taste. He indulges the fashion of the time for elaborate ornamentation, but not to excess. He is at once grave and carefree; some pieces are slight; the chaconne of the G minor suite is serious, sterling, sincere. § His output also includes a substantial number of short pieces, marches, airs, grounds, trumpet tunes and the like. Chips off the work-bench though many of them are, there is often both freshness and originality in the music; several of the chaconnes and grounds have an entirely Purcellian nobility and expressiveness.

§ Purcell's teacher, John Blow, also wrote a set of 'Lessons' for the harpsichord. It is, however, as a composer of vocal music that he is remembered.

§ (b) The French school

Amongst the French, the most remarkable contributor to instrumental music is François Couperin, descendant of a long line of musicians. We are indebted to him on many counts. He wrote an important work on the art of the keyboard, and taught performers to use their thumbs; he was the first, in the compositions for two violins and bass, to write chamber music for three players; he made of the 'suite' something more than a collection of oddly assorted fantasias. These very valuable contributions to the art of the time do not fall, however, within our scope; our concern is with his music for the harpsichord.

Couperin left a good number of compositions for harpsichord; the most important are the four sets of *Pièces de Clavecin*, divided into *Ordres*, and *L'Art de Toucher le Clavecin*. Some of these bear bold, provoking titles – 'La Dangereuse', 'Les Baccanales'. He is, however, no revolutionary. Even 'Les Baccanales' falls very far short of one's conception of a bacchanalian orgy. He is the courtly composer *par excellence*, who found court atmosphere as congenial as the convent is to the mystic and the ascetic. His gentle melodies are his own; the heavy ornamentations with which they are overlaid are of his time. He held an appointment at the court of Louis XIV and was a polished and highly successful courtier. His art is very remote from life as we understand it, rather precious and artificial. The little pictures, whether inspired by the pseudo-pastoralism which celebrated Phyllis and Corydon, or by types of womanhood – La Manon,

La Diane, La Diligente, La Voluptueuse – are sometimes beautiful, often vague, always fictitious. They represent not so much the music of a people as of a class which exercised a very powerful influence on the military history of the world, and one in which the musician was of value only in so far as he could add to its splendour; a class with an etiquette, a mode of life and an art all of its own, as far removed from the world of men and lively passions as a company of Trappists.§ Yet in a work such as the magnificent B minor passacaille, with its highly chromatic harmonies matching the intensity of the exceptionally rich decoration, there is human passion struggling to express itself. Just as the conventions of the time and the court repress the real world of humanity, so the restraints of the passacaglia form and the musical style contain the emotion and restrict it to a latent position, always seeming likely to burst out into the open, but never quite doing so. Nowhere in the early French music is there a clearer musical parallel to the subterranean growth of revolutionary feeling among the people.

The compositions of Rameau are similarly elaborate and picturesque, yet here too there is an occasional sense of emotion simmering beneath the surface. The famous gavotte and variations in A minor shows this, for the poised, ornate surface has a growing sense of dark nobility running through it.

(c) The Italian school

The first great Italian master of keyboard writing, Frescobaldi, produced a large output for harpsichord and for organ, ranging from dance-movements to more substantial contrapuntal essays. The strength of these works lies as much in the powerful rhetoric of the music, which is always strong and vigorous, as in the outstanding quality of Frescobaldi's formal control. There is often a free improvisatory feeling to the structures, but this is kept under careful control by the composer, allowing the music's innate feeling to make its effect without unbalancing the form.

Ralph Kirkpatrick's description of Domenico Scarlatti as 'without question the most original keyboard composer of his century' might seem a startling one, but it is surely true. Scarlatti's story is a curious one. The son of Alessandro Scarlatti, one of the founders of the Italian, as opposed to French, overture style, he spent his first thirty years or so imitating his father in producing vocal works, both secular (including operas) and liturgical. At the age of thirty-four he left his native Italy to enter the service of the Portuguese court, and ten years later, in 1729, moved to Spain. It was during these foreign years, which lasted until his death in 1757, that he produced the more than 550 keyboard sonatas for which he is best remembered, and which represent his art at its most distinctive.

The form he adopted was a straightforward binary one, with each half of the piece repeated; there are few exceptions to this format. What is so striking is not simply the range of invention in the music, or the subtleties of structure which he managed to elicit from such a narrow and small-scale shape, but rather the astonishing range of keyboard textures and of harmonic and rhythmic patterns. The influence of Spanish guitar music undoubtedly played a part, for the remarkably high level of dissonance in some of the works (which still sound modern to many ears) results in a distinctly Spanish textural tinge, and a Spanish rhythmic earthiness can also be discerned. As his style developed, the charming, extrovert air of the earliest sonatas (which were for a long time the only ones familiar to us) gave way to a far greater intensity of emotion, and an even more astonishing range of imaginative inspiration. Small though they are, Scarlatti's sonatas contain many works of enormous power, whose sheer originality never loses its capacity to amaze and move us.

§ (d) Bach and Handel

The early instrumental music of Germany is entirely dominated by the genius of J. S. Bach. If nothing of his had come down to us beyond the compositions for organ, clavier and violin his fame would stand no less high than it does. We should indeed be poorer without the Passions and the B minor Mass; but the concertos, the fugues, the suites, would still entitle him to a place amongst the greatest prophets of music.

Two impulses have been noted in him – the emotional and the practical. No doubt, his work derives its monumental qualities from the technical, practical mastery of the medium that he uses with such consummate ease. But even more striking is his combination of gentleness and strength which is, in my view, the hallmark of the great composer. Not a few minor composers have excelled in one character or the other, as lyrical or dramatic, as singers of tender romances or as designers of bolder musical structures. Bach reaches both poles and his lyrical melodies are all the more moving because they are the expression of an essentially manly, robust nature.

Bach came at the end of a period; he did not set out to modify the art of his time but to enrich it. He did not avoid ornamentation as the

Italian Benedetto Marcello did in his sonatas; he controlled it and used it for a more correct purpose. The slender French courante would seem overweighted by ornament that the more solid structure of a Bach prelude can carry with ease. He did not invent the fugue; he carried it to its highest peak of perfection. The greater bulk of his output is choral, yet he understood perfectly the genius of instrumental music and was one of the first to see how the well-tempered clavier (see Book 1, Glossary) opened up a store of rich harmonies undreamt of in the days when instrumental music still bore the signs of its vocal origin.

It is not too much to say that, whereas his predecessors and successors wrote inventive preludes and fugues, Bach alone made great works of them. Couperin looked upon preludes as a poet, if he is not himself a prose writer, may look upon prose. He wrote them for an eminently practical purpose, to help – as he said – players who had not the gift for improvisation, and he warned them not to obey strictly indications of time, so as to be able to give the impression of a free, fanciful excursus – a preparation for the real piece, which was to follow. In Bach's hands, the prelude makes as great a demand on our faculties as the following fugue. It does not predicate an audience that has to be conjured into a state of alertness, but one already alert. 'There is not one prelude in the collection,' says Parry, 'which does not appeal to the hearer's feelings as much as, if not more than, to his intelligence, and with infinite variety.' Parry also remarks upon the unity of the E flat minor prelude of the '48', the underlying basis of whose harmony is not presented in figurate form but in chords. 'The effect of coherence,' says Parry, 'is attained by these chords being systematically grouped in threes ... which serves as the unifying principle throughout the long rhapsodical melody.' This is but one example of that spiritual unity, against the unity of balanced formulae, found also in the concertos and suites.

This spiritual unity, frequently met in other works of Bach, the outcome of intellectual discipline as well as of a sure instinct, is entirely at the mercy of the interpreter. The last movement of the B minor suite for flute and strings, for instance, consists of a set of dances of different cast and measure. Rightly interpreted they appear as a chain, every link of which, outwardly varied, is of equal strength. When their pace and proportions are not accurately gauged they seem unequal, unrelated, and we resent the disproportion between them. The relation between some of the preludes and fugues is of a similar character. The apparent link is that of tonality and nothing

594

more; yet we cannot but feel that they complete each other in an organic whole. The truth is that the real unity of any great work of art is not given by adherence to a pre-conceived, infallible plan. A true sense of measure and unity is as much part of that elusive faculty called genius as is the ability to write lyrical or dramatic music. No one can ever sound the depth of the problems connected with the construction of a shapely piece of music, any more than account for its beauty.

A few facts about Bach may be usefully recalled here. Bach never knew the nationalism of a later day. His music, thoroughly German, owed a good deal to Italian influence. The sonatas and concertos of Italian composers he heard at Weimar opened his eyes to the superiority of the Italian models over those of Buxtehude, and he attained perfection, says Schweitzer, by the devoted study of Vivaldi, Albinoni, Legrenzi and Corelli. All he did was touched by the same modesty. He had written a good deal before he published his first composition – a partita – at the age of forty-one, feeling, no doubt, that the work he was to do was 'not to be raised from the heat of youth or the vapours of wine'. He certainly never thought the day would come when his *Art of Fugue* was somehow to be orchestrated and performed before an admiring audience. Present-day technique and tastes alike have brought about a marvellous revival. Enthusiasm, however, can be carried too far. The organ was Bach's instrument and a Bach fugue well performed is to us what it was to him and to his contemporaries. The high standard of modern technique has brought even the variations written for his pupil, Goldberg, within reach of any average solo pianist. Of all composers he stands to gain most by close, intimate study. His instrumental music is all chamber music in the most literal sense. § Indeed, it is worth recalling that the vast majority of Bach's keyboard works, especially those for harpsichord or clavichord, were written for private use, not public performance. The forty-eight preludes and fugues that make up *The Well-Tempered Keyboard* were written as a vast pedagogic exercise, for use by his pupils, as were the two- and three-part Inventions. In the English and French suites and the partitas (six of each), Bach produced music for use at the semi-private court functions, but even here the music's essence is intimate in its meaning; the dance-forms which make up the predominant types of movement are handled with intense imagination but a complete lack of conscious public display. They are, however, a magnificent display of compositional inventiveness, for Bach's handling of these conventional forms is supremely

595

resourceful, not least in its polyphonic richness and in its dramatic, almost orchestral exploitation of sonority. It can be said that it is here, with the sense of growth and drama, rather than in the bipartite sonatas of earlier periods, that the roots of the classical sonata form lie.

In, for example, the chromatic fantasia and fugue in D minor, he looks forward, in the incredibly wide-ranging fantasia, to the bursting of the bounds of baroque and rococo styles in the music of his son, Carl Philipp Emanuel. Equally, in a work like the Concerto in the Italian Style, for solo keyboard without orchestra, he looks back and pays tribute to the Italian masters from whom he had learnt so much. Bach's position in musical history, standing as he does at a watershed, has been much misunderstood. While coming at the end (some say, after the end) of one tradition, he nevertheless exploited new developments of his time, not in any narrow way, but by assimilating them into his own techniques, and his influence on composers of the future, even if not the immediate future, was profound. Mozart and Beethoven were deeply influenced by him, and during the romantic era, a knowledge of Bach's music was a *sine qua non* for any composer worth his salt.

§ The death of Bach passed almost unnoticed, however, and the very place of his burial was soon forgotten. When his great contemporary, George Frederic Handel, died in London, he was carried to a grave in Westminster Abbey by a mourning nation. § Yet, while Bach's keyboard music is of prodigious importance, Handel's far smaller output has sunk into almost total neglect. If it does not represent his art at its greatest, the eight suites at least contain much fine and typical music. There is all his characteristic rhythmic genius, which sustains the form of the music strongly and enables him to develop his own individual and quite often dramatic style of keyboard writing, in which wide leaps and octave displacements occupy an important place. Even if Bach remains the supreme master of fugue *per se*, Handel's subjects are sometimes more striking and memorable, judged simply as tunes, than those of Bach. There is an added dramatic element to them, which reveals the essentially public nature of his art.

There are other composers who demand attention, too. In the six sonatas called *Musical Representations of some Biblical Stories*, Kuhnau composed some of the earliest substantial pieces of programme music, each of the sonatas being carefully marked off in sections that denote stages of the story. This is music of charm and vivacity, often with an overtly emotional content that anticipates the exploitation of this aspect of music by C. P. E. Bach and others.

The keyboard works of Telemann are concise and often attractive, relaxed but finely wrought works by a master of his craft. The Spanish master Soler composed a good many sonatas of a Scarlattian vivacity, and of his solo pieces the fandango in F sharp minor is an extraordinary piece; built on a large scale, it has a wildness of textural imagination that bursts out of the confines of convention.

2 MUSIC FOR SOLO PIANO

(a) Haydn

It has become customary to couple the names of Mozart and Haydn, though with no more justification than the equally frequent coupling of Bruckner and Mahler, to name two other totally dissimilar composers. But whereas this century has seen vastly increased recognition of Mozart's genius, that of Haydn has made slower progress, at least partly because of the notion, carefully fostered by many critics, that the divine Mozart is infinitely 'superior' to jolly old Papa Haydn. As to the myth that Haydn's music was full of jokes, but that he was incapable of expressing the deeper feelings in music, one need only refer to the sublime late Masses, forty or so of the symphonies, and many of the quartets, not to mention some of the remarkable piano trios, in order to refute it. Nevertheless, many of his major works remain neglected, and in no medium is this more true than in that of the piano sonatas, which form one of the most striking parts of Haydn's entire oeuvre. Indeed, as a writer of piano sonatas, Haydn sustained his highest level of invention and personal commitment to a much greater extent than did Mozart. The Mozart sonatas, of course, are all fine, and include a number of powerful masterpieces, but for sheer imagination, and the technical ability to carry through with absolute conviction strikingly original ideas, Haydn's convey a much more adequate impression of their composer's true worth.

From the sonatas, quite a clear picture is gained of the progress of Haydn's career as a composer, from the early divertimenti and partitas (both titles used for early works which are now numbered among his sonatas) of simple, direct style and form; through a period in which the *Sturm und Drang* emotionalism of his symphonies and quartets has its counterpart for keyboard; and closing with the majestic sonatas in C, D and E flat, probably written for Haydn's second London sojourn (1794–95). Despite the similarities of the

597

first twenty or so sonatas, many of them already show an entirely personal flavour, and several are remarkably fine. The G major sonata (Hob. 6; UE 13),[1] thought to have been composed by 1760, is especially striking; characteristically inventive and tightly organized in the first movement, it continues with a delightful minuet followed by a hauntingly beautiful G minor slow movement; a brilliant, joyous finale closes a genuinely ambitious work. The sonata in B flat (Hob. 2; UE 11) is also marked by a deeply-felt slow movement in G minor, with a finely-wrought, forthright first movement, and closing with a perky minuet joined to a B flat minor trio of great loveliness. The charm of the E major sonata (Hob. 13; UE 15) lies largely in the suave elegance and repose of the first two movements, with a vigorous peasant-dance finale bringing the work to an infectious conclusion. But most of the early sonatas have at least one movement of high quality and resource, and many of them retain this level throughout, hinting strongly of the Haydn to come, not least in the astonishingly early formulation of his individual approach to sonata form. The development of his personal monothematic technique can perhaps more strongly be seen in the quartets and symphonies, but even in these apparently – though deceptively – slight works it can be clearly perceived.

In the sonatas after 1766, Haydn's style expands considerably, and the emotional penetration of the music is deeper: indeed, several of his masterpieces belong to the period immediately following this date, which is clearly influenced by the concerto style of C. P. E. Bach with its great intensity, emotional variety and rich decoration. (For example, in the appearance of cadential points at which the performer is to improvise a short cadenza: not new, but on a bigger scale now.) The A flat sonata (Hob. 46; UE 31) is ascribed by Christa Landon to 1767–68, but for once one suspects that Hoboken's later numbering is more correct, for otherwise the extraordinary change in Haydn's style, with its sudden immensity, is completely out of context. This magnificent sonata integrates features of the baroque and galant which had hitherto largely been contrasted in his piano output. The lyrical first movement has a fantasia-like freedom certainly influenced by C. P. E. Bach, and controlled by an acute thematic working;

[1] The numbering of Haydn's sonatas has been complicated over the years by the appearance of a number of incomplete editions. I have adopted the course of using two numberings, indicated by 'Hob' (the familiar Hoboken/Haydn Society list) and 'UE' (the more recent catalogue compiled by Christa Landon for her edition, published by Universal Edition).

while the heavenly slow movement has a J. S. Bach-ian contrapuntal complexity – a song-like movement of the utmost serenity and gravity. The finale is one of his finest virtuoso pieces, full of high spirits and strength of purpose, and with considerable harmonic power. The grand intimacy of this work contrasts with the smaller scale of the delicate two-movement sonata in G minor (Hob. 44; UE 32), which has a Dresden china-like fragility, yet, miraculously, an underlying strength of organization that gives it a uniquely moving character.

The emotional undercurrent of this remarkable piece comes to the fore in the C minor sonata (Hob. 20; UE 33) of 1771, one of the few to have established themselves in the regular repertoire of leading pianists. This symphonic work is the most powerful statement in Haydn's piano music of the world of *Sturm und Drang*, and remains one of Haydn's biggest sonatas, in ideas as well as length. The superbly-wrought first movement, with its unusually extensive development section, is followed by an equally large-scale, flowing and deeply expressive slow movement; while the finale returns to the emotional drama of the first movement, this time with added turbulence, and no consolatory ray of hope to soften the stark, defiant ending. This most moving work must have sounded disturbing indeed to Haydn's contemporaries, and in few of the sonatas written in the following years does he attempt anything like the same sustained vehemence of utterance. Apart from the two fine minor key sonatas, in B minor (Hob. 32; UE 47) and C sharp minor (Hob. 36; UE 49), the composer relaxes, effortlessly enjoying his skill and imaginative resource. Many of the sonatas are brilliant and delightful pieces, often marked with that pure serenity which is so typical of Haydn.

The last sonatas exemplify Haydn's range admirably. In the E flat sonata (Hob. 49; UE 59) he gives us one of his most Beethovenian first movements, full of forthright character; the slow movement has a spacious, majestic main theme, and the finale is a sprightly, effortlessly relaxed, but always tightly controlled minuet and trio. In the three sonatas written for the London visits of 1794–95, Haydn explores new gestures. There is amazingly imaginative use of the pedal in the first movement of the C major sonata (Hob. 50; UE 60), while the finale is clearly from the same imaginative world as the later scherzos of Beethoven. The first movement of the next, D major, sonata (Hob. 51; UE 61) has an elaborate, wide-ranging freedom; there is much of the improvisatory origins of the fantasia about this piece, reminding one of Haydn's achievement in reconciling this type of writing with the stricter formal controls demanded by sonata form.

The finale is again Beethovenian, but this adjective can with even more justice be applied to the great E flat major sonata (Hob. 52; UE 62), probably his last. This noble work sums up his achievement in this medium. The first movement is possibly the greatest in his keyboard output – an intricate, yet seemingly simple manipulation of ideas to form a massive and imposing piece. The affectingly serene adagio, with its powerful central section anticipating Mussorgsky at one point, is set with brilliant inspiration in the remote key of E major; while the finale is a high-spirited combination of sonata and rondo forms, filled with Olympian wit and resource.

It is notable throughout Haydn's output of piano sonatas how he avoids descending to the use of mere formulae. But more to the point, perhaps, would be to remark on his amazingly sustained level of imagination. It is sad that he wrote little else for solo keyboard apart from the sonatas; but even so there are some gems, notably the moving variations in F minor, written in 1793 (and headed 'sonata' in the autograph), and the brilliant fantasia in C of 1789. The former is a characteristic series of alternating variations on two themes, one in F minor and the other in F major, and it has established itself firmly in the repertoire; not surprisingly, for its haunting loveliness is long sustained until, in the final section, there is a sudden and powerful outburst of impassioned harmonic development. The fantasia, one of the most difficult pieces technically in his piano output, is also full of startling harmonic changes, but the difficulties of the variations are, if more subtle, almost as severe; and few of the sonatas fail to present a real challenge of style and technique to the interpreter.

(b) Mozart

Perhaps one of the reasons why most pianists fail to come to grips with Haydn's sonatas is that they are approached as if they were Mozartian. But the difference between the composers is total, and extends to the relative stature of their sonatas and shorter pieces. With Haydn the sonatas are by far his most significant contribution to the keyboard repertoire; he explores and stretches his resources almost continuously in them. With Mozart the reverse is true, for while the sonatas are almost uniformly finely made and full of good things (with a few standing out particularly) it is in the shorter pieces that he extends his imagination, and reveals the depths of expression of which we know him to be capable.

This is particularly true of the late pieces such as the rondo in A minor, K 511, and the adagio in B minor, K 540. Both are perfectly formed structures (the adagio in sonata form), and both are imbued with a spirit of resignation, and an overt, subjective emotionalism that had always been the hallmark of Mozart's most expressive slow writing, yet had never before been expressed in his keyboard music with such haunting perfection. But the earlier pieces contain much that is equally fine: the D minor fantasia, K 397, with its improvisatory freedom contained within a strongly controlled format of two main sections; the C minor fantasia, K 396, completed from Mozart's unfinished manuscript by Stadler, and even in this hybrid form one of the most powerful of all his keyboard utterances; the D major rondo, K 485, based on a theme of J. C. Bach, and full of the spirit of delight; and the fantasia and fugue in C, K 394, an immensely strong and forthright composition, all demand attention. Even in so slight a piece as the enchanting gigue in G, K 574, Mozart's individuality and depth of feeling are conveyed miraculously by the subtlest of means.

Of these short pieces, one outstanding masterwork remains to be named: the C minor fantasia, K 475. It was composed in 1785, but Mozart published it together with the C minor sonata, K 457, of the previous year, and the two form an infinitely satisfactory unit. The sonata came after a gap in Mozart's output of keyboard sonatas, the previous one, in B flat, K 333, dating from 1778. During the intervening years Mozart had managed to free himself from his father's dominance and had also left the slavery of the Archbishop Hieronymus in Salzburg and settled in Vienna. His increasingly successful career as virtuoso and composer undoubtedly left its mark on the sonatas that were to come, but so, too, did a new depth of feeling. The C minor fantasia and sonata have a new range of expression, symphonic expansiveness and richness of resource, the latter being perhaps the greatest of all Mozart's piano sonatas. Texturally there can be no doubt of his increasing familiarity with the fortepiano, and technically his mastery of composition is now at its peak. Both in this and the succeeding sonatas there is an astonishing versatility and subtlety in his handling of harmonic change and contrapuntal devices. Even in so apparently light a sonata as K 570 in B flat, one of the most serene in his output, every bar reveals new wonders of imaginative artistry; and in such a noble piece as the neglected sonata in F, K 533/494 (the rondo K 494 added by Mozart to form a finale to the two movements labelled K 533) there is great strength of purpose underlying the surface charm of the music.

It must not be thought, however, that the earlier sonatas are in any way unsatisfactory. Only if one expects the Mozart of the concertos

601

can one occasionally be disappointed. The early sonatas, though 'earlier' is a better word, since his output of keyboard sonatas started surprisingly late, show the master in relaxed mood, enjoying his craft, without forcing himself to think deeply. The prevalence of Alberti basses, used without the point that Haydn usually brought to this device, gives the game away, so to speak. But on this level, Mozart being virtually incapable of writing poor music, there is a constant flow of lovely melody, and occasionally one work stands out as being especially gracious. Such is K 333 in B flat, a life-enhancing stream of glorious melody.

The A minor sonata, K 310, stands outside the trend of these earlier works, however. An extraordinary outburst of passion sustaining in the finale a bleak air of tragedy right to the end, the sonata may well have been inspired, as Einstein suggests, by the death of Mozart's mother. Whatever the cause, this astonishing piece, so shattering in the context of the general urbanity of the surrounding sonatas, remains one of the most deeply felt of all his works. Seldom did Mozart bare his soul so powerfully throughout an entire work. Only the C minor sonata, a transmutation of these feelings into more symphonic, almost Beethovenian terms (perhaps as a result of the influence of Haydn) reveals something of the same spirit. In the remaining sonatas he regains his urbanity, yet I have no doubt that their stature, for all their apparent simplicity, is the greater because of the experience of the two great minor key sonatas.

Like the other Viennese classics, Mozart produced numerous sets of variations. Without achieving the depth of feeling of Haydn's great F minor set, and without essaying the symphonic style to be developed in this form by Beethoven, Mozart produced several enduring masterpieces of this type. The most familiar are those on Gluck's *Unser dummer Pöbel meint*, K 455, and on a minuet by Duport, K 573, richly decorative and full of the most marvellous colouring and variety; but most of the sets have rewards for both player and listener. Often it is as though Mozart were using the decorative elements of this technique to try out textural ideas for use in his sonatas and concertos. Only in the major sets does he reveal anything like his true capabilities when it comes to treatment of harmonic development and rhythmic variety.

(c) *Beethoven and the early romantics*

With Haydn and Mozart the Classical era reached its close; the Romantic was about to start. The composers who provide the greatest link between the two are Beethoven and Schubert, with a host of satellites of varying importance surrounding them. It is perhaps significant that whereas the Classical era was marked by the concept of the composer as employee, either of the aristocracy or the Church, in the Romantic era he came into his own as his own master. Beethoven's familiar brushes with authority were often the result of his desire to assert this new self-awareness on the part of the composer, in the face of the reactionary attitudes of the authorities. In passing one might note that with this new self-awareness and self-consciousness, the composer became much more prone to lapses of taste. Though they may sometimes have been relatively uninspired, one can hardly say of Bach, Haydn or Mozart that they wrote any bad music. But Beethoven most emphatically wrote some bad music, and when the Romantic era really got under way one can see that every composer was capable of the most colossal lapses of taste. Self-awareness, self-confidence – these things were a salutary change, allowing music to develop naturally and inevitably; yet they led at times to a self-consciousness that brought about an inflation of the composer's aims.

In Beethoven's huge output of piano music, however, there is hardly a piece that merits this criticism, and certainly not even a movement in all the thirty-two piano sonatas. This monumental collection is perhaps his most startling single achievement, for, even more than in the symphonies, quartets and duos, starting with the Haydnesque form, and faithfully returning to develop it throughout his career as his own form developed, he ultimately made it something far removed from the essentially self-contained structure he had inherited. Nobody viewing in its historical context Beethoven's first piano sonata, the F minor, op. 2 no. 1, could reasonably be expected to deduce that from this essentially classical (though entirely personal) work, its composer would, within twenty years, have produced the Hammerklavier. Yet the path from one to the other, and on to the last three glorious works, is logical and consistent.

Several factors contribute to this line of development. One, naturally, is the rapid improvement of the pianoforte, for no composer has been more responsive to, or demanding of, instrumental development than Beethoven. His deafness, turning him increasingly on his inner self, is another important factor; the intensity of the late sonatas, and the power with which they create so strongly the sense of intense personal thought breaking the barriers of established musical style, must surely derive at least partly from this physical limitation. Seldom can such a personal tragedy have been of such lasting value to mankind. The growth of Beethoven's technical development and imagination would, however, have been startling enough without these two added stimuli. Even the very first sonata (disregarding the three juvenile ones, un-numbered among the established thirty-two, despite their undeniable interest and merit) proclaims in its first phrase the presence of a new master. The three sonatas of op. 2, written in 1796, two years after Haydn had composed his final group of sonatas, adopt the classical sonata as established by Mozart and Haydn; in the first at least there is little that ventures as far formally as some of the features of Haydn's last works in this medium. But the voice is defiantly Beethoven's, and by no. 3 of the set, the approach to form is entirely his own.

It is indeed remarkable how, throughout his sonata output, Beethoven tackles each work as if it were a completely new challenge. The range of structures and techniques is extraordinary. Take the two sonatas labelled 'Quasi una fantasia' (the two op. 27, in E flat, and the well-known 'Moonlight' in C sharp minor), the first of which is especially fascinating and unusual, with its condensation of several sections into a single movement – a synthesis of the elements of the classical fantasia, transformed into a genuinely symphonic structure. Into the usual elements of a sonata he brings extra movements; his minuets have, following and developing Haydn's example, become scherzi, and he introduces a massive and powerful funeral march into the A flat sonata, op. 26. The same work starts with a set of variations, not an unfamiliar element of the classical sonata, but here handled with vastly more symphonic technique and resource.

Even in so great a range of masterworks several sonatas stand out. The D minor, op. 31 no. 2 (known these days as the 'Tempest', because supposedly inspired by Shakespeare's play) emphasizes, especially in the recitative passages of the first movement, the dramatic element that lies behind Beethoven's art. The F minor, op. 57 ('Appassionata') is, as it were, a consummation of the spirit of *Sturm und Drang*, the hesitations, gropings, dramatic outbursts and wide emotional variety, the transformation of a line going right back to C. P. E. Bach. When one comes to the last sonatas, too, the music is not only forward-looking, but also aware of its own roots. Beethoven's handling of the fugue, that eminently baroque form, gives it a new lease of life here. One thinks of the finales of the A major sonata, op. 101, the Hammerklavier in B flat, op. 106, and the A flat, op. 110; in each of these fugal form is treated with the utmost respect technically, yet with the most amazing imaginative and emotional power. Variation form, too, undergoes a transformation typical of Beethoven, not least in op. 111, the second and final movement of which uses the essentially decorative nature of the classical variation, but metamorphoses it into something of infinitely greater significance. The first movement of this work, too, is one of the finest examples of Beethoven's fugal technique, being superbly integrated with his other technical resources. It is not merely that he takes classical, baroque, or other old techniques and develops them; rather he changes their essential meaning, through the intensity of his own vision, and makes them something entirely new.

Outside the sonatas, Beethoven's output for piano is still enormous. There are numerous sets of variations, the earlier ones of a largely decorative nature, but several of the later ones demanding special attention. The remarkably varied *Six Variations on an Original Theme in F*, op. 34, of 1802, is unusual in that each variation is in a different key (D, B flat, G, E flat, C minor, and finally F again), as well as being more markedly different in character than has been the case with his variations hitherto. In the same year he wrote the more substantial and well-known *Fifteen Variations with a Fugue*, op. 35, in E flat. The theme is taken from his ballet *The Creatures of Prometheus*, and was later used for the finale of the 'Eroica' Symphony, so that these variations are nowadays known, somewhat inaccurately, as the 'Eroica' variations and fugue. The intellectual power of Beethoven's manner is more pronounced in this work; brilliant virtuoso music though it is, there is a rigorous pursuit of the thematic material which foreshadows the next two masterpieces in this genre, while the final fugue has all the grandeur and uncompromising integrity of those in the final sonatas.

But perhaps finest of all are the *Thirty-two Variations in C minor* (1806, without opus number) and the *Thirty-three Variations and Fugue on a Theme of Diabelli*, op. 120 (1823), the latter his last large work for piano solo. The *Thirty-two Variations* are, taken individually, miniatures of astonishing range; but they add up to an immense, dramatic passacaglia. The *Diabelli Variations*, written as Beethoven's contribution to an album in which fifty-one composers were asked by Diabelli to write one variation on a theme by himself, have as their basis a naïve little waltz tune. Whether he intended it as a typically fierce joke or not, is not known, but Beethoven's response, this massive, complicated structure lasting for nearly an hour, certainly puts Diabelli's tune in its place! The wealth of invention he derives from what seems a most unpromising basis is quite

605

extraordinary, culminating in arguably the noblest and most fiery of all his fugues, and then a final *Tempo di Menuetto* which reaches once again to the purity and serenity of the finale of op. 111.

Beethoven's large output of shorter pieces again contains many remarkable works, not least the various sets of bagatelles, which though as miniature as the title suggests, indicate no lessening of his imagination. The two sets, op. 119 and 126, contain some of the essential features of his late manner, expressed in the subtlest sketches. But it is in the sonatas and variations that Beethoven made his mark most powerfully. Small wonder that he cast such a profound shadow on his successors (a shadow still felt today).

Mendelssohn, for instance, showed his debt clearly in his youthful E major sonata, which is obviously modelled on the master's op. 101. But Mendelssohn's talent is more clearly revealed in his shorter works. The *Songs without Words*, once standard salon fare and today unjustly underestimated on that account, contain much of typically fragile beauty; that Mendelssohn could be made of sterner stuff can be seen in the fine preludes and fugues, op. 35, the sonorous *Variations Sérieuses* in D minor, and perhaps above all, in the magnificent fantasy in F sharp minor, op. 28, fully worthy of the great traditions of the title.

Most of Beethoven's fashionable competitors, some of whom were deemed far more important composers at the time, have faded. Hummel, Czerny and Spohr have more or less disappeared from the repertoire, and so also, with less justification, has the work of Muzio Clementi. The advocacy of a few (regrettably few) pianists, such as Horowitz, has continued to remind us of the truly remarkable qualities of many of Clementi's sonatas, but they are otherwise seldom encountered in recital programmes. Perhaps Mozart's unkind remarks, following the famous, indecisive competition between the two, have affected history's judgment of the music; if so, this is a pity, not least because Mozart was notoriously ungenerous about his competitors. Clementi's sonatas are clearly written for the pianoforte; even more than Beethoven's early ones, they exploit the technical brilliance available on the instrument. But they also have great expressive range, as well as genuine melodic and harmonic inspiration. There is, too, a distinctive, clearly recognizable personality behind the music. If the masterpiece of the series is certainly the great *Didone Abbandonata* Sonata in G minor, there are many which reward closer attention than they have received in recent years.

(d) Schubert and Weber

Beethoven's true successor as a writer of piano sonatas, however, is none of these, but Schubert. It is strange how long it has taken for this point even to begin to be recognized. The mistake has often been to look in them for some kind of Beethovenian style, and to regard Schubert's highly personal style of piano writing as clumsy. Neither of these attitudes is logical. Schubert's way of writing for the piano is unlike any other, but he uses it in the sonatas with even more richness and variety than in the songs (which, though equally difficult, have always been praised for the keyboard writing, as Harold Truscott has pointed out).

Furthermore, to regard Schubert's sonatas as attempting to continue Beethoven's line is to miss the point entirely. Indeed, I would go so far as to suggest that if Beethoven had not lived, Schubert's sonata output would have remained remarkably as it is, for his approach was entirely different. There is, of course, a marvellous flow of melody (which has been adduced as evidence that he could not sustain a large form – though it is not so used in connection with Mozart's sonatas!). There is, too, Schubert's highly individual handling of tonality, full of the most moving changes of key, often enough a simple key-shift producing a heart-rending effect.

Far from being the loose, unwieldy but charming structures they are too often considered, Schubert's sonatas are almost without exception superbly wrought pieces, tightly held together (his handling of tonality is important in this) and sustained by the sheer power of the composer's vision. Only one of them is markedly Beethovenian in feeling, the C minor, D 958, the first of three sonatas written in September 1828, the year of his death. Here the brusque opening gesture reminds one strongly of Beethoven, while the finale's basic tarantella motion is equally reminiscent, especially of the finale of Beethoven's E flat sonata, op. 31 no. 3. Yet there is still a world of difference; Beethoven never wrote so inexorable a Dance of Death as this Schubert finale, while the first movement is Schubertian through and through. The other two of this final trilogy are, like the C minor, among the greatest of all piano sonatas; the A major, D 959, with its powerful first movement containing one of Schubert's richest development sections, and its lonely, wandering slow movement, interrupted in the middle by a terrifying burst of passion; and the serene B flat major, D 960, as moving and other-worldly a valediction as any composer has penned.

But the earlier sonatas contain a number of masterpieces too, such as the three magnificent works in A minor, of which the central one (D 784) achieves an almost Sibelian grandeur and bleakness in its first moments. Then there are the energetic, massive and extrovert D major, D 850, the equally large-scale, but much gentler G major, D 894, and the finest of the many unfinished ones, that in C major, D 840. Of this only two movements were completed by Schubert, though he sketched sizable portions of the other two. But as it stands, it is as satisfying a masterpiece as the 'Unfinished' Symphony, with a first movement of symphonic power, and a slow movement of large-scale passion, closing with such finality that a scherzo and finale somehow seem superfluous.

Of Schubert's other contributions to the piano repertoire, the 'Wanderer' fantasia in C – a sonata in all but name, with four movements played without a break – has deservedly won popularity for itself. Each main theme is derived from Schubert's song 'Der Wanderer', the fantasia being a symphonic working out of the ideas derived from this, ending with a finale that essays a full-blown fugue. This is Schubert's perhaps most avowedly virtuosic piano work, but an equal amount of technical competence is needed to play even the famous impromptus, of which there are two main sets. The four impromptus, D 899, are charming miniatures, the first being a most impressive piece, of large proportions. The second set, D 935, amounts almost to another sonata, with an impressive first movement, an allegretto in A flat that might be regarded as an intermezzo, the popular B flat third piece (a set of variations on a theme from Rosamunde), and a fiery, scherzo-like finale. There are also the Three Piano Pieces, D 946, published after Schubert's death, with the title 'Impromptus': these, though often criticized for being too long, seem to me masterpieces of large-scale thought. Nor must one omit mention of Schubert's vast number of dances – Ländler, waltzes and écossaises in the main – which contain many gems; nor the fairly small number of other piano works he wrote, including two delightful sets of variations, two lilting scherzi, and a number of flowing small pieces.

Few composers since Schubert have shown such prolific interest in the piano sonata. The four examples by Weber, less familiar nowadays than they were during the 19th century, deserve special mention, however. They inhabit very clearly the world of the early Romantic era; the fourth, in E minor, has a particularly emotive programme attached to it, about the last thoughts of a dying hero. But it is a magnificent work, with a distinctly Chopinesque first movement, and an unrelenting, whirling, final tarantella. Each of Weber's sonatas has some feature of special attraction: the famous *moto perpetuo* finale of no. 1 in C, the verdant, pastoral beginning of no. 2 in A flat, with its suggestions of distant horn-calls; and the power of the D minor's (no. 3) first movement. These works, perhaps more than his more conventionally virtuosic sets of variations and other display pieces (written under the influence of the growing demand for pyrotechnics from the performer) demand a thorough revival of interest, not least for the sheer poetry of their invention. They are very much, one feels, the sort of music Chopin might have written had he been German.

(e) *The romantics*

Despite the romantic elements in the music of Beethoven and Schubert, however, and despite the high achievements of Clementi and Weber, it was perhaps inevitable that the form of the piano sonata as such should appeal less to the Romantic era. It bespeaks, after all, a limitation of form and content which, for all Beethoven's expansion of these, was taken to be the essence of the sonata. Thus, even Schubert's 'Wanderer' piece is entitled a fantasia rather than a sonata; his G major sonata, too, was originally published under the title 'Phantasy', a misnomer if ever there was one. With what might be described as the cult of the personality growing in importance, composers felt free to express themselves in looser forms, with the programmatic connotations or pictorial elements that typify the romantic approach.

Thus, 19th-century piano music is far more diverse in its approach to form, and when so eminently romantic a composer as Liszt chose to write a sonata, it predictably turned out to be an immensely passionate, virtuoso work, its emotional content apparently bursting out of the music's seams. But this superficial impression gives a far from complete picture of his B minor sonata, for despite its seemingly improvisatory nature it is most closely bound together by a few motifs; the technique of thematic metamorphosis which it reveals so clearly had an immense influence on music after Liszt, but it was not an altogether new feature of sonata-writing, for the second and third sonatas of Chopin (the first, in C minor, is a far finer work than is usually conceded, but also more conventional in form, despite its fascinating $\frac{5}{4}$ slow movement) are subtly inventive in this respect. The B flat minor sonata, nicknamed after its funeral march slow movement, is often regarded as typically romantic (i.e. poetic and emotional), and indeed it is. The relentless, truly Napoleonic funeral march, with its heart-rendingly personal trio section, is a romantic conception. Even in its outer sections, full of a sense of homage, and the pageantry of mourning, there is a feeling of national identification with an individual; this might be the funeral of a beloved statesman, who represents the national aspirations of every one of his countrymen. The finale, that astonishing flurry of quiet quavers without rhythm or apparent melody, sends a shiver down the spine – another truly romantic conception. Chopin breaks all the rules in giving this large sonata so short, and so entirely different a finale; and yet, miraculously, it falls into place as an inevitable conclusion to the work, while the earlier movements, including the powerful scherzo (like an elephantine minuet), have as much classical poise as they have romantic feeling. Much the same can be said of the equally fine, B minor sonata, his third; here too the passion and apparent freedom of the music cannot hide the composer's ability to think in a large, thoroughly-worked-out format.

For all this, the essence of Chopin lies in his shorter pieces – 'shorter' rather than 'smaller', for a work like the F minor fantasia, or any one of the ballades or scherzi, displays to the utmost an ability to construct out of seemingly diverse materials a sense of unity and organic growth, without losing one iota of the spontaneity or freshness that marks his miniatures. Even some of these have a sense of size quite surprising for a composer who is too often regarded solely as a miniaturist: think of the D flat major prelude from op. 28, for instance. A composer incapable of writing sonatas could never have conceived or carried out such a powerful single piece, whose implications go far beyond the five minutes or so of the music, with its sense of inexorable growth not unlike some of Schubert's grander conceptions.

From an emotional point of view, perhaps the very heart of Chopin can be found in the mazurkas and polonaises, the latter tending to be on a fairly large scale, culminating in the glorious A flat polonaise, op. 53, the apotheosis of brilliant ceremonial familiar also from the earlier 'Military' polonaise in A, op. 40; and then in the great polonaise-fantaisie, op. 61, in which a more subjective note is touched in terms akin to those of the fantasia and the ballades. In the mazurkas, Chopin shows most directly his incredible imagination which derives from the colours, and even the physical properties, of the keyboard, as in his handling of the textures obtained by discreet use of the pedal; and he extends his harmonic, rhythmical and

610

textural resources as nowhere else. Such features as the extraordinary chain of descending sevenths at the close of the C sharp minor mazurka, op. 30, no. 4 are the hallmark of the master.

The other great pianist-composer of the romantic era (disregarding for the moment Schumann, whose pianistic career was short-lived) was, of course, Liszt, to this day seen by many as the embodiment of all that is inherently bad in romanticism. Certainly he presents a puzzling enigma as a personality. There are innumerable stories of his egotism. His extraordinary life itself, in which he was both libertine and religious (not that the two have always been so far removed) at one and the same time, serves as further fuel to those who would detract his music on the grounds of personality alone. And there are undeniably compositions of his which go beyond the bounds of reasonable taste, however these are computed. Yet there are at the same time innumerable instances of his generosity to his fellow-composers, both contemporary and younger – Smetana, for example, among many others, benefited from his warm advocacy. No mere egotist would have been capable of acts like these, which included conducting many works of his fellows. Perhaps, after all, Liszt was merely a realist who knew his own worth, and it is surely unjust to castigate his works as those of a self-centred poseur. The B minor sonata could not have been written by such a one, for its musical qualities are masterly.

Liszt found his inspiration in many sources: poetry (the lovely Petrarch sonnets), landscape (so many of the *Années de Pèlerinage*), heroic personalities of the past ('Mazeppa'), the sounds of the world, such as the tolling of bells, and, inevitably, the keyboard itself, with his massive, brilliantly conceived *Studies of Transcendental Execution* (of which 'Mazeppa' is one). He also found inspiration in folk-music (he is revered to this day in Hungary, as one of the great figures of Hungarian nationalism), and, in keeping with the romantic virtuoso tradition of operatic fantasies, in the music of others. Some of his operatic fantasies, such as those on Mozart's *Don Juan* and Verdi's *Simon Boccanegra* seem almost extensions of the opera, showing profound psychological insight into the characters they portray; while his transcriptions from Wagner's operas, and perhaps above all, the entire series of Beethoven's symphonies, remain to this day the summit of the transcriber's art. In his *Paganini Studies*, too, he took six of Paganini's violin caprices and made them entirely his own.

The romantic flamboyancy attributed to Liszt certainly does not apply to those piano pieces of his declining years. The famous

'Mephisto' waltz had three successors from this period, ever more strange and unearthly, and such works as the two pieces entitled 'La Lugubre Gondole' (The Funeral Gondola), the Elegies, and the numerous memorial pieces of this period, concentrate on the exploration of new harmonic structures derived largely from the tritone, the interval of an augmented fourth, known in the Middle Ages as 'the Devil in Music'. Perhaps in preparing to meet his God, Liszt had decided to finish his business with the Devil? At any rate, in these last piano pieces he essays into new worlds of harmonic colouring, with a novel austerity and sparsity of texture that looks forward to Bartók and, if one extends the implications of the fragmentary nature of some of the music, almost to Webern. It is a cold weird world that these works inhabit, yet a compelling one, revealing once again the astonishing resources of Liszt's mind.

If Liszt, save in his last years, represents the romantic era at its most public (an incomplete view, it is true, but the standard one), Schumann represents it at its most intimate and personal, more so than even Chopin. For Schumann, who put an end to his pianistic career by his attempt to stretch his hands to an even wider span, saw his piano music as a vehicle for some of his most intimate and directly personal messages; his use of ciphers, addressed to particular people (usually young ladies) reveals this. Schumann is regarded as a miniaturist, but with even less cause than Chopin; there is, after all, no finer or more satisfying piano concerto than his, while his symphonies are surely masterpieces. That he was capable of writing for solo piano on a large scale is shown by the three sonatas – all striking, dramatic and powerful works, with moments of fancy and intimacy. They are youthful pieces, all except the finale of the G minor, being composed in 1835, when he was twenty-five, and they inevitably show the spontaneity and impulsiveness typical of Schumann throughout his career, but especially at this stage.

The forms adopted are largely classical, and the restriction this imposed might have been crippling to Schumann, were it not for his inspired flow of melody and idiomatic handling of the keyboard, which is both thoroughly pianistic, and utterly unlike that of any other composer. So individual is this style that the sonatas retain their interest as a unique contribution to the literature; but they also have, in sympathetic performances, great power of utterance. Perhaps the most successful is the second, in G minor. None of the movements seems to sprawl quite as much as in the other sonatas, and perhaps that is why performers tend to prefer this one. Yet the F sharp minor sonata (no. 1), and the F minor (no. 3, printed first, at the publisher's suggestion, as 'Concerto without Orchestra') are, in the right hands, rich and pulsating works, despite being, perhaps, not ideal by textbook standards. (But then textbooks seldom allow for such a vivid, unrestrained imagination.)

The two greatest abstract creations of Schumann's piano output are, however, the three-movement fantasia in C, op. 17, dedicated to Liszt, and the symphonic studies, op. 13. The fantasia owes its inspiration to Clara Wieck, whose father had at that time attempted to cut off communication between Schumann and his daughter. It is a passionate work, especially in the magnificent first movement, perhaps Schumann's most subtly achieved large-scale movement for piano solo. The symphonic studies, like the fantasia, represent Schumann's compositional skill at its finest; variation form, which allowed the composer room for keen musical characterization within a strict format, yet without the restraints of a larger structure, was highly suited to the romantic temperament, and these variations on a theme by Baron von Fricken are both concentrated and volatile.

Even so, Schumann was most himself in the enormous number of sets of short pieces he produced throughout his career: groups of pieces with titles like *Fantasiestücke* (of which there are two sets, at opposite ends of his career), *Carnaval*, *Kreisleriana*, *Davidsbündlertänze*, and the two remarkable sets of pieces concerned with childhood, the *Scenes from Childhood*, and the *Album for the Young*. His extraordinary power of musical characterization is seen at its peak in these works, as also in the *Faschingsschwank aus Wien* (Carnival Jest from Vienna) and the *Forest Scenes*: naïvety and sophistication go hand in hand, just as do the world of the romantic era and a delight in mythical characters, such as the Davidsbündler and the figures of the Commedia dell'Arte (whose spirit is never far away even from the lighter moments of the sonatas). And the world of romantic literature as typified by Hoffmann's tales and the writings of Jean Paul Richter was an invaluable inspiration.

The story of Schumann's championship of the young Brahms is well known, yet Brahms is a totally different type of composer. Here is a romantic expressing himself in much more strictly classical terms, not least in the sets of variations which occupy a central position in his output and culminate in the two great masterpieces, the *Variations and Fugue on a theme of Handel*, and the two books of variations on a theme of Paganini. The *Handel Variations* are the epitome of classicism brought up to date; this is as rigorous and finely worked a

613

set of variations as any by Beethoven or by Bach, whose spirit is powerfully conjured up in the glorious final fugue. In the *Paganini Variations* the virtuoso element, though present in the previous work, is here paramount; Paganini's fascination, which affected such composers as Liszt and Berlioz, here exerted an equal spell on so apparently sober a composer as Brahms, drawing from him a work of coruscating brilliance, a *sine qua non* of pianistic virtuosity.

Brahms's output for solo piano falls into three distinct groups. In his early years he produced three massive and remarkable sonatas. Of these, only the third, in F minor, has achieved anything like a regular place in the repertoire, yet one cannot help regretting that the timidity of pianists has led to the neglect of its predecessors, no. 1 in C and no. 2 in F sharp minor. All three are magnificently symphonic works, huge in scope, and full of the most memorable ideas. Only in the outer movements does one occasionally feel that the composer's exuberance is getting the better of his control of form, though it should be said that the first movement of the C major is a startling achievement for so young a composer. These sonatas, great despite their faults, seem to have been essays towards a symphonic style of composition, for their lessons are applied in the first concerto, in D minor; and having achieved mastery of this aspect of composition, Brahms turned his attention to the development of motifs in a more concentrated form, as seen in the sets of variations.

Having, in turn, achieved the peak of this technique in the two sets discussed above, he left piano composition for a while, returning to it later in life with the various sets of short pieces, beginning with the eight pieces, op. 76, and the two rhapsodies, op. 79, and going on to the flowering of his most personal musical impulses in the sets of pieces, op. 116–119 inclusive. In these short works, vehicles for his most intimate thoughts, especially in the last sets of all, Brahms shows himself to be as fine a miniaturist as he was a symphonist. Each piece is a perfect expression of subtle feeling, expressed in terms of the most acute pianistic sensibility. Mention should also be made of Brahms's pedagogic work; his studies are still invaluable exercises, and among his arrangements, that for left hand alone of Bach's unaccompanied violin chaconne is an astonishing *tour de force*.

(f) The romantics outside Germany

Apart from Liszt and Chopin, the solid core of the romantic era tends to be the German tradition; but throughout the period, composers from outside this tradition enriched its music, from Clementi's Irish pupil, John Field, whose nocturnes provided a model for Chopin's pieces in this genre, and continue to give elegant, expressive pleasure, to the large number of virtuoso composer-pianists whose names have disappeared somewhat from the repertoire now, but who in their day were lionized almost as much as Liszt: Scharwenka, Kalkbrenner, Tausig, Moscheles, Henselt, Thalberg, Gottschalk, Reinecke, von Bülow, Anton Rubinstein. The list is almost endless, going on to the early years of the 20th century with those who, like Rosenthal, Godowsky, Paderewski, Albeniz, Busoni, Hofmann and Rachmaninov, carried on the tradition. It was the high peak of pianistic virtuosity as such. Not all these performers were composers to any extent. Leschetitsky is remembered, with Liszt, as one of the greatest teachers of all time; von Bülow as a great pedagogue. Some, such as Busoni, Albeniz and Rachmaninov, are still known as fine composers; but the majority made their fortunes touring Europe and America as show pianists (Clara Schumann and Teresa Carreño outstanding among the women), of varying degrees of musical integrity. In recent years there has been an attempt to rekindle interest in the music of these and other romantic composers whose charms seem to have faded, an attempt successful in only a handful of cases, and then mostly with concertos.

But one of the most extraordinary of all these musicians, and one with a special claim to immortality as a composer is Alkan, whose real name was Morhange. His life was spent very largely as a recluse – though not entirely, since he had an illegitimate son – yet his reputation as a pianist seems to have been formidable. He must indeed have been a phenomenal performer, for his piano music, which seems to have constituted virtually his entire output, is of almost superhuman difficulty. His set of *Studies* in all the minor keys, op. 39, includes two enormous works of great importance: the Symphony (nos. 4–7 of the set) and the Concerto for solo piano (nos. 8–10). The advocacy of pianists like Busoni, Egon Petri, John Ogdon and Ronald Smith has kept his name alive, but it is unlikely that his music can ever enter the regular repertoire, masterly as it is, for it is far too difficult for most pianists to contemplate.

The organization behind these vast spans of music is as formidable as its technical difficulty; and, moreover, it is genuinely pianistic in conception. The *Grande Sonata*, op. 33, is another masterpiece from the same source. Subtitled 'The Four Ages of Man', each movement depicts a stage in life, of a man at twenty, thirty, forty and fifty years respectively. Typical of Alkan's grandiose ideas is the second movement, given a further title, 'Quasi-Faust'. Developing with Lisztian thoroughness a *leitmotif* of four notes, it culminates in a fugue of no less than eight real parts. Even Alkan's 'Sonatine', op. 61, is a far more imposing piece than the title might suggest. But Alkan was also capable of writing miniatures, though these are not all as soft and gentle as the barcarolle; the 'Song of the Madwoman on the Shore' is surely one of the most eerie short pieces in existence.

The Belgian, César Franck, committed himself with more sustained imagination to the organ repertoire than to that of the piano. But his *Prelude, Chorale and Fugue* is a notable application to the piano of Franck's immense contrapuntal skill, allied to his individual chromatic, harmonic style, influenced to a large extent by Wagner.

(g) France

However, neither Alkan nor Franck belongs to what we somewhat mistakenly tend to call the French tradition, which despite the many charming pieces of such composers as Chabrier, Saint-Saëns and Hahn, really came to the fore in the early years of the 20th century, with Debussy and Ravel. To replace the Romantic movement came the Impressionists, who saw themselves, in music as in painting, reacting against the overblown, overloaded canvasses of their predecessors. Now there seems a distinct and logical line between the two; yet at the time, Debussy's washes of tonal colour must have seemed a startling innovation.

Actually, despite Debussy's early individuality, there is little in the essence of his youthful style which cannot be seen in embryo at least in earlier composers. Wagner's influence, filtered through Franck, is there; so too is the particular kind of superior salon music developed by Chabrier and Massenet. To these he added more exotic, Russian and oriental influences; oriental pentatonicism and the whole-tone scale became an important feature of his style, as he pursued his own path, ignoring the classical-romantic sonata tradition and deriving his inspiration from nature and legend. Works like *L'Ile Joyeuse*, *Reflets dans L'Eau* (continuing the tradition of 'water' music inspired by Liszt's highly influential *Les Jeux d'Eau à la Villa d'Este*), the two sets of *Images* for piano, and the two books of preludes – all these testify to his sensitive response to the world of nature. Antiquity, too, held a fascination for him, as it did for the romantics, and continues to do for composers today. Yet all these pieces are perfectly satisfying abstract music. 'Voiles', from the first book of preludes, is a vivid, shimmering picture of sails at rest on a still sea; yet Debussy, by placing the titles of his preludes at the end of each piece rather than at the beginning, emphasizes the essentially musical nature of the basic impulse, and in this he was certainly reacting against the romantic predilection for recreating some explicit picture in musical terms.

Nevertheless the *Children's Corner* suite is as vivid an evocation of childhood as the *Scenes from Childhood*, and, as with Schumann, the world of masks and carnivals is often close at hand, for example in the early *Suite Bergamasque*. One of the most curious manifestations of this new French tradition, from Chabrier's orchestral *España* onwards, was the ability of the composers to penetrate to the very depths of the Spanish spirit (as did the Russians, Glinka and Rimsky-Korsakov). In his piano music, Debussy's *La Soirée dans Grenade*, *La Serenade interrompue*, and *La Puerto del Vino* are far more convincing portrayals of the Spanish spirit than anything by indigenous composers, save, perhaps, De Falla.

In 'Hommage à Rameau', one of the *Images*, Debussy paid tribute to one of the great French composers of the past; that he was capable of writing abstract music is shown by the great *Twelve Studies*, dating from 1915, three years before his death. These pieces, inspired by particular pianistic problems, are as evocative as the earlier preludes, the Study in Fourths (for example) revealing clearly the subtlety of his structural methods.

Debussy's colleague and close contemporary, Ravel, produced two great piano suites whose inspiration was extra-musical. In the *Miroirs* (1905), arguably his greatest single piano work, he draws from a wide source of inspiration: we encounter the natural world (in 'Moths' and 'Sad Birds', the first and second pieces), a seascape ('A Ship on the Ocean'), a Spanish genre piece ('Alborado del Gracioso'), and finally 'The Valley of the Bells'. His music inhabits an extraordinary dream-world, for all its clarity of outline. In the suite *Gaspard de la Nuit*, inspired by the prose poems of Aloysius Bertrand, Ravel approaches even nearer to the world of Expressionism, while in pianistic terms recreating the spirit of Lisztian fantasy. But in other works he concerns himself with a re-creation of the spirit of Couperin; there is *Le Tombeau de Couperin*, and also an even more purely abstract, clear-eyed, subtly organized recreation of the spirit of classicism in the 'Sonatine'.

However, another distinct French school existed side-by-side with that of Debussy and Ravel, the more classically-minded trend represented by D'Indy and Dukas. The latter's two major works for piano, the enormous and, until its rather bombastic finale, satisfying sonata in E flat minor, and the fine *Variations, Interlude and Finale on a theme of Rameau*, show this second side of the French character at its peak. The music of Eric Satie, which has in recent years enjoyed considerable vogue, represents a third element, which was to burst out in the ethos of *Les Six* during the 1920s: humour. Satie and his disciples thought the current trends too serious and self-conscious, and their attempts to prick the bubble of academic complacency led to some curious manifestations. Many of Satie's titles alone show a deliberate surreal jokeyness: the *Sonatine Bureaucratique*, a parody of a Clementi Sonatina; the *Three Pieces in the form of a Pear* (actually seven, a typical joke), or the titles he made up for himself (*Gymnopédies, Gnossiennes*) – all these point to a degree of wilful eccentricity which might be dislikeable were not the music itself so distinctive and original. He explored often quite startling harmonic territory, as well as areas of expression – or rather, deliberate lack of expression – developed, if that is the right word, more recently by the static 'non-events' of composers such as Cage. But Satie's handling of the static feeling is not negative; there is a limpid grace about such works as the early *Sarabandes*, the well-known *Gymnopédies*, the *Gnossiennes* and the late *Nocturnes* that can, in sympathetic performance, enfold the listener in a unique, magic world.

There is a similar cool elegance in the piano music of Fauré, perhaps Chopin's direct descendant in both his handling of keyboard sonority, and the apparent modesty of his aims. Fauré's piano output consists largely of groups of nocturnes, barcarolles, preludes and impromptus. He wrote also a fine *Theme and Variations*, and the *Ballade* (better known in its piano and orchestra version), but it is in his shorter works that the heart of Fauré's art can be most deeply appreciated. His style changed little in essential detail through his career, though there is a gradual paring-down of excessive decoration towards the end, and the stylistic influences on him are as clear at the end of his career as at the beginning: Chopin, Mendelssohn, Schumann, of the romantic tradition, and Franck and Chabrier, of the Gallic school. Yet his voice is subtle and personal, and his music remains among the most rewarding and affecting contributions to the repertoire by any French composer.

(h) *Italy and Spain*
The Italian tradition has been so much concerned with vocal music that it is not surprising to find piano music occupying only a small part of the output. But one of the most outstanding, and enigmatic,

figures of the turn of the century is the pianist-composer, Ferruccio Busoni, who tempered his Italianate warmth and lyricism with a strongly disciplined intellectual conception derived from the German tradition. His compositions for piano are typically fascinating, such as his *Fantasia Contrappuntistica*, a massive completion of Bach's *Art of Fugue*, in which Busoni exploits to the full his architectural and contrapuntal mastery. Then there are the six *Sonatinas*, ranging from the exploratory, almost atonal 'Sonatina Seconda', to the sixth, a 'Chamber Fantasy on themes from Bizet's *Carmen*', in which Busoni takes the principle of operatic fantasy and carries it further in terms of sheer individuality and free handling of the motifs. In his *Elegies, Indian Diary* (based on American Indian folk-music) and numerous other short pieces his style ranged equally widely, encompassing neo-classicism, Brahmsian romanticism, and approaching the developments of Schoenberg. If Busoni's music has over-all a weakness, it is that he seldom found a consistent, personal idiom; only in his unfinished masterpiece, the opera *Doktor Faustus*, did he achieve consistency of purpose and manner.

The Spanish composers of the same period, notably Albeniz and Granados, restricted themselves in the main to music descriptive of scenes in Spanish life. Each produced one major suite representing the composer at his best. Albeniz's *Iberia* is a set of twelve pieces each deriving its inspiration from a particular Spanish location. Not mere postcards; in their luxurious, but sharp-edged keyboard brilliance they represent a recreation of the spirit of Liszt, with an accent drawn from the Spanish folk-music that provided Albeniz's essential stimulus. Granados's *Goyescas*, six pieces written in homage to Goya's paintings, has a closer link with the traditions of salon music, but imbued with refinement and sensitivity, and, once again, an acute awareness of the piano's capabilities.

De Falla, perhaps the greatest composer (with Roberto Gerhard) Spain has produced since her Golden Age, wrote sparingly; but his piano output includes the *Iberia*-like *Four Spanish Pieces*, evocative and sensuous, and the brilliant *Fantasia Baetica*, a powerful expression of the Andalusian spirit, and a remarkable, highly original work.

(i) The Slavs

The movement towards nationalism in music inevitably left its mark on the music of the Slavonic races, and the Czechoslovakian repertoire is richer, perhaps, than any other of these, save for the great

Russian tradition. Composers such as Dussek and Voŕisek (who produced at least one masterpiece – his B flat minor Sonata – during his regrettably short life) were distinct ornaments to the classical era; but it was with Dvořák and Smetana that Czech music found its first figures of lasting, international importance. Of the two Smetana is perhaps the most striking figure, a man of defiant pugnacity and almost Bartókian fierceness of patriotic nature. His musical mind was more adventurous, also, than that of the more comfortable Dvořák; and though his greater experiments lie in the orchestral field, one must certainly point to his superb series of ten Czech dances as a masterly suite, expressed in terms derived from Chopin and Liszt, but with a distinct and original personality. In his many other dance pieces, also, such as the numerous polkas, Smetana reveals the breadth of his imagination; even his *salon* pieces occupy a high place in his output, for they seldom show any cheapness, or lowering of sights.

Dvořák's piano music is on the whole more conventionally romantic, and too often feels like orchestral music reduced to the keyboard. But his flow of melody and characteristic touches of affecting harmony make his best piano works highly attractive. But for sheer individuality, and an entirely personal approach to the keyboard, one must go to Janáček, whose piano music is as characteristic of his essential personality as are his operas. One must except from this the early *Theme and Variations*, written under the influence of Schumann; but in his profoundly moving sonata in E flat minor, and in his suites *From an Overgrown Path*, and *In the Mist*, Janáček's humanity, and response to nature, are vividly conveyed.

The Pole Szymanowski possessed an equally characteristic voice, influenced to some extent by his native folk-music, but also by an increasing absorption in eastern music. He shares something of Scriabin's perfumed world, especially in the sonatas, which demonstrate the same fine sense of organization and lusciously refined colouring as those of the Russian. His piano textures are complex, even at times self-indulgent, such as in the fine third sonata, whose complexity is self-defeating despite the music's fascinating soundworld. His sets of shorter, though still substantial, pieces, such as *Métopes* and *Masques*, with their freedom of form and fantastic lyricism, are more successful; but perhaps his greatest piano work is the set of twenty mazurkas, op. 50. Based on music from the Tatra region, these superbly colourful and varied pieces display not only his sensitivity to pianistic and harmonic colouring, but also a wonderful ability to convey an entire world within a short span of music. In these pieces Szymanowski reveals himself to be the heir of Chopin.

(j) Scandinavia

The first Scandinavian composer to make a lasting impact on the repertoire was Grieg, whose early music, naturally enough, shows signs of various influences, including Schumann and Mendelssohn from Germany, and the outstanding Danish composer, Gade, whose importance in the history of Scandinavian music is too easily over-looked; for his music has, not altogether with justification, dropped out of circulation. Grieg's output for piano consists largely of col-lections of short pieces, among which the six books of lyric pieces have achieved a special degree of popularity. So familiar, indeed, are pieces like 'Butterfly', 'Little Bird', 'To the Spring' and the 'March of the Dwarfs' that they are too easily taken for granted, but they stand high in the repertoire of *salon* music for their individuality and high level of invention. As Grieg's career progressed, both his own musical personality and (linked with this) his interest in Norwegian folk-music intensified, and his piano oeuvre is dotted with collections of beautifully wrought arrangements of folk-tunes, culminating in the remarkable *Slåtter* (Norwegian Peasant Dances), op. 72, which con-jure up vividly a rustic atmosphere and anticipate Bartók's style of folk-music arrangement by some years. Here too the apparent sim-plicity of the music should not lead us to underestimate the imagina-tion and insight of the composer's mind. It is more fully expressed here than in the early E minor sonata, op. 7, which has some charm, but also some note-spinning; a far more totally convincing large-scale canvas appears in the fine *Ballade*, op. 24, a notable set of variations on a theme of melancholy folk flavour.

Undoubtedly the greatest contribution to the piano repertoire from Scandinavia has been that of the Dane, Carl Nielsen. His early piano pieces, such as the *Five Pieces*, op. 3, and the Symphonic Suite, op. 8 (1894), show clearly two of the strongest influences at work on him (Grieg and Brahms – though Gade's influence on his music was also profound). Yet in both compositions Nielsen's attractively forth-right, deeply human character is expressed with much individuality. His output divides itself neatly into major works and collections of short pieces. Among the latter, the set of *Humoresque-Bagatelles*, op. 11, have wit and variety, and his last piano work of all was a collection of five-finger exercises, *Music for Young and Old*, which represent one of the most striking compositional triumphs of his career in their miniature way. These are genuine compositions, full of invention and personality, not mere didactic studies.

The mature major works range from the set forms of the great *Chaconne*, op. 32 (1916), with its inexorable progress to a massive climax, and the immensely resourceful, brilliantly inventive *Theme and Variations*, op. 40 (also 1916) to the briefer, but more fantasia-like *Three Pieces*, op. 59 (1928), in which he explores tonality and piano textures even further than hitherto. Perhaps his masterpiece for piano, if one alone must be singled out, is the Suite, op. 45 (1919). It is surprising that Nielsen, one of the great masters of symphonic form and of piano writing, should have written no piano sonata, but the 1919 Suite comes arguably nearest to it. The six movements pursue an entirely logical course, the changes of key carefully controlled to fulfil their own expressive purpose, the music exploring an astonishing emotional range. This is certainly one of the most powerful and moving piano works of the century, entirely individual in every way and the product of a profound human thinker.

(k) Russia

One of the strongest and most enduring traditions to spring up during the last two centuries, despite the political upheavals of the country, is that of Russian piano music; but although Glinka's position as Father of Russian Music holds firm, it was not until the later years of the 19th century that Russian composers began to make significant contributions to this particular genre. Many of these were in the *salon* tradition; Borodin's admittedly delightful works are the least important part of his output, and it was left to Mussorgsky to provide the first major masterpiece of his school. His *Pictures from an Exhibition*, inspired by a show of paintings by his friend Hartmann, is a series of descriptive pieces of tremendous range and variety, linked by intermittent versions of a ritornello marked 'Promenade', and culminating in the formidable 'Great Gate of Kiev': a colossal achievement.

Tchaikovsky's output of piano music is variable. His two sonatas, an early work in C sharp minor, and a later Grand Sonata in G, are sadly inflated, the composer's sense of pianistic colour insufficient to compensate for the overblown form. More satisfactory are the twelve delightful pieces forming the suite *The Seasons*, and, of his many other compositions, a large-scale Dumka and a splendid set of variations. The outstanding body of piano music from this period, however, comes from Balakirev. His Oriental fantasy *Islamey*, is a magnificent display-piece; at the same time it is an extravagant, yet compelling tone-poem, bearing in every bar the impact of a brilliant imagination. He also wrote a particularly fine sonata, large-scale and with four movements, in which an expressive, almost neo-classical andante is followed by a revision of one of his loveliest earlier mazurkas. A lyrical slow movement is succeeded by a brilliant finale imbued with the spirit of a folk-dance. It is a superbly satisfying work which deserves more attention than it receives. Balakirev also wrote three scherzi, modelled, no doubt, on Chopin, but full of individuality; while his output of mazurkas, nocturnes and waltzes, though uneven, contains a number of haunting pieces.

The great Russian tradition was continued by two fellow students and contemporaries, who went vastly different ways – Scriabin and Rachmaninov. The former's ten sonatas form perhaps the most striking body of works in his entire oeuvre. The earliest are typical in relying on influences from the past, Chopin especially, but with the fourth and fifth sonatas (in C sharp minor and F sharp minor) he really found himself in this medium; the style is consistent and personal and the form tightly integrated. The sound of Scriabin's music, with its tritonal feeling and increasingly chromatic technique, is extraordinarily vivid; even in the piano works, with an ever-increasing multiplicity of interpretative directions, his ear for instrumental colour was acute. Moreover in his last sonatas, nos. 9 and 10, he achieved maximum compression of form, these single-movement pieces being astonishingly varied within their terse format. His immense output of separate and grouped pieces shows something of the same stylistic progression, from Chopinesque early work to the last preludes, op. 74, with their atonal and fragmentary sparseness.

Rachmaninov's contributions to the repertoire lie in his two sonatas, two sets of variations and various sets of shorter pieces. His first sonata (1908) is a massive, three-movement piece, originally intended to have a Faustian programme which was, however, never fully revealed. Vast in span and full of purpose, like the Second Symphony it gains rather than loses from an uncut performance. The second sonata, revised in 1931, is considerably more economical in form, and full of powerful ideas; only the inferior second subject in the finale prevents it from being a complete success. Of his variations, the earlier set, on a Chopin prelude, is luscious and beautifully written, but essentially decorative in nature. The *Variations on a Theme of Corelli*, however, written before the famous Paganini Rhapsody, show an increased compression of thought, a touch of

623

austerity which gives the music added strength of purpose; the final climax has a classical authority and the closing epilogue is hauntingly beautiful. Rachmaninov's preludes have become standard repertoire material. Apart from the notorious early C sharp minor prelude there are two sets. Those of op. 23, ten in number, are characteristic in their range of moods, and the writing, though individual, derives from the Lisztian tradition. The later set, op. 32, is even more striking, for the thought is more economical and the style more refined. The two sets of *Etudes-Tableaux* contain many fine things, expressed with more expansiveness and even more decorative textures.

Prokofiev's contribution to the piano repertoire is even more substantial than Rachmaninov's. His nine sonatas range from the youthful, often humorous and high-spirited early works, such as the 3rd, in A minor (which uses material from his music note-books of studentship and even childhood) through to a more serious vein of thought culminating in the great trilogy of so-called 'War' sonatas (nos. 6–8) written from 1939–45. The psychological depths revealed by these works are far removed from the magical, entertaining world of the early sonatas; but his vision has deepened without losing its lightness of touch or expression. Such things as the pounding first movements of nos. 6 and 7, the diabolic finale of the latter, and the uncanny first movement of no. 8 achieve a directness of expression and variety of insight remarkable in any composer's output of sonatas. In the ninth sonata, however, he returns to the straightforward world of the earlier works, allowing only the slow movement to rise to an impassioned, typically clangorous climax. Just as his sonatas provide a conspectus of his career, so do his collections of short pieces. The *Sarcasms*, op. 17, typify his early, brittle wit; while his life-long feeling for childhood receives magical expression in the *Grandmother's Tales*.

Shostakovich's output includes two sonatas, the first an early work of quite exceptional wildness and originality, and the second a wartime piece of power and beauty, as well as greater simplicity of style. Perhaps his greatest achievement in piano writing, however, is the monumental series of twenty-four preludes and fugues. This remarkable set is perhaps uneven in inspiration, but it contains many fine pieces. The composer ranges widely in stimulus: the Russian choral tradition clearly influences a number of preludes, there are several pastiches of such composers as Scarlatti and (inevitably, in this context) Bach. The set culminates in a superb D minor prelude and fugue, a profoundly impressive conclusion.

(a) *Twelve-tone technique*

The main revolutions of 20th-century style have yet to be touched on, and of these Schoenberg's development of twelve-tone technique has had perhaps the most profound effect. During the late romantic era the increasing chromaticism of the music had led to what Schoenberg saw as a weakening of the strength of classical tonality. Thus a work in, say, G major, would no longer have so strong a pull towards that key as in Beethoven's day simply because the high proportion of notes disturbing this tonal centre weakened its dominance.

After a period of atonality (i.e. lack of any key at all) Schoenberg formulated an idea which would carry this tendency to its logical conclusion: instead of having one key as the centre of the work, he would make the structural basis a series containing all twelve notes of the chromatic scale, treated equally. Thus, instead of one dominating note, all twelve would form a unit serving the same binding purpose. All melodies would be derived from this series of notes, or twelve-tone row, and by playing several notes together the harmonies would be similarly arrived at; the essential element was to keep the notes in the right order.

Critics of the technique have objected to its apparently mathematical (and therefore unspontaneous) nature, but if one compares Schoenberg's earlier atonal pieces such as the *Three Piano Pieces*, op. 11, or the *Six Little Pieces*, op. 19, with such a fully-twelve-tone work as the Suite, op. 25, there is in fact very little difference in style between the scores. What difference there is lies largely in the nature of his rhythmic invention, which had developed along his own lines involving a greater use of dance rhythms such as the gavotte and the waltz; but the organization behind the music is remarkably similar.

In both op. 11 and 19 Schoenberg's handling of small groups of notes is similar to his handling of the more formal twelve-tone row in op. 25. Development of small motifs was always an important element in his music, even in his very earliest days when he wrote in a typically luscious, but definitely tonal late romantic style. Of the *Five Piano Pieces*, op. 23, it is interesting to note that only the last piece is written along serial (i.e. twelve-tone) lines; the remaining four are freely chromatic pieces of atonal music, yet there is no discrepancy whatsoever of style between the first four and the fifth piece. Twelve-tone technique, thus, becomes not an abstract idea thought up on the spur of the moment, but rather a rationalization or formal embodiment of the tendencies already inherent in Schoenberg's music, and a way out of what he saw as the impasse of romantic music which could be passed on as a viable technique to others.

As with all music, it is the character and feeling of Schoenberg's music that is what matters to the listener; the architectural or organizational procedures are a means to this end, not an end in themselves. Although his piano works are all short, and mostly collections of miniatures, the feeling behind the music is large-scale, expressed with intense compression and concentration. The *Six Little Pieces*, op. 19, show this clearly; here each piece lasts only one page, except the first, which has two pages. The sixth piece is typical of the intensity of his vision; inspired by the sound of bells tolling at Mahler's funeral, it is a brief glimpse of infinity, vast in the implications of its few notes.

It is this extraordinary compression that marks, also, the work of Schoenberg's pupil, Webern, who developed his own austere, precise technique following along this line of stylistic development. His one major piano work, the Variations, op. 27, is a storehouse of characteristic devices, marked by the prodigious use of canonic and mirror techniques, and by his typical economy of means. Webern's music compresses the melodic lines into a few notes, often spaced widely over the keyboard (a parallel to his orchestra technique of sharing the notes of a brief melodic phrase between various instruments). In his mature works he abandoned the romantic love of a lengthy melodic line which Schoenberg himself retained to the end of his life. Webern's music thus has a sparseness and glittering precision of outline that is both austere and moving. In fast music, his displacement of rhythm has its own vitality of impact, and on the rare occasions when he permits himself the luxury of a rich chord, this casts a glow over the whole work.

Schoenberg's other most famous pupil, Berg, took an opposite line of development. He began to reconcile the twelve-tone technique with the idea of classical tonality, so that in his mature work there is always a sense of an underlying key at any given point in the music. Berg's sonata, however, is an early work, cast in a richly romantic B minor and pre-dating his adoption of Schoenbergian techniques. Its single movement is one of the loveliest of all late romantic piano pieces, full of passion and a sense of lush nostalgia.

(*b*) *The Schoenberg tradition*
Almost every country has had many composers who have followed Schoenbergian traditions without going very much further with them.

The sonatas of the American, Roger Sessions, for example, are deeply musical, well-thought-out works along these lines. He combines this technique, with its almost inevitable intensity of emotional feeling and its frequent changes of dynamics and texture, with a classically rigorous approach to form.

In Britain, Hugh Wood's *Three Pieces* are an outstanding and individual contribution to the tradition. The vigorous central piece has a Stravinskian pungency of rhythmic bite, while in the outer sections, Wood applies a serial control to music which in its highly pianistic, often decorative nature owes much to the example of Chopin, thought out afresh in a modern context. Two works by Alexander Goehr also demand attention. In his sonata, op. 2, he pursues a single-movement form with power and energy, while in the more recent *Nonomiya* (the title derives from a Japanese Noh play) the austerity of his serial style is enriched by a strong element of rhetorical drama.

More advanced are the sonatas of Anthony Gilbert, both influenced by Boulez's extensions of serial techniques. The first sonata, for solo piano, is colourful, rhythmically vital and occasionally highly poetic. The second, for piano duet, in which one player frequently plays on the inside of the piano, is an incredibly difficult virtuoso work continuing the same line of development. In the several works by Richard Rodney Bennett, a straightforward twelve-tone technique is characterized by lightness of touch and an infectious rhythmic liveliness, notably in the fantasy (really a three-movement sonatina in style); his *Five Studies* have more dramatic power and great bravura panache.

The solo piano works of Henze include an early set of variations and a later sonata. The Variations have a hard-edged richness, while the sonata's intellectual austerity is more marked. In the work of the Italian, Dallapiccola, we have some of the most lyrical and warmly expressive of twelve-tone writing. His *Quaderno Musicale* (Musical Notebook) is a collection of short pieces of great charm as well as intellectual variety.

(c) *The Avant-garde*
The most influential figures of modern times, Boulez and Stockhausen, both started from Webernian principles of compression and rigour, but they have pursued entirely different paths. Stockhausen's concern has been increasingly with problems of time and space, coupled with an increasingly mystical approach to the meaning of

music itself, and a fascination with the properties of sound for its own sake. His series of eleven *Klavierstücke* exemplifies this. From the rigorous intellectual qualities of Piano Pieces I–IV, in which dynamics and register are controlled with as much strictness as the notes themselves, his piano works have become freer and more expansive. The range of sonorities in them is quite extraordinary. Piano Piece IX, for instance, repeats the same chord 140 times, the sound's repetitious regularity becoming hypnotic, but the sound also changing as one listens to it.

In Piano Piece X, Stockhausen uses the full range of the piano with extreme virtuosity. Glissandi clusters are an important element in the staggering variety of texture he obtains from the instrument. Piano Piece XI offers the interpreter freedom of choice. It is printed on a large sheet of paper, and consists of a number of short sections of music. The pianist can play these in any order that is chosen during the performance, and each section indicates the style of performance for whatever is chosen next (dynamics, tempo, type of attack and so on). This particular attempt to bring the interpreter into the creative act is not entirely successful, a view that would seem to be supported by evidence that Stockhausen and his devoted interpreter, Aloys Kontarsky, have actually arrived at what they consider the 'best' order for performance of the sections – which suggests an inconsistency in the ideological basis of the music.

In many of these pieces Stockhausen adopts a spatial notation; that is, he abandons time-signatures and bar-lines, and instead asks the performer to keep in mind a particular time-scale and to fit the notes into this in accordance with their spatial relationships on the printed page. In Piano Piece VI he even indicates a constant fluctuation of tempo by means of a graph drawn above the notes of the stave.

In the music of Boulez there are three notable sonatas. The first two pursue Webernian techniques to their utmost. No. 1 is the shorter and lighter of the two works, though immensely complicated, while no. 2 is a staggering display of pianistic virtuosity as well as compositional resource. His third sonata offers the interpreter a degree of freedom akin to that in Stockhausen's Piano Piece XI, in so far as the sections can be played in various orders and within each order some of the events can be played in a variety of sequences. Only two movements of this work have been published, and the remaining three have been long awaited.

Boulez's writing demands the utmost virtuosity from the performer, and an acute sensitivity to his complex rhythmic techniques. The same can be said of the piano sonata of his disciple, Barraqué, which is a formidable intellectual achievement. As with Boulez, the writing seems to be almost anti-pianistic, yet in the hands of a sympathetic interpreter its power comes across.

The music of Berio takes avant-garde techniques in a different direction, for in his *Sequenza IV* he exploits the superimposition of sounds and textures by a complex, clearly indicated use of pedals, and the result is a fascinating, often sensuous string of flickering, glittering sonorities. In America, John Cage has used the piano in his characteristically free way. *Music of Changes* derives its inspiration from the use of chance elements, resulting in music of static, almost ritual expansiveness.

(d) Neo-classic

However, Schoenberg's answer to the late romantic dilemma was only one of many. In the music of Hindemith, Bartók and Stravinsky, there is a profound and emphatic realignment with traditional tonality, arrived at by different means. Hindemith formulated his own musical language, based (like classical technique) on the natural harmonic series, and expressed in music of contrapuntal power and rhythmic vigour influenced by baroque procedures. Of his three sonatas, the first is an elaborate, romantic work, the second a lighter, sonatina-like piece, and the third an impressive architectural sonata, closing with a vigorous and sonorous fugue. In all three sonatas, as in his masterly series of interludes and fugues, *Ludus Tonalis*, the music combines a high degree of chromaticism with a strong feeling of key.

During the 1920s and '30s Stravinsky adopted a deliberately neo-classical approach, typified in his two major piano works. In the sonata, the lines have a Bachian clarity and in the faster movements the character of a two-part toccata is the dominating impression. In his Serenade in A, there is a similar feeling, but its lyrical freshness and more decorative textures are more communicative. Elsewhere, in his *Piano Rag Music*, *Ragtime* and the delicious *Tango*, he revelled in the influences of jazz and dance music.

Bartók's sonata is a dramatic, uncompromising work. The two pounding outer movements and the central slow movement of vehement austerity make this one of his most impressive piano works. His output also includes a large number of delightful folk-based pieces, the superb suite *Out of Doors* (in which his earlier flirtation with Impressionism results in a mature transformation of colourful textures in his own strikingly personal way), and the six books of *Mikrokosmos*, a vast series of carefully graded teaching pieces from the simplest up to concert standard. Brief though they are, the *Mikrokosmos* pieces contain many pages of Bartók at his finest, and in them many of his techniques can be seen in compressed form.

(e) America and Britain

Both British and American composers have contributed invaluable piano works to the repertoire. Among the American compositions, the two sonatas of Ives stand out especially. The first, in five movements, draws its roots from a typically wide range of sources – hymn-tunes, early piano jazz, folk-music of all kinds – and Ives's own extraordinary sense of harmony, which, varying wildly between extreme simplicity and extreme complexity, is invariably convincing. The second sonata, known as 'Concord', and consisting of four movements named after great New England philosophers and writers, is equally remarkable. Like its predecessor, it makes tremendous demands on the performer (and, characteristically, contains an optional part for flute for a few bars towards the end). Apart from mere technical considerations, there is a vivid, almost Beethovenian personality behind both these hypnotic works.

Samuel Barber's four-movement sonata, dating from 1949, is one of his finest pieces, romantic, wide-ranging and technically demanding, while Copland and Elliott Carter have similarly composed one sonata each. Copland's is clear, direct and most moving, with a memorable slow last movement. Carter's, written in 1944/5, and thus pre-dating the complexities of the works that have made his name internationally famous, has two movements, the first scintillating, with great rhythmic subtlety, and the second an arch-form, with a superb fugue of cumulative excitement as its centrepiece. Two other works by Copland are also notable. His 1930 Variations are a moving, powerfully architectural exploration of a four-note motif handled with almost Schoenbergian rigour; while in the much later fantasy the clarity of rhythmic life of the sonata is re-expressed in more austere terms. Here Copland directly uses twelve-tone technique, without losing one iota of his individuality, and the music is massive and convincing.

There is nothing quite like the Ives sonata in the repertoire of British music, but a number of composers have written works of major importance. Bax's four sonatas, for instance, display great virtuosity of keyboard writing together with full-blooded and colourful imagination. Indeed, the first three at least have a genuinely orchestral feel to them that demands a performer of infinite tonal control. The fourth sonata is lighter in texture, with an especially lovely slow movement.

Ireland's sonata in E minor is, like Bax's works, massively virtuoso, though with a less distinctly orchestral cast. This too is rewarding music, as is his far more terse and perhaps even more poetical sonatina, arguably one of the finest works in his output. Bliss, Lambert and Berkeley have all contributed a sonata each to the repertoire, while the entertaining and moving sonatina by Rawsthorne is highly successful, as are his early *Bagatelles* and the fine, late *Ballade*.

In more recent years two composers have shown particular interest in this medium. Tippett's three sonatas stem from different periods of his career, and reflect clearly his style at the time of composition. The first, one of the earliest piece she acknowledges, is large-scale, ornate and relatively conventional in form. The second, dating from the same period as the opera, *King Priam*, adopts a more severe structural method of juxtaposing and contrasting blocks of material in a kind of mosaic technique. The third, written in 1973, is vital, urgently boisterous and filled with quicksilver rhythmic fluctuations.

The Welsh composer Alun Hoddinott, has produced no less than six sonatas to date, ranging from the Lisztian first sonata of 1959, a four-movement work of great brilliance, to the fine sixth sonata of 1972, written in memory of Rawsthorne. Here, having worked through the increasingly economical nature of the intervening sonatas, Hoddinott has achieved a full integrated single-movement structure, in which the various sections add up to a satisfying whole. His delight in palindromic techniques is revealed in many of the sonatas, notably the subtle second and the more extrovertly virtuosic fourth.

The two sonatas of John Joubert are a courageous and powerfully muscular restatement of the ideals of classical tonality; while Kenneth Leighton's large output includes a particularly fine 'Fantasy on two themes', entitled *Conflicts*, and several sets of variations and studies, all emphatic and expressive avowals of faith in the continued validity of tonality, allied to an individual use of twelve-tone technique.

(*f*) France

Since the deaths of Debussy and Ravel, French music has largely been dominated by the figure of Messiaen, and later by that of his pupil and disciple, Boulez (who is discussed elsewhere). Messiaen's output is enormous, not necessarily in number of works, but in their sheer size. His piano oeuvre includes two enormous collections of pieces. The earlier *Vingt Regards sur l'enfant Jésus* (Twenty Glances at the Infant Jesus), is a collection of twenty works often large-scale in themselves. His musical language is made up of many diverse elements: the rhythms of Indian classical music, bird-song, influences from Debussy, Mussorgsky, Massenet, serial techniques – all these play an important part in his style, which also involves a high degree of religious mysticism.

In the *Vingt Regards*, the whole is set in a profoundly religious context, and the music is a summation of his development up to that date (1944), full of intellectual power as well as colourful keyboard writing. In the *Catalogue des Oiseaux* (Catalogue of Birds) completed in 1958, Messiaen more closely examines bird-song; the seven books of the massive undertaking are a monument to his intense powers. A shorter, single work is *Canteyodjaya*, a masterly concert piece in which Indian rhythms play an important part, the whole being a complex ritornello structure showing clearly the influence of the mature Debussy's formal methods.

The music of most other French composers pales into insignificance by the side of this extraordinary figure, but Jolivet's sonata, and, more satisfactorily, his *Mana* Suite are typical of his rich, complex style, with its powerfully erotic elements. Roussel's piano works are typically elegant and strongly made, while the two Swiss composers, Honegger and Frank Martin, have written valuable works. The latter's *Eight Preludes* are an especially fine set, full of grave beauty and all his characteristic textural subtlety.

4 PIANO AND ORCHESTRA, PIANO DUO, ORGAN, HARPSICHORD
(a) Bach and Haydn

The title Concerto has a long history, and from the earliest days of the instrumental concerto, there were several types of this genre: the Concerto Grosso, in which a group of instruments is pitted against the larger body of the main orchestra; the concerto for a group of players among whom none is specifically a soloist (Bach's Brandenburg concerto no. 6, for example), and the solo concerto, for one predominant soloist against an orchestral setting. The title is still used in various ways; the 20th century has seen many concerti grossi, especially in the neo-classical movement, while works like Bartók's Concerto for Orchestra, in which the whole orchestra is treated as one large solo body, develop the principle of the *concertino* group (placed in concertante fashion as soloists from within the basic ensemble) and extend it to the whole band. There are also, of course, numerous works for solo instrument, especially keyboard, without orchestra, such as Alkan's Concerto for solo piano, and Bach's familiar Italian Concerto.

It was above all the development of public concert-giving and the increasing demand for virtuoso star performers, with its corresponding demand for virtuosic music, that led to the rise of the solo concerto. One simple formal feature indicates this – the stabilization of solo concerto structure in three movements during baroque and classical eras. It was, significantly, the minuet movement that came to be omitted out of the previous set of four; for while the other movements could all be developed along virtuosic lines, this could hardly be done with the essentially self-enclosed minuet. This argument is supported by the fact that the minuet was retained in the symphony through the classical era, developing finally into the scherzo form that, in turn, and once more significantly, became incorporated into the concerto by composers such as Liszt and Brahms. During their time the scherzo had so transformed minuet style as to provide full opportunity for concerto-style writing; but the gradual transformation had to be accomplished within the confines of symphony and string quartet, not in the concerto.

The three-movement concerto form was only firmly established as the norm by Haydn, Mozart and Beethoven; until their day it had alternated between four- and three-movement schemes. Bach's solo concertos had the latter shape. Indeed, his Italian Concerto, though for keyboard alone, is a perfect example of his concerto style, with its lively, virtuosic outer movements and a slow movement devoted to the development of a long-breathed, richly decorated melody above a steadily moving bass line. Bach's famous harpsichord concertos in D minor and F minor are equally representative of his style at its finest. In the first movements of each, the orchestra opens with the ritornello material which forms the bedrock of the music, returning between the soloist's episodes in slightly varied but always recognizable form to provide a binding element in the structure. The solo part is predominantly one of elaboration and decoration, sometimes developing the main material by taking it into new keys, but more often simply contrasting with it or, on occasion, weaving contrapuntal embellishment around an orchestral statement of it. (The rondo-like nature of the form, with its constantly recurring main theme, is complicated by the high degree of development and variation of the main material.)

It is worth commenting on the key scheme of this music, for one of the primary elements in the classical concerto is the relationship of the chosen tonic key to the others. In Bach's case the music seldom strays far from the tonic and a few of the most closely related keys; yet here and there during the development of the material he does go into relatively remote keys, and in so doing he anticipates very strongly the form of the classical concerto's first movement.

In the slow movements the music sings its glorious melody above the steadily pulsating bass line. In the D minor concerto this bass line is repeated, with some alteration throughout the movement, giving it something of the character of a chaconne; while its initial statement is in unison by the orchestra. By this latter means it achieves the status of a main theme, and its reappearances as a theme (as opposed simply to a free ground bass) give it the character of a ritornello, once again binding the form together. This is an unusual procedure for Bach's concerto slow movements, though not unique.

In the finales Bach pursues a course similar to the ritornello form of the first movements, though a shade lighter in tone; the finale of the F minor is especially dance-like.

The concertos of Haydn are far less significant than his sonatas. The element of virtuoso display was evidently not to his taste, nor did it inspire him creatively. But his keyboard concertos contain a good deal of delightful material, cast in the form that was to become the conventional classical concerto structure. The D major concerto is best-known, and it is the only one in which, momentarily, he sounds a profound note. The influence of C. P. E. Bach, whose passionate D minor concerto is surely one of his finest works, is felt in the sonatas rather than in the concertos, even this one. But the slow movement especially has a deeply-felt lyricism. Beside Mozart's great series of concertos, however, those of Haydn seem small beer indeed.

(b) Mozart

Mozart wrote twenty-seven piano concertos, of which the first four are arrangements by him of other composers' works, made when he was (relatively speaking) a child. The first piano concerto, actually written for a harpsichordist, in which the great master of this medium reveals himself fully is the ninth, in E flat (K 271). Written in 1777 at the age of twenty-one, this is still one of the most striking of the whole series. The by-now-established concerto first movement (or sonata) shape – exposition of two main themes, development of these and recapitulation of the exposition in much its original form, with a cadenza for the soloist placed before the closing section of the recapitulation – this structure was retained, but with immensely added richness. Instead of two main themes only, Mozart elaborated the structure with a host of lesser themes and motifs, and these were developed along with the main material.

Furthermore, he was almost the first composer to allow the soloist to introduce new material as the music progressed; hitherto this had nearly always been the orchestra's task. He also deepened the character of the music; deriving a strong impulse from his natural affinity with opera, he allowed a dramatic element to enter the music, so that many of the movements are operatic dramas in miniature. This is especially true of his first movements, for though more complex and subtle, his slow movements and finales continue the basic pattern of arioso style and rondo or variations respectively, that had already been set down.

K 271 exemplifies all this admirably, as well as the increased subtlety of the orchestral colouring used by Mozart. The dramatic element is present at the very start, where Mozart, with complete originality, divides the main theme between orchestra and soloist. This orchestral statement/pianistic comment device immediately sets up the quality of a dramatic dialogue, which is sustained right through this glorious movement. In the finale which follows the passionate, sombre andantino central movement, Mozart breaks the flow of high spirits by interpolating a slow, stately minuet with four variations of great decorative complexity into the presto's headlong course, though it is the quick tempo that leads the work to its brilliant finish.

Both the device of interrupting the finale and that of dividing the first movement's opening between orchestra and soloist are rare in Mozart's concerto output; the latter is indeed unique. But after this remarkable work his output of piano concertos was regular and unfailingly inspired. Among the most impressive are no. 19 in F (K 459), containing what Charles Rosen has described as 'the greatest of all Mozart's concerto finales'; the sunny A major (no. 23, K 488); the brilliant 'Coronation' concerto in D major (no. 26, K 537); the massively symphonic C major (no. 25, K 503), and the most touching perhaps of all, the last one, in B flat (K 595), with its extraordinary sense of resignation – a beautiful, lingering sunset.

Two others demand some special comment, the two great minor

key concertos, both far from the idea of 'social music' for simple entertainment that had generally prevailed until Mozart's day as the basis behind concerto music. The D minor (no. 20, K 466) has an epic force, and though the first movement's symphonic tension is relieved by the outer sections of the slow movement ('Romanze'), the central section is passionate and turbulent, and the tensions rise again in the tempestuous finale. Only the martially cheerful close banishes the sense of nervous emotion. A similarly emotional mood occupies the C minor concerto, no. 24, K 491, but here it is more withdrawn. If the D minor is an expression of public emotion, the C minor is devoted to a more private world, yet its restraint cannot disguise its deep feeling. Mozart gradually builds up one of the grandest of all his symphonic works by the subtlest means, and though the slow movement brings serene repose, the finale this time fails to banish tragedy. In this glorious set of variations, possibly the finest in his entire output, moments of lightness or optimism are swept aside by the increasingly passionate nature of the music until its defiant close.

(c) Beethoven

At the time of Mozart's death Beethoven had not yet written any of the five concertos which have become so famous. He had, however, written an E flat concerto in 1784, at the age of fourteen; this was the year in which Mozart wrote no less than six of his masterpieces, culminating in K 459. Mozart's greatest were, on the whole, still to come. It is necessary to remember this, because although Beethoven's youthful essay still owes much to the *galant* style of the concerto before Mozart, it does contain much that is startlingly prophetic of the mature master to come, especially in the first two movements.

The first of the series of familiar numbered concertos dates from 1795, the first version of the B flat major concerto now known as no. 2. This was revised in 1798, the year after he had composed the C major concerto known as no. 1. Both these works are enchanting; the brilliance of their piano writing betrays the hand of a distinguished executant, and their formal mastery is superb. This is especially true of the C major – the very opening, with its witty, cheerful vigour, has a Promethean strength of purpose which the music's classical scale cannot hide. In the slow movement Beethoven starts with the piano almost entirely alone, playing one of those consolatory, almost hymn-like tunes which are so typical, and the interplay between soloist and orchestra is notable for its subtlety. Even in the finale, which is basically a lively dance-rondo, the sheer muscular strength of the music expands the Haydn–Mozart tradition into something altogether more epic.

In the third concerto, in C minor (1800), a new note of passion enters the music. The dramatic opening theme is obviously influenced by the example of Mozart's C minor concerto, but Beethoven's is a more heroic, optimistic work; for all the almost operatic implications of the opening, and the tension of much of its working out, the predominant note is one of grandeur. It is in the slow movement that Beethoven achieves his most advanced style so far in the concertos. As in the C major concerto, it has a chordal, sublimely simple main theme, from which the music expands through an astonishing range of keys and elaborate keyboard textures until simplicity again ends the movement. In the sheer originality of the piano writing, the movement foreshadows the slow movements of the late sonatas.

Between the third and fourth concertos, Beethoven's life had drastically changed, with, among other things, the onset of his deafness. Yet the G major concerto (1805) is the most eloquently lyrical of all; it is music of vision beyond personal troubles, expressing something sublime in the human spirit. The opening is a stroke of the utmost genius, a gentle, chordal theme given to the piano alone. Yet the note of intimacy, of spiritual communion struck from the start and sustained throughout is combined with the most marvellous intricacy of development; this is in some ways the most complex of all his concerto first movements. The slow movement is simplicity itself – a dialogue between the hectoring orchestra and the contemplative solo piano. The movement has been given many literary allusions: Cordelia gradually softening the anguish of Lear is perhaps one of the most pertinent. Only towards the end does the piano itself express any suggestion of passion, but this is brief, and the close is calmness itself. Into this serene, still atmosphere the finale steals like a gentle sunrise; with consummate artistry Beethoven only gradually allows a dance-like spirit of exuberance to gain control.

The last of the five piano concertos, in E flat, followed four years later, and provides a startling contrast. Its nickname of 'The Emperor' is well-earned, for the magnificent opening, with its powerful orchestral statement of E flat, and storming solo cadenzas, has a royal majesty. This is as public an expression as that of the fourth concerto is private, yet even in the outer movements, with their thrust and drive, there are moments of tenderness, and the slow movement, placed in the remote key of B major (a touch that immediately sets it in a different world from the other movements) has a fragility and

637

exquisiteness unparalleled in the other concertos. It is linked to the finale by a passage of supreme beauty, the rondo's main theme foreshadowed ruminatively by the soloist before it breaks out in all its powerful energy.

It is worth pondering for a moment the matter of the cadenza, which during the progress of the classical concerto had become more and more a subject of concern to composers. In the early concertos after Bach's it was a section, usually in the first movement, but occasionally in one or other of the remaining ones, in which the soloist improvised on the material of the movement. As concerto form developed, composers began to write down their own cadenzas, trusting less and less to the compositional skill of performers other than themselves. A good many of Mozart's have come down to us. Beethoven wrote cadenzas for his first four concertos, and significantly, in the finale of the fourth movement (where there is a pause for an improvised cadenza) he stipulated that it should not be too long. A concern not to overbalance the music's form is apparent here, and the next logical step was taken in the 'Emperor', where there are no cadenzas as such, but rather cadenza-like passages. In this work, the function of the cadenza, that of bravura display, is no longer necessary, for its essential elements are built into the musical material itself.

(d) Mendelssohn, Chopin, Schumann, Liszt
It was perhaps inevitable that the rise of the romantic virtuoso should lead to an intensification of this line of development, and that the display element should to a considerable extent take over the place of symphonic argument during the course of the 19th century; in the concertos of the great travelling virtuosi, naturally it was of paramount importance, but there were other composers for whom the demands of musical form and argument continued to be primary.

Mendelssohn's concertos illustrate this very well. He wrote two well-known ones, as well as a charming early concerto for piano and strings in A minor. The first, in G minor, typifies his approach to the form. After a brief orchestral introduction the piano enters with ferocious ebullience – a far cry from the standard orchestral exposition of the classical concerto. The three movements are played, as in his violin concerto, without a break – a move in the direction of the single-movement work. It is a characteristically entertaining work. The music has little subtle thematic argument, but the form is beautifully balanced, and if it deals with charm and entertainment rather than anything more profound, entertainment is seldom so beguiling as this. The second concerto, in D minor, is a finer and more profound work; again the three movements are played without a break, but there is a more symphonic approach to the relationship between the themes.

Chopin's concertos, judged simply as concertos, are less convincing. He relegated the orchestra severely to a supporting role, and relied largely on the piano writing to carry the music through. Yet in the hands of a sympathetic conductor the orchestral writing can be made to sound velvety and delicate, while Chopin's revolutionary style of piano writing is as skilful as ever. It is not his ability to write on a large scale that is in question, simply the unsuitability of his personal style to the demands of concerto form. The concertos have nevertheless held a secure place in the repertoire, for their vivacity and inspiration.

The real masterpieces of the romantic virtuoso tradition are, if one accepts Brahms as more of a classicist, the concertos of Schumann and Liszt. The A minor concerto of the former is one of his inspired orchestral conceptions. I stress the orchestral side because Schumann, like Brahms, is often accused of being a poor orchestrator. The criticism is just, insofar as his symphonic works tend to demand a conductor of rare sensibility to make their orchestral sound completely coherent (though when this happens one is aware of the 'rightness' of the sound). But in the piano concerto the orchestration is translucent, vigorous and indeed remarkably original. So too are the themes, the development of which is thorough and yet seemingly spontaneous. The element of display, too, seems to arise out of the character of the themes; in its apparent waywardness, the work is the epitome of all that is best in romantic music.

Liszt's two concertos are more dramatic than this – more melodramatic one might almost say. The sensational aspect of their writing, the grandiose dramatic poses, the outbursts of violent virtuosity, the overt emotionalism of the lyrical tunes – all these cannot disguise Liszt's complete command over his compositional resources. Both concertos are integrated by the characteristic use of motto themes, in the familiar Lisztian cyclic manner, and the music's variety never breaks the tautness of the structure arising from this. The first, in E flat, is in four movements played without a break, and tied closely together by inter-relations. The opening takes off from the 'Emperor', but here the orchestral phrases are not an emphatic statement of E flat but a powerful move away from it (the first phrase ends on D flat, straightaway disrupting the tonic key), and the piano's opening flourishes maintain the sense of heroic struggle.

This is the work once dubbed a 'triangle' concerto, because of Liszt's prominent use of the instrument in the scherzo, but this is really a marvellous touch of aural imagination. There is nothing quite so startling orchestrally in the second concerto, in A major, which contains a touch more sheer lyricism, though it is the demonic-heroic element that comes out on top.

(e) Lesser romantics and shorter works

Before going on to the later romantics, this is perhaps the place to say something about the lesser figures of the 19th century, and also about the rise of the shorter piece for piano and orchestra. There are often good things in the concertos of composer-pianists like John Field (whose work needs a thorough revaluation), Hummel, Moscheles and Scharwenka. Not in every case is there the ability to sustain a convincing musical argument; but on the other hand their very ability to write grateful bravura music enabled them often to produce concertos which are highly successful at doing what they largely set out to, i.e. to dazzle with soloistic pyrotechnics set off by orchestral colour. One of the finest of them is Scharwenka's first concerto, in B flat minor. It dates from 1877, that is a quarter of a century after both Liszt's concertos had appeared, and has two particular merits: the tunes are exceptionally good and the orchestration is equally engaging.

The concertos of Rubinstein were at one time inordinately popular. The fourth, in D minor, kept the longest hold on the repertoire, and its impressive qualities owe much to the composer's real mastery of large-scale composition. Only a sense of 'manufacture' about the concerto – as though he were deliberately setting out to write an impressive work – prevents it achieving a higher status.

Parallel with the development of the grand virtuoso concerto was a rise in the number of shorter pieces for piano and orchestra. The rondo was a particular favourite – Mozart himself had written two such. Mendelssohn's several creations in this field are outstanding. The *Capriccio Brillante* in B minor is particularly splendid, bounding along with inexorable vivacity. But the greatest works are again by the composers of the most outstanding concertos. The orchestral parts in Chopin's four shorter pieces are even more perfunctory than in the concertos, but both the *Krakowiak* (a rondo on Polish ideas) and the *Andante Spianato and Grande Polonaise* have such tremendous impetus and abound in such good tunes that all can be forgiven.

Schumann's two works in this medium follow the same course: a fairly substantial slow section followed by a predominantly fast and rather longer part. The *Introduction and Allegro Appassionata* in G is the better-known, but the *Introduction and Allegro* in D minor is an equally exciting and moving piece. More striking than any of these, perhaps, is Liszt's *Totentanz*, in my view his masterpiece for piano and orchestra. This vivid symphonic fresco is a Dance of Death formed as a set of variations on the mediaeval Plainchant melody, the 'Dies Irae' (Day of Wrath), highly remarkable from its pounding, violent beginning to its defiant close.

(f) Brahms, Tchaikovsky

The main shape of the piano concerto as developed by Mozart and Beethoven had become changed by later composers, notably Liszt, into something more continuous. It was Brahms who, as in the case of the violin concerto, took up the classical thread again. His first concerto, in D minor, is a massive symphony for piano and orchestra; there is plenty of virtuoso writing, but it is always at the service of the development of ideas. It was a bold stroke to devote the first five minutes to a vast, passionate orchestral exposition, and when the piano does enter, it is with a pleading, lyrical theme of great beauty: a far cry indeed from conventional romantic habit. For all the passion and expressiveness of the music, however, it is set in a highly classical context, the themes being explored and developed with great rigour.

In contrast with the intensely heroic struggles of the first movement, the slow movement withdraws into a quiet, prayer-like mood; it is a calm benediction in memory of Schumann, whose death had been a tragic blow to Brahms. The sense of striving is renewed in the finale, an epic rondo of vast proportions. The skill with which Brahms introduces and develops his themes is remarkable, especially notable being the fugal section, which takes one of the more lyrical tunes and transforms it into a spiky, threatening theme. The influence of Liszt's methods of thematic metamorphosis can be felt here.

If the Brahms first concerto is a great work, youthful in its impetuosity and masterly in conception, the second, in B flat, is even more immense and in some ways even more masterly. To three movements equivalent to those of the earlier concerto, he adds a gigantic scherzo. His handling of form and approach to concerto form are both more subtle than before; in the D minor he was flexing his muscles. Here he is more relaxed, more completely confident of his own abilities, and the youthful dramas have given way to a more serene wisdom. The work gains intensity only gradually, for the opening is deceptively simple. Yet the giant is stirring, and with a lengthy section for piano alone the music is whipped up into a triumphant statement of the opening material by full orchestra. The concerto is thus given an expansiveness, the listener an awareness of its true dimensions from the start. This movement has all the character of a far-ranging philosophical discussion, while in the scherzo, placed second, something of the passion and turbulence of the earlier concerto returns. The slow movement's opening theme for solo cello is famous, one of the most serenely beautiful of all Brahms's melodies, and though the movement has moments of drama, this flowing loveliness dominates it. The finale's lightness of touch is, like the concerto's opening, supported by an underlying strength.

There is little Lisztian rhetoric in either of the Brahms concertos, but Liszt's example lies behind a good many of the late romantic concertos which have remained popular, not least those of Tchaikovsky. Of his three concertos, only the first has really established itself – the B flat minor, regarded by many people as more of a sporting event! (A result of too many performances slashed through as loudly and quickly as possible by both soloist and conductor.) An application of real musical integrity to the performance reveals what a powerful and imaginative work it really is. The notorious opening theme is a bold stroke, a resounding theme which once stated is repeated and developed at some length. But this whole section is a snare and delusion, for the first movement itself is quite different, with material of a more folk-like nature and a much lighter touch. It really is an astonishing piece, and the boldness and thoroughness of its conception and working-out are thrilling and masterly.

The other movements of this work are less startling, though no less inspired or attractive; one of Tchaikovsky's lyrical, canzonetta-like slow movements, followed by a peasant-dance finale. Neither of Tchaikovsky's remaining piano concertos sustains quite this level of inspiration, but the second concerto, in G, has much to recommend it. More consistently muscular, it is notable for a lengthy but beautiful slow movement in which violin and cello soloists play an important part; the chamber music texture of this duo, which dominates the movement, adds a new dimension to Tchaikovsky's concerto style. The third concerto exists only as a single movement – which however makes a satisfactory piece structurally on its own and has some splendid moments. There is also a highly attractive Concert Fantasia in G, a thoroughly enjoyable bravura work.

(g) *Later romantics*

Grieg's A minor concerto, like the Tchaikovsky B flat minor, is also influenced by Liszt and has become a warhorse; but the freshness of Grieg's inspiration, and his remarkable success in handling the large form are so great that it never loses its charm. Dvořák's G minor concerto is less spontaneous in invention, nor is it quite so satisfying in form; but it has passion and life, and in the hands of a sympathetic interpreter it can reveal great qualities. Later than any of these comes the remarkable concerto of Busoni, one of the longest of all piano concertos, in five movements, the last of which uses a male-voice choir. It is a virtuoso work, but more primarily an extension of the philosophical side of the Brahms concertos writ even larger.

The greatest series of piano concertos in the romantic idiom comes from the pen of Rachmaninov, who like Busoni was one of the greatest of all pianists, as well as a composer of exceptional originality and skill. Common to all four of his concertos, and to the *Rhapsody on a theme of Paganini*, are ever-increasing structural skill, and a marvellous sense of orchestral colour. The passionate, high-spirited first concerto, in F sharp minor, is a youthful work, written when he was eighteen, but revised in 1917, just before he left Russia. The second concerto, the immensely popular C minor, is far more mature, and is both satisfying and highly original.

Rachmaninov's mastery of symphonic concerto form is even more clearly shown in the D minor concerto, no. 3, written eight years later. Here there is great strength of construction, as well as even deeper emotional penetration, from the evocative opening, through the first movement's elaboration of its basic motifs and the slow movement's juxtaposition of basic variation-form with scherzo elements, to the dancing, powerful vigour of the finale. The fourth and last of his concertos, in G minor, is less striking at first acquaintance. It was written at the end of a ten-year silence in composition which followed Rachmaninov's emigration from his beloved native land, and the sense of bitterness at his loss of cultural identity makes its mark. Yet it is a moving piece. The lyrical sections cry straight from the heart, and the brilliance of the finale has a tragic ring to it.

In his *Paganini* Rhapsody Rachmaninov achieved his tautest concerto structure. The theme is that famous Paganini violin Caprice, the inspiration of so many composers, and from it Rachmaninov fashioned an elegant, witty, immensely resourceful score. The use of the 'Dies Irae' Plainchant tune, which is found embedded in almost every one of his major works, is unusually overt in this one, and exceptionally effective. This scintillating score justly retains its popularity, and was one of his own favourites from his output.

(h) France and Germany

The best way to continue this discussion of the piano concerto forms is to split the grouping into nationalities, for each nation has produced its own characteristic styles. France's tradition is predominantly one of elegance and charm, and the diverse titles often indicate the less formal preoccupations of their composers. Saint-Saëns, however, wrote five concertos of quite classical proportions; the most familiar are the second, in G minor, which has a finely Bachian first movement and a scintillating scherzo, and the fourth, in C minor, where the Lisztian technique of thematic metamorphosis is adopted with real nobility. One of the most lasting sets of variations for piano and orchestra is the *Symphonic Variations* of the Belgian, César Franck; again influenced by Liszt's thematic technique, it shows poetry and drama, as well as a fine sense of over-all structure. D'Indy's *Symphony on a French Mountain song*, for piano and orchestra, is a fine, three-movement work, which derives all its themes from a lovely folk-song; though less taut than the César Franck, it is music of great attractiveness.

In his *Ballade*, op. 19, and *Fantaisie*, op. 111, Fauré composed two quite substantial works, characteristic in their limpid grace and harmonic subtlety. Debussy's *Fantaisie* is an early piece, but its three movements have a vernal freshness that makes its neglect incomprehensible, the more so as the piano writing offers considerable opportunity for varied display. Ravel's two concertos, however, are late works, among the finest of his last decade. That in D, for left hand alone, was written for the one-armed pianist, Paul Wittgenstein. Its single movement encompasses dark drama, a glittering chinoiserie and a rattling, ferocious jazziness; while the G major concerto, written in a spirit of Mozartian clarity, shares a certain jazzy quality in its almost Gershwinesque finale. There could hardly be greater contrast between the two works, however.

During the 20th century, wit has become almost the most important element of French concertos. Only Roussel's tough, knotty piano concerto sustains a more serious mood; the delightful concertino, and rather less successful (because rather inflated) concerto of Jean Françaix, and the charming works of Poulenc, are more characteristic, though the latter's *Aubade* has deeper moments. Swiss composers with French affiliations have produced excellent works.

Honegger's concertino exploits jazz idioms with point and wit; while Frank Martin has written two concertos, the second of which is an impressive, powerful work, as well as his magnificent *Ballade* for piano and orchestra.

But it has been left to Messiaen to produce the most significant French concertos after Ravel, though they bear exotic and far from formal titles. Both *Oiseaux Exotiques* (Exotic Birds) and *Reveil des Oiseaux* (Awakening of the Birds) are, as their titles suggest, dominated by the birdsong which so fascinates him. Their scoring is exotic, mostly chattering wind sounds and an incredible array of percussion sonorities, but for all the programmatic and pictorial elements in the music, Messiaen's control of form is masterly, and in his contrasting of orchestral sections with solo piano passages, and in his placing of the larger sections for the two together, he shows an inspired sense of balance.

The German tradition has been less consistent in its approach to the piano concerto than the French, Russian, British or American; though the great concertos of the 18th and 19th centuries are predominantly German or Austrian, the 20th century has seen a dispersal of this tradition through many countries. Richard Strauss's early *Burlesque* in D minor is a marvellous, lively work, full of muscular but effective piano writing, rich orchestral colouring and considerable subtlety of formal manipulation. The concertos of Reger and Pfitzner are typically complex and powerful. Only Hindemith and Henze have contributed concertos of symphonic size and yet more than local appeal. In Hindemith's output there are the biting, cleanly outlined Kammermusik concerto from the 1920s and two works from his years in America during the 1940s – a fine concerto (1945) of contrapuntal richness and lyrical warmth, and the slightly earlier *The Four Temperaments* for piano and strings. This last is one of his most lovable works. Of Henze's two concertos the first is early and eclectic, whereas the second is one of the most satisfying and rewarding of all his large-scale abstract structures.

(i) Britain

British music is richer in piano concertos. That of Delius, in C minor, is an early and perhaps overlong work, though it contains some hauntingly beautiful pages. Bax's *Symphonic Variations* is more idiomatic, but again its length tells against it, and the work as a whole is uneven. More familiar is the E flat concerto by John Ireland, with its predominantly lyrical tone and perky finale. There is much lyrical writing in Bliss's concerto in B flat, but here the key note is heroic rhetoric; this fine piece, built on a Brahmsian scale, is one of his most inspired. The concerto of Vaughan Williams is a gritty, powerful work, better known in its two-piano version; in the original solo version the piano writing is thick and apparently unidiomatic, yet the uncompromising toughness of the style matches the work's dynamic force, and in the poetry of the slow movement and the close of the finale the mood of contemplation is deeply affecting.

One of the earliest works to bring Walton's name to prominence was his *Sinfonia Concertante*. Nowadays it seems light and entertaining rather than the tough nut it at first seemed. Its present neglect is unjust, and may be partly due to the relative simplicity of the piano part which does not offer the virtuoso much with which to dazzle. More substantial are the two concertos of Rawsthorne. The first, both in its original scoring with strings and percussion, and in the later version for symphony orchestra is an athletic work of classical elegance and much wit. The second concerto has a more Brahmsian scale, though written with Rawsthorne's customary economy and integrity, and ends with a finale of down-to-earth tunefulness which never fails to delight an audience.

Britten and Tippett have both written concertos, the former an early and uneven work in D, and the latter a most original one dating from 1956. Inspired by the lyricism of Beethoven's fourth concerto, it is full of colour and has a florid beauty which makes great demands on all the performers. Many composers have written concertos in recent years. Among the most successful are the bravura concerto by Richard Rodney Bennett, three brilliant works by Hoddinott (the powerful first with orchestra of wind and percussion only, and the third a modern counterpart of Liszt's virtuosic concertos), the third concerto by Malcolm Williamson, full of splendid tunes, and fine thoughtful concertos by Leighton (three) and Joubert.

(j) *Bartók, Stravinsky, Schoenberg*

Like Rachmaninov and Hindemith, three of the century's most important figures spent some or all of their last years as emigrants to the USA. Of these, Bartók and Stravinsky wrote most of their concertos elsewhere. Bartók's three concertos stem from different periods of his life. The first two date from 1926 and 1931 respectively. In no. 1, written when he was undergoing his most intense exploration of percussive textures and an almost baroque concentration of line, his rhythmic vitality, fascinating sonorities and contrapuntal vigour combine to produce a work that is only now coming into its own.

The second concerto, in G, has a more lyrical element, and a more clearly baroque toccata-like figuration in the outer movements. In the slow movement, outer sections of static beauty frame a central, flickering scherzo of extraordinary fascination. The increasingly lyrical tone of Bartók's last years is uppermost in the third concerto, in E. The last eighteen bars of score were completed by his pupil, Tibor Serly, from the sketches, Bartók dying before finishing the concerto; yet this is not the music of a dying man, save in a sense of reconciliation and unearthly beauty.

Stravinsky's three contributions to the genre are different in character. The Concerto for Piano and Wind Instruments is sternly neo-baroque in its directness and rhythmic pulsation. The *Capriccio* for piano and orchestra has a more Mozartian touch, though here, too, the slow movement has a high degree of Bachian decoration. Both these works date from the 1920s. 1960 saw the first performance of 'Movements' for piano and orchestra, a short work exploiting the serial techniques that fascinated Stravinsky in his last period, though this seems to me one of the more arid productions of Stravinsky's last phase.

Schoenberg's only piano concerto was written in the USA in 1942. It is a thorough-going example of his twelve-tone technique, but it has a greater sense of spontaneity than is often the case; the work as a whole is imbued with a spirit of warm lyricism that makes it one of the most approachable of áll his major works. The writing is complex, but always clear, and though the highly polyphonic piano part is demanding, it is set in an orchestral context full of subtle colourings.

(k) *The United States of America*

The USA has itself produced a fine crop of indigenous piano concerto works, stretching back to the days of Macdowell's energetic, slightly Griegian concertos. Of these the second, in D minor, has been successfully revived in recent years. One of the greatest geniuses in the field of popular music, Gershwin, made several essays into composition for the symphony concert, including three outstanding ones for piano and orchestra. The *Rhapsody in Blue* is perhaps the most popular, followed closely by the F major concerto; in both the idiom derives from jazz and popular song, but is set in a classical context, the former being a kind of concertante symphonic poem. The variations on 'I got rhythm' for piano and orchestra is, if anything, an even more fascinating, imaginative work.

The world of jazz is not far away from the early two-movement concerto of Copland, nor from the music of Leonard Bernstein, whose masterly Second Symphony, subtitled 'The Age of Anxiety' after a poem by Auden, is really a piano concerto. The more recent concerto of Samuel Barber is an uneasy combination of his innate lyricism with grandiose gestures that fit unhappily into his style, but the 1964–65 concerto of Elliott Carter is one of the most fascinating of all modern works in this medium, and typically original. Carter's music has increasingly included a dramatic element, and here the conception is that of a scenario in which the soloist and the orchestra each work out their instrumental dramas, inter-acting on each other but maintaining their separate identities; a concertino group of seven instruments acts as a link between the two. This imaginative idea is carried out in terms of the utmost virtuosity, though the display element is never simply dazzling extroversion but rather an inherent part of the work.

(*l*) *Russia*

The Russian concerto tradition after Tchaikovsky is dominated by Rachmaninov (who has already been discussed) and Prokofiev. There are others, of course. Arensky's concerto is tuneful and enjoyable, while Scriabin's early example is a richly melodic, often Chopinesque piece. In more recent years Khatchaturian's D flat major concerto, of thoroughly Russian character, has been very popular; while the two concertos by Shostakovich represent the lighter side of his character. The first, for piano, trumpet and strings, is an entertaining piece including a great deal of what one can only describe as 'circus' music, while the second is relaxed and tuneful, with moments of greater intensity. But the five concertos of Prokofiev must take pride of place.

The first, in D flat, is a student work, but what an assured student! The style is recognizably that of Prokofiev already, and in his handling of an inventive approach to form he shows real mastery. The second, in G minor, is an even more astonishing achievement, thoroughly mature and individual, even though Prokofiev was still only twenty-two. Its four movements deploy the full range of the keyboard, and it remains one of the most difficult of all piano concertos. The scherzo is a brilliant toccata, in which the piano plays fast semi-quavers throughout, and the work as a whole seldom relaxes. Only in a folk-like interlude in the finale does lyricism take the stage, but the concerto's basic power and aggression return to replace this. Perhaps there is too much piano and not enough orchestra, but this is such an exciting, dramatic work that one hesitates to criticize it.

The third concerto, in C, has become the most popular. In this Prokofiev achieved the perfect balance between pianistic virtuosity, orchestral ingenuity and formal qualities. Here the orchestra takes part in the thematic discussion, which is more elaborate and genuinely large-scale than in the preceding concertos. All the main themes are memorably inspired, and the final display of fireworks, leading up to the rip-roaring close, is exhilarating.

Neither the fourth concerto (for left hand alone) nor the fifth has achieved anything like this success. The fourth is a fine piece, however, resourcefully laid out for the left hand, and beautifully formed. In the fifth, Prokofiev's ironic sense of humour becomes somewhat sarcastic and perhaps rather mannered, though there are fine things here too. But the achievement of the first three, and possibly four, concertos is colossal, and it is good to see them increasing their place in the repertoire.

(m) Piano duo

Works for keyboard duo, either for two or more instruments, or for two players at one keyboard, are mostly for the piano. There are a number of interesting pieces for organ duet, and Bach's concertos for two, three and even four harpsichords have long been appreciated as wonderful works, written in his concerto style without any drastic modification save the natural enrichment of the contrapuntal technique. But the first outstanding masterpieces for two pianos and for piano duet come from Mozart's pen. The concerto in E flat for two pianos (K 365) is one of his noblest creations, full of epic joy. His D major sonata for two pianos, K 448, is just as brilliant and exciting. Mozart gives both players an equal opportunity for display, as in the concerto, but the virtuosity is magnificently integrated into the material, and indeed is an embodiment of its innate high spirits.

Mozart's contribution to the literature of piano duet is as fine. The last two of his four piano-duet sonatas, those in F (K 497) and C (K 521), have a symphonic scale and grandeur, while the *Theme and Variations in G* (K 501) are captivating.

Schubert's immense output for piano duet (he wrote nothing for two pianos) is of musicological interest, for in his early youth he wrote a number of strange, exploratory fantasias of great length, essays in large-scale form that are immature but highly revealing. There are many enchanting pieces of a lighter character from his later years, and two great masterpieces. Of these, the F minor fantasia (D 940) is a hauntingly beautiful work, in linked sections; its scale is large, and despite the vigour and brilliance of much of the music, the work has something of the valedictory quality of his last solo sonata, in B flat. The Grand Duo in C, D 813, was for some time thought to be a version of the lost 'Gastein' Symphony; be that as it may, this is one of the noblest of all Schubert's symphonic forms, music of grandeur and epic sweep.

During the 19th century the output of duos for piano was vast; the piano duet in particular was a common domestic pastime, and many original works were written for the combination, as well as arrangements of popular symphonies and overture. (Nowadays the best way of getting to know the overtures of such composers as Spohr and Lindpaintner is to come across an old volume of such duets.)

Schumann wrote a number of sets of charming duets, though his masterpiece in the medium is the fine set of variations in B flat for two pianos. Weber's sets of duets contain some of his most delightful pieces, while Mendelssohn's early concerto for two pianos and orchestra is lively and enchanting. Two major works by Brahms are better known in his other versions, but the two-piano versions of both the F minor piano quintet and the orchestral *Variations on the St Antoni Chorale* are extremely effective.

French composers of the latter half of the 19th and early 20th centuries were prolific duo composers. The piano duets of Chabrier and Fauré (the charming *Dolly Suite*) are elegant miniatures, while Ravel's *Mother Goose Suite* has an air of innocence and delicacy that goes straight to the heart. The *Variations on a Theme of Beethoven* for two pianos, by Saint-Saëns, has much wit and invention, while his *Carnival of the Animals* for two pianos and orchestra continues to delight audiences.

Debussy's output includes a number of miniatures, including the well-known *Petite Suite*, and two works of major importance. The gravely sensuous, spare, *Six Epigraphes Antiques*, for piano duet, derive their inspiration from the classical art of Greece, while the great two-piano suite, *En Blanc et Noir*, is a broad canvas which contrasts energy with sadness, even bitterness. It is significant that it was written shortly after the outbreak of the First World War.

In Poulenc's sonata for two pianos and concerto for two pianos we have works of size, wit and vigour; his sonata for piano duet is simple, straightforward and often very funny. Wit is also to be found in Milhaud's immensely popular tuneful suite *Scaramouche*. More recently, *Visions de l'Amen* is a fascinating, complex exploration of Messiaen's mystical interests, and his concern with musical colour;

650

while in the two books of *Structures*, Boulez displays at its most rigorous and formidable the technique of total serialization which occupied him during the 1950s.

Among the masterpieces of their entire outputs are the concerto for two pianos (alone) by Stravinsky, and Bartók's sonata for two pianos and percussion. The latter is a complex work, in which the second and third movements (a slow nocturne and a vital, often humorous peasant dance) balance the first, where a slow introduction climbs gradually out of nothing and bursts into a magnificently sustained and varied contrapuntal movement. The Stravinsky is well named concerto rather than sonata, for it, too, has immense contrapuntal vitality, and if anything even more brilliance *per se* in the writing. Its intellectual concentration makes a powerful impact, and the same can be said of the glorious sonata for two pianos by Hindemith, in which bell sounds and textures play an important part. The slow movement, entitled 'Recitative', is a musical counterpart to the mediaeval English poem, *This Worlde's Joie*, and its solemnity and deep feeling form the heart of the work, which ends with an exciting double fugue closing with clangorous polyphony.

Rachmaninov's output for two pianos includes three fine creations. Of the two suites, the first is an early work, in the finale of which he conjures up a vivid picture of a Russian Easter, with bells resounding. The first three movements are luscious and perhaps overlong, their freedom of form supporting the suite's subtitle, 'Fantasy'. In the second suite, op. 17, written shortly after the second piano concerto, there can be no doubts about his mastery of the structure: it is a large work, but its four movements are perfectly proportioned, culminating in a wildly exciting tarantella. Rachmaninov's final composition was the set of three *Symphonic Dances*, of which both orchestral and two-piano versions were written concurrently. In the keyboard version some of the superb orchestral colouring is lost, but the tensile strength of this awe-inspiring work is retained.

(n) Organ repertoire

A study of the repertoire for organ alone would make this survey totally unassimilable. Suffice it to say that the neglect by the non-organist, non-church-going musical public of this vast repertory causes them to miss music often of great quality. The output of composers such as Buxtehude from the baroque, Widor and Rheinberger from the romantic era, and a whole host of 20th-century composers contains many masterpieces. Buxtehude's organ music, indeed, is as rewarding an oeuvre as that of Bach, who learnt much from him.

The music of Rheinberger, whose many sonatas are superbly written for the instrument, consciously takes up the mantle of Bach. His eighth sonata includes a passacaglia of Bachian complexity, couched in the richly chromatic terms of the late romantic era. With composers like Widor, and his French successors Dupré and Duruflé, the music is more dramatic in concept. Widor, of these men, is the most fulsomely romantic, his successors composing in a clearer, more open-textured manner. If not all these men reach the status of great composers, their music often has great appeal. The immense amount of music written by organists for their own use seems somehow an offshoot of the general musical tradition (certainly the music is often written in a manner which is out of date by the time it reaches the organ loft), and much of the music is decidedly second-hand. But to say this is not to dismiss all organ music, save that of Bach, as inferior. Indeed, the romantic era, which saw some of the worst pieces for organ, also saw some of the finest.

Written along Lisztian models, Reubke's Sonata on the 94th Psalm is both a piece of virtuoso organ writing and a finely integrated large-scale construction, in which the emotional power never bursts the architecture of the music asunder. Liszt's contributions to the repertoire, apart from a handful of small, but austerely fascinating pieces, lies in three works of Gothic grandeur: the *Prelude and Fugue on the name of Bach*, the *Fantasia and Fugue* on the 'Ad nos, ad salutarem undam' theme from Meyerbeer's opera *La Prophète*, and the *Variations on Bach's 'Weinen, Klagen, Sorgen, Zagen'*. Essays in the monumental and virtuoso, these works have a firm basis in the procedures of the classical and baroque periods, and represent Liszt's formal mastery at its most stunning.

It is odd that between Bach and Messiaen the majority of the most significant organ works should have been written by non-organists, or at least musicians who were not generally noted as organists. Mendelssohn's six sonatas, for example, though not so dazzling as the Liszt works, have great dignity and breadth. Perhaps organists themselves were too prone to fall into the easy mannerisms induced by their frequent improvisations. But in the music of Messiaen we find a composer and organist who perhaps achieves his most sustained and consistent level in this very medium. His organ works stem from all periods of his career, from the short, intensely slow-moving early piece *Le Banquet Céleste*, through various large-scale collections of short pieces (among which 'La Nativité du Seigneur' and 'Les Corps Glorieux' are outstanding) to the massive mysticism of *Meditations sur la Mystère de la Trinité* completed in 1971. In these, as in the *Messe de la Pentecôte* of 1933, Messiaen combines immense technical resource with astonishing communicative power.

The literature of organ concertos is much less notable than for organ solo, yet opportunity must be taken to dwell on Handel's contribution to this genre. Alone among the great figures of the baroque he wrote a large number of concertos for organ with orchestral accompaniment, varying from strings only, to the so-called concerto in *Judas Maccabeus*, where the scoring adds oboes, horns and bassoons. Not all of the organ concertos were originally written for the instrument, for some are arrangements of his own concerti grossi, and others use other composers' material, as was often done at the time. In his D minor, Handel is credited with having provided the soloist for the first time with an opportunity for display and development of the material: the first concerto cadenza.

Handel's harmonic vigour, and the memorable nature of his melodic lines, are supported by his large-scale rhythmic vitality. The rhythms do not simply set the foot tapping, they play an active, almost structural part in the music's form. This is an essential cause of the success of his greatest oratorios, but it is an equally important element in the achievement of his concertos, of all kinds. With this rhythmic grounding they attain the status of substantial works of real grandeur. It is this status that the organ concertos of Haydn, charming though they are in their rococo elegance, miss; more than his other concertos, they demonstrate that the concerto was not his most suited field.

Guilmant and Rheinberger wrote powerful organ concertos, the former's in the luscious, French organists' tradition of the latter half of the 19th century; the latter's typically elaborate contrapuntal works in his Bachian manner. During the 20th century organ concertos have occasionally been produced, but few of them have entirely succeeded. Malcolm Williamson's concerto is for organ and full orchestra, an exuberant essay in the grand virtuoso manner. Hindemith's two concertos, as might be expected, pursue a more neo-baroque style. The first one is the last of his seven Kammermusik concertos, with an orchestra of wind instruments, cellos and basses. Written in 1928, it is a more consistently serious, abstract work than its companions in his Kammermusik series. Towards the end of his life, in 1962, he wrote a second organ concerto, this time with full orchestra. This imaginative work is typical of his later years, in that his style, always strongly contrapuntal, and now often thicker in texture, is imbued with an extra sense of struggle – a new element of Beethovenian inner turbulence.

In complete contrast, possibly the most popular organ concerto of recent years is that in G minor, with orchestra of strings and timpani, by Poulenc. His style is as individual as ever, with its echoes of Mozart, Stravinsky, Johann Strauss and many others, yet this is one of his most serious and personal works; the lightness of touch cannot disguise the deep feelings. Kenneth Leighton has also written a more severely contrapuntal, more intensely passionate concerto, with the same orchestration.

(o) Modern harpsichord

The revival of interest in the instruments of the baroque has led to a renascence of the harpsichord above all others, and 20th-century composers have written many valuable works for the instrument. Frank Martin's concerto is one of his most successful pieces, with a spirit of grave elegance. of classical purity, that is deeply moving. He avoids the pitfall of writing too much 'knitting' music for the instrument. Martinů's concerto, with small orchestra, is equally resourceful; its distinctly Bachian opening gives the clue to the neo-baroque style, but his rhythmic vigour and expressiveness of line make this a particularly fine example of his mature manner.

Poulenc's *Concert Champêtre* is also performable on the piano, on which instrument it gains a Mozartian glow; played as originally intended on the harpsichord, it has a Scarlattian directness of tone which is suited to the music's wit and wistfulness.

The concerto of Gerhard is possibly the most difficult of all to perform; the Spanish element in his style is important here, integrated most satisfactorily with a grave contrapuntalism derived from his studies with Schoenberg. Another great Spanish work is the brief but powerful concerto of De Falla, scored for an ensemble of only five instruments. Typically rhythmical and lively overall, the music has also a grave beauty, especially in the statuesque slow movement. Far lighter is the delectable little Concertino of the British composer Walter Leigh, a miniature of delicious charm.

5 VIOLIN SONATAS

(a) The Italian school

The rise of the duo sonata closely parallels that of the violin, and the earliest home of both was Italy. Just as the great master violin-makers (Stradivarius, Amati, Guarnerius) were predominantly

Italian at that time, so the greater quantity of sonatas was written both for the violin and by Italians. The first to use the title for this kind of piece, as opposed to Giovanni Gabrieli's famous use of it for his brass music, was Biagio Marini, in 1617. Several features can be noted straightaway about these early pieces. In the first place they were not strictly duo sonatas as we know the form today; they were often for two violins playing inter-weaving melodic lines, and they were also for one or more violins plus continuo. This last consisted of two players, one a viola da gamba or cello playing the bass line, and the other a harpsichordist doubling the bass line and filling in the chords that were indicated by the figures under it.

Thus a sonata for single violin and continuo would consist of two lines only, a top melodic stave, and a bass line, with the harmonic figurations beneath the latter. There were two basic kinds of sonata, both of which resembled suites in their succession of short movements: the sonata *da camera* (chamber sonata), in which each movement had a dance character, and the more serious sonata *da chiesa* (church sonata). Even during Marini's lifetime the character of the music became more substantial, from the toccata or fantasia nature of the earlier movements to more firmly established identities for each movement within the context of the sonata, and a more clearly marked alternation of tempi between the movements.

The greatest achievements of this period are concurrent with the emergence of the great Stradivarius himself, in the late 1660s, and the corresponding emergence of the great Italian virtuoso violinist-composers. Corelli is perhaps pre-eminent among these, for though little of his music has come down to us, it includes a number of fine sonatas *da chiesa* for two violins and an important volume of sonatas for one violin. Slightly later, Tartini made invaluable contributions; among his sonatas, the *Devil's Trill* Sonata, in G minor, is famous, both for the long trill in the last of its four movements and for supposedly being dictated to Tartini by the Devil in a dream. His *Didone Abbandonata* Sonata, also in G minor, is another splendid work, exemplifying the standard procedure for this kind of sonata and including in its lyrical first movement the kind of advanced violin technique that these composers demanded of their soloists even in their slower music.

(b) Bach, Handel, Mozart

The sonatas of Bach were the first in which the keyboard part was fully written out, though it must be remembered that the players would probably have added further elaboration of harmony or texture during performances. The formal scheme of the Italian sonata was retained, but in the quicker movements Bach's polyphonic writing for the two instruments is more elaborate, and in the slow movements the harmonies and textures tend to be richer. The third sonata, in E major, is particularly masterly, with two slow movements of haunting beauty.

The sonatas of Handel rely to a greater extent on the beauty of the melodic writing in the slow movements and, though Handel used polyphonic techniques occasionally, a more thorough-going dance character in the quicker sections. His slow movements, too, often tend to be, as it were, preludes or interludes rather than movements in their own right. This is especially true of his third movements, which sometimes act simply as a link (often very beautiful) to the finale, and tend to end not on their tonic, but on the dominant or the mediant, to emphasize the continuity into the finale.

Whereas Bach and Handel sustained the violin-plus-accompaniment tradition, this was severely upset by Mozart, whose earliest violin sonatas were described as being 'for Harpsichord or Pianoforte with Violin Accompaniment'. There is much charm in these early works (though they lack appeal to violinists because of their simple violin parts) and there are some surprises. But the first Mozart sonata in which the instruments are treated pretty well as equals is the E minor sonata, K 304, of 1778: a magnificently worked out sonata-form followed by a minuet, but this time with its dance feeling overladen by a sense of restrained grief. Shortly after this Mozart was to produce one of his most passionate piano solo works – the great A minor sonata, K 310.

The E minor, though by no means lengthy, remains one of the most moving of Mozart's violin sonatas, but having found a viable technique of writing in this medium, he produced a large number of masterpieces for it. Several stand out even in this great output. The two sonatas in B flat, K 378 and K 454, are marvellously lyrical works, the latter displaying a somewhat more symphonic stature. The slow movement of K 481 in E flat is also a superb piece, with an astonishing harmonic resource that leads Mozart (unusually) into several changes of key signature. Another elaborate slow movement comes in the A major sonata, K 526, a work which perhaps achieves his most perfect balance between the two instruments; but fine though this slow movement and the first movement are, it is the finale that takes the listener's breath away – a virtuoso whirlwind of quavers, marked presto, that has more than a touch of the influence of Clementi's keyboard writing, and achieves the massive feeling of a Beethoven scherzo.

(c) Beethoven

Beethoven's ten sonatas were also described as being for 'Piano and Violin', but even more than in the mature Mozart's case this is a ludicrous statement of their instrumental balance. Throughout all ten works the instruments are partners, taking part equally in the statement and development of the themes. Taken in chronological order, the sonatas convey vividly a sense of Beethoven's own stylistic and technical development up to 1812, when the last of the series, op. 96, was written. They also reveal just how deeply Haydn influenced him.

In the first set of three sonatas, op. 12, no. 1 in D includes a central set of variations of Haydnesque simplicity, while the delight in off-beat accents and pauses, sometimes dramatic, sometimes humorous, which he shared with Haydn, continues throughout this part of Beethoven's oeuvre. These early works, published in 1799, are entirely characteristic of their composer in every way, though occasionally his relative inexperience is revealed by a touch of awkwardness in the structure or formal balance. But Beethoven's mastery of this medium was soon achieved, with the A minor sonata, op. 23, and the F major, op. 24. The former is given a start of such impetus, in its opening tarantella, that even the 'slow' movement (actually an *andante scherzoso, più allegretto*, and thus of moderate pace only) is nervous and edgy, while the finale is astonishingly original, full of pauses and strange seekings for the right key. Op. 24, familiarly known as the *Spring* Sonata, is a complete contrast, sunny and open in nature, the first and last movements both opening with soaring, almost Schubertian melodies, and the slow movement a pastoral idyll of almost uninterrupted reflection. The scherzo and trio, brief and to the point, are supremely witty and concise.

Beethoven's resources continue to be deeply mined in the three sonatas, op. 30, of which the C minor, no. 2, and the G major, no. 3, are especially striking. The C minor is dramatic, full of extraordinary tappings and mutterings, and outbursts of violence; any lyrical softening of tension is left to the heavenly slow movement, while the light relief of the scherzo is underpinned by the nervous tension which dominates the work. The good-humoured, rippling, flowing G major is in complete contrast.

The two remaining sonatas, however, are perhaps Beethoven's supreme achievements in this medium. He himself described the

Kreutzer Sonata in A, op. 47, as being 'like a concerto'. From the very opening, with the unaccompanied violin stating the striking first theme, the *Kreutzer* is a summation of the dramatic side of Beethoven's art, full of shifts of key, mood or tempo, and totally uncompromising thematic development. In the central variations the element of instrumental decoration is seen as an essential part of the variation technique, while the unrelenting tarantella finale sweeps all before it. His last sonata, in G major, op. 96, on the other hand, is an idyllic, poised summation of the more intimate aspect of his art.

(d) The romantics
The output of sonatas and other works for violin and piano continued unabated during the 19th century, though few composers have so consistently given of their best to it as did Beethoven. But the neglect of Schubert's contributions is surprising. The three sonatinas, in D, A minor and G, are familiar to most violin students, and like the bigger, though by no means massive, Duo (or sonata) in A, do occasionally appear on concert programmes or gramophone records; yet their stature is still far from realized. The sonatinas are quintessential Schubert in miniature, so to speak, while the A major Duo is a marvellous work, generous in melodic invention, and with a formal perfection of Mozartian elegance. His B minor *Rondo Brillante* is perhaps over-long for non-Schubertians, but his admirers find it a fascinating, highly imaginative piece; while the C major Fantasy, his last work for violin and piano, is an astonishing achievement, with far more subtle thematic formation than the Rondo and great originality of harmonic thought.

The sonatas of Weber and Mendelssohn, charming early romantic works though they be, are lightweight compared to the efforts of the later romantics. Schumann's two sonatas are seldom played, perhaps because their complex piano writing demands a pianist of soloist calibre, which type tends too easily to dominate this kind of partnership. But there is much fine invention here, nor are the works so unsatisfactory formally as they are often considered.

However, the three sonatas of Brahms are acknowledged masterpieces. The G major, op. 78, known as the *Regenlied* because its finale uses the theme of this Brahms song, has one of the most beautiful openings of any violin sonata, a series of slowly repeated soft piano chords over which the violin sings its lyrical melody. As in all these works, but especially here, Brahms's typical combination of romantic warmth with classical grace and symmetry governs the music's character. There is even more poise and serenity in the second sonata, in A major, in which it might be noted that Brahms links the three movements by a subtle thematic inter-relationship. The opening movement has an imposing sense of grave contentment, imbued with a feeling of spacious wisdom, and nowhere in his sonatas is his 'scoring' for the two instruments more striking than in the sonata's finale. The central movement shares the alternating functions of both slow movement (andante tranquillo) and scherzo (vivace).

His third sonata, in D minor, is of a more dramatic cast than its predecessors. The sombre opening, akin in feeling, though lighter in texture than the *Four Serious Songs*, sets the mood. Dynamic and emotional contrasts are greater than before, and the work as a whole is on a bigger scale. Even the lovely simplicity of the slow movement, and the delicacy of the third movement do not disguise the sonata's basic seriousness.

So far, after the early Italian days, the history of the violin sonata has been predominantly Germanic, though composers like Mondonville and Leclair occupy an honoured place in the early days of this medium. In the latter half of the 19th century, however, the field suddenly spreads much wider. The single sonata, in A, by César Franck is one of his greatest works, totally satisfying from every point of view. The opening movement is a lovely, lilting piece of gentle poetry, and the dramatic, almost demonic scherzo which follows is in turn succeeded by a remarkable movement headed 'Recitativo-Fantasia'. Here the music has a genuinely improvisatory feeling, yet it is fully balanced in the context of the work as a whole. Miraculously the sonata's diversity succeeds, for the finale's cheerful, sonorous canons provide precisely the right kind of conclusion to tie the whole together.

Both Grieg and Fauré produced attractive sonatas which deserve to be heard more often. Grieg's are typical of his style, with its undertones of Norwegian folk-music inflecting his spontaneous melodic gift. Fauré's two sonatas date from opposite ends of his career, the first a fresh, ebullient early work, while the second, dating from 1917, is characteristic of his later works in its sweetness and elegant nostalgia. Richard Strauss's vigorous early sonata in E flat, though immature, gives more than a hint of the forceful personality to emerge in the symphonic poems.

(e) The 20th century

Two French sonatas that have been undervalued by critics, though they are played quite frequently, are those of Debussy and Ravel. These are both late works, and in both cases the critical assumption is that the composers' gifts were on the wane. Certainly they are economical, almost sparse pieces, sharing a degree of austerity and a touch of bitterness (particularly in the Ravel) that immediately sets them apart from the composers' more popular works. Yet they are both superbly wrought. Debussy's especially is remarkable, breathing an attenuated, infinitely subtle air, through which the ghosts of Pierrot, Harlequin and Columbine flit hardly less pervadingly than in his cello sonata. Only in a brief, *Iberia*-like interruption of the finale does he depart from the sonata's basic style (with an acidity contradicting the work's apparent lushness) and this is done for an admirably judged dramatic effect.

Ravel's sonata is, if anything, even more austere in texture; the first movement has a limpid detachment, seeming altogether to repel emotional connotations. These, however, rise to the surface in the slow movement, a 'Blues' of increasingly terrifying hollowness, and again in the perpetuum mobile finale, where the dazzling virtuosity serves to express a desperate anguish.

The two fine sonatas by Carl Nielsen are the most striking Scandinavian contributions to the genre. The first, in A, dates from 1895, a period when the influence of Brahms and Dvořák can still be detected in the music, though the personality behind the music is entirely Nielsen's. It is typical and apt that the first movement should be headed 'allegro glorioso', and the whole work inhabits a fiery, but sympathetic, human world. The second sonata, 1912, is not in any very fixed key; indeed, one of its structural elements is, as usual with Nielsen, a search for the music's home key. This turns out to be C major, but even at the end, a series of hammered B flats on the piano attempt, unsuccessfully, to disrupt this final resolution. As in several of his other major compositions, the first movement begins placidly enough, but soon gains terrifying momentum; the awesome undercurrents burst to the surface and are only subdued at the cost of a frozen conclusion. This is a remarkable, powerful work, whose very toughness fascinates and rewards the listener.

Among British composers of the early 20th century, Elgar, Delius, Bax and Ireland all provided notable examples of the genre. Elgar's E minor sonata is a late work, one of the three chamber pieces written just before the valedictory cello concerto. It typifies what we call the Elgarian manner, full of grandiose, sweeping tunes, yearning phrases, and underpinning all, a sense of personal sadness more marked than usual in this intimate medium. Delius's sonatas are typically profuse in harmonic riches and melodic beauty, as are those of Bax. The latter's first two are often darkly coloured, and full of that curious personal melodic flavouring, compounded of various influences including Russian music and Celtic folk-song. His third sonata, 1927, has an added athleticism and clarity of texture characteristic of his later music. Ireland's two sonatas are more straightforward in their simple romanticism; the power of the second, in A minor, must owe much to its being written during the First World War. Unlike Ireland, Vaughan Williams waited until his last years to write a violin sonata; the heaviness of the piano writing makes it awkward to encompass with clarity, weighing against the work's effectiveness, and so too does the over-long nature of the final variations. But there are many fine things here, especially in the flowing first movement, and the demonic scherzo.

The two sonatas by Busoni, both mature representatives of his art at its most thoughtful, are occasionally heard, as are the powerful Poulenc sonata (written in memory of Lorca) and those of Honegger, Milhaud and Enesco. However, Russian composers have provided some of the most famous modern works. Stravinsky's Duo Concertante, 1932, which stems from the peak of his neo-classical phase, as the Grecian titles given to the movements testify, is poised and clear-eyed, its lines enunciated with the coolest grace. Prokofiev's two sonatas are both masterpieces. The second, in D, is equally familiar in its version for flute and piano; this is Prokofiev at his most delightful and charming. In the first sonata, in F minor, he deals with sterner things; indeed, this is one of the toughest and most profound works of his entire output. Even the peasant-dance nature of its scherzo and finale have a sense of power rare in such music, and it comes as an eminently satisfying catharsis when, at the height of the finale's boisterousness, the music turns a corner and reverts to the mood of the opening movement, the dance being replaced by a flickering snowscape and, finally, a most haunting cadence.

Shostakovich's single sonata, op. 134, was written only in 1968. It too is powerful; for all the economy of much of the writing, the music gives an impression of symphonic size, borne out by its brilliant central scherzo and the final passacaglia, one of the finest of his explorations of this form.

Of the other great figures of this century, Bartók and Hindemith have both produced fine violin sonatas. Both of Bartók's date from the early 1920s, and therefore represent that period of his career when he was trying to synthesize the influence of folk-music with all the abstract influences that went to make up his musical character.

Neither is easy to listen to, but their extraordinary power is undeniable, the apparent wildness of the music shaped by an acute inner ear.

Hindemith's various violin sonatas are more classically polyphonic; one should call this a baroque polyphony to be exact, since the C major sonata (1939), the finest of them, is a masterly exploration of baroque techniques in modern terms. Schoenberg, in his *Phantasy* for 'violin with piano accompaniment' (his title) written towards the end of his life in the USA, composed one of his most concentrated works, a rigorous exploration of his serial technique and a constant challenge to performers.

American composers themselves have produced several fine essays, notably Copland's sonata, 1943. This clean, lithe piece is marked by a subtle warmth of expression, and has retained its place in the repertoire. The four numbered sonatas of Ives (there is at least one earlier, unnumbered work) typify his tendency to utilize bits and pieces from earlier compositions and place them together in a new format. They are consistently inspired by the music of urban America: ragtime, and the music of revivalist camp-meetings dominate these imaginative, often elaborate sonatas.

From British composers of recent years, two violin sonatas take pride of place. Walton's (1950) is a lusciously romantic work in two movements, his innate melodic gift set in a context of Mediterranean warmth; the piano writing is exceptionally difficult, and as rewarding as the violin part. Rawsthorne's violin sonata (1959) is one of his finest compositions, in which the central pair of movements, a haunting waltz and a brilliant, toccata-like scherzo respectively, are framed by two movements of lyrical beauty, the finale especially moving with its dying clash of E flat minor and D minor echoing into the distance. Roberto Gerhard's *Gemini*, originally entitled Duo Concertante, demands attention, too. Like many of his other late works it combines his adventurous approach to sonorities and structure with an immediately accessible sense of colour and rhythm.

(f) Violin unaccompanied, and two violins

Among the jewels of the violinists' repertoire are a number of masterpieces for violin alone, or two violins only. The former is best served by composers, and Bach's great set of sonatas and partitas (three of each) stands head and shoulders above the rest. Their respective titles indicate approximately the bases from which they spring. The partitas are largely collections of dance-movements, akin to suites (which title is given to his equally masterly set of six solo cello works), and close in spirit to the early Italians' sonatas *da camera*. The sonatas, on the other hand, invariably follow the basic, four-movement outline established so firmly by Corelli's sonatas *da chiesa*, and their feeling is more serious and thoughtful.

This should not be taken to mean that the partitas are lightweight in comparison, however. They are, on the contrary, as noble, dignified and elaborate as the sonatas, even given the different formal bases of the two types of movement. And even in the partitas there are movements with a large-scale organization akin to that of the sonatas. The most notable example of this comes in the second sonata, where Bach suddenly breaks off the sequence of dance movements and interpolates the great Chaconne, a massive, visionary movement, in which his creative ingenuity and inspiration are at white heat.

It has often been thought that polyphonic writing for the violin is impossible, at any rate for a lengthy stretch of music, but in this Chaconne above all, and in the fugues which invariably form the second movement of the sonatas, Bach proved the falsehood of this view. The basis of his art is contrapuntal, and the skill with which he sustains a melodic line and, often by implication, a bass line as well on the single instrument is astonishing. Of the fugues in the sonatas, the most extraordinary is that in the third sonata, where the difficulty of the writing nearly stretches the player's technique to the breaking-point; the intensity of expression achieved by this sense of challenge and strain is exciting and moving. But even in the more decorative movements of the partitas, where contrapuntal technique is more subservient, the music attains great power through its very complexity. These six works are as much a summit of baroque polyphony as is, say, the *Art of Fugue*. Few composers since have dared to challenge Bach in this medium, though the twenty-four *Caprices* for solo violin of Paganini have both inestimable value as technical exercises and great musical worth. But the Belgian violinist and composer, Ysaÿe, also wrote six sonatas for solo violin, published in 1924. As a composer he was no Bach, but the sonatas should not be under-valued. Indeed the third, in D minor, is in its own way a powerful and exciting work; and while it was probably inevitable that the element of bravura display should be uppermost in the mind of a composer who was one of the greatest executants on the instrument, there is something freely expanding, almost improvisatory about the work (as the sub-title 'Ballade' might suggest) which in its intensity and sense of drama reminds me of nothing so much as the English ballad poetry of the Middle Ages.

From more recent years, Prokofiev's light, lyrical and entertaining sonata for solo violin, op. 115, is not perhaps one of his most profound pieces, but it is full of infectious gaiety. The major 20th-century work for unaccompanied violin remains Bartók's sonata. Commissioned by Menuhin, and written in 1944, only a year before Bartók's tragic death, this is one of the toughest of his pieces for the listener as well as for the player, exploiting to the full all the potential of the instrument. He seems to have chosen to challenge Bach on his own ground, for the second movement is a fugue, though not so rigorous as the Bachian model and more fantasy-like in its freedom, while the first movement is headed 'Tempo di ciaccona'. This, however, is not a true chaconne in form; the heading simply indicates tempo and character, though its sonata-form structure is worked out with great intensity. The third movement is in ternary form, with elements of variation technique, and the finale is a scherzo-rondo, full of the bounding rhythmic vitality which is such an important element in Bartók's style. None of the other 20th-century solo violin works attempt such massive exploration of the medium, but the sonatina of Honegger, the invigorating sixth sonatina of Jean Martinon, and the two inventive, imaginative works by Nielsen (*Prelude and Theme with Variations*, 1923, and *Preludio e Presto*, 1928) demand attention. These latter, like the magnificently wrought Chaconne by Gerhard, are the nearest thing outside Bartók to a 20th-century re-examination of Bach's approach to the genre.

The tradition of writing for two violins with accompaniment was strong in the early days of the sonata. But after the baroque few composers have written for two violins, either with accompaniment or without. Bartók's forty-four Duos for two violins alone are a typically resourceful set of miniatures, based on folk-song in much the same way that his piano pieces 'For Children' are. These duos, however, are often technically demanding, despite their pedagogic basis. A more substantial work is Rawsthorne's *Theme and Variations for two Violins*, one of the first to bring his name to prominence – music of inexhaustible variety and ingenuity.

6 VIOLIN CONCERTOS

(a) Bach

The enormous explosion of interest in the music of the 17th and 18th centuries has resulted above all in a tremendous expansion of the solo violinists' repertoire. Musicological research has contributed to this renascence of the early concerto, too, so that far more works of this period are known to us.

The most prolific master of the period was surely Vivaldi, whose vast output includes hundreds of concertos. His concerto style is the epitome of the period's approach to the form: ritornello sections for the orchestra providing a steady, structural bed-rock against which the soloist's more decorative episodes, with their florid, often almost operatic character, form a contrast in their fantasia-like freedom. The four concertos which make up Vivaldi's set *The Four Seasons* exemplify this format admirably. This dramatic quality derived from contrast in the vital outer movements is heightened by the arioso-like character of the slow movements.

The great number of other composers who contributed fine works to the genre is too big to be encompassed here. The dominant nationality, as in the case of the sonata, was Italian, though Leclair's elegant, fastidious concertos from France demonstrate the spread of the genre. But though the element of soloistic display was important (inevitably, as a result of the preponderance of violinist-composers) and though the orchestral ritornello/solo episodes contrast was equally basic, it was only with Bach that the real capabilities of the concerto began to appear. His violin concertos, though they continue the Vivaldian tradition to some extent, use the orchestral ritornelli with a far more thorough intent of binding together. This is a distinct movement on the way towards the tightly integrated element of discussion between solo and orchestra that is such an important feature of the classical and modern concerto. Contrast is still of paramount importance, however, and the slow movements retain the aria style.

Many of Bach's violin concertos have been lost, though a reconstruction of the famous D minor harpsichord concerto in what is supposed to be its original form as a violin concerto adds a fine work to the canon. The situation with Bach's concertos is remarkably complicated; apart from his many arrangements or recompositions of concertos by other composers, there are various transcriptions by him of his own concertos. Thus the famous E major violin concerto was also rewritten as a harpsichord concerto in D, in which version it works very well. But the scope of this essay must restrict us to the 'pure' violin concertos by Bach. All three of these are among his most popular works. The D minor concerto for two violins is especially fine, with its marvellous contrapuntal dexterity, the two solo lines interwoven from first to last with consummate artistry. The two concertos for solo violin, in A minor and E major, are if anything a touch slighter in scale, but equally beautifully written.

(b) Mozart and Beethoven

With the advent of the early classical era, the violin concerto became momentarily a lighter piece. In the concertos of Haydn and Mozart, the process of integrating the soloist and the orchestra is taken a step further; the principle of orchestral statement of the main theme followed by a solo restatement of it is retained, but the onset of sonata form, with its thematic development, began to replace the decorative freedom of the solo part, and the whole structure is closely woven. However, neither Haydn nor Mozart stretched his resources very far in his violin concertos. Haydn's are delightful, tuneful pieces, in which an operatic element is distinctly discernible.

Mozart's concertos are more often played, and contain some surprising things, even though they are all relatively early works. The three most popular, in G (K 216), in D (218), and A (219), all have finales in which the progress of the music is suddenly interrupted by a complete change of mood or character, as in K 219, where the elegant minuet feeling is dispelled momentarily by an extraordinary episode of Turkish or gypsy character. The wit, grace and charm of Mozart's violin concertos owe less to earlier models than to Haydn, more to the development of the classical style. With the single concerto in D by Beethoven we reach the peak of this particular musical development.

From the remarkable opening, with its four quiet drum-beats setting the moderate pace, to the close of its joyous finale, this is one of the most sublime of all Beethoven's symphonic works. Just as in his piano works he had achieved a new style of writing for the keyboard, here he developed a new manner of violin writing. The solo part is certainly of virtuoso difficulty from the technical point of view, with a certain amount of bravura (though never gratuitous) but the clear and exposed nature of its setting offers another challenge to the performer, one of the most acute musicianship. It is interesting to compare this work with his violin sonatas, for whereas each sonata has a distinct character (as a rule the odd-numbered ones are fiery and dramatic; the even, more gentle and purely lyrical), in the concerto these two aspects of Beethoven's musical character go side by side. The opening itself combines them, with the sense of latent drama in the drum-beats and then the heavenly lyricism of the wind theme

666

which follows. The entry of the violin, too, contains both elements: after the way has been prepared by a sudden drop in dynamics following the orchestral climax, the soloist enters with a rising series of octaves that would, in the hands of a lesser composer, have probably been made the excuse for a short bravura cadenza. Beethoven restrains the drama, and by so doing makes it all the more subtly effective; the violin slowly winds down again, to ascend once more into the solo version of the main theme.

This subtle interweaving of the dramatic and the lyrical is a hall-mark of the entire concerto. Even the most powerful moments have a sense of airiness, of a clear, but not harsh, light diffused over the world. The slow movement, marked by a withdrawn, rapt beauty, is linked to the finale, a bold stroke for the period. Here the spirit of the peasants' merry-making of the *Pastoral* Symphony is transfigured into something transcendental. There is all the heroic innocence of Haydn, all the nobility of the Greek pastoral poets in this enchanting music.

(c) The romantics

Beethoven's influence on his successors in the field of violin concerto composition was profound, at any rate in external matters. But the next work to attempt to reach the same expressive heights was the concerto in D of Brahms, who in many ways is Beethoven's true successor anyway. This must be dealt with in its proper place, for between these two peaks of the violin concerto repertoire lie a good many foothills, some of which perhaps deserve greater attention than they usually receive, and one of which has certainly won the hearts of all listeners: Mendelssohn's E minor concerto, in three linked movements. It is often dismissed as trivial, if entertaining; yet the inspiration of the melodies is supreme. Mendelssohn's handling of the orchestra (by now, of course, a much fuller band than in the baroque concerto, and therefore more of a problem to the composer in terms of aural balance) is equally inspired. Like several others of his greatest works, it has an almost Mozartian grace in its formal perfection, and if it does not achieve the spiritual heights of the Beethoven concerto, it must in fairness be conceded that it does not aim for them.

The arrival of the romantic era meant, as with piano music, that violinists were given more music of a predominantly bravura nature. Most of this, as in the early Italian days, was composed by violinists themselves. The concertos of Spohr were at one time regarded as among the greatest of all, though now we seldom hear any of them. Yet they had great influence, and often great imagination. No. 8, in A minor, lasted longest in the repertoire, and its sub-title ('Gesang-szene') indicates Spohr's individual idea of writing a violin concerto in the style of an operatic scena. In the brevity of its various linked sections it is an important step on the way to the single-movement concerto, and its great melodic charms are worth seeking out.

Of equal stature is Paganini, that flamboyant figure. The number of concertos by this supposedly Devil-possessed violinist are occasionally increased by a new discovery or reconstruction. The works are marked by the exceptional virtuosity of the solo writing, and the large number of tunes which are instantly memorable, though their formal properties are not very great; the orchestra (though handled with great skill) is relegated to a decidedly subsidiary role. Another great violinist, Joachim, wrote music of a more substantially wrought character; his Hungarian Concerto contains many fine pages.

Along with concertos, many of these composers wrote genre pieces of the type so familiar from the romantic era. The Polish Wieniawski, for example, wrote two concertos of fiery character which remain in the repertoire, and also a hauntingly melodic *Legend* and some polonaises. The *Fantasy on themes from 'Carmen'*, and the *Gypsy Airs* of the Spaniard, Sarasate, are typical of the period in their wild solo exuberance, enormous variety of violin techniques and emotional directness.

In the concertos of the Belgian Vieuxtemps a more classical element is retained. The scherzo of his fourth concerto, in D minor, for instance, has strong echoes of the pastoral jollity of Beethoven's finale; while his own finale has a Mendelssohnian lightness of touch. His approach to concerto form was original; typical of it is his fifth concerto, in one movement, rather like a condensed version of the Mendelssohn three-movement plan. These works are among the most musicianly of these compositions, for Vieuxtemps more easily integrated the demands for display with the creation of musical ideas than did many of his colleagues.

With the Brahms concerto, however, the tradition of the great classics is taken up once more, with resounding success. Just as the Beethoven concerto perfectly reconciled the dramatic and lyrical sides of his art, so here Brahms's two essential qualities – the lyrical and the architectural – are superbly joined. The melodic invention has all the warmth and flow of his song-writing, and the concerto is also wrought on a massive, symphonic scale. And despite the bravura

668

of the solo part, it is not, like so many romantic concertos, written for soloist with intermittent accompaniment, but is a fully worked score in which the orchestra is an equal partner. After the balm of the wonderful slow movement, the distinctly gypsyish high spirits of the finale come as a tribute to Brahms's friend Joachim (who was of Hungarian birth – gypsy music then being regarded as the indigenous Hungarian folk-music), and as a triumphant conclusion to one of the composer's finest works.

Tchaikovsky's D major concerto stands in something of the same relation to that of Brahms as Mendelssohn's does to Beethoven's: a lesser peak of the mountain range of violin concerto masterpieces, but masterly nonetheless. Alone of the major works of this repertoire, it is still usually performed with some cuts and alterations, some of which are slight improvements, others merely perverse. The concerto has long been accused of all kinds of vices: unevenness of inspiration, over-thick orchestration, structural imbalances and the like. Its admirers can only presume that it is being decried by Beethovenian ideals in this respect. For the orchestration is as brilliant as Tchaikovsky's usually is; and why, in a work where his melodic inspiration was at its most spontaneous, should his customary skill in orchestration suddenly disappear? True, there is little of the supreme symphonic integration of motifs that marks the Beethoven and Brahms concertos, but if Tchaikovsky is aiming at a simpler kind of structure, who is to fault him for that? The music's qualities have communicated with audiences, however, and it retains its popularity.

Dvořák's A minor concerto is not so vastly inferior to the Tchaikovsky that it has deserved the neglect from which it has suffered. If it does not touch the great heights of his cello concerto, it contains a characteristic prodigality of tunes, and there is much strength in the music's core. The D minor concerto of Sibelius (who was himself a violinist) is much more remarkable, however. There are hints of the influence of Tchaikovsky here and there, especially in the slow movement, but this is a mature and individual work, written with a typically original approach to form. There are three movements, of which the second is a melting romance and the finale, perhaps, the epic homeward ride of one of his beloved Finnish folk-heroes; but neither of these, fine though they are, demonstrates his originality. This is seen in the first movement which, from its atmospheric start, moves forward in a series of symphonic steps closely inter-related in true Sibelian manner, but in a way which had so far not been applied to concerto writing.

The violin concerto of Schumann, though containing much inspired music, also includes some material unworthy of so great a composer; the onset of his fatal illness is betrayed at times. But other romantic works sustain a higher level. Of Max Bruch's three concertos, the first, in G minor, is still an important part of the violinist's equipment, as, to a lesser extent, is his inventive *Scottish Fantasy* for violin and orchestra. The broad, nobly shaped themes of the concerto are inspired, while the finale is a fiery piece not unlike that of Brahms's concerto. The element of display arises quite naturally from the melodic content, as it does also in the gorgeously Russian A minor concerto by Glazunov.

Two French works also reward attention: Lalo's *Symphonie Espagnole*, and the last of Saint-Saëns's three concertos. Lalo's work, one of the few of his to remain familiar to us, is a beautifully coloured series of five, instead of the usual four, movements, with the character of vivid genre pieces in which the Spanish element is perhaps more notable than the symphonic. Saint-Saëns's third violin concerto is a vigorous, athletic work in B minor. It is conventionally structured in three movements, but is marked out by the inspired nature of its themes. Nor should one forget the refined, meltingly lovely *Poème* of Chausson, a work of perfect proportions.

(d) The 20th century

But, together with the Sibelius, perhaps the finest violin concertos of the early 20th century are those of Delius and Elgar. Delius's is refined and flowing, full of those luscious strings of rich chords that tend to make his music a very acquired taste. The criticism that he was unable to maintain a large form is finely answered in this concerto, for its structure is beautifully held together. The elements of ritornello and orchestral partnership in thematic development are observed, and the rhapsodic freedom of the solo writing, often cadenza-like in style though still accompanied, is soaringly lovely. If its intimate tone is likely to prevent it from becoming a 'pop' item, it is currently undervalued and underplayed.

Elgar's B minor concerto is also underplayed, for a different reason. Though it is in the repertoire of a few international soloists (Menuhin and Heifetz are both closely associated with it), most of them, one senses, are almost afraid to tackle a work that is not only one of the greatest of all violin concertos, but also probably the longest (nearly fifty minutes) and arguably the most difficult. In purely technical terms, it is a colossal achievement to have written a concerto which

670

encompasses so much human experience, from the most intimate of feelings to the expression of public grandeur. Its unique stature derives from the innermost depths of the composer's spirit; the inscription at the head of the score ('Herein is enshrined the soul of . . .') suggests a deeply personal impulse underlying the music, and though we do not know who (several ladies have been suggested) or what (some argue that it is the soul of the violin) is thus enshrined, there can be no doubting the essential intimacy of the inspiration. For all the seemingly extrovert splendour of much of the outer movements, this is as personal a concerto as has ever been written. The infinitely subtle, reflective slow movement is the direct expression of the composer's deepest feelings; we are privileged to take part in this act of communion. And even in the final allegro molto, with its brilliance and verve, the essential clue to the work's character comes in the miraculous cadenza, where Elgar softly, gently accompanies the soloist's rhapsodies: the most sheerly musical of all cadenzas.

The more revolutionary figures of the first half of the 20th century have all produced fine violin concertos. Stravinsky's, in D, is an attractive, pungent exercise in his neo-classical vein. Schoenberg's complex concerto is one of his most striking orchestral pieces. It is formidably difficult for the performer, as it is for the audience, but the writing is recognizably an extension in terms of the composer's own technique of the traditional style of the concerto, and the work is a tour de force of Schoenberg's manner. Ravel's *Tzigane* is a short explanation of gypsy-like ideas, with a minute part for orchestra: an enjoyable, if not significant work (but why need significance always be essential for quality?).

Bartók's two concertos differ considerably from each other. The first, an early work written before he had reached full compositional maturity, is in two movements: one a richly harmonized slow movement of considerable emotional intensity, and the second, derived from one of his piano bagatelles, a bitter waltz parody. The second concerto is one of his mature masterpieces. The first and last movements, both in sonata-form, though the latter has a dance-rondo atmosphere, are closely related thematically, while the central movement is a set of freely rhapsodic variations on a theme of folk-like simplicity.

Like Bartók, Prokofiev wrote two concertos, both among his most successful orchestral works. The first, in D, dates from 1913, when Prokofiev was twenty-two, and it has astonishing maturity and individuality, together with genuine originality of approach. For both first and last movements are predominantly slow or slowish, while only the typically brittle scherzo adopts a genuinely fast tempo. His second concerto, in G minor, was written after his return to his native Russia, in 1935, and is equally lyrical in impulse, though here the three-movement form more conventionally places a slow movement in the centre, with a leisurely first movement and a breezy finale.

Hindemith's concertos are sharply contrasted. The earliest is the fourth in the previously mentioned Kammermusik series, and is one of the finest of the group, with music of splendid, full-blooded purpose and imaginative textural variety, dominated by the sound of wind instruments. There is a mediaeval directness about this music which is instantly accessible. His 1939 concerto, with full orchestra, is equally accessible; here, though the music is as strong and lusty as ever, there is more lyricism.

Two of the finest 20th-century concertos after Elgar's could hardly be more different. Berg's concerto, written in 1935, the year of his death, was composed under the profound shock of the death of the young actress, Manon Gropius, the daughter of Mahler's widow by her marriage to the architect Gropius, and a dear friend of the Bergs. Just as Elgar's great concerto is a personal utterance, so is Berg's, inscribed 'To the memory of an Angel'. His use of Schoenberg's twelve-tone technique to create a fresh viewpoint on traditional tonality is inspired, and the music's emotional qualities have continued to move audiences since it first appeared. The concerto was written at white heat, yet everything in it is masterly and considered, while the final fade-out of the music at the close has the heart-rending ethereality of the end of Mahler's *Song of the Earth*.

Walton's B minor concerto, on the other hand, is a true bravura work. Yet, as with the Elgar, the element of public display it contains cannot disguise an essential intimacy of tone. The many glorious melodies in which the work abounds (for Walton is one of the 20th century's finest melodists) have a sense of yearning which is personal, and the opening of the concerto is more like chamber music than a display piece. The central scherzo is a quicksilver capriccio, while the finale is governed largely by its perky main theme, though in both its soaring second subject, and in the Elgarian accompanied cadenza, the private voice comes to the fore again.

It is a matter for regret that Vaughan Williams wrote no major violin concerto. But he did contribute two excellent pieces. The *Concerto Accademico* in D minor for violin and strings has a lively, Bachian air: there is nothing academic about this vital essay in the spirit of the baroque. In *The Lark Ascending* he explores a more intimate world. The spare writing for small orchestra is wonderfully subtle in its delicate colouring, while the violin's serene roulades, vividly conjuring up the song of the lark, express something more than a picture; in its simplicity and wisdom, this is a truly spiritual work.

The concertos of Moeran and Bax have suffered neglect in recent years, but one hopes that their day will come again. Moeran's is one of the loveliest of all, and the most consistently personal; the influence of Delius cannot disguise Moeran's own personality, and this is the least overtly virtuoso of all concertos. Bax's is among his strongest major works, full of fire and brilliance as well as some of his loveliest slow tunes. Britten's early violin concerto is one of his finest abstract works, written with great imagination, and Bliss's is a characteristic exploration of his Elgarian side.

The violin concerto by Gerhard is a scintillating piece, serious but joyous in its exploitation of orchestral and solo textures. The two concertos by Rawsthorne are especially successful, the first in particular having both passion and wit.

In recent years, several British composers have written major violin concertos. Fricker's two are both craftsmanly, that by Don Banks is always musicianly, and the second of Gordon Crosse's concertos (the first is with chamber ensemble) has great originality.

Russian composers have had special success with the violin concerto form. Apart from those by Tchaikovsky, Glazunov and Prokofiev, there is the perennially fresh and popular one by Khatchaturian; while both of Shostakovich's have rare stature. The first is the more immediately impressive. Its four movements alternate between the intense, sombre moods of the opening nocturne and the third movement (a passacaglia of massive power) and the more extrovert vigour of the second and fourth movements. In 1967, twelve years after the completion of the first concerto, Shostakovich produced his second, to less public acclaim in the West. Its relative austerity may account for this, for it is as finely wrought as the earlier piece and, if a shade more withdrawn, equally moving and exciting.

Of Szymanowski's two concertos, it is the first which has become most familiar. This magically scored, exotically coloured work casts a spell over the listener. The second concerto has a more folk-like character, and a greater economy of means. It too is immensely rewarding. Mention must also be made of the Swiss master, Frank Martin. His entirely individual adaptation of twelve-tone technique to his own needs has resulted in an idiom in which the key is constantly shifting yet always has a firm tonal base. This can be perceived from the start of his violin concerto; the atmospheric, sinuous orchestral lines have an inner strength that prevents them from merely meandering. The three movements have their own distinct characters, Martin's deep emotional commitment controlled by a pure, classical balance. The same can be said of the fine, toughly argued, but always communicative second concerto of Jean Martinon.

Among American composers, Barber has written a typically tuneful work, and William Schuman's concerto, which has been twice revised, is among his most memorable works, reconciling a sweet lyricism with the hard-edged dynamism characteristic of the composer. There is, too, an exciting and highly imaginative concerto by the Argentinian, Ginastera, in which his mastery of the orchestra and original approach to concerto form are at their best. The early violin concerto of Roger Sessions is something of a curiosity, for it is almost neo-classical, written before the adoption of serial techniques that released his full potential as a composer. But if it is a curiosity, it is also a remarkably fine work.

The avant-garde have shown less interest in this genre than in some others. Penderecki's Capriccio for violin and orchestra is, however, one of his happiest pieces. Quite short, it revels in its orchestral virtuosity, provides the soloist with an exciting display piece, and has both colour and wit. Of Henze's two concertos, the first is early and largely derivative, while the second, a recent work with electronic amplification of the soloist, is music of great sonic virtuosity, if at times seemingly desperate in its trendiness.

7 VIOLA, CELLO, DOUBLE-BASS, HARP, GUITAR

(a) Viola

It is not surprising that the lion's share of music for solo strings should be taken by the violin, so much more 'public' an instrument is this than its colleagues. And there have been far fewer virtuoso soloists on the others, though cellists have emerged in considerable numbers in the 20th century. But there is still a large repertoire of fine music for viola, cello and double-bass, and in some cases major works by composers who contributed little or nothing to the violin repertoire. An example of this is Berlioz, whose *Harold in Italy* Symphony is as near to a concerto (with viola soloist) as he ever got. The

674

idea for the symphony came from Paganini, but it is a typically Berliozian design, on a vast scale. Its emotional character, for all the fury of the 'Brigands' Orgy' finale and other sections, is dreamy and lingering. The viola solo part is that of a concertante instrument rather than that of a bravura soloist, which is why Paganini refused to play the work ('too many rests', as he succinctly put it).

During the baroque, of course, viola and viola d'amore were well catered for by characteristic concertos; Telemann's viola concerto in G is a particularly fine example of the conventional work of this period at its best. But it was not until the 20th century that works of major importance arose, largely because of the persuasive advocacy of a new breed of viola soloists. Tertis and Primrose are honoured names, and so too is that of Hindemith, whose main instrument it was (though he was said to be able to play every orchestral instrument). It was Hindemith who gave the first performance of what is still the greatest of all viola concertos, by Walton.

This dates from 1929 in its original form for full orchestra; in the 1960s Walton re-scored it for slightly smaller, though still full, orchestra, adding harp and softening its outlines somewhat. It is an interesting result. The work has lost none of the bounce and athletic vitality of its quicker sections, but the new scoring enhances the warmth of its lyrical invention and sets the viola tone in a context which is more of a balance with its innately intimate sound. In both versions it is a masterpiece.

Hindemith himself wrote several viola concertos. Two of these come in his Kammermusik series – a lively work for viola, and a further, more hard-edged and elaborately contrapuntal one for viola d'amore. For viola and full orchestra he wrote his later concerto, *Der Schwanendreher* (The Swan-Turner), in which the ebullient high spirits and bold wit conjure up vividly the basic subject of a mediaeval minstrel embellishing a variety of folk-songs before the assembled company.

Bartók's viola concerto was commissioned by William Primrose, but tragically Bartók did not live to complete it; the concerto as we know it was finished by Tibor Serly from the composer's often confusing sketches; but even if, like Mozart's Requiem, it is only partially authentic, it has a convincingly Bartókian air.

Other notable viola concertos come from a variety of sources. Fricker's, also written for Primrose, is an imaginative, thoughtful piece. The American Walter Piston has written a typically serious and likeable concerto, imbued with that cool lyricism which is a hallmark of his style. Henze's *Compases para preguntas enismades*, sub-titled (more intelligibly, if no more memorably) 'Music for viola and 22 players', is a subtle exploration of the lyrical, sensuous side of his musical style. While not really a concerto, it gives the viola a true solo part. The ensemble includes harp, harpsichord, piano and a wide variety of percussion.

Outstanding sonatas for viola and piano, or viola alone, are rare. The two by Brahms, his own versions of the clarinet sonatas, are of prime importance here. Powerful sonatas have been written by Rawsthorne (one of the finest of his early works) and Iain Hamilton (another early work, in his dark, turbulent mood), while Britten's elegiac *Lachrymae*, a set of variations on a theme by Dowland, is a moving piece. Hindemith's contribution is, as might be expected, more substantial. There are several sonatas for viola and piano, of which the early, vigorous op. 11, no. 4, is often heard. He also wrote several sonatas for viola alone. Reger's three solo viola suites are late works, of greater linear and harmonic simplicity than is often the case with him.

(b) Cello

Like the viola, the cello has a private, more soulful sound than the violin, and neither is so capable as that instrument of virtuosic display. But the cello's mellowness, and its greater penetration compared to that of the viola, has often led composers to write major works for it. From the earliest periods of the concerto, the name of Leonardo Leo stands at the head of several fluent, attractive works of the 18th century, while C. P. E. Bach's A major concerto is warmly lyrical. Two concertos by Haydn are familiar. That in D major was for some time thought to be by Anton Kraft, one of Haydn's instrumentalists at Esterhazy; the C major concerto is a recent discovery. Both are enjoyable, the D major predominantly lyrical, while the C major is more brisk and lively.

The cello's highly emotive tone was bound to make a strong appeal to the romantics, and while Tchaikovsky's *Variations on a Rococo Theme* are an inventive and classically poised set, and Saint-Saëns in his concertos explored equally fastidious matters, both Schumann and Dvořák plumbed deeper emotional waters. Schumann's concerto in A minor is perhaps not as perfectly judged as his piano concerto in the same key. Its form has a tendency to sprawl. But what an ardent opening theme it has, and what eloquence there is throughout the score! Even more moving, and certainly finer from the compositional standpoint, is Dvořák's B minor concerto. Indeed, this is the first complete masterpiece in this genre, and one of his greatest works. From first to last the noble, passionate nature of the music is perfectly attuned to the sound of the cello solo, and it is set in a beautifully judged orchestral context.

The E minor concerto of Elgar stands with the Dvořák as a peak of this repertoire. Nothing reveals more clearly his superlative stature as a writer for orchestra than his skill in writing a scherzo movement which has nothing of the galumphing clumsiness which might so easily have marred a work for this medium. His lightness of touch here is masterly, but the essential heart of the work, as with his violin concerto, lies elsewhere. The very opening, with its heart-felt cry from the solo instrument, reveals the concerto's basic character. It was Elgar's last major score; after this valedictory, even tragic work, the will to create all but left him. It is music which speaks of disillusion, of the sadness of man's folly (Elgar was profoundly upset by the First World War), yet is transfigured by an innate nobility of spirit. Few other concertos strike home so directly.

Neither Delius's nor Bax's concertos achieve quite the same consummate mastery, but both include so much beautiful music that they must be retained on the edge of the repertory. Walton's concerto, 1956, is more satisfactory, full of rich colourings and perfectly balanced between orchestra and soloist. He also achieves a convincing scherzo of quicksilver brilliance, but again the heart of the work, as in so many cello concertos, is in the predominantly slow and lyrical music of the outer movements.

Two of the most powerful cello concertos are by Hindemith. The earlier, another of his Kammermusik series, has both wit and richness; while the later concerto, 1940, scored for full orchestra, is among his greatest works. The theme of the slow movement has been further immortalized by being taken as the basis for Walton's fine orchestral *Variations on a Theme of Hindemith.*

Honegger has provided a delightfully sentimental and witty concertino, and among other composers who have major works in this medium are Milhaud (with two concertos), Martinů (two), Prokofiev (two versions of the same work, and a vastly inferior concertino), Rawsthorne (a fine piece, marked by a sombre, dramatic slow movement), and Hugh Wood, whose concerto is a romantically expansive example of Schoenbergian traditions. More familiar than these is the first concerto, in E flat, of Shostakovich. (His second has been far less successful.) This reverses the by now customary approach to a cello concerto and, while it contains a memorably personal slow movement, is dominated by the driving motor-rhythms of the outer fast movements.

The avant-garde have not neglected the cello. Ligeti's concerto and Penderecki's sonata for cello and orchestra are typical examples of their individual styles, both of which depend on different types of cluster formations for their effect. These are short pieces, with little or no thematic development of the traditional kind. Instead the music decorates apparently static chord-structures and gradually changes them. The ebb and flow of sound is fascinating, as it is in the concerto by Lutoslawski, written for Rostropovich. Here the degree of freedom afforded the players by the composer is, as usual with him, carefully controlled, so that a genuine sense of growth and progress can be perceived. The same player has inspired Britten to write a symphony for cello and orchestra, and three unaccompanied suites.

These latter take up once again the challenge of the solo suite set by Bach, whose violin works have already been discussed. Bach's set of six solo cello suites maintain the same inspired standard, though unlike the violin works they are consistently sets of dance movements, and do not include any of the supreme contrapuntal writing of the violin sonatas or the Chaconne of the D minor partita. But they are just as memorable and as engrossing. The first of Britten's three solo suites is the most Bachian in its scope and intensity, though the remainder are equally resourceful and idiomatic.

Between these two composers come a succession of fine works for cello and piano. Beethoven's five sonatas range from the two op. 5 sonatas, in which the cello is relegated to a subsidiary role, to the far more challenging pair of sonatas, op. 102. Here the fugal technique of his late works, and his innate sense of drama are powerfully expressed. But the most popular sonata is the third, in A major, op. 69, which has a more consistently lyrical mode of expression.

The two sonatas of Mendelssohn are often dismissed as merely fluent, yet like those of the mature Beethoven, if less strikingly, they have a real strength of purpose. Brahms also wrote two sonatas. The earlier, in E minor, is a gritty piece, with some superb contrapuntal writing; in the later F major sonata he achieves some of his most glorious melodies, and the tone of the work as a whole is more lyrical and expansive.

In Debussy's sonata in D minor we have one of the most subtle and masterly of all cello works. In it he deliberately sets out to recreate the spirit of the Commedia dell' Arte, and the ghostly humour, moments of lyrical expansion, and superb formal grasp place this among his masterpieces, despite its brevity. Kodály was particularly attracted to the cello, and in his unaccompanied sonata, op. 8, he achieved a Bachian strength. His sonata for cello and piano, op. 4, is pleasant, but not nearly so remarkable.

The single sonata of Delius is more striking, for in its brief span it encompasses elements of both a sonata-form movement and an over-all sonata shape. The seemingly uninterrupted flow of lovely tunes is cunningly organized. Equally cunning is Rachmaninov's G minor sonata, built on a large, four-movement scale and replete with gorgeous melodies. It dates from his recovery from a nervous break-down, like the second piano concerto, and shares that work's lyricism and brilliant colouring.

It was perhaps inevitable that Hindemith should write both for cello and piano (sonatas, and a delightfully light-hearted set of variations on 'A Frog he would a-wooing go') and for solo cello. His unaccompanied sonata, op. 25 no. 3, is a commanding achievement, in which his ability to hold the listener's attention to a single line of music for some length of time is never better shown. Ireland, Bax and Moeran have all written fine cello and piano sonatas, but in the British repertoire Rawsthorne's concise but tremendously varied sonata perhaps takes pride of place. Its cyclic form is perfectly judged, and each movement is characterized by a memorable main theme.

Two important works have been produced by American com-posers. Barber's early sonata is attractively tuneful, gratefully written for both instruments, while Elliott Carter's is one of the most im-pressive of modern sonatas. His approach, rather than trying to in-tegrate the instruments or conceal their differences, deliberately stresses the independence of their natures. Thus the cello writing is predominantly noble and lyrical; that of the piano more percussive and colouristic. The sonorous interplay of the instruments, rhythmic freedom and vitality of line make this the work of a master.

Both Prokofiev and Shostakovich have written admirable cello sonatas, the latter's being especially fine. Written in 1934, and pro-phetic in style of the forthcoming Fifth Symphony, it contrasts an elegiac lyricism with sharp wit and vigour. Prokofiev's sonata, op. 119, dates from 1949, and is a typical product of his late years – simple and straightforward in style, with much invention of balletic grace.

Outside the concerto sphere, few of the more advanced composers have shown interest in the cello. Webern's *Three Little Pieces*, op.

11 are miracles of his condensed, polished art; while the solo sonata of Bernd Alois Zimmermann is a remarkable exploitation of the artistry of Siegfried Palm, the cellist who is to the avant-garde what Casals was to earlier generations in opening up to audiences and composers the possibilities of the instrument.

(c) Double-bass

The double-bass must be the hardest instrument of all for a composer to feature in a solo capacity, for apart from the difficulties of balancing its gruff tone satisfactorily with other instruments, the huge stretches from one note to the next make virtuosity uncommon if not impossible. Yet Dittersdorf wrote an E major concerto and Bottesini an entertaining Grand Duo for violin, double-bass and orchestra. One of Haydn's many lost works is a double-bass concerto, and there is always the possibility that it will turn up one day! In more recent times, the Russian conductor (and, in his early days, bassist) Koussevitzky wrote a concerto for the instrument, and so has Henze. A number of American and British composers have very recently written pieces for bass and piano, solo bass, or two basses together, and the repertoire for the instrument is growing all the time.

(d) Harp

Harp concertos are less common than one might suppose, though the difficulties of balancing this far-from-penetrating instrument in a solo capacity are considerable. There are several attractive concertos from the early classics, including a number by Albrechtsberger (as well as a partita in F for harp and orchestra) and a mellifluous one in G by Wagenseil. Some of Handel's organ concertos, op. 4, have been arranged for harp. The concerto in A by Dittersdorf is only attributed to this composer, but Eichner's concertos are original, as is the famous C major concerto (1795) by Boïeldieu.

In more recent times many composers have produced either concertos or solo works with orchestra. The mild, romantic tone of Glinka's concerto belies its late composition (1938), but though pleasant, it is hardly outstanding even in his uneven output. It is not surprising that French composers, whose treatment of the harp within the orchestra is so superb, should have been attracted to it as a solo instrument. Saint-Saëns wrote his *Morceau de Concert* for harp and orchestra in 1919, towards the end of his career, and it is really, despite its modest title, a four-movement concertino, classical to a degree rare even in his style. This enjoyable piece is less familiar than the two dances by Debussy, *Danse Sacrée et Danse Profane*. In these enchanting, mature works the harp is treated as a concertante soloist rather than given opportunity for bravura display, and the grave, poised tone of the music places them high in Debussy's output.

The Spaniard Rodrigo has graced the repertoire with a lilting *Concert-Serenade* (really another concertino in form) and more recently a harp version of his popular guitar *Concierto de Aranjuez*. There is a strong Spanish element in the music of Ginastera, whose harp concerto pulsates with life, energy and colour.

But possibly the two finest harp concertos are by modern Welsh composers. Hoddinott's, written in 1958 and rescored a decade later to include more percussion, is subtly coloured, harmonically rich and organized with typical tautness and economy. William Mathias's concerto, written in 1970 for Osian Ellis, is simpler in style. The outer movements are lyrical and joyous, while the central slow movement has claims to be the finest, most deeply felt single movement yet written for harp. Mathias's *Three Improvisations* are an essential part of the repertoire for harp alone, too, and Hoddinott has also contributed an effective, brief sonata.

The vast majority of pieces performed by solo harpists, however, tend to be transcriptions from either keyboard or guitar literature, and this is especially true of the baroque and classical periods. Nevertheless, the 18th-century Welsh composer John Parry's sonata in D is original, and testifies to the great tradition of Welsh harp-playing, as well as to the tradition of 'Penillion' singing (the singer accompanying himself or herself on the Welsh harp).

French composers again contributed a number of striking works for harp alone during the 19th and 20th centuries. Among these, Fauré's and Roussel's Impromptus, and Saint-Saëns's *Fantaisie* are outstanding. Also significant is Hindemith's limpid, graceful sonata; while the charming Intermezzo from Britten's *Ceremony of Carols* is often taken out of context and used successfully as a concert solo.

(e) Guitar

The guitar and its ancestors the mandoline and the lute are well served by baroque composers and moderns for concertos. Those of Vivaldi, Giuliani, and (a real curiosity) Hummel's Mandoline Concerto, are in the repertoire of most virtuosi. In the 20th century a number of composers have written outstanding works. Villa-Lobos, in both his concerto and his large number of pieces for guitar alone; Rodrigo, whose *Concierto de Aranjuez* has achieved the status of a classic, and whose *Fantasia para un Gentilhombre* is not much less popular; Stephen Dodgson, with two concertos, and a series of beautifully idiomatic solo works; and Berkeley, with a fine recent concertino and a string of solo pieces, are among the most notable exponents of the instrument.

Among less frequent composers for the guitar, Malcolm Arnold has produced a searching concerto; written in memory of the jazz guitarist, Django Reinhardt, it has an especially moving slow movement. The concertos of Castelnuovo-Tedesco, Ponce, Previn and Richard Rodney Bennett (the latter a particularly inventive piece) are notable, inspired in many cases by the playing of virtuosi such as Julian Bream, John Williams, and the immortal Segovia, while the great German guitarist Siegfried Behrend has performed an invaluable service in inspiring the more advanced composers to write for him; the Korean, Isang Yun, the Pole, Penderecki (whose imaginative solo *Capriccio for Siegfried Behrend* is one of his most appealing works), and many German composers have written music which exploits admirably these new developments in guitar technique.

8 WIND INSTRUMENTS

(a) Flute

It is interesting to note the extent to which the wind instruments, both wood and brass, have been well represented by a large amount of solo music in the 17th, 18th, and 20th centuries, but hardly at all in the 19th. Undoubtedly one of the main reasons for this was the rise of soloistic virtuosity during the romantic era. Apart from being by their very nature the solo instruments most likely to cope with music of immense difficulty, the piano and violin also provided more of a performance spectacle than any others.

But in earlier years all the wind instruments were given some important work to do, and the flute was particularly well favoured, especially during the late baroque and early classical periods, along with its relatives, the recorder and the piccolo. Among Vivaldi's hundreds of concertos there are many for flute, piccolo or recorder, for instance, and the contribution of Frederick the Great's flute-teacher, Quantz, is of paramount importance; for although he wrote a good deal of other music, his output is dominated by over 300 concertos for one or two flutes, as well as by a famous treatise on flute-playing. Nowadays few of the concertos are heard, though those that are reveal an elegant, craftsmanly talent. But the influence of Quantz, and Frederick himself (no mean composer for the flute) spread far and wide.

The immensely prolific Telemann wrote several concertos, some for solo and some with other instruments; there are, for example, concertos in E for flute, oboe d'amore, violin and strings, and in F for recorder, bassoon and strings. Telemann's most famous flute work, however, is surely the great Suite in A minor for flute and strings, today often performed by recorder instead of flute, throughout which his inspiration is at its finest; full of superbly shaped melodies and vital rhythmic invention, it remains one of the glories of the flautist's repertoire.

Apart from important flute parts in his Brandenburg concertos and suites (notably the second suite, in B minor), J. S. Bach refrained from flute concertos, but his son, Carl Philipp Emanuel wrote several, including two fine dramatic works in D minor, one of his favourite keys. By its very nature, the flute was not an instrument easily capable of expressing great passions or turbulence; even C. P. E. Bach was forced to express his innate emotionalism more overtly elsewhere. It is hardly surprising, therefore, that Mozart's two concertos should be amiable, but lesser, works in his canon. They were commissioned by a Dutch amateur, De Jean, and though no. 1 in G, K 313, was brand new, for no. 2 in D, K 314, Mozart reworked an earlier oboe concerto. This was a thorough recomposition, not merely an arrangement, with the solo part rewritten in thoroughly idiomatic terms for the flute, but still De Jean must have known about the circumstances, since he refused to pay Mozart's full fee! The flute concerto in D attributed to Haydn for many years has now been re-attributed to Hoffmeister; this too is an elegant, enjoyable work, which is still occasionally heard.

In the 20th century there has been a renascence in writing for the flute, as is the case with all the wind instruments. The first important concerto of this era remains among the most remarkable, that written in 1926 by Nielsen. Though composed after the onset of the heart disease which was to kill him, and after the Sixth Symphony in which he expressed a vein of bitterness and tragedy unique in his output, there is little trace of these things in the music, which explores a mood of relaxed, amiable wit, tempered with a keen edge of irony. Characteristically the work is a search for the right key, but in this instance it is the bumbling, clumsy trombone who beats the flute to it, while the soloist is still wandering in rather distraught fashion. The comfortable chortling of the trombone at the close epitomizes the charm of a piece which, though as tautly written as any by Nielsen, impresses most by its human sense of friendliness.

Since then many composers have written for flute and orchestra. The French composers Ibert and Barraud have contributed notably to the repertoire, and Frank Martin's *Ballade* is particularly successful. In Britain, Sir Lennox Berkeley has written concertinos for both flute and recorder, while of Malcolm Arnold's two flute concertos, the first is especially delightful, full of wit and poise.

In more recent years, new developments in flute-playing, led by the great Italian flautist Gazzelloni, have produced a great interest among avant-garde composers in exploiting these new resources. The flute concerto of Petrassi is a major work, utilizing the orchestra with great imagination; and such pieces as Nono's *Y su sangre dah vieni cantando* for flute, strings and percussion, and Fukushima's *Hi-kyo* for alto flute, piano, strings and percussion, treat the instrument in solo fashion, with a more chamber-like texture overall. The Nono, though often performed as a separate item, forms part of his triptych *Epitaph for Garcia Lorca*, and in it gentle washes of string and cymbal sound provide a soft background for the delicate display of flute sonority. The Fukushima, one of his many works featuring solo flute, has a similarly fragile texture, using silences and pauses with creative judgment.

One of the most remarkable pieces of the post-war period is Boulez's early sonatine for flute and piano. Of phenomenal difficulty, and written in a toughly argued post-Webern style, it is an astonishing *tour de force* of virtuosity (both compositional and interpretative) and textural variety.

The history of flute sonatas is similar. There are many sets from the pens of composers such as Leclair and the two Bachs, J. S. and C. P. E., and apart from isolated pieces there is then a gap until the 20th century is reached. Then, however, there are many significant works. Hindemith, who has written at least one sonata for almost every conceivable instrument, has contributed a particularly charming one to the flute repertoire. Martinů's first sonata is an important, substantial work in three large-scale movements, music in which this composer's often uneven inspiration is sustained at its finest. The Dutch composer Pijper has contributed a beautiful sonata, and Messiaen's short *Le Merle Noire* for flute and piano, one of his explorations of bird-song, is a particularly fine concert piece. Nicholas Maw's sonatina, an early but engaging piece; *Three Episodes* for flute and piano by the Australian Don Banks, communicative despite its economy; Poulenc's haunting late sonata – all these have an important place.

There are, too, several outstanding pieces for flute solo, of which three, Debussy's *Syrinx*, Honegger's *Danse de la Chèvre* (Dance of the Goat), and Varèse's *Density 21·5* (the density of platinum, the work being written for a new platinum flute) exploit the instrument's lower register especially. Berio's *Sequenza V*, one of a series for different solo instruments, is a remarkable piece in which avant-garde techniques of performance and composition are handled with great assurance to positively dramatic effect.

(b) Oboe

The extraordinary richness of the early concerto repertoire opened to us by recordings and the increase of chamber orchestral concerts, is nowhere more clearly shown than in the case of the oboe. Vivaldi, inevitably, and Telemann contributed fine concertos, as did Leclair, and in his three concertos published in 1740, Handel. These last are especially beloved of oboists, and they represent Handel's concerto style at perhaps its purest and most mellifluous.

Less often performed, but a magnificent work, is C. P. E. Bach's E flat concerto, Wq 165; this contains a deeply expressive slow movement, as well as faster movements of great dramatic impetus. Mozart's oboe concerto in C, K 314, is, as previously mentioned, the earlier version of his charming, lightweight second flute concerto. Though J. S. Bach wrote no straightforward oboe concerto as such, his oboe d'amore concerto in A is a fine vigorous work. With the advent of the 19th century, of course, the output of oboe concertos more or less dried up, though from the early years of the century come two surprises by Italian composers best known for their operas. Both Bellini's concertino in E flat for oboe and Donizetti's concertino in G for cor anglais have a melodic charm which continues to appeal to performers and players.

But it was not until the advent of such great 20th-century soloists as, above all, Léon Goossens that the oboe was once again considered as a soloist. Vaughan Williams wrote a charming, if minor, concerto for this instrument, and among many other British works the concertos by Malcolm Arnold and by Rawsthorne demand mention; all these are with string orchestra.

Richard Strauss's oboe concerto, written in that glorious Indian summer of his during the 1940s, uses a classical orchestra, and breathes a distinctly Mozartian air. Tougher music comes in

Martinů's lively concerto, again with small orchestra which includes a harpsichord, and in the busy concerto of the American, Benjamin Lees. Few composers have dared to pit the tone of the solo oboe against a full orchestra, but in recent years Maderna's three concertos have to some extent done this, and the distinguished oboist Heinz Holliger, who has extended the frontiers of oboe technique, has composed the striking *Siebengesang*, in which the oboe is sometimes amplified electronically, and the orchestra, of full size, includes a large percussion section; a women's chorus is also employed. The power and fascination of this work is tremendous, with an immense range of textures, from full ensembles to sections for small chamber groups.

Although the romantic era produced a few works for oboe and piano, notably Schumann's *Three Romances*, op. 94, and Nielsen's early but delightful *Two Fantasy Pieces*, op. 2, it is again the 20th century that has contributed most significantly to the genre. Hindemith's sonatas for oboe and for cor anglais are remarkable, particularly the latter, with its darker harmonic colouring, while Poulenc's moving sonata, completed shortly before his own death, is an eloquent tribute to the memory of Prokofiev. The sonatine of Berkeley is typically Gallic in style, with a cool freshness of expression. Few avant-garde pieces have made much of a mark, though Berio's *Sequenza VII*, written for Holliger, is resourceful. Works for oboe alone remain a rarity, though Britten's *Six Metamorphoses after Ovid* are frequently heard.

(c) Clarinet

The later development of the clarinet means that there is no baroque music for solo clarinet, but with Mozart we suddenly acquire three masterpieces, all written towards the end of his life: the trio in E flat, the quintet in A, and the concerto in A. Like the others, the concerto, K 622, was written for Anton Stadler, and it was one of his last completed compositions. It is a work of supreme resignation, imbued with heart-rending simplicity of expression and line. In its acute judgment of solo and orchestral texture, its extraordinary combination of major key serenity with ineffable sadness, and its formal perfection, it remains one of the most completely personal utterances of its composer. Not until Nielsen, in 1928, was the clarinet to receive another concerto of such depth.

In the intervening years, however, quite a large number of major works were written, for the clarinet, luckier than most wind instruments during the 19th century, found several virtuoso performers able to encourage composers to write for them. Mühlfeld was one; it was for him that Brahms, like Mozart and Nielsen nearing the close of his life, composed his trio, quintet and the two magnificent sonatas of op. 120. Earlier than this, Spohr had written four, and Weber two clarinet concertos, full of florid solo writing, and a good deal of early romantic charm. The same can be said of the F minor concerto of the Finnish composer Crusell.

Nielsen's concerto, however, strikes much deeper. It is more irascible and forceful than his flute concerto, and a tougher piece for the listener, though in the end the humanity of the composer's character wins through. In its handling of the volatile clarinet part, and in its orchestration (with a side-drum recalling the astonishing writing for this instrument in the Fifth Symphony), and formal subtlety, playing without a break, it is a remarkable achievement; few wind concertos are as genuinely moving as this. Lighter in tone, but thoroughly inspired, is the concerto of Aaron Copland, written in 1948 with orchestra of strings, piano and harp. This is perhaps the apotheosis of Copland's twin fascinations with jazz and American folk-music. On a smaller scale, Debussy's rhapsody for clarinet and orchestra, written as a competition test-piece, is resourceful and enjoyable, without being in any way very striking.

A remarkable work of more recent date is the concerto by Thea Musgrave, in which the soloist is required to move about the platform, or even direct groups of the orchestra at times. It is exciting and dramatic, and exploits the entire range of the clarinet.

Works for clarinet alone are seldom found; Stravinsky's Three Pieces remain perhaps the only familiar contribution to this part of the repertoire. But both 19th and 20th centuries are rich in duos for clarinet and piano. Weber's Duo Concertante in E flat and his *Variations on a theme from Silvana* are invigorating virtuoso pieces, and Schumann's three *Fantasiestücke*, op. 73, with the two Brahms sonatas, occupy a prime place in the repertoire. Nearer to our time, Hindemith's sonata, a mellow work, and Poulenc's witty, pungent sonata are strikingly successful. Many other composers have contributed smaller works; Hoddinott's imaginative sonata, Honegger's entertaining sonatine, and Hamilton's dark, richly worked sonata stand high in any list.

(d) Bassoon

The bassoon is widely regarded as the buffoon of the wind family, yet composers as different as Haydn and Rachmaninov have demonstrated in their orchestral scores that it is capable of great expressiveness. Nevertheless, by far the greatest contribution to the bassoon concerto literature has been by composers of the baroque and early classical periods. Often enough the works have been for 'bassoon or cello', as in Vivaldi's E minor concerto, Pincherle 137, and many of them are for bassoon with another solo instrument or instruments; but there are still a large number of perfectly respectable concertos for the bassoon itself. Though some of these are performed from time to time, few have established for themselves a strong place in listeners' affections. Mozart's, K 191, is perhaps the only one, though it is a conventional, if likeable, piece. One wonders in passing what his several lost bassoon concertos were like. A curiosity is Weber's *Andante and Hungarian Rondo*, written in 1813 when he was twenty-seven.

Even in our imaginative 20th century, the bassoon has been somewhat neglected as a solo instrument. Gordon Jacob and Eric Fogg have both produced elegant, entertaining concertos for bassoon, and in his Duet Concertino for clarinet, bassoon, strings and harp (1947), a witty, charming work, Richard Strauss composed one of the most substantial, sympathetic contributions to the bassoon repertoire, yet all these seem to be almost totally neglected at present.

(e) Horn

Of all wind instruments the horn has perhaps the most romantic appeal, and its history is a curious one. Starting out as a simple, straight piece of tube, on which the notes of the harmonic series were the only ones available, it proceeded through several clear stages of evolution: it was curved round, to give the shape we know today; a bell was added to improve the tone, and it also enabled players, by altering the position of their hand inside the bell, to obtain some of the notes hitherto unavailable. Crooks (pieces of coiled tubing of different lengths to be inserted between mouthpiece and instrument) were invented, to give different sets of harmonics (thus enabling the player by changing the crook to change the key in which he was able to play), and finally valves were added to do the work of the cumbersome crooks instantly, thus enabling the player to revel in a completely chromatic instrument.

The valves, however, came after the classical era, so the enormous horn repertoire of previous years was limited, in the choice of notes used, to those obtainable from the harmonic series of the instrument plus those intermediate notes achieved by the movement of the hand in the bell. The Mozart concertos were played in this way; the quicker music, with its scalic passages being limited mainly to the upper octave, would have involved only a small amount of flapping about with the hand in the bell; but the sound in the slower passages would not have been entirely consistent, for notes obtained in this way have a more constricted air than those made with the bell open.

Nevertheless there is an immense amount of music for the horn from the baroque and classical era. Often the concertos are for two horns; Telemann and Handel wrote masterpieces in this medium. But there are many for one horn alone. The sonatas for horn and strings of Cherubini are attractive, as is the concerto of Leopold Mozart, Wolfgang's father. Haydn's two concertos contain some fine things, especially the deeply moving slow movement of no. 2. But most familiar are the four concertos and the separate *Concert Rondo*, K 371, by Mozart. The earliest of these is the *Concert Rondo*, which was presumably intended, like the four concertos, for Mozart's horn-playing friend, Leutgeb, and very likely formed the first movement of a concerto. At any rate, in its $\frac{2}{4}$ motion it is unlike the finales of the complete concertos, which invariably pursue the $\frac{6}{8}$ 'hunting rondo' style which is such an inevitable and essential part of the horn's image.

The concertos, especially the third and fourth, have become justly popular, and are still among the handful of wind concertos that can actually fill a hall, if the soloist is a virtuoso such as Barry Tuckwell, Ifor James, Alan Civil or the late Dennis Brain. Indeed, in recent years the horn has been fortunate in having so many famous soloists – more perhaps than any other wind instrument – the majority of whom seem to be British.

One of the few horn-players whose name still holds meaning, between the ages of Leutgeb and of the Brains, father and son, is that of Franz Strauss, Wagner's favourite horn-player and father of the famous Richard. Franz Strauss was himself a good composer; his horn concerto, op. 8, is as fine a piece of sympathetic romantic writing as the equally virtuosic concertino by Weber. But undoubtedly we owe to his influence, and the knowledge of the horn gained during his childhood years, the two magnificent concertos by Richard Strauss. The first, written in 1882–83, is an early work, but every bar is stamped with the composer's personality. The second concerto,

1942, comes from the other end of Strauss's career, and again it is lively and rich, with that degree of extra clarity typical of his late music; it ends with what must be the apotheosis of the 'hunting rondo' finale.

The concerto (1950) by Hindemith, was written for Dennis Brain, and in the opinion of many horn-players is the finest yet written for the instrument. Certainly it is one of his greatest works. In recent years both Don Banks and Thea Musgrave have produced fine horn concertos; that of Banks is tightly written, with an extraordinary sense of orchestral colouring, while Musgrave explores the dramatic element of musical performance to great effect.

The repertoire of horn and piano duos is rich, too. Beethoven's early, Haydnesque sonata in F is delightful, though hardly as powerful as his later years would have made it. Among romantic works is Schumann's glorious *Adagio and Allegro*, which, though separate, has the feeling and scope of a sonata. Hindemith, who gave of his best to this instrument, wrote two sonatas, one in F for horn and piano (a powerful, heavy work) and one in E flat for alto-horn and piano. The latter, more economical in style, but no less brilliant or varied, is unusual in that after the third movement, the players declaim a poem by the composer before going on to the finale.

Poulenc's *Elégie*, written in memory of Dennis Brain, is one of his most touching pieces, while the fine, Hindemithian sonata of the Dane, Niels Viggo Bentzon, the fascinating, dialogue-like *Music for Horn and Piano* of Thea Musgrave, and the dark, hard-edged *Sonata Notturna* of Iain Hamilton stand out as especially significant.

There are, too, many lighter or shorter works. Nielsen's *Canto Serioso* ranges widely in its small span, and French composers in particular have produced many entertaining pieces, such as Bozza's *En Forêt* and Dukas's fine *Villanelle*.

(f) Trumpet, trombone, tuba, harmonica

Above all other instruments the trumpet was perhaps best served by composers of the baroque. With its ringing tones, so suited to the open-air character of much of their faster music, it inspired them to much of their most vigorous work. There are innumerable concertos for trumpet, or sonatas for trumpet and strings, or works for more than one trumpet by composers of that era. Albinoni, Telemann, Torelli, Giovanni Gabrieli, Loeillet, and many others contributed with resounding success. So too did British composers, for there are fine pieces by composers like Richard Mudge, Capel Bond, Jeremiah Clarke and of course Henry Purcell.

As music became more personal, more emotional in nature, so the output of significant works for trumpet dropped considerably. The earliest classical composers, men like Leopold Mozart, Michael Haydn and of course the great Joseph Haydn himself, wrote fine concertos; Joseph Haydn's indeed remains one of the most popular trumpet concertos, though hardly striking in the context of his output. Hummel's concerto in E flat, too, is often heard today, a tuneful exercise by a composer who anticipated the high virtuosity of the romantic age.

In more recent years few composers have written substantial trumpet concertos, and as far as I know no composer has risen to the challenge and produced one of genuine weight and importance. Jolivet's concertos are predominantly light in tone, far removed from the solemnity of his more important works. There are a number of excellent concertos by composers such as Grace Williams, Horovitz and Sauguet. There is only a limited repertoire for trumpet and piano, too, though Hindemith's sonata (less memorable than those for horn) and the early sonata of Peter Maxwell Davies stand out for their basic seriousness of approach.

Inevitably the trombone has been less well served. Indeed trombone concertos are a genuine rarity, though two demand attention. The concerto in E flat by Wagenseil (Maria Theresa's court composer for over thirty years from 1741) is a charmingly melodic piece; Rimsky-Korsakov's concerto is typically tuneful, though hardly outstanding, and remarkable above all for being one of the astonishingly few wind concertos by Russian composers.

It would be predictable that if the trombone is so poorly served, the tuba hardly enters into contention at all; yet it has been granted one masterpiece, the tuba concerto by Vaughan Williams. A relaxed, marvellously inspired product of his fluent old age, this work reveals expressive potentialities of the instrument with great resource.

One more wind instrument remains to be mentioned, the harmonica. Thanks largely to the advocacy of Larry Adler, this instrument, hitherto largely associated with light music, has inspired several composers to write for it. The *Romance* by Vaughan Williams, another product of his old age, is a heart-easing miniature; Milhaud's suite for harmonica and orchestra is also delightful and short, while Malcolm Arnold's concerto, brief though it is, charms our ears with its wit.

One of the most striking developments during the 20th century has been the sustained extension of percussion, both in terms of the instruments used and the methods of playing them. This naturally has played an important part in the attainment of an astonishing range of orchestral sonorities, but the percussion themselves have also been used on occasions in a solo capacity. Milhaud's ballet *La Création du Monde* is a chamber score which treats all the instruments including the percussion in a concertante manner, and his percussion concerto is a virtuoso display for both composer and performer. Unlike his concertos for vibraphone and marimba, it has remained in the repertoire. Another marimba concerto, by Paul Creston, is occasionally heard.

There are a few works for solo timpani; a sonata by the Welsh composer Daniel Jones, and more recently a set of Studies by Elliott Carter reveal in their different ways extraordinary imagination.

But the majority of percussion pieces have been written for one or two players utilizing a variety of instruments. American composers have led the way in this field. Varèse's *Ionisation* (1931) is for thirteen players confronting an enormous battery of instruments; music of urban civilization, this is a strongly architectural work which never loses its hypnotic fascination for the listener. The *Canticles* of Lou Harrison, and the many works by Harry Partch (often using instruments of his own invention) inhabit a more withdrawn, almost ethereal world.

John Cage has explored percussion sonorities extensively, both in works for percussion instruments, and in his music for prepared piano (which surely comes under this instrumental heading). The prepared piano was his invention; it entails placing objects such as screws, pieces of wood, rubber or glass between the strings of the piano, and in his sonatas and interludes the sonorities obtained enhance the inward-looking character of the music.

Further outstanding contributions to percussion literature have in recent years been inspired by the virtuosity of the young Japanese performer Stomu Yamash'ta, for whom works have been written by, among others, Henze, Takemitsu and Peter Maxwell Davies. The latter's *Turris Campanarum Sonantium* (Bell-Tower) is a large-scale piece, testifying to the obsession with bell-sounds (and bell-ringing techniques) that was an important element in Davies's work at one time, and it is an outstandingly successful exploitation of these sonorities. Yamash'ta's art is almost as much choreographic as instrumental, and his own compositions, of a free, improvisatory character, are as much to be seen as heard. The element of drama in performance which is currently occupying the minds of many composers here reaches the status of a new kind of music theatre. Stockhausen's *Zyklus* is a notably successful example and has already attained the status of a classic. Here the element of drama is important in the music, and though it is an exciting work to see in performance, it is equally satisfying to listen to; in its varied and often subtle exploration of this medium, it remains perhaps the most notable work for percussion so far produced.

10 CONCERTOS FOR MORE THAN ONE INSTRUMENT

The great Italian tradition of concertos for two or more violins (think of Vivaldi's great concerto in B minor for four violins) and the baroque tradition of the concerto grosso have both been sustained, or transformed from recognizable roots. During the late baroque, the Sinfonia Concertante became a significant form. Its element was an extension of the concerto grosso principle, in that a number of instruments took a primary role without achieving quite the dominating status of the virtuoso. This generalization has exceptions, of course, for example, Mozart's marvellous Sinfonia Concertante in E flat, K 364, for violin, viola and orchestra is really a particularly fine Mozart concerto with two genuine soloists instead of the usual one. It is a near neighbour, chronologically speaking, of his two-piano concerto, and it shares that work's nobility, but with an added depth of feeling, or pathos, in the beautiful slow movement.

His C major concerto for flute and harp, K 299, is an enchanting piece, but by no means as searching. Both Mozart and Haydn wrote a further outstanding example of the Sinfonia Concertante, Mozart's (in E flat, K 297b) for clarinet, oboe, bassoon and horn being immensely satisfying, while Haydn's (in B flat, for oboe, bassoon, violin and cello) is one of his most richly worked concertos. Another of Haydn's most rewarding concertos is that in F, for violin, piano and orchestra, a substantial work, with a nobly expressive largo movement.

Beethoven's triple concerto, for violin, cello and piano, is one of his least memorable creations, largely because the piano writing is surprisingly unimaginative and because although some of the themes are fine, there is little of the concentrated development and majestic interplay that we expect from him. Brahms's double concerto in A minor, for violin and cello, however, is a magnificent piece. Built on large-scale proportions, it has a powerful sense of suppressed energy, even in the slow movement, with its singing themes. Brahms was more successful than Beethoven in solving the problem of balancing these solo instruments against the full orchestra, and though there are times when the violin and cello have to struggle to penetrate the texture, the sense of striving is an essential part of the music's impact.

Schumann's *Concert Piece* for four horns and orchestra is the quintessence of romanticism: the bounding impetuosity of the opening, in which the four horns are used as a virtuoso ensemble, sweeps the music irresistibly forward, and throughout its three movements a mood of ebullient romantic ardour is maintained. The idea of using a solo ensemble rather than a number of separate soloists with different identities is a rare one. More usual is the approach of Delius, whose beautiful double concerto for violin, cello and orchestra is far removed from Brahmsian rhetoric.

Among the many 20th-century revivals of concerto grosso form (as in Bloch's Concerto Grosso no. 1, where string orchestra is added to by an important piano part) two works by Frank Martin stand out. Both his concerto for seven wind instruments, timpani, percussion and strings, and the more familiar *Petite Symphonie Concertante* for harp, harpsichord, piano and double string orchestra are masterly in their exploitation of striking sonorities as well as their typical restraint of expression. The *Petite Symphonie Concertante* has well earned its popularity, for its concision does not cramp Martin's slightly acidulous lyricism, and from start to finish it is an exciting piece.

Martinů's deeply moving double concerto for double string orchestra with piano and timpani gives the piano especially a genuinely concertante role, so that it is sometimes part of the ensemble and sometimes spotlit as a soloist. Written under the shadow of the Second World War, the intense slow movement leaves no doubt about the composer's compassion.

More recently, Elliott Carter's double concerto for harpsichord and piano with two chamber orchestras (including a fair amount of percussion) concerns itself with the characters of each instrument; a highly complex musical dialogue is developed, with a glittering, flickering brilliance all of its own.

Book 8

An Essay on Listening and Performance
by Eric Blom

Listening and Performance Now
by David Atherton

Of performance in general and of conducting in particular

And now, what does all this reading about various aspects of music amount to for those who have sought enlightenment from this volume? The question is sure to be asked, for nobody can go on accumulating knowledge merely for the sake of keeping it in cold storage. The possession of facts means a craving for their application, even if only negative or amateurish, and I take my task to be, in this final summing-up, to give a series of indications to those who listen to music of how they may hear it to the utmost possible advantage, though without any professional insight on the one hand or professional detachment on the other.

I take it for granted that readers of this volume are all, in some way or another, listeners to music, and if any by some mischance are not, they will be people worth converting, or they would have no use for these pages at all. I shall therefore as a matter of course address those who have at least a mind to listen. How they do it is of no consequence to me, though I hope it will be to them by the time they have come to the end of this section. Every form of listening has its merits and its problems, and I can do no better than begin at once to deal with each in succession. As there can be no listening without performance, I shall have to discuss that too; but as this is not a book for executive musicians nearly so much as for their audiences, the former's problems will never be touched upon here without reference to those of the latter.

Concert performance must come first. Despite the gramophone and the radio it is still of the utmost importance; indeed more so than ever, precisely because of these inventions, as will be seen later. No doubt the most vital concerts nowadays – it was not always so – are the orchestral ones, not only in London, where several orchestras give extended series all through the winter season, but also in some of the larger provincial towns.[1] Symphony concerts without a soloist were unthinkable until not long ago; now it is perfectly possible, thanks mainly to a vast improvement in the standard of orchestral playing, to give a whole programme without the assistance of any executive artist apart from the members of the band and the conductor.

It is true that the latter is often himself the star performer, which

[1] Though I make conditions in England the basis of my discussion, much of it will, I think, be capable of a wider application.

can on occasion be extremely annoying. A conductor like Sir Thomas Beecham without the genius of that supreme master of the orchestra would be a constant irritation. Beecham would do no music he felt to be uncongenial to him – to which one must add that he continued to enlarge the range of his sympathies; he conducted conspicuously and with some mannerisms that seemed superfluous; he sometimes exaggerated a tempo either on the slow or on the fast side; occasionally he overpointed music that should have been kept quite simple; in short, he had his little perversities which were saved, which indeed could become fascinating, only because after all one knew from the intoxicating beauty of his musical shaping and phrasing that he was passionately interested in and in love with music as an art. He cultivated it as someone else might cultivate a vineyard that has the twofold value of growing an exquisite vintage and of being a precious family heirloom. Thus, in spite of occasional eccentricities, he compelled one to listen to music, not to watch him. So did Toscanini, who could distil the very essence of a composer's meaning from the orchestra. Many other great conductors could be mentioned, some as all-round masters, some as specialists, but they must be left to speak for themselves in music.

To watch the conductor is dangerous, unless we have trained ourselves very carefully to be sure of listening to the music intently at the same time, which is not a natural thing to do or an easy thing to achieve. It is perfectly possible, unfortunately, to take the interpretation from the sight of a conductor who has the gift of gesture, instead of from the sound of the music. I remember a performance of Tchaikovsky's Fifth Symphony a good many years ago during which I wished the conductor, no other than Koussevitzky, had been placed behind a screen, for I felt certain that a stone-deaf man could have seen from his extremely telling antics exactly what the work was all about. But as stone-deaf people do not as a rule frequent concerts, the danger of Koussevitzky's method (which I found to have become much modified at a later performance of his of the same work, though the musical effect remained telling as ever) was greater than its advantages. The music was splendidly done; the trouble was that it was not at all necessary to listen to it, and I am certain that many people in the audience were so captivated by the conductor's extremely fine histrionic display that they really did not listen.

What is infinitely worse, of course, is to be engrossed by the sight of a conductor who merely attitudinizes, without obtaining any convincing musical effect at all. This happens quite frequently, for orchestral performers, who are very shrewd people indeed, invariably play as badly as possible for a mountebank. They would rather turn out a pleasant performance off their own bows, so to speak, for a respectable dullard who merely beats time for them, and perhaps cannot even do that properly. In which case again the audience might judge badly by merely looking at the conductor, and so it might, once more, where the permanent conductor in charge of a rigorously governed orchestra – a man like Furtwängler, let us say – obtains with a minimum of outward show a variety of sensational effects that have been carefully drilled into the players beforehand. It is thus a good rule for concert-goers to beware of watching the conductor unless they are quite sure that they can listen intently at the same time.

Of scores and when to use them

A sure way of keeping one's eyes off is to follow the performance with a miniature score. However, whether from a purely musical point of view this is always to be recommended is debatable, to say the least. I think one may safely say: no, not always. It depends a good deal on how frequently a work is likely to be performed whether the acquisition of a miniature score of it is to be advised. A novelty or rarity that may not be heard again for years is on the whole better listened to without a score, unless a quick critical estimate has to be made of it, in which case it is undoubtedly easier to get hold of the more concrete aspects of the music at once by having it under one's eyes. But something of the general impression, of the mood, is apt to evaporate, and the average hearer is better left with that alone for a beginning.

On the other hand a library of classical works that are in the regular repertory is very much to be desired. The term 'classical', in the sense in which I use it here, embraces, of course, such now established works as Debussy's *Prélude à l'après-midi d'un faune*, or Strauss's *Till Eulenspiegel* or Elgar's violin concerto, to give only three out of a hundred possible examples. Probably the best way of getting to grips with a repertory work and engraving it upon one's mind is to hear it the first time without a score, to follow it in print carefully the second, and then to go on as one feels inclined. There is no sense in laying down hard and fast rules.

One precept, however, should be heeded. Never try to follow a score you cannot be sure of reading reasonably well. I do not suppose that anyone nowadays would be caught committing the classic blunder of the old lady who very carefully followed a performance of Berlioz's *Faust* with a vocal score of Gounod's; but the distracted roving of the eye up and down a page of full score and the desperate attempt at catching up a passage farther ahead after being left behind, snared in an entanglement of staves and notes, is a distressing spectacle that one is always sorry to witness at a concert. For in his frantic effort at seeing in print what is being played the earnest student quite forgets to listen to it.

Of scores and how to read them

Perhaps the reader will ask what it is that constitutes fairly useful score-reading. Much could be said; but as it will already have been gathered from other parts of this book, I will content myself with pointing to merely two or three accomplishments to be desired; the eye should be trained to take in the convergence of all the parts at any point from top to bottom of the page, with a certain amount of what is about to happen to each part farther on; the reader should understand the nature of the transposing instruments and not be put off by their playing other notes than those written, remembering that relatively they follow the composer's intentions like the non-transposing parts; there should be no feeling that the violas are playing at the wrong pitch merely because they do not happen to be written for in the familiar treble or bass clef.

The hearer should test himself with such things. If they are beyond him, score-reading at concerts had better be dropped for a time. It can, however, be learnt by anyone for whom the reading of a single instrumental part, or, better still, a work for piano, presents no difficulty. No teacher is needed. Self-instruction had best begin with a string quartet, or any not too complicated work; the score should be taken to a performance and followed as closely as possible, unless the reader has the courage to worry it out at the piano until the parts in some of the easier passages fit together. The alto clef, in which the viola part is written, is learnt quite easily for reading purposes if it is remembered that it has middle C on the central line of the stave and that the Cs an octave above and below both look alike, as though one were the other's reflection in a mirror. The tenor clef, sometimes used for the cello, has middle C on the fourth line from the bottom, which is less convenient, but not really difficult to learn.

From quartets it is advisable to go on to orchestral works with few wind parts, such as the first two of Bach's Brandenburg Concertos, and from those again to the more lightly scored symphonies of Haydn and Mozart. After that there will be no holding the reader until he has come to such lavish scores as those of Stravinsky's *Sacre du Printemps* or Holst's *Planets*.

Score-reading quickly makes for instant recognition of the different qualities of sound produced by orchestral instruments, but such a knowledge, acquired first, also makes for greater ease in reading. The eye, which may be about to miss a phrase given out by the oboe, for instance, will quickly catch it if reminded by the ear where to look for it.

If a work followed with the score refuses to impress itself on the listener as a whole, he should not worry, unless it is one he is not likely to hear again for a long time, in which case he had better drop the music and listen. But in the case of a familiar composition, it will do him no harm for once to let go of the total impression and concentrate on details in the musical texture, perhaps one single strand throughout. It is excellent training to fix the eye entirely on the second violins and violas throughout a whole movement of a symphony, on the horns only during the next and on the clarinets and bassoons for another. That sort of thing should not be done habitually, of course, and never in the case of a work that is wholly new to the hearer; but it will help much to train the ear to disentangle inner parts from the symphonic web.

Of hearing more things than one
This brings us to an accomplishment even the most amateurish of music lovers must at all costs acquire if his love is to bring reward. It is of the most vital importance to be able to hear a number of things going on simultaneously. When I say 'going on', I mean it literally. Anyone, needless to say, hears the incidence of the notes of a static chord or of a series of chords in succession; but not everybody, I imagine, is able to make out several melodic lines played or sung at the same time. Tests I used to make with myself in early years showed that it is quite possible to concentrate on a treble melody alone and to let all the rest recede into the background, and I do not doubt that this is the kind of way in which music is listened to by people who will tell you that much of Bach's work, or anything else of a polyphonic nature, has no 'tune'. If they hear a melody on the top, the music is tuneful for them; if a melody happens to be in a middle part, it is tuneless, because they never hear middle parts continuously. They are like shortsighted people who do not see the

whole charm of the sight of a girl standing in a beautiful landscape, because they see only the human figure, and the rest is out of focus. If the girl happens to be pretty (i.e. if the tune pleases them) they are satisfied; if not, the beauty of the landscape (the rest of the musical fabric) fails to compensate for her plainness.

The easiest part to pick out, next to the treble, is the bass. Those who cannot do so had better make a point of listening to that first and see what melody they can find there – a great deal in some music (e.g. Bach and Handel). As soon as that becomes plain, without the top melody being lost to the ear, the inner parts should be concentrated on, still always with reference to the more obvious lines of treble and bass. Thus music will constantly gain in plasticity and life; orchestral concerts will become more and more of an adventurous delight. And almost the only thing that will become difficult about a big symphony concert will be to find it tiring or tiresome.

Of singing together

An excellent incentive to taking notice of the importance of hearing single strands in a polyphonic musical texture is, for those who can sing a little, to join a choral society. Even anyone who can sing more than a little has no business to assume a superior attitude, which I am afraid is only too common among gifted amateur singers, and often not even gifted ones, who regard it as below their dignity and as possibly injurious to their precious voices to go and sing in a choir. Dignity can well survive such condescension, provided that it be there from the beginning, and a good voice is not harmed by being made to work. Even if there were some slight dangers of this kind, the positive gain in musical experience would still outweigh them enormously. Nothing cultivates musicianship, both practically and in the matter of taste, more markedly than taking part in a performance, and choral singing does so particularly in Britain, not only because it is generally on a high level of achievement, but also because the bad Continental habit of singing from chorus parts is rarely indulged in, the choristers reading nearly always from vocal scores and so having the work as a whole continually before their eyes.

Choral singing is almost a sport in this country, indeed wholly so where choirs take part in the competitive festivals, one or two of which are held at some town within reach of most choral societies. It may be debatable whether, from a purely aesthetic point of view, a sporting attitude towards music can ever be desirable; but friendly competition is so natural to Britons that, so long as any kind of music-making remains a fit subject for contest, it is sure to show vitality and a considerable degree of skill.

Many of those who frequent choral concerts, and more especially the large festivals, do so in a sporting rather than a musical frame of mind. They may have friends or relatives in the choir, in which case that body of superlative musicians can do no wrong. Again, there may be some local axe to grind. I was once solemnly assured by a frequenter of the Three Choirs Festival with plenty of county loyalty but no more than the haziest idea of how that venerable organization was run, that the choir at Hereford was infinitely superior to those at Gloucester and Worcester.

Of all concerts, I am afraid, choral ones are most often attended for other than musical reasons. It is not merely a matter of limited taste, but a matter of indifference and utter lack of curiosity that at festivals and elsewhere the changes are eternally rung on *Messiah* and *Elijah* in many places, though it must be acknowledged that choral enterprise has advanced greatly in recent years. I have no wish to disparage these two works. They became standard works, in the first place, because they deserved it. But the concert-goer may just as well be recommended not to accept them uncritically merely for that reason. In the concert room, as in life, far too much is accepted simply because it is among the 'things that are done'. It is as well, while taking as much pleasure as possible in these two oratorios, to remember that Handel wrote many others containing an astonishing wealth of splendid music which are scarcely ever heard, and that Mendelssohn did better work in other musical spheres than even in his best choral composition, to say nothing of the desirability of hearing works by other composers, old and new. If choral concerts can teach us one thing more convincingly than another, it is the advantage of an open mind.

Of recitals

Although one may be glad that choral concerts have improved in quality, one would not be sorry to think that recitals had decreased in quantity, even if this is due in part to economic conditions generally. Artistically nothing is lost. Recitals used to be far too frequent, at any rate in London. Twenty-five of them in one week was once by no means an uncommon thing, and one often felt this continuous parade of artists before the public to be a sort of grotesque tragedy on a gigantic scale. For alas! to give a recital requires no artistic qualifications, or at any rate not more than can be comfortably eked out with self-confidence. It is only necessary to be able to afford the very considerable expenses, or, if not to afford them, at any rate to pay them somehow. So it comes about that week after week new artists appear in the smaller concert halls, performing generally to rows of yawning seats, which is only less bad than rows of yawning people, to be warmly applauded by a handful of friends, a little less warmly by a number of other deadheads, and benevolently but non-committally mentioned by the Press, only to disappear again, more often than not, into heaven knows what limbo of disillusion. If now and then a young performer makes a recital pay, it is most likely thanks to an energetic mother who has sold tickets to reluctant but polite friends at tea-parties. Artistically the result is equally null. Occasionally an artist of quite exceptional gifts gets somewhere through that channel; she (it is more often 'she') would have done so in any case and less expensively.

So altogether the giving of recitals is hopeless. Our music lover may thus just as well make up his mind not to patronize them on an every-little-helps principle. The proverb is misapplied here: it is the drop-in-the-ocean one that fits. Even a charitable principle to buy a ticket for every recital that is going would not help. If anyone wished to be really useful on a lavish scale, it would be far better to buy up the whole hall for one single recital by a really promising beginner; but such a good deed would avail little in a naughty world in which there is so much talk, and talk too often justified, of 'influence' and 'push', unless it were done anonymously. That is being visionary. There are more recitalists than idealists.

Artists who have already made their names frequently give recitals that may be very much worth hearing. But let not the name alone be your attraction. It is always a good plan to look at the programme before one goes to hear any performer, however celebrated, and people who issue handbills of recitals without giving a fully detailed list of what they propose to do are to be invariably regarded with suspicion. A perfectly unknown artist who has the enterprise to give an unusual and exceptionally well-planned programme is nearly always worth supporting, even if the performance itself should turn out to be far from satisfying. Those in search of guidance in the matter of musical experience cannot be too strongly enough urged always to go and hear music, never, or only in quite exceptional cases such as the farewell appearance of a great artist, a performer, however eminent. Perhaps this is an austere view, but for anyone who professes a genuine interest in music as such it makes a perfectly good rule, the more so because it modifies itself automatically in the case of very great executive musicians, who invest a comparatively conventional programme with an interest that attaches legitimately to the hearer's expectation of a model performance on their part. Even if it turns out a disappointment, there is at least the satisfaction of seeing an idol tottering on its pedestal. That, too, is legitimate.

Of song recitals

Much the most frequent recitals are those of singers, and it is here that one comes most often across more or less shocking exhibitions of incompetence. To go on a platform without some sort of an adequate technique is simply not possible for an instrumentalist, but a singer who has been complimented on possessing a beautiful voice often feels that to amount in itself to a vocation, which is almost as absurd as if I who, like the Irishman, have never tried whether I can play the fiddle or not, were to announce a recital merely because I happened to have become the owner of a Stradivari violin. But then, I am afraid some singers *are* absurd.

All the same, song recitals can be very interesting indeed, and their programmes are worth watching. When all the feeble or pathetic upstarts and all the vain dabblers in and on the borders of the profession who misuse opportunities for public appearance have been discounted, there remain a number of highly intelligent vocalists, both British and foreign, capable of filling an evening unaided, except by an accompanist. (Of the latter, who is very important, more anon.) Singers who deserve the music lover's attention are those who do not merely throw together a number of songs which happen to exhibit their voices and natural capacities to the best advantage, but group their material in some order that presents the whole programme as a definite, shapely scheme. The plan may be historical and the order chronological; the aim may be to show the differences between various national expressions through the medium of song; there may be some literary unity, such as a whole evening of settings of Shakespeare or Goethe; the development of a single school may be demonstrated; and so on and on. Anything of this kind should be looked for as sure to yield an experience, and it may fairly be taken for granted that a singer who has had the intelligence to devise a programme of the sort will not be likely to present it in an entirely futile manner.

Songs, not arias, should as a rule be looked for at vocal recitals. Despised once by many of the most famous singers, who never dreamt of rendering service to music by submitting to the composer's requirements, but on the contrary expected it to provide them with material for their own display, songs in a programme are now to a great extent an index to the intelligence and artistic sincerity of a vocalist. A vocal recital is a matter of partnership between a singer and a pianist, and it follows that works written for voice and piano ought at least to predominate in its programme if not to fill it exclusively. As to vocal pieces not originally so written, there is no need to proscribe them altogether and on principle. An aria from a Handel oratorio or a Bach cantata or a Mozart opera, or a group of such things, may serve two very good purposes at a recital. It may discipline the performer by a series of difficulties of a technical rather than an interpretative order, and it may be of such intrinsic beauty and so impossible to hear anywhere else as to make its performance, even in a makeshift version with a piano accompaniment, a true benefit for the hearer. What is undesirable is to feel that any and every recital must needs open with a set of classical arias as a sort of introductory rite demanded by a noble tradition. There is no noble tradition about this; it is merely an ignoble convention. A person who set out to perform a feat of mountaineering by first crossing the main street of Innsbruck or Zermatt high up on a tightrope would never reach the mountains at all, for he would either break his neck or be locked up as a lunatic first; but foolhardy singers are still seen trying an exactly similar exploit without anyone in the audience turning a hair. Perhaps, though, that accounts to a great extent for the persistence of the bad habit of arriving late at concerts: people with nerves avoid the ghastly rope-dance in a sort of agony of artistic vertigo.

However, it all depends on the concert-giver. Most singers nowadays are better at interpretation, which indeed is an art that has vastly improved, than at technical accomplishments, which those who had the miraculous achievements of Patti and the de Reszkes and the rest from their own mouths, in one way or another, assure us have sadly deteriorated. Arias being, broadly speaking, vehicles for technical exhibition and songs for realization as much by intelligence as by voice, it is generally safer to frequent recitals that lay stress on the latter.

Of the words of songs and their translation
Song recitals are not easy to listen to. More than anywhere else in the whole range of the singer's art is good enunciation wanted here.

Not only is a song meaningless if its words are not caught; a singer who does not make clear verbal articulation the first condition of performance cannot possibly hope to be regarded as an adequate interpreter. Only in the shaping of the verbal phrases do the musical ones acquire their full meaning.

There is this to be said, though; song recitals are very rarely given in one language only, and that language the vernacular of the audience, so that even if the singer is thoroughly familiar with the three or four different languages represented in the programme, which is comparatively rarely the case, every member of the audience can hardly be expected to understand them all. Indeed, the more idiomatically they are sung, the harder they become to catch by the English ear. Some of the mediocre German, the dreadfully diphthong-al Italian and the altogether atrocious French – to put them in order of difficulty – we are often condemned to listen to in our concert-halls it would seem almost impossible not to understand, so considerably is it approximated to an English pronunciation; but the real thing is a very different matter, and even that is rarely articulated so ideally as to be readily understandable by the initiated without artificial help.

Such help comes, with rare exceptions, from the programme notes. The concert-goer may ask whether he is not likely to have his attention distracted from the music if he follows the printed words. Unfortunately, yes. It is much more difficult to lend an attentive ear if the eye is otherwise occupied at the same time. But since words are essential and yet cannot be expected to be always heard, it is better to follow them in the programme than to let them escape. Singers who give a recital and provide no printed words cannot eschew the reproach of dealing unfairly both with their audience and with themselves, unless they happen to sing a whole programme in the vernacular and have made quite sure by previous experience that their enunciation is wholly above suspicion.

These printed words must be really useful, though. For foreign songs the original is desirable, if not essential, and a translation into the audience's own language indispensable.[1] These translations ought

[1] Since Eric Blom wrote this essay, the following volumes of song-texts with translations have appeared: *The Penguin Book of Lieder* edited and translated by S. S. Prawer (paperback, Penguin Books, London) and *The Fischer-Dieskau Book of Lieder*, translated by George Bird and Richard Stokes (hard cover, Gollancz and Pan, London; Knopf, New York), *The Interpretation of French Song* by Pierre Bernac (Gollancz, London; Norton, New York).

to be as good as possible. They need not be in verse; indeed the turning of a fine poem into doggerel merely for the sake of versification is to be deprecated. Far better good prose versions, such as those made by Richard Capell for his book, *Schubert's Songs*, or those by Winifred Radford in the booklets accompanying the records of the Hugo Wolf Society and of Schubert's *Winterreise*. For a great many classical German Songs A. H. Fox Strangways and Sir Steuart Wilson have provided inimitable English versions, and these might just as well be sung, not merely put into the programme to elucidate the originals. What should not be reproduced without careful thought are certain translations that paraphrase the original poem loosely in order to fit the music more or less faithfully. A bald literal translation is better than that, though it should preserve something of the spirit of the author, or at any rate his meaning. It will not do to pursue the line of least resistance quite so strictly and to be quite so scrupulously literal as was done on one occasion, when a famous German soprano sang an aria from Bach's *Phœbus and Pan* and gave in her programme a translation on the following lines: the opening words are 'Patron, das macht der Wind', of which one of those free English versions which are no use for programmes begins 'Yes, yes, just so'. But in order to be quite faithful the translator simply said 'Patron, that makes the wind', from which anyone not acquainted with the pitfalls of the business might have concluded that nothing was easier than the turning of German verse into English.

Of pianoforte recitals

This, however, as the observant reader will have noticed, is a digression. Let us return to recitals, with which we have not yet done. Instrumental executants require some consideration, in fact often deserve more than singers, their standards being higher all round. By far the most interesting, as a rule, are the pianists, not by any means because they surpass others in personal achievement, but because they have beyond all comparison the richest scope of music at their disposal. There is practically no limit to the number of things they can do in public, even if they made an organized effort never to duplicate each other's performances. It is the more distressing to find that every other manipulator of the keyboard must needs include Chopin's B flat minor sonata in his repertory, whether because it is regarded as an irresistible attraction or because each player thinks that he or she will at last give the exemplary reading, I shall not venture to determine. I will not lay myself open to the charge of Chopinophobia by suggesting that all public performances of any music by that composer ought to be forbidden for at least three years, though I do feel that the most hackneyed of his works, such as this sonata, and the first, third and fourth ballades, all deserve a rest. The distressing fact is that precisely his best compositions, being ideal pianists' material, are apt to hang an atmosphere of staleness over a concert room, unless they happen to be played by a latter-day Paderewski or Rosenthal, when it is the personality at the instrument rather than the composer who creates the spell. Through no fault of the composer's – no, curiously enough, rather owing to his peculiar merits – it has come about that Chopin recitals are generally better avoided and single groups of Chopin in a programme put up with only because they can be cut out by the hearer if the performance does not prove exceptionally good.

So much of the harm which the ordinary run of pianists must be said to have done to music. It is sad to think that they should have made some of the most congenial music for their instrument hard to listen to with patience – and by no means Chopin alone. Now let it be said that much gratitude is due to them also. Not only is their range of music as good as illimitable; it gives them infinite chances for the exercise of personality. Interpretation may vary almost as much as the music itself, and there is endless fascination in following the play of the executant's imagination on the composer's invention, provided it be neither too feeble nor too perversely individual. Of all instrumental solo performers the pianist has much the greatest latitude here; but questions of interpretation not being exclusively applicable to him, I will deal briefly with other instrumentalists' chances of public display first and then revert to matters of musical presentation.

Of violin recitals, and others

Violin recitals tend much more to become exhibitions of executive personality than of music as such. The repertory is surprisingly small compared with that of the piano and tends to be made to look even smaller than it is by a certain traditionalism that seems to be ingrained in most fiddlers, who would rather play Bach's Chaconne for the hundredth time than dig out an almost certainly less imposing but fresher work. And the Chaconne itself has often shown that violinists are too apt to expect their public to find fiddling interesting in itself, simply as a feat and a science, for they seem to be quite oblivious of the fact that unless this masterpiece is performed with the utmost perfection it remains a lifeless abstraction and, it must be confessed, a sore trial to the mind and the ear alike. It is no less true that the numerous sonatas by the Italian violinist–composers of the 17th and 18th centuries, to which most recitalists almost invariably resort, are less interesting to those who have come for the sake of music rather than of fiddling, unless they are handled by a supreme master of style. They are only too apt to sound all very much alike, a fact which must however be attributed not so much to lack of personal enterprise in the composers themselves as to the disastrous shorthand system of thorough-bass which, too often imperfectly understood by modern editors, has caused the accompaniments to all these sonatas to be written out far too unenterprisingly and uniformly to bring the old music quite to life again. Italian sonatas and unaccompanied Bach are things to be avoided by all but master-performers, and generally by concert-goers too unless played by such performers. It is only kind, however, to bear in mind how limited violinists are in their choice.

Cellists are even more so, though enough fine music is written for them to make a programme worth hearing, if they know how to find it. Even viola recitals are possible, as such a player as Lionel Tertis has shown, and can occasionally be attended for the music's sake, though the player will almost certainly have to fall back on a number of transcriptions. Other instrumentalists can hardly venture before the public with only an accompanist. Plenty of solo music is written for most of them, but nearly all of it is by specialists who know very well how this or that instrument should be played, but have too little taste and inventive power to give it something worth playing. The repertory of all wind instruments suffers from an astonishing pre-dominance of the most meagre fare, with perhaps a few exceptionally valuable things thrown in here and there.

The nadir of ineptitude is probably a harp recital, partly because the instrument, unaccompanied by others, is too monotonous and insipid to make tolerable company for any length of time, partly because as a rule only those who have been trained to play it write really effectively for it, and they do not happen to be fertile as well as mechanically resourceful composers.[1]

[1] In recent years several superlative performers have emerged, and this has led to a number of excellent works for the harp by modern composers.

Of organ recitals

The organ, too, takes most of its repertory from performers who happen to compose chiefly for the sake of demonstrating its infinitely varied capacities and enlarging its library. Even the best of them, such as Guilmant and Widor in France or Rheinberger and Karg-Elert in Germany, remain almost unknown to lovers of music who do not happen to care for the organ. If it were not for the singular good fortune of organists that Bach happened to be one of them, and for a few composers of genius like César Franck and Max Reger, who really cared for and understood the organ, there would be extremely little in organ recitals to attract the musician. Isolated works of exceptional value written by composers who do not cultivate the organ particularly, but take it in their stride now and again, would be swallowed up in a spate of arrangements of music heard to better advantage in its original form and of pieces by organists more anxious to feed their instrument than to sustain the art of music.

Music lovers are well advised to look for Bach in an organ programme first of all, but not to give up an intended visit to a recital merely because he may happen to be absent. Some arrangements may be put up with as an unavoidable part-solution of the organist's dilemma, and the best of the specialist composers certainly deserve to be heard. The presence of a good composer's name should be regarded as an attraction even if he is not known particularly as a writer for the organ. For the rest, one may well go and hear a performer of repute in a spirit of adventure, always remembering that to listen to an organ must remain something of a matter of taste and its enjoyment to a great extent dependent on associations. It is a curious fact that numbers of people who would never think of going to any other concert will attend organ recitals with every outward sign of the most concentrated attention, which they will display even during a work like Bach's Passacaglia that taxes the hearer's musicianship to the utmost, though they may secretly much prefer a pretty gavotte in which the organist will tickle the ear with the carillon stop. It is difficult to see what precisely it is that attracts crowds of undiscerning listeners to the organ. Perhaps some sort of exceptionally pleasant church-going that is all amenity and free from duty. The sheer sound of the organ may somehow make the listener satisfy his conscience about attending church without imposing on him the necessity of going through the service and being exhorted by a sermon. If so, this is rather touching in its ingenuous unconsciousness; but it is hardly an attitude to be commended to those who frequent concerts for the pure love of music.

Of programme-making and the curse of encores

Organists more than any other recitalists are faced with the difficult problems of programme-making, about which something may perhaps be said here in a general way, though I have already referred to it in passing, under the head of singers' recitals. How is the concert-goer to tell a good programme from a bad one beforehand, from the mere look of it? Broadly speaking, he will make up his mind without difficulty as to whether it contains music worth hearing. But it is quite possible to make up an unsatisfactory scheme with nothing but fine music. A recitalist cannot simply throw together a number of songs or pieces that happen to be congenial. There must be contrast, but not confusion. A certain harmony in the composition of each group must be aimed at, and even the groups themselves must make some sort of shape between them. Styles should not be mixed too much, except possibly for certain purposes which may well disregard unity of period and possibly even chronological presentation. Again, a programme, like a single piece, should have a climax, or a series of graded climaxes, the placing of which ought to be very carefully considered. The most significant contribution may be gradually worked up to towards the end of the concert, or better still, since people so often discover that they have a train to catch or a supper to eat before the end, in the middle of the programme. In the latter case it is as well to observe the rule that the descent towards the close should be less steep than the ascent has been at the beginning, and it is also well worth the artist's pondering whether it ought to take him back to quite as low a level again as that from which the recital started. To end with a flashy group of show pieces seems to me the height of folly, for that is simply asking the more cultivated section of the public to depart early and only the indiscriminately omnivorous to remain to clear up the leavings of the feast, and rapaciously to demand more and more.

That brings me to the matter of encores. They are a ridiculous convention, and the artist who conforms to it too readily is to be regarded with suspicion. The abuse has grown so widespread that all programmes have nowadays to be deliberately shortened from the beginning in order to be afterwards artificially lengthened by these extras, which the public has come to expect as a matter of course, one hardly knows whether through its own exorbitance or through a particularly stupid mixture of vanity and compliance on the performers' part. The only sensible thing to do is to include everything in the printed programme that is really meant to be performed, even such displays of virtuosity for its own sake as may seem desirable. The public must know what to expect, or if it does not, be taught a lesson in moderation again and again until it has learnt to do so. This can be done quite graciously. Instead of ruthlessly cutting out encores altogether, the artist may produce a sobering effect by the simple expedient of giving something short and quiet by way of an extra, instead of a gratuitous exhibition of brilliance that only excites a craving for still more. If a singer has the sense to show that no further adventures are to be expected, by merely adding such a thing of hearteasing simplicity as Bach's song, 'Bist du bei mir', or a pianist playing very calmly one of the gentle numbers from Beethoven's later sets of *Bagatelles*, all would be over in a moment without any vulgar fuss, and sensible people would be able to go away refreshed. What is more, they would gradually learn that it is not necessarily degrading to stay to the end of a recital.

The accomplishment of accompaniment

A word is due to the accompanist, of all executive musicians the most unjustly treated. He has in some respects to be more accomplished than a solo pianist; yet he rarely gets his due. All those who go to recitals, and particularly recitals given by star performers who take all the efforts made on their behalf by the rest of the world calmly for granted, cannot be strongly enough exhorted to do justice, at any rate in their own minds, to the man 'at the piano', as the programme has it. If they will only listen, they will find that this man very often is not merely at the piano, but actually plays it, and sometimes extremely well. Great deftness is expected of him, moreover, in various ways. If the soloist misses a bar or a page, he has to catch up with the offender without giving him away. He is expected to cover up a multitude of his more conspicuous partner's sins by a variety of subterfuges, and even to take them upon himself, if they cannot be covered. Supposing a singer suddenly finds on the night of the concert that she cannot possibly produce that high B she sang so penetratingly at the rehearsal, he is asked at the last minute to transpose a possibly very difficult accompaniment at sight into E flat minor. And so on and on.

What is more, the accompanist sometimes improves out of all knowledge what without him would have been a thoroughly shapeless, flaccid performance. He can, if he is musician and man enough, be the real maker of a fine interpretation. This does not only mean an amount of moral courage for which a musical distinction equivalent to the V.C. ought to be specially created; it is an uncommonly noble act of heroism, for it does not even draw attention to itself, but lets all the credit go elsewhere. There are songs – Schubert's 'Erlkönig', for instance – of which even the finest singers can make nothing without an accompanist with the keenest sense of rhythm. Yet, if they have succeeded, who thinks of thanking the pianist?

To ask concert-goers to make at least an attempt to recognize a good accompanist is to ask only for a simple act of justice. The difficulty is that it is often very hard to tell whether the merits of the performance are really his. It can sometimes be told only negatively, and listeners may well begin to train themselves by merely trying to determine whether this or that accompanist is bad or not bad. That will be something towards a discovery, for at least it will not take them long to know a bad one. We all know the type of accompanist of whom the critics say the next morning: 'Mr Timiddy Meek accompanied discreetly.' Beware of that discretion which, whatever it may be the better part of, is certainly not that of a performance with rhythmic life in it. These good people have for years and years been so submissively following singers and players who have not a notion of what a rhythmic performance means, instead of imperceptibly leading them, that in the end they play with a lamentable flabbiness even when the artist they accompany happens to be gifted with a rhythmic sense.

A word about rhythm and 'rubato'

That rhythmic sense, perhaps the rarest quality in performers, is nevertheless the one to be looked for first of all by those who wish to become good judges. Rhythm is not mere time or metre. Jazz, popularly supposed to be much the most rhythmic music, is not rhythmic at all, but rigidly metrical. True rhythm has the fundamental regularity, but also the quick, responsive variability, of the human pulse, not the mechanically precise beat of the metronome. It feels time and goes in time, but not *dead* in time. Yet the jazz fever – if anything so cold-blooded and machine-pulsed may be called fever – has been allowed to invade the concert room. One has heard performances of Mozart concertos sound as though their composer were indeed the 'Austrian Gershwin'.[1]

[1] Ernest Newman's joke! Some musical patriot in the USA called George Gershwin the American Mozart, whereupon Mr Newman ironically suggested that this was doing scant justice to the composer of the *Rhapsody in Blue* and that Mozart ought henceforth to be called the Austrian Gershwin.

On the other hand, the fetish of the *rubato* is responsible for much ill-considered performing, especially piano playing. *Rubato* means literally 'robbed'; but the wholesale pilferings that go on in the concert room are sheer wanton destructiveness that do music infinite harm. The true musician does not rob with violence, but rather in the spirit of Robin Hood, taking something from time in order to give it to rhythm, as it were.

Interpretation – and the virtuoso

This is laying down no more than a broad principle. It cannot be uniformly applied. Mozart must be played much more strictly in time, for instance, than Chopin; one modern composer may require the loosest treatment, another the most rigid. Still, a principle it remains, though subject to many varieties of style. Not style only, either. Everything does not depend on the composer in the ideal partnership of creator and executant that makes for a good performance. It is an exceedingly delicate relationship, the more so because the opinion of the hearer, who is a kind of sleeping partner, carries some weight too. That is why it is so important that the hearer should understand the problem of interpretation which arises between the composer and his exponent. How much does the former impose or suggest? How much may the latter assume and take upon himself?

A great deal depends on the performer's individuality. An artist of strong personal convictions can read much more into a work without danger of warping it than one who is content to mirror the music as he sees it without holding very strong views on it. Many of Busoni's interpretations used to go to the very edge of perversity; yet even while protesting with all one's might there was no helping one's admiration of such superb wilfulness. For in spite of his all-conquering technique Busoni was anything but a mere virtuoso. He was always felt to place himself at the service of the music, often wrongheadedly, but never without passionate sincerity. Thus one accepted all sorts of things from him which would have seemed alike repugnant in the virtuoso pure and simple – if purity and simplicity are not too fantastically inappropriate terms – and in the earnest interpreter of smaller mentality and weaker conviction.

Virtuosity in itself is one of music's curses. The sooner lovers of the art make up their minds to that the better. The artist who thinks only of personal display is an enemy to the fine things he does not even pretend to serve, but arrogantly takes to exist for his own glorification. He will sing or play bad music shamelessly, so long as it exhibits his technical attainments, and choose a good work only if by accident it lends itself to the same end. As a rule he will do his best to spoil it – yes, quite honestly what does happen to be *his* sort of best. Merely to bring his overweening mind to bear on the music is enough to warp it, ludicrously if not tragically. The one thing that redeems the out-and-out virtuoso is, to put it paradoxically, that he is doomed to perdition. He has his day, vanishes, and does not take long to fall into oblivion.

Fortunately the musician who is a virtuoso and nothing else is comparatively rare. Although one would not go out of the way to recommend an assiduous cult of the celebrities who fill the largest concert halls, there are nevertheless few of them who cannot be heard at any rate once or twice without some profit. If there is no positive musical gain, there is at least the general one of a new experience, of a fresh exercise of the critical faculty. For the rest, there is no need to fall into the inverted snobbery that insists on discrediting any artist who has made a resounding name. Even while fame is being exploited to the full, it is still possible to give a valuable performance, and indeed one may often hear from artists who have attained to widespread popularity the model performances their reputations would naturally lead one to expect. They are at least worth trying. But if they are found supercilious in their attitude towards music, they had better be dropped at once.

Liszt, Rubinstein, Paganini

The value of virtuosity thus remains disputable even after its most self-centred representatives have been ruled out as public nuisances. For that very reason, though, its possible merits must at least be considered. A few typical figures of the past may serve to show how the virtuoso may help music, since to discuss living artists would be too uncomfortably invidious. Liszt as pianist is sufficiently distinct from Liszt as composer to serve for a shining example of beneficent virtuosity. In spite of the disconcertingly vulgar streak of the showman in his oddly contradictory personality, he made a vast amount of great piano music accessible to an almost limitless public, and even his numerous arrangements did more good than damage to the music they exhibited, for, shallow as they often were, they by no means always betrayed the spirit of the originals. Another composer–pianist who scarcely counts any longer as a creative musician, but whose influence as an interpreter has lasted, was Rubinstein, whose historical recitals did a great deal to show younger players how to exercise virtuosity for the benefit of art.

Even virtuosi who dazzled the world by technique alone, or almost alone, contrived at times to advance music, at any rate as a medium for more lavish and varied writing on the composer's part. We may smile at the amazement of Paganini's contemporaries who thought that his tricks, which can nowadays be performed by dozens of virtuosi without turning a hair on their heads or ruffling one on their bows, were possible only because he was in league with the devil, who supplied him with strings made of human intestines, and whatever all the romantic stories are that circulated at the time; it is nevertheless a fact that if he had not shown these apparently supernatural powers, it might not for a long time have occurred to anybody that they could ever become quite natural. Once it had become clear that undreamt-of things were possible for violinists to play, it also became habitual for composers to apply new technical acquisitions to their works.

Not only composers, but instrument makers as well, advanced under the influence of virtuosi. Liszt, with his thunderously sonorous transcriptions of organ and orchestral works, demanded more of the piano of his time than it could give. The result was that piano makers, urged by these new requirements in the first place and by competition in the second, developed the instrument's power of sound to the utmost of which it is, and indeed need be, capable.

Of celebrities, and how one hunts them

As for the evils of virtuosity, it must be said, quite brutally that they have sprung very largely from the public's attitude. The low sport of celebrity-hunting is responsible for the most appalling things that go on in the concert world. Unfortunately it is a kind of chase that has the peculiarity of being enjoyed as much by the hunted as by the hunters, which means that nobody, not even the tiny minority of humanitarians this wicked world contains, ever cries out vigorously against it. Critics, it is true, occasionally do so, being the only victims of this monstrous traffic in enslaved music; but as in sheer self-defence they have to cultivate a blend of humour and resigned cynicism, their protests are apt to be somewhat ineffectual. The rest of mankind is divided into the indifferent and the enthusiastic. The latter, though very much in the minority, make up a public quite large enough to fill the biggest concert halls up and down any country which a musician who has somehow achieved celebrity may choose to visit.

No doubt that celebrity may have been legitimately gained by genuine musicianship; still, it remains only too true that notoriety of one sort or another invariably affects the box-office returns to the concert-giver's advantage. Anything from spontaneous eccentricity (which soon enough loses its spontaneity and grows into a pose) to downright charlatanry will serve, and if only a performer who had murdered his wife and then bigamously married two others were allowed a concert tour before being forcibly seen off into the next world, he would without doubt depart on his last journey with the peculiar satisfaction of having first gained immense popularity and made a fortune.

Those who want to cultivate music sincerely for its own sake had better be warned to approach all but half a dozen of the popular virtuosi warily, and even the half-dozen with a mind unprejudiced by their reputation. It is always a good plan to judge for oneself. Even a Paderewski, a Gerhardt, a Kreisler, a Casals may not be to one's individual taste, in which case, though it will be impossible not to respect such artists' gifts, it is as well not to be guided merely by their fame, but to maintain a sturdy independence of judgment – that is, if one can be sure that there is a judgment. As for people of renown whom one has not previously heard, a trial may be made if curiosity is strong enough and sufficient cash is available. If not, one may safely make it a rule to distrust virtuosi about whom the more popular newspapers go out of their way to print what they call 'stories', in other words interviews by which they tell the world through the medium of a reporter exactly what they want it to know about themselves. For it is not unreasonable to expect of famous persons who are about to give concerts that they should be good musicians rather than breeders of dogs, lovers of parrots (three dozen of which are always taken about by special train), owners of race-horses, collectors of stamps, authorities on interior decoration or personal friends of exiled royalty.

However, some mild fun may occasionally be got out of the spectacle of celebrity-hunting by the mere onlooker. If a visit to one of the meets at the Albert Hall or elsewhere seems really indicated, it may turn out a success of sorts, even if the results are artistically too dreary for words. The levity with which great music is at times treated, equalled only by the solemnity with which these self-sufficient people dish up inferior pieces; the ever-fresh surprise with which performing ladies greet a wholly unexpected floral tribute previously examined by them in the green-room, matched possibly by a perpetual grievance on the part of performing gentlemen at being by nature debarred from similar attentions (these vexing distinctions of sex have so far disappeared only at ballet perform-ances); the elaborately modest reluctance to give encores carefully prepared beforehand until the requisite amount of applause has been forthcoming; the mechanical readiness on the part of the audiences to furnish such applause; all this and much more should be enough to gladden the heart of anyone who has not been nauseated by the perennial repetition of these invariable manifestations. If it is, the quality of the actual performance is a matter of comparative un-importance.

The haven of chamber music

Celebrity concerts are apt to be both arid and restless. In these turbulent deserts it is always refreshing to find an oasis of chamber music, and fortunately such rest for the nerves and food for the ear may be found frequently enough. Not that public performance of chamber music is in itself the ideal way of presenting it. Greater intimacy and, so to speak, greater collaboration on the hearer's part is required to make it yield all its friendliness and emotional nearness. The finest works in its repertory do not seize upon the hearer with the pouncing effect that is characteristic of orchestral and choral works in varying degrees. They require more familiarity, more constant devotion. It is not enough to hear this or that Beethoven quartet once and then to go on to something else. Such a work wants to be sought out, pursued and wooed again and again before it will allow us to boast of its conquest. There is at once a coyness and a richness of feeling in the best chamber music which makes a kind of natural selection among its lovers, sifting out the cruder and more impatient ones, but retaining the finer and more discerning with an enduring hold that is unlike anything exercised by other species of music. Among those who are attached to the art, worshippers of chamber music are fewest, but also most constant.

They are a little shy about coming out into the open. The most devoted of them do not very much care to attend public perform-ances. Still, these are to be welcomed as the only means whereby new attachments are to be formed, and anyone who has never been to a chamber music concert can be urged to attend one at the earliest opportunity. He may not find himself a case of love at first hearing, but if only the tiniest spark is kindled in him, it will be more than worth nurturing, since ere long it may warm his heart more steadily than he has ever found love for any other music to do.

Even so, he will have to regard public performance as more or less of a makeshift. It will never quite satisfy him. The more aware he becomes of the Muse in her most intimate moods, the more he will in fact feel the need of seclusion. He will want to offer her his home. In time even a gramophone record of a quartet will satisfy him more in his own room than a brilliant performance about town. Like a true lover, he will be far from sure whether he would not rather sit at his fireside and gaze upon a photograph of his charmer than see her out at a dinner or a dance, in the half-frivolous detachment which the world demands. It is such an attitude of correctness and unconcern that chamber music always seems to assume directly it is played in public. Half the charm of its true self is lost there.

However, one may at least be introduced to it in the concert world and hope that such a meeting will be the first step to friendship, perhaps love. If only a grain of pleasure has been found in the first meeting, it will be well to cultivate the acquaintance assiduously. To drop all else in order to concentrate on chamber music is a good plan to adopt for a time, until one is fairly bitten by love of it. After that, it will keep its hold of itself. Indeed, it may then become necessary to beware of adoring it too exclusively. In this attachment, as in that to any other ideal, it is possible, dangerously possible, to become priggish. It will then be time to remember that to pride oneself upon an exceptionally select taste is itself a lapse from taste.

Of reading and playing for oneself

The habit of score-reading is especially to be recommended to those who have made up their minds to frequent chamber concerts. At least the current classical works should be listened to with their scores, which can be bought relatively cheaply and are, of course, comparatively easy to read, the parts being few and transposing instruments absent except in rare cases where wind parts are a feature of the music. It will be found that the standard works are absorbed by the mind and retained by the memory far more quickly if the music has been seen as well as heard. Another advantage of score-reading is that chamber music, thus listened to, greatly helps in the training of the ear to listen to single parts through the whole fabric of sound. Once a particular work has become fairly familiar as a whole, the eye should for once in a way be made to follow an inner part throughout and the ear induced to pick it out all the way. The second violin in a string quartet, being the part most likely to escape the ear, had better be chosen; but in order to acquire the practice of reading the alto clef it is also advisable to concentrate on the viola part at some other performance.

Here is some sort of preparation for the home cultivation of chamber music – the true and final aim of its most ardent devotees. No musical pleasure is more enduring than that of playing this essentially domestic form of music in its proper environment. Even to hear it thus performed, if with no more than reasonable competence, is a treat of which a musical nature cannot soon weary. But the supreme joy is that of taking part in it. That is the natural thing to do, for chamber music, except in freakish cases, is written to be played rather than to be listened to passively. Anyone who can scrape a fiddle or strum on a piano should try to make something of a part in a quartet or trio or other combination. For it is an incontrovertible fact that this, of all musical delights, is the one not to be spoilt by incompetence. No doubt it is the charming domesticity of chamber music that makes it immune from blame even at its clumsiest. Affection sees only the attractions and fondly disregards the faults. As a cake over which a young wife has bungled hopelessly seems more delicious to the infatuated husband than the confection devised by a Brillat-Savarin, so lovers of music at home rejoice more over a Beethoven quartet mangled by themselves than over a crack performance of it by the finest quartet team in the world. And the wonder is that even those who are normally most inimical to amateurishness in music cannot but say that this is as it should be. Provided, it should perhaps be added, that they do not have to listen to these ardent fireside efforts. But that is not the point. The point is that such efforts should be made by all who can possibly do so.

Of opera

In England music lovers are perhaps more constrained to rely on their own resources at home than they are elsewhere. In London, it is true, there are more concerts than the public needs, and some of the larger provincial cities are well enough provided; but concert-going is not for all moods of musical entertainment, and from one of the means of satisfying these moods, by far the most popular one in most other countries of any musical pretensions, the British public outside London is all but cut off. I need hardly say that I refer to opera.

Nothing could be remoter from the playing of chamber music at home than a more or less regular habit of frequenting opera. Nevertheless, there is no very great dissimilarity between these two forms of musical relaxation. For that is what they are. Neither is so strictly concerned with music for music's sake as concert-going is bound to be. In the former case sociability plays its part, in the latter the

721

excitement of an evening out. The German, the Frenchman, the Italian who regards himself as a patron of music if he does nothing for it but visit the opera, more or less frequently and regularly, labours under one of the most agreeable self-complacent delusions it is possible for human vanity to discover, but a delusion without a doubt, and one of the easiest at that. It is perfectly possible to be very fond of opera without either knowing or caring more than two top notes about music. So long as one does not actually dislike it, there is enough going on in opera apart from the sound to engage all the attention there is to spare, during an evening following a busy day and a good dinner, for the spectator merely to regard it as a duck does water – a necessary and agreeable element, but one that leaves no mark on him.

No doubt there are differences. *Tristan*, I suppose, attracts the better musician or the greater snob than *Tosca*; *Figaro* and *Falstaff* appeal to finer tastes than *Faust*; if a gorgeous spectacle be the main attraction, *Turandot* would still find a better audience than *Thaïs*; and if tense drama be the test, *Carmen* will have a more cultivated following than *Cavalleria Rusticana*. However, it is certain that music alone is practically never the sole enticement of opera.

But now that we have consoled ourselves with the welcome truth that opera is not the whole of music, and indeed a devotion to opera not necessarily a proof of musical intelligence, we may proceed to smite our breasts a little for not being in this matter as other nations are. To have no permanent opera houses in at least a dozen of the larger towns is decidedly a loss. To allow one or more of the country's permanent opera organizations to pay short visits to provincial cities is something nowadays, but it is still not enough.

Of the five opera companies in Great Britain, Covent Garden no longer gives performances outside London, except occasionally abroad. Touring is shared by the other four, Sadler's Wells (now called the English National Opera), the Welsh National Opera, the Scottish Opera and Glyndebourne (only its 'reserve team' for three or four weeks each year). None of the theatres outside London are really adequate for opera. Conditions backstage are often primitive, as are the stage machinery and lighting facilities. Acoustics, almost without exception, are unsympathetic and the lack of an orchestra pit is commonplace. In short, the majority of the 55 million people in this country never have the opportunity to see professional opera productions under proper conditions.

Of the language problem

In London opera can usually be heard in the original language at Covent Garden and in the vernacular at the English National Opera. Sometimes in one season it is possible to hear the same work at both these houses, although in general this is avoided through the co-operation of the two managements. (Certainly there has never been a case such as in 1975 when *Manon Lescaut* could be seen at the Metropolitan Opera and the New York City Opera, a few hundred yards from each other, on the same night in the same language.)

Until recently English operatic translations were often better unheard. They were too apt to make one weep where all should be joy and laugh where one ought to remain serious. Consider this from *Il-Trovatore*:

Soon to the dread stake
(Beldam) they bound her,

which raises the nice problem of singing a word in parentheses. Or this from *Tosca*:

Ah! I have baulked them! Dread imagination
Made me quake with uncalled-for perturbation.

No doubt life would have been sadder without these gems; but operatic performances would have been less disconcerting.

Good translations of opera, however, are no longer as rare as they were, though the standard version of *Carmen* still lingers on – with humble *brigadier* José raised to the exalted British rank of Brigadier! – and that of *Faust* (with its 'Loving smile of sister kind' and so on) cries aloud for a new translation.

Of Covent Garden

Before the establishment of a permanent opera company at Covent Garden in 1946 the performances by foreign artists were only too often the more or less haphazard results of throwing together people with various degrees of talent on to the stage without any proper control, much less with any aim at unity. The point is, though, that without any intensive training at home they could not even have been thrown together. It was the experience of each individual that made some sort of adequate performance possible at all, from the point of view of stage-management. Even those singers who looked upon their appearances here as star turns, and were delighted to give a holiday airing to their autocratic instincts, had in their own countries to do very much as they were told, and the discipline they had thus acquired could alone save productions in which they were allowed to run wild on the stage. So that, although the lesson was an indirect one, they still taught us the immense value of team-work in opera.

This team-work was gradually cultivated with our own artists and reached a landmark with Kleiber's *Wozzeck* in 1952. Whilst this performance illustrated how the company's sense of ensemble had grown, the Callas–Stignani *Norma* in the same year reintroduced the excitement of Grand Season singing for the first time since the war. From 1946 up to this point all operas had been sung in English, but the inevitable internationalism of the house gradually forced a relaxation of this rule. The policy of giving British singers a share in this internationalism achieved its most spectacular success with Joan Sutherland's *Lucia di Lammermoor* in 1959 and, since then, Covent Garden singers, conductors and producers have been in demand throughout the world.

Covent Garden's repertoire, however, has remained extremely conservative. Although it does not include any of the four Tippett operas written for Covent Garden or the *Ring* cycle which was a feature of Solti's reign as Musical Director (1961–71), the following list is typical:

1973–74

Composer	Operas	Performances	Composer	Operas	Performances
Beethoven	1	5	Mussorgsky	1	7
Bizet	1	9	Puccini	3	23
Britten	3	13	Strauss (R.)	3	15
Donizetti	1	11	Tchaikovsky	1	6
Gluck	1	6	Verdi	7	47
Janáček	1	7	Wagner	1	8
Mozart	2	20			
Totals				26	177

This lack of adventurousness can be traced directly to the dependence upon box-office returns. Although Covent Garden receives the highest state subsidy of all arts organizations in Great Britain, it is only a paltry sum compared with other European opera houses, such as those in Germany. Ticket prices are in danger of reaching the point where, as in America, opera becomes the pastime of the rich.

Of the English National Opera
(*formerly Sadler's Wells*)

Since Strauss's *Der Rosenkavalier* (1911), only one opera, Berg's *Wozzeck*, has established itself in the *regular* international repertoire. At the same time the 'old' repertoire has been considerably reduced. Before the First World War you could often see such pieces as Auber's *Fra Diavolo* and *La Muette de Portici*, Adam's *Postillon de Lonjumeau* and *Si j'étais roi,* Bellini's *Sonnambula*, Meyerbeer's *Les Huguenots, Le Prophète* and *L'africaine,* even Wagner's *Rienzi.* Sadler's Wells, whilst not reviving these curiosities, has gone a long way to providing London with a balanced operatic diet. Although its grant from the Arts Council of Great Britain is only a proportion of that received by the Royal Opera, its running costs are similarly smaller. Within its limited framework it has produced a remarkable variety of works. Consider the following, chosen at random:

Bartók *Duke Bluebeard's Castle*
Berlioz *The Damnation of Faust*
Dvořák *Russalka*
Flotow *Martha*
Handel *Semele*
Henze *The Bassarids*
Janáček *Kát'a Kabanová, The Cunning Little Vixen, The Makropoulos Case, The House of the Dead*
Massenet *Manon, Werther*
Monteverdi *The Coronation of Poppaea*
Penderecki *The Devils of Loudun*
Prokofiev *War and Peace*
Stravinsky *The Nightingale, Oedipus Rex, The Rake's Progress*
Tchaikovsky *The Queen of Spades*
Wagner *Lohengrin, The Mastersingers*
Weill *The Rise and Fall of the City of Mahagonny*
Weinberger *Švanda the Bagpiper*

Of opera production

Production in opera, though it is not strictly a musical matter is vitally important. It is true that the complete musician who simply wants to hear the music of a great opera may be willing to shut his eyes to a hideous and incompetent setting and still able to enjoy himself. But if opera appeals to complete musicians only, it is doomed to failure, for there are not enough of them to keep it going.

That the general public in England will not go to 'see' operas, as it would certainly put it, unless they are beautifully and interestingly produced, may be taken for granted. It is in fact now being considerably pampered in this respect, so that one need no longer priggishly reproach those who talk about 'seeing' operas, especially when so many operatic performances are heard, and heard only, over the air. Scenic design for opera is doubtless England's most distinguished contribution to this form of art. Such things as Oliver Messel's amazingly beautiful sets and dresses for Tchaikovsky's *Queen of Spades* at Covent Garden, or Osbert Lancaster's enchantingly witty ones for Donizetti's *Don Pasquale* at Sadler's Wells, made unforgettable experiences of works not in themselves absolutely in the front rank. John Piper's designs for most of Benjamin Britten's operas have also been most remarkable, and several other excellent artists have been at work to make opera enticing to the eye as well as to the ear (e.g. Tanya Moiseiwitsch for Britten's *Peter Grimes*, Alan Barlow for Verdi's *Masked Ball*, Loudon Sainthill for Rimsky-Korsakov's *Golden Weathercock*, Sir Hugh Casson for Walton's *Troilus and Cressida*, and so on).

The model performances given, more exclusively and expensively, at Glyndebourne each summer, and by the Glyndebourne company at the Edinburgh Festival, are said to be barred to the general public, the theatre in Sussex being small and a visit to either place costly. But they are such rare experiences that many people of small means have discovered them to be worth saving up for once in a way, and there too the eye is nowadays as much flattered as the ear. Casson's designs for Gluck's *Alceste*, Messel's for Rossini's *Barber* and *Le Comte Ory* and Strauss's *Ariadne*, Lancaster's for Stravinsky's *The Rake's Progress*, for instance, were all things of exquisite beauty and style.

Of deportment at the opera house

The potential opera-goer, having been told what he has a right to expect at performances, may now without offence be reminded of a few things that can be reasonably expected of him. Some bad habits still prevail which, by eradicating in himself, he may perhaps help to exterminate in others, though of course it remains true that, as Oscar Wilde said, 'Vulgarity is the behaviour of other people.' One of the most primitive and at the same time offensive is that of arriving late, a transgression equalled only by that of leaving before the end. It must be admitted that both are complicated by a tragic possibility of misunderstanding. It may well be that a late-comer, who tries desperately to present a brazen front before all the glowerings that assail him on all sides, is actually consumed with shame at making a disturbance and vexed at not being able to explain to everybody how his car was unexpectedly delayed by a policeman who may know all about point duty, but has no regard whatever for opera. Those who leave early, too, may possibly have found that the performance is taking longer than they expected and that the last train on which they depend will be missed if the fall of the curtain is not.

With such cases one may sympathize theoretically; but the fact remains that in practice late coming and early going are among the foremost things to make one hate mankind and all its blundering ways. Quite plainly, it is the duty of all who attend a musical function, a duty to art, to other people and not least to themselves, to be punctual. It is quite possible to make doubly sure about cars, trains, dinner and other nuisances of civilization in planning an evening at the opera. Those who do not must be prepared to be looked upon, possibly unjustly, as among the barbarians who do not scruple to disturb a whole audience by turning up late and those who start that exasperating avalanche of early leavers – for there are always plenty of sheepish people ready to follow the bad example – merely because they cannot be bothered to get into a bit of a crush at the end of the performance. I believe that is the real reason for most of the early leaving that goes on in our theatres. It is not, I am sure, that people suddenly begin to be so intolerably bored by a performance that they cannot possibly endure another five minutes of it, after having sat through it for a whole evening. For are we not a nation of clubs and tea-parties and school sports and prize-givings and what not – a nation trained to the most stoical endurance of boredom in some of its most subtly cruel forms?

Another trespass that is still too frequently committed at opera performances is that of creating disturbances in the middle by misplaced outbursts of enthusiasm or at least benevolence. It is true that this sort of annoyance used to be far more rife than it is nowadays. I shall never forget the horrors of a performance of *Don Giovanni* at Covent Garden at which not one of the wonderful instrumental postludes to the arias could be heard for the clapping that burst immediately upon the singer's final note.

Happily such atrocities seem to be a thing of the past. As a rule opera audiences have the good sense to wait at least until an aria they are aching to applaud is really finished, orchestra and all, and if the work happens to be one composed of a string of set pieces and of a lightish character – say *The Barber of Seville* – there is really no harm in a little demonstration of pleasure in the middle of an act, provided it be sincere and well-conducted. In fact I am not sure that it does not enliven the performances and put spirit into the singers. But where the music is continuous, any interruption before the end of the act is a lapse of taste, and it is always well to remember that an operatic act is not finished when the curtain begins to descend, but only when the music has stopped. You may find to your embar-rassment – embarrassment, that is, if you have been clapping too rashly – that though the curtain may have dropped, the music does not stop at all, but leads on to the next scene, as in *Götterdämmerung* for example. Nothing could be more humiliating than to be found smiting one's hands together with a resounding smack while the rest of the audience gasps and glares, and then to look artificially unconcerned, as though the fly had been successfully killed at the first attempt. Therefore, if you do not wish to look like the abject hero of a *faux pas* in a Bateman cartoon, you will be well advised never to applaud at an opera until you are quite sure that the proper moment has arrived. There is not always a vainglorious singer present who will be prepared to acknowledge an encouragement at any stage of the performance, however inopportune.

Of deportment in the concert hall

It is perhaps needless to say that in the concert room too the attitude of an audience makes a great deal of difference to the impression made by the music. But although, as music is being taken more and more seriously by the public at large, concert manners are steadily improving, the behaviour of some people – invariably 'other' people – still makes it desirable to advise all frequenters of concerts to make a firm stand against abuses, if not by protests, which un-fortunately have a way of being at least as disturbing as the offences themselves, at any rate by example. Punctuality should be raised to the dignity of the first concert-goer's virtue and observed especially in cases of performance of long works at which late-comers cannot be kept waiting outside, as fortunately they almost invariable are nowadays at miscellaneous concerts.

That talk during the music is a bad habit hardly requires pointing out; but it is perhaps worth remembering how difficult it may become at times to resist passing a remark to a friend if one is truly interested, keenly appreciative or passionately indignant. I am not so sure that in such cases a forcibly kept silence is always desirable. It is better that music should rouse feelings too strong for restraint than that it should leave us indifferent. If you cannot keep a remark to yourself without the danger of bursting, one can only say that to utter it will be less troublesome than to burst. To make an observation in an undertone during a not too quiet passage of music is not likely to be noticeably disturbing. Only let it *be* an undertone and on no account a whisper. Ordinary speech kept very low does not carry beyond your immediate neighbour's ear; a whisper, with its sharply exaggerated sibilants, can cut through a concert room like a sudden gust of wind through the rigging of a ship. The historic remark of 'we always fry ours in dripping' that is said to have once reverberated through the whole enormous nave of the Crystal Palace in the middle of the performance of some solemn classic was not delivered in a shout: it was a whisper.[1]

Of applause and its abuse

The intelligent concert-goer could do much to help rescue applause from the silly convention it has unfortunately become. One would think that applause ought to have something to do with the public's reaction to a performance, but only too often one suspects it to be a purely mechanical response. At certain concerts which attract a select audience – I mean musically, not socially select – differences in the quality of the applause may sometimes be detected which an analytical ear may bring into accord with the quality of the performance; but too often the same thick, nondescript noise of hand-clapping greets any and every sort of music-making and induces one to ask despairingly whether audiences are really as dense as they seem or merely misguidedly kind-hearted.

Occasionally one has cause to suspect the latter more strongly. It is a psychologically interesting if artistically distressing fact that when for once in a way an audience in this country goes to quite extravagant lengths of generosity in the matter of applause, it is usually after some ghastly blunder on an artist's part, some accident too obvious to have escaped even the most impercipient listener. The British sporting spirit, admirable even where it is most grossly out of place, asserts itself on such occasions with fervour that is humanly touching, but both ludicrous and exasperating from an aesthetic point of view.

[1] Mr Blom has forgotten to protest against those who tap time audibly with foot, or even finger. There are few habits in the concert-hall more infuriating to other people whose rhythmic sense may need no such artificial inspiration. – Ed.

I shall be haunted to my dying day by a performance, I think it was of one of the Bach Passions, in which a singer who was more admired in fashionable drawing-rooms than in the concert world found himself a bar ahead in one of the arias. Found himself, that is, after jogging along out of step for a couple of pages and meeting frantic signs from the conductor with a stony stare of non-comprehension. When at last it began to dawn upon him that something was wrong, he attempted to fall in with the orchestra at the precise moment at which the conductor had succeeded in cutting out a bar of accompaniment, with the result that he was then a bar behind. Being by this time near the end, he appeared to regard any further adjustment as superfluous, if indeed he was not beyond noticing the necessity for it, and arrived at his final cadence too late, with excruciating effect.

Well, except perhaps at events like the farewell of Melba or the reappearance of Paderewski, I do not think I have ever seen an artist receiving such an ovation, or for that matter receive it with such condescending complacency. The sporting spirit was working at high pressure that evening. The singer had suffered a double accident and yet gone through his task without a breakdown, and so he had to be rewarded for his pluck and compensated for his misfortune, according to the ethics of the racecourse and the football ground. That a frank interruption and a clean new beginning would have been much more admirable did not occur to anybody, nor was the audience seemingly annoyed by the thought that more likely than not the singer really did feel as though he had performed a valiant deed and richly deserved this outburst of popular enthusiasm.

The whole incident was utterly absurd and I can only advise those who go to concerts to leave their sporting spirit at home if they do not wish to become involved in ridiculous demonstrations of this sort. Where sports and games are concerned nothing could be finer than the principle that approbation should be offered for an attempt rather than an achievement, and indeed such a principle may well be applied to musical performances by amateurs. But professional performers are to be judged only by the results of their work and on no account by shows of pluck. An attempt not properly carried out is simply a bad performance, and there is no excuse for applauding this from any consideration whatever. It is an excellent rule for any concert-goer to regulate his outward response entirely by the impression which the performance as such makes on him, not by the performer's personality. And really, he ought to take the trouble to train himself to measure his applause by what he feels about the music-making. If he is stirred to the point of wanting to shout for joy, let him shout by all means; but if he is left cold, no mere sense of politeness should move him to stir a hand. Much less ought he to be induced to clap merely because others clap and it seems rather churlish not to join in. Enough goes on at concerts, goodness knows, at which one *ought* to feel churlish. But there would probably be less of it before very long if only everybody were to learn to deal out applause according to feeling, and not merely for the sake of keeping up a stupid habit.

Of lions and the press

Much of the emptiest and artistically most meaningless applause comes from the even worse habit of personality-worship. Indeed this amounts to a positive vice, which the lover of music cannot be strongly enough urged to shun. Although the cinema provides an excellent outlet for the shallowest seekers after entertainment, perhaps fortunately for music, there is no denying that the latter too suffers to some extent from the film fan mentality of the less desirable of its patrons. There are people who will listen to anything from a prima donna who has to have half New Scotland Yard on the stage of Covent Garden to watch her jewels, from a fiddler who has swum the Channel or from a pianist who has married first a peer and then a prize-fighter and is the mother of triplets. Beware of being caught by the glamour of such fascinating irrelevances.

Some newspapers, unfortunately, will do their best to spread what they call stories about an executive artist, particularly those who do not even pretend to take the slightest interest in their actual work. There are editors in Fleet Street who will welcome any indirect advertisement of an executive musician, provided only that it be sensational enough as news, while they will cut down the critic's notice of the same person's concert, supposing they do have a music critic at all and have not replaced him by a writer of musicians' gossip, to a minimum, if indeed he is lucky enough to escape having it reduced to nonsense for the sake of precious space, occupied more likely than not by the latest murder. Musical performers who are really anxious to endear themselves to the editors of the more popular and therefore presumably more useful Press might do worse than try their hands at some other than concert-room crimes. I would even go so far as to suggest to the most ardent seekers after notoriety among them that they might usefully put their own heads into the nearest gas-ovens. To people who do not perform, but who wish to show a sensitive appreciation of the best performers, I can only recommend that they should take no notice whatever of newspaper and other stories circulated about artists, but try them for what they are worth as musicians and form an independent judgment from that.

Of professional critics

If anyone does not trust himself entirely, that judgment need not remain wholly uninfluenced, at any rate at first. There is something to be said for seeking guidance from professional criticism which, though variously competent, need not be despised on principle. Rather would it be advisable to determine for oneself whether it is despicable or not. The one way of reading it unprofitably is to make up one's mind to agree with it on the assumption, all too meekly made, that after all the critic, who is bound to have had some kind of training, naturally knows better. So he may; but even the best critic sees things only from his own angle, and it is precisely the best who would not dream of asking anyone else to agree with him all the time.

What the reader of criticism should ask first of all is that it should be stimulating, not that it should be right. One critic may write brilliantly or entertainingly without being in the least convincing; another may be judicious and informative but comparatively dull to read; both will be worth attention, and if their views are diametrically opposed, all the more so. Even if the reader disagrees with either, he will still profit from his writing because he will have been compelled to articulate his dissension, if only to himself. In other words, he will have used his brain, which never does any harm.

Criticism, however, comes after the performance, which has the advantage of at least not sending anyone to a concert with a bias, but does not do everything for the listener that musical writers might do. Especially where it is desirable to read something about the music heard, rather than the way in which it is presented, it would often be a great advantage to do so beforehand. It is a pity that there is not enough opportunity of this sort. Newspapers are far too reluctant to help the musical public in this way. Only the few critics who are still fortunate enough to have a weekly column set aside for them in which they may deal with any subject they please are able to write an occasional article on an important work before its appearance or reappearance. Such articles ought to be eagerly looked for by the public and as eagerly read when found, unless they reveal themselves as mere pieces of news or propaganda.

The latter shows usually more intelligence than the newspaper stories and it has at least the greater claim on our attention that the sincere passion for a cause confers. Nevertheless, propaganda in all its forms had better be distrusted. The hitherto obscure German professor suddenly discovered by his countrymen to be a great creative artist need no more be taken on trust than the young English composer about whom another young English composer writes an enthusiastic article. It may only be that the former happens to have acquired some particularly impressive academic distinctions of no special interest to the world at large and that the two latter are entitled to wear the same public-school tie. Every interest, from politics to friendship, may be productive of propagandist writing on music, and at the slightest sign of it the reader had better desist from his perusal unless he scents some satisfaction to his sense of fun or feels in himself a firmer determination than ever to use his own judgment. In either of which cases propaganda may be quite a welcome stimulant.

Of programme notes

One way of obtaining information about a work to be performed is to read programme notes beforehand. Unfortunately they are as a rule obtainable only too immediately beforehand. The now extinct Courtauld–Sargent Concert Club, was so far as I am aware, the only musical organization that circulated its programmes with excellent notes a few days before the concerts – a procedure that might well be adopted by other institutions. To scan programme notes hurriedly just before the music begins is not very helpful, and the sight of people reading them actually during the music is a distressing one. It is too obvious that they can take in neither the work nor the annotations properly, and certainly the musical impression cannot merge with the literary commentary. The temptation to do so much as glance at programme notes during the music should be firmly resisted. Even where a purely technical analysis with musical examples is given, no exception should be made, for although these quotations in music type are immensely useful to the analyst in his attempt to elucidate the structure of a movement, nothing could be worse for the listener than to glue his eye to the first example and wait until the theme shown duly pops out of the orchestra for the first time, then to lie similarly in wait for the next tune, and so to the end. He will be highly elated over the clever piece of detective work he has done, but he will certainly not have heard the music.

It depends, of course, very much on the quality of the notes whether they will do the listener a service or not. If he finds that they tell him nothing he needs, he may put them down without compunction and hope that the music may do without help. It must also be said, in fairness to the writers, that the best music does not by any means always call forth the best commentary. A symphonic poem that may be poorish music but is based on a good subject may be quite exciting to write about, whereas a great symphony, speaking for itself alone in terms of absolute music may yield nothing beyond a competent formal analysis. Sometimes notes on the most poetical music imaginable may positively have to make dull reading, because the poetry may not be interpreted in definite terms, lest they should fail to express the meaning of the composer, who may never have intended to be definite. It does not do to praise or condemn programme notes for their literary merits or shortcomings. They are not meant to be satisfying primarily as literature, but as signposts on a musical journey of adventure. Signposts are not expected to be beautiful in themselves; they are prosaic objects showing the way into a land where one hopes to find poetry.

Of gramophonic aids
For a public hearing of the more familiar works the best preparation is, beyond a doubt, some kind of a hearing at home. Mechanical reproduction has made that not only possible, but often perfectly easy. Gone are the old times when one used to play through piano duet arrangements of orchestral and chamber music with an aunt or a sister, though let it be said quite firmly that this is still one of the ways of making its acquaintance most pleasantly and profitably, quite apart from the fact that the partner *need* not be an aunt or sister. All those who can play reasonably well and, what is more important, who can read at sight with some ease, must be urged most earnestly to play in duet form any mortal music they can possibly get hold of – and more particularly the immortal music. For the others there is the gramophone and the radio, not to mention the pianola, nowadays grown too much out of use to be discussed here more than casually.

The gramophone, to deal with that first, can by this time hardly be said to have any defects at all, at any rate in itself. It may be productive of abuses, as I will show in a moment; but the reproduction of the best discs available on the best instruments may be said to have come as near living performances as one may well desire.

Most of what is worth studying may be obtained, and the immense advantage of the gramophone over the radio is that we may always make our own choice of the music we wish to hear and may repeat anything we want to know intimately as many times as we like. The difficulty is that the expense of buying records means that the accumulation of a library of respectable size is a slow business for most people. Until it has grown to a fair size, the gramophone owner is in danger of either tiring of his stock of records or of limiting his musical experience unduly. There is also the danger that long-playing records restrict the number of shorter works we can afford to have in our personal collections.

As few people can make endless purchases of records, it is important to make a very careful choice. Their quality, which can sometimes be tested at record shops, should be the first consideration. But only the very first. What should take much more thought is the music that is worth keeping at home. This matters far more than the quality of the performance, though naturally one will get the best singing and playing that is procurable, if one's resources run to it. I should certainly advise all those who buy records always to set out with the intention of acquiring this or that work, not such and such performers, however eminent. Even if Beethoven's B flat major trio, let us say, were obtainable in a performance by the Archangels Gabriel, Michael and Raphael, it should still be bought for the sake of Beethoven.

What I have said earlier about the advantages of listening to music with the score applies even more forcibly to the hearing of gramophone records. Here, in fact, score-reading can be practised most usefully, so that full scores and records perform a kind of mutual service the twofold benefit of which goes to the owner of both. In following the music with the score, you will acquire a much more intimate knowledge of it; at the same time you will almost automatically become an accomplished score-reader, or at any rate a follower of the printed music, which is not quite the same thing.

Of broadcast music
As for the radio, it has technically very much the same advantages and disadvantages as the gramophone. They vary somewhat according to conditions and the quality of the instruments used, but for the listener's purpose there is not much in these differences. When it comes to the question of usefulness, however, radio reproduction is quite another matter. A slight advantage lies in the fact that the

performance is more direct, although still obtained at second hand by transmission, and consequently rather more alive and engrossing. One listens with a degree more of respect and less of detachment. Not that there is very much in it, for it still remains difficult enough to concentrate on a radio hearing and to treat it really like a performance, not merely like a household commodity turned on like water or gas – sometimes, it must be confessed, gas without either light or heat, but merely a lethal element.

That music by radio should be so easy to procure is something to think seriously about. Any quantity of it obtainable free of charge: that cheapens it perilously. Of course, the best things in life being free, this should make us hold it in contempt; but it would not be like human nature to be able to think of it quite apart from terms of cash. This is a pity. Those who wish to make a companion of music, not a slave, must be enjoined to rid themselves of this bad habit.

How is this to be done? Most safely, I think, by making up one's mind quite firmly never to have the radio going unless one means to listen. There is no harm, of course, in tapping the supply idly, from mere curiosity to see what happens to be 'on', for there is always the chance of an adventure. But there is no point whatever in keeping it going if the adventure has not materialized. If what is broadcast is not to one's liking, or if it is found to be something for which one has not time enough, it should be left alone.

But even this adventure is rather unprincipled, though I would insist again that I have no wish to be so priggish as to advise against it. What is to be viewed with disfavour is only the probability that, if there happens to be something going which one really wishes to hear, one may hit upon it in the middle. Incomplete performances are always vexing, and increasingly so in proportion to the rising value of the music performed. This pecking and nibbling between meals should therefore be reserved for occasional delectation, not allowed to interfere with a regular diet, and the latter should be worth some attention. Those who wish to make the best of their radio supply cannot do better than devise a programme for themselves. Let them sit down once a week with the *Radio Times* and draw up a calendar of what they intend to hear during the next seven days. If other engagements interfere with something unusually enticing, they may be worth changing; if not, then the music may go. There is, it should always be remembered, too much of it in the world to be absorbed, and the mere fact that an only too plentiful supply now happens to lie to our hand is not a good enough reason for us to plunge into a surfeit. If many interesting or thrilling experiences tempt us one week, it is as well to resist some of them. But they may as well be set down in the preliminary programme, provided that we can promise ourselves to cut them out ruthlessly if they will not fit in with whatever else is there to fill life. If we have work to do, or friends to see, or are perhaps only tired, then the music must withdraw. Nothing is worse than to listen with half our attention, unless it be to sample just a bit of some work or another and then cut off the rest.

Of fixing the mind

It is at the best of times not at all easy to listen to a radio performance with attention. In fact, speaking for myself, I find it amazingly difficult. I cannot tell what it is, but somehow it does not seem sufficiently absorbing just to sit there and let the music stream at you out of an apparatus. A score in my hand will help me to concentrate, it is true; but without that I soon begin to grow restless, however compelling the music may be. I find myself looking at the clock, getting up to help myself to a cigarette, stretching out my hand for a book, only to withdraw it again with a sense of shame, stroking the cat, worrying over a word in that morning's crossword puzzle, discovering a subject for an article – I don't know what else. A hundred trivialities and irrelevancies come into my head, until I feel as guilty as though I were eavesdropping and as often as not give up any attempt at paying attention, which for me is the same thing as turning off the music.

I speak quite personally for a moment because I cannot know whether many readers have the same experiences with radio performances. From what various friends tell me about their own, I should imagine they do. What I am quite sure of is that nobody ought to keep the radio going unless he is really interested, or at least determined to be interested, in what it emits. To try and concentrate on a large amount of music each week simply because it is easily available is to be unnecessarily conscientious, not to say heroic; to keep the radio always going, whether anybody heeds it or not, simply because it costs no more to let it yield a lot than a little, is downright vulgar. You may as well keep all the taps in the house constantly going for the sake of getting the most out of the people who make you pay water rate. In either case you gain nothing for yourself.

As an accompaniment to any other activity, except dancing,

radio music is pernicious. Some people like to eat, talk, play cards or chess, even read to music, which means, of course, that they are incapable of giving their minds to anything properly. Nothing could be more deadening to the imagination and the intelligence than this duplicating of impressions on the mind, for it means not the redoubling of agreeable experiences, but the halving and thus utterly ruining of two of them that can be enjoyed only separately and whole. I have just said how hard it is in any case to give one's full attention to radio performances; there is no need, to be sure, to go out of one's way to train oneself to inattention.

Of hearing, overhearing and listening

The larger question arises now how we do pay attention to music – not merely to mechanically reproduced music, from which it is time to get away, but to any sort of performance. Let us return to the concert room and see what happens there. Well, a great many things happen, perhaps as many different ones as there are people in the audience. For our present purpose they may, however, be reduced to three main categories, which I will for convenience call hearing, overhearing and listening.

The most primitive form is hearing; but though primitive, it is also most common, as a glance round any concert hall will reveal in a moment. There are always numbers of people who yawn or cough, ladies who fidget with their handbags and fan themselves, gentlemen who read the advertisements in the programme or whisper to their friends, and so on and on. Within certain genteel limitations the possibilities for betraying a mere aural function unconnected with any mental process are infinite. For that is what hearing, in the sense in which I use it here, amounts to. It is a scientific fact that, if the mental faculty is wholly engaged, such reflex actions as coughing or sneezing are for the moment out of the question. People sometimes wonder what would happen if a singer or player were suddenly seized with a fit of coughing, sneezing or yawning in the middle of his performance. But this is precisely what cannot possibly happen. Or has anybody ever seen it happen? If so, the performance must have been an extremely slovenly one.

Even a member of the audience who is entirely absorbed by the music cannot be caught doing anything of the kind. If he does, he has momentarily ceased to listen and taken, at the most, to overhearing, for it must of course be borne in mind that the three functions are very easily interchangeable. That is also why a careless performer *may* find himself caught in a coughing fit; my point is that one who is anxious about his work cannot by any chance be so caught.

Listening, it will now have become obvious, is what I mean by a total absorption in the music, not merely a soaking up by the ear, but its penetration through that channel to the brain. While that process is going on, no other impression or reaction but that produced by the music can impose itself. The hearer, for instance, may think of a beloved person while receiving a separate aural impression of sorts that remains distinct from the fond recollections; the listener will not be capable of thinking even of that person unless there is something in the musical impression as such to produce the thought and to make it commingle with what is being played.

It is much the same with reactions. It is always possible for the listener suddenly to become aware of intense heat in the room, the physical impression thus taking precedence over the musical one, and then begin to fan himself with his programme for coolness. But that will mean that he has ceased being a listener and become a hearer, if indeed he still pays any attention to the music at all.

Overhearing is more difficult to define and the definition, once made, more debatable. It may be said to take an intermediate place between hearing and listening. I do not, of course, take it in the sense of an apology for listening. I leave that to the person who tells you confidentially: 'I could not help overhearing Mrs Jones giving her husband a piece of her mind', which plainly means that she has been listening with strained ear and an unusually concentrated attention. Overhearing music is a kind of hovering on the brink of receptiveness, an absorption of the musical impression without any conscious effort. We may be keen, but tired. Nothing else will hold us more than the music, as it would a mere hearer, yet the music cannot quite move us out of our listlessness. But once the lassitude has worn off, we shall find that the impression has remained – nothing very definite, perhaps, only a sort of afterglow, but something compelling and endearing just the same. It is rather a blessed state to find oneself in at a concert, and afterwards the felicity, felt to be undeserved, is perhaps for that very reason the more welcome. The only trouble is overhearing cannot be cultivated. It is a delight that comes rarely, a gift of the gods to accept thankfully, but it must not be expected too often. When most expected it will be least likely to produce itself. What can be cultivated is listening, and if that is done that delicious sense of effortless absorption which overhearing can give will now and again come as a reward.

Needless to say, there are different ways of listening. Let me mention two, both of which are valuable in their way. It is sometimes good to listen with complete emotional detachment, merely for the way in which things are done by a composer or for the place occupied by his work in the history of music. At other times passionate listening is indicated – indeed it should always come to that again. The charm or beauty, the emotional significance of the music, the composer's sensibility will then sway the listener: he will be in love with music.

It ought to be possible to mix these two attitudes to some extent; but it is also very useful to be able to separate them and then to try and assume them in turn before different works which may at first seem to call exclusively for the one or the other. For instance, one would think it impossible, to begin with, to come to *love* an opera by Monteverdi or to take any real and detached intellectual *interest* in one by Verdi. Nothing could be more fascinating and revealing, however, than the discovery that in the former is, given an understanding of its period, a vast deal of sheer sensuous beauty, while the latter shows, apart from its fiery melodies, sumptuous harmony and dramatic aptness, a musicianly ingenuity that, studied quite dispassionately, yields a surprising amount of interest.

Of interest and taste

Interest, yes. The listener must have that as well as a fund of affection for music. It will help him not only to discriminate and weed out inferior works, but also to add others to this store which he would never have discovered by mere loving. The great thing, then, is to listen with attention to anything that presents itself. Only so can an intelligent choice be made and a large stock of music of varied appeal accumulated. To hear everything with an open mind, to accept nothing too gushingly and dismiss nothing hastily, is to lay the foundation to a true musical culture. Taste is formed by browsing, and if a bad weed occasionally spoils one's digestion, there is no permanent harm done.

By training a wide sympathy, by forming no prejudices, taste will be made comprehensive. For the lover of music must beware of acquiring too individual an outlook. To become so fastidious as to be able to tolerate only half a dozen composers or the music of only one period or one country is to become a bore to others and in the end a nuisance to oneself. On the other hand, it hardly requires saying, a taste that has no individuality at all, and no little spice of perversity, is too commonplace and dull for words. Only, if you do possess idiosyncrasies of outlook, beware of always indulging your peculiar taste, lest it should grow into a mere affectation. It must always remain possible to listen with interest even to distasteful things. If one truth is worth remembering more than another, where concert-going is concerned, it is that everything is worth hearing, at least once. It should be impossible to find a work intolerable to listen to the first time, however much one may wince at the bare idea of repeating the experience.

Of the historical sense

One way of acquiring a wider outlook is to cultivate the historical sense. There is much music, even great music, that does not become palatable until one has learnt the fine art of placing it mentally into a picture of its period; and it is astonishing how much of the world's smaller music becomes delightful, at least temporarily, once it is perceived against its proper background. It is possible, to take a great instance, to regard much of Purcell's music as irritatingly florid and repetitive and stilted, though his supreme mastery could hardly escape notice. But it will be found that all vexation will vanish and give room to the keenest appreciation directly it has been realized that Purcell's music is the ideal expression of the baroque style in music. To this end it is obviously necessary to come to know something of baroque architecture and painting and sculpture, though there is fortunately no need to have seen Salzburg and Dresden or the work of Bernini in Italy, desirable as such experiences are in themselves. The study of a few monuments of the late 17th century, lovely examples of which can be found in almost every church of any importance in England, is sufficient to reveal the reason for the amusingly naïve over-ornateness, the graceful excrescences often found in Purcell's music and to show that, far from disfiguring it, they stamp it with characteristic features of its time without which it could not reveal the whole flavour of the man's personality. For great men express their time as well as their individuality, and only the perception of both emanations from their work can yield the fullest enjoyment.

Every time an old book is read, a picture gallery is visited, an ancient building is examined, a chapter of history or an essay is perused, in fact anything connected with any form of art is considered imaginatively, a richer store of musical experience is laid by for the future. For all aesthetic apprehensions hang together. Let me try to find another instance. I will create for myself an imaginary friend

741

who is incapable of taking that keen-edged delight in Domenico Scarlatti without which any lover of music misses something in life. He may, for argument's sake, be made to object that Scarlatti's sonatas are merely the expression of a cynical swaggerer and give no emotional satisfaction. My answer to him would be that one should not invariably ask for emotional satisfaction, at any rate not without first inquiring whether the artist in question intended to give it. I should then recommend him to read one of the works of Smollett and to study the drawings of Rowlandson. When he had done so, I should invite him to lay his hand on his heart – his all too exacting heart – and swear that he derived no pleasure whatever from these deliciously stylish things merely because they left his emotions high and dry, as of course they would, and should. Having then, as I think he could hardly fail to do, admitted that he did find some enjoyment in them, I should ask him to go back to Scarlatti and say whether he did not now feel that there was some room in music for that master's particular brand of rather frigid and heartless but immensely vital and nimble wit. I should regard even the most grudging and fragmentary admission as a triumph and consider that my limited friend had made great *musical* profit from two enforced excursions into literature and graphic art which were, of course, beneficial in themselves as well.

Of the eclectic ideal

Only the very greatest musical works stand, as it were, detached from time. Everything else has a period-value that requires appraisement by the listener, an appraisement that can be attained only by an understanding of artistic life in all its phases, not necessarily by profound study, but by a kind of casual, opportunist training of all one's faculties of perception. They can be exercised almost everywhere, not only in museums and theatres and churches, by the reading of books, and so on, but in the streets and in conversation with other people, who are as a rule more intelligent and critically alert than one would suppose from their preliminary remarks about the weather, which only too often are allowed to clog any further progress of the conversation.

Now it must be remembered that very great experiences do not come often. Indeed it is not desirable that they should. One neither can get, nor should one wish, for a Matthew Passion, a *Don Giovanni*, a Beethoven quartet with an opus number in three figures, week by week any more than one wants to read nothing but the *Divine Comedy*,

Paradise Lost and the two parts of *Faust*. The rarer the occasions are on which the most elevating artistic experiences come the better, for there must be plenty of time for the countless minor edifications and delectations which the exploring of the arts offers. A lifetime is not enough to encompass them all.

It is nevertheless advisable to husband one's opportunities for artistic delight – or let me say musical enjoyment, since it is time to return to our immediate sphere. While as many different works as possible should be heard, it ought to be remembered that their enjoyment should never become a mere indulgence. It is good to listen to a great variety simply to satisfy one's curiosity, which again need not be extended to everything that is going in the way of new fashions and crazes. Curiosity being given its due, there must be room for that on which one can fasten a lasting affection. Have as many acquaintances as possible among composers, but be sure to retain a chosen number of them as friends. It is not worthwhile, however, to become attached to any of them simply from a sense of duty, because they happen to be universally recognized as outstanding figures. If you have no taste for Wagner or Brahms, for instance, do not pretend to any, though you will have to make quite sure of your disinclination by a most searching trial and a constant renewal of tests.

Of human judgments

To ask anyone to become an impartial listener would be absurd. Likes and dislikes add to the music lover's zest and interest, although it is true that there can be satisfaction both in the dismissing of the former and in the overcoming of the latter. It all depends on the quality of the music and on one's capacity of developing and refining one's taste. The great thing is to remain human in one's attitude to music, in other words not to come to imagine that there are any absolute values which one is in duty bound to learn to appreciate, perhaps against one's will. It may be admirable to attain to a kind of divine judgment of right and wrong by allowing no personal associations of memory, sentiment, historical knowledge and so forth to interfere with a cool and collected appraisement; but such utterly dispassionate listening is altogether too aloof to be desirable. Far better to be occasionally carried away by a second-rate work than to go about with an exalted air of one in a million who is always quite sure of what is good and what only seems so to the other 999,999 vulgarians.

That is speaking of works. In the case of performances it is as well to try and determine as positively as possible whether they are satisfactory or not. The only caution that must be offered here is that there are various kinds of satisfactoriness. It will not do to condemn a singer or player for not achieving something that was obviously not meant to be attempted, nor to praise another who may perform a work very pleasingly as far as sheer execution goes without entering in the least into the composer's mentality.

Of personality and performance

This leads once more to the very difficult question of how far the performer may project his personality into the interpretation, and at the risk of repeating myself, I let it. Those who wish to answer that question for themselves will have to bear two things in mind: it depends, for one, on the magnitude and significance of the interpreter's personality and, for another, on how far the projection is consciously made. I have already dealt with the first point. Much wilfulness may be forgiven an artist of outstanding character, an interpreter of the type of which I have mentioned Busoni as being representative. As for the conscious or unconscious influence of the performer on the music, the attentive listener will not find it too difficult to learn to distinguish between them. Those who let their own character come through uncontrolled will invariably give a performance of a too plainly tell-tale badness. A careless or flabby pianist will make any music sound slovenly or flaccid; a hectoring conductor will make Bach's B minor Mass or Delius's *Mass of Life* appear equally harsh and rigid; a conceited singer will give a touch of arrogance to Mozart and Debussy alike. In all such cases it will require little training in listening to detect that it is hopeless to look for truth about the music. The facts about the performer are too glaringly revealed.

With the conscious obtrusion of personality it is quite otherwise. Here the finest judgment is needed, and a great fund of sympathetic adaptability. Values may temporarily alter and, what is more, be found to have been worth the change. It was all very well, for instance, to think of Chopin as one of the most feminine of composers; but when a woman like Teresa Carreno came and made his music sound masculine, and doubly unexpectedly so, yet played it with superb conviction and persuasiveness, there was nothing for it but to capitulate admiringly. What was most amazing was that the music did not seem to have been in the least perverted. One simply felt that Chopin had facets that had remained unsuspected before. Thus does the great interpretative artist, in superimposing another individuality on that of the composer, often illuminate rather than obscure the latter's work. In fact, whenever that happens, the hearer may be sure that the interpretative personality really is a great one. Conversely, when the music does seem to have been wantonly perverted, the performer may be written down as inferior.

To draw the distinction here is not easy, as there are many borderline cases in which one cannot always immediately decide whether the performer belongs to the sheep or the goats. Short of discussing particular performers, for which this is not the place, I can only suggest as a general principle that the first test should be whether the artist delivers something that impresses one as being the truth – one of the many possible truths – about a composer and his work. If he does, the performance must be called a good one. Not necessarily a great one, though, which is another matter. Greatness comes in, I think it may be said, where the performer adds an imaginative quality that is quite his own and could not be reproduced just like that by anyone else, but does so – please remember – without in the least warping the aforesaid truth, but on the contrary enlarging and clarifying it.

Whether this happens in a performance or not must, failing actual examples that can be discussed on the spot, be left to the decision of each hearer, though I may perhaps add as a last warning that individual taste, let alone personal prejudice, should not be allowed a free rein here, if breadth of sympathy and sensitiveness of apprehension are aimed at.

2 LISTENING AND PERFORMANCE NOW
by David Atherton

The composer and his environment

Music has invariably been an expression of the age that produced it. For instance, in the 16th century we had the gay madrigals of 'Merrie England' expressing the sentiments of a relatively prosperous age, whilst in 18th-century continental Europe there were much more polished emotional expressions and refinement (e.g. Gluck's melodies). Most composers of the following century showed immense devotion to detail in keeping with the decorative and elaborate architecture of the day but, as the influence of the princely patrons of music diminished, compositions began to show more clearly the personal views of the composers themselves. Nowadays life is much more complex. Science and invention have taken a senior position in our lives and we ourselves are living at a nightmarish pace. Instead of stately minuets we now have the feverish rhythms of modern dances and the blare of high-powered record players in our trendy discothèques, machines which produce so many decibels as to be positively harmful to our hearing mechanisms. Just as modern life has become noisier, so too has our present-day music. We counteract the many aural disturbances, such as ever-increasing motor traffic, by switching up the volume controls of our amplifiers and by creating more and more aggressive noises. For example, the acceptance of transistor radios in public places is now a part of our everyday existence, just as the incessant use of 'atmospheric' background music in restaurants is a major irritant to people with any musical sensibilities. Psychologists tell us that the 'canned music' played before aeroplanes take off is a useful means of soothing people's nerves; for me it has the adverse effect. Is it any wonder then that music composed in this climate mirrors these conditions? The contemporary composer, as in past centuries, is simply reflecting the background of the civilization in which he is living.

Composers have generally dealt with the sights and sounds of their own era when writing descriptive music. When Honegger wished to portray a gigantic locomotive in *Pacific 231* he had to conjure up new combinations of sound, for the harmonic, melodic and rhythmic vocabulary of, let us say, Mozart would not have been sufficient to describe such a monstrosity of our modern civilization. Similarly Mossolov, in his *Soviet Iron Foundry*, could obviously not use the kind of material employed by Handel in the 'Harmonious Blacksmith'. Music must always acquire, just as languages do, new words and expressions, although in so doing it will possibly run the risk of obtaining rather negative reactions from audiences and critics. Indeed history shows that we should not pay too much attention to them. For instance, Monteverdi's music was at first considered to be quite shocking and Mozart's later string quartets were criticized as being 'too highly spiced'. Even Schubert, Schumann, Chopin, Mendelssohn and Wagner were all resisted by the conservatives and reactionaries of their time. It is therefore not very surprising to find fierce response to certain 20th-century devices, such as Schoenberg's twelve-tone system, which many regard as not even a logical development of the music of the past. Let us always remember however the remarks of Edgar Varèse, the French–American composer, who, commenting on the traditional view that every composer is ahead of his time, pointed out that the composer is in fact 'an *observer* of his time and that it is his audience who is usually about fifty years behind him'.

The composer and his audience

The ever-increasing gap between composer and audience is often attributed to the preoccupation of many present-day composers with experimentation and their apparent lack of concern for communication. There is much truth in this, for music, like technology, has developed in the present century at a pace unprecedented in musical history, so much so that 'the public', who have always historically been some way behind the composer, have now been left completely stranded. The composer has begun to live and work in his own ivory tower, seemingly oblivious of his failure to communicate with all but a fraction of his public.

To be fair the extremely conservative tastes of concert-going audiences do not help him. As all orchestral managers know to their cost, the inclusion of just one contemporary work in a programme probably means a drastically reduced audience and, since box-office returns are always a major factor in the continued solvency of an orchestra (more so in England than in, say, Germany where public subsidies are considerably higher), a play-safe policy is generally pursued. The results of this over a long period are less responsive audiences and poorer performances of the modern orchestral repertoire owing to players' lack of stylistic expertise and idiomatic familiarity.

In London there are five major symphony orchestras: the London Symphony, London Philharmonic, Royal Philharmonic, Philharmonia and BBC Symphony. All of them (with the exception of the BBC) have a dismal track record as far as the representation of the living composer is concerned. Take, for example, a typical season at the Royal Festival Hall. Statistics compiled by the Composers' Guild of Great Britain show that, in 1973/74, these five orchestras gave a total of 155 concerts – surely too many – and played 453 different works. Only a meagre twenty-seven living composers were represented, sixteen of them British, and, of the forty-seven works by living composers, no less than nineteen were by Britten, Walton and Shostakovich. The rest of Great Britain fared slightly better, with Wales, Scotland and the regional BBC orchestras showing the most originality, but even here a certain adventurousness was lacking. Is it any wonder, then, that the composer turns more and more towards the smaller art form and utilizes chamber ensembles of a specialist nature? If a society does not encourage contemporary art, then it deserves the artistic sterility that will almost certainly result.

Like drama, music requires an alert audience. Stravinsky writes, in *Poetics of Music*, of 'the listener who gives himself up to the working out of the music – participating in and following it step by step . . .'. This exceptional participation gives the partner such lively pleasure that it unites him in a certain measure with the mind that conceived and realized the work to which he is listening, giving him the illusion of identifying himself with the creator. That is the meaning of Raphael's famous adage: 'To understand is to equal.' But of course many listeners will feel they have neither the technical knowledge nor the experience to be able to participate in this way. Eric Blom's perceptive essay suggests a number of ways in which the intelligent listener can improve his know-how; these apply just as much to music of the 20th century as to a Mozart or Beethoven symphony. He will want to learn more about such elements in composition as serialism, pantonality, polytonality, neo-classicism, tone-clusters, quarter-tones, etc, but, although the acquisition of such knowledge will undoubtedly be of immense assistance in the appreciation of a new work, one must always remember that it is not *essential* to the enjoyment of it. After all, you don't need to know how a Rembrandt was painted in order to enjoy its beauty.

Inattentiveness
Audience reaction, whether to Mozart or Stockhausen, is a good barometer of the performer's/composer's ability to communicate. Undoubtedly an epidemic of uncontrolled coughing is an indication of the listeners' wandering attention. For the performer's sake, as much as the listener's, there should be strict observance of the notice posted in all the programmes of the Royal Festival Hall. Headed 'MIND THAT COUGH', it asks the listener to 'consider others' and informs them that 'during a test in the Hall, a note played *mezzoforte* on the horn measured approximately 65 decibels of sound. A single "uncovered" cough gave the same reading. A handkerchief placed over the mouth when coughing assists in obtaining a *pianissimo*.'

A fair hearing

As far as is humanly possible the listener should approach new works with as open a mind as possible. He should try to listen with the same degree of awareness that he would bring to a Bach cantata, a Beethoven symphony or a Strauss tone poem. The aim of all composers (and for that matter performers) is, or should be, to *communicate*, but they will not be able to begin making their point if they are not afforded the possibility of a fair hearing. They must be allowed ample opportunity to state their case and then, and only then, should conclusions be drawn.

Repetition

Unlike a statue which obligingly stands still whilst being examined, music is constantly moving away from one. To have the opportunity of only one hearing of a difficult piece of music is like viewing an art gallery from a moving car. Just as the performer rehearses the music, so must the listener. He must choose the most difficult passages for closer examination and repeated study, but only after a complete viewing of the work as a whole. As a conductor, at the first rehearsal of a new piece I always encourage the musicians to play through an entire work (or at least a complete movement) before commencing the detailed surgery, so that we are all aware of the general symmetry, character and mood of the piece. The same applies to listening, particularly to a modern work. If there is a recording of the work available, use it to familiarize yourself with the general architecture and sound-world before coming to grips with the inner detail. A recording has the advantage of allowing you to repeat a passage over and over again until the clauses become clearer, gradually turning into sentences, then into paragraphs, then chapters, etc.

Selection

There is so much 20th-century music to choose from that the serious listener must be puzzled as to where to begin. Might I suggest one or two works which could be used as starting points. They all date from the composers' earliest years and were written by probably the three most important figures of this century:

Schoenberg   *Verklärte Nacht* (Transfigured Night) 1899
             Gurrelieder 1900
             Chamber Symphony no. 1 1906
             Pierrot Lunaire 1912

Stravinsky	*The Firebird* 1910
	Petrushka 1911
	Le Sacre du printemps (The Rite of Spring) 1913
Bartók	*Duke Bluebeard's Castle* 1911
	The Miraculous Mandarin 1919

Familiarity with one or more of these pieces will perhaps pave the way to examining the more 'inaccessible' works by these composers. In most of the above you will find elements that you associate with pre-20th-century music (e.g. 'tunes', recognizable thematic and harmonic links, etc.), but also an abundance of colours, shapes, textures and atmospheres. It is these last qualities which have gradually assumed a more important role and have now become, in the work of Penderecki and Ligeti, the most dominant factors in their music.

If, after a great deal of persistence, you decide it is not for you, then try something else, for there are many people who adore, say, Tchaikovsky, but who find Brahms extremely boring, or who prefer Handel to Bach. Indeed you may find that you enjoy the early works of Schoenberg, but detest his serially-orientated pieces. Or again, Stravinsky as far as *The Rake's Progress*, but not beyond.

Of present-day composers the listener may be able to identify more closely with figures who write music in order to communicate philosophical ideas (Tippett, Nono) rather than those whose compositions are written on a more abstract canvass (Berio, Ligeti). Try some of the following for repeated listening:

Penderecki	*Threnody to the Victims of Hiroshima* 1961
	St Luke Passion 1966
Lutoslawski	*Trois Poèmes d'Henri Michaux* 1963
	Paroles tissées 1965
Messiaen	Turangalîla Symphony 1948
	Et exspecto resurrectionem mortuorum 1964
Henze	*Elegy for Young Lovers* 1961
Stravinsky	*The Flood* 1963
Tippett	Symphony no. 3 1972
Ligeti	Chamber Concerto 1970
Berio	*Sinfonia* 1969
Nono	*Epitaffio per F. Garcia Lorca*

Musical overcrowding

It is very simple now for the listener to suffer from acute musical indigestion. In London alone it is normally possible to choose from five or six events every evening in addition to having serious music on the radio throughout the day. Pop music, good and bad, is constantly available at the touch of a button, and even jazz, which is not as popular as many would believe, seems to be coming out of the wilderness. Unless you are extremely selective you run the risk of allowing your ears to be constantly bombarded with musical noises, to the point where *effective* listening becomes increasingly difficult. By all means play a Schubert symphony as background music whilst writing a letter, but always differentiate between this form of listening and that when you devote 100 per cent of your concentration to the work in question.

In the contemporary field musical overcrowding often takes a different form. The present trend is to build programmes of entirely modern works. This is normally economically sensible and provides much wider opportunities for the composer to have his music performed, but for the poor listener it is too often counter-productive. By the time the seventh work in the programme is to be heard he can no longer listen with the degree of awareness and acuteness that most new pieces demand. It also makes for divisiveness, your tiny specialist audience on the one hand and your traditional concert-going one on the other.

Participation

The awareness of the listener can be greatly enhanced by active participation in the making of music. If you are a member of an orchestra, try persuading the conductor to programme a 20th-century work composed in a slightly more advanced idiom than he might normally have attempted. As starters, suggest pieces which are not too frightening or enigmatic, works such as Bartók's *Rumanian Dances* or Stravinsky's Suites nos. 1 and 2 (orchestrations of the *Eight Easy Pieces* for piano duet). For the more enterprising, the Viennese School (Schoenberg, Webern and Berg) offer tremendous scope, although unfortunately they all composed cruelly exposed orchestral music. One exception is Webern's *Im Sommerwind,* an early tonal work (1904) for large orchestra, not too technically difficult and a good starting point for the uninitiated as it begins and ends firmly in D major.

For singers there are now many local amateur choral societies whose repertoire extends beyond the annual *Messiah* and carol concert. In recent years the best choirs have developed to the point where almost anything is tackled. To take part in exhilarating performances of such works as *Les Noces* (Stravinsky) and the *Glagolithic Mass* (Janáček) is probably more exciting and stimulating than listening to them.

School teaching

Musical education in the majority of schools has tended to be based on the music of the past. Most readers will have memories of sitting through periods of class-singing, or maybe discourses on rudimentary harmony or history. More enlightened schools may have provided extra-curricular instrumental lessons. In virtually all cases school teaching was founded on the traditional concept that it is the composer's function to specify the rhythms, pitches and tempi, and the performer's to translate them into sound. Applied to school activities this certainly develops skill at reading and, if well presented by the teacher, perhaps enables the child to enjoy a real musical experience, but it does not allow the pupil to recognize and develop the language of his own time.

The inquisitive teacher will be aware of recent developments in the classroom, particularly the work undertaken by Peter Maxwell Davies at Cirencester Grammar School during the mid-1960s. In a climate where pupils generally left school with scant knowledge of even the existence of most modern works (with the influential exception of the latest pop music), Davies introduced avant-garde idioms into his classroom and wrote a number of pieces for children without significantly watering down his style of composition (except in so much as he made them technically playable or singable by young people). Other composer–teachers like Harrison Birtwistle, David Bedford, Bernard Rands, Wilfrid Mellers and the Canadian, R. Murray Schafer have also written interesting works for schools, many of which allow the children, through very simple notation and improvisation, to become co-creators (as opposed to simply co-interpreters). Eventually some are able to create little compositions of their own in the same way that Art and English students are able to produce their own paintings and poetry. The composer of Example 1, for instance. This piece, entitled 'The Storm', was written by a class of average secondary modern boys under the guidance of their teacher, George Self. At a time when composers are tending to be more preoccupied with texture and tone-colour than they are with melody and diatonic harmony, this little piece is worth examining in some detail, as the different types of notation used are typical of many devices being employed today. First, the conductor indicates

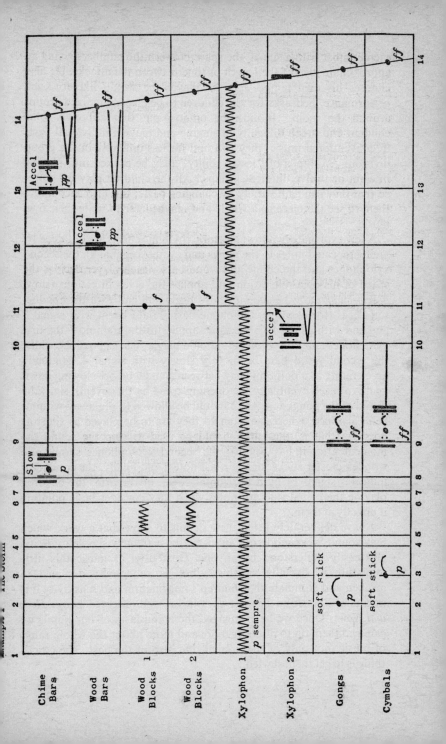

each number with a signal, the space between the numbers giving an approximate idea of the length of time between the attacks. He also chooses his own tempo and the players he would like for each performance. Self asks for the children to be placed in mixed groups around the room. 'It must be pointed out that although some children find much difficulty in singing and playing individual parts in conventional music, they will find far less difficulty in the group division. ... Pupils of "lesser ability" may be coaxed into playing in eight or twelve different groups.' All the children play off scores so that they can gain variety by changing parts; this also encourages them to see the piece as a whole and maybe later to write their own music.

A few explanatory notes: aleatoric rhythmic effects are obtained by giving repeated notes to the gongs and cymbals (signal 9), the second xylophones and the chime and wood bars – each player decides the speed of his own reiteration and applies the given directions (slow, *accelerando*, etc.); he/she must also begin and end with the conductor's beat (for example, the chime bars should begin with signal 8 and end with signal 10); the same applies to the tremolo – the first xylophones and first wood bars should play as fast as possible, whilst the second wood bars begin very slowly with signal 4, gradually accelerating to a point midway between 5 and 6 before slowing down again to reach eventually the opening speed by the seventh sign; the sound of the gongs at signal 2 should be allowed to die away without being damped, whereas at sign 14 they are to be played as short as possible (that is, the hand should be used to stop the sound the moment after it has begun); the second xyolophones should use wooden cluster sticks for their last notes; and finally, the conductor indicates signal 14 by a horizontal sweep of the arm, the children playing their final staccato notes when they consider he is pointing it directly at them.

I have deliberately listed these details to show that a work which may sound 'very modern' can in fact be extremely simple in design and easily understood by anyone. Obviously, as music this little miniature is virtually worthless, but as an activity designed to awaken and stimulate the children's imagination and sensitivity it is invaluable. As John Paynter says in his well-observed book, *Hear and Now*: 'Once we have engaged the enthusiasm of our pupils we can lead them on to discover more and more about the whole range of music, not only of the present, but also of the past. The crucial thing is to get them started.'

Notational developments

We cannot here examine the numerous notational developments that have occurred since the 1950s. Let us however examine two short extracts which the average score-reader would initially consider impossible to comprehend, but which, with understanding and patience, are actually easier to follow than many large-scale orchestral pieces such as *The Rite of Spring*.

First, *Tempi Concertati* by Luciano Berio, a work completed in 1959 and scored for solo flute, violin, two pianos and four groups of instruments spaced as far as possible from each other, preferably around the audience. I have conducted it a number of times and, even with the most sympathetic and technically capable of players, it has always proved to be a treacherously difficult piece requiring a vast amount of rehearsal time. Berio in his introductory list of instructions states that 'in a public performance the work should always be performed without a conductor, even though a conductor is always necessary for the preparation and rehearsals of the work'. In practice even the composer himself has found this to be totally impracticable. As far as I know there has never been a conductorless performance of the piece owing to its extreme complexities, although undoubtedly a more dramatic and theatrical presentation would result if the conductor was found to be dispensable. Berio asks that the gestures strictly necessary to co-ordinate the performance should be made by the solo flautist and sometimes by the violinist and either of the two pianists. In Example 2 these gestures are indicated in the flute part: ↓ for a downward gesture, → for a gesture to the right, ↖ for an upward gesture. They take the form of cues for specified instruments. During the work the ordinary rhythmic notation is gradually superseded by a proportional one where the absolute rhythmic values are not indicated but rather the relative time proportions. Berio asks that the notes ♪ should be performed freely; their actual duration being determined by the manner of attack, whilst the ♩ notes should last until the succeeding notes or silences, in proportion to the length of the cross-bar ⌐. Unless otherwise indicated (such as by the sign ↓ at the beginning of a bar), an exact synchronization of the parts written in proportional notation is not required or intended. The degree of approximation of the synchronization should, however, be prepared and predisposed during the rehearsals in accordance with the technical capabilities of each performer. Finally, the vertical dotted lines constitute a visual point of reference and thus suggest the average degree of approximation.

Example 2   Berio: *Tempi Concertati*

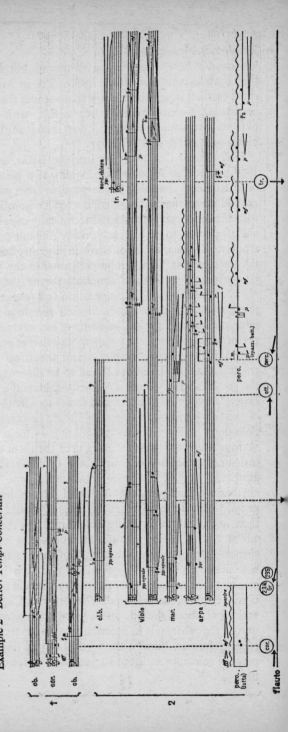

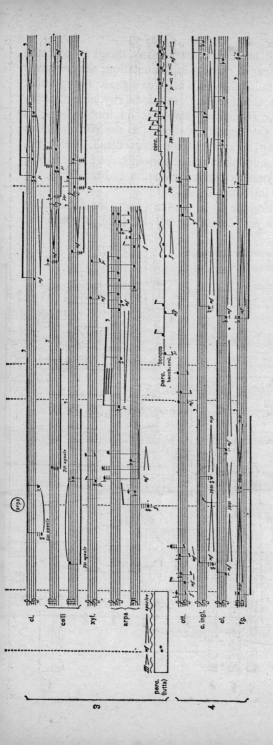

This short extract will be seen to have many things in common with Example 1: the spacial element in the notation; the deliberate gathering together of musical strands at given signals; the resultant flexibility and freedom; the absence of traditional rhythmic patterns, melody and harmony; the strong emphasis on tone-colour and instrumental texture; the opportunity given to the performers to determine the make-up of some of the inner detail. Above all, neither piece will ever sound the same at two different performances because of the employment of spacial notation and the element of indeterminacy thereby introduced.

At the risk of digressing too far let us take a hasty look at another example from *Verses for Ensembles* by the English composer,

Example 3   Birtwistle: *Verses for Ensembles*

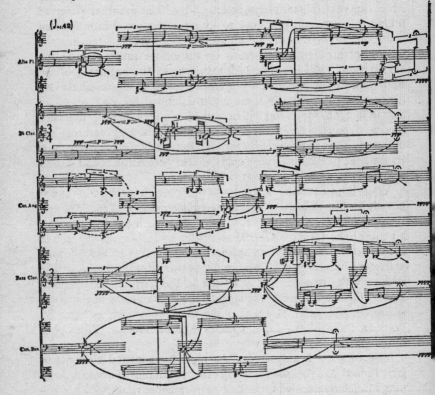

Harrison Birtwistle (1969). Here the five woodwind players are asked to play from three staves at once, although, as a catalogue of instructions at the front of the score shows, at no point is a player expected to perform a trio with himself. Each woodwind instrument has a choice of notes. He may start on any of the three lines offered at the beginning of the passage and must then continue with the same line until an indication that he may change to another line is given (↗); if there is a choice, the player may take any of the alternatives (⇐).

Improvisation

As we have seen notation is the shorthand by which a composer indicates to the players what to play and how to play it. It is a very inexact method of communication and yet it is this very inexactitude which appeals to many composers today. The eventual result of taking this unscientific science to its inevitable conclusion is often controlled improvisation, in which the composer still remains the captain of his ship, but remains on the bridge rather than in the engine room. Take Example 2 for instance. At the beginning of the Berio extract the percussion players are asked to improvise on *any* instruments. 'Aren't they being given unlimited licence?' you may ask. In fact, no, for as you will observe, Berio very carefully indicates precise dynamics for both players and meticulously controls the duration of the improvisation through the use of a rectangular box. By the time the flautist gives signal 295, the percussion sound should have completely disappeared (*sparire*).

As the diligent reader of this book will know, improvisation is not new. It is older than even the *basso continuo* practice of the 17th and 18th centuries (see pp 124, 128, 148). Anyone listening to stylish attempts to perform the *Messiah* as written by Handel, as opposed to the versions with added instruments and harmonies by first Mozart, and later Ebenezer Prout – strange bedfellows I always think – will be struck by the freedom and flexibility in the harpsichord continuo and by the elaborate embellishments and colourations in the vocal and orchestral parts. (I am thinking of editions such as those by Watkins Shaw, Basil Lam, Charles Mackerras and Christopher Hogwood.)

Improvisation is also one of the most fundamental elements in jazz. Indeed jazz performances will often retain only the barest skeletons of melody and bass, the best performances resulting when the improvisatory sequences are inventive and exciting. So too in much 'serious' music being written now. The more a composer leaves to the non-interpretative imagination of the performers, the more dependent he must be upon having players with equally creative minds.

Between the 17th and 19th centuries the pendulum definitely swung towards the use of more exact notation and less improvisatory performances, probably reaching its zenith in the 1950s with works which required (and still require) the performers to have almost mathematical, computerized brains: works such as *Structures* and *Le Marteau sans Maître* by Boulez and *Punkte, Kontra-Punkte* and *Gruppen* by Stockhausen. The performing musician has never since been held in such a strait-jacket. The degree of liberty given to him by the development of improvisatory techniques has afforded him a freedom of expression such as he previously enjoyed only during the baroque era.

The performance of contemporary music

In much avant-garde music the performer's role is partly creative as opposed to interpretative. I am thinking of works such as those we looked at earlier where he is directly involved in the construction of the piece's overall architecture. Interpretative freedom, as in Puccini, rarely exists. The opposite is often the case, for the two most important elements in the successful performance of most new music are faithfulness to the printed page and a high level of accuracy. Aligned to this is the degree of technical brilliance that is often demanded. Frequently the boundary between what is, or is not, possible becomes extremely blurred and performers find themselves being pushed beyond what they previously considered to be the limits of their capabilities.

The regular all-Tchaikovsky concerts at the Royal Albert Hall are usually done on one three-hour rehearsal. One twenty-minute contemporary piece for full orchestra might require four rehearsals. Add to this the fact that many modern pieces call for unusual instruments which cannot be used anywhere else in the programme, and you can easily see the problem facing the orchestra's administrator and accountant, particularly since they can expect a fall in the box-office returns.

The preoccupation of present-day composers with tone-colour is exaggerated by those who use electronic means to expand the sound-range at their disposal. The most successful of these employ electronically produced sounds as an extension of the existing material rather than as a substitute for it. In such pieces the performer may find problems of synchronization between the live sounds and those on tape and, where the transmutation of these live sounds is involved, by means of microphones and potentiometers, the conductor may find that he no longer has control over the final balance heard by the audience.

Our obligation to history

If, after a genuine effort and after becoming extremely familiar with a wide-ranging amount of contemporary music, the reader finds that he enjoys little of what he hears, then he may justifiably question the amount of time and money spent on presenting new works. My reply would be similar to the reasoned response of Charles Munch, the conductor of the Boston Symphony Orchestra, when answering one of his audience:

You reproach me for playing too much contemporary music, and I understand your point of view since you come to concerts for amusement or distraction or perhaps for consolation – surely for pleasure. But we are asking you to do something, to participate actively in an exchange between performer and public when we want you to listen to something new, something difficult to understand, even difficult to listen to especially at first encounter.

It is our duty to the young to give them the opportunity to be heard. Music written on paper must be realized and considered. The painter's work or the sculptor's work, when completed, exists for all to see. Music to exist must be played and who is to play it if we do not? I tell you frankly that it would be easier for us to play only older music just as it would be easier for you as a listener, but if we impose this restriction on ourselves, we should be abandoning our obligation to history.

Envoi

And now I daresay that all readers of *The Musical Companion* have been preached at quite enough, considering that what they are in search of is, I fancy, the acquisition of an independent judgment. I can only hope that the foregoing pages of this final Book may have helped a little to this end, if only by laying down a few principles, and I may perhaps be allowed to add on behalf of my colleagues, as I happen to be the last to address those in search of musical companionship, that we all trust to the whole of this volume or, more modestly put, to each other, for a certain amount of useful suggestion that shows music to be as approachable by all those who seek it sincerely. if not quite so cheap for those who regard it as a mere commodity, as modern conditions tend to make it.

INDEX

by Michael Gordon

Musical expressions are given page numbers only for their first appearance or definition and where the reference may be of particular interest.

Abel, Karl F. (1725–87):
  influence on English music of 312
Abraham, Gerald, *A Hundred Years of Music* by. on Russian music 283
accent and rhythm 59
accompanist, the 713–14
Adler, Larry (b. 1914) 691
Afanasiev, Nikolay (1821–98) 549
African music:
  percussion 228
  polyrhythms 56
Agincourt Song 442
Alabiev, Alexander (1787–1851):
  realism in songs 488
Albéniz, Isaac (1860–1909):
  folk-song, and 474
  operas 426
  piano music 615, 619
Albert, Eugène d' (1864–1932) 409–10
Alberti basses and Mozart 602
Albinoni, Tomasso (1674–1745) 690
  Bach's study of 595
Albrechtsberger, Johann G. (1736–1809):
  harp concertos 680
aleatory music 205, 351, 498
Alfano, Franco (1876–1954) 417
Alfvén, Hugo (1872–1960) 309–10
Algarotti, Francesco (1712–64) 396–7
Alkan, Charles H. V. (Morhange, 1813–88):
  piano music 615–16, 633
amateur participation in music 702–3, 751–2
Amati family, violin makers (16th–18th cent.) 149
Ambrose of Milan, St. (c. 339–97) 437
amour courtois (courtly love) 440
amplification 500, 501, 686
Anerio, Giovanni Francesco (1567–1630) 449
antiphony 40, 90–1, 438

in early Baroque music 70
Apollinaire, Guillaume (1880–1918):
  libretto by 416
'Apollonian' and 'Dionysian' music 27
applause, occasions for 729–31
Arabia, instruments of 150, 159
Arcadelt, Jacob (c. 1514–75) 446, 447, 454
arco (strings) 206
Arensky, Anton S. (1861–1906):
  piano concerto 648
aria:
  da capo, standardised by Scarlatti 373, 385
  development in opera of 44
Aristoxenus of Tarentum (fl. c. 350 BC), treatise on modes and keys by 140
Arne, Thos. A. (1710–78) 476
Arnold, Malcolm (b. 1921) 335
  chamber music 581
  concertos 684, 685, 691
Arriaga y Balzola, Juan (1806–26):
  chamber music 534–5
ars nova 441, 442
'art-anti-art' movement 351–2
Arts Council of Great Britain 433
Asantchevsky, Michel von (1838–81) 549
Asia, ancient:
  instruments of 142, 150, 159, 161
    woodwinds 151
  Mesopotamia 24, 28, 29, 33
Assyrians, ancient, instruments of 150, 159, 161
atonal music 77, 78, 79–81, 89, 341
  see also Twelve-note scale
Attaignant, Pierre (?–1552) 507, 511
Atterberg, Kurt (1887–1974) 310
Auber, D. F. E. (1782–1871):
  opera 393

Auden, W. H. (1907–73):
  libretti by 421, 423–4
Audran, Edmond (1842–1901):
  operettas 344
aulos (reed-pipe) 26–7
Avignon, Papal Court at 441

Babbitt, Milton (b. 1916) 326
  chamber music 577, 578
  rhythmic series 60
  vocal works 500
Bach, Carl Philipp Emanuel (1714–88)
    596
  cello concerto 676
  continuo, on 513
  flute, works for 683, 684
  Neapolitan operas, influence on 378
  influence on Haydn 598, 634
  motives, and 106
  oboe concerto 685
  symphonic form in chamber music
    518
Bach, Johann Christian ('English
    Bach', 1735–82):
  chamber music 518
  English music, influence on 312
Bach, Johann Christoph (1732–95):
  chamber music 518
Bach, Johann Sebastian (1685–1750):
  background to work 349–50, 593–5
  brass, and 156
  'broken work', use of 158
  cantatas, church 461–2
  cello, works for 678
  chamber music, and 514
  Christmas Oratorio 461
    and tempo 58
  chromatic harmony, and 79
  concertos:
    Brandenburg:
      'broken work', non-use of 158
      concerti rossi, as 632
      counterpoint 202
      flute 683
      dissonance 76
      ritornello 45–6
      syncopation 54–5
      timbre 70
    harpsichord 633

  'Italian' 633
  oboe d'amore 685
  solo 633
  violin 665–6
  violins, two 64
  death of 596
  'Du bist die Ruhe' ('You are my
    peace') 98
  flute sonatas 684
  fugues 44, 107–8, 594–6
  Handel, compared with 460–1
  keyboard music 593–6
  '48' 41, 107
  Mass in B minor 462
    dance tunes, and 45
    fugues in 107
    romanticism 110
    modulation 98
  orchestration 172, 202
  Passions 462
    harmonization and 79
    intervals, and 75
    motives, and 87
  preludes 594–6
  programme music, and 336
  religion of 461–2
  suites, orchestrated 46, 100,
    328
  trumpet music 114
  violin sonatas 655–6
  violin, unaccompanied 662–3
  woodwinds 151
Baird, Taduesz (b. 1928) 343
bagpipes 29
Balakirev, Mill Alexeivich (1836–
    1910) 338, 350
  influence on Russian composers 285,
    286–7
  piano music 623
  songs 488–9
  symphonies 283, 287
Balfe, M. W (1808–70):
  The Bohemian Girl 414
Balinese Gamelan orchestras 51, 71,
    141–2, 228
ballad, 475
ballade 440
ballata 442
ballet form in madrigals 453

Banks, Don (b. 1923):
  horn concerto 690
  Three Episodes, flute and piano 684–5
  trios 579–80
  violin concerto 673
Bantock, Granville (1868–1946):
  'Hebridean' Symphony 313
Barber, Samuel (b. 1910):
  cello sonata 679
  opera 430
  piano concerto 648
  piano sonata 679
  songs 499
  symphonic works 326
  violin concerto 674
Barberini family (17th cent. opera
      patrons) 364
Bardi, Count Giovanni (1534–1612),
      circle of 362–3
bar-lines 36, 456
Barnett, J. F. (1802–90):
  operas 413–14
Barraqué, Jean (1928–73):
  piano music 629
Barraud, Henry (b. 1900):
  flute, music for 684
Bartók, Bela (1881–1945):
  chamber music 572–4
  concertos:
    orchestra, for 75, 632–3
    piano 646–7
    viola 675
  Duke Bluebeard's Castle 425
  Duos for two violins 664
  folk-music, and 335, 347–8, 349, 474,
      492, 573, 629–30, 664
  harmony 80
  intervals 75
  melody 64
  Mikrokosmos and rhythm 56–7
  Music for Stringed Instruments,
      Percussion and Celesta 60–1, 226
  piano music 629–30
  random rhythm 60–1
  sliding notes 67
  sonatas:
    2 pianos and percussion 651
    violin 661–2
    unaccompanied violin 664

suites 330
Bassani, Giovanni Battista (c. 1657–
      1716), violinist-composer 512
bassoon 151–2
  compass of 213–6
  double 216
  mute, and 210 n
  origin of 151–2
bass tuba 219–20
  compass of 220, 223
Bax, Arnold (1883–1953):
  cello concerto 677
  chamber music 560–1
  sonatas:
    cello 679
    piano 630–1
    violin 660–1
  Symphonic Variations 645
  symphonies 316–18
  violin concerto 673
Bayreuth, opera house at 398–9, 400
  timbre, and 69
Beaujoyeulx, Balthazar de (?–1587),
      impresario 366
Beaumarchais, Pierre-Augustin C. de
      (1732–99), *Marriage de Figaro* by
      386
Beecham, Thomas (1879–1961) 698
Beethoven, Ludwig von (1770–1827):
  analytical criticism of 532
  antiphony and Leonoras 90
  'broken work', use of 158
  cadenzas 638
  chamber music 173, 527–33
  Cherubini; mutual admiration 387,
      533
  chromatic harmony 79
  concerto form 103
  concertos:
    piano 89, 104, 633, 636–8
    triple 693–4
    violin 666–7
  dance-like movements 104
  development, and 89
  discords 77
  Fidelio (1805 and 1814) 387
    Leonora overtures 90, 209
  form 45, 47, 82, 84
  Handel and Bach, re-discovered 50

Beethoven, Ludwig von *continued*
keys, development of choice 248 ff
Masses 467
motives 86
orchestration 172
Oulibicheff (19th cent.) on 19 and n,
22
parameters, manipulation of 91–2
piano, on the 116
piano, solo, works 603–6
Rasumovsky, Count, and 530
Rondino for wind 335
Rossini; mutual influence 390
sonata form, and 102
sonatas:
cello 678
horn 690
piano 603–6
violin 657–8
Songs 478
Sturm und Drang 604
symphonies 246–52
no. 3 (Eroica) 45, 102–3, 158, 164
brass 216
fugues 108
ground bass 88
harmony 64, 79
syncopation 55
no. 5, 19, 41, 105, 164, 248–50
melody 62
motives 86–7
timbre 69–70
no. 6 (Pastoral) 109, 326, 337
no. 9 (choral) 251–2, 467
form 84
motives 86
syncopation 55
thematic development 48
use of:
instruments (Fig.) 165
timpani 160
trombones 164
trumpet 215
variations 87
Wagner, influence on 397–8
Beggar's Opera, The, by John Gay 379,
420
folk-song, and 472, 476
bel canto operas 392

Belaiev, Mitrofan (1836–1904):
publisher of *Les Vendredis* 552, 555
Bellini, Vincenzo (1801–35):
concertino for oboe 685
operas 391–2
Benedict, Julius (1804–85) 414
Benedictine order 437, 439
Benjamin, Arthur (1893–1960):
operas 428
Bennet, Richard Rodney (b. 1936):
chamber music 577, 580–1
opera 429
piano concerto 646
piano music 627
symphonies 322
Bennett, Sterndale (1816–75):
chamber music 557
symphonies 312
Bentzon, Niels V. (b. 1919) 311
horn sonata 690
Berberian, Cathy (b. 1928):
vocal music 500
Berg, Alban (1885–1935) 341–2
'Lyric Quartet' 570
operas 174, 175, 421–2
orchestration 174
piano music 626
songs 491
violin concerto 213, 672
Berio, Luciano (b. 1925):
chamber music 582
Circles 582
influence of 580
piano music 629
Sequenza V (flute) 685
Sequenza VII (oboe) 686
Tempi Concertati, performance of
755–8
vocal works 500
Berkeley, Lennox (b. 1903) 631
choral works and songs 497
concertinos for flute and recorder
684
harp, works for 682
oboe sonatine 686
symphonies 321
trios 579–80
Berwald, Franz (1796–1868) 301–3
chamber music 548

Berlioz, Hector (1803–69) 912
  choral works 469
  cymbals, antique, use of 159
  Gluck's *Orfeo*, rearrangement of 381
  Harold in Italy (solo viola) 674–5
  harp, use of 227
  influence on: Russian music 285
    Wagner 398
  'motto theme' (*idée fixe*) 106
  operas 405–6
  orchestration 167, 168–71
  programme music 336–7
  Requiem and timbre 70, 71
  Romeo and Juliet 70
  saxophone, eulogy on 587
  songs 485–6
  symphonies 70, 262–3, 264–6, 336–7
  Traité de l'instrumentation by 168
Bernart de Ventadour (12th cent.
    troubadour) 440
Bernstein, Leonard (b. 1918):
  musicals 55, 430
  operas 430
  symphonic works 326, 646–7
binary form 43, 45, 46, 86, 100
Binchois, Gilles (c. 1400–1460) 443–4
Birtwistle, Harrison (b. 1934):
  operas 433
  schools, works for 752
  Verses for Ensembles, notation of
    758–9
  vocal works 501
Bizet, A. C. L. (1838–75):
  brass, use of 171
  Carmen 225, 406
  suites 329, 330
  symphony 266
Blacher, Boris (1903–75):
  operas 421
  serial rhythm, and 57
  vocal works 498
Bliss, Arthur (1891–1975) 631
  chamber music 561
  'Colour' Symphony 314
  piano concerto 645–6
  violin concerto 673
Bloch, Ernest (1880–1959).
  chamber music 567
  Concerto Grosso 694

Blomdahl, Karl-Birger (1916–68) 425
Blow, John (1648–1708) 335, 457
  keyboard music 591
Boccherini, Luigi (1743–1805):
  chamber music 525–6, 540
Boieldieu, François A. (1775–1834):
  harp concerto 680
Boito, Arrigo (1842–1918):
  librettist 392, 404
  operas 405
Bond, Capel, (b. ?–1790) 690
Bořkovec, Pavel (1894–1972) 262
Borodin, A. P. (1834–87) 302, 334, 622
  chamber music 531, 550–1, 552
  songs 488
  symphonies 283, 287–8
Bottesini, Giovanni (1882–89):
  music for double bass 680
Boughton, Rutland (1878–1960):
  The Immortal Hour 414
Boulanger, Nadia (b. 1887) 324, 563, 564
Boulez, Pierre (b. 1925) 229, 583
  conductor, as 195
  Le Marteau sans Maître:
    influence of 580
    orchestration of 178–80
  piano music 627, 628–9, 631
  sonatina for flute and piano 684
  vocal works 498
bow, hair, introduction of 147
bowing of strings 113
Boyce, William (1710–79):
  sonatas 513
Braein, Edvard F. (b. 1924) 312
Brahms, Johannes (1833–97) 335
  chamber music 173, 540–2
  choral works 469–70
  clarinet, works for 687
  concerto form 103
  concertos:
    double 694
    piano 639, 641–2
    violin 63, 641, 667, 668–9
  double-bassoon, use of 214
  folk-song, and 414, 474–5, 477, 481–2
  forms, and 47
  orchestration 170
  piano music 613–14
    two pianos 650

Brahms, Johannes *continued*
  St Anton Chorale 215, 333
  sonata form, and 102, 105
  songs 481–2
  variations, and 87
  viola sonatas 676
  violin sonatas 658–9
  symphonies 185, 223, 277–82
    choice of keys 279–81
    no. 2 and motives 87
    no. 4 and ground bass 88
brass:
  baroque composers' use of 156–8
  devices 217–19
  instruments:
    compass of 219–23
    mediaeval 154
    Roman 154–5
  music for orchestral 581
  muted 218–19
Brian, Havergill, (1877–1973):
  orchestration 173
  symphonies 318–19
Bridge, Frank (1879–1941):
  chamber music 558, 561
  suite, *The Sea* 331
'bridge' passage 102
Britten, Benjamin (1913–76):
  cello, works for 678
  Ceremony of Carols (harp) 681
  chamber music 559, 562, 575
  choral works and songs 469,
    496–7
  harp, use of 227
  Lachrymae for viola 676
  operas 87, 428
  orchestration 175
  piano concerto 646
  saxophone, use of 213–14
  Six Metamorphoses after Ovid (oboe)
    686
  suites 331
  timpani, use of 226
  violin concerto 673
  War Requiem 175
  Young Person's Guide to the Orchestra
    and cross-rhythm 55–6

'broken work' 158
Bruch, Max (1838–1920) 565
  Scottish Fantasy 670
  violin concerto 670
Bruckner, Anton (1824–96):
  chamber music 543
  choral works 470
  symphonies 49–50, 269–74
    revisions (Fig.) 270–3
Bruneau, Alfred (1857–1934) 407
Brustad, Bjarne (b. 1895) 312
buccina 154
Bull, Dr John (1563–1628):
  fantasias 510
  keyboard music 590
Bülow, Hans von (1830–94) 615
burden, the 442
Burnacini, Giovanni (?–1656):
  stage scenery of 365
Burney, Dr Charles (1726–1814):
  History of Music by 372, 375
Bush, Alan (b. 1900):
  operas 427
Busoni, Feruccio (1866–1924):
  interpretations by 715
  on Beethoven 532
  operas 418
  piano concerto 643
  piano music 615, 619
  violin sonatas 661
Butt, Clara (1872–1936) 493
Butterworth, G. S. K. (1885–1916) 333
Buus, Jacques (?–1565) 508
Buxtehude, Dietrich (1637–1707) 595
  organ music 651
Byrd, William (1542–1623) 32, 42, 450,
    451
  fantasias 510
  Ferrabosco, and 589
  keyboard music 590
  madrigals 452–3
  Mr Byrd's Battell 108, 589
  remained Catholic 451–2
  solo-songs 455
  virginals, music for 589
Byström, Oskar (1821–1909) 303
Byzantine Church 437

Byzantium and notation 33

Cabanillas, José (?–1725) 460
caccia (chase, hunt) 441
cadences 42, 43
  discords, and 77
  'Landani' 64
cadenza 103, 638
  Handel for organ, by 653
  use by C. P. E. Bach and Haydn 598
Cage, John (b. 1912) 93, 231, 327, 351,
    583
  chamber music 578, 580
  percussion and prepared piano, work
      for 692
  piano music 629
  vocal music 501
Camerloher, Placidus von (1718–82)
    515
Campian, Thomas (1540–81) 456
Campria, André (1660–1744):
  operas 377
canons 29, 41–2, 54, 441, 465
  beginnings of 439
  'crab', resurrected 48
cantata and Gabrieli 588
cantus firmus (fixed song) 31, 32, 41, 57,
    443, 508, 509
canzona;
  da sonar 507
  instrumental 444
Cardew, Cornelius (b. 1936):
  Scratch Orchestra of 583
  vocal music 501
Carissimi, Giacomo (1604–74) 459, 464
Carl Rosa opera company 414
carols 442, 475–6
  see also folk-songs
Carreño, Teresa (1853–1917) 615,
    744–5
Carter Elliott (b. 1908) 326
  cello sonata 679
  chamber music 577–8, 580, 581
  double concerto 694
  piano concerto 648
  piano music 630
  songs 499

Studies (solo timpani) 692
Casella, Alfredo (1883–1947):
  chamber music 565–6
  operas 418–19
Castiglione, Baldassare (1478–1529),
    The Book of the Courtier by, on
    fashion and music 360, 362
castrati 83–4, 375–6, 378
Caurroy, Eustache du (1549–1609) 511
Cavalieri, Emilio de (c. 1550–99):
  Anima e Corpo 363
  oratorios 459
Cavalli, Francesco (1602–76):
  operas 364–5
Cazzati, Maurizio (1620–77) 512
celebrity concerts, warnings on 717
cello as continuo 513
Cerha, Friedrich (b. 1926) 230–1
Cesti, Marcantonio (c. 1620–69):
  operas 365
Chabrier, Alexis Emmanuel (1841–94)
    335, 487
  piano music 616, 617, 650
chaconne 88
Chadwick, Carole S. (b. 1939) 563
chamber music:
  amateur playing of 721
  listening to 720
  with singers 517–18
'chance' music 230–1
chansons 473, 477
  collections of (16th cent.) 507
  de geste 440
  mediaeval four-part 444, 445
chansonnier 477
Chapel Royal (Household Chapel)
    musicians (15th cent.) 443
Charles II, King of England (1630–85),
    favourite music of 457
Charpentier, Gustave (1860–1956) 407
Charpentier, Marc-Antoine (1636?–
    1704) 463
Chausson, Ernest (1855–99):
  chamber music 554
  Poème for violin and orchestra 670
  songs 487
  symphony 266, 267

Chavez, Carlos (b. 1899):
  chamber music 566
  operas 427
Cherubini, M. L. C. (1760–1842):
  Beethoven, and; mutual admiration
      387, 533
  chamber music 533, 553
  Masses 467
  operas 387, 388, 389
  sonata for horn and strings 689
  quartets 525
  The Water Carrier 387, 389
Chinese music 24–5
  notation 33
  percussive instruments 228
Chopin, Frédéric, F. (1810–49):
  Bellini's influence on 391
  chromaticism, and 66, 79, 98
  interpretation of 715
  nocturnes 66, 79
  piano and orchestra, works for 640
  piano concertos 639
  piano music, 609–11
  rubato, and 59–60
  Waltz in A flat, op. 42 and cross
      rhythm 55
choral singing, participation in 702–3,
    751–2
chords and chord patterns 75–80
chromatic scale, introduction of 36
chromaticism 98–9
  melody, and 65
Cimarosa, Domenico (1749–1801):
  operas 389–90
Ciprian de Rore (1516–65) 447
Church, the:
  drama, and 359, 360, 361, 368–9
  mediaeval:
    puritanical control of music 30, 31–
        2, 35, 54, 142–3, 159
    modes, and 438, 441
    vocal music, and 142
    woodwinds, and 149–50
    worldliness and unpopularity of
        439
  post-Reformation and puritanism
      450, 451, 457
  post-Restoration (English) music of
      457

clarinet:
  compass of 215
  glissando and jazz 212
  invention of 153
Clarke, Jeremiah (c. 1659–1707) 690
clarion (*claro*) 155
'classical' music, meaning 110
Claudel, Paul (1868–1955):
  libretti by 416
clavichord 115
Clementi, Muzio (1752–1832):
  Field, John, and 614–15
  sonatas 606
Clements, A. J. and South Place
      concerts 559
close, half and full 84–5
Coates, Eric (1886–1958) 331
Cobbett, Walter Willson (1847–1937):
  chamber music 558
  *Cyclopaedic Survey of Chamber
      Music* by 558, 565
  influence of 558
Cocteau, Jean (1889–1963):
  libretti by 416, 417, 423
Colette, Sidonie (1873–1954):
  libretto for Ravel 415
Coliseum (English National Opera
      Company) 433, 723, 725
coloratura 376
comedy, *see under* opera
composers:
  early social history of 110
  modern, and audiences 747
Composers' Quartet (Boston, U.S.A.)
      578
concertato style 459
concerto:
  derived from *aria* 383
  form 103
  history of 632–3
  three-movement form 633
concertino 111, 240
  group 632–3
concerto grosso 110, 632–3
  20th century revival of 694
concerts, listening to 738–44
conductors 697–9
  Berio, and 755
  combination of several 232

role of, 191–8
Connolly, Justin (b. 1933):
  chamber music for brass 581
consorts 152–3, 154, 155, 157, 161,
  509–12
contemporary, *see* modern music
continuo 200–2, (Fig) 201
  chamber music, in 513, 520
Cooke, Derycke and Mahler works
  275
Coperario, Giovanni (John Cooper,
  c. 1570–c. 1627) 510
Copland, Aaron (b. 1900):
  chamber music 563–4
  clarinet concerto 687
  operas 430
  piano concerto 647
  piano sonata 630
  songs 499
  violin sonata 662
  symphonic works 325
cor anglais: compass of 215
  mute, and 210 n
Corelli, Arcangelo (1653–1713) 328,
  512
  binary form, and 45
  'Christmas Concerto' and tempo 58
  concerti grossi 512
  sonatas 512
    da chiesa 663
    violin 655
Cornelius, Peter (1824–74):
  Barber of Baghdad 409
cornet 171; compass of 220
cornett 153 n
Cornyshe, William (c. 1465–1523) 450
Corsi, Jacopo (c. 1560–1604) 363
counterpoint 107
  origins of 30
  rules of 76
Couperin, François (1688–1733) 335
  chamber music 591
  fantasias 511
  harpsichord, music for 591–2
    teaching for 590
  preludes 594
  vocal music 463
Covent Garden, *see under* opera-
  houses

Cowell, Henry (1897–1965):
  note-clusters, and 80
Cowen, Frederick (1852–1935) 330
  symphonies 313
Cranmer, Thomas, Archbishop (1489–
  1556):
  puritanical attitude to music 451,
    589–90
Creston, Paul (b. 1906):
  marimba concerto 692
Cristofori, Bartolommeo (1655–1731):
  piano, invention of (1711) 588
critics, professional 732–3
Cromwell, Oliver (1599–1658), and
    English music 457
'crooners' and *rubato* 59
Crosse, Gordon (b. 1937):
  vocal music 500
  violin concertos 673
cross-rhythm 55–6, 59
Crumb, George (b. 1929) 327
  Black Angels 579
  vocal works 500
Crusell, Bernard H. (1775–1838):
  oboe concerto 687
Cui, César A. (1835–1918) 550
  songs 488–9
cuivré ('stopped' horns) 219
cyclic form 106; Beethoven and 532
cymbals 159
Czerny, Karl, (1791–1857) 606

D'Albert, *see* Albert, E. d'
Dallapiccola, Luigi (b. 1904) 343
  chamber music 566
  operas 418
  piano music 627
  twelve-note scale, and 418
  vocal works 498
dance bands 176–7
dance tunes:
  mediaeval songs and 39, 453
  16th and 17th cent. 45–6
Dancing Master, by Playford 472
D'Annunzio, Gabriele (1863–1968):
  libretto by 417
Danyel, John (1565–1630) 456
Dargomizhsky, A. S. (1813–69) 549
  songs 488

Darmstadt school of composers 230–1
'Dashing away with the smoothing
    iron':
  melody 62
  rhythm 51–3
D'Avenant, Sir William (1606–68),
    masques by 367
Davies, Hugh, 'The Gentle Fire'
    group of 181
Davies, Peter Maxwell (b. 1934):
  chamber music 580, 582
  operas 429
  school teacher, as 752
  trumpet sonatas 691
  Turris Campanarum Sonantium
    (bells) 692–3
  vocal works 501
Debussy, Claude (1862–1918) 91–2,
    334, 339–43
  atonal music, and 78
  Balinese gamelan orchestra, and 71,
    141–2, 228
  brass, use of 171
  cello sonata 678–9
  chamber music 551, 554–5
  cymbals, antique, use of 159
  Danse Sacrée et Danse Profane (harp)
    681
  dissonance, and 77–8
  harmony, and 76
  harp, use of 227
  La Mer 71
  melody, and 64
  Nocturnes for Orchestra 71
  Nuages (Clouds) 71
  Pelléas et Mélisande 415
    and whole-tone scale 78
  piano music 616–17, 650
  rhapsody for clarinet and orchestra
    687
  Russian influence on 339
  songs 486
  suites 330
  timbre, and 70
  violin sonata 659–60
  Voiles (Sails) and whole-tone scale 78
  woodwind, works for 685
Delibes, C. P. L. (1836–91):
  suites 330

Delius, Frederick (1863–1934) 334
  Brigg Fair and chromatic
    harmonization 79
  choral works 494
  common chords, and 78
  concertos:
    cello 677
    piano 645
    violin 670
    violin and cello 694
  operas 427–8
  sonatas:
    cello 679
    violin 660
Dello Joio, Norman (b. 1913) 326
Denner, Christopher (1655–1707):
  invention of clarinet by 153
Desormière, Roger (1898–1963) 137
Destouches, André (1672–1749):
  operas 377
development 87, 88–9, 102
Diamond, David (Leo, b. 1915):
  symphonies 326
diatonic melodies supplant modes 456
diatonic scale 94, 98–9
Dibdin, Charles (1745–1814) 476
Dieren, Bernard van (1884–1936) 561
D'Indy, Vincent (1851–1931):
  chamber music 554
  Schola Cantorum, founder of 554, 566
  symphonies 267, 644
'Dionysian' and 'Apollonian' music
    27
discant, origin of 439
dissonance (discord) 76–81, 441
Dittersdorf, Karl von (1739–99) 379
  concertos 680
divertimenti 518
divisi 208–9
Dobias, Vaclav (b. 1909) 262
dodecaphonism, *see* twelve-note scale
Dodgson, Stephen (b. 1924):
  harp, works for 682
Dohnányi, Ernst von (1877–1960) 333
  chamber music 566
  suites 330
Dolmetsch, Arnold (1858–1940) 203,
    506
'dominant', the 96

Donizetti, Gaetano (1797–1848):
  chamber music 565
  concertino for cor anglais 685
  operas 392
double-bassoon 216
Dowland, John (1563–1626) 455–6
  Book of Ayres 455
  Lachrymae (1605) 509
Draeseke, Felix (1835–1913) 337
drama, the (15th–16th cent.) 360–2
drone, the 29, 42, 93
drums
  kettledrums, introduction of 160
    see also timpani
  20th century innovations 176, 228–9
Dufay, Guillaume (c. 1400–74) 32,
    91–2, 145–6, 443–4
  melody, and 64
Dukas, Paul (1865–1935):
  Ariane et Barbe-Bleue 415
  piano music 617–18
Du Mont, Henry de Thier, known as
    (1610–84):
  fantasias 511
Dunstable, John (?–1453) 443
  motets 32, 40
Duparc, Henri (1848–1933):
  songs 487
duple time, origin of 439, 441
Dupré, Marcel (1886–1971):
  organ music 652
Duruflé, Maurice (b. 1902):
  organ music 652
Dussek, Jan L. (1761–1812) 620
Dutilleux, Henri (b. 1916):
  symphonies 268
Dvořák, Antonin (1841–1904) 333, 335
  chamber music 545–7
  choral works 470
  concertos:
    cello 676–7
    piano 643
    violin 669
  folk-song, and 414, 474
  piano music 620
  Schubert, on 252
  symphonies 256, 258–61
    no. 5 ('New World') 210
    numbering of 256–7

Dylan, Bob (b. 1941) 475
dynamic and rhythm 59

Egge, Klaus, (b. 1906) 312
Egk, Werner (b. 1901) 420–1
Egypt, ancient:
  instruments 142, 158–9, 160, 161
  music of 25–6, 33
  woodwinds, use of 150
Eichner, Ernst (1740–77):
  harp concertos 680
Einem, Gottfried von (b. 1918):
  operas 423
Einstein, Alfred (1880–1952), on
    Mendelssohn 263
Eleanor of Aquitaine, m. Louis XII
    (c. 1122–1204) 440
electronic music 37, 61–2, 80–1, 144,
    180–2, 582–3
  antiphony, and 90–1
  instruments and 116–17
  Messiaen, and 175, 181
  performance problems of 760
  pitch, and 67
  timbres, and 73–4, 91
Eliot, T. S. (1888–1965), *Murder in the*
    Cathedral, Pizzetti opera based on
    417
Elizabeth I, Queen of England (1533–
    1603), as musician 589
Elgar, Edward (1857–1934) 335
  cello concerto 677
  chamber music 559, 561
  choral works and songs 493–4
Elgar
  Enigma Variations 333
  Falstaff 339
  Introduction and Allegro and
    statistical rhythm 61
  suites 331
  symphonies 313–14
    no. 1 and muted brass 218
  Violin Concerto 670–1
  Violin Sonata 660
Ellington, 'Duke' (1899–1976) 91–2
  encores 712–13
Enesco, Georges (1881–1955) 348, 661
English National Opera Company 433,
    723, 725

'ensemble of perplexity' and
    Scarlatti 373
episodes 105, 107
Esterhazy, Prince Nicholas (1765–
    1833):
  Haydn, and 240, 519–20
Evangelisti, Franco (b. 1926) 231
Evelyn, John (1620–1706):
  diary of 152, 457
  on 'Opera' 371
exposition 107

fagott (bassoon) 151–2
Falla, Manuel de (1876–1946):
  folk-song, and 474
  harpishord concerto 654
  operas 426–7
  piano music 619
  songs 490
  suites 330
'Fancy', the 558
fantasias 509, 510
Farnaby, Giles (c. 1560–1600):
  music for virginals 110
Fauré, Gabriel Urbain (1845–1924)
    335
  Ballade op. 19 644
  chamber music 553–4
  Fantasie, op. 110 644
    Impromptu for harp 681
  piano music 618
    duets 650
  Requiem 470
  songs 486, 487
  violin sonatas 659
Fayrfax, Robert (1464–1521) 450
Feldman, Morton (b. 1926) 231, 327
  chamber music 570, 582, 583
Ferrabosco, Alfonso II (1575–1628):
  Byrd, and 589
  fantasias 509, 510–11
Fibich, Zdenek (1850–90):
  chamber music 547
Field, John (1782–1837):
  nocturnes 615
  piano concertos 640
figured bass 513
film music 423
Filtz, Anton (c. 1725–60) 515

final, the 42, 95–6
finales 105–6
  operas, in 385–6
Finck, Heinrich (1445–1527) 446
Finney, Ross Lee (b. 1906):
  chamber music 578
Fischer-Dieskau, Dietrich (b. 1925) 497
  Book of Lieder by 707
Fitzwilliam Virginal Book 472, 589
'Five, the Big', *see under* Russian
    music
Florentine school (*musiche nuova*) 587
Flotow, F. von (1812–83) 409
flute:
  compass of 215
  crosswise played (*flauto traverso*)
    150–1
  introduction of 150–1
flutter-tonguing of woodwinds 212
Foerster, Josef Bohuslav (1859–1951):
  symphony no. 4 261
Fogg, Eric (1903–39):
  bassoon concerto 688
folk-music, folk-songs:
  cantus firmus 32
  Elizabethan settings of 589–90
  form, and 40–1, 83–4
  heterophony 28
  influence of:
    American 475, 687
     Appalachian 619
     Indian 471
    carols 473–4
    Czech 474
    dances 620
    English 471–2
    French 473
    German 474–5
    Hungarian 474
    Italian 473
    Norwegian 621
    Russian 474, 620
    Spanish 473–4, 619
     Moorish 473–4
    Welsh 472–3
  influence on:
    Albeniz 474
    Bartók 335, 347–8, 349, 474, 492,
     573, 629–30, 664

Beethoven 528–9, 530
Brahms 414, 474–5, 477, 481–2
Busoni 619
Copland 687
Dvořák 414, 474
English opera 414, 427
Falla, de 474
Granados 474, 490
Haydn 475
Ives 630
Janáček 547
Kodály 335, 347–8, 474, 492
Liszt 611
Mahler 477
Milhavd 557
Prokofiev 552
Russian music 412–13
Spanish opera 426–7
Tchaikovsky 550
20th century music 347
Vaughan Williams 494–5
melody 62, 63
modes 95–7
motives 86
numerical 471, 473
pentatonic scale 25
rhythm 51–3, 58
tempo 59
Ford, Thomas (c. 1580–1648) 456
form 81–5
'aria' 83
binary 43, 45, 46, 86, 100, 593
growth of musical 40–3
instrumental 43–50
key or tonality, and 85–6
'open' 340
'song' 83
ternary 83–4
variation 44, 45
forme fixe 440
Fornsete, John, of Reading Abbey
      (13th cent.) 143
Forqueray, Antoine (1671–1745) 511
Forsyth, Cecil, Orchestration by 155,
      207, 216–17, 224
Berlioz's chords, on 71–2
Fortner, Wolfgang (b. 1907):
vocal works 498
Foss, Lukas (b. 1922) 327, 575

Foulds, John (1880–1939) 331
Françaix, Jean (b. 1912):
chamber music 557
piano concertino and concerto 644
Franck, César (1822–90):
brass, use of 171
chamber music 553, 554
piano music 616
sacred works 468
songs 480
Symphonic Variations 644
Symphony in D minor 266–7
violin sonata 659
Franco of Cologne (13th cent.) and
      notation 143
Frankel, Benjamin (1906–73):
symphonies 321
Frederick Barbarossa (1123–90) 440
Frederick II, the Great, of Prussia
      (1712–86), and the flute 514, 682–3
Freemasons, influence of 465
Frescobaldi, Girolamo (1583–1644):
improvisations of 590
keyboard music 592
Fricker, Peter Racine (b. 1920):
symphonies 321–2
viola concerto 675
violin concertos 673
Vision of Judgment 497
Friskin, James (1886–1967):
chamber music 558
frottola 446–7
fugue, the 44, 107
Furtwängler, Wilhelm (1886–1954)
      195, 699

Gabrieli, Giovanni (1557–1612) 368,
      690
antiphony, and 90
family, and 448
grouping of players 189
motets and chamber music 508
orchestration, instruction of 156
sonata, first, 'Pian e Forte' 587–8
Gade, Niels (1817–90) 301, 621
chamber music and nationalism 544–
      5
Galuppi, Baldassare (1706–85) 379,
      380

gamelan orchestras, Balinese 51, 71, 141–2, 228
Gardner, John (b. 1917):
  chamber music for brass 581
Gay, John (1685–1732), *The Beggar's Opera* and *Polly* by 379, 420, 472, 476
Gebrauchmusik (workaday music) 571
Geminiani, Francesco (1667–1762) 328
Gentle Fire Group, the 181
Gerhard, Roberto (b. 1896) 343
  Chaconne for solo violin 664
  chamber music 577, 580–1
  Gemini (Duo Concertante) 662
  harpsichord concerto 654
  violin concerto 673
  vocal works 498
Gerle, Hans *Musica Teusch* (1532) by 512
German, Edward (1862–1936) 333
Gershwin, George (1898–1937):
  An American in Paris 176–7, 213, 219
  Mozart, and 714 n.
  piano and orchestra 647
  Porgy and Bess 430
  Rhapsody in Blue 212–13, 647
Gervais, Claude, Dances for viols (1555) by 511
Gesamtkunstwerk and Wagner's theories 396
Gesualdo, Prince of Venosa (c. 1560–1613) 447
  chromaticism and 65
  dissonance, and 459
Gibbons, Orlando (1583–1625) 454
  fantasias 510–11
Gieseke, Karl L. (Mozart librettist) 388
Gilbert, Anthony (b. 1934)
  sonatas 627
Gilbert, W. S. (1836–1911), and Sullivan Operettas 401–2
Ginastera, Alberto (b. 1916):
  harp concerto 681
  operas 427
  violin concerto 674
Giordano, Umberto (1867–1948) 407, 417
Giovanni da Firenze (14th cent.) 441
Glazunov, Alexander K. (1865–1936):

Borodin, re-scoring of 287–8
  chamber music 551–2
  suites 329
  symphonies 289
  violin concerto 670
Glière, Rheinhold M. (1875–1956):
  symphonies 291
Glinka, Michael I. (1804–57) 282, 622
  chamber music 549
  harp concerto 680
  operas 411–12
  orchestration 172
  songs 488–9
glissando 38
  clarinet, trombone and jazz 212, 223
Glockenspiel 160
Gluck, Christoph W. (1714–87):
  development of *bowed tremolo* 208
  operas 380–3, 395, 396
  orchestration 382–3
  trombones, use of 156, 163
Glyndebourne 433
  repertoire 726
'God rest you merry, gentlemen' 95–6
Goehr, Alexander (b. 1932):
  chamber music 577, 579
  piano music 627
Goetz, Hermann (1840–76):
  chamber music 543
  Taming of the Shrew 409
Goldoni, Carlo (1707–93), as librettist 380
Goliards (wandering scholars) 439
gong, sound of 82
Goossens, Eugene (1893–1962) 561
Goossens Leon (b. 1897) 685
Gossec, François J. (1734–1829):
  chamber music 553
Gottschalk, Louis (1829–69) 322, 615
Gounod, Charles, F. (1818–93) 335
  operas 405
  sacred works 468
  songs 485, 486
  symphonies 266
Grainger, Percy (1882–1961) 334
  gramophone, music on the 734–5
Granados, Campina E. (1867–1916) 335
  Goyescas 426

folk-song, and 474, 490
piano music 619
Greece:
  ancient 26–7, 33, 437
   instruments in 140–2
   notation and 33
  modern, and rhythm 57
Gregorian chant 28, 437–8
Grétry, A. E. M. (1741–1813) 553
  chamber music 553
Grieg, Edvard Hagerup (1843–1907)
    303, 306, 311, 330, 335
  chamber music 548
  piano concerto 643
  piano music 621
  songs 490
  violin sonatas 659
Griffes, Charles T. (1884–1920) 563
ground bass (*basso ostinato*) 88
Groupe des six 268
Gruenberg, Louis (1884–1964):
  operas 429
Guarnieri family (17th–18th cent.)
   149
Guerre, Michel de la (1605–79):
  opera production by 366
guerre des bouffons 378
Guido d'Arezzo (c. 990–1050) 439
  notation, and 34–5
  tonic sol-fa, and 99
Guilhem VII, Count of Poitiers, Duke
   of Aquitaine (c. 1071–1127) 440
Guilmant, F. A. (1837–1911):
  organ concertos 653
guitar, influence on Scarlatti of 593
Gung'l, Joseph (1810–89) 335
Guy, Barry (b. 1947) 579
gymel, the 442

Hahn, Reynaldo (1875–1947) 616
  songs 486–7
Halévy, J. F. F. (1799–1862):
  operas 393
Hamilton, Iain Ellis (b. 1922):
  clarinet sonata 687
  Sonata Notturna (horn) 690
  viola sonata 676
Handel, George Frederick (1685–
   1759) 328, 463–5

Bach, compared with 460–1
brass, and 156
'church sonatas', and 47
concertos:
  harp 680
  horn 689
  oboe 685
  organ 653
concerti grossi 202
cosmopolitanism of 463
death of 596
Gluck, on 382
'Harmonious Blacksmith', nickname
   111–12
hemiola 55
keyboard music 596
Messiah 464–5
  intervals 75
  rhythms 58
  romanticism 110
  tempo 58
operas 375–6
  arias and ternary form 84
oratorios 463–5
orchestra of 161
Purcell, and 463
ternary form, and 84
violin sonatas 656
Water Music, nickname 112
Hanson, Howard (b. 1896):
  operas 429
harmonic series and brass 214, 217–18,
   223
harmonics:
  explained 114–15
  strings, and 207–8
  wind, and 209 n
harmony 74–81
  melody, and 64
harp, 149, 226–7
  Ravel, and 555
  Wagner's use of 170
harpsichord 115
  continuo, and 200–2, (Fig) 201
  scales played with 2 fingers (17th
   cent.) 590
Harris, Roy (b. 1898):
  chamber music 564
  symphonies 324

Harrison, Lou (b 1917):
 Canticles (percussion) 692
Harty, Hamilton (1880–1941):
 'Irish' symphony 312
Hasse, Johann Adolph (1699–1783)
 380
Haydn, Franz Joseph (1732–1809):
 bassoon, and 688
 brass, use of 158
 canzonets 477
 chamber music 516, 519–21, 523–5
  attributions to Hofstetter 519
 choral works 465–7
 clarinets, and 153
 concertos:
  cello 676
  double-bass (lost) 680
  horn 689
  keyboard 634
  trumpet 691
  violin 666
  violin, piano and orchestra 693
 dance-like movements 104
 Esterhazy, Prince, and 240, 519–20
 folk-song, and 475
 influence of C. P. E. Bach on 634
 Mozart, and 519, 520, 521–3
 operas 242
 orchestration 202–3
 piano:
  sonatas 597–600
  use in chamber music 516
  works, other 600
 polyphonic development, and 89
 sonata form 101–2
 string quartets:
  'Emperor' and variations 87
  origin of 515
 Sturm und Drang 597, 599
 symphonic form in chamber music 518
 symphonies 240–3
  nos. 44–9, *Sturm und Drang*, and 241
  nos. 82–7 'Paris' 241–2
  no. 94, 'Surprise' 88
   binary form 86
   motives 86
   tonality 85
  no. 101, 'The Clock' 242–3
  sonata da chiesa, and 240–1

 variations, and 87–8
 timpani, and 160
Haydn, Michael (1737–1806) 691
hemiola 55
Henry VIII, King of England (1491–
 1547):
 composer 450
 dances 507
 instruments at the time of 507
Henselt, Adolf von (1814–89) 615
Henze, Hans Werner (b. 1926):
 concertos:
  double-bass 680
  piano 645
  violin 674
 'Music for viola and 22 players' 676
 operas 421
 percussion, works for 692
 piano music 627
 symphonies 320
 vocal music 501
heptatonic scale 25
Hervé, Florimond (1825–92):
 operas 401
heterophony 28–9
hexachord 36
Hildegard, St. (1098–1179):
 music dramas 359
hill-billy songs 475
Hiller, Johann Adam (1728–1804) 379,
 477
Hindemith, Paul (1895–1963) 345–7
 chamber music 543, 571
 concertos 645
  cello 677
  horn 690
  organ 653–4
  viola 675
  violin 672
 operas 419–20
 piano music 629
 sonatas:
  cello 679
  clarinet 687
  cor anglais 686
  flute 684
  harp 681
  oboe 686
  trumpet 691

two pianos 651
  viola 676
  violin 661–2
songs 491
symphonic works 277
The Four Temperaments 645
viola player, as 675
historical sense of music 741–2
hocket, the 31, 54, 441
Hoddinott, Alun (b. 1929):
  clarinet sonata 687
  harp concerto 681
  piano concertos 646
  piano sonatas 631
Hoffmann, E. T. A. (1776–1882) 418
Hoffmeister, Franz (1754–1812):
  flute concerto (form. attr. Haydn)
    683
Hofman, Josef (1876–1957) 615
Hofmannsthal, Hugo von (1874–1929),
    and Richard Strauss 408, 410
Hofmusik 505
Holborne, Anthony (?–c. 1602):
  Dances (1599) 509
Holliger, Heinz (b. 1939) 213
  Siebengesang (oboe amplified) 686
Holmboe, Vagn (b. 1909) 311
  chamber music 549
Holst, Gustav (1874–1934) 335, 560
  choral music 494–5
  operas 428
  orchestration 173
  Planets, The
    rhythms 56
    timbre 70
  suites 331
  symphonies 314, 319
Homer, Sidney (1864–1953) 499
homing note 95 ff
homophonic 42, 446
Honegger, Arthur (1892–1956) 632, 661
  chamber music 556
  clarinet sonatine 687
  concertino for cello 677
  Danse de la Chèvre (flute) 685
  operas 416
  sonatina for solo violin 664
  symphonies 268
horn 166, 183

ancestry of 155
compass of 220–1
stopped (muted) 218–19
Horovitz, Joseph (b. 1926) 691
Horowitz, Vladimir (b. 1904) 606
Howells, Herbert (b. 1892):
  vocal music 496
Humfrey, Pelham (1647–74) 457
Hummel, J. N. (1778–1837) 606
  chamber music 533
  piano concertos 640
  trumpet concerto 691
Humperdinck, Engelbert (1854–1921):
  operas 409
Hurlstone, William Y. (1876–1906):
  chamber music 558

Ibert, Jacques (1890–1962):
  flute, music for 684
Imbrie, Andrew (b. 1921) 326
improvisation:
  art of (16th cent.) 590
    re-emerges 49
  modern and old 759–60
  'indeterminacy' 49, 92
Indian music 24
  influence of 141–2
  instruments of 159
  Messiaen and 632
In Nomines 508, 509, 589
instruments:
  defined 112–16
  form, and 44
International Composers' Guild 563
interpretation of music 715–16, 744–5
intervals 75
Ireland, John (1879–1962) 333
  cello sonata 679
  chamber music 558, 561
  piano concerto 645
  piano music 631
  violin sonatas 661
Isaac, Heinrich (c. 1450–1517) 32, 42,
    446
isorhythm 31, 41, 57, 443
Italian influence, spread of 372–3,
    378–80, 460
Italy, audiences in 392
Ives, Charles (1874–1954) 37

Ives, Charles *continued*
  antiphony, and 90
  chamber music 563, 580
  From the Steeples and Mountains 90
  note-clusters, and 80
  piano sonatas 630
  polyphonic works 49
  songs 499
  symphonies 232, 318, 322–3
  The Unanswered Question 90
  violin sonatas 662

Jacob, Gordon (b. 1895):
  bassoon concerto 688
  on Berlioz's chords 71–2
Jacopo da Bologna (14th cent.) 441
Janáček, Leoš (1854–1928):
  chamber music 547
  choral works and songs 492
  operas 426
  piano music 620
  Sinfonietta 261
Jannequin, Clément (c. 1475–c. 1560)
      335, 445
  Battle 108
Jarnach, Philipp (b. 1892) 418
jazz 49, 141
  American composers, and 647–8
  Bach and 54
  Copland and 687
  glissando: clarinet 212
    trombone 223
  Honegger and 645
  improvisation, and 759–60
  influence of 175–6, 212
    on: Ives 630
    Janacek 547
    Milhand 557
    Ravel 223, 644
  metrical, not rhythmic 714
  opera, *Jonny spielt auf*, by Křenek 422
  syncopation, and 54
Jenkins, John (1596–1678) 510
Jensen, Ludwig Irgens (1894–1969) 312
Jewish music:
  ancient 27–8
    percussion 158–9
  ritual 437
Jew's (jaw's) harp 22–3

jig (gigue), the 46–7, 105, 143
Joachim, Joseph (1831–1907) 669
  Hungarian Concerto for violin 668
Joio, *see* Dello Joio
Jolivet, André (b. 1905):
  piano music 632
  trumpet concertos 691
Jommelli, Nicola (1714–74) 380
Jones, David (b. 1912):
  sonata for solo timpani 692
Jones, Robert (16th–17th cent.) 456
Jones, Sidney (1861–1946):
  The Geisha (1892) by 402
jongleurs (jugglers) 143, 439
Josquin des Près (c. 1445–1521) 32, 42,
      145–6, 444–5, 450
  El Grillo 43
  melody, and 64
Joubert, John (b. 1927):
  piano concerto 646
  piano sonatas 631
Juon, Paul (1872–1940):
  chamber music 543

Kabalevsky, Dmitry (b. 1904) 300
  operas 424
  symphonies 299
Kajanus, Robert (1856–1933) 306
Kabélač, Miloslav (b. 1908) 262
Kagel, Mauricio (b. 1932):
  chamber music 580–1, 582
Kalabis, Viktor (b. 1923) 262
Kalinnikov, Vassily (1866–1901):
  symphonies 288–9
Kalkbrenner, Friedrich (1785–1849)
      615
  Kammermusik 505
Karayev, Kara (b. 1918):
  symphony, no. 3 301
Keiser, Reinhard (1674–1739) 369, 372
Kern, Jerome (1885–1945):
  songs 499
Ketelbey, Albert (1875–1959) 331
key:
  Aristoxenus on 140
  change (modulation) 98, 99
  choice of, development by:
    Beethoven 248 ff
    Brahms 279–81

chromatic 97–8
dominant, of the 97
form, and 85–6
home 97
major and minor 42, 98
note meaning 'final' 97
signatures, introduction of 36
system, development of 42–4, 97
keyboard instruments as continuo 513, 516
Khachaturian, Aram Ilyich (b. 1903) 300
  piano concerto 648
  violin concerto 673
Kilpinen, Yrjö (1892–1959):
  songs 490
kickshaw ('quelque chose' – dance) 509
Kiel, Friedrich (1821–85) 518
Kirnberger, J. P. (1721–83) 477, 514
Klemperer, Otto (1885–1973) 92
Knox, John (c. 1513–72), puritanism of 451
Kodály, Zoltan (1882–1967):
  cello sonatas 679
  chamber music 566–7
  choral works 492
  folk-music, and 335, 347–8, 474, 492
  Háry János 330, 425
Koessler, Hans (1853–1926):
  chamber music 566
Kokkonen, Joonas (b. 1921) 311
Kontarsky, Aloys 628
Koppell, Hermann D. (b. 1908) 311
Korngold, Erich (1897–1957):
  film music 423
  operas 422–3
Koussevitzky, Sergei (1875–1951) 698
  double-bass concerto 680
Kraus, Joseph Martin (1756–92) 301
Krauss, Clemens (1893–1954) 411
Krebs, Stanley Dale, on Miaskovsky 292
Křenek, Ernst (b. 1900):
  operas and jazz 422
  vocal works 491, 498
Krennikov:
  symphonies 299
Kuchka see under Russian music

Kuhnau, Johann (1660–1722):
  Bible pieces 108
  keyboard sonatas 596–7

Lacombe, Louis (1818–84) 330
lai 440
Lalande, Michel de (1657–1726) 462–3
Lalo, Victor A. E. (1823–92):
  chamber music 553
  Symphonie Espagnole 670
Lambert, Constant (1905–51) 631
  choral music 496
  Music Ho! 352
Landini, Francesco (c. 1325–97) 441–2
Landon, H. C. Robbins, and Haydn 240
Langgard, Rued:
  symphonies 318
Lanner, Joseph F. K. (1801–43) 335
Lassus, Orlandus (Orlandi di Lasso, 1524–94) 32, 42, 447–8, 451
Laub, Ferdinand (1832–75) 550
Lawes, Henry (1595–1662) 456, 510
Leclair, J. M. (1697–1764) 659
  flute sonatas 684
  violin concerto 665
Legrenzi, Giovanni (1625–90) 512
  Bach's study of 595
Lehár, Franz (1870–1948) 335, 402
Leigh, Walton (1905–42):
  Concertino for harpsichord 654
Leighton, Kenneth (b. 1929):
  organ concerto 654
  piano concerto 646
  piano music 631
leitmotiv and Wagner 87, 398
Le Jeune, Claude (1528–1600) 511
Lekeu, Guillaume (1870–94):
  chamber music 554
Leo, Leonardo (1697–1744) 385
  cello concertos 676
Leoncavallo, Ruggiero (1858–1919) 407, 416
Léonin (12th cent.), *Liber Magnus* by 439
Leschetitsky, Theodor (1830–1915) 615
Liadov, A. C. (1855–1914) 552
librettos, bad 397

Liebermann, Rolf (b. 1910), works for theatre 421
lieder:
  collections of 707 n
  origins of 477
  see also songs
Ligeti, György (b. 1923):
  cello concerto 678
  chamber music 580, 582
  note-clusters, and 80
  orchestration 231
  vocal music 501
Lindpainter, Peter J. von (1791–1856) 650
Liszt, Franz (1811–86):
  choral works 468
  forms, and 47
  generosity of 612
  harp, use of 227
  influence of Bellini on 391
  influence on Wagner 398
  Liebestraum and chromatic harmony 78
  metamorphosis of themes 532
  organ music 652
  piano concertos 79, 633, 639–40
  piano music 609, 611–12
  programme music 337
  Samson et Dalila, recognition of 406
  'symphonic poems' 47
  symphonies 265–6
  Totentanz 641
  virtuoso, as 716–17
Locke, Matthew (c. 1630–77) 457, 510
  concerted music by 367
Lodizhensky, Nikolay (1843–1916) 488
Loeillet, Jean Baptiste (1680–1730) 690
Loewe, J. C. G. (1796–1869):
  songs 480
Lortzing, G. A. (1801–51), operas 395
Loussier, Jacques (b. 1934) 141
Lucas, Charles (1808–69):
  symphonies 312
Lully, Giovanni Battista (1633–87) 328, 462–3
  operas 366–7, 377, 395
Lupo, Thomas (16th–17th cent.) 510
lute accompanies solo-songs

Lutoslawski, Witold (b. 1913) 351
  cello concerto 678
  orchestration 232
  quartet 578–9
  vocal works 499
Lutyens, Elisabeth (b. 1906) 343
  vocal music 500
lyre (*kithara*) 26–7

McCabe, John (b. 1939):
  chamber music 581
  symphonic works 322
Macdowell, Edward A. (1861–1908) 322, 563
  piano concerto 647
  songs 499
Mace, Thomas, *Musick's Monument* by (1676) 511
McEwen, John B. (1868–1948):
  chamber music 558
  music, on 110
Macfarren, George A. (1813–87):
  chamber music 557
  symphonies 312
Machaut, Guillaume de (c. 1300–77) 145–6, 441
Mackenzie, Alexander C. (1847–1935):
  chamber music 557
Maderna, Bruno (1920–73):
  oboe concertos 686
Madetoja, Leevi (1887–1947) 311
madrigals 36, 335, 362, 363, 441–2, 505, 507, 508
  chromatic harmony and melody 79
  England, in 452–5
  Italy, in 446–7
  Triumphs of Oriana, The 453
Magnard, Alberic (1865–1914):
  chamber music 554
Mahler, Gustav (1860–1911):
  conductor, as 274
  Das Lied von der Erde 228, 275
  folk-songs, and 477
  orchestration 72, 173, (Fig.) 179–80, 229–30
  songs 274, 276, 484–5
  Sibelius, conversation on the symphony with 275
  symphonies 269, 274–6

no. 7 (1908), orchestration, (Fig.) 178–80

Malipiero, Gian F. (1882–1973):
chamber music 565
operas 417

Mangeot, André (1883–1970) 506

Mannheim school of violinists and string quartet 514–15, 518

Marais, Marin (1656–1728) 511

Marcello, Benedetto (1686–1739):
sonatas 594

Marenzio, Luca (1560–99) 335, 447, 449

Marini, Biagio (1597–1665):
violin sonatas 655

Marschner, H. A. (1795–1861):
operas 395, 397

'Marseillaise', the, and melody 63

Martin, Frank (1890–1974) 343
Ballade for flute 684
concerto grosso (style) 694
Eight Preludes for piano 632
harpsichord concerto 654
Petite Symphonie Concertante 694
piano and orchestra 645
violin concerto 673–4

Martinon, Jean F. E .(b. 1910):
sonata for solo violin 664
violin concerto 674

Martinů, Bohuslav (1890–1959):
chamber music 547–8, 556
concertos:
cello 677
double 694
harpsichord 654
oboe 686
flute sonata 684
operas 426
symphonies 261

Mascagni, Pietro (1863–1945) 407–8, 409, 416

masques 361–2, 366, 456

Massenet, J. E. F. (1842–1912) 339, 616
operas 406
songs 486
suites 330

Mathias, William (b. 1934):
harp, works for 681

Maugars, André (17th cent. violist) 509

Maw, Nicholas (b. 1935):
quartet 577
opera 429
sonatina for flute 684
symphonic works 322
vocal music 500

mediaeval European music 57–8
instruments 143–4

Medtner, Nicholas (b. 1935):
songs 489

Méhul, Etienne Henri (1763–1817):
operas 387

Meistersingers 39, 440

melisma 42, 439

mélodies, French 485–6, 488

melodrama, origins of 371

melody 62–7
harmonized single, introduced 42

Mendelssohn-Bartholdy, Felix (1809–47) 335
cello sonatas 678
chamber music 537, 538–9
Chopin, on 60
concertos:
piano 638–9
two pianos 650
violin 667
forms, and 47
Handel, and 468
Midsummer Night's Dream, and timbre 70
oratorios 467–8
organ music 652
piano and orchestra, works for 640
piano music 606
serpent, use of 157
songs 480
Songs Without Words, nickname 111
symphonies 262–3
violin sonatas 658

Mennin, Peter (b. 1923):
symphonies 326

Menotti, Gian-Carlo (b. 1911):
operas 430

Merbecke, John (16th cent.), settings for First Prayer Book 451

Mersenne, Marin (1588–1648), treatise on viols 509

Mesopotamia, music in ancient 24, 28, 29, 33

Messager, André S. P. (1853–1929) 330, 402

Messiaen, Olivier (b. 1908) 37, 229
  chamber music 557
  electronic music 175, 181
  Indian music, and 632
  La Merle Noire for flute and piano 684
  ondes martenot, and 117
  organ music 652–3
  oriental music, and 142
  piano and orchestra 645
  piano music 631–2
  polyrhythm, and 56
  scales, and 99
  Structures 651
  Turangalila Symphony 175, (Fig.) 178–80, 181, (Fig. 196–8), 268
  Visions de l' Amen 650
  vocal works 498

metamorphosis of themes, initiated by Liszt and Wagner 532

Metastasio, Pietro (1698–1782), librettist 376

metronome marking, introduction of 38

Metru, N. (fl. 1642) 511

Meyerbeer, Jacob (1791–1864):
  operas 393, 394

Miaskovsky, N. Y. (1881–1950):
  symphonies 291–2

microtonal:
  harmonium 36–7
  scales 36–7, 67, 99

'Mighty Handful', *see under* Russian music

Milhaud, Darius (1892–1974) 661
  cello concerto 677
  chamber music 556
  harmonica and orchestra, suite for 691
    operas 416
  percussion, works for 692
  Scaramouche 650
  suites 330, 691
  symphonies 268

Millöcker, Karl (1842–99) 402

Milner, Anthony (b. 1925):
  vocal music 496

Milton, John, music for *Comus* by 456

minim, origin of 35

Minnesingers 39, 440

minstrels, court 439

minuet 70, 104, 237, 239
  introduction of 46–7
  omission in concertos of 633

modern music:
  audiences, and 747–9
  introductory programmes of 749–50
  listening to 748–50
  performance of 760–1

modes 94–8
  Aristoxenus on 140
  before 17th century 42
  plainsong, and 437
  rhythmic 35–6
  modulation meaning 'key change' 98

Moeran, Edward J. (1895–1950):
  cello sonata 679
  chamber music 561
  symphony 314
  violin concerto 673

'moment' form 92–3

Mompou, Federico (b. 1893):
  songs 490

Mondonville, Jean J. de (1711–72) 659

Moniuszko, Stanislaus (1820–72) 412

Monn, Georg Matthias (1770–50) 515

monody:
  development of 89
  re-emergence of 32
  secular 39–40

monothematicism 524

Monteverdi, Claudio (1567–1643) 449, 460
  concertato style, and 459
  grouping of players 189
  operas 364
  Orfeo 364
    hemiola, and 55
    orchestration, and 200
  orchestra, and the 161, 200
  tremolando, introduction of 587

Montsalvatge, Xavier (b. 1912):
  songs 490

Morley, Thomas (1557–1603) 509
  ballets 453
  fantasias 510
  First Book of Consort Lessons by 509
  madrigals 452–3, 455
  'Mistress mine well may you fare' 97,
    98
  'Now is the month of maying' 43
  Shakespeare songs, setting of 455
Moscheles, Ignaz (1794–1870) 615
  piano concertos 640
Mosolov, Alexander (1900–74):
  The Iron Foundry (music or symphony
    of machines) 224, 293
Moszkowski, Moritz (1854–1925) 335
motet, beginnings of 439
  and chamber music 508
motives 86–7, 106
Mottevilli, Madame Françoise de (*c.*
  1621–89), on Italian opera 366
Mottl, Felix (1856–1911) 406
motto theme (*ideé fixe*) 106
Moussorgsky, *see* Mussorgsky
mouth-bow 113
Mozart, Johann Wolfgang Amadius
  (1756–91):
  Alberti basses, and 602
  'Apollonian' music of 27
  brass, use of 158, 163
  chamber music 521–3
    use of piano in 516–17
    wind, for 523, 529
  clarinet, works for 686
  Clementi, on 606
  chromatic:
    decorations 98
    harmony 79
    melody 78
  concerto form 103
  concertos:
    bassoon 688
    flute 683
    flute and harp 693
    horn 689
    oboe 685
    piano 104, 633, 634–6
      C minor (K 491) and chromatic
        harmony 79
    violin 666

Eine Kleine Nachtmusik and harmony
  64
flutes, and 153
Gershwin, and 714 n
Handel, on 463–4
Handel and Bach, re-discovered 50
Haydn, and 519, 520, 521–3
instrumentation and timbre 69
interpretation of 715
Masses 467
melody, and 63
operas 383–6, 389–90, 393, 395
  arias and abridged sonata form
    104
  castrati 376
  Don Giovanni 163–4
  The Magic Flute 163–4
orchestra, father of modern(?) 163
orchestration 203
phrasing, and 63–4
piano:
  duo 649
  music 597, 600–2, 656
  orchestra, and, works for 640
polyphonic developments 89
sonata form 102
songs 478
suites 328
symphonies 243–4
  no. 38 ('Prague') 89, 102
    chromaticism 65–6
    melody 62–3
    timbre 69
  last three 102
    sonata form, and 105
  no. 40 (G minor) 89
    melody 62
    motives 87
    romanticism 110
  no. 41 ('Jupiter') 89
Sinfonia Concertante 693
timpani, and 160
trombones, re-discovery of 163, 167
trumpet music 114–15
variations, and 87
violin sonatas 656–7, 666
Mozart, Leopold (1719–87) 691
  horn concerto 689
Mudge, Richard (1718–63) 690

Mühlfeld, Richard (1856–1907):
  clarinetist 542, 687
Munch, Charles, (1891–1968) on
    contemporary music 761
Munrow, David (1942–76), on
    Machaut 441
Musgrave, Thea (b. 1928):
  chamber music 577, 581
  clarinet concerto 687
  horn concerto 690
  Music for Horn and Piano 690
musica da camera 505
Musica enchiradis (10th cent. treatise)
    439
musica ficta 43–4
musical comedy 401–2
musicals, 55; Broadway 430
musiche nuove (Florentine school) 587
'music theatre' 92
musique concrète 18
Mussorgsky, Modest P. (1835–81) 283,
    339, 550
  Boris Godunov 530
  piano music 622
  songs 488, 489
mute and:
  brass 218–19
  strings 207
  woodwind 209–10 and n
mystery-dramas 438

Napoleon Bonaparte (1769–1821),
    operatic favourites of 387
nationalism in music 347, 411–12,
    544–5
  see also folk-music
Naylor, Bernard (b. 1907):
  vocal music 496
Neapolitan operas, influence on
    C. P. E. Bach 378
neo-classicism 345–7, 418, 419, 572
  piano, and 629 ff
Neri, St. Philip (1515–95):
  origin of oratorio 459
neumes (form of notation) 33
Niccolo da Perugia (14th cent.) 442
nicknames of compositions 111–12,
    284
Nicolai, Carl Otto (1810–49) 409

Nielsen, Carl (1865–1931):
  chamber music 580
  clarinet concerto 687
  flute concerto 683–4
  piano music 621–2
  symphonies 304–6
    no. 5 225 n
  Two Fantasy Pieces (oboe) 686
  violin sonatas 660
  violin, works for solo 664
  violinist, as 303
Nijinsky, Vaslavy (1890–1950) 344
Nikisch, Arthur (1855–1922) 194 n
noise 73–4
Nono, Luigi (b. 1924) 229
  vocal works 500
Norman, Ludwig (1831–85) 303
notation, musical 30–40, 118–21, 441
  beginnings of 143
  Berio, and 755–8
  Birtwistle, and 758–9
  breakdown of traditional 498
  Chinese 33|
  development of 33–9
  graphic 38
  modern adaptions of 581–2
  twelve-note scale, and 37
  visual 38
note-clusters 80–1
'note mixture' distinguished from
    electronic music 80
Notra Dame School 439

oboe:
  compass of 212
  history of 151
  mute, and 210 n
  new techniques 213
Obrecht, Jacob (1453–1505) 444
Ockeghem, Jan (c. 1430–c. 1495) 444,
    445
'O come all ye faithful' (*Adeste
    Fideles*) 85
Odington, Walter de (13th–14th cent.):
  notation 143
Offenbach, Jacques (1819–80):
  operettas 401, 402
ondes martenot 117, 175, 181
'open form' 340

opera:
  aria: *da capo* standardised by
      Scarlatti 373, 385
    development of 44
  arrival of (c. 1600) 33
  ballad 476
  bel canto 392
  bouffe 387
  Britain, in 428–9, 432–4
  comic, 364–5, 377–80, 387, 395, 400
    influence on instrumental music of
      379
  comique 387
  finales in 85–6
  financial problems of 431–4
  French (18th century) 378
  Italian, spread of 372–3, 378–80
  orchestra, and the 395–6
  origin of word 371
  performance of 721–2
  recitatives and form 47
  scenic design for 725–6
  stagione system 434
  translations of 723
  U.S.A., in 429–30, 434
opera-houses:
  Bayreuth 69, 398–9, 400
  Coliseum 433
  Covent Garden (Royal Opera) 433
    repertoire of 723–4
  first, at Venice 364–5
  Glyndebourne 433, 726
  Paris 393
  Sadlers Wells, repertoire of 723,
    725
opera seria 386
operetta 395, 401–2
ophicleide 155, 157
oratorio:
  origin of 459–60
  English 463
orchestras:
  before 16th century 140 n., 143–6
  19th century 166 ff
  20th century 172–80, (Fig.) 179–80
    financing of 177–8, 231
  chamber, 20th cent. development of
    231–2
  evolution of 160–2

6th cent. B C–18th cent. A D (table)
    161–2
platform, on the 186–91, (Fig.) 188
repertoires of London 747–8
versatility of 178
orchestration:
  baroque 203–4
  brass 214–222, Figs. 216–22
    compass of instruments 219–22
  Gabrieli and introduction of 156
  percussion 222–5
    20th century, in the 226–8
  strings 204–8, (Fig.) 205–7
  20th century 228–31
  woodwind 208–14, (Figs.) 208–9, 210
Orff, Carl (b. 1895) 420
  choral works 499
organ 116
  concertos 653
  early 30–1
  electronic 117
  recitals 711
  solo works 651–3
organum (organising) 30, 438–9
oriental music:
  influence of 140–2, 176, 339
    see also gamelan orchestra *and*
      Chinese music
Oulibicheff, A., on Beethoven 19 and
    n., 22
overtones 68
overtures:
  composers of (listed) 332
  types of 332

Pacius, Frederic (1809–91) 306
Paderewski, Ignace Jan (1860–1941)
    615
Paër, Ferdinando (1771–1839) 382
Paganini, Nicolo (1782–1840):
  Berlioz's *Harold in Italy*, and 675
  Caprices for solo violin 663
  inspired:
    Berlioz 614, 675
    Brahms 613
    Liszt 611, 614
    Rachmaninov 623, 643
  violin concertos 668
  virtuoso violinist, as 717

Paisiello, Giovanni (1741–1816) 382, 387
Palestrina, Giovanni Pierluigi da (1525–94) 32, 42, 349–50, 447–9
  Masses 190
palindromes resurrected 48
Palm, Siegfried (b. 1927) 680
parameters and Schoenberg 91
Paris (19th cent.), musical life of 391
Parker, Charlie (1920–55) 213
Parker, Horatio (1863–1919) 563
Parry, Charles Hubert (1848–1918) 330, 506
  chamber music 557
  choral music 493
  sacred works 468
  symphonies 312
Parry, John (?–1782):
  harp sonata 681
Partch, Harry (b. 1901) 36–7
  chamber music, 580
  microtonal harmonium of 36–7
  percussion, works for 692
  quarter tones, and 36–7
passacaglia 88, 89
Passion-dramas 438
pastorale, rhythm of 58
Pears, Peter (b. 1910) 497, 499
Pedrell, Felipe (1841–1922) 566
Penderecki, Krzystof (b. 1933) 426
  bowing of strings 232
  Capriccio for violin and orchestra 674
  operas 426
  quartets 578
  sonata for cello and orchestra 678
  vocal works 499
'Penillion singing' 681
pentatonic scale:
  Chinese music and 25
  folk-songs and 25
percussion 145, 158–60, 222–8
  African music 228
  orchestration of 224–6
    for schools (Fig.) 752–4
  20th century, in the 176, 226–8
  See also timpani
Pergolesi, Giovanni Batista (1710–36) 465
  operas 378, 385

sonatas 513
Stabat Mater 463
Peri, Jacopo (1561–1633):
  operas 363–4, 368
Perle, George (b. 1915) 326
Pérotin, 'le Grand' (c. 1160–1220) 439
  notation 143
Petrassi, Goffredo (b. 1922):
  chamber music 566
Pettersson, Allan (b. 1911) 310–11
Pfitzner, Hans (1869–1949):
  operas 409, 419
  piano concertos 645
Phoenicia, woodwinds, use of 150
phrasing 63–4
pianoforte:
  Beethoven's criticism of 116
  chamber music, and 516–17, 520
  development for virtuosi (19th cent.) 717
  invention of 587–8
  meaning 115
  recitals 708–9
Piccini, Nicolo (1728–1800) 328
piccolo, compass of 215
pifferari (pipers) and tempo 58–9
Pijper, William (1894–1947):
  flute sonata 684
Piston, Walter (b. 1894):
  chamber music 564
  symphonies 325
  viola concerto 675–6
Pizzetti, Ildebrando (1880–1968):
  chamber music 566
  operas 417
pizzicato 208
Plainsong (plainchant) 28, 30, 443
  drama, in 359
  form and 40
  melody, and 64
  modes, and 437–9
  notation of 33
Plato on musical rules 26
player-pianos 92
polka introduced 547
polyphony 439–49 *passim*
  Bach, writing for violin by 663
  Bruckner, influence on 270
  dance tunes, and 45–6

development, and 88–9
dissonance, and 76
England, in 442, 450
form, and 41, 43–4, 50, 82–3
history of 28–32, 35, 39–40
melody, and 64
re-discovered 48
rhythm, and 57–8
secular 42
17th cent., losing fashion in 508, 509
songs in Florence 441
vocal (madrigals), chromatic
   harmony and melody 79
polyrhythm and African music 56
Ponte, Lorenzo da (1749–1838):
  libretti 384, 385
Porter, Cole (1891?–1964):
  songs 499
Potter, Cipriani (1792–1871):
  symphonies 312
Poulenc, Francis (1899–1963) 268
  Aubade 644
  chamber music 556
  Concert Champêtre 654
  Élégie (horn) 690
  operas 416
  organ concerto 654
  piano duo 650
  sonatas:
   clarinet 687
   flute 685
   oboe 686
   violin 651
  songs 488
Pousseur, Henri (b. 1929):
  vocal music 501
Power, Leonel (?–1445), and *cantus
   firmus* 443
Praetorius, Michael (1571–1621):
  Organographia by 148, 150, 230
pre-historic music 22–4
prepared piano 692
programme:
  making of 712
  music 108–10, 335, 538
   chamber works, in 545
  notes 733–4
Prokofiev, Sergei (1916–53):
  ballet, *The Prodigal Son* 293–4

chamber music 552, 556
concertos:
  cello 677
  piano 648–9
  violin 671–2
operas 424
  The Angel of Fire 293–4
piano music 624
sonatas:
  cello 679
  solo violin 664
  violin 661
songs 490
suites 329
symphonies 268, 292–6
Prout, Ebenezer (1835–1909) 759
Psalms, the 27–8
Puccini, Giacomo (1858–1924):
  operas 402, 408–9, 415
Purcell, Henry (1658–95) 328, 457–8,
  690
  Chaconne for strings 88
  chromaticism, and 65, 79
  fantasias 511
  kettledrums, use of 160
  keyboard music 590–1
  key-relationship, sense of 458
  operas 367–8
   Dido and Aeneas 367
    chromaticism 65
    ground bass 88
   King Arthur (1691) 367
  sacred music 458
  secular choral works 458
  sonatas 513
  songs 458
  trombones, and 156
Puritans and English music 457
Pythagoras on musical theory 26, 32

Quantz, Johann J. (1697–1773):
  flute concertos 682–3
  teacher of Frederick the Great 682
quarter tones (microtones), use of 36–
  7, 67
Quilter, Roger (1877–1953) 335

Rachmaninov, Sergius (1873–1943):
  bassoon, and 688

Rachmaninov, Sergius *continued*
  cello sonata 679
  piano concertos 643–4, 648
  piano music 615, 623–4
  songs 489
  suites for two pianos 651
  Symphonic Dances 651
  symphonic works 290–1
radio broadcast music 735–8
radiogram, music on the 734–5
Raff, Josef Joachim (1822–82) 337
  chamber music 540
raga 24
ragtime 141
Rainier, Priaulx (b. 1903) 497
Rameau, Jean Philippe (1683–1764):
  clarinets, and 153
  keyboard music 335, 592
  operas 377, 378, 380, 385, 395
random form 92–3
random rhythm 60–1
Rangström, Ture (1884–1947) 309–10
Rasumorsky, Count, and Beethoven
  530
Ravel, Maurice (1875–1937) 339, 340
  Balinese gamelan music, and 141–2
  Bolero and trombone 223
  chamber music 551, 555
  harp, use of 227
  Mother Goose Suite 650
  piano concertos 644
  piano music 617
  operas 415–16
  orchestration 173
  songs 488
  suites 330
  Tzigane for violin and orchestra 671
  violin sonata 659–60
Rawsthorne, Alan (1905–71):
  chamber music 561–2
  concertos:
    cello 677
    oboe 685
    piano 646
    violin 673
  piano music 631
  sonatas:
    cello 679
    viola 676

  violin 662
  Theme and Variations for two violins
    664
  symphonies 321
reading music 117–22
rebab (Egyptian) 161
recitals:
  doubtful value of 703–5
  organ 711
  pianoforte 708–9
  song 704–6
  strings and harp 709–11
recitative:
  accompanied, invented by Scarlatti
    373
  harmony, and 65
  in opera, invention of 44
recitativo secco 373, 381
'reciting note', the 96
refrain principle, the 45–6
Reger, Max (1873–1916) 333, 345
  chamber music 543
  piano concertos 645
  viola, solo, suites 676
rehearsals, time required for 760–1
Reich, Steve (b. 1936):
  chamber music 583
Reicha, Anton (1770–1836):
  wind chamber music 534
Reinecke, Carl Heinrich (1824–1910)
    615
  chamber music 543
Reinken, Johann (1623–1722):
  Horticus Musicus (1704) by 514
Reizenstein, Franz (1911–68):
  chamber music 581
Respighi, Ottorino (1879–1936):
  chamber music 566
responsorial singing 40–1, 96
Reubke, Julius (1834–58):
  organ music 652
rhapsodies 333–4
Rheinberger, Josef Gabriel (1839–
  1901):
  chamber music 543
  organ music 651–2, 653
rhythm 51–62, 714–15
rhythmic series 60
ricercar, the 507–8

Richard I, King of England (1157–99) 39
Richter, Franz Xaver (1709–89) 515
Rigveda 24
Rimsky-Korsakov, Nicholas A. (1844–
    1908) 283, 344
  bassoon concerto 691
  Berlioz's influence on 285
  Borodin, re-scoring of 287
  chamber music 551
  Coq d'or and double-bassoon 216
  operas 413
  Principles of Orchestration by 172,
    204, 210, 216
  Scheherazade 329
  songs 488
  symphonies 288
  The May Night 214, 216
Rinuccini, Ottavio (1562–1621), poet
    363–4, 368, 381
ripieno 111, 240
ritornello (refrain) 45–6, 54, 103, 457,
    665
  Stravinsky, and 48
Rochberg, George (b. 1918) 326
Rodrigo, Joaquin (b. 1902):
  harp, works for 681–2
Roman, Johan Helmich (1694–1758)
    301
Roman de Fauvel (14th cent.) 441
Romans, ancient 437
  instruments of 142
    brass 154–5
    woodwinds 150
Romantic Movement 108–9, 110
  Bach's influence on 596
  Beethoven, and 602–3
  chamber music, and 537 ff
  'classical' and 'romantic' meaning
    110
  composers of, and form 47
  opera, and 393 ff
  sonata form, and 609
rondo (rondeau) 105, 240, 440, 444 640
  dance ('Round O') 509
  form 46
Rosenberg, Hilding (b. 1892) 310
Rosenthal, Manuel (b. 1904) 615
Roslavetz, Nikolai (1882–1930) 293
Rosseter, Philip (c. 1575–1623) 456

Rossini, Gioacchino (1792–1868):
  Beethoven, on 390
  brass, use of 171–2
  chamber music 565
  influence of 390
  operas 390–1, 393
  sacred works 468–9
  songs 476–7
Roussel, Albert (1869–1937) 335
  chamber music 555–6
  Impromptu for harp 681
  piano concerto 644
  piano music 632
  songs 487
  symphonies 267, 268
Royal Academy of Music 312
Royal College of Music 312
Royal Opera, Covent Garden 433
  repertoire of 723–4
rubato:
  'crooners' and 59
  rhythm and tempo 59
  use of 715
Rubbra, Edmund (b. 1901):
  symphonies 319–20
Rubinstein, Anton (1830–94) 615
  chamber music 549
  piano concertos 640
Ruggles, Carl (1876–1971):
  chamber music 564
Russian music:
  cadences, and 43
  'Five, the Big' ('the Mighty
    Handfull', *Kuchka*), composers
    283, 339, 448–9, 550, 555
  influence on French music 339
  symphonic music 282–301
    influence of Berlioz 285

Sacchini, Antonio (1734–86) 382
Sachs, Curt (1881–1959), on musical
    sounds 23
Sachs, Hans (1494–1576) 39
sackbut 154, 155
Sadlers Wells, repertoire of 723, 725
Saeverud, Harald (b. 1897) 312
Saint-Saëns, Charles Camille (1835–
    1921) 338, 616
  chamber music 553

Saint-Saëns, Charles Camille *continued*
  concertos:
    piano 644
    viola 676
    violin 670
  Danse Macabre and *col legno* 207
  Fantaisie for harp 681
  Morceau de Concert (harp) 680
  Samson et Dalila 406–7
  suites 330
  symphonies 266
  two pianos, works for 650
Sauguet, Henri (b. 1901):
  trumpet concerto 691
Satie, Erik A. L. (1866–1925):
  piano music 617
Sax, Adolphe (Joseph, 1814–94) 213
saxophone 587
  compass of 213–14
  invention and use of 216
scales:
  chromatic 97–8
  diatonic 94–6, 98–9
  heptatonic 25
  microtonal 36–7, 67, 99
  whole-tone 99
  see also twelve-note scale
Scarlatti, Alessandro (1659–1725) 459–
      60, 465
  cantatas, oratorios 459–60
  operas 373–4, 375, 377–8, 385, 459–60
Scarlatti, Domenico (1685–1757):
  binary form, and 45, 593
  career of 592–3
  'ensemble of perplexity' and 373
  keyboard sonatas, 100–1, 592–3, 742
  sonata form 105
  vocal works 463
Schalk, Franz (1863–1931):
  Bruckner's symphonies, and 272
Scharwenka, Xaver (1850–1924) 615
  piano concerto 640
Schedrin, Rhodion (b. 1932):
  Symphony no. 1 301
Scheidt, Samuel (1587–1654) 460
Schein, Johann H. (1586–1630) 460
  Banchetto Musicale 512
scherzo 104, 237, 239, 246
  development of 633

Schikaneder, Emmanuel,
      commissioned *Magic Flute* 388
Schmidt, Franz (1874–1939):
  symphonies 276–7, 317–18
Schmitt, Florent (1870–1958) 340
Schoenberg, Arnold (1874–1951):
  atonality, and 79
  chamber music 543, 568–70
  Chamber Symphony 515–16
  chromaticism, and 66
  dissonance, 'emancipation of' 77
  Five Pieces for Orchestra 68, 230
  Klangfarbenmelodie (tone-colour-
      melody) 68
  Moses and Aaron and *Sprechgesang* 65
  Ockeghem, affinity with 444
  operas 421–2
  orchestra, and 72
  orchestration 173, 229
  oratorios 491
  parameters, and 91
  Phantasy for violin and piano
      accompaniment 662
  piano concerto 66, 647
  piano music 625–6
  Pierrot Lunaire:
    influence of 568, 571, 580
    Sprechgesang and 65
  Quartet no. 2, op. 10 with soprano
      solo 517
  songs 490–1
  Sprechgesang 65, 490, 498
  tone-poems 338–9
  twelve-note (-tone) scale (row or
      series) 48, 60, 79–80, 89, 341 and
      n., 342, 344, 569
  Verklärte Nacht 338–9, 568–9
  violin concerto 670
Schola Cantorum 554, 566
schools, music teaching in 752–4
Schrecker, Franz (1878–1934):
  operas 422; songs 491
Schubert, Franz (1797–1828) 335
  chamber music 173, 535–6, 590
  chromaticism 99
  Dvořák on 252
  form 82
  Masses 467
  piano music 607–8

duets 649–50
Rossini, influence of 390
songs 478–80
  modulation, and 98
symphonies 252–6
  no. 8 ('Unfinished') 89, 99, 210, 254–6
    development 88–9
    dissonances 77
    form 85
    woodwinds 212
  no. 9 212, 254–6
  trombones, use of 165
  violin and piano 658
  woodwinds, use of 212
Schuller, Gunther (b. 1925) 327
  chamber music for brass 581
Schultz (Sultetus), Johann (?–1653) 477
Schuman, William (b. 1910):
  symphonies 325–6
  violin concerto 674
Schumann, Clara (1819–96) 613, 615
Schumann, Robert (1810–56):
  Adagio and Allegro (horn) 690
  chamber music 539–40
  choral works 468
  Fantasiastücke (clarinet) 687
  Concert Piece (4 horns and orchestra) 694
  concertos:
    cello 676
    piano 639
    violin 670
  on: Mendelssohn trios 539
    Schubert 255
    Schubert piano trios 536
  songs 480–1
  piano and orchestra, works for 641
  piano music 611, 612–13
    duo 650
  Three Romances (oboe and piano) 686
  violin sonatas 658
Schütz, Heinrich ('Sagittarius', 1585–1672):
  baroque style, and 460
  grouping of players 189
  opera 368
Scontrino, Antonio (1850–1922):
  score:

chamber music 565
  miniature, use of 699–701, 720
  writing of full 183–5, (Fig.) 184
'Scotch Snap' 472
Scott, Cyril (1879–1971) 561
scratch activities 583
Scriabin, Alexander (1872–1915) 339
  piano concerto 648
  piano music 620, 623
  symphonies 289–90
Sculthorpe, Peter (b. 1929):
  operas 429
Searle, Humphrey (b. 1915) 343
  on Liszt 337
  symphonies 321–2
secular music:
  growth in Italy of 446
  origins of 439–40
Seiber, Mátyás (1905–60):
  chamber music 577
Self, George (b. 1921), and music teaching 752–4
semibreve, origin of 35
serial rhythm 57
serialism, *see* twelve-note scale
Serly, Tibor, and Bartok's work 647, 675
Serov, Alexander (1820–71) 549
serpent 155, 157
Sessions, Roger (b. 1896) 343
  chamber music 564
  symphonies 325
  violin concerto 674
Shakespeare, William (1564–1616):
  music for plays, by 367
  operas from plays by 425
  theatre in times of, music for 153
Shaporin, Yuri (1889–1966):
  operas 424
Sharp, Cecil (1859–1924), and folk-song 471
shawms 151–3
Shebalin, Vissarion (1902–63) 300
Shnitke, Alfred (b. 1934) 301
Shostakovich, Dmitri (1906–77):
  cello sonata 679
  chamber music 574–5
  concertos 299
    cello 676–7
    piano 648

Shostakovich, Dmitri *continued*
  violin 673
  Mahler, influence of 276
  operas 424
    The Lady Macbeth of Mtsensk 297,
     424
  piano music 624
  songs 490
  symphonies 292, 295, 296–300
  violin sonata 661
Sibelius, Jean (1865–1957) 334
  form, and 48
  Mahler, conversation with, on the
    symphony 274
  quartet, *Voces Intimae* 548
  songs 490
  suites 329
  symphonies 304–9
    no. 7 and motives 87
  Tapiola 309
  tone-poems 338, 339
  violin concerto 669
siciliana, rhythm of 58
Simpson, Christopher (?–d. 1669):
  on viols 509, 511
Simpson, Robert (b. 1921):
  symphonies 321–2
sinfonia 46, 236, 331
  avanti l'opera 236–7
  concertante 693
sitar, Indian 29
Sitsky, Larry (b. 1934):
  operas 429
Six, Les (French composers) 416–17,
  556, 618
Skalkottas, Nikos (1904–49) 343
Smetana, Bedřich (1824–84):
  chamber music
  folk-song, and 474
  operas 412
  piano music 620
  Schubert's influence on 256
  tone-poems 338
Smythe, Ethel (1858–1944):
  The Bo'sun's Mate 414
snares 225
Sokolov, Nikolay A. (1859–1922) 522
Soler, Antonio (1729–83):
  keyboard music 597

Somers, Harry (b. 1935):
  operas 429
sonata:
  classical, deriving from Bach 596
  da camera (chamber) 47, 512–13, 655
  da chiesa (church) 47, 240–1, 512–13,
   655
  dissociated from cantata 588
  form 100–3
   'abridged' 104
   chamber music, in 518 ff
   development 88
  -rondo 46
Songs:
  lieder: collections of 707 n
  origins of 477
  recitals of 704–6
  solo: 'art' 454–5
   early 39
  'spirituals', Negro 475
  strophic 40
  translations of 706–8, 723
  see also folk-music *and* chansons
Sousa, John Philip (1854–1932) 563
  on march tunes 51
South Place concerts 559
space 90–1
Spanish music, European composers'
  interpretation of 617
Sperontes (Johan S. Scholze, 1705–
  50) 477
'spirituals', Negro 475
Spohr, Louis (1784–1859) 468, 606,
  650
  chamber music 173, 537
  clarinet concertos 687
  quartets 525
  violin concerto 667–8
Spontini, Gasparo (1774–1851):
  operas 387, 388
Sprechgesang and Schoenberg 65, 490,
  498
Stamitz, Johann Wenzel (1717–57):
  chamber concerts by 514
  sons of 514
Stanford, Charles V. (1852–1924):
  chamber music 557
  choral music 493
  operas 414

sacred works 468
symphonies 312–13
'Star-Spangled Banner, The', and
  harmony 64
statistical: rhythm 61
sound 81
Stenhammer, Wilhelm (1871–1927)
  310
Stevenson, Ronald (b. 1928):
symphonic works 322
Stockhausen, Karlheinz (b. 1928) 583
antiphony, and 90–1
  Carré (square) 90, 232
  chamber music 581–2
  electronic music 67, 91, 93
  Gesang der Junglinge (Song of the
    Youths) 91
  Gruppen (Groups) 90, 190, 232
  Kontakte ('Contacts') and 'moment'
    form 93
  melody, and 66
  oriental music, and 142
  piano music 627–8
  Studie II (electronic) and melody 67
  vocal works 498
  Zyklus (music theatre) 693
Stradivari *or* Stradivarius, Antonio
  (c. 1644–1737) 149, 161, 587, 654,
  655
Strauss, Franz (father of Richard):
horn concerto 689
Strauss, Johann (1804–49) 335
Strauss, Johann (son, 1825–99) 335
operettas 401, 402
  The Blue Danube and harmony 64
Strauss, Richard (1864–1949) 339, 341
  Also sprach Zarathustra and string
    devices 208–9
  Burlesque in D minor 645
  Cosi fan tutte re-interpreted by 384
concertos:
  bassoon 688
  horn 688–90
  oboe 685
  Don Quixote variations 333
  Duo Concertante 651, 661
  operas 410–11, 415
  songs 484
  Till Eulengespiel 109

muted brass 219
tone poems 338
violin sonata 659
Stravinsky, Igor (1882–1971) 339,
  344–5, 346
Bach's instrumental writing, on 203
chamber music 570, 571–2
choral works 491–2
neo-classical forms, and 48
  Octet for Wind 556
  influence of 580
operas 423–4
orchestra, and 72
orchestration 228
piano and orchestra 646, 647
piano music 629
rhythm, and 53
  Rite of Spring (1913) 37, 174, 229
  dissonances 78
  random form 93
  random rhythm 60
  rhythm 53
  ritornello 48
  Soldier's Tale, The (*Histoire du
    Soldat*) 173, (Fig.) 179–80
  influence of 580
  rhythm 53
songs 490, 491–2
suites 329
  Symphony of Psalms (1930),
    orchestration 72
  Symphony in Three Movements
    (1945):
    orchestration 72
    'swing band' chord 78
  Three Pieces (clarinet) 687
  twelve-note-serialism 80
  violin concerto 670
  Wedding, The, and rhythm 53
strings:
devices and expressions defined (table)
  206–9
modern devices 205
orchestration 204–8
recitals 709–11
16th–17th century 148–9
tuning of 208
viol family 148–9
violin family 149

Sturm und Drang music 241
  Beethoven, and 604
  Haydn, and 597, 599
style mécanique 293
suite, orchestral, origin of 46–7
Suk, Joseph (1874–1935):
  Asrael Symphony 261
Sullivan, Arthur (1842–1900):
  'Irish' Symphony 313
  operettas 374, 401–2
'Sumer is icumen in' 29, 35, 36, 143,
    442
Sumerian music 24
Suppé, Franz von (1820–95) 402
Susato, Tielman (?–d. 1561–4),
    (Antwerp music publisher) 507
Sutermeister, Heinrich (b. 1910):
  operas 425
Suzuki method of violin teaching 33
Svendsen, Johan Severin (1840–1911)
    303, 306, 334
Sviridov, Georgii (b. 1915) 300
Swannee River ('The Old Folks at
    Home') 84
'swing' bands 78, 176, 219
Swingle Singers 141
symphonic form in chamber music 518
symphonic poem 338
symphony:
  development of 46
  finales, influence of opera 385
  origins of 236–7
  plan of, (Fig.) 238–40
  table of dates (1866–1911) 270–1
syncopation 54–5, 61
  accent, and 59
synthesiser 182
Szymanowski, Karol (1883–1937) 348,
    349
  chamber music 566
  choral works and songs 493, 499
  operas 426
  piano music 620–1
  symphonies 277
  violin concertos 673

tablature 33
'keyboard', and microtones 36–7
Takemitsu, Toru (b. 1930):

percussion, works for 692
Tallis, Thomas (c. 1508–85) 450–1
  motet 96
  Spem in alium (forty-part motet) and
    antiphony 90
tambourine 159, 225
tape recorder 37, 190–1, 500–1
Tartini, Giuseppe (1692–1770):
  violin sonatas 655
Tausig, Carl (1841–71) 615
Taverner, John (c. 1495–1545) 450
  conversion of 451–2
  In Nomines, and 508
  vocal music 501
Taylor, Deems (1885–1966):
  opera 429
Tchaikovsky, Peter Ilitch (1840–93)
    333, 335, 338
  bassoon, and 215–16
  chamber music 550
  Concert Fantasia in G 642
  influence of Bellini on 391
  operas 412–13
  piano concertos 642
    no. 1 and melody 62
  piano music 622–3
  songs 489
  suites 329
  symphonies 257, 282–7
    no. 4 and rhythms 58
    no. 6 ('Pathetic') 104
    and rhythms 56, 58, 215–16, 225
  Variations on a Rococo Theme (cello)
    676
  violin concerto 669
Telemann, Georg Philipp (1681–1767)
    336, 690
  cantatas and oratorios 462
  chamber music, and 514
  concertos:
    horn 689
    oboe 685
    viola 675
  flute, works for 683
  keyboard music 597
tempo and rhythm 58–9
Teplov, Grigori (1711–79):
  songs 488
Thalberg, Sigismond (1812–71) 615

thematic development 48
theremin, the 117, 181
Thomas, Ambrose (1811–96):
  Mignon 405
Thomson, Virgil (b. 1896):
  operas 430
  songs 499
Thuille, Ludwig (1861–1907):
  chamber music 543
Tibbett, Lawrence, baritone 429
timbre 68–73
timbrel (tambourine) 159
time signatures, introduction of 36
timpani (kettledrums) 226
  introduction of 160
  trumpets, and 160
  tuned 228
Tippett, Michael (b. 1906):
  A Child of our Time 320
  chamber music 562
  choral works and songs 496, 497
  operas 320, 429
  piano concerto 646
  piano sonatas 631
  suite in D 331
  symphonies 320–1
Tishchenko, Boris (b. 1939) 301
toccata 331
Toeschi, Carlo (c. 1722–88) 515
tonality and form 85–6
tone poems 337–9
tonguing of wind instruments 115
tonic sol-fa 99–100
Torelli, Giacomo (1608–78), scene
  painter 690
Torelli, Giuseppe (1658–1709),
  violinist-composer 512
Toscanini, Arturo (1867–1957) 195,
  698
Tovey, Donald (1873–1940)
  on: continuo 513
  Haydn quartets 519, 525
  Schumann 264
  Tchaikovsky 286
transients 68
transposing instruments 215
trautonium 181
tremolando introduced by Monteverdi
  587

tremolo 208
  bowed 208
  sul ponticello 207
trio 104; origin of 70
triple time, origin of 439, 441
Tristan and Yseult (troubadours' song)
  440
Triumphs of Oriana, The (1601) 453
trombone 163–5, 171–2
  ancestry 154–5
  Beethoven and 164
  compass 220–21, 222–3
  double-bass 222
  glissando 223
  tenor-bass 220
troubadours 39, 143, 439–40
trumpet 155, 171, 216
  ancestry of 154–5
  Beethoven and 215
  compass of 221–2
tuba, bass 219–20
  compass of 220, 223
'Tubas, Wagner' 170
tucket (*toccata* – dance) 509
Turina, Joaquin (1882–1949):
  chamber music 566
  songs 490
Turkish instruments 159, 228
twelve-note (-tone) scale (-row)
    (dodecaphonism, serialism) 48,
    79–80, 89, 341–4, 418, 491, 492,
    569, 577
  Babbitt's adaptation of 60, 577
  Dallapiccola and 418
  notation, and 37
  piano music 625 ff
  rhythmic series 60
  see also under Schoenberg
Tye, Christopher (c. 1500–72) 450, 508

'unexpectedness' and modern music
  230
unison, singing in 30

Vainberg, Moïshe (b. 1919) 300–1
Valen, Fartein (1887–1952) 312, 331,
  343
Varèse, Edgar (1883–1965):
  chamber music 564

Varèse, Edgar *continued*
  Density 21·5 (flute) 685
  electronic music 91
  founder of International Composer's
    Guild 563, 564
  Ionisation (1931) for percussion 228,
    232, 692
  Poème electronique 91
  variation 87–8
  form 332–3
Vaughan Williams, Ralph (1872–1958)
    333
  chamber music 559–60
  concertos:
    oboe 685
    piano 645
    tuba 691
  choral music and songs 494, 495–6
  operas 427
    Hugh the Drover 414
  polyphonic composition 43
  Romance for harmonica 691
  symphonies 314–16, 319
  violin and orchestra 672–3
  violin sonata 661
Vecchi, Orazio (c. 1551–1605):
  L'Amfiparzano 363
Venice and opera 364–5, 369
Verdelot, Philippe (early 16th cent.) 447
Verdi, Giuseppi (1813–1901):
  brass, use of 171–2
  operas 225, 392, 396, 408
  Requiem 469
  string quartet 565
  Wagner, and 404–5
  Verismo 406, 417, 430
Victoria, Tomás Luis da (c. 1535–1611)
    447, 448
Vieuxtemps, Henri (1820–81):
  violin concerto 668
Villa-Lobos, Heitor (1887–1959) 347
  chamber music 566
villancico 460
Vinci, Leonardo (1690–1730),
    composer 376
viol 508–12
  accompanies madrigals 454–5
violas, da braccio and da gamba 147
violin:
  early use of 508–9, 512 ff
  'great period of making' (Parry) 587
  introduced to England 457
  see also strings
violone (double-bass viol) 147
virelai 440, 442
virginal 589 ff
virtuosity, dangers and values of 715–
    19
Vitali, Giovanni Battista (c. 1644–92)
    512
Vitry, Philippe de (1291–1361),
    treatise by 441
Vivaldi, Antonio (1678–1741) 328, 463
  Bach's study of 595
  concertos 336
    bassoon 688
    four violins 693
    oboe 685
    violin 665
    wind 682
  ritornello, and 45
Volkonsky, Andrei (b. 1933) 301
Voltaire, François de (1694–1778),
    librettist for Rameau 377
Voříšek, Jan V. (1791–1825):
  piano sonata 620

Wagenseil, Georg Christoph (1715–77)
    515
  harp concerto 680
  trombone concerto 691
Wagner, Richard (1813–83) 335
  anvils, use of 224
  Beethoven's 9th Symphony, on 251
  bowed tremolo and the 'Ring' 208
  chromaticism, and 66
  development 89
  dissonance 77
  'Dionysian' music of 27
  forms, and 47
  influence:
    of Liszt 265
    on Dvořák 257–8
    on Franck 616
  instrumental form 47
  melody 65
  metamorphosis of themes 532
  operas:

dates of composition 396
Die Meistersinger:
  brass 218
  motives 87
  woodwinds 211
Gotterdämmerung and brass 218
leitmotiv 87, 398
Lohengrin and timbre 69
Parsifal and woodwinds 211
Tannhäuser:
  bassoon 216
  harmony 64–5
Tristan and Isolde:
  brass 218, 219
  chromaticism 66, 79
orchestration 167–71, (Fig.) 169, 173
Siegfried Idyll 173
thematic development 48
timbre 69
woodwinds, use of 210–11
'Wagner Tubas' 170
Waldteñfel, Emil (1837–1912) 335
Walter de Odington (13th–14th cent.):
  notation 143
Walther von der Vogelweide (c. 1170–
  1230) 440
Walton, William (b. 1902):
  chamber music 559, 562
  choral works and songs 496
  operas 428
  Sinfonia Concertante 646
  suites 331
  symphonies 314
  viola concerto 675
  violin concerto 672
  violin sonata 662
  waltzes 335
Ward, Robert (b. 1917) 326
Warrack, John (b. 1928):
  Tchaikovsky, and 287
Weber, Carl Maria von (1786–1826):
  Andante and Hungarian Rondo
    (bassoon) 688
  chamber music 534
  clarinet, works for 687 *bis*
  horns, and 156
  influence of Rossini 390
  operas 394–5, 397
  piano music 608–9

duets 650
romanticism 109
violin sonatas 658
Webern, Anton von (1883–1945) 341
  chamber music 570
  concerto for 9 instruments 230
  Klangfarbensmelodie 174–5
  melody, and 66
  orchestra, and 72
  orchestration 174–5, 229
  percussion 228
  piano music 626
  songs 491
  symphony form, and 50
  3 Little Pieces for cello 679–80
Weckerlin, Jean-Baptiste (1821–1910):
  song collection of 477
Weelkes, Thomas (1575?–1623) 453
Weill, Kurt (1900–50):
  operas and musicals 420
Weinberger, Jaromir (1896–1967):
  Schwanda the Bagpipe Player 426
Wellesz, Egon (1885–1974):
  chamber music 577
  symphonies 277
  Viennese school, on 2nd 342–3
Welsh music, early 40
Werle, Lars Johan (b. 1926) 425
Wexford Festival and opera 433
whole-tone scale 339, 340
  see also twelve-note scale
Whyte, Robert (c. 1530–74) 450–1
  fantasias 510
Widor, Charles M. J. A. (1844–1937):
  organ music 651–2
Wilbye, John (1574–1638) 453
Wilkmanson, Johan:
  chamber music 548
Willaert, Adrian (c. 1480–1562) 446,
  447
  Fantasie e Ricercari collected by 508
Williams, Grace (b. 1906):
  trumpet concerto 691
Williamson, Malcolm (b. 1931):
  chamber music 581
  operas 429
  organ concerto 653
  piano concerto, no. 3 646
  vocal music 499

Wirén, Dag (b. 1905) 310
Wolf, Hugo (1860–1903):
  chamber music 543
  Der Corregidor (The Magistrate) by
    409
  songs 482–4
Wolff, Christian (b. 1934):
  chamber music 582
Wood, Haydn (1882–1959) 331
Wood, Henry (1869–1944) 187
Wood, Hugh (b. 1932):
  cello concerto 677
  chamber music 577
  piano music 627
  symphonic works 322
Wood, Ralph, on Sibelius 308
woodwinds:
  ancient 145
  compass of (table) 215–16
  flutter-tonguing 212
  mediaeval 144, 150

17th–18th cent. 151–3
  tongued or slurred (Fig.) 211–12
Wuorinen, Charles (b. 1938) 327

Xenakis, Iannis (b. 1922):
  Bohor 190–1

Yamash'ta, Stomu (b. 1947):
  percussionist 692–3
yodelling 64
Ysaye, Eugéne (1858–1931):
  sonatas for solo violin 663–4
Yun, Isang (b. 1917) 232

Zach, Jan (1699–?1773) 515
Zandonai, Ricardo (1883–1944) 417
zarzuelas (operettas) 426
Zemlinsky, Alexander (1872–1942):
  songs 491
Zimmermann, Bernd A. (1918–70):
  cello sonata 680

A number of recent dates in the index which follows have
been supplied from *The New Grove Dictionary of Music and
Musicians* edited by Stanley Sadie, to be published in 1979,
by courtesy of the publishers Macmillan Publishers Ltd,
London